Rudolf Steiner

EURYTHMY
AS
VISIBLE SINGING

Anastasi Ltd
meaning 'rebirth'

Publisher
Established 1994

First Impression of the 4th English edition June 2013

Part I

Rudolf Steiner

EURYTHMY

AS

VISIBLE SINGING

Verbatim report of a course of lectures held in
Dornach 19 Feb. 1924 – 27 Feb. 1924

newly translated, including a facsimile, transcription and translation of the
Lecturer's Notes, with an introduction and index

Part II

A COMPANION to *Rudolf Steiner's*
Eurythmy as Visible Singing
compiled and expanded by
Alan Stott

together with *Josef Matthias HAUER*
"INTERPRETING MELOS" (1923)

EURYTHMY as VISIBLE SINGING

English Language Translation of GA 278

Chronology of previous editions of this publication:
From shorthand reports unrevised by the lecturer.
The German text published under the title
Eurythmie als sichtbarer Gesang.
1st German edition Dornach 1927
2nd German edition Dornach 1956
3rd German edition, revised and enlarged, Dornach 1975
4th German edition Dornach 1984 (editor Eva Froböse)

GA 278 (Bibliographic Survey 1961, No. 278)

First published in English (including a lecture given at Penmaenmawr, 26 Aug. 1923) by Anthroposophical Publishing Co., London, and Anthroposophic Press, New York 1932, as *Eurythmy as Visible Song*, translated by V. & J. Compton-Burnett; Foreword and Synopsis of Lectures by Marie Steiner; Introduction to eurythmy performance, Dornach 24th June 1923, "The Festival of St John" by R. Steiner.

Second English edition, *Eurythmy as Visible Music*, Rudolf Steiner Press, London 1977; a reprint translation of the lectures.

Third English edition 1996, corrected 1998; a fresh translation of the fourth German edition. Drawings in the text from the lecturer's blackboard sketches, executed by Assja Turgenieff. Sketch (Fig. 1) from a photograph of the blackboard drawing. Fig. 2 derives from the 1st German edition. A figured bass has been added to Fig. 22.

Previously published in two volumes by The Anderida Music Trust ISBN for complete set of 2 volumes 0-9527454-0-2 ISBN for volume I 0-952745-1-0 and volume II 0-9527454-2-9 Part 2 contains study material to Rudolf Steiner's *Eurythmy as Visible Singing* (GA 278), which, with the lecturer's personal Notebook NB 494, forms Part 1.

This edition © Alan Stott 1996-2013

This combined edition is published by Anastasi Ltd

ISBN 978-0-9569266-1-6

Page layout designed by: Anastasi Ltd Typeset in Adobe Garamond and Minion Pro
Cover Cover design by: © Anastasi Ltd **Design Studio 2013**
Anastasi Ltd Leominster, Herefordshire, HR6 8TA, England.
<www.anastasiltd-book-matters.com> <info@anastasiltd-book-matters.com>
Printed and Bound in Great Britain by:
Lightning Source UK Ltd

TABLE OF CONTENTS

Part I

N. 223-247

255-275

Skip

v

Part II

Part III

Publisher's Acknowledgement

For expanding, editing and correcting this edition, the publisher thanks Alan Stott for the many hours he spent in updating this publication, over the last two years.

Part I

Rudolf Steiner

EURYTHMY

AS

VISIBLE SINGING

Verbatim report of a course of lectures
held in Dornach 19 Feb. 1924 – 27 Feb. 1924,

newly translated, including a facsimile,
transcription and translation of the Lecturer's
Notes, with an introduction and index,

translated by

Alan Stott

Foreword
by Dorothea Mier

The study of music is the study of the human being. The two are inseparable, and eurythmy is the art which brings this most clearly to expression. In these lectures, Rudolf Steiner guides us along a path toward an understanding of the human form as music come to rest – the movements of eurythmy bringing this music back to life.

I would like to express my deepest gratitude to Alan Stott for the enormous undertaking of translating these lectures. He has taken great care to keep as close as possible to the original. I feel the effort made here in translating to be of tremendous importance, because it is very difficult not to shift slightly, or to make concrete formulations of that which holds a true mystery, thus limiting the reader's access to the path of discovery inherent in the original formulation. Steiner's characterisations are often challenging, but spiritually vital. They are like gems that have a depth which is unending.

The translator has achieved a great deal, in my opinion, in keeping Rudolf Steiner's work intact as far as possible. He has tried to accommodate, using copious notes, the different terms used in the various cultures, and he gives many references for further study. I appreciate his logic in translating *Ton-Eurythmie* as "music-eurythmy", yet am deeply grateful that [for the 3rd edition] he has accepted the term "tone-eurythmy" used worldwide over the past decades.

It soon becomes apparent when studying these lectures, that there are many enigmas, and many baffling statements. As yet, there is much that is not completely understood, but over the years people may come to a greater depth of understanding that will unlock the secrets hidden within the various indications. When reading these lectures, I think it is very important to remember that they were lectures, spoken to an intimate group of invited eurythmists and musicians – unrevised by the lecturer. Regarding the Lecturer's Notes (which in themselves are so valuable), I feel we also need to be very careful to remember their context. These Notes, included in this edition, were Rudolf Steiner's personal notes in preparation for the lectures. I am filled with questions, for instance, in connection with Lecture 5, on Cadence. What prevented Steiner from bringing some of the aspects of his notes into the lecture? As you read, you will find your own questions which can stimulate lifelong research.

This is a real handbook for active eurythmists and musicians, a text for advanced study. It is not meant for the casual reader, because (as with any "time art") eurythmy cannot be self-taught. I can only encourage the reader to work deeply into the questions that arise when living with these lectures, because it is through delving into the mysteries contained here that we will come further into the unfolding of tone-eurythmy.

Dorothea Mier, Spring Valley, Michaelmas 1994

Translator's Preface and Acknowledgments

"A translation has to be made out of the spirit of the language of the country just as if the respective book were written in this language." R. Steiner. Soul *Economy and Waldorf Education*. Lecture 14. 5 Jan. 1922, GA 303. RSP/AP 1986. With this sentence, Steiner encapsulates the translator's ideal. It is echoed by Gerald Vann: "Translation must always of course be a rendering not of word for word but of idea for idea; to be content to transliterate is merely illiterate." G. Vann. "Translator's Note" to Teilhard de Chardin. *Hymn of the Universe*. Collins. London. 1965. I do not think any translator believes a fixed "fundamentalist" view concerning Steiner's terms is a tenable position. Words with Teutonic roots are not automatically holy or accurate, whoever the author might be. Nor does anybody claim *pommes de terre* has anything to do with apples! We have all heard of "anthrospeak", that habit of jargonizing which we try to avoid in serious discourse. We all know that language is a living reality, and we try to be sensitive to its development.

These remarks arise from a perception that general awareness of our use of language is not as precise as it might be, that several factors are involved, and that a translator of a text on music faces a difficult and controversial situation from which, nevertheless, I am convinced much good can result. Questions of terminology began to be aired at last in the Association of *Eurythmists U.K. Newsletter*. Aberdeen. Winter 1993. Potential critics may care to know that the aims expressed in Anna Meuss' article "Translating Rudolf Steiner's lectures" in *Anthroposophy Today* No. 20. RSP. Autumn 1993, match my own. Translators working in English owe much to her example. With the question of spelling and what to italicise, I have followed *The Oxford Dictionary for Writers and Editors* (1991). The few alternative American musical terms are included.

The course of lectures on music-eurythmy translated here was held in February, 1924, for an audience of eurythmists and musicians. It represents the greatest of Steiner's contributions to music, and should interest all artists. Other lecture-courses were planned, including one for musicians, but Steiner's death in 1925 prevented this. Nevertheless a rich fund of insights was offered with which artists can begin working: the lectures published under the title *Das Wesen des Musikalischen...* GA 283; most of which are published in *The Inner Nature of Music and the Experience of Tone*. AP. 1983, also *Art as seen in the Light of Mystery Wisdom*. GA 275. AP. 1984, and *The Arts and their Mission*. GA 276. AP 1964. Lea van der Pals, a leading eurythmist in Dornach, has achieved a creative synthesis of what Steiner gave on the subject in her book *The Human Being as Music*. Stourbridge. 1992 (distrib. <eurythmywm@gmail.com>).

Eurythmie als Sichtbarer Gesang (GA 278) was first published in English as *Eurythmy as Visible Song* in 1932. In the second edition (1977) this title was changed to *Eurythmy as Visible Music*, presumably on the grounds that eurythmy is not practised with singers (for reasons Steiner gives in Lecture 7 below). However, the original designation *sichtbarer Gesang* is unusual in German, too. The literal translation "visible singing" is what Steiner had in mind, more active than either "visible music" or "visible song". Steiner sometimes said *sichtbares Singen*, "visible singing" (14 Feb. 1920 in GA 277 and Tb 642, and in the essay "Das Goetheanum…" IV, 1924 in GA 36 and Tb 635. 142); and in Lecture 6, in connection with instrumental music, he said *Gesangseurythmie* – "a singing eurythmy" (64). *Gesang* is translated as "singing" because it points to three central issues:

(1) the human being as the creative source of music;

(2) the origin of all instrumental music in singing, intrinsically and historically;

(3) the possibility of expressing this human essence in artistic movement.

Steiner sums it up: "Eurythmy is a singing through movement; it is singing. It is not dancing; it is not mime." Lecture 7; see also GA 277. 337. Ralph Kux explains:

> The eurythmical artist… perceives instrumental music through the ear and straight away transforms it into an inwardly heard singing, and fashions this singing into visible movement. Consequently we can speak of a "visible singing" and not of a "visible music" (R. Kux. Erinnerungen an Rudolf Steiner. Melinger Verlag. Stuttgart. 1976. 52; tr. A.S.).

It also seems reasonable that a conscientious translator should be consistent in following the use of one of the main branches of the English language. Clarity of meaning is thereby encouraged. As this translation aims, in the first place, for accuracy in English as it is used in Britain, we should clarify three words. The German *Ton* means "sound", more specifically "musical sound", and "note". In the U.S.A. the term "tone" might cover some, but not all, of the uses: both English and American musicians sing and play "notes". To British musicians, the word "tone" denotes a major second; it also refers to the quality of sound. Interestingly, Shakespeare's Titania begs, "I pray you gentle mortal, sing again/ Mine ear is much enamoured of thy note"; Don Pedro advises: "do it in notes." Steiner, too, sometimes uses *Note* and *Noten* in his lectures. Eurythmy employs sound as its raw material: *Laut* – speech sound, *Ton* – musical sound. For *Lauteurythmie*

Sp '19 X-over w/ Coursework!

we rightly say "speech-eurythmy", and for *Toneurythmie*, logically "music-eurythmy". This term suggests itself as one which avoids misunderstanding and consequently one which could be internationally acceptable. But it may genuinely not be desirable to have an "internationally acceptable" term.

Incidentally, Steiner uses the expressions *musikalische Eurythmie* ("musical eurythmy") and *musikalisches Eurythmisieren* (literally "musical eurythmising") in Lecture 5; *musikalische Eurythmisierende* ("the person engaged in music eurythmy") in Lecture 6, and *Musikgebärde* ("gestures of music[-eurythmy]") in Lecture 1. Owen Barfield, in his article "The Art of Eurythmy", in *The Golden Blade.* RSP. London 1954, speaks of "speech-eurythmy", "musical eurythmy", and simply "eurythmy".

The Romance languages use the words "music" and "musical": *eurythmie musicale* (French), *euritmia musicale* (Italian), *euritimia da musica* (Portuguese), *eurythmia de la musica* (Spanish). Hebrew possesses only one word for both musical and speech sound (*tzlil*), and so uses "music" too: *oritmia im-musica.* Eastern Europe uses the word "musical", for example: *muzikalaija evritmija* (Russian), *musikalna evritmia* (Bulgarian). The Japanese, too, use their equivalent word for "music". Since this translation uses English as it is spoken in Britain, *Ton* is translated as "sound", "musical sound" and "note" according to the context. Here, as in general, I have been guided by *The Oxford Dictionary of Music* (1985) and *The New Oxford Companion to Music* (1983), *The New Grove Dictionary of Music and Musicians* (1980), and *Collins Encyclopaedia of Music* (1976). Those who feel they are closer to the Teutonic tradition, and who prefer the earlier terms "tone" and "tone-eurythmy" that have been hallowed by use, will realise that these terms sound like jargon, at least in Britain. It should also be said that the modern meaning of the word "tone" for acoustics and electronics, for example, as implied in "a musical note, without its harmonics" (from the first sentence of the entry "Tone" in *The International Cyclopaedia of Music and Musicians.* Ed. Oscar Thompson. Dodd, Mead and Co. New York and Toronto/ Dent, London; 10th edition 1975. 2293), is the opposite of what Steiner means by *Ton*. For the fourth edition of this work, I have decided to be consequential, whatever people decide for themselves locally.

Eurythmists, Steiner explains, have to "raise" their bodies "through work", so that their bodies (their instruments) can appear as if moving in the etheric realm. Translators, similarly, have to "raise" their thinking. In fact, anyone who manages to do this can "approach [the archangel] Michael" (lecture 13 Jan. 1924. GA 233a). "Christology", Steiner says elsewhere (Lecture 1 Aug. 1915), "has nothing to do with any division of man and mankind." But he does emphasise that realisation comes only from within. The "raising" mentioned above is also attempted by all those who have contributed their labour of love to the present work. No translation, of course, can claim to be "perfect". Even were this translation good, it could still be better. Any comments in this direction would be appreciated. Endnote numbers in square brackets refer to the section "Notes to the Lectures". In addition to the Appendices on specific subjects, this 4th English edition includes an English translation of J.M. Hauer's manifesto which helped Rudolf Steiner in so many ways.

Eurythmists will be for ever grateful to Marie Steiner for her incalculable contribution to eurythmy. Her main concern, however, was the speech work. Her synopsis of the present lectures which appeared in the first edition (*Eurythmy as Visible Song*) even contains an occasional misleading statement. Her original titles for these lectures have been slightly revised here. The third edition of *Eurythmy as Visible Singing* appeared during the bicentenary of Schiller's *Aesthetic Letters* (1794) and the centenary of Steiner's own *The Philosophy of Freedom* (1894). Both books are recommended by Steiner for eurythmy students. What worthier companions could be imagined for the present lecture-course, which is an attempt to blaze a trail between naturalism and abstraction in art, in order to get beyond materialism? Hopefully that edition, appearing in 1994 (seventy years after the lectures were held), could encourage a further step in bringing about that which Goethe called "Nature's worthiest exponent, Art". The same wish accompanies this fourth edition, appearing 100 years after the birth of eurythmy.

Acknowledgements

Two eurythmists in particular have helped with many valuable suggestions regarding this translation, for which I am deeply indebted. Dorothea Mier lent me the translation notes she kept from study groups held throughout the years she has spent in training eurythmists. Her colleague, Barbara Schneider-Serio, provided me with copious and detailed suggestions both before and after the editing stage. She is responsible for felicitous solutions to several difficult translation problems, and the final result should be termed a collaboration. Both of these artists helped me to keep as close as possible to Steiner's expressions (sometimes even at the expense of "smooth" English) and to beware of making slight "interpretations". The reader's access to Steiner's meaning should be as direct as possible. [Translator's additions are included between square brackets.] Margaret Miles and Maren Stott also spent time checking the translation, and they made many valuable suggestions at several stages of the work. Suggestions from some of my own students have been included. Katherine Stewart's, an American eurythmist, editing and exemplary professional attitude, I took to be another positive sign for international relations in the world of eurythmy as we approached the millennium. I am indebted to her for the interest and support she unstintingly gave. Dr David Rycroft kindly edited the Introduction and Endnotes at an earlier stage. Terry Boardman, a eurythmist and historian who has lived in Japan, helped with Appendices 4, 5 and 8, and checked the text. Naturally I am responsible for certain choices in this translation (such as keeping to English as spoken in England), and I am responsible for all the defects of the final version. I am grateful to all those people who helped me to realise how important it is today to know what we are doing. I might also be allowed to express here my gratitude to all the performers, eurythmy students, and pupils of the Waldorf Schools for whom I have played, and from whom I have learned. Thank you, all of you.

Written on 20 Sept. 1993, the eightieth anniversary of the laying of the foundation stone of the First Goetheanum, Dornach, Switzerland; revised 2011, the centenary of the birth of eurythmy.

Alan Stott, Stourbridge

Note to corrected 3rd and 4th editions

My grateful thanks go to a colleague, Julian Clarke, for several improvements to the section concerning the bar line (Lecture 4) and for his contribution of Endnote 32, also to Werner Barfod for the readiness with which he complied to my request for Endnote 66. Numbers in 00 boxes refer to the Endnotes to the Lectures. Other suggestions for improvement have not reached me. Very few other changes have been made to the translation. *"Ergreifen"* is now rendered (p. 47) more accurately as "laying-hold", rather than simply "understanding" (previous ed., p. 14), which I argue now acquires the status of a technical term (truth be told, "understanding" in eurythmy really *is* a "laying-hold"! "Devotion" (86/122) is a more correct rendering of *Hingeben*; the translator's addition [ ] on p. 52/88 is revised; the *"e"* (previous ed. 68, l. 10) is now corrected to *"ee"* (58, 3 lines from below; this 4th edition 92, 4 lines from below). I am grateful to *Rudolf Steiner Nachlassverwaltung* for the opportunity to study NB 494, to publish the missing entries and to report my discoveries (forthcoming).

Further small corrections were made in 2013, particularly in Lecture 4: p. 74 para 2, third sentence, now reads: "As physical human being marking the *beat*; as etheric human being expressing the *rhythm*; as astral human being evolving the *melos*; it is thus that I appear before the world"; and in Lecture 5: "freedom to carry out the movements beautifully" is now correctly "freedom to carry out each individual movement beautifully" (53/89); Lecture 7: "left and right sides of the collar-bone" becomes (twice) "left and right collar-bone" (68/102). An arrow is added to Fig. 18, and an arrow moved in Fig. 20. The adopted pagination system, admittedly cumbersome, solved a computer problem – hopefully but a trifling inconvenience.

Alan Stott, Stourbridge, Easter 1998, rev. 2013

PLEASE NOTE

The forthcoming 6th German edition of *Eurythmie als sichtbarer Gesang* will contain the results of a detailed examination of the original shorthand report of the lectures. Further impressions of the present English edition will contain details and any necessary revisions to the English translation. The passages in question will also be avalible for download on my website <www.alansnotes.co,uk> and the publishers <www.anastasiltd-book-matters.com> as soon as possible after the German revisions have become available.

A.S. June 2013

Pronunciation

A,	"ah",	as in	*father*
E,	"a",	as in	*mate*
I,	"ee",	as in	*meet*
O,	"o",	between	*ought* and *obey*
U,	"oo",	as in	*moot*
Ö,	"ir",	similar in	*birth*
Ü,	"eu",	similar in	*feud*
AI,	"ei",	as in	*height*
AU,	"ow",	as in	*how*
W,	"v",	as in	*volume*

The above are approximate English equivalents (for example, "*a*" and is actually a diphthong). The vowels of German resemble Scots pronunciation of English, rather than that of some English as spoken in America, Australia, New Zealand, South Africa, and so on. The eurythmy gestures for the vowels, it should be noted, are archetypal gestures, standing behind local and national variations of pronunciation, including those of the German language.

To avoid possible confusion in the text, phonetic spelling has been reproduced in italics. In Lecture 4, where a poem by Goethe is discussed, some German sounds are also given, with phonetic reminders as listed above.

Abbreviations

AP   Anthroposophic Press, New York.

GA   *Gesamtausgabe*; Bibliographic Survey numbers of Steiner's complete works (Dornach 1961).

MS   Manuscript translation awaiting funding for possible publication.

OUP   Oxford University Press, Oxford.

RSP   Rudolf Steiner Press, London.

Tb   *Taschenbuch*, paperback edition, Dornach, Switzerland.

INTRODUCTION TO THE THIRD ENGLISH EDITION

The musical element

When speaking of the arts, Rudolf Steiner (1861–1925) emphasises that the musical element increasingly belongs to the future of humanity. [1] In the following words [2] he points to the mission of music:

> Fundamentally speaking, music is the human being, and indeed it is from music that we rightly learn how to free ourselves from matter. For if music were to become materialistic, it would actually be false: it is not "there"! Every other form of matter is present in the world and is insistent. But musical sounds are not to be found in the material world in their original form. We have to devise a means of producing them; they must first be made. The soul element that lives in the human being lies between the notes. But today, because the world has become so unmusical, people are scarcely aware of it.

This passage also witnesses to Steiner's own particular mission at the beginning of the twentieth century: to sow seeds in the cultural life which could enable humanity to find its way from estrangement to co-operation with the world of spirit. This concept is of immense practical importance in a century which has allowed the forces of technology and finance to encroach into the realm rightly belonging to the free human spirit. About the time of these lectures, Steiner was responding to requests from many professional quarters for advice which would provide creative stimuli. Lecture-courses were given to experts seeking renewal in their particular fields: science, medicine, agriculture, religion, the arts, education and therapeutic education. "The development of anthroposophical activity into the realm of art resulted out of the nature of anthroposophy." The art of eurythmy, however, occupies a unique position as the newly-born daughter of anthroposophy itself. [3]

For Steiner, it is not only music; all the arts are to become more musical. Steiner is concerned with living, creative activity. He communicated this vision most succinctly in a far-reaching lecture in Torquay. [1] Like J.M. Hauer (1883–1959), whose theoretical writings he knew, Steiner uses the Greek *Melos* ("tune", "musical line") for pure pitch (*Melodie* – "melody", of course, includes rhythm and beat. See also Steiner's Notebook 494. 11). Both Hauer and Steiner use "melos" to indicate the actual creative principle in music. "Melos is the musical element", Steiner claims (Lecture 4). In this translation I have retained the word "melos" where it is employed. One might mentally paraphrase "melos" as "inner Voice".

In speech, melos only "peeps through". But it "poured into" oriental architecture, which "really did transpose music into movement". "Oriental architecture has within it a great deal of eurythmy", we read in Lecture 5. The word "rhythm" comes from the Greek *rhuthmos* (measured motion, time rhythm), from *rhe-ein* (to flow). The word "eurhythmy" is an architectural term: "beautiful proportion, hence beautiful, harmonious movement" (*Oxford English Dictionary*). Laurens van der Post mentions the "eurhythmic grace" of certain beautiful animal movements in his African writings. "Eurythmy" and "melos", accordingly, have existed and still exist both in nature and in human culture. Both worlds unite in the art of eurythmy, which cultivates melos, and was brought to birth through Rudolf Steiner. Otto Fränkl-Lundborg claims the spelling of "eurythmy" without the "h" is philologically correct; *rho* as suffix loses its aspirate. (See *Das Goetheanum*. 49. Jg. Nr. 30. 26 July 1970. 246).

Steiner, like Hauer, uses the expression *das Musikalische* ("the musical") more often than *die Musik* ("music"), and in this way emphasises the inner activity before the technicalities of the craft come into consideration. This is a supremely important detail. In English we have to extend this to phrases like "the musical element", or "the realm of music", which may be clumsy, but they are accurate. What Steiner has in mind and continuously refers to is the musical essence. This is not only the concern of musicians, for it is the underlying creative, transforming force of life itself, present in all vital human expression. (We may justly remark that "music" does not exist solely for musicians!) Moreover, music bears a direct relationship to the path of mankind's inner development. This development can be prepared and assisted by the inner activity of individuals on the path of initiation, [4] which is described by Steiner [5] as a process of development through God's grace, involving Imagination, Inspiration and Intuition (spiritual vision, inner hearing and a higher life):

> Long, long before the human being enters consciously into the stages of initiation, he is able to express these experiences in his own way in images, and this is done through music! In the final analysis genuine music is essentially a developing drama of life taking its course in musical sounds, which are an external picture of what the soul consciously experiences in the life of initiation.

We may sense that Steiner channelled his own musicality into his work as a teacher of humanity, and this he confirmed [6] more than once:

> It gave me particular pleasure to be told one day by one of our artistically-gifted

friends that some of the lecture-cycles I have given could be transcribed into symphonies purely on the basis of their inner structure. Some of the courses are indeed based in their structure on something very like this. Take for instance the lecture-course given in Vienna on life between death and a new birth: you will see that you could make a symphony of it.

The art of eurythmy has been given to us as a gift from the future. Its evolution depends upon each individual eurythmist, musician and speaker developing an inner listening with his or her artistic feeling. This must be developed, not in an ecstatic way, but as a spiritual path the individual undertakes while within the body. This inner activity, Steiner insists – in answer to Hauer –, can be revealed in art by raising sensory experience. [7] The present lecture-course may prove to be the best companion on such a path, which is akin to the practising of a musician. This is a demanding exercise, but however small the progress, it forms the substance of true art, and can be offered as nourishment to a world in need. [8]

One of the questions today concerns recorded sound (see Appendix 6). After following the arguments concerning recordings, it can be refreshing to return to the present course of lectures. Though modestly described as "only a beginning", Steiner begins where many of the great musicians of his time, and the ensuing decades, leave off. [9]

Music's turning point

Steiner characterises music as the art which "contains the laws of our ego". [10] If we could consciously dive down into our astral body, the musician in us, we could perceive the cosmic music that has formed us: "… with the help of the astral body, the cosmos is playing our own being… The ancients felt that earthly music could only be a mirroring of the heavenly music which began with the creation of mankind." Modern humanity has been led into the muddy, materialistic swamp of darkness and desire, which obscures this music. But there is a path of purification leading to perception of the music of the spheres once again. When we hear a symphony we dive with soul and spirit into the will, which is usually asleep in daytime consciousness. Art – "even the nature of major and minor melodies" [10] – can bring life to the connection between man and cosmos – in other words, anthroposophy –; to what might appear as dead form. Steiner warns "that these things are not a skeleton of ideas!" hinting that his *Theosophy* was written musically, not schematically.

The present lectures on eurythmy represent Steiner's greatest contribution to musical studies. When he gave them in 1924, he advised the eurythmists to study Hauer's theoretical writings. J.M. Hauer was a musician who discovered atonal melody, or twelve-note music, at the same time (or even just before) as Schönberg did by a different route. Both composers endeavoured to get beyond the materialistic swamp through spiritual striving. [11] By 1924, Hauer had published his own attempt at a Goethean theory of music, [12] and his *Deutung des Melos*. English translation ("Interpreting Melos: A questions to the artists and thinkers of our time") includes an appreciation of Goethe's *Theory of Colour*. [13] In these eurythmy lectures, Steiner appears to agree with Hauer's diagnosis of the modern situation as "noise"; Wagner's music, for example, is "unmusical music", though justified. Steiner seems to agree with Hauer's spiritual principle of melos, "the actual musical element" (to Hauer "movement itself", or the "T A O", the interpretation of which is "the only true spiritual science"). He reproduces Hauer's correspondence of vowels and intervals, writing in his notebook Hauer's list of examples (Notebook 494. 11, left), and he retells the story of the Arab listening to a contrapuntal piece, who asks for it to be played "one tune at a time". But Steiner certainly does not agree with Hauer's answer to the challenge of materialism. "Those who deride materialism are bad artists, bad scientists," Steiner declares. [14] Instead of criticism, he offers help.

In his profound study on Bach, Erich Schwebsch suggests that eurythmy arrived just at the right time in the evolution of mankind. [15] His justification of music-eurythmy is unlikely to be supplanted. With the founding of music-eurythmy, a new beginning opens up for the art of music too. This thought was also expressed by the musician and eurythmist Ralph Kux. [16] It remains for me to draw attention to the counter-phenomenon accompanying this new beginning.

The counter-tendency, so strongly marked in Hauer's thought and life, artificially separates itself from the human roots of music. Steiner's answer to Hauer's dissatisfaction with western culture was to give a further impetus to music-eurythmy (already born but still in its infancy) by tracing the origin of music back to the human being. Through a conscious "turning inside out" within the organism, at the point of departure in the collar-bone, the cosmic music that formed us (flowing in between the shoulder-blades) is released and made available for artistic ends. [17] Music today, he implies, is not a purely spiritual, meditative affair, leading (as later in Hauer's career) a reclusive life. The music of the spheres sought along the old paths "out there" in the cosmos leads to an abstract caricature today. The living connection is to be found on earth, in the human being. [18] Steiner was in all things concerned with living, creative activity. The arts are the means whereby inner activity and experience become outer expression "to present the soul and spirit in fullest concentration… is basically the highest ideal of all art". [19] The arts remind us of the meaning in our earthly destiny. Steiner's meditative verse, written for Marie Steiner at Christmas 1922, begins: "The stars once spake to man" – but what leads to the future is "what man speaks to the stars". [20]

Albert Steffen expresses it clearly: there is a splitting of the way "concerning the life or death of music as such… The whole of humanity stands before this alternative. There is no way back. Every individual has to go through it or come to grief". [21] In one of his most inspired articles, Hermann Pfrogner – a musicologist and authority on twentieth-century developments – characterises the one path of experience as the way of "universal concord", and the other as "ego concord". [22] The former path leads to universal spirituality, to a dissolving of the self. The latter path leads to a maturing of the self. Pfrogner accociates the former spirituality with the impulse emanating from the conspiracy of Jundi-shapur (seventh century AD – further details can be found in Ruland), [29] which echoes on in Islamic culture; the maturing spirituality he associates with the Christian west. Inclinations to dissolve the ego, as a "blossoming (*Aufgehen*) of the individual", [23] spiritually subscribes to Arabism, whereas all steps toward strengthened responsibility follow the latter path. But this latter path leads to an extension of the diatonic system, "that resounding image of the human being pure and simple" (Pfrogner).

The path to overcome materialism, further elucidated by Pfrogner, [24] will not be reached by avoiding the swamp of man's egotism and hastily "reaching for the stars" (the arrangement of twelve) to the exclusion of the diatonic system (based on the number seven). Lurking in such a counter-reaction to romanticism (which, like Viennese classicism, arose in the age of materialism as a protest) is an implied denial of the Christ-event. "Christ Jesus inaugurated an evolution in human nature, based on the retention of the ego's full consciousness. He inaugurated the initiation of the ego," Steiner explains. [25] "With Christ," Friedrich Rittelmeyer reminds us in his last book, "the whole orientation of humanity is changed. And from now on we no longer look back with longing to the past, to a 'golden age' of the primal beginning, but look forward toward fulfilment, creating the future…" [26] There is a path through the swamp which has been trodden by composers such as Bartok, Hindemith, Messiaen, Martinu, Sibelius, Vaughan Williams, Shostakovich, Britten, Tippett, Hartmann, Henze, Schnittke, Gubaidulina, Pärt and many others – following in their own ways the example of the modern "Prometheus", Beethoven. [27]

Musical art of the future

On more than one occasion, Steiner, speaking of the future of music, pointed to "finding a melody in the single note". [28] In the eurythmy lectures he points out that this does not mean listening to the acoustic "chord of overtones" in *a* single note – on which Hauer and Hindemith base their theoretical work. It is a supersensory experience. One of the climaxes of the investigations of Pfrogner and Heiner Ruland (one of the former's successors), is the working out of Steiner's hints of a development of our tonal system. [29]

Here mention should be made of two other pioneers in musical studies whose work is acknowledged by Ruland in his *Expanding Tonal Awareness*. Ernst Bindel developed the relationship between mathematics and music. [30] Without some mathematics there can be no responsible step towards a musical future. The other pioneer is H.E. Lauer, [31] whose account of the evolution of tonal systems has subsequently been considerably developed by Ruland.

We conclude with a suggestion regarding "artistic longing", made by Steiner some months before the lectures translated here:

> If someone feels that here on earth he does not fulfil what lies in his arche-type, with its abode in the heavens, there arises in him an artistic longing for some outer image of that archetype. Whereupon he can gain the power to become an instrument for expressing the true relation of man to the world by becoming a eurythmist. The eurythmist says: "All the movements which I ordinarily carry out here on earth do less than justice to the mobile arche-type of man. To present the ideal human archetype I must begin by finding a way to unite with its movements." These movements, through which the human being endeavours to imitate in space the movements of his heavenly archetype, constitute eurythmy. [32]

Steiner wrote in his Notebook (see p. 197, below) for the present eurythmy course:

> In the *musical element* the spatial human being
> is transformed into the non-spatial human being –
> the spiritual human being is the *inner* origin
> of the musical element.

Artistic people often think more naturally in evocative images, rather than with philosophical or technical concepts about "the spiritual human being" or "the heavenly archetype". And ultimately the inner life cannot express itself other than in images. Artistic readers looking for direction to surmount materialism may be able to grasp the necessity for decisive action more directly in the form of a picture. It may be appropriate to recall a passage from one of Selma Lagerlöf's novels to show the precision of Steiner's statement. An image of the Christ-child is kept in a basilica run by Franciscan monks. An Englishwoman plans to steal this image and replace it with a cheap imitation.

> When the copy was ready she took a needle and scratched into the crown: "My kingdom is only of this world." It was as if she was afraid that she herself would not be able to distinguish one image from the other. And it was as if she wished to appease her own conscience. "I have not wished to make a false Christ-image. I have written in his crown: 'My kingdom is only of this world'." [33]

Stourbridge, Michaelmas 1993 Alan Stott

---

[1] R. Steiner. *True and False Paths in Spiritual Investigation*. GA 243. RSP 1975. An accurate translation of the section on music (last part of the final lecture of 24 Aug. 1922) appears in Lea van der Pals. 1992. 71ff. Compare: "The basic mood of the new world conception [since the Mystery of Golgotha] is musical, whereas the basic mood of the old world was sculptural. The basic mood of the new age is really musical, and the world will become ever more musical. In order to continue rightly on the path of human evolution, we must know the importance of striving towards a musical element and not repeating the old sculptural one" (R. Steiner. "Der Baum des Lebens und der Baum der Erkenntnis des Guten und Bosen" ["The tree of life and the tree of knowledge of good and evil"] lecture, Dornach. 31 July 1915. GA 162 [tr. A.S.]; see also Appendix 4, "R. Steiner. Torquay. 22 Aug. 1924").

[2] R. Steiner. GA 278. Lecture 3; 67 below.

[3] The name "anthroposophy" ("wisdom of the human being") is not used in any of Steiner's basic books. It appeared before the world for the first time one year after the founding of the Anthroposophical Society (1913), in the final chapter of R. Steiner. *Riddles of Philosophy* [original ed. 1914, E.T. AP .1973], "A brief outline of an approach to anthroposophy". In this chapter, reference is made to the author's *Truth and Science* (1882), *The Philosophy of Freedom* (1894), and the lecture "The psychological foundations and epistemological position of spiritual science", delivered before the Philosophical Congress, Bologna, 18 April 1911.

"Eurythmy has grown out of the soil of the anthroposophical movement, [originating] like a gift of destiny" (R. Steiner. "Eurythmy: what it is and how did it come into being". Lecture, Penmaenmawr. 26 Aug.1923 in *Eurythmy as Visible Singing*. Anastasi. 2005. 172-83). "The artistic element will be an elixir of life of the anthroposophical movement" (R. Steiner. Intro. to a eurythmy performance on the occasion of the founding of the General Anthroposophical Society. Dornach 5 Jan. 1924. GA 277. 423). See also R. Steiner. "Das Goetheanum in seinen zehn Jahren" ("The Goetheanum, ten years in retrospect"). Essay 14 Jan. 1924. GA 36 & Tb 635. 131. For a detailed account, see R. Steiner. *Eurythmy: Its Birth and Development*. GA 277a. Anastasi. 2002; R. Steiner. *Eurythmie – die Offenbarung der Sprechende Seele* ("Eurythmy – revelation of the speaking soul") GA 277. Dornach 1972;

a paperback mainly consisting of selections is published: *Eurythmie*. Tb 642. Dornach. 1986. Some introductions are translated in R. Steiner. *Eurythmy: an Introduction*. AP. 1984; lecture 14 Feb. 1920. E.T. R. Steiner. *The Inner Nature of Music…* AP. 1983.

[4] Rational thinking is not jettisoned in favour of "mysticism" or something else. The spiritual activity within thinking itself can be strengthened for investigating and creating within the realm of the spirit. The spiritual activity of pure thinking, the higher union of science and religion demonstrated by Steiner, was prophesied, for example, by Emerson: "No man ever prayed heartily without learning something. But when a faithful thinker, resolute to detach every object from personal relations and see it in the light of thought, shall, at the same time, kindle science with the fire of the holiest affections, then will God go forth anew into the creation" (R.W. Emerson, tract on "Nature", Chapter VIII [1836]. See also, Richard G. Geldard. *The Esoteric Emerson*. The Lindisfarne Press. West Stockbridge, Mass. 1993).

[5] R. Steiner. *Art as seen in the Light of Mystery Wisdom*. GA 275. Lecture, Dornach 30 Dec. 1914. RSP 1996. 60, slightly corrected.

[6] R. Steiner. *Practical Advice to Teachers*. GA 294. Lecture, Stuttgart 28 Aug. 1919. RSP. 1976. The lecture-course referred to is R. Steiner. *The Inner Nature of Man and the Life Between Death and a New Birth*. GA 153. Vienna 9-14 April. 1914. RSP. 1959. Steiner aimed at a marriage of form and content in his work, which is the lofty artistic ideal. After the Christmas Foundation of 1923/4, he reached a new level in this respect. In connection with the subject matter of GA 153, *cf.*, "Contrary to the works of architects, sculptors and painters, musical works must be repeatedly generated anew; they flow onwards in the surge and swell of their melodies, a picture of the soul, which in its incarnations always has to experience itself afresh in the progressive stream of time. The soul flows down from its spiritual homeland and returns thither – likewise its shadow-images: notes and harmonies. Hence the intimate effect of music on the soul" (R. Steiner. Lecture, Berlin. 12 Nov. 1906. *The Inner Nature of Music…* AP. 1983).

Steiner confirmed that, "[f]or anyone who would read my *Occult Science* as today one would read a novel or any other book, passively giving oneself to it, it is really only a thicket of words – and so are my other books. It is only someone who knows in every moment of reading that he must create out of his own soul's depths, and through his most intimate will – which the books should stimulate – only this person is able to regard these books as musical scores from which he can experience the true music. This active experience of the individual soul, moreover, is what we need" (R. Steiner. *Heilfaktoren für den sozialen Organismus*. Lecture, Dornach 2 July 1920. GA 198. Tr. A.S. See also R. Steiner. *The Gospel of St John*. Lecture XI. Hamburg. 30 May 1908. GA 103. RSP. 1978; GA 278. Lecture 6 below, and Endnotes to the Lectures 39).

The implications for the musician are discussed by Erich Schwebsch in his pioneer study on anthroposophy and music. He concludes: "The cosmology of *Occult Science* contains in its thoughts the best exercises for a meditative musician who is searching for new forms today." E. Schwebsch. *J. S. Bach und Die Kunst der Fuge*. Stuttgart. 1988. Chapter 4. "Musik als Offenbarung des Geistes. Aphoristische Betrachtungen". 193 ("J. S. Bach and The Art of Fugue"; Chap. 4. "Music as revelation of the spirit. Aphoristic observations").

[7] In his first lecture (before the Goethe Society. Vienna. 9 Nov. 1888), Steiner said: "Beauty is not the divine in a cloak of physical reality; no, it is physical reality in a cloak that is divine. The artist does not bring the divine on to the earth by letting it flow into the world; he raises the world into the sphere of the divine" (R. Steiner. *Goethe as Founder of a new Science of Aesthetics* [London c.1927; reissued Botton ND]; and included in R.

Steiner. *Art as Spiritual Activity.* Ed. M. Howard. AP. 1998. 113-34). Steiner claims that this lecture, already in 1888, contains "a sound foundation for anthroposophy and the anthroposophical way of thinking" (Preface to the 2nd ed. 1919). The lecture suggests an acid test for what is truly new. Movements exist today which bear the adjective "spiritual" but do not attempt any transformation. Indeed, it is often stated that "no musical knowledge is necessary"! Is not the call for courage against despondency and inadequacy met right here with every individual?

[8] See Schwebsch, Endnote 6. Pfrogner, in the chapter "und was nun?" ("and what now?") in his extensive study on "the living world of music", presents a clear vision of tasks for the future: "No longer *l'art pour l'art*, but simply and solely: *l'art pour l'homme* will be the saying of the hour. This "art for human beings", however, will have to be an art totally "from human beings", an art in the above-mentioned sense "raised" from the human being, if it should be true "nourishment for life"" (H. Pfrogner. *Lebendige Tonwelt.* Langen Müller. München/Wien. 1981. 474, tr. A.S.).

[9] For example: John Foulds. *Music Today.* Ivor Nicholson and Watson. London. 1934; Cyril Scott. *Music.* Rider. London. 1933/58; Aquarian. Wellingborough. 1976; Bruno Walter. *Theme and Variations.* Hamish Hamilton. London. 1947, and *On Music and Music-Making.* Faber. London. 1957; W. Furtwängler. *Concerning Music.* Boosey & Hawkes. London. 1953; Artur Schnabel. *My Life and Music.* C. Smythe. New York and Gerrards Cross/ Dover. 1988, and *Music and the Line of Most Resistance.* Princeton 1942/ Excellence in Music, Inc. 2007; Edwin Fischer. *Reflections on Music.* Williams & Norgate. London. 1951; Ralph Vaughan Williams. *National Music and other Essays.* OUP. Oxford. 1987; J. Ma. Corredor, *Conversations with Casals.* Duddon. New York. 1956.

[10] R. Steiner. *Art as seen in the Light of Mystery Wisdom.* Lecture, Dornach. 29 Dec. 1914. GA 275. RSP. 1996.

[11] For the best introduction to this perspective, see H. Pfrogner, *Zwölfordnung der Töne.* Zürich/Leipzig/Wien. 1953; reprinted in H. Pfrogner, *Zeitwende der Musik.* Langen Müller, München/Wien 1986; tr. in MS "Music's turning point of time".

[12] J. M. Hauer. *Vom Wesen des Musikalischen.* 1920/ later ed. Robert Lienau. Berlin-Lichterfelde. "The essence of music".

[13] J. M. Hauer. *Deutung des Melos.* Tal & Co. Verlag. Leipzig/ Wien/ Zürich. 1923. "Interpreting Melos". Germ. original held at R. Steiner Library, 35 Park Road, London NW1 6XT e-mail: <rsh-library@anth.org.uk.> ET Part III, below.

[14] R. Steiner. *The Arts and Their Mission.* Lecture Oslo. 18 May 1923. GA 276. AP. 1964. 111.

[15] Schwebsch presented his eloquent conclusion already in 1930: "But all inner experience of the soul when it is ripe to that end, wishes to become visible, perceptible. The soul world desires to become objective. The first beginning for this becoming visible of vitally filled musical movement, from the All rising up behind the Nothing [an echo from Goethe's *Faust*, Part 2, 6256. Tr. note.] of the vanishing past, at the exact nadir of time, is the art of music-eurythmy: visible singing, newly created by Rudolf Steiner." E. Schwebsch. 1988. 211. Chapter 4 is more than the title suggests. It is an anthroposophical musician's "credo", which applies to Steffen's essay (see Endnote 21 below), too.

[16] R. Kux and W. Kux. *Erinnerungen an Rudolf Steiner und Eurythmie und Musik.* Mellinger Verlag. Stuttgart 1976. Tr. *EA Newsletter.* Aberdeen 1997. "Recollections of R. Steiner"; "Eurythmy and music".

[17] See R. Steiner. *The Essentials of Education.* GA 308. Lecture 10 April 1924 a.m. RSP. 1982. 58. The physiology is explained in Armin Husemann. *The Harmony of the*

Human Body. Floris Books. Edinburgh. 1994; Germ. latest ed. *Der musikalische Bau des Menschen.* Verlag Freies Geistesleben. Stuttgart. 4th ed. 2003. Note, for example, with what careful scholarship Dr Husemann explores what *beim Auftreten* ("by stepping", or "with the first step", from Lecture 7) must mean (Section 31. 189ff.). See also Endnotes to the Lectures 55 on *Ansatz.*

[18] Compare Steiner: "Since the Mystery of Golgotha we cannot speak of the music of the spheres as did Pythagoras, but we can speak of it in another way. An initiate might even today speak as Pythagoras did, but the ordinary inhabitant of the earth in his physical body can speak of the music of the spheres and of the cosmic life only when he experiences in his soul, 'Not I, but Christ in me', for the Christ within him has lived in the music of the spheres and in the cosmic life. But we must go through this experience in ourselves; we really must receive Christ into our souls" (R. Steiner. Lecture, Norrköping. 16 July 1914. *Christ and the Human Soul.* GA 155. RSP. 1984. 69-70). The harmony of the spheres is heard "in deep sleep" by the initiate "as if they were the notes of trumpets and the rolling of thunder" (R. Steiner. *An Esoteric Cosmology.* GA 93a. St George Pub. Spring Valley. New York. 1978. Lecture, Paris 30 May 1906. Report by E. Schuré. 45). Steiner's proclamation of Christ rests on knowledge. By the turn of the century, he could say: "The unfolding of my soul rested upon the fact that I had stood in spirit before the Mystery of Golgotha in most inward, most earnest solemnity of knowledge" (R. Steiner. *The Course of my Life.* GA 28. AP. 1951; closing sentence of Chapter XXVI. 276). "Spiritual science is concerned not merely to talk about the Christ, but to declare what the Christ wishes to say to people in our time, through the medium of human thoughts" (R. Steiner. Lecture, Zürich. 4 Feb. 1919. *The Inner Aspect of the Social Question.* GA 193. RSP. 1950. 16).

Steiner indicates what amounts to 84 (= 7 x 12) meditations for musicians: "You have in the fixed stars a wonderful cosmic instrument, and the players of this instrument of the zodiac and fixed stars are the gods of the planets beyond." Lecture, Dornach. 2 Dec. 1922. *The Inner Nature of Music...* GA 283. AP. 1983. 42-3; see also R. Steiner. *The Gospel of St Matthew.* GA 123. Lectures, Berne. 3 & 4. 10 & 12. Oct. 1910. RSP. 1965; R. Steiner. *Universe, Earth and Man.* Lecture, Stuttgart. 12 Aug. 1908. RSP. 1987. 118ff. See also Appendices 3 and 5 below.

[19] R. Steiner. GA 277. 320.

[20] R. Steiner. *Verses and Meditations.* RSP. 1961. 96-97 In this connection, *cf.,* Beckh's definition of "cosmic": "the revelation of the spirit within the earthly realm." Tr. H. Beckh. *Die Sprache der Tonart.* Urachhaus. Stuttgart. 1975. 54; E.T. "The language of tonality", in MS.

[21] Albert Steffen. "Musik" in *Der Künstler und die Erfüllung der Mysterien.* Dornach. 1964. Tr. held by R. Steiner Library, London. An artist could base his life on this astonishing essay.

[22] Hermann Pfrogner. *Zeitwende.* Chap. 17.

[23] Hauer speaks (1922) of "subduing the whole personality for the sake of the problem in hand", an attitude that could be laudable but could also threaten to become fixed and limiting. J.M. Hauer, *Vom Wesen des Musikalischen.* Lienau, Berlin-Lichterfelde 1966. 40. Compare: "When the human being became a personality, God also had to become a personality in order to save him, to give him the possibility of rising again." R. Steiner. *Egyptian Myths and Mysteries.* AP. 1971. 139. Another twentieth-century scientist, comparing his life to that of Goethe's, declared that his goal was "to penetrate into the secret of the personality"; the "central concept" of his psychology is "the principle of individuation". Tr. C.G. Jung. *Memories, Dreams and Reflections.* Fontana. London. 1967.

232 & 235. Sir Julian Huxley summarises Teilhard de Chardin, the scientist-seer: "persons are individuals who transcend their merely organic individuality in conscious participation" (Intro. to Teilhard. *The Phenomenon of Man*. Collins. 1959/ Fontana. 1965. 20/21). A vague pantheism is avoided: "Union differentiates", and "the more "other" [grains of consciousness] become in conjunction, the more they find themselves as "self"" as they make for the "Omega point" of evolution. 261/88. See Endnotes to the Lectures 25.

[24] See Hermann Pfrogner, *Zeitwende*. Langen Müller. München/ Wien. 1986; and *Lebendige Tonwelt* for informed views on musical development right up to the twentieth century.

[25] R. Steiner. *The Gospel of St Matthew*. Lecture, Berne 9 Oct. 1910. RSP. 1965. Steiner explains the meaning of the atonement: "The One suffered for all, so that through the world-historic initiation a substitute has been created for the old form of initiation… Through inner vision, through true mysticism, community with Christ is possible." R. Steiner. *Foundations of Esotericism*. GA 93a. Lecture, Berlin. 27 Sept. 1905. RSP. 1983. 14.

[26] Friedrich Rittelmeyer. *Christus*. Urachhaus. Stuttgart. 1936. 38 (tr. in MS). Rittelmeyer's mature relationship to John's Gospel, with its hidden music, informs his major works. See Alan Stott: "Friedrich Rittelmeyer and the "Song of the earth's perfecting"" in *The Threshing Floor*. May/June 1988. Floris Books. Edinburgh. Another study on the Christ-Impulse is C.E. Raven. *Jesus and the Gospel of Love*. London. 1931/49. See Chapter XV, "Christ in the Twentieth Century".

[27] The following reference to Beethoven's entelechy is the only one that has come to my notice: "I was deeply impressed when a while ago I heard from a famous musician that in a personal conversation Rudolf Steiner said 'Beethoven is Prometheus.' E. Kolisko. "Beethoven", from a series of articles under the title "Reincarnation" in *The Modern Mystic*. September 1938; reprinted, E. Kolisko. *Reincarnation and other Essays*). No doubt the inspiration of Prometheus is meant.

[28] See Endnote 22, in Endnotes to the Lectures.

[29] See Heiner Ruland. *Expanding Tonal Awareness*. Tr. John Logan. RSP. 1992.

[30] Ernst Bindel. *Die Zahlgrundlagen der Musik im Wandel der Zeiten*. Stuttgart. 1985; "The numerical basis of music in its development".

[31] H.E. Lauer. "The Evolution of Music through Changes in Tone-Systems" in *Cosmic Music*, ed. J. Godwin. Inner Traditions. Rochester, Vermont. 1989. Lauer also wrote *Musik und Musiker*. Selbstverlag. ND.

[32] R. Steiner. *The Arts and their Mission*. Lecture, Oslo. 18 May 1923. GA 276. AP. 1964.

[33] Selma Lagerlöf. *The Miracles of Antichrist*. Gay & Bird. London. 1899. 14.

Rudolf Steiner on the Music-Eurythmy Lecture-Course

Report from the *Nachrichtenblatt* (News sheet) of 2nd March 1924 [1]

... Now in the Section for Speech and Music, of which Frau Marie Steiner is the director, it was felt intrinsically necessary to arrange a course on music-eurythmy. The practising artists and eurythmy teachers living in Dornach, and those living elsewhere who were able, took part, in addition the Council Members of the Anthroposophical Society and some personalities interested in music and eurythmy.

So far as is possible in a corresponding manner, the content will be reported in a suitable way. Here in only a few sentences the aims and intentions should be reported. In the art of eurythmy, speech-eurythmy has been developed to a certain extent. We are our own most severe critics, and realise that whatever we manage to achieve in this realm is merely a beginning. But what has begun must be developed further.

Less progress has been made so far with music-eurythmy, "visible singing", than with speech-eurythmy, "visible word". So that the beginning which we have achieved can be continued in the right way, the stage at which music-eurythmy is now practised had to be taken a step further. This was the purpose of the lecture-course. Consequently, the nature of the musical element had to be indicated, too. For in eurythmy, music is made visible, and we have to feel where music has its true source in the human being if its fundamental essence is to be made visible.

Music-eurythmy makes visible that which is invisible, but lives audibly, in music. It is just here that we are in the gravest danger of becoming unmusical. I hope to have demonstrated in the lectures that when music flows over into movement, the urge arises to reject all that is unmusical in music and to make visible only "pure music". Those who hold the view that music ceases when the audible is carried over into visible movement will certainly have reservations about music-eurythmy as such. This view, however, is not in the deepest sense an *artistic* one, for someone who inwardly experiences art must take delight in *every* extension of artistic sources and their forms. It is a fact that music, like all true art, springs forth from man's innermost being. His life can reveal this in the most varying ways. What wants to *sing* in the human being wants to be presented in forms of movement too, and only those possibilities of movement that lie in man's organism are called forth in speech-eurythmy and music-eurythmy. It is the human being himself who reveals *his* essence here. The human form is only truly understood as arrested movement, and only the movement of the human being reveals the *meaning* of his form. It may be said: Someone who disputes the justification of music-eurythmy and speech-eurythmy refuses to allow the human being to appear in his totality. Materialism does not permit the spirit to appear in human understanding, and the rejection of eurythmy as an art that can justifiably stand on a par with the other arts no doubt has its origin in a similar conviction.

It is to be hoped that the eurythmists have received some inspiration from this course, and thus some contribution has been made towards the further development of our art of eurythmy.

Eurythmy figure for the major triad, or cadence

The Eurythmy Figures

In 1921 the sculptress Edith Maryon endeavoured to make models of the eurythmy gestures. However, it was found that eurythmy could not be suitably represented in this medium, and Steiner then designed the wooden eurythmy figures that have since become well known. He gave indications regarding the production and colouring of these figures, some of which remain extant in the original and some in copies by Edith Maryon. The complete set was published as Skizzen zu den Eurythmiefiguren *Dornach. 1957 ("Sketches for the eurythmy figures").*

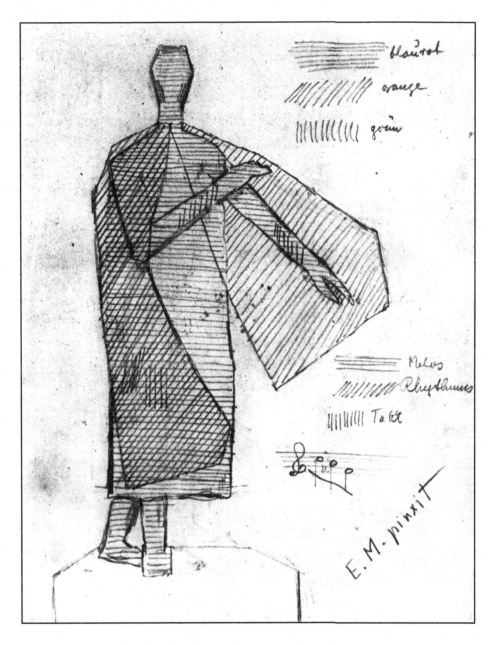

Eurythmy figure for the minor triad, or cadence

The two following examples (the only ones for music) for the major and minor chords (strictly speaking, cadences) are reduced in size by about a half. The figures have been redrawn and newly coloured by Annemarie Bäschlin, and are published as Die Eurythmiefiguren von Rudolf Steiner. *Dornach 1989 ("Rudolf Steiner's eurythmy figures").*

The words written in the two sketches are : orange—*orange,* violet—*violet,* rot-Karmin—*carmine red,* blaurot—*bluish red,* grün—*green,* Melos—*melos,* Rhythmus—*rhythm,* Takt—*beat (see also Endnotes to the Lectures* 59*).*

Lecture 1:
The Experience of Major and Minor

Dornach, 19 Feb. 1924

Speech-eurythmy has been developed up to a certain stage, and it may be said that we have achieved something in this domain. Until now music-eurythmy has only been developed in its very first elements, and due to a remarkable fact which has recently come to my notice, I have been led to give this short course of lectures. From various quarters it is strongly apparent that people have frequently found music-eurythmy more pleasing than speech-eurythmy and comparatively easy to appreciate, whereas speech-eurythmy has seemed much more alien to them. This sad fact, that more significance is attached to something still in its infancy than to something more fully developed, is really a proof that at the present time the understanding 2 for eurythmy has not made much headway. It is of the utmost importance that this understanding should be fostered, and consequently I should like today to begin with certain introductory remarks, which in the light of such understanding may enable you to work for eurythmy.

If we try to develop music-eurythmy out of eurythmy in the more general sense, the opportunity will arise of speaking about this understanding at least in an introductory way. It cannot be denied that on the part of eurythmists themselves, much can be done with a view to increasing a right understanding of eurythmy, for above all what is perceived by the onlooker must be borne in mind. The onlooker not only perceives the movement or gesture that is presented by the eurythmist, he also perceives what the eurythmist is feeling and inwardly experiencing. This makes it essential that the eurythmist actually experiences something while engaged in eurythmy, and especially that which is to be presented. In speech-eurythmy this is the portrayal of the sound of speech, and in music-eurythmy the portrayal of the musical sound.

So far [1915–24], with the exception of the forms 3 which have been created for certain pieces of music, this portrayal of musical sound has consisted of nothing but the bare notes, nothing but mere scales. 4 If in speech-eurythmy we had no more than we have today in music-eurythmy, this roughly would amount to the range of the vowels *ah, a, ee, o, oo*.

Just think how little we would have achieved artistically in speech-eurythmy, if until now we had only been able to make use of the vowel sounds, *ah, a, e, o, oo*! But so far artistically we have actually had no more than this in music-eurythmy. This is why there is something depressing about the kind of judgements about music-eurythmy that reach us, which I have mentioned. And this is also why I believe it to be necessary that now we should at least begin to lay down the foundations of music-eurythmy.

It is necessary, above all, that in eurythmy we should get beyond the mere making of gestures and producing of movements, and that in the realm of music-eurythmy, and in speech-eurythmy too, the actual sounds should be really felt. You must permit me to make this introduction, for in our speech today, and especially in our writing, we no longer have any conception of what a speech sound really is. This is because we no longer give the sound a name, but at the most briefly touch it.

We say *ah*. The Greek language was the last to say alpha. Go back to the Hebrew – aleph. The sound as such had a name then; the sound was something real. The further back we go in language, the more essentially real we find the sounds. When we name the first letter in the Greek alphabet, alpha, and trace back the significance of this word alpha (it is a word which really encompasses the sound), we find that even in the German language many words still exist closely related to what lies in the sound alpha or aleph – as, for instance, when we say *Alp, Alpen* – Alp, the Alps. And this leads us back to *Alp-Elf*, [the] Alp, [the] elf, ⑤ to a being in a state of constant activity, of becoming, of coming-into-being, of lively movement. The *ah* sound has completely lost all this because we no longer say "alpha" or "aleph".

If the alpha or aleph is applied to the human being, then we can really experience the sound *ah*. And how do we experience *ah*? A snail could neither be an aleph, nor yet an alpha. But a fish could be an alpha, an aleph. Why? Because the fish has a spine, and because the spine is really the starting point for the development of such a being as an aleph. It is from the spine that those forces proceed which embrace an alpha-being.

Now try to understand that the spine is the point from which rays forth that which constitutes an alpha or aleph. Then you could roughly experience it by imagining that, as a human being, you could not receive much benefit from your spine [alone], if there were no ribs that go out from it, forming the body. If you then picture the ribs

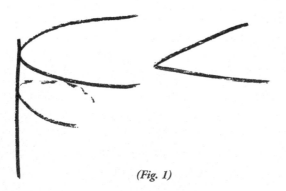

(Fig. 1)

as detached and capable of movement, you get the arms. And then, if you consider it, you arrive at the eurythmic *ah*.

Now you must not think that anyone watching eurythmy sees only this forked angle; if this were so, instead of stretching out your arms you might just as well open out a pair of scissors, or the firetongs! You cannot do this, however, for the onlooker must have a human being before him. And the human being has really to feel the alpha, the aleph, inside. He has to feel that he is opening himself to the world. The world approaches him and he opens himself to it. How do you open yourself to the world? You open yourself to the world most purely when you stand before the world in wonder. All knowledge, said the Greeks, begins with wonder, with amazement. And when you stand before the world in wonder you break out with the sound *ah*.

When you have made the eurythmy movement for *ah*, you have brought your astral body into that position which is indicated by the angle formed by the stretched arms. But this gesture will not ring true if you have never tried to experience the feeling of this fork-like movement of the arms, as has already been mentioned in earlier instructions. Feeling must be in it. You actually have to feel that the sound *ah* is an abbreviation in the air, some sort of abstraction as opposed to the living reality which the human being experiences.

When, let us say, we encircle something with rounded arms, we encircle it with love. When we open ourselves in the form of an angle, we receive the world in wonder. And this mood of wonder is felt by the astral body (contained as it is within the physical body, within the whole human being). This mood of wonder must be felt in practising, once or even repeatedly, if the *ah* is to be true. The making of signs is not the essential thing, but the feeling that it cannot be otherwise (corresponding to a specific inner experience) than that the arms assume a forked angle as you stand confronting the world.

Let us pass on to the sound *a*. [Presenting this sound accurately] depends on being able to feel the *a* – which means holding yourself upright while facing something. In *ah* we open ourselves to the world in wonder; we let the world approach us. When we experience *a* we do not simply allow the world to approach us, but we offer some resistance; we confront the world. The world is there and we stand facing it. This is why the movement for *a* demands that we touch ourselves (crossed hands [in Austrian dialect *die Hand* can begin at the shoulder; consequently it can mean "arm". Tr. note.]). We touch ourselves. We say, as we experience the *a* sound, "I too am here confronting the world". And you will learn to understand the *a* when, in making the gesture, you feel, "I too am here confronting the world, and I want to feel that I too am here". The bringing of one limb into contact with the other awakens this feeling that I too am here.

Now I would have liked things to have developed so that first what we call [the gestures of] the letters or sounds would have been given, and then the urge would have inwardly arisen to develop these experiences out of the letters themselves, for then you would get hold of it. And certainly this has frequently happened subconsciously with many people, though it is not always definitely apparent. But the study of eurythmy must proceed from such things as these, too.

Let us take *o*. In making the gesture for *o*, you form a circle with both arms. You must feel that while experiencing the *o*-gesture, you cannot experience *a*. With *a* you confirm your presence: I too am here confronting the world. With *o* you go out of yourself, enclosing something within yourself. You embrace something. It is important in the *a* that that which you are addressing stays outside and you are inside, within yourself. With *o* there is a kind of falling-asleep-while-staying-awake, in that you allow your whole being to go for a little walk into the space which you enclose with the *o*-gesture. But now that other thing you are addressing is also within this space. Thus, when experiencing the *o*, your feelings are such as these: I approach a tree; I embrace this tree with my arms, but I myself am the tree; [6] I have become a tree-spirit, a tree-soul. There is the tree, and because I myself have become a tree-soul, because I have become one with the tree, I make this gesture. I go out of myself. That which is important for me is enclosed in my arms. This is the feeling of *o*.

The feeling of *oo* is that of being bound up with something, yet wishing to get away from it; following the movement you make and going somewhere else, leaving yourself and preparing your way. I run along my arms when I make the movement for *oo*. I am convinced of it, that in *oo* I stream away, away, away – away in this direction.

You see that this is speech. Speech poses questions. "How does the human being relate to the things of the world?" Speech always asks: "How does the human being relate to the things of the world? Does the world fill him with wonder? Does he stand upright confronting the world? Does he embrace it? Does he flee before it?" Speech is the relationship of the human being to the world. Music is the relationship of the human being, as a being of soul and spirit, to him- or herself.

When, in the way I have just indicated, you try to enter into what may be experienced in the vowel sound *o*, let us say, or *oo*, then you have a distinct going-out of the soul from the body. This is also expressed in the pronunciation. Think of the way in which the sound *o* is spoken, right forward on the lips and with the lips clearly rounded: *o. Oo* is spoken with the lips pushed somewhat outwards: *oo* = away. We have, then, in the gestures made in the air by speech, this going-out-of-ourselves in the sounds *o* and *oo*.

The musical element presents the exact opposite of speech. When you are going out of yourself in speech, the astral body and ego leave the etheric and physical bodies, even if this only occurs partially and imperceptibly. It really is a falling-asleep-while-still-awake when we utter *o* or *oo*, or when we do *o* or *oo* in eurythmy. It is a falling-asleep-while-staying-awake. When you are going out of yourself in *o* or in *oo*, you really are going with your soul into the element of soul. And when I say that with the sounds *o* and *oo* I am going with my astral body out of my physical body, I am speaking in terms of speech.

When I say: "In what I am now experiencing I am going with my soul into my spiritual being" (for in spite of the fact that I go out, I am entering into my spiritual being; just as when falling asleep I enter into my spiritual being too, while forsaking my physical body), this is just the opposite [of what happens in speech]. Thus when I say: "I am entering into my spiritual being in *o* or in *oo*", I am speaking in musical terms. [7]

Now when I reflect upon the sound *o* or *oo*, I am naturally denying the musical element. But the point in question is: what is the musical experience in this going-out-of-ourselves of *o* and *oo*? What is it in music itself that corresponds to the out-going connected with *o* and *oo*? The musical experience which is contained in *o* and in *oo* is, in the most comprehensive sense, the experience of the major mood.

In speaking of the experience of the major mood, it is certainly true that we experience this in the sounds *o* and *oo*. I cannot say that we change our interpretation into an experience of speech, but we change the way we live in this experience. Whenever the sounds *o* or *oo* are uttered, or when a word is uttered in which either of these two sounds is predominant, then, underlying the speech, we musically experience the major mood.

When we reflect upon *ah* and *a*, where we may very clearly perceive the experience, underlying the sounds, of the astral body remaining within the physical body (indeed, we are here made particularly aware of the physical body), this produces a different musical experience. Pay attention, then, to this growing awareness of the physical body. When you speak the sound *ah*, or fashion it in eurythmy, you cause your astral body to sink down as much as it can into your physical body. This entails a feeling of well-being. It is as if you could feel your astral body flowing through your limbs like – I will say "sparkling wine" for the less abstemious people, while for the more abstemious I ought perhaps to say "lemonade"! Thus in uttering the sound *ah* you actually sense something like the flowing of some sparkling fluid through your physical body. What is the kind of feeling that now arises in the physical body? *Ah* – a feeling of comfort or well-being arises.

Let us take the other sound. You stand upright confronting your surroundings and say, "I too am here". Now it is as if, let's say, you were to shelter from the cold by means of a protecting garment. You increase the intensity of your own existence. This feeling of being aware of something outside yourself and defending yourself against it, this reliance on yourself in the face of some other element, lies in the sound *a*. In both cases, in *ah* and in *a*, the physical body is taken hold of by the astral body.

The same thing can be experienced musically, too. Musically this can occur in the experience of the minor mood in the most comprehensive sense. The minor mood is always a retreat into yourself with the soul and spirit part of your being; it is a laying hold of the bodily by the soul and spirit. You will most easily discover what is to be felt in the eurythmic gestures as the differentiation between the major and the minor moods when you draw the experience of the major out of the living experience of the sounds *o* and *oo*, and when you draw the experience of the minor, again with feeling, out of the experience of the sounds *ah* and *a* – not out of the sounds themselves, but out of the experience.

When you enter into these things you will feel how little people today know about the nature of the human being. It must be said that in our modern world the understanding for such things is remarkably limited. But without this understanding, absolutely nothing productive can be achieved in so many realms. Unless such understanding is acquired, we shall never be able to stand with our whole being within the realm of art. Something artistic which has not been permeated with the whole human being is nothing; it is a farce. Something artistic can only endure when the whole human being has poured himself into it.

But then we really have to feel the connection between the world and the human being; we must feel how speech brings us into a relationship with the outer world, and music into a relationship with ourselves; how, in consequence, all the movements of speech-eurythmy are, as it were, drawn from the human being and transplanted into the outer world, whereas the gestures of music [–eurythmy] have to flow back into the human being. Everything which goes out in speech-eurythmy has to lead back into the human being in music-eurythmy. **8**

Today, as you know, the whole world of thought is chaotically fragmented. There is no living picture of anything. Take a person of what we call a sanguine temperament, one who lives intensely in what is outside himself. A sanguine person pleases us, that is, he makes an agreeable impression upon us, only when he utters the sounds *o* and *oo*. We get quite a bitter taste in the mouth when anyone of sanguine temperament speaks the sounds *ah* and *a*; it doesn't quite work. But people today do not possess such vivid perceptions, and this is why contemporary people create so little from the depths of their being.

Now let us take a person of melancholic temperament. To anyone who has understanding for such things, a melancholic person seems to be an absolute caricature when he speaks the sounds *o* and *oo*. It only seems right when he speaks the sounds *ah* and *a*. Here we have the going-over into the everlasting major mood of the sanguine person and into the everlasting minor mood of the melancholic person.

Now let us think of a person who is simply bursting with health, as we say. Such an overwhelmingly healthy person is in the major mood, and for the most part his astral body makes movements which correspond to *o* and *oo*. His step is light; that is to say, he lives in a continuous *oo*. He takes on everything, because it pleases him; he can endure anything. He is continually in the feeling of *oo*; he is the major mood incarnate.

Let us take a sick person. He is continually in a state in which, without the element of wonder, but through the very fact of his illness, he imitates the mood of *ah* or the mood of *a* – more especially the latter. A sick person is perpetually in the minor mood. And it is not exactly a metaphor or something of an analogy when we ask: What is fever? Fever is the sound *ah* transposed into the physical realm, which a eurythmist or someone who speaks the *ah* produces in the astral realm. The mood of the minor projected into the physical plane produces fever; it is the same process which takes place when you utter the sound *ah*, but in speaking this process takes place on a higher level – the level of soul and spirit. The sound *ah* is a fever. Either it is fever or it is tears, but it is always a process which the human being produces in himself.

These things lead to a true knowledge of the human being only when they are understood through the feelings. And because the human being is partially healthy and partially ill, the development of that which is superabundantly healthy (which must be inherent in art) and the development of movements imbued with the power of healing are closely interwoven. The latter exists in the case of ill people. This close relationship exists because, in reality, the major and the minor moods are, on a higher plane, the same as health and illness – that is to say, the experience of health and illness. Now we must not think that because the minor mood is [connected with] illness, it is therefore something bad or in some way inferior. Being ill in the soul-world always signifies something quite different from being ill in the physical world. From all this, you will see that the moods of major and minor, when developed eurythmically, may in time bring about therapeutic results.

So you see there is actually a bridge between speech-eurythmy and music-eurythmy. And when in speech-eurythmy we experience the vowel sounds rightly, in the way I have described for *ah* and *a* on the one hand and for *o* and *oo* on the other hand, we really have something that leads us towards the experience of major and minor. But the important fact we could seriously bring home to ourselves is that we tend to push (*schieben*) the musical element more inwards, whereas the movements of speech-eurythmy we have to push away (*abschieben*).

Imagine the following: Take a step forwards with the right foot, trying to feel this step as vividly as you can; do it in such a way that you also express in feeling the involvement of the head: you take a step forward (your head not too far back, but more forward). This is the first gesture. Now we carry out a second gesture. Try to accompany the gesture you have just made with a movement of the right hand, palm outwards, as much as possible in the direction of the foot taking the step. Now you have made a second gesture.

Take the first gesture: the stepping. Take the second: the movement. And now try to add a third gesture by making a light movement of the left arm, touching the right arm as if you wanted to push it away (left arm slightly pushing the right). You take a step forwards, following in the same direction with the right arm, and finally pushing the right arm with the left. Here you have a certain gesture in its most extreme form. You have the step and the movement, with what you add with the left arm bringing about a forming gesture – for when you follow on with the left arm, you arrest what you have poured into the movement in the right arm and hold fast the movement. We then have:

> Step,
> Movement,
> Formation.

Here you are really involved in something threefold, and you are so much within this threefold occurrence that you will actually be able to feel this as a threefold occurrence. In the stepping you are in a position to discover an intimation of the outgoing of your astral body. In the following on of the movement, which you make with the right arm, this outgoing feeling is intensified. And in what I have described as the formation, you can feel how the movement is held fast. Now if you really feel what I have indicated in this gesture, if you put yourselves into it, having no other wish than to enter with your whole being into this step, movement and formation, then you have something that is threefold. And you will easily realise that the step is the foundation of everything; it is the starting point. The movement is felt as the continuation, and must be in harmony with the foundation. And the formation establishes the whole process.

You must experience all this yourselves. You can experience it in the most varied ways if you take the notes into consideration; you can make the gesture in the upper, lower or middle zones. If you do it in such a way as to have C below, the E in the middle (thus beginning with the step, leading the movement over into E, and trying to confer the G in the formation) then in this step, movement and formation you have presented the major triad. Fashion the major triad quite naturally and objectively, and put the experience of the major triad into what you yourself present as a human being in the world. Just as in the gestures presenting the sounds of speech you have to feel the inner content of the sound, so here, in step, movement and formation, you have to experience the chord. This is a first element.

> Step: C
> Movement: E
> Formation: G

Now let us try to step backwards with the left foot, allowing the head to follow [in the same direction]. And now try to follow this with the left arm. You must follow your backward step with the left arm, taking care to hold the palm of the hand inwards. Be really relaxed as you start. Make the backward step together with the movement of the head and arm (hand on the chest) trying to achieve completion by putting the right arm across. Try to hold fast this position. The whole gesture should be done in such a way that it can actually be seen how the left arm is led inwards towards the body, the left hand being brought to the body, and how the right hand is carried over towards the left hand as though to hold it fast [*Hand* is probably Austrian dialect for "arm". Tr. note].

> Here you have presented in the step: C
> in the movement: Eb
> and in the formation: G

You have presented the minor triad, and when you keep these gestures in view and have repeatedly tried to keep them in view, you will come to the conclusion that these basic elements of music, the major triad and the minor triad, can be presented in no other way. It is only when you have become convinced that there is absolutely no other way of expressing the matter that you will really have felt it. You may try as you like to find some other way of doing it; it is only when another method pleases you less than the gestures shown here that you can really be said to have realised what dwells in them.

Now you see, you have basically expressed in the realm of music what is expressed for the vowel sounds in speech-eurythmy. If I ask you to produce an *ah* in speech-eurythmy it is really the same (in speech-eurythmy) as when I asked you just now to produce a major, or a minor, triad. It is simply doing vowels.

Now there is one thing which I have not yet characterised. I said that we can experience the major mood as such in *o* and *oo*, and the minor mood as such (which unlikely as it appears, is really the case) in *ah* and *a*, but I have not yet mentioned the fact that there can be something which lies between. Consider the transition. Try to experience the transition from the mood of wonder to the embracing feeling in the sound *o*, or, vice versa, the transition from the embracing feeling of *o* to the mood of wonder. Here you go from without inwards; you pass from the "going out" of the astral body to a "diving down" of the astral body. Here you pass from illness to health, from health to illness. This is the *ee*. *Ee* is always the neutral feeling of yourself between the experience of going outwards and the experience of being within – both in relation to the physical body. Thus *ee* stands between *ah* and *a* on the one side, and *o* and *oo* on the other side.

And now (you can think these things over before tomorrow and apply them for yourselves) try to pass over from the experience of minor to the experience of major by simply changing [direction]. You first produce the experience of the minor, then you change it by placing yourself forward. Simply incline the head somewhat forward (in the minor experience it lies in a backward direction), and incline yourself forward, thereby changing the whole movement of the muscles. Instead of the step backwards with the left leg, you would now have to step forwards with the right leg; you simply bring that which you have in front out of the minor into the major; that is to say, you pass out of the major into the minor mood, or out of the minor into the major mood. The experience underlying this transition corresponds to the experience of *ee* in speech-eurythmy. You will already sense the interesting variety of life underlying this transition from the major to the minor mood if you really carry out what I have just indicated.

You see, the point is this. When we initially enter into the nuances which lie in the major and the minor moods and the transition between them, we are really entering into what, in the realm of music, corresponds to the vowel sounds. You must take deeply into your soul this first principle, as I have described it. The gestures you have made for the major and the minor moods and the transition from the one to the other are the musical way of doing the vowels. The starting point is taken from the major and the minor moods.

The musical realm carries the fundamental moods corresponding to the vowels throughout its entire tonal configuration, through tension, resolution, and so on. ◼9 And just as we can pass over from the spoken vowel sounds into words, so we may also pass over from the laying-hold of the elements of music (as, for instance, the simple chordal nature of the major and minor triads) into eurythmical laying-hold of the musical realm, the inner musical configurations.

Tomorrow at this time we shall continue.

Lecture 2: Experience and gesture; the intervals

Dornach, 20 Feb. 1924

Gesture which is to be used for the expression of music must be gesture rising out of actual experience, and this can only be an experienced gesture if the underlying experience is there first. You will understand this if you once more place before your soul the origin of music and speech in the human being. [10] Music and language, that is to say, the sounds of music and of speech, are connected with the whole human being. When the human being sings or speaks, the experience of the singing or speaking is in the astral body and ego.

Now everything that lives in the astral body and ego has its physical manifestation in air and warmth. Let us suppose that someone is singing or speaking. Imagine to yourselves as vividly as possible how the sound-formation of speech or music comes about. The formations of speech and music live purely as soul-element in the astral body and ego. Along with the astral body and ego they are then imparted to the air, to the organs of breathing and everything connected with them; they are imparted to the air and the organs of breathing by and through the astral body.

But you know that when any body, [like] a volume of air, is compressed, it becomes warmer. It becomes inwardly warmer. Compression causes an increase of inner warmth. When such a body expands, it uses this warmth again in the process of expansion. In the oscillating air, that is to say, in the alternation between condensed and rarefied air, there are continual fluctuations of temperature – warm, cold; warm, cold; warm, cold.

Thus there enters into the stream of singing or speaking the element of warmth. The ego lives in this element of warmth, and singing and speech gain their inwardness through this. Musical sound and the sounds of speech actually acquire their inner quality of soul from the warmth that, as it were, is carried on the waves of this air (which form the sound purely outwardly); warmth is carried on the actual flowing waves of the air. The astral body is active in the flowing air itself, and the ego lives in the warmth which flows on the waves of the air. But the astral body and ego are not only present in the air and warmth, they are also present in the fluid and solid elements of the human body. When a human being speaks or sings, the astral body and ego are partially withdrawn from there, and limit themselves to the air and warmth. Singing and speaking do in fact entail a withdrawal of the astral body and ego from the structure of the human body, but not completely, as in sleep. This is a partial withdrawal from the solid and fluid elements of the human body, which then remain behind. From this you will see that when someone speaks or sings, something takes place in his whole body.

We will now try to become aware of how the human being perceives what is taking place here. We know that the sounds of speech and of singing are activated by the larynx and all that is connected with it. The human being perceives by means of the ear. Here we have two organs clearly placed at the periphery of the body. Feeling is poured into these organs. In the senses there is the actual active feeling, active feeling of the soul. We feel with the eye; we feel with the ear. But it is also feeling which stimulates activity in the larynx and its neighbouring organs. Feeling is at work here. The imagination (*Vorstellung*) is merely pushed into the feelings. It is feeling which is at work. The human being, as it were, is specialised in the organs connected with hearing, speech and singing when he sings or takes in what is sung, or speaks or takes in what is spoken. Hence the actual experiences remain in the ear and larynx, and do not really enter into consciousness. `11`

Everything that can be laid hold of by the senses, and everything that can be expressed through the organs of speech, can also be expressed by the entire body, by the entire human being. In the movements of eurythmy, the whole human being becomes a sense-organ. The whole range of feeling, as it streams and strongly pulsates through the body, becomes incitement and an organ of perception – the whole range of feeling with the human being as the instrument. And so what otherwise remains an experience of the ear or larynx only, now has to become an experience of the whole human being. When it becomes an experience of the whole human being, it quite naturally becomes gesture. Once the experience is understood, is laid hold of, then the experience becomes gesture. Let us make this clear with a few examples. Think of a musical sound as such, and in order to have a starting point, take any note as keynote.

The connection of the sound with feeling will become clear to you when you recall that the animal (which is of a lower order than man) breaks forth into sound as the result of a sensation of well-being, of pleasure, or of some sort of pain. Now pleasure, comfort and pain are experiences of feeling. Ultimately every sound uttered by the human being originates from some such basic source. When the human being experiences pleasure or well-being, he feels impelled to utter sounds. Why? Why does the human being utter sound? You might say he could also remain silent. Why does the human being break out into sound when he is overcome with delight?

What does a feeling of pleasure imply? To be overcome with pleasure really means that we lose ourselves in our surroundings. Everything which induces pleasure means that the human being is losing himself. And everything painful means an excessive awareness of himself. You are aware of yourself too strongly when you are in pain. Just think how much more aware of yourself you are when you are ill, or experience some kind of pain, than you are when the whole body is free from pain. When we are in pain we are too strongly within ourselves, and we are excessively aware of ourselves. In pleasure, on the other hand, we nearly, or even utterly, are losing ourselves. Harmonious feeling is brought about by the balance between pleasure and pain, by giving ourselves up entirely neither to the pleasure nor to the pain.

Why does the human being give vent to sound when experiencing pleasure, pain, or any other nuance of feeling – each of which in the last resort leads back either to pleasure or to pain? Why does he produce sound? He does so in order to keep a hold on himself when he is at the point of losing himself in pleasure. The sound enables him to keep hold of himself; otherwise in this pleasure his astral body with his ego would leave him. By giving vent to sound he is able to keep hold of himself. This is at the root of all phenomena in which sound is produced by a living being. (For instance, the moon works very strongly upon certain creatures, such as dogs. It threatens to tear away a dog's astral body. And the dog barks at the moon because by this means it anchors its astral body.)

When the human being gives vent to sound for itself (and any note may be regarded as the keynote) it means that he is resisting this tendency to lose himself in pleasure. He is holding fast to his astral body. And when the ego and astral body sink down into pain, then, because the human being is too intensely aware of himself, he quite rightly tries to tear himself away from himself by the utterance of some note or sound. In the plaintive sound of the minor mood there is an effort to tear free from an excessive awareness of self.

When we think of it, by saying this we are already speaking in gesture. There is not the least need to interpret anything artificially, because we speak in gesture. We need only to understand what occurs here, and we speak in gesture. If I say: "I have sunk too deeply into myself and must tear myself out of myself" – then indeed it is beyond doubt that some sort of gesture which proceeds from me is a natural gesture, and is the actual expression of what I experience. It expresses what the experience is. And so the understanding of such an experience already indicates the gesture. You cannot do otherwise when describing the experience than to describe the gesture. For this reason the movements of eurythmy are not arbitrary, but actually reveal what is experienced.

Now let us suppose that someone, either in pleasure or pain, has produced a sound which we will regard as the keynote. The underlying mood is unfinished; it cannot stay like that, for if it did, the person in question would be constantly obliged to sing the keynote or to utter a sound. When experiencing pleasure he would never be able to cease uttering this sound; he would have to sustain it forever if the sound itself did not exert a certain calming influence. The human being cries out into the world as a result of pleasure or pain, and here is an incomplete condition of human experience, an unfinished condition of soul for human experience.

Let us now take the transition from keynote to octave. In the transition from keynote to octave, the octave simply falls into the keynote. It is as if you stretched out your hand and came into contact with an object. Through this external touch the longing you felt for something outside yourself is satisfied. In the same way the octave comes to meet you from the world in order to calm the prime within itself. That which was unfinished to begin with is now complete. When the octave is added to the prime, a wholeness is created again. In the course of these lectures you will see how the gestures come about by themselves if we penetrate to a true understanding of the underlying experience. 12

Let us consider [the interval of] the fifth – the fifth which is united in some way to the keynote. It is essential here truly to acquire the experience of the fifth. The remarkable thing about the fifth is that when the human being holds the keynote and the interval of the fifth from it, he feels he is a completed human being. The fifth is the human being.

Naturally such things can only be expressed in the language of feeling – nevertheless, [we can say] the fifth is the human being. It is exactly as if the human being inwardly extended as far as his skin, as if he laid hold of his own skin and enclosed himself off within it. The fifth is the skin as it encloses the human being. And never, in the realm of musical sounds, can the human being feel his humanity so strongly as he does when he is experiencing the fifth in relation to the keynote. What I have just said may be more intelligible in the following considerations.

Let us now compare the experience of the fifth with that of the seventh and the third. The experience of the seventh (sounding either harmonically or melodically) involves those sounds which were especially favoured in the world of ancient Atlantis; 13 it was the interval that gave them special delight. Why was this? It was because in the epoch of ancient Atlantis, people's experience of going outside themselves was still a positive one. In the seventh we really do go out of ourselves. In the fifth we go as far as the skin; in the seventh we are outside ourselves. We leave ourselves in the seventh. Indeed in the seventh as such there is absolutely nothing soothing. It might be said that when a person cries out in the keynote because he is being hurt, and then adds the seventh to it, he is really crying out about the crying, in order to escape from it again. He is completely beside himself. Whereas the fifth is experienced at the surface of the skin, and the human being feels his humanity, in the seventh there is the feeling of breaking through the skin and going into his surroundings. He goes out of himself; he feels he is in his surroundings.

In the third there is a distinct feeling of not reaching as far as the skin, but of remaining within yourself. The experience of the third is very intimate. You know that what you settle with the third you settle with yourself alone. Just try out how unfamiliar the experience of the fifth is compared to the experience of the third. The feeling of the third is an intimate one which you settle with yourself in your heart. In the fifth you feel that other people too can see what you experience, because you go as far as the skin. It is only by means of feeling that such things can be experienced. And in the experience of the seventh you are outside yourself.

And now recollect what I said yesterday. The gesture that characterises the keynote is the step. This step gives us the position. The third is characterised either by an accompanying or a following gesture of one arm, indicating an entering into movement, while following in the direction of this gesture. The direction of the gesture is followed in such a way that if it is the major third, you still remain within your arm. You remain within it. I have characterised the fifth as something that you form. You return, just as the skin forms the human being on all sides. In the triad, regardless of whether it is major or minor, we have:

Inner activity: the step
Remaining within yourself: the movement
Closing off what is outside: the formation

Now the point is this: When trying to give clear expression to the remaining-within-yourself in the third, it is possible to vary the movement. In order to introduce some variety, you might, for instance, stretch out your arm and, while continuing the direction of the gesture, move in some way such as this (right arm stretched out, the hand moving up and down). Now you are within yourself. Thus the interval of the third is well expressed when you first take up the position, and then make the movement – continuing, however, to move within the movement. Now you have inwardness.

Suppose that you are dealing with a major third. Then you will show inwardness by making the arm movement go away (out) from yourself. If you express the minor third, you remain more within yourself, which you indicate with your arm back towards yourself (inwards). You have a gesture that really expresses the experience of the third. 14

If you want to experience these things you must repeatedly practise the corresponding gesture and try to see how the experiences of the intervals actually flow from the gesture, and how they are within it. Then the corresponding experience will grow together with the gesture, and you will possess that which makes the matter artistic. The experience will grow with the gesture. Only then will the matter become artistic.

In the experience of the seventh this is especially apparent. With the seventh, the essential thing is that you go out of yourself, for it is a going-out-of-yourself. Somehow the gesture has to show that you go out of yourself (you stretch out the arm, turning the hand while shaking it). The natural expression of the seventh is a movement which you do not follow, but in which the hand is allowed to be shaken. And when you compare the experience of the fifth with that of the seventh, you will feel in the fifth the necessity of closing off, of giving it form, of making so to speak an enclosing movement. This is not possible in the experience of the seventh, for in the seventh it is as if your skin disappears while experiencing the seventh, and you stand there as a sort of flayed Marsyas. 15 The skin flies away and the whole soul goes out into the surroundings. If you want to introduce the other arm as well into the movement to support the seventh experience, you can do so, of course, for there is never a question of pedantry or retaining something schematic. In such a case you would have somehow to indicate the seventh with the other hand. Of course this must be beautifully done.

Thereby you will experience, when you enter deeply into the matter in this way, that the experience itself becomes gesture. And eurythmy will only flourish when the experience itself becomes gesture.

A eurythmist must become in some respects a new human being compared to what he or she was before, because in general, through the fact that we speak or sing, we have brought about a certain attentiveness to what we actually want in the gesture. We lead over what we want in gesture into speech and song. When we retrieve it, gesture arises. And a professional eurythmist (if I may use such a philistine expression)[1] has to feel it absolutely natural to translate everything into gesture. Indeed, when mixing in ordinary, polite society, a eurythmist cannot help feeling a sense of restraint and restriction at not being able to eurythmise all sorts of things in front of people. Isn't it true, that just as the painter itches to paint when he sees something and is unable to (for he would like to paint everything but cannot always be at it, and thus has to restrain himself), so too a tired eurythmist is actually something terrible? A eurythmist cannot manifest

---

1   It has a bourgeois ring in German. (Translator's note.)

fatigue as something natural. It is really dreadful to see a eurythmist sitting down tired during a rehearsal, for it is exactly — isn't it? — as if someone suddenly became rigid or got paralysed. I have sometimes observed in eurythmy rehearsals that eurythmists sit down when there is a little pause. Such things do not, I believe, happen in Dornach, but here and there it does occur. I probably turn quite pale, for my blood runs cold at this quite impossible sight of a tired eurythmist. There is no such thing! In life, of course, there is such a thing, that is the paradox, but you must sense that this is so. So I do not say you must not sit down if you are tired, but I do say: "If you do, you must regard yourself as a caricature of a eurythmist!" `16`

These things must be said in order that the fundamental mood of the artistic process may be brought into the matter, for art has to be based upon the mood, upon that which runs through everything like a connecting thread. And especially such an art as eurythmy, where the whole human being is involved, can never prosper if this mood is lacking, if this mood does not permeate everything.

When these things have become real experiences, you will simply and truly feel eurythmy as you do speaking and singing. You must accustom yourselves, however, just as you experience the sounds of language, to experience singing too for the activity of eurythmy. It is quite true to say that the eurythmist must experience the musical element in a fuller sense than, for instance, a singer does. With a singer it depends upon his entering right into the musical sound, taking hold of it, being able to hear it, and living in an element in which his body comes to his assistance to a marked degree. The body does not come to the assistance of the eurythmist; for in eurythmy it is the soul that has to engage in the gesture of what the senses or larynx have to do in singing and speaking.

It is necessary to preface the description of the actual movements by this somewhat lengthy introduction, for these things are especially important for the whole feeling of the eurythmical element. The eurythmical element will not be understood if such things are not entered into with intensity. An understanding must be acquired by the eurythmist for all that I have stressed when giving introductions to performances, but which in the present time is rarely correctly understood. I often say that the prose content of the words do not make for the poetical element, the artistic and poetic element. There are people today who read a poem as though it were prose. You do not have the poem there. The prose content does not constitute the poem. The poem is what lives in the musical, sculptural and pictorial element of the words, in their melodic motifs, rhythm and beat, and so on. Anyone who wishes to express what should be expressed in poetical form, must be vividly aware that the words must not be used merely on account of their meaning, but arranged according to the beat, the rhythm, the melodic motifs, or that which is pictorial in the formation of the sounds, and similar things.

We have, consequently, to go one stage beyond the mere content of language, for in so far as its actual content is concerned, language is inartistic. It exists for prose. This is the inartistic element in language. Not until language is fashioned, not until it is given shape and form, does it become artistic.

What has been said here about language is quite obvious for singing, of course. We can see that our age does not care much for real artistic creation, for it happens that modern music [1924] too exhibits the tendency that does not allow the actual music, the progression of notes, to speak for itself, but tries to express something quite different by this means.

Now you must not misunderstand me, for it is not my intention to make any anti-Wagnerian propaganda. Time and again I have emphasised Wagner's significance in the culture of our age. This, however, is not because I regard his music as being "musical music", but rather because we have to admit the demand of the present age for "unmusical music". It is apparent to me that unmusical music has its justification in our age. Fundamentally speaking, Wagner's music is unmusical. [17] And it is really necessary in an age like ours, when music should also become gesture, to point the way to musical experience as such, when musical experience is to be expressed in gesture, and to show how the interval of the third represents inwardness, and the fifth a boundary, the seventh a going-out-of-yourself. And what is it that gives the feeling of inner satisfaction in the octave? The inner satisfaction in the octave is due to the fact that here, I would like to say, we get away from the danger inherent in the seventh. We escape from this danger inherent in the seventh and re-find ourselves outside.

With the octave it is like this, as if – with the seventh – you had become a flayed Marsyas, without your skin, the soul departing, the skin flying off and is getting away; but now you feel in the octave: "I am stripped of my skin, but it is coming, returning, I'll have it in a moment, it is about to return, it is there approaching and yet it is still outside." You have indeed grown somewhat, you have expanded and become fuller. It is as though you grow while experiencing the octave.

Obviously, then, the movement for the experience of the octave is not the same as that for experiencing the seventh. The experience is attained by turning round the whole hand outside yourself. The interval of the octave is expressed by turning the hand, starting with the palm facing outwards. If you wish to give full expression to the octave, you can of course make the same movement in this way too (in the same way, but carried out with both arms and hands). Here again it is self-evident that these things must be practised so well that they become second nature. Just as the musician has to get the producing of the notes into his fingers, so the eurythmist must get the corresponding gestures into his or her whole body.

This is why it is so necessary for the basic elements of eurythmy to be repeatedly practised. Such elementary movements as those I have briefly indicated (and shall develop further in the course of the next few days) must become second nature so it is no longer necessary to think about them, any more than it is necessary to think about the letters of a word that is spoken. If we say the word "letter" we do not need to think, for we know quite well how its component sounds have to be pronounced. And so we have to reach the point where the movements for the intervals, triads, and so on, are produced out of ourselves quite naturally. You will then see how easily the other things arise. And above all you will increasingly realise how the experience passes over into gesture.

In order to understand this, let us deal with the difference between concords and discords. As you know, triads are concordant or discordant; a four-note chord is actually always discordant.

You will have realised yesterday from the movements for the triads, that in order to give expression to the experiences of the triad, the assistance of the whole human being must be invoked. In the first place we have what I characterised as the step. The step essentially entails the use of one leg. Then, with both major and minor chords, we have the movement with one arm, and the forming with the other. You may say, "I have nothing else to use". Well, as you do have two legs, you have a means of expressing a chord of four notes. And now you may say, "I really cannot step forwards with one leg and backward with the other, simultaneously". And yet you can do this if you jump. You see, we arrive at this quite naturally.

There is no other means of presenting a four-note chord than by jumping somewhat, moving one leg forwards and the other backwards. This is how a four-note chord is presented. But think for a moment what happens here. It would be difficult, as well as not looking particularly beautiful, to jump without bending the knees. You cannot jump easily with totally stiff legs, quite apart from the ungraceful appearance. In jumping you must bend at the knees, so that in the jumping movement necessary for the four-note discord (because of the nature of the body and its relation to the environment) you really get the bending of the knees as the gesture for the discord. The natural movement for a discord is the bending of the knees entailed by jumping.

From this, however, something else arises. If you have a discordant triad you can again apply the same principle. With a concordant triad you take a step forwards; with a discordant triad you must also make a bending movement. There is no necessity to bend as with jumping, but you can bend. And so you express the discordant triad by moving with bended knees. You can discover this from the fact that a four-note chord – which is always a discord – can only be done by a jump in order to set both legs into movement; for you just do not have four members of your body in order to express a discord of four notes, so you have to jump, coupled with bending. This gives us, therefore, bending as the expression of the discord.

Now just as a musician has to practise his exercises, a tremendous inner liveliness is attained by practising the alternation between discords and concords, passing from one to the other simply with a view to experiencing in their gestures the change of mood, the change in the actual feeling.

If you think of all I have just said, you will find the experience of the fourth of particular interest. In the third we are intimately within ourselves. In the fifth we come just to the boundary of the body. The fourth lies between. And the fourth has this striking characteristic, that here the human being experiences himself inwardly, although not so intimately as in the third. But he does not even reach his surface. He experiences himself beneath this surface. He remains, as it were, just beneath it. He separates himself from the surrounding world, and creates himself within himself. He does not form himself, as in the fifth, where the external world also compels this forming, but he forms himself out of the needs of his own soul. The experience of the fourth is such that the human being feels his humanity through his own inner strength, whereas in the fifth it is through the world that he feels his humanity. In the fourth he says to himself, "You are really too big; you cannot experience yourself because you are so big. Make yourself a little smaller, yet stay as important as your size". In the fourth you make yourself into a snug, comfortable dwarf. Thus the fourth demands a very strong relation to yourself. You can achieve this when, instead of simply going outwards or inwards as in the third, you draw the fingers sharply together as if to concentrate the strength of the hand in itself. In this way the fourth is expressed and revealed.

These, then, are the principles that have to be considered before entering more deeply into the gestures of the musical element, for without the experience of these principles no truly artistic gestures can come about. I am sure you will have plenty to do when you come to work through all these details. It is better therefore not to give too many gestures in one session, for what has been given must first be assimilated.

So we shall continue tomorrow.

Lecture 3: Melodic movement; the ensouling of the three dimensions through pitch, rhythm and beat

Dornach, 21 Feb. 1924

Let us first see if you can manage the following exercise. With the right arm, try to make a movement similar to the one I gave for the forming of the seventh; now try to hold the arm still whilst stepping forwards, so that the arm remains stationary, the body following the direction of the arm. To do this you must bend your arm as you step. The arm, the hand that is, must remain in the same place while you step forwards. This exercise must be carried out in such a way that the arm, the hand, remains where it is, while you come up and join it. This must be practised.

Now try another exercise: While stepping forwards try to draw the hand back somewhat – not too strongly, however. Now we have two exercises. Try to experience in succession seventh and prime, and sixth and prime. The first movement just shown expresses the succession of notes: seventh – prime; and the second movement for the experience sixth – prime; the sound [of each interval] imagined in succession. They can, however, also be imagined simultaneously; I will speak about this a little later on. In this way you are able to bring movement into the gesture.

The movement first shown is one which, in a certain way, throws life back into the lifeless. And indeed, as may be seen from yesterday's description of the seventh, this is also the case in regard to its relationship to the keynote. If you picture the keynote as the embodiment of calmness and quiet, and the seventh as actually lying outside the physical body, so that in the seventh the human being goes out of himself, then it will be possible for you to imagine that by your going out, the seventh brings back the spiritual quickening element into the resting, bodily part.

You see, these things become vividly real when we pass over from the musical element to the eurythmical element. Music naturally is something perceived, as it is produced in the first place in order to be heard, whereas eurythmy brings the whole human being into movement. And you will best recognise the inner reality of what has just been said about the relationship of the seventh to the keynote, from the fact that this can be therapeutically effective. When for instance a hardening process in the lungs or some other organ in the chest is diagnosed, it will be found that this very exercise, as it has now been demonstrated, will have a healing, re-vitalizing effect, helping to bring the condition back to normal.

It is precisely music-eurythmy in all its elements, when suitably carried out, which is a factor in eurythmy therapy. Only it is necessary to penetrate into the nature of the musical sounds in a really living way, as we endeavoured to do yesterday, and as we shall try to continue.

In this connection let me also say the following. If, in a similar way to that which I have just indicated, you go on from the seventh to the sixth in relation to the keynote, you will find in this interval a noticeably weakened relationship, and it is strikingly characteristic that the hand, which is held stationary from outside in the case of the seventh, here goes backwards. This does not express the relation of the living to the lifeless, but the sixth in relation to the keynote is so expressed that you feel it merely as motion, as a setting into activity. It may be compared to a stimulation of feeling rather than to something which imparts life. The sixth in relation to the keynote induces a picture of feeling. The seventh in relation to the keynote induces a picture of life; it imparts life to the lifeless.

And now, bearing in mind these gestures (which will have shown you that in its essential being, music-eurythmy must be movement), I will ask you to consider how music-eurythmy, just as speech-eurythmy, may after all provide a correcting influence upon art as a whole.

It was necessary to tell you that speech-eurythmy has a corrective artistic influence upon recitation and declamation. In introductions to public performances, for instance, it is difficult to make use of the necessary drastic expressions which are demanded if we are to describe the inartistic nature of our modern age, for people would only be shocked, and very little would be gained. Things have to be put mildly, as indeed I try to do. But the truth of the matter is that in our inartistic age, recitation and declamation have become completely degenerate. The laws of true art are no longer observed in recitation and declamation. Everything is read like prose in a thoroughly materialistic way. People think it must be felt out of the gut instinctively; emphasis is determined by pathos, or something of the sort, indeed by anything that makes an appeal to sensation or sense-impressions. Now true recitation and declamation must be based upon the forming and shaping of the actual language, upon making speech musical, and upon a sculptural, pictorial treatment of speech. 18 And when on the one hand we have a eurythmy performance, and on the other hand recitation, then it is not possible to make use of recitation and declamation in their present degenerate state. Attention must be paid to speech formation. I always describe this as a "hidden eurythmy", for eurythmy is indicated in recitation and declamation. Attention must be paid to the shaping and forming of speech. In such a way eurythmy can also exert a corrective influence upon everything that is musical.

We are actually living (this is naturally still more shocking) in a terribly inartistic age where music is concerned, too. This cannot be denied – we are living in a terribly inartistic age. For today there is an exceedingly widespread tendency to drive music as such into mere noise. [19] We have gradually ceased to be musical in the real sense, and instead we now make use of music in order to portray all sorts of sounds which are meant to represent something or other; the listener cannot always be sure what actually is intended, but at any rate it is a question of portraying something or other. Now please do not regard me as one of those Philistines who are only out to denegrate all that is being produced today in the sphere of music – doubtless with the most honest intentions! But it is necessary, when dealing with an art such as eurythmy, to raise it upon the foundations of what is really artistic, and to be able to speak about such things radically, too. It is impossible to do otherwise. Thus it is easy to see how eurythmy can work correctively upon musical taste.

You must forgive me if I now introduce something in the nature of an exercise; I have to do so in order to show how something can be built out of the fundamentals of art. Try first of all to become inwardly completely quiet, indifferent to sense impressions, as well as to any inward passion. Having achieved this state of indifference, sit down at the piano and play one of the middle notes – any note will do – and try while going up the scale to the octave really to experience the progression of notes. [20]

Having experienced this in peace and quiet, stand up and try to realise in eurythmy gestures what you have experienced. You will arrive at much, both in regard to what I have already mentioned and to those things about which I have still to speak. Endeavour, when attempting to reproduce in gesture what you have just played (single notes in an ascending progression) to bring into the eurythmy gestures (into the gestures for the triad, for instance) something similar to the gestures we have been discussing during these last few days. You will find it comparatively easy to feel a very strong connection between what you produce, feel and experience as gesture, and the notes as you play them successively on the piano.

Try striking a chord and try to reproduce in eurythmy the harmony of the notes. You will now discover that something within you does not want to go along with this. When striking a chord you are faced with the problem of having to carry out the step and movements of both arms simultaneously, as I indicated, let's say, for the movements for the major triad.

You are impelled to do this, but it will certainly arouse in you a feeling of inner opposition. A certain tendency will become apparent in your soul to transform the chordal, harmonic element into the melodic element, to transform the notes sounding simultaneously into a progression. And you will only feel really satisfied when, as it were, you release the chord, when you actually lead it over into melos, making three movements for the three notes, one after the other.

It may be plainly stated as a law that eurythmy actually compels us to release continually the harmonic element into melos. This is the corrective element about which I now want to speak. When you feel this in the right way you will come to the conclusion that, drastic as it sounds, the chord is really a burial. The chord may be likened to a burial. The three notes which are played together, and which are thus dependent upon space and not upon time – these notes have died in the chord. They only live when they appear as melody. When you really feel this you will discover the actual musical element is only to be found in the melodic element, the effect of the notes living in time.

You will then realise how senseless it is to ask, "What do the notes express?" Today people have gone so far in this direction that they try to make music represent the rippling of water, the sighing of the wind, the rustling of leaves, and all sorts of things. This, of course, is really appalling. Naturally, it is not my intention to campaign against this kind of thing, neither to detract from the pleasure anyone may take in it; I am only concerned that we correctly understand the matter out of the fundamentals. The notes, or progressions of notes, speak for themselves. They are indeed only there to speak for themselves, to express what the third says to the fifth, what the third says to the prime, or what the three of them say together when played in succession. Otherwise we find ourselves in the position of the distinguished European musician who once played a most complicated piece of many voices to an Arab. The Arab got into a terrible state of agitation, and said: "But why go so quickly? I should like to hear each song in its turn." He wanted each voice to be played separately, for he could not take in that the piece represents something quite other than a basically unmusical, noisy conglomeration of quite different things. [21]

I want to make clear to you the fact that in the musical element a real world is present, wherein we rediscover the impulses of the rest of the world.

Let us consider one fact. We die. The physical body remains, but it disintegrates. Why does it disintegrate? Why does it dissolve? The process of dissolution begins after death; up to that point the body does not disintegrate but remains intact. Why? Because previously we bore time within ourselves. From the moment when death occurs, the corpse exists only in space; it cannot participate in time. Because it can no longer participate in time, because it exists only in space and is subject to the laws of space, this fact makes it dead, this makes it fade away. We become a corpse because of the impossibility of bearing time within ourselves; we live, during earthly existence, because we are able to carry time within ourselves, to allow time to work within ourselves, because time is active in the material which extends in space. Melody is manifest in time. The chord is the corpse of melody. Melody dies in the chord.

As far as the understanding of music is concerned, our present age is in a sorry state. All these discussions about tone-colour in the overtones, and so on, are really only an attempt to make the single note into a kind of chord. People today have an innate tendency to find the harmonic element even in a single note. In reply to various questions as to how music ought to be developed, I have frequently answered that we must become aware of the melody in the single note; 22 in the single note we must become aware of the melody, not of the chord, but of the melody. One note conceals within itself a number of notes – every note at all events contains three. With the one note that you actually hear as sound, which is produced by an instrument and is actually audible, we have the present. Then there is another note within it, which is as if we recalled this second note. And there is a third note within it, which is as if we expected this third note. Every note really calls forth recollection and expectation as adjacent, melodic notes. This will come to be presented one day. 23 People will surely discover the possibility to deepen music by the single note becoming deepened into melody. Today people look for the chord in a single note and think about how this chord exists in the overtones. This, however, actually points to their materialistic conception of music.

Now the following question is unusual, but from the point of view of eurythmy it is fully justified: Where does the musical element really lie? Today there would be no doubt that the musical element lies in the notes, because such a terrific effort is required in the schools to put down these notes correctly, to arrange them in the right way. As you know, it all depends on mastering the notes. But the notes are not the music! Just as the human body is not the soul, so the notes are not the music. The interesting thing is that the music lies between the notes. We only need the notes in order that something may lie between them. The notes are necessary, of course, but the music lies between them. It is not the C nor the E which is essential, but what lies between the two. Such an element lying in-between, however, is only possible in the melodic element. In the chord it would be quite senseless. In harmony, such a lying in-between would be quite sense-less. The transition from melos to the harmonic element is really a stepwise transition from the musical to the unmusical realm. For through this the music is buried, through this the music is killed.

I could give you a somewhat peculiar definition of music. Naturally I should not want to give it in a music school, but I have to give it to euryth-mists, for anyone really wishing to promote music-eurythmy has to under-stand these things. It is a negative definition, certainly, but nevertheless correct: What is the musical element? It is what you do not hear! 24 That which you hear is never musical. If you take the experience which exists in time, which lies between two notes of a melody, then you hear nothing, for it is only the notes themselves which are audible. What you inaudibly experience between the notes, that is music in reality, for that is the spiritual element of the matter, whereas the other is the sensory manifestation of it.

You see, this enables you in the most eminent sense to bring the human personality, the human personality as soul, into the musical element. 25 The more you are able to bring out that which cannot be heard, the more you use the audible as the vehicle for the inaudible, so much the more is the music permeated with the soul. To feel this in the musical element is precisely the task of the eurythmist. And this is why, in the gestures of eurythmy, in the manner we saw earlier (or as we have otherwise already seen them, or shall be showing them) with these gestures he or she should feel delight not in the position, but in the bringing about of the positions, that is, in the movement. In the whole extent of eurythmy, the essential thing is not in the making of poses, but in the movement.

You may never say (I have frequently emphasised this, but frequently see the opposite conception in practice), you may never say, "This is an *ee*" (stretched arm). For now it is an *ee* no longer. It is only an *ee* as long as it is being formed, as long as the arm is in movement; so long is it *ee*. Nothing in eurythmy ever retains its meaning once it has come into being. In eurythmy, the significance lies in the process of coming-into-being.

Consequently, the eurythmist has to pay great attention to the forming of the movement, directing the greatest care to that movement through which a form arises. And consideration must be taken, as soon as one form arises, to transform it as quickly as possible, to lead it over into the subsequent form. The eurythmist regards movement as his element, neither standing in, nor holding on to, the form.

Anyone sensitive to these things in eurythmy will especially feel the sort of things which we have already done, in the following way. Some piece of music has just finished; the piece is over and you stand in the last position until the curtain falls. (I have asked for this to be done in performances, but it must be felt too.) It is quite finished. The final position, the final figure has come to rest, and the curtain is drawn. What feeling should live here; what should we feel? That the eurythmist seizes up! We actually arrive at the annulling of the artistic, eurythmic activity. It is finished. We say, as it were, to the audience, 26 "Friends, we have now killed the performance so that you may come to yourselves and think about it a little". Standing still may certainly have this significance. That is why it is justified in relationship to the audience, but only in this relationship.

All this serves to show you how much it matters in every possible form to make a study of the human being in movement. There are three observations we can make about the human being. We know the human being exists in space, but that which is spatial in him does not belong to eurythmy. But what can manifest in space as movement; that is what belongs to eurythmy. And it is clear that the human being lives in space in a threefold manner.

First he lives in space in the direction from above downwards, and from below upwards. We know that above we have the head and below the feet, and that they differ from one other. Whoever makes a deeper study of the human being will discover this as being of equal importance, let us say, to what is described more externally in anatomy, namely the fact that in the foot there are the bones of the heel, the toes and the instep, and so on, and in the head the frontal bone, the parietal bone and the occipital bone, and so on. Then, moving further inwards, the brain is described; the muscles of the foot are described. These things are described as if somebody or other had chanced to put them all together, and thus the human form came into being by accident. In reality, the head is the octave of the foot. And there is just as much truth in this (in the fact that the head is the octave of the foot) as there is in the other facts contained in the books on anatomy. For if you take the activity of the feet as your starting-point, and take what the head has done for it (for the head has something to do with the fact that you are able to walk with your feet), and if you really grasp the activity of the head and *(Fig. 2)* the activity of the feet, then, in the relationship between the two, you have quite literally the feeling of octave and prime. It is nothing other than this. We may go through the whole human being in this way, for the human being is a musical scale. 27

We have thus the human being extended from above downwards, and from below upwards. But we have also the human being extended in the directions right-left and front-back, back-front. The other directions of space may be related to these three directions, which are so clearly to be distinguished in the human being. [28]

When the human being carries musical experience over into eurythmy, he carries it into movement. And he has no choice in his movements but to enter, in some way or other, into these three different directions. He has to find some way of making use of these three directions if the musical element is to be carried into movement, for they represent him and [all] his possibilities of movement. In eurythmy [all] the human possibilities of movement should become apparent.

When you take the directions of up-down and down-up (you will have gathered this from the still relatively primitive music-eurythmy we have had hitherto), when you take the directions up-down and down-up (also taking into account what I have said about the major and the minor triads, and so on, and in connection with the foot and the head), then you will be able to feel: The height of the human being, the up-down and the down-up, corresponds to pitch. We have no other means of expressing pitch than the upwards and downwards movement of the arms, of the hands, and indeed, if you like, the upwards and downwards movement of the legs or head. When making pitch visible, we move in the vertical direction (see *Fig. 3*).

Now let us take right-left. This direction immediately carries us over into the gesture of movement. Where is it that the direction right-left makes itself especially apparent? The right-left is especially apparent when someone walks. Walking really is the bringing-into-movement of the right-left: right leg, left leg, right leg, left leg. And the direction right-left will remain lifeless just so long as you walk in life in a philistine manner; there will be no life in the right-left. But life is immediately introduced when we make some differentiation between the right-left, as nature does in that people usually write with the right hand and not with the left. A differentiation may also be shown simply by taking a strong step with the right leg, the left leg being drawn back, before placing it again. Everything that comes about in this way through the differentiation between right and left is connected with beat (see *Fig. 3*). Beat in music is carried over into eurythmic movement by means of the right-left.

There still remains the front-back. The point here is that the front-back is inwardly taken hold of, and in order to do so we must look at the human being a little more closely.

Now, you know, the front-back is not merely, let's say, as if some sign-board is written with "front" on the one side and "back" on the other. The essential element of the front-back is that we see in front of us, but do not see behind us. Behind us is a world of darkness, in fact, of which we have scarcely an

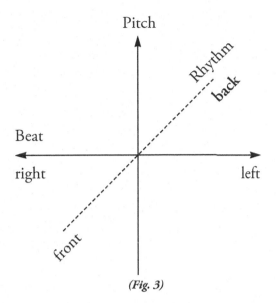

(Fig. 3)

inkling, whereas in front of us lies the whole visible world opening out. And in our movement, we can turn the "front" to the whole visible world, and then we are dealing with that which is in front. And when we turn to this "front", it means that we make the movement short. We are right in the midst of the world. We make the movement short.

When we are not able to enter this world, when we are held back, stuck, as it were, to the darkness lying behind us and unable to get out of it, we make the movement long. And so we may simply differentiate the relationship between front and back by means of "short-long". We have then U— or —U, iambus and trochee (see "rhythm" in *Fig. 3*). That means, we have rhythm; front-back confers the rhythm.

Now we possess three of the musical elements, and these may be used in your musical forms. If I may thus express it: you step the beat, you express the rhythm by means of quick-slow, and you express the actual musical element, melos, leading the movements up or down accordingly. The entire human being is engaged in eurythmy by means of beat, rhythm and melos.

Fundamentally speaking, music is the human being. And indeed it is from music that we may rightly learn how to free ourselves from matter. For if music were to become materialistic, it would actually be lying: it is not "there"! Every other form of matter is present in the world and is insistent. But musical sounds originally were not to be found in the material world. **29** We have to devise a means of producing them; they must first be made. The soul-element, which lies between the notes, this lives in the human being. But today, because the world has become so unmusical, people are scarcely aware of it.

This will once again be taken into account when people realise that the musical sound (*der Ton*) corresponds to the calm posture of the eurythmist. Let us now look at the major triad. (This was demonstrated.) Now you are no longer engaged in eurythmy, for eurythmy lies in the process of arriving at this position. The major triad lies in the going-forwards, in the tending-towards, the coming-into-being, not in the accomplished fact. But the musical sound, the note as such, corresponds to the completed posture. That means, the very moment a note is completed, the musical element ceases.

In this connection the following is of special interest: We have to be able to feel a relationship between the musical element and speech. If you endeavour in your listening to draw out the scale from the main vowels, most interesting things result:

> C may be said to correspond to u ('*oo*')
> D to o ('*o*')
> E to a ('*ah*')
> F to ö ('*ir*') (English equivalent as in 'birth')
> G to e ('*a*')
> A to ü ('*eu*') (English equivalent as in 'feud')
> B to i ('*ee*')

This is the approximate correspondence between the scale and the main vowels, purely according to their sound. 30

Now I would like you to make an *oo* with the legs. That is the keynote, as you all know. And now try to make the movement of a major or minor triad in the way we have already discussed, marking the third with its completing fifth. If you relate the movements and push them somewhat across, the fifth will be expressed in the movement of the *a*; it will become an *a* of its own accord.

After this try to make an *ah*; and now try most strongly to make a third, not with one hand as we otherwise do, but do the movement for the third with both arms, after imagining the keynote. Then you will find yourself in the eurythmy movement for the sound *ah*, with the third.

You see something very striking from this. If we listen very attentively it is almost possible to hear approximately this correspondence between the main vowels and the scale; if the sounds are articulated properly they do approximate to the scale. The movements of eurythmy bring this about of themselves. These movements rendering the formations of the musical sounds, also indicate those of the formations for the sounds of speech. This means that we cannot do otherwise in eurythmy than, when doing the right movements, to introduce the right conditions between the musical sounds and the sounds of speech, too.

We have never considered this other aspect of the movements that we have been studying all these years from the point of view of the sounds of speech and their formation; now we must try to realise them in their relationship to the form of the musical sounds. We have to become clear about the approximate correspondence between the scale and the formation of the sounds of speech. And when we compare the formation of the musical sounds with those for the sounds of speech, we find that their resemblance corresponds to the same degree as that between the musical sounds and the speech sounds as such. Of course, it's not the same; there is simply a resemblance. Neither in eurythmy are the two identical.

You see from this how naturally what we call eurythmy arises out of the very essence of speech on the one hand, and of the musical element on the other. That is quite plainly to be seen. And when you have entered into these things, you will be able to feel in no other way than: A musical sound or sound of speech can have only one gesture; it cannot be expressed in a variety of ways.

Let us continue tomorrow.

Lecture 4: The progression of musical phrases; swinging-over; the bar line

Dornach, 22 Feb. 1924

As you will have gathered from yesterday's lecture, a proper eurythmical presentation has to take its start from melos, from the melodic element, or, we could also say, from the motif or phrase. 31 It is the progression of the motif, the musical motif in time, which indicates the path which eurythmy must take on the basis of the musical element.

Let us concentrate on this today. Here again you will see how necessary it is to pay special attention to the actual musical element. Now, the musical element makes sense in the progression of the motifs – that is, the musical element as such, not as it manifests in expression. And this sense has absolutely to be brought out in a presentation of eurythmy. The question, then, is how the progression of a musical phrase must be treated in eurythmy. Usually in music itself, even when listening to it, people fail to observe the musical sense progressing within the motif itself. You all know that a motif frequently includes the bar line [American: bar]; indeed this is generally the case. The bar, the change of bar that is, interrupts the motif. And when passing from one completed motif to the following formation many people feel that something like a "dead interval" lies between them (musicians frequently even use this expression). 32 It is further said that such a "dead interval" corresponds to the progression from the end of one spoken word to the beginning of the next. The matter is frequently regarded in this way. But this very comparison, as I said yesterday, demonstrates that people have no feeling for the fact that the true musical element actually is that which is inaudible. When the "dead interval" is spoken about, and is compared with what lies between two spoken words, the comparison is not valid. Anyone wishing to speak out of an understanding of art really should not speak of the "dead interval" between two words, but on the contrary should place the greatest value upon the way the transition proceeds from one word to another.

Just think that in speech, in the treatment of speech, we can observe the following fundamental difference between good and bad treatment. You can treat each word separately, but this is quite different from a clear feeling that one word ends in a specific way and the next begins in a specific way. And you look for meaning between what is apparent to the senses (that is to say, between the end of one word and the beginning of the next), where the spirit lies, which you are endeavouring to express. The spirit also lies between the words. Furthermore, the sounds we hear in words are only the sensory impression; when we speak, too, the spirit lies in the inaudible realm. It is sad that people today have so little feeling for the inaudible realm, and are no longer able to listen between the words. A lecture on spiritual science can never be understood when you follow merely the actual words; you have to listen between the words, even listen into the words, discovering in the words what lies behind them. In this case words at all times are an aid to express that which cannot be heard.

The question, then, is to find different eurythmic movements for the position of a bar line in a motif, and for the transition from one motif to the next. This difference may be shown by holding back the movement at the bar line; so that whoever carries the movement does it, so to speak, within himself, possibly indicating through the position of the arms and hands that he is pressed together, and especially in moving a form by contracting the movement of the form into himself – in other words, becoming stuck whilst in the form. Conversely, in the transition from one motif-metamorphosis to the next, we are dealing with a swinging-over (*Schwung*) from the one metamorphosed motif to the other. We swing in a spirited manner from one metamorphosed motif to the next; in the actual bodily movement itself we have a kind of upward swing. And where the bar line appears within a motif we aim for a rigidly upright posture.

Try to practise this until it becomes a matter of course when moving. This will be of great significance. It would be quite good to make sure that the matter is clear. Let us take the following to clarify this. (At the moment we are only trying to work out the simplest rudiments, and it doesn't matter if this simplicity is somewhat home-spun.)

Here, then, we will select as simple a phrase as possible to make clear to ourselves the real significance of what I have been speaking about. The phrase starts, let's say, with a G and progresses to B, returns to G, the next motif progresses to F#, and so on. Thus we have the first motif, then the second, third, fourth, fifth and sixth, and the question is: How should this progression of motifs be carried out in eurythmy? In the first motif we hold ourselves back, then we boldly swing onwards to the next motif: the first motif rises, the second falls, and each time we have the bar lines between. The phrase continues (see *Fig. 4*) with holding ourselves back, boldly swinging onwards, holding ourselves back.

Thus, if I draw the whole thing: up, down, up, down, up, down – we always find the bar line during the motif, and in the fifth and sixth motifs, two bar lines each. The progression is one, two, three, four, five, six, seven, eight restraining-ourselves, and one, two, three, four, five swinging-onwards. Try to be quite upright, but go together with the whole movement; to be upright at the bar line and boldly swinging onwards at the transition from one motif to its following metamorphosis. The bar line must be strongly indicated by means of a strong holding-on to yourself. This may never take place simultaneously with the notes, however, but must always occur between them.

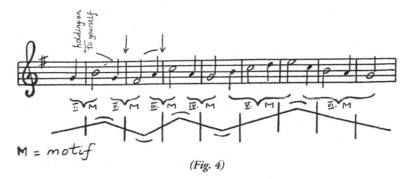

(Fig. 4)

This, hopefully, is clearly understandable. Always show the bar line, and its holding-on movement, very distinctly. This, of course, is something I ask you to ponder about, what it means for the various forms of phrasing. I wanted to show you this with as simple an example as possible. You see, the presentation of eurythmy quite especially reveals that the melody takes up the actual spirit and carries it on. Fundamentally speaking, everything else does not add the spirit of the musical element, being at all events a more or less illustrative element. But in order to gain a real conviction of this for yourselves, I ask you to try first and foremost to seek the whole human being in the musical element. The eurythmist is really obliged to study the way in which the human being streams out, as it were, into the musical element.

It is a fact that when we stand with our physical form, whether slim or short, fat or thin (that part of us which is actually visible), this is really the very least part of us. It even remains, in fact, for a short period after we have gone through the portal of death. But yet how much of the human being is present in the corpse? When we look at the human being as he stands before us in the physical world it is only the corpse, or hardly more than the corpse, that may be seen. Now in music, the physical form of man corresponds to what may be called the least significant of the musical elements; it represents the beat. It is therefore quite natural that with the bar line there should be an emphasis of the bodily form, a holding-on to yourself. 33

When you pass over to rhythm, presenting the "short-long", you already go beyond what is represented by the human bodily form. In rhythm you already show a very considerable part of the life of your soul. With beat in eurythmy, you always feel that a person's heaviness is the determining factor in its expression. When the beat is shown in eurythmy, you always feel (as you just saw from these attempts) that it becomes evident how heavy a person is. A heavier person will be able to mark the beat in eurythmy better than a lighter person. This is less apparent in the case of rhythm. Rhythm brings the human being into movement. And here already it is quite easy to differentiate whether the movement has artistic taste or is tasteless, whether the movement is permeated with soul: slow – quick, slow – quick. You see, here the etheric element in the human being makes its appearance. It is the etheric human being which is revealed in rhythm.

If, however, we turn our attention to melody, which conveys the actual spirit in the musical element, then the astral being of man is revealed. When you are active in the musical element the whole human being, with the exception of the ego, is brought into play. It is really true to say: "As physical human being marking the *beat*; as etheric human being expressing the *rhythm*; as astral human being evolving the *melos*: it is thus that I appear before the world." And, you see, the moment when you pass over from the musical realm to that of speech, the ego steps in. Naturally, speech is then transmitted into the astral element and even into the etheric, but its original impulse lies in the ego. 34

At the end of yesterday's lecture I indicated the hidden parallel between the scale and the vowels, and we even saw how the musical element enters eurythmically into the vowel element. Now we must also be clear about the fact that in singing the realm of the pure musical element is already exceeded. The pure and real musical element is expressed in the astral make-up of the human being. This is why singing becomes more essentially musical in proportion to the degree in which it holds to what is purely musical – the more it follows melos. And indeed this following of melos will be the most sympathetic in singing.

Passing from singing to speech (to declamation and recitation), we find marked disharmony between melos and something that has also to be borne in mind by the reciter, namely the sense of the words. It ought to be emphasised that the musical element has to be active in recitation and declamation, but an inner conflict will always exist, a conflict which the singer can only solve in the musical element. The more musical a singer, the more he will enter into the sphere of the astral, into melos, thus solving for himself the problem of how to remain musical in singing. Consequently it requires greater skill to remain musical in singing than for instance it is to remain musical in instrumental music.

But now let us consider the following. I think everyone must feel that a certain poem of Goethe's produces an extraordinarily musical effect. I refer to the poem:

> *Über allen Gipfeln*
> *Ist Ruh;*
> *In allen Wipfeln*
> *Spürest du*
> *Kaum einen Hauch;*
> *Die Vögelein schweigen im Walde.*
> *Warte nur, balde*
> *Ruhest du auch.* 35

Let us take the principal words from this poem: *Über allen Gipfeln ist Ruh: Gipfeln, ist Ruh, Wipfeln, Hauch, auch, warte, balde.*

If you enter into this poem with your feeling, you will find that what is appealing and musical (for it is extraordinarily appealing and musical) lies in the use of the words *Gipfel, Wipfel, ist Ruh, Hauch, auch, warte, balde.* It is in these words that the actual musical element lies. Now I ask you, what have we got here? Let us compare this with what I told you yesterday of the correspondence of the vowel sounds, with the scale. I always write the scale thus (naturally any note can be written on a C [*i.e.* tonic]) but I write C in the usual way, as the note from which the scale starts. Of course, the matter is not dependent on this way of writing it, but when you write in the way I did yesterday, then we have in the word *Gipfel* B G, B A G – a descending third. It has the effect of a minor third (*Moll-Terz*). It is the mirror image of a third. And it is the repetition of this mirrored third in *Wipfel* and *Gipfel* which initially renders this wonderfully subtle musical effect.

Going further, we have *ist Ruh*. In *ist Ruh*, according to the model I described yesterday, we first have a B, and the *u* ['*oo*'] represents C: B C. We find the seventh relating back to the prime, and in this relationship we have an example of everything I said both yesterday and the day before. When the human being enters into the seventh he goes out of himself. There is a relating back when he returns from the seventh to the keynote; he regains himself, as it were. You can feel this in *ist Ruh*, because it is inherent in the words.

Now it is especially interesting that in *balde* and *warte* we have E G – once more a kind of third, but the other third which moves in the opposite direction; it is the mirror image of the previous third, a kind of major third (*Dur-Terz*). Consequently we have a marvellous correspondance here: thirds which relate to each other as mirror images and the descending seventh chord, seventh harmony, in which the human being is given back to himself.

And now we will go further. *Hauch* and *auch* are words in which the diphthong makes its appearance. What are diphthongs? Where may we look for them in music? Here, you see, we may reverse our usual process. We have often found a transition from music to speech, and now we will pass over from speech into the diphthong element, into the musical element. If you possess an ear for such things, applying the principle about which I have often spoken, you will ask: Where does the essence of the diphthong lie? – of *ei*, for instance, or *au*? Does it lie in the *e* or the *i*, in the *a* or the *u*?[2] No, it lies between them. The actual sounds *ei, au*, are uttered (*Ausgesprochene*), but the "essence" (*Ausgegeisterte*, lit. "spirited out") of the diphthong lies between them, and for this reason we must look in the diphthong not for notes, but for intervals. Diphthongs are always intervals. And the interesting thing about Goethe's poem is that *Hauch* (*au*, that is to say) is truly the interval of the third. You only need call to mind yesterday's model *Wipfel* – B G, *ist Ruh* – B C, *Gipfel* – B G, *Hauch* – third, *auch* – third, *warte* – E G, *balde* – E G. In this way Goethe not only makes use of clear thirds and their mirror images, but in order to employ every possibility in this matter, he adds true intervals of the third in the diphthongs. Here you have what matters.

When someone reads or recites this poem of Goethe's, it does not matter that he should think it contains intervals of the third and even the seventh. Of course he does not think about it! Nevertheless, when the poem is rightly felt, something of this will be expressed by the reciter. It will find its way through. But what have we here? What is it that is almost as spiritual as the meaningful utterance of the ego, and which yet remains unknown? It is the astral element. And so behind the meaning of the poem there is a deeper, unconscious meaning for the human being, which is the musical meaning to be found in the astral element; this is especially effective in this poem. In this poem Goethe has transferred the effect of the poem, as far as this is possible, from the ego back into the astral realm.

Now you will best express this poem in eurythmy when you actually manage to emphasise the separate sounds less, but rather to indicate them wherever possible, without finishing them. Thus the *i* ('*ee*') in *Wipfel* and *Gipfel* is not quite finished, but left hovering in the air. This whole poem is most beautifully expressed, both eurythmically and musically, when the movements for the vowels are left hovering, and the eurythmist pulls back before completing them.

These are the things I have in mind when I say that eurythmy should be

---

2   For pronunciation of German vowels, see p. 18 (Tr. note).

studied with feeling. Feeling should not be allowed to disappear while you are engaged in eurythmy, but rather cultivated. For the onlooker can clearly differentiate (he is not aware of this, for it does not reach his consciousness, but unconsciously the onlooker can tell quite clearly) whether a eurythmist automatically goes through the motions in eurythmy, or whether feeling is poured into the forms he or she creates. And two eurythmists, one of whom is an intellectual, only presenting the meaning of what has been learned, whereas the other feels through everything down to the details of curved or stretched arm movements, feeling through the finger movements – two such eurythmists will really be as different as the virtuoso is from the artist. A person can know perfectly well how to be a virtuoso, but is not therefore an artist. These things, when brought to full consciousness, will be apparent in the beauty of your eurythmical movements. Consequently it should not be a matter of indifference whether or not you know the relationship that exists between a eurythmical presentation of music and a eurythmical presentation of recitation. Through a knowledge derived from feeling-experience you will assume the attitude which must be embraced if eurythmy is increasingly to develop into a real art. 36

Just consider how the sense of the words actually destroys melody. It might be said that the necessity of attending to the meaning of the words entails a certain fear lest the melody be destroyed. The result is that speech does violence, as it were, to the musical element. These words are naturally somewhat drastic, but speech does do violence to the musical element. Must this be so? Can it be confirmed anywhere in the world?

Yes, how this is confirmed in the world may be seen from the following: Speech consists, on the one hand, of the vowel sounds, which mainly serve to express what lives within. In the vowel sounds, as we have seen, it is easy to see that the musical element leaves its mark, whereas in the consonants this is very difficult to find. But you also know how often I have emphasised the fact that the vowels have been wrested from man's inner being. They are the direct expression of feeling, of the inner essence of the soul; wonder, amazement, shrinking back in fear, holding yourself in relation to the outer world, self-assertion, giving way, loving embrace – all this is clearly expressed in the vowels.

The consonants are entirely adapted to the outer world. If you study a consonant you will find that it always imitates some thing or process existing in the outer world. When someone speaks *i* ['*ee*'], you can feel quite definitely that here someone asserts himself. Certain German dialects even use *i* instead of *ich*, and here the human being feels his own being the strongest, as I know, for until my fourteenth or fifteenth year I myself spoke in dialect:

"*Na, nit du, i!*" ["No, not you, me!"]; I know how one's own being asserts itself when one says *i* ['*ee*']. When speaking this sound *i*, you first jump into the air and then you stand on the ground. This is what has to be felt.

Now for the consonants – let us take *l* – you can picture the sound, but *i* has to be heard; *ah* has also to be heard. At most they may be pictured astrally. But you can quite well picture *l* or *r*. L – if someone creeps along, you straightaway have *l*. The *r* – someone skips while running; you have *r*, which is a process. An ordinary wheel creeps along, it *l*'s, so to speak, but a cog-wheel *r*'s along! You can immediately picture it. If you have ever noticed a stake being driven into the ground with a hammer, you cannot picture anything else but a *t*; it is a *t*. An external process is a consonant. It is always an external process. Thus the consonantal formations of speech plainly point to the world outside. The vowels fit themselves into the consonants. `37`

You know, of course, that in [certain] languages the consonants are interchangeable with the vowels. Every consonant has something of the vowel about it, and every vowel something of the consonant. We need only remember that in some languages the *l* becomes *i*; a consonant becomes a vowel. In certain German dialects, for instance, the final *l* is always pronounced *i*. When speaking dialect "*Dörfl*" is always pronounced "*Dörfi*" [approximately, "Dirfee"]. The sound is *i*, and the *l* is very softly indicated in it; it is the *i* which is really pronounced.

But this also brings the vowel sounds towards the outside, towards the outer world. Speech is something which comes into contact with the outer world; in a certain sense it may be said to be an image of the outer world.

This is why speech does violence to the musical element, and why great skill is necessary if we are to retrieve the musical element in recitation. Great skill is necessary in order to strive back to the musical element, and we will only find the melodic element in speech if the musical element in the poet comes to meet us; indeed rhythm and beat have to be taken into account when reciting any passage of poetic language. If we neglect this, we sin against rhythm and beat (which in the musical realm itself do tend, of course, more towards the outside), and this results in incorrect recitation. The nearer you approach the musical element itself, the more you enter into melos. Melos is the musical element.

When you examine everything I have just said, you will find that in the world outside the human being, the musical element is only present to a limited degree. By proceeding from within outwards, passing from musical experience to the experience of speech, we ourselves retreat ever further from the realm of music. Why do we retreat ever further? Because speech has to lean on external nature. But external nature can only be laid hold of by speech when an element is introduced into speech which is really foreign. For nature scorns beat, rhythm, and indeed our melodic speech. And a purely naturalistic materialist deems poetic speech of any sort, that is, artistic speech, affected and sentimental.

I once knew a fellow student, for example, who regarded himself as highly gifted. This was at the time of certain lectures held by Schröer, of which I wrote in *The Course of My Life*. 38 The classes took the form of practical exercises in lecturing and essay-writing. This student arrived one day, saying that he was prepared with subject-matter of the very greatest, indeed world-shaking, importance. He went on to tell us what these world-shaking ideas were. They amounted to the following: All metrical, poetic language is fundamentally wrong. People write in iambic, trochaic rhythms; they write in rhyme. This, however, is entirely wrong, for it is not natural but artificial. It must all be abolished from poetry. Such was the discovery he had made. He declared that a new poetry must make its appearance – without rhythm, without iambus or trochee, and without rhyme. Later on I even experienced that such poetry is actually written. At that time my fellow student only put it forward as theory. We thrashed him so thoroughly that he never held his lecture!

You will see from all this that it is perfectly obvious that what comes from nature does not form the basis of the musical element, for the musical element itself is [a/the] creation of the human being. And if we examine the inner nature of music and speech, we shall realise why it is that the musical element is so far removed from anything naturalistic. It is the self-creating [power] in the human being, and imitating nature is an aberration of the musical path.

As I said before, I do not mean to cast aspersions on the imitation of "rustling forests", soughing winds, bubbling springs, "a brook in March", 39 and so on. It is far from my intention to criticise these things in any way; but there does lie behind them the urge to pass out of the actual musical element, to enrich music by the introduction of something unmusical. In certain circumstances the result may be very agreeable, for it is possible to enlarge the sphere of every art in every direction, but because eurythmy demands that music be taken still more musically than it already is, terrible difficulties will arise if attempts are made to express in the right way in eurythmy something that is not purely musical.

Yet another thing can be understood from this, and that is the beneficial effect of music-eurythmy therapy; for this must gradually be developed side by side with usual music-eurythmy. Why is this? Fundamentally speaking, a large number of illnesses are caused by the fact that people have an inward tendency to turn into nature in some way, instead of remaining human. We always turn into a piece of nature when we are ill. Now we are human beings through the very fact that we inwardly do not tolerate natural processes to remain as they are, but instantly subject them to an inner transformation; we instantly make them inwardly human. There is no process in the human being (with the exception of the dissolving of salt, the metamorphosis of salt) [40] which is not a transformation of some process of nature. We become ill when we are powerless against natural processes in this inner transformation, if we cannot metamorphose them – a process they have to undergo within the human being –, and when they still run their course as natural processes. If in any part of the human organism a natural process preponderates over the human, and we then make the person practise music-eurythmy, this is a therapeutic factor; for by this means we lead the part of the body in question away from nature and back into the human realm. When we let someone do music-eurythmy because nature in him is too strong, it is as though we said to the natural process in the organ: "Out you go!" – for these movements are solely human and have nothing of nature about them. The musical element belongs only to man, not to nature. [41]

In earlier times the musical element itself was recognised as a means of healing, and music in such times did bring about many cures. But because the musical element comes especially to the fore in eurythmy, so the thera-peutic forces of the musical element must also come to the fore with an efficient therapy. This is what I wanted to tell you today.

Tomorrow at the same time we shall continue.

Lecture 5: Choral Eurythmy

Dornach, 23 Feb. 1924

You will have seen that it is quite possible for a single individual to express in eurythmy the essence of the musical element as musical element. We have tried to show how, for instance, the triad and the progression of the phrase may be mastered by a single person.

But the eurythmical expression of the musical element by a single person, from a certain point of view, is necessarily rather primitive, and is somewhat meagre when presented on the stage – although most beautiful and impressive performances can be given by a solo eurythmist. It is to be hoped that these solo performances will be valued, for they are a means whereby the actual essence of musical eurythmy may be revealed. In spite of this, it cannot be denied that a musical impression can also be given by means of the concerted working of a number of persons, in other words by means of choral eurythmy. The point, however, is that we must not merely take these things schematically, but also enter somewhat into the quality of people working together in artistic presentation. 42

I have emphasised what doing eurythmy entails: it is work to raise (*herausarbeiten*) the physical human being (which really only "sounds" in beat) to the etheric and the astral human being. And if we seek for melos as such in the astral organisation of the human being (whereas we seek for speech in the ego-organisation), then we can perceive that which forms the fundamental basis of musical eurythmy. What you experience as astral human being usually remains stuck in a state of repose. But when you proceed a step further and present to the world that which otherwise remains in repose in the astral human being, you show, as it were, your spirit- and soul-nature. And it is this power of making things manifest which constitutes the most predominant element of all artistic endeavour.

At this point I will take the opportunity of alluding to a very, very remarkable contemporary phenomenon. My reason for doing so is, that if as eurythmists you can awaken a feeling for it, it would do much to help you in the actual artistic development of eurythmy.

During this course of lectures on music-eurythmy, I have often found myself thinking of a very significant Austrian musician of the present day. This musician, who was born in Wiener-Neustadt, opposes all modern music with extraordinary vehemence, denouncing it as "bad European music". This in itself is an interesting phenomenon, and should be of special interest to eurythmists. Hauer 43 began to study music at a very early age, between his fifth and eighth to ninth years, by playing the zither, and he progressed far, coming to the view that it does not take much to acquire all that we presently call music. We can feel in Hauer's whole manner of expression that in a certain respect he is inwardly extraordinarily honest. On the one hand, he came to the conclusion that what goes by the name of music today is exceptionally easily come by, but, on the other hand, that precisely the musical element is missing, that we are led away from the musical realm. Indeed, very much of what I have to say about the eurythmic presentation of the musical realm can be found in Hauer's writings, although he expresses it in a stark and radical way. He speaks, for example, about atonal music.

I have said that the actual musical element, the spiritual element in music, lies between the notes, in the intervals, constituting that which we do not hear. In speaking about atonal music Hauer touches on something that is very significant and true. He is of the opinion that the production of a note or chord is nothing more than an appeal to the emotions or the senses – merely a means to express externally the inaudible melos, which presents the inmost life of the human soul.

Now there is something so decadent and chaotic in the culture and civilisation of the present day, especially where the arts are concerned, that your heart may well warm towards anyone who, with a certain instinctive flair, realises that the music of today [1924] is not really music, but simply noise, and perceives that on which the musical element depends. It is, moreover, not difficult to understand that a man who has developed by himself out of all this can be absolutely furious with all European art. And this is true of Hauer. European art is absolutely repugnant to him.

All this is very interesting, and I have long been interested in this man Hauer. At the time when I was trying to lead over the musical element into eurythmy, I had to seek for some things that appear in Hauer, and I had to say to myself, "It is certain that you could never take Hauer's atonal melos as a basis for the gestures of eurythmy". The movements of eurythmy could not be found in this way. I had to ask myself, "Why is this so? Why is it not possible to come to eurythmic movements in this way, when Hauer undoubtedly feels the movement of melos with such inwardness, and sees so clearly what is essential in the musical realm?" In the case of Hauer, the explanation is simple. Hauer hates that civilisation which marks the beginning of European culture – a civilisation which the rest of humanity admires tremendously. He hates the civilisation of Greece. He is a man who hates to excess the civilisation of Greece.

Now it is interesting for once to come across a man who honestly and truly hates Greek civilisation. There are any number of people who venerate it insincerely, by which I do not mean to imply that there are not others who venerate it with sincerity. To honour Sophocles and Aeschylus is a matter of course today, whereas to find anyone abusing Sophocles and Aeschylus as destroyers of art is an interesting phenomenon, and one that should not be overlooked. Hauer's view of the Greeks is based on the fact that, in his opinion, they brought everything that is related to art into the theatre, thus pouring everything that is audible into visibility. Now, after all, that is quite true. The question is whether we can also love the visible realm. If we are to find our way to eurythmy, we must of course be able to love what is visible. If we do not love the visible realm, honestly do not *love* it, preferring to remain in the audible realm, to stop with melos, then we shall never be able to find any satisfaction in Greek culture, where everything was transferred into the sphere of what can be seen and understood.

Now among the Orientals there were inspired teachers who truly wanted to listen to the audible realm. Oriental architecture was really music in space; it has within it a great deal of eurythmy. You actually see melos pouring itself into movement. Europe possesses very little understanding for a musical architecture, as has been built with the Goetheanum here in Dornach, for the Goetheanum was, in a sense, a revolt against Greek architecture. There was very little suggestion of Greek architecture about it; but the Goetheanum was musical, it was eurythmical. 44

Now, you see, Hauer actually hates speech, too, because speech does not stop with melos, but (as I have already shown) does violence to it, pushing it into the outer world. For from the moment we utter sounds (and in so doing give ourselves up to what is demanded of us by the meaning of the sounds), from that moment onwards we become in a certain sense unmusical. The speaking of sounds is an art that in fact can only indicate a sounding of melos. Melos may thus peep through, but it cannot be fully developed. You cannot form words according to the arrangement I proposed, as if the vowel sounds contained in them were really thirds or other intervals. You cannot do this, for the world does not permit it.

When, let us say, you feel wonder, an *ah*, and just after experiencing this sound you experience some feeling, let's say, which lies in the interval of the third compared to the former feeling, the world does not allow you to feel it. It's not possible, wouldn't you agree? – Life continually destroys that which is musical. Nature too is unmusical, and it is not from nature that we are able to derive that which is musical.

This destruction of what is musical extends to recitation and declamation. If there were only vowel sounds in speech, there would be no recitation or declamation, for the human being would always be yielding up his inner being (through pronouncing the vowels) to the outer world. There would be no declamation or recitation, for we would have to go along with the experiences of the world, and it would not be possible to conserve the musical element. That is why we have the consonants. The consonants are, as it were, the apology for the vowels. Man apologises to himself for the fact that, in the vowel sounds, he follows his own experiences. And when he fits in the consonants between the vowels, it is an apology for having become so foreign to himself. When you make the sound *a* follow an *ah*, forming thus either *warte* or *balde* (I have already spoken about these things) you have at the same time, in the consonants fitting themselves in between the *ah* and the *a*, an apology for the succession of the vowels.

In the case of that particular poem by Goethe, however, the vowels really make a musical effect, and consequently this apology of the consonants is not so much needed. When listening to this poem, a subtle, musical impression would be received if the speaker could achieve a swallowing of the consonants as much as possible, so that only the vowels were audible, with the consonants merely indicated.

Many other poems, however, really need the consonants. It may be said that the less musical a poem is, the more careful you must be to make the right use of the consonantal instrument (palate, mouth, lips, teeth, and so on). Then, in recitation and declamation, we have the apology for the offence committed by the vowels.

This will demonstrate that with the vowel sounds, which are an externalisation of what is inward, the human being places a kind of caricature into the world. He is no longer himself. The human being is himself as long as he remains musical. When he becomes a vowel sound, he places a caricature in the world. With the consonants he once again recasts this caricature into the human form, and is then outside. He lays hold of an image of himself. This corresponds to the vowel when framed by the consonants. In music we go more and more inwards. In speech we go further and further outwards. It is infinitely important for eurythmists to feel and experience these things, to develop a rounding-off of the artistic process, which is more than simply making or copying movements.

Taking this as your starting-point you will also be able to feel how choral eurythmy can be effective. In choral eurythmy we are dealing with a number of people. Let us first take the musical case: [i] We have a metamorphosis of the motif, or phrase. We might express this metamorphosis of motifs in choral form by somehow grouping people together – three, let us say. We will let the first person present the first motif in eurythmy by moving in the form to the place of the second person, who will now take over the second metamorphosis of the motif. The first person remains standing. The second person moves on, passing the next metamorphosis of the motif over to the third person, who now continues the form to the place of the first (see *Fig. 5*). A kind of round dance can be brought about in this way.

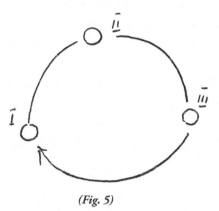

(Fig. 5)

It is only necessary in such a case for those who remain to continue to carry out the corresponding motifs while standing. In this simple way (where one person develops the motifs by moving, while the others retain their original motifs in standing), we have introduced a new variation into the motifs by means of eurythmy. By means of the motif which is in motion and the motif which is formed, in eurythmy we are able to introduce into the musical realm something which could never be expressed by the pure musical element, for in the pure musical element the previous chord or motif can no longer be retained after the new one has begun to sound.

Only think how often I have observed that, in the spiritual world, the past remains. In this development of the motifs through the chorus, the past remains (becomes engraved, so to speak, hardened), through the fact that the bearer of the motif in question carries out the movements while standing. This is one way.

[ii] Another variation appears when we have chords in the progressions of the motif. Here you can arrange the chorus in such a way that the chord is carried out by several people, and the motif is carried over to another group of people. In this way, one group expresses the harmonic element, and the harmonic development is then expressed by letting the harmony flow over from one group to another. Here we reach something very significant and totally different in its effect. When the progression of the motif is expressed in movement (the chord can also be represented by a single person, and the progression of the motif can also be expressed in movement by an individual), the space in which the movement occurs, and all the metamorphoses and transformations of the music are filled out by the physical human being.

[iii] When making use of a chorus, however (we will suppose that you have one group of three people, and three more, and a further three, each carrying the progression of the motif from one group to the next), the element of visibility ceases to be [paramount], for when the motif is passed from one group to the next an invisible element wends its way through this

choral dance. Here we approach very near to making this invisible element musical, very near especially to atonal music. Thus, by transferring to a chorus, the whole matter takes on quite a different aspect [from the atonal conception]. In this way the aspect of the musical element which is becoming progressively unmusical, may be made musical once again by means of eurythmy, because precisely movement makes it possible for you to appeal to that which is invisible. Thus, in this direction too, we shall possibly find that music-eurythmy is able to exert a corrective influence upon the musical element [*i.e.*, the conceptions of practising musicians].

Now in the continuation of a motif everything will naturally depend upon the movement, but when the chord is being represented by a group, the relative positions of the people are of importance. The people in question (even when their group is moving) must endeavour to retain their relative positions. Your feelings will have to tell you this. Let us now suppose that we have to represent a triad. You can't place yourselves one behind the other (left of the diagram). You can and have to feel that you place yourselves in such a way that the first person stands here, the second here and the third in the middle (see *Fig. 6*).

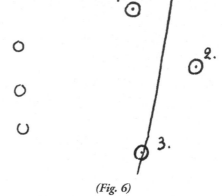

(Fig. 6)

Then, when the lowest note is taken by the first person, the next highest note by the second person, and the third note (if you wish, the fifth) by the third person, then you can tell by looking at it that the right thing has happened. The motif, when brought into movement, is carried over to the next group of people. And when the whole chorus is moving, each individual must endeavour to retain the right position in relationship to the others, so the whole design of the form (which is determinded by the relative positions of the people) may be expressed through this.

If we have a combination of two notes, the people can only be placed in this way (see *Fig. 7*). We can feel that this is incomplete.

But now for the four-note discord. When you consider the artistic effect of placing three people as we did for the triad, and observe the complete grouping (which really does make the triad stand before us), then you will say to yourself: "Where

(Fig. 7)

shall I put the fourth person?" Whoever has artistic feeling will not find a place for a fourth person. Indeed no such place can be found. The fourth person can only be provided for by letting him or her move around the third person. There is no other way of doing it. You come to this by direct intuition. So now you already have an indication for the discord in the grouping. The group, the fixed configuration, can only express concords. The moment a discord enters, movement must be introduced into the grouping (see *Fig. 8*).

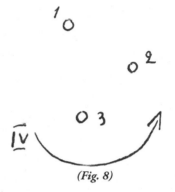

(Fig. 8)

When you introduce movement into the grouping, you bring a challenge, and you can no longer remain still. The movement made by the fourth person (a movement necessary to the progression, to the resolution of the discord) is disclosed by its own nature.

You see, we have to look at things in this way if we are to gain insight into the gestures as the essential matter. Having gained this insight, you will say to yourselves, "What we do is the outcome of an intrinsic necessity". This is no infringement of freedom, although it does not open the door for purely arbitrary ideas. What always remains is the freedom to carry out each individual movement beautifully.

Choral eurythmy may be developed from the usual eurythmy which the individual presents. In particular, however, the following can be done. Let us suppose that in some piece of music we have the tonic, the dominant and the subdominant. To present this we take three groups of people and place the tonic with the first group, the dominant with the second group and the subdominant with the third, making those presenting the tonic have larger movements, whereas those presenting the dominant and subdominant make smaller ones. Now try to imagine how this would look. The frequent recurrence of the tonic is shown by the larger forms. The tonic is given prominence by the larger movements. It follows that the eurythmist who is moving these larger forms will quite naturally make larger gestures too, prompted by his or her feeling. The tonic, which recurs time and again, also recurs in the eurythmy forms. If these things are well practised in the way that has been explained, you will find that the character of each individual key 45 will be revealed, for you will be obliged to make the corresponding movements in the transitions.

The difference between major and minor keys appears very clearly with this interplay between the different groups [see Steiner's lecture notes. NB 494. 10]. And when, in addition, you take into consideration the fact that every time a sound goes higher there should be the feeling that the eurythmist has to approach nearer to the audience, whereas when the sound goes lower the eurythmist has to move more towards the back of the stage – when all this is added you will have the whole musical element in a visual image. There is still another point which belongs to this, that when a group comes to high notes, there must be a feeling that the movement has to be made more pointed, whereas when it is a question of lower notes, then it has to become rounder. Thus it may be said that a movement carried out with this gesture is lower, and a movement with this gesture is higher.

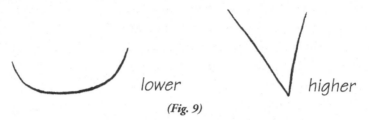

lower   *higher*

(Fig. 9)

You will say, "These things present us with a great deal to learn, for in actual practice they are very complicated". Quite true! But they are no more complicated than learning to play the piano, or learning to sing.

I have indicated how the transition can be made from solo eurythmy to choral eurythmy. Real difficulties only make their appearance when we come to polyphonic music, but we shall speak about this tomorrow. In movement the whole affair will become even more disjointed than in the musical element as such. When we have a piece with many voices, therefore, we also have to make use of different people, and the quality of belonging together can only be achieved by means of a certain relationship in the form.

At this point I should like to develop a brief, esoteric "intermezzo" for you. It has to do with the fact that the eurythmist has to use his or her body as an instrument. Only think of all that goes into the making of an instrument and how we appreciate certain violins which today can actually no longer be made.[3] Think of everything that is involved in an external musical instrument. Now it is true that the human being is, in a certain way, exempt from these demands, for the divine-spiritual powers have already built him as an exceedingly good instrument. But actually the case is not so rosy, for otherwise every individual would find his body were the most perfectly suitable instrument. The eurythmists sitting here will be well aware of the great difficulties they have in overcoming bodily hindrances and impediments, if it is a question of arriving at eurythmy that is really worthy of the art.

The fact is that quite a bit can be done in order to work inwardly upon

3   Instruments made by Stradivarius, Guarnerius, and so on. (Translator's note.)

your body so that eurythmy to the sounds of speech and of music may gradually appear out of this body in a truly artistic, complete form. There is very little opportunity for this in the civilised life of Europe. European civilisation has developed a view towards outer nature, but has not developed that which is necessary to give the human being a place in the world commensurate with true human dignity. And so people today have great difficulty feeling their real humanity within themselves.

Now what I have to say in this direction will not be immediately clear. It will become apparent through doing it. What I want to say in this connection is as follows. Listen to this progression of notes, which will at first seem very strange to you:

And now (to the pianist): Play the first two notes together and the next

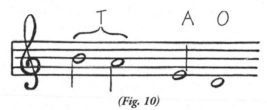

(Fig. 10)

two notes consecutively, sustaining the last note for a long time. The first two notes, accordingly, played together and the last two notes one after the other, the final note sustained for a long time.

Now will someone who can do it well show this in eurythmy, simply in standing: B, A, along with E and D; the E short, and sustaining the last note for a long time.

And now I need somebody who will sing a word to this progression of notes; for there is a word which rings true when sung to this peculiar progression of notes, namely, the word "T A O". We are dealing here with the following: When expressing this in eurythmy (and here you must apply what has been given in these lectures) you have the seventh, the sixth, and only then the other notes. But you also have to feel the descending progression of notes, and then try to express this in eurythmy, not merely the notes. Hitherto you have become stuck in what is elementary, but you really have to express what I have said and then you will see that in the T A O you have a wonderful means of making your inner bodily nature flexible, inwardly supple, and able to be artistically fashioned for eurythmy. For when you lead the seventh and the sixth, as I have indicated them, down into the E and the D (that is to say, you come into this second), you will see how by carrying this out you will gain an inner strength which you will be able to carry over into all your eurythmy. This is an esoteric exercise, and when it is carried out it means meditation in eurythmy.

And when you ask someone else (either singing or speaking in a reciting or declamatory way) to accompany these gestures with declamation or singing of T A O, you will see that in connection with singing, eurythmy and recitation, this is something like that which meditation is for general human life.

What I have given here is indeed an esoteric "intermezzo", and it points the way to eurythmic meditation. We must go very far back, back to the ancient civilisation of China, if we are to find our way into this meditation in eurythmy. [46] And you will understand that we can exercise a certain sympathy for someone who wants to get back to the ancient Orient in order to re-discover music, and whose feeling leads him to say: The Greeks have totally ruined music, and that is why the Greeks really had no proper musician – with the exception of the mythological figure, Orpheus. [47]

On the other hand, we can love the Greek civilisation for its way of entering into the sculptural, plastic element. But one thing is true, that the Greek culture with its sculpture gradually was led away from eurythmy. Here we must compare the forms of oriental architecture, which really did transpose music into movement, with the forms of Greek architecture, which basically exhibit a dreadful symmetry. Here this dreadful symmetry rules. This, too, had to make its appearance in the world at some point.

The Greek culture did – I might almost say – tragically suffer the consequences of its civilisation. It was a short-lived civilisation, bringing about its own dissolution. The fault does not lie in the Greek culture: the fault lies in the fact that Greek culture is supposed to be forever reproduced in European civilisation. It is, however, a kind of dissolution of this Greek element when we derive our movements directly from speech and singing, from the realms of speech and of music themselves. The difficulty people have in understanding eurythmy lies in the fact that European understanding has been, as it were, frozen into the reposing form, and is fundamentally no longer able to live in movement. The reposing form, however, should be left to nature. When we come to the human being, we have to enter into movement, because the human being transcends the reposing, purely sense-perceptibly visible form.

That is what I wanted to say to you today.

Lecture 6: The sustained note; the rest; discords

Dornach, 25 Feb. 1924

If, in the forthcoming lectures, we are to become acquainted with a few things in further detail, today we have to put the question: If music essentially is the flow of melos, and if it is melos in particular which should be expressed in the gestures of eurythmy, what then is the musical element as such, the music shown in eurythmy, meant to express?

Here we meet with two extremes. On the one hand it may be said that the melodic element is tending more and more towards what is thematic, towards the expression of something that is not in itself musical. I have often mentioned that, especially in recent times through a Wagnerian influence, as well as other influences, music on the one hand has become expression, expression of something that is not music. On the other hand, especially in the beginning of the age of Wagner, we also find pure, absolute music (the musical element as such, simply the weaving of musical sounds) – of which it was said (not without a certain justification) that it made music into a tonal arabesque, a progression of notes without content.

Naturally these are both extreme cases. To put forward the idea that music embodies nothing and is merely a tonal arabesque 48 is nonsense, utter nonsense. But such nonsense may very easily arise when there is no real understanding of where the essential musical element lies. It cannot lie in the notes themselves, as I have repeatedly emphasised. The person engaged in music-eurythmy has constantly to bear in mind the necessity for expressing in the movements, in the actual gestures themselves, that which lies between the notes, regarding the notes as merely giving him the occasion for the movement.

It may help you to carry out these gestures I have already indicated, with inner correctness, and the right inner feeling, if we make a certain basic provision. And the provision should consist that you, as eurythmists, regard the actual note, and in a certain sense the chord too, as that which pushes you into movement, causes you to move, and gives the impetus (*Ruck*: "jolt") towards movement. You must continue the impetus between two notes and again regard the next note as the impetus which is given to you. In this way the movement will not express the note, and will not emphasise the note, but will express in the fullest possible way everything that lies between the notes and what comes to the fore, for instance, in the intervals. This is of great importance.

Now, why is there such a strong urge in our modern age to deviate from the purely musical realm? Something quite beautiful may sometimes result from this deviation from what is purely musical, but why is the urge to deviate from it so strong? It is because the contemporary person has gradually acquired an attitude of mind in which he is no longer able to dream, no longer able to meditate. He has nothing within to set him into movement, and wants to be set into movement from outside. But this being-set-into-movement from outside can never produce a musical mood. In order that modern civilisation could furnish proof of its unmusical nature, it has laid hold of a drastic means to do so. It is really as though, in its concealed depths of soul, modern civilisation wanted to provide the clearest proof that it is unmusical. And the proof is given in that it has produced the film (Am. movie). The film is the clearest proof that those who like it are unmusical. For the whole basis of films is that they only permit those things to be active in the soul which do not arise out of the inner life of the soul, but which are stimulated from outside [see Appendix 6].

It must be admitted that a lot of modern music-making [1924] tends to lay special stress upon that which is stimulated from outside. Attempts are made to imitate what is external – not by means of the pure melodic element, but rather by employing some subject matter as far remote from the melodic element as possible.

There is a very simple way, once more a kind of meditation (I recently spoke to you about the T A O-meditation, which may be helpful to eurythmists in the way I have already explained), whereby you may gradually accustom yourself to seek for that which is musical even in what lies outside the musical sphere. It consists in comparing a sequence of vowels, such as: *Lieb ist viel* or *Eden geht grell*. There need be no meaning. Compare these for instance with: *Gab man Manna* or *Ob Olaf warm war*.

And now repeat such sentences one after the other:

> *Lieb ist viel… Eden geht grell…* : does not resonate
> *Gab man Manna… Ob Olaf warm war…* : musical

You will most certainly feel that the second examples are musical, whereas the first exist as if they would not resound. Just try to repeat these sentences one after the other: *Lieb ist viel. Gab man Manna. Eden geht grell. Ob Olaf warm war.* You will easily recognise that the vowels *ah*[4] and *o* lie within the musical sphere, whereas the vowels *ee* and *a* depart from it. This is an important matter for eurythmists to observe, for eurythmy must, of course, represent a wholeness. When in music-eurythmy you wish to express something very inward, the movements may be led over into *ah* or *o*, or likewise

---

4   Phonetic spelling, see p. 18 (Tr. note).

into *oo*. But the gestures of music-eurythmy may not readily be led over into *ee* or *a*. Thus the sounds *ah, o, oo* may be employed in pieces of music for eurythmy in order to emphasise the mood, but *a* and *ee* should only be used when it is definitely intended to pass, at some point or other, out of the musical realm. This is important.

These things are of such a nature that we have to acquire a consciousness of them above all. It is interesting, for example, when we follow the German language through several centuries, to observe that it has gradually dropped many *ah, o,* and *oo* sounds, and has taken on many *ee* and *a* sounds. In other words, the German language has become progressively more unmusical in the course of centuries. (I am speaking now of the vowels, not of the intervals.)

It is really important to bear this in mind in music-eurythmy, and indeed in other eurythmy too. For the knowledge that the German language has a marked tendency towards a distorted phonetic imagination may be quite valuable. With the western Germanic languages this is even more the case. But all this rightly leads us to put the question, "What does music really express?" This question cannot easily be answered by anyone who is unable to dream. For, you see, in very truth the poet, the artist, must basically be able to dream, to dream consciously – that is to say, to meditate. Either he must hold dream-pictures in recollection, or be able to find dream-pictures of the realities of the spiritual world.

But what does this mean? It means leaving behind everything that makes sense in the sensory world. Take a dream (I have often spoken of these matters). Take a dream: if we are to get at its nature, we must not look at it as an interpreter of dreams does. For the interpreter of dreams takes the dream's content. Anyone who really understands the nature of dreams does not take the dream's content, but considers whether the dream rises up in fear and calms down, whether the dream stirs up an inner uneasiness which is intensified to anxiety, ending perhaps in this anxiety, or whether there is a state of tension which is afterwards resolved. This is really the decisive thing in a dream. And in the description of spiritual processes this becomes even more necessary.

It is, of course, exceedingly difficult today to speak to humanity about the things which spiritual science has to impart. For instance, when I described the progression of world-evolution (Saturn, Sun, Moon and so on), people thought the very things important that were unimportant to me. It is certainly correct that the processes on Saturn were as I described them. But that is not the essential point. The essential point is the inner movement that is described. And I have always been most delighted when somebody said that he would like to compose in music what has been described in the evolution of Saturn, Sun and Moon. Of course, he would have to leave out some of it, leave out the colour element, as I described, the warmth phenomena, even the smells on Saturn (for apart from the "smelling-harmonium" 49 we have no musical instrument functioning to smells, do we!). Even so, particularly Saturn evolution is such that its essence could be expressed quite well in music and could be composed. 50

When anyone dreams, and (setting aside its content) takes the tension and relaxation, the culmination of the picture sequence, or the culmination of bliss when flying, and so on; if he takes all this movement and says: "I am quite indifferent to the meaning of the dream; for me it all depends on how its movements take place" – then the dream already is a piece of music, then you cannot write it down except in musical notation. Once you feel that the dream can only be written down in musical notation, then you are just beginning to understand the dream, I mean really to understand it by looking at it directly.

From this you will see that the musical element has content – not the thematic content, which is taken from the sensory world, but a content which appears everywhere when something is expressed in terms of the senses, but in such a manner that everything sensory can be left aside, revealing the essence of the matter. You have to treat the musical element precisely in this way. And the eurythmist has above all things to bear this strongly in mind. And he will bear it strongly in mind when he pays more attention than is usual in listening, when he pays attention to the sustained notes and the rests.

For the eurythmist, the sustained note (the pedal-point) and the rest are of special importance. And it is a serious question whether a pedal-point or anything that recalls in some way the sustained note (this really is of great importance) is being adequately treated. It will be adequately treated if, every time he or she comes to a held note, or to something which either is a pedal-point in germ, or might become such, the eurythmist carries out the eurythmy in the greatest possible calmness, emphasizing standing calmly, in other words not proceeding further in space as long as the sustained note is heard.

On the other hand, it is important for the eurythmist to penetrate inwardly into the musical significance of everything connected to the rest. And so it will be good to take an example. Here (see musical example) you have the opportunity of moving up after the descending mood, with a corresponding rest which even contains a bar line, something which may seem a contradiction, from the point of view of the eurythmist.

I mention this because after what I just said it must appear contradictory to the eurythmist. I previously said that the bar line signifies a holding-on, doing the movement in yourself; that the transition from one motif to another signifies moving in space, if possible with a swinging movement – naturally suited to the notes in question. As a eurythmist you may say, "Now here I really do not know what to do. I am supposed to move forwards and yet at the same time remain standing". That is in fact just what you should do! You should move forwards two steps and remain standing between them. You should accomplish this when you want to express anything similar to this example, taken from Mozart's *Piano Sonata* in F major, where you can have a longer rest during which the bar line occurs – then you should move with a swing from one note to the next, but calmly stand still in yourself in the middle of this swinging movement, in the rest. Here you will see how you radically indicate, precisely through eurythmy, that the musical

(Fig. 11: From Mozart's Piano Sonata in F major (K.332), III, bars 58-61)

element lies between the notes, for in such a case it is the rest which you specially emphasise through eurythmy. It is this that is so very important.

And now consider I said on the one hand that when a note is sustained, you should try as far as possible to stand still, remaining within yourself. Now, the pedal-point, the sustained note, frequently lies in a second voice and of course it may be aesthetically expressed when the two parts are taken – as they always have to be – by two people, each moving a different form. In this way a very beautiful interplay (*Variation*) may result between the two people. When the one proceeds in the movement, the other remains standing with the sustained note. The movements are carried out so that the person remaining standing moves a shorter curve, during which time the person moving onwards in the form makes a fuller curve – and they re-encounter each other. In this way the whole thing is brought into a satisfactory movement, which on the one hand may be shown between the swinging-over, between the interval (which may go as far as the rest), and on the other hand in the pedal-point or the sustained note in general (see *Fig. 12*).

It is in this way that the actual quality of music-eurythmy has gradually to develop. Only when you feel things in this way will you be able to bring out the actual quality of music-eurythmy.

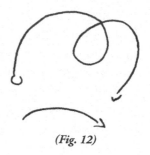

(Fig. 12)

This shows you at the same time that music of several parts will essentially be expressed by a number of people moving a number of forms. The forms must be carried out in such a way that they really correspond to each other, just as the different voices correspond in the music itself.

When you further develop the feeling of which I have spoken (the realisation that the musical element lies in the tension, relaxation, in the rising and falling of the movement), you will indeed have something which the music expresses. For music does not express that which creates the meaning of words, but it expresses the spiritual element itself living in the movement of musical sound. It is consequently specially important for eurythmists to pay great heed to what the movement expresses quite inwardly in the greatest sense, that is discord and concord. Now, you know, a composer will never make use of a discord unintentionally, and indeed music without discords is not really music, because it is without inner movement. Composers and musicians in general make use of discords. Concords are actually there in order to calm the discords, to bring the discord to some sort of completion.

In the experience of discords and concords something makes its appearance which approaches the mysteries of the world closer than we can put into words. Let us suppose that we hear a discordant phrase which resolves into a concord. Let us observe what the eurythmist does. He or she of course can bear in mind all that I have indicated, and shall possibly still indicate, with regard to forms. He or she will go on to a concord and may use as form the various intervals that I have indicated. But the transition from a discord to a concord, or vice versa, should be brought out in the presentation. It should be that the eurythmist, while moving on in a discord, at the moment of going over from a discord to a concord, must insert an abrupt movement (*Ruck*) into the movement itself (*Fig. 13*).

Fig. 13

Something very significant is expressed in this way. By this means we express the fact that here, with the transition from discord to concord, or vice versa, something is brought about which the human being places outside of himself. What I have drawn above could also be drawn like this (*Fig. 14*).

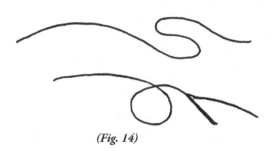

(*Fig. 14*)

Observe how I erase a small part. That is where you go back. You will feel that a small part has been erased. It is a passing over into the spiritual. When you erase a piece of your path you annul all musical sound [that is present] in the movement, and you indicate: "Something is present that is no longer possible to express in the sensory realm. Here I [the eurythmist] can only suggest the bounds to you [the onlooker]; your imagination must take you further."

You see, it is only when we come so far in doing such things that we reach the point where the arts should be. Philistines may think, when they see something of this kind (see *Fig. 15*, drawing on the left), that it is a face. It is not a face; it is a line. A face is as follows: I must manage in such a way that no actual line is drawn, but a line, as it is, is allowed to arise out of the light and shade (see drawing on the right). Anyone who draws these lines, from the very moment he begins to draw, is no painter, indeed no artist at all. Only someone who allows the lines to arise either out of the colour, or out of the chiaroscuro [light and shade], is an artist.

(*Fig. 15*)

Sky

Sea

(*Fig. 16*)

You can draw in a philistine fashion, like this (*Fig. 16*). This represents the boundary between sea and sky. But in reality it does not exist! It is absolutely non-existent. The sky exists: blue. The sea exists: green. The boundary between them both comes about because they touch each other (see *Fig. 17*).

If you want to paint a picture

(*Fig. 17*)

of a house, surrounded as it is by air, leave room for your colours within the area which the air leaves free. The house will come about. That's what art has to work for! In this matter one can indeed sometimes reach a fine state of despair. [51]

You see, such despair is very difficult for someone of today to understand. Now, many and various are the types of people who apply for teaching posts at the Waldorf School [Stuttgart], amongst them, teachers of drawing. They have certainly learned something (namely drawing) that is quite useless at the Waldorf School. They say, "I can draw". Indeed there is no such thing as drawing! It is damaging when children are taught to draw, for there really is no such thing as drawing. [52]

When you reach the point of understanding this erasing of your line in eurythmy, you will also have reached the point when this understanding of the musical element in doing eurythmy really leads into the artistic realm. Thus whenever transitions occur, try – once again without being pedantic – to develop a movement which goes back over itself so that the onlooker is obliged to go back, so that he says to himself, "He or she was already further and is now going back". He will notice all this unconsciously, but he will at that moment be urged out of the sensory realm, to enter into the spiritual realm where everything to do with the senses is erased.

In this way you will discover the possibility of looking for the essential nature of eurythmic movement in the rest (*Pause*: "rest", "pause"), even bringing more and more into the rest. Let us once more consider our example (see *Fig. 11*). Here you have a transition which, in its note values, already presents a marked feeling of going-out-of-yourself, of going with your inner being out of your skin. With the interval of the fifth there is still the feeling of being just at the boundary of the skin. The fifth is the human being. Going further, we actually pass over into what lies beyond the human realm, but in this case, because we are dealing with music, into the spiritual realm. If you achieve this emphasis of the rest by means of specially pronounced movement, and yet introduce into this movement a momentary calmness (as I have indicated), you will express the whole meaning of this ascending passage in a really satisfactory eurythmical way.

When you are practising, try to find examples of musical phrases containing long rests and very pronounced leaps in pitch, and then try to make the movement as characteristic as possible. This will result in a eurythmy perfectly adapted to the expression of instrumental music; I might say, a singing eurythmy. This will also affect your eurythmy as a whole. For by this means you will feel the very marked contrast which lies between the vowels and the consonants for eurythmic expression. Even if it is true that *ee* and *a* actually tend towards a distortion of phonetic imagination, they are nevertheless vowels, and remain within the sphere of music, whereas the consonants are merely noises and lead away from the musical realm.

I have also said that the consonants are really the apology for using the vowel sounds for something in the outer world. This will closely concern you, for in speech-eurythmy it will cause you to introduce as much of the vowel element as possible into the consonants. This means, in other words, that you should try in eurythmy to make the consonants as short and the vowels as long as possible.

Now this is not what I wanted to impress on you (for this will arise from your feelings) that there must be a certain parallel between declamation and recitation, and eurythmy. What I do want you especially to take to heart is that for speech-eurythmy, too, it is most important to bear in mind that it is also the task of the speaker not only to say something when he speaks, but at times to say something even more essential when he doesn't speak. I do not mean by this those dashes of which recent poets are so enamoured, presumably because they have so much spiritual matter to communicate that they are compelled to express it in continual dashes! I expect you are acquainted with an ironical poem by Morgenstern, consisting only of dashes. 53 It does not contain a single sound, not a single word – simply dashes. I do not mean these dashes, then, but rather the fact that, in order to bring out certain effects in a poem, it is absolutely necessary, just as necessary in declamation as in eurythmy, to understand how to make proper pauses.

Think of the hexameter, with its caesura, where a pause has to be made, and you will realise that something is actually said by means of the pause. Sometimes the pauses need only be short, but it is important that they should also be given their place in declamation and recitation. Imagine the phrase: *Was hör ich draussen vor dem Tor was auf der Brücke schallen?* recited without any pause – appalling!

> *Was hör' ich draussen vor dem Tor –*
> *Was auf der Brücke schallen?*

is correct. Now as eurythmists, when you are concerned with the expression of a rest, and in speech-eurythmy too, the effect will be eminently correct and aesthetically good as well as intrinsically justified, if you cultivate the going-back-into-yourself (going back in the form) which you have been able to learn from music-eurythmy. So that at times even in the short pauses of speech-eurythmy, this retracing, this erasing the form, should by all means be seen.

In conclusion I only want to add something which will serve to complete what was left out in the preceding lectures. It is this: You know that the keynote is best expressed by the position, or also by means of the step: position, step (as I explained in connection with the triad). Now imagine that you have to form the interval of the second. The second in music is something which actually does not quite express the musical element, but in which the musical element makes a beginning. It stands at the gateway of the musical realm. The second is a musical question. Thus it is necessary (and you will feel the necessity) when forming a second, which follows any keynote, that you as second (whilst the second follows from another note) strive to turn the palms of the hands upwards. Any sort of movement you like can be produced while trying to arrive with the palms of the hands turned upwards, when ascending from one note to the next, or just a movement upwards, straightening the palm of the hand. Of course you must see to it that the hand does not appear in this position beforehand. The important thing is always to acquire a view of the whole. Through this, it [the second] manifests itself.

Now, on the basis of what I have said, we have still to arrange the next two sessions.

Lecture 7: Musical physiology; the point of departure; intervals; cadences

Dornach, 26 Feb. 1924

I have often stressed that eurythmy is drawn from the nature of the human organisation, from the possibilities of movement prefigured in the human organism. The human organism on the one hand contains the musical element, which in fact is built into it, and on the other hand (as should be especially mentioned in connection with music-eurythmy) it contains music translated into movement. It will doubtless be obvious to you that the musical element is situated, so to speak, in the human chest structure, above the chest. If we put the question, "How are we to find in the actual human organisation the transition from singing, and from the inner musical organisation upon which the human being is founded, to the 'organism of movement' of eurythmy?" – then (as is immediately apparent) we must turn to the limbs attached to the chest structure, which reveal themselves as limbs of movement out of the chest organism. 54

Now in regard to the whole human organisation, the hands and arms are the most wonderful human "organs". And you need only exert your intuitive vision a little to recognise that that which is latent in the human singing apparatus through the palate, jaw, and so on appears as limbs. In a certain respect it is like arms and hands that have become solidified and brought to rest. Try the following: Bring your arms and hands into movement before you by means of an interlocking of the fingers (folded hands), and now compare this with what happens when the lower and upper jaws are interlocked, as may be observed in the skeleton. If you take into account the muscles stretched across this, you will easily begin to discern the process of metamorphosis from a mobile state to a state of rest.

Now we see how that which serves the musical element in singing is continued below. That which is connected to voice-production and to initiating the sound is actually surrounded by the muscles and bones which end in the arms and hands. And because movement depends upon making use of these muscles and bones, it is consequently a question of learning to feel how the muscles and bones have to be used in order to do eurythmy in the musical sense.

In voice production, the singer seeks the point of departure for initiating the sound. Can we too find a point of departure in eurythmy, where we make use of those most expressive "organs", the arms and hands?

The human being possesses a singular "organ" which may be said to form the anatomical, physiological starting point between the chest and the arms. This is the collar-bone. It is S-shaped – truly a most wonderful bone. At one end it is connected with the human middle system, and at the other end (after making the S-form) it goes out towards the periphery, towards directing the movements of the arms and hands. Now I must ask you to consider the following. Animals which make use of their fore-legs and their fore-paws for dexterous climbing – the bat, for instance, or the monkey – have quite an ingeniously formed collar-bone. Beasts of prey, animals such as cats or lions, which do not exactly climb but make use of their fore-paws when tearing their spoil to pieces, possess a less well-formed collar-bone, but they do have one. The horse, which only makes use of its fore-legs for the purpose of running, has developed no skill in their use, and their formation permits no mobility in itself; the horse has no collar-bone. Now, it is in the collar-bone that we may feel the starting point from which music-eurythmy originates. It is located there. And when you become conscious that a force goes out from your collar-bone with its muscles into the arms and hands, then vitality will be brought into your music-eurythmy. Then you have the point of departure. It really has to do with livingly feeling your limbs so that they can be used for such movements as we have done. Anyone who is unable to feel at a specific place will never discover the right point of departure.

The most necessary preparation for music-eurythmy, therefore, is a concentration of your consciousness to the left and right collar-bone. And when starting to do music-eurythmy, with the first step, transfer your consciousness to the left and right collar-bone. Feel that all the subtle possibilities of movement which you pour into your arms and hands really proceed from your collar-bone, just as the voice proceeds from its starting point. 55

Then feel that you pour this feeling, which you consciously stimulate in the collar-bone, first into the socket of the upper arm. And feel too when you express the keynote with the legs, with the step, the following: Already while unfolding the arm, the force which causes the arm to be unfolded goes to the keynote from up here, proceeding from the point of departure of the arm. Feel as if the whole forearm (and indeed the upper arm too) together with the hand and fingers were quite light, as if they had no weight, as if they really were not there, as if you were dealing with them quite casually. But here, at the point of departure, feel a strong unfolding of force; then you have held fast the keynote in the arm.

And now feel a raising or turning of the upper arm, in connection with the movement I have already shown for the second. Feel the second itself, by holding the hand in a certain way so that the force enabling you to retain this position of the hand starts in the upper arm. Then you have the right unfolding of the second; then it really is a second.

The stream flowing out from the collar-bone passes by way of the upper arm and on into the forearm; and only then does the flowing into the forearm become the third. And here something extremely remarkable makes its appearance. In order to form the third, you unfold the movement as I described it in the first lecture. For this, you need the forearm, both hands [probably Austrian dialect for "arms". Tr. note.], and the right or left hand [arm], depending on where you will form the third. When you allow the feeling which you have already made use of in the upper arm to stream on further, it will pass over the elbow and flow into the back part of the forearm. This is possible. When you go by way of the elbow, you come to the starting point for the third. Now you can ask yourself: "Can I also allow the feeling to stream hither (along the inside of the arm towards the hand)?" Here, if your feeling is sound, you will say: "This is not possible. I can let the feeling stream forth up to the back part of the hand. But if I try to let it flow down the inner part of the arm, this is not possible. I have to imagine it as coming towards me, from below upwards. I have to imagine to myself as though I were laying hold somewhere with my hand, as though the feeling were flowing over along this side." And so we have two possibilities. If the beginning of the upper arm is here (see *Fig. 18*), the feeling streams in this direction (downwards). We pass from the second to the third. We can also unfold the feeling that comes towards us, and here we have to think of it as flowing from the hand inwards (direction of the arrow).

Now, you see, isn't this something wonderful! The human arm possesses one bone in the upper arm, for [the interval of] the second, and it possesses two bones in the forearm (radius and ulna) because there are two thirds. The bone at the back of the forearm [ulna] presents the major third, and the inner bone of the forearm [radius] the minor third. The way the scale is active in the bones and muscles of the arm is simply marvellous. When you now reach the place where the hand begins (where the small bones are) you still feel exactly as if you were inside yourself.

It is only when coming to the hand itself that you go out of yourself. The fourth is still within. It is here at the place where the hand begins. Here you have to feel the movement that gives you the fourth. The fifth is here on the hand itself. Feel the sixth here in the base of the fingers [proximal phalanges], and the seventh – as I showed you – you can produce in particular with the ends of the fingers [distal phalanges]. You must send your feeling into the ends of the fingers.

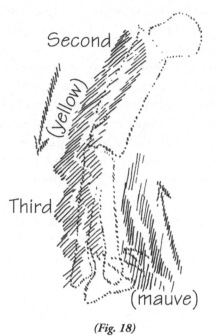

Second

(yellow)

Third

(mauve)

(Fig. 18)

You see, it is not a mere figure of speech to say that eurythmy has been drawn out of the organisation of the human being. So strongly is this the case that you can keep completely to the structure of the human form. There are the two bones in the forearm for the major and minor thirds, and here too you have to develop the feeling corresponding to a major key and a minor key. The major key is felt in the feeling flowing downward, passing by way of the elbow into the ulna and from there into the back of the hand. **56** When you feel this stream as flowing down into the back of the hand, the feeling is of the major mood.

When, however, you feel a slight current of air or a feeling coming towards you, passing through the palm of the hand and here at the lower arm into the inner bones, then you have the feeling of the minor mood. If you acquire a sensitivity for this transference of feeling in the human organism you will find yourself becoming inwardly musical, for you yourself are really living the scale.

Take some opportunity of observing two people engaged in eurythmy, of whom one makes the movements as if they were being carried out by an artificial, papier maché, mechanical human being, whereas the other really feels the origin in the collar-bone, feels the keynote at the point of departure of the upper arm, the second proceeding from here (upper arm), the third in the forearm, and further out in the hand itself the fourth, fifth, sixth and seventh. We have to get out of ourselves in the hands. We are out of ourselves the most at the ends of the fingers. It is here that the seventh arises. The goal in eurythmy is not to invent worked-out movements, but rather to draw out the possibilities of movement that are inherent in the human form itself. This is where eurythmy differs from every other modern attempt to develop an art of movement. In none of these attempts do we find in what is practised the movements drawn out in this way from the human being himself. For it is necessary, in the first place, to know that the human arm with the human hand, from the point of departure through the collar-bone, is precisely the scale itself.

If you look at a horse, you will feel that it actually could not do eurythmy.

A horse engaged in eurythmy would be an appalling sight! A kitten would make a more charming impression, and a little monkey better still. The eurythmy of a little monkey might be quite pleasing. Why? Because the horse has no collar-bone. A kitten has a collar-bone, even if less perfectly formed than that of a monkey, which possesses the most perfect collar-bone [of the three]. The eurythmic movements of an animal, if you could imagine them, would be pleasing in proportion to the development of its collar-bone.

Everything arising from the appendage of lungs, larynx, and so on, when metamorphosed and correspondingly projected outwards, is represented in the conglomeration of collar-bone (the shoulder-blade serves as a completion) collar-bone, shoulder-blades, upper arm, forearm, and the bones of the fingers.

Now when the first four notes of the scale are played, or shown in eurythmy, you will undoubtedly feel them as a progression. Play the scale up to the fourth: prime, second, third, fourth; it is a progression. With the fifth you feel that something is changing. And with the sixth and seventh you will distinctly notice at the same time a spreading out; the whole scale expands. Even this is reproduced in the hand. If you consider the simple structure of the upper arm and the two bones of the forearm, you find there the entire musical image of the first stages of the scale. When the scale widens out (from the fourth onwards), everything is indeed situated in the hand itself; and here [hand and wrist] there are twenty-seven bones designed for inner mobility. Thus, when you ascend to the upper notes of the scale, you can develop considerable powers of expression, especially in the use of the hands.

You know, however, that from the anatomical point of view there is much similarity between the arm and the hand, and the leg and the foot even if such points of departure are not present. And it is possible to transfer the movements – which we have used to express the notes/tones – to the legs and feet, harder though they are to carry out, and necessarily remaining as an indication. When you transfer the gestures for the notes to the legs and feet, the effect will be less beautiful, but you have here a different means of expression for the legs and feet from dancing, as we have already tried in the most various ways in speech-eurythmy and the like. Now you will easily gather that in the case of legs and feet, the beginning of the thigh-bone, the whole thigh-bone, corresponds to the keynote, when you flex the muscles. When you try to produce a movement in which the lower part of the leg hangs, to a certain extent, while strong movements are made by the upper part of the leg, then you are in the sphere of the keynote and the second. Passing over the lower part of the leg to the fibula and tibia (shin-bone and splint-bone), you again find the major and minor thirds – the major third in the tibia and the minor third in the fibula. In this way the thirds may be expressed once again by means of the leg. But essentially such movements will be differentiated very strongly from those most expressive movements the human being is capable of – the movements, that is to say, of the arms and hands –, just as the double-bass differs from the violin.

When, with two people, a piece of music is so carried out that the notes down to the C two octaves below middle C are strongly articulated with the arms, while the bass notes beyond the C two octaves below middle C are correspondingly expressed by the legs – either by the same or another person – you will find this renders a remarkably expressive possibility.

Thus it is really possible today that all the musical elements may be included in eurythmy. It is, of course, impossible to work out the actual exercises during these lectures; you will, however, understand how matters lie, and in the future it will be a question of thoroughly practising all the things that I am putting before you. It is only through practising that you really get into it. Then you will see that this is precisely the method of music-eurythmy.

Now if a person wishes to show the lower notes (the notes two octaves or more below middle C) by emphasising them as strongly as can be done with feet and legs, at the same time only slightly indicating the same notes with the arms, the effect will certainly be fine, too. This is one possibility.

Another possibility is this. While carrying out the movements with feet and legs, the arms may in a certain way retain confirming movements enveloping the whole thing, varying according to the degree of liveliness in movement that you wish to express (see *Fig. 19a*), or, when stronger and more lively, a movement of this sort *(b)*, or, when specially lively in mood, a movement of this sort *(c)*. You see, it is quite possible to say to yourself: "Yes, there are different possibilities of expressing the notes." For this is the case. Eurythmy will never lead anyone into pedantry.

If you have thoroughly practised the things we are discussing here, many different variations and possibilities of expression will be revealed – but only if you base your work on the realisation that everything does actually depend upon being conscious of the point of departure, of developing the consciousness: seconds are in the upper arm, thirds are in the forearm. With your awareness correspondingly transferred to the upper arm or forearm, you will create aesthetically beautiful movements. Then your soul is brought into play.

Just imagine one of you carrying out the movements of eurythmy. Eurythmy is a singing through movement; it is singing. It is not dancing; it is

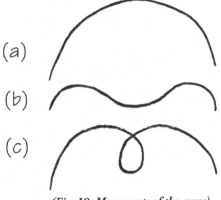

(a)

(b)

(c)

(Fig. 19: Movements of the arms)

not mime; it is singing. This is why you cannot sing and do eurythmy at the same time. Instrumental music can be expressed in music-eurythmy, but not singing. Anyone who imagines that this is possible has not yet grasped what eurythmy is. He is not looking upon it as an autonomous art, but is making use of it in order to illustrate what is being sung. In such a case eurythmy would only be an art of illustration, and this, of course, is a complete misunderstanding. A better understanding may perhaps be furthered by mentioning something in this connection. Imagine that one person is expressing in eurythmy something that another person is singing, both exactly the same thing. Anyone possessing spiritual vision would see in the etheric body of the singer precisely the same movements; it would be as though a spirit were perched on the singer's shoulders, making the very movements that are being made by the eurythmist. Singing is nothing other than a carrying out with the etheric body of the same movements resonating in the vocal organs, which you permit the physical organism to perform in eurythmy. That is why it is difficult to bear the sight of anyone doing eurythmy whilst singing to it at the same time. For then you are aware of the same thing duplicated; you perceive with the physical eyes, and then you see another, etheric being, with his legs dangling on the shoulders doing these movements up there, doing the very same thing! 57

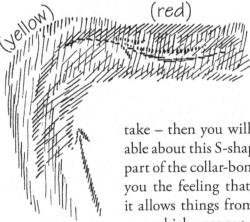

(Fig. 20)

Should you ever have the opportunity of examining a collar-bone — perhaps managing to acquire some knowledge of the surrounding muscles, and especially studying the direction they take — then you will notice something very remarkable about this S-shaped collar-bone. The form of that part of the collar-bone which tends outwards will give you the feeling that it is receiving something, that it allows things from outside to approach it. In that part which goes out from the middle you will feel an out-streaming tendency. In the collar-bone (see *Fig 20*) you really have an out-streaming and an in-streaming. The outward stream passes through the back part of the arm, via the ulna, down into the back of the hand. The inward stream passes through the palm of the hand, up the radius and back again here [to the collar-bone]. Here two streams continually exist, the one flowing upwards this way, and the other outwards (see arrow). The one gives something out, the other is receptive. Following this, you arrive directly at a real understanding of the major (*Dur*) and minor (*Moll*) moods.

The things that are said about major and minor and which are found in books on music are actually appalling. ⬛58 Many such theories with regard to major and minor have been put forward in recent times. If people, in such a case, did not listen in a sounder way than they think, the fate of music would be the same as the fate that would undoubtedly overtake the art of eating if the numerous physiological theories had to be followed instead of the instincts. It is a mercy that in music – and consequently in eurythmy – we can, up to a point, follow the instincts; for the real secret of the difference between major and minor lies in the fact that everything of the nature of major streams out from the will, that is, a streaming-out from the fullness of the human being. Everything that is major is related to action (*Tat*). Thus a certain activity must be introduced into all motifs in the major mood. All phrases in the minor mood are receptive. They possess something of recognition, of acceptance, of laying hold of something. All phrases in the minor mood are related to feeling. When passing over from a phrase in the major mood to a phrase in the minor mood, we must definitely show that this is a transference of activity from the outer structure of muscle and bone to the manipulation of the inner structure of muscle and bone in the arm and hand of the eurythmist. It is from feeling and experience of the impulse towards action that all eurythmy has to proceed.

It is a fact that anything based on the musical element may be expressed in music-eurythmy. To be convinced of this, you need but to remind yourselves, for instance, not only of how this or that occurs in the musical phrase, but also in the musical element that which brings about a close/ cadence for musical feeling as such (where the progression of a phrase leads in a certain direction, resulting in a feeling of being checked). In the cadence we have something (the expression is somewhat crude, but I think it is applicable) which dams up the flow of the music.

When you experience the cadence and the whole progression towards the cadence, you will find the following to be quite obvious. As an example, let us take the cadence in the major mood (see *Fig. 21*).

How would you express this in eurythmy? In the fashioning of your

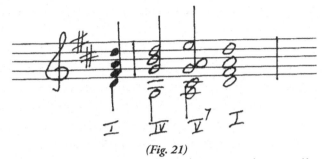

(Fig. 21)

movement you have to bring it to a conclusion, and you will certainly feel a tendency to lead the movement over towards the right, stopping it. This gives the effect of a close. Thus a cadence in the major mood leads you to move in a turning from left to right; the eurythmic movement is made in this way, towards the right side.

If, instead of this, we have a cadence in the minor mood, the process is reversed; the stopping movement would then proceed from right to left, for now the element of feeling has to be present. It is only the ignorance of our civilisation which gives rise to the wish to teach children to write with both right and left hands. This differentiation in the human organism is fundamental. For there is a great difference – is there not? – whether the heart is situated on the right side or the left. (Cases are known in which the heart lies on the right side, but they are exceedingly rare; in such a case the person in question would differ from all his fellow-men.) Now, this fundamental difference does indeed exist. It is based upon the inner organisation of the human being. And so, when approaching a close it is necessary that you feel: cadence in the major mood (towards the right side), cadence in the minor mood (towards the left side). And when, in the progression of the music, at the moment when you reach a close in the music itself (where you cannot imagine continuing), then at this point you have to introduce something into your movement whereby this movement is inwardly brought to a conclusion. You will feel the necessity of expressing the cadence in eurythmy in just this way.

You see, in this course of lectures it has been my full intention to direct your attention precisely to those things relating to the inner feeling of the movement. For I have been struck by the slight attention paid by eurythmists to that aspect of the eurythmy figures designated as "character". 59 I have always emphasised that a real attempt has to be made to concentrate the feeling and to stimulate a strong muscular tension at those parts of the eurythmy figures where the "character" is applied. This makes quite a different impression upon the audience from that which is created when – if you will pardon the expression – the matter is carried out phlegmatically to the utmost. Eurythmy is fundamentally based on the possibility that these things can be used.

Now, because speech-eurythmy is more bound up with the sense of the words, it will not be quite so noticeable if feeling does not accompany the activity. But if the movements of music-eurythmy are not permeated through and through with feeling the whole thing becomes utterly meaningless. If your feelings are not incorporated just as I have indicated today for the scale, the audience will feel the movements as arbitrary and disjointed. Everything depends upon your feeling: Here the upper arm begins, and you form the keynote – or you feel: A humanly-felt impulse is situated here in the upper arm, and you fashion the second in the way I told you yesterday. These feelings determine whether the movements which you carry out for any progression of notes appear filled with human motivation or whether they appear unmotivated. For in everything artistic, nothing is as important as motivation.

From this, however, you see (and this is a point I would like to touch on at the end of this lecture) that eurythmy has to develop gradually in such a way that auxiliary subjects are studied, just as in other forms of art. 60 The painter and sculptor are obliged to acquaint themselves with sculptors' and painters' anatomy. They cannot get on without it. The eurythmist should endeavour to acquire a thorough knowledge of the human being, and should study such things as the physiology of the collar-bone, and so on, as an auxiliary study (or whatever you'd like to call it).

When you now consider this intimate connection between eurythmy and the whole organisation of the human being, it will no longer seem strange to you that in the case of music-eurythmy too (although perhaps with occasional variations) we are able to speak of a eurythmy therapy. Only think of all that lies behind what I have discussed today! We have realised that there is both an inner and outer organisation in the formation of arms and hands (see *Fig. 22*). They fit each other as does the nut to the nutshell; they are built up out of the same forces. Consequently, if we have to treat a diseased lung, it is possible to work back on this lung by encouraging the patient to do music-eurythmy in a certain way, as eurythmy therapy.

(Fig. 22)

It is in afflictions of the throat, however, that music-eurythmy can work with particularly far-reaching results. For the whole muscular and bony structure of hand and arm is in reality nothing but an outer, concave image of what exists in inner, convex form in the lungs, and proceeding further, in the heart-organisation and in everything concerned with speaking and singing right out as far as the lips.

And so, a really practical awakening of the eurythmy that is within you, will enable you to gain deep insight into the human organisation; indeed, I would like to say, the study of eurythmy may lead over into the esoteric realm if a practice is made of transferring the inner impulse of feeling from collar-bone to upper arm, radius, ulna, and so on, or correspondingly in the legs and feet. 61

Tomorrow, then, at the same time, we shall begin by adding what is still lacking, and in retrospect complement our studies.

Lecture 8: Pitch (*Ethos* and *Pathos*), note values, dynamics, changes of tempo 62

Dornach, 27 Feb. 1924

Today, I will try to pass on some things which will bring our studies of music-eurythmy to a provisional conclusion, so that a stimulation for the advance of the substance of music-eurythmy will have been given. The first step in this direction will be to digest those things I have given. Then, a little later on, it will be necessary to hold a further series of lectures, either on music-eurythmy or speech-eurythmy, 63 for it is quite clear that a living stream of development has to be maintained. I have frequently said that eurythmy is only just beginning – perhaps only an attempted beginning –, and it must be developed further.

From yesterday's study, which dealt more with the bodily aspect of the human being, and with the way in which the body is brought into activity in the movements of eurythmy, I should like to pass over today to the aspect of soul, and make clear to you how the life of the soul is brought to expression in every single movement or gesture. Your attitude to eurythmy must always be such as to prevent any form of pedantry. You will realise more and more that many things can be expressed either in one way or another, and that in art it is a question of taste. And with several things you will have to consult your own feelings, "What special means must I employ to bring this or that to expression?"

Let us consider an effectual means of expressing that most essential element of music, the phrase in melos. Let us consider the progression of the phrase (since it really is the phrase which truly carries music into being), and direct our attention to that which gives the phrase its actual content, and makes it a true means of expressing the musical element: pitch. Further, we must distinguish note values and dynamics. The three elements of pitch, note values and dynamics really give us the inner content of the musical phrase. The more external aspect will be considered later.

Now everything musical, in so far as it is wrought out of the inner nature of the human being, comes from the feelings, from the realm of feeling. And it is true to say that nothing is musical which is not in some way rooted in human feeling. Similarly, when music streams over into eurythmical movement, everything which is brought to life in this movement must also be rooted in the feelings. When we studied the anatomical, physiological aspect of the matter yesterday, we saw that in its more physical, bodily aspect, movement springs from the feelings. The scale is the human being, but actually the human being as he encloses his chest, or in so far as his chest is able to be revealed outwards via the collar-bone. The chest is connected with the feelings, and carries within it the central organ of the feelings, the heart. And the physical characteristic we touched upon yesterday simply points to the fact that in music we have to do with the feelings.

If I may put it in this way, feeling can be coloured either more towards the head-organisation or more towards the limb-organisation. Should feeling tend in the direction of the head, it is expressed so to speak in the rounda-bout way of the intellect. Now I must beg you not to misunderstand this, and think that it is my intention to intellectualise the musical element. I have no such intention! It is a fact, however, that precisely in the element of pitch, something is manifest which causes feeling to tend in the direction of the intellect, only it does not reach the intellect, but remains in the realm of the feelings. And so a musician need not in the least be interested when the intellectual physicist comes along and speaks of the frequency and the pattern of sound-waves. The musician can justifiably answer: "This may be all very well, and so on, but it has nothing to do with me. I am not interested in this." An intellectual conception of music leads away from the sphere of music. It may be left to the physicist. 64 That element of music which tends towards the intellect is also felt. Pitch, in all its differing manifesta-tions, is an experience of the feelings. And it is just because music inclines away from the intellect that the head has so little to do in music-eurythmy. Indeed in speech-eurythmy, too, the head should play practically no part, though naturally it should humanly accompany the movements carried out by the speech-eurythmist.

Of course, in a humorous poem it would not be good for a eurythmist to make a face as if he had drunk a pint or so of vinegar! This would obviously be out of place. Generally speaking, the whole mental attitude should be suited to the content of the words. But if anyone attempted to do eurythmy with the face (and some people miss mime or a special play of the facial features), we could well answer that this would be equivalent in real speech-eurythmy to someone accompanying his speaking with grimaces.

In music-eurythmy, exactly the same as in speech-eurythmy, the head need not remain inactive. But just where it is a concern of manifesting the intellectual tendency of the musical element, that is pitch, the activity of the head should be restrained as much as possible. Otherwise interpreta-tion, or the element of seeking meaning, enters into the musical element, and this is its ruination. This introduces thinking into art, and the moment you begin to think, artistic activity ceases. I am not saying that art may not present thoughts, but thoughts must be there already in a finished form, they cannot just be made up on the spot. A majestic, elevated thought may, for instance, be contrasted with lesser thoughts, or an idea may frequently recur in a train of thought, just as a musical motif may recur, for then the musical element is effective in the train of thought. This is certainly possible. But you must not be thinking! 65 The same even applies to poetry. When a poet begins thinking he ceases to be a poet. Certainly he may embody thought in artistic form – but that is a very different matter.

Now as we have already seen, pitch (which lives in the musical phrase) initially finds expression in movements made in the upward-downward direction. The expression of pitch is up-down. Why should the movements be upwards and downwards? What lives in pitch?

You see, in the case of ascending pitch we feel a rising up into the spiritual element, in the musical element a rising up into the spiritual, rising with the ascending pitch. This is exceedingly significant. What really happens here is that the astral body and ego ascend. The human being is freed from his physical and etheric bodies. If he were to do this in an inartistic or even an anti-artistic manner, then he would faint. If he were to go out of his physical body without sufficient preparation, he would faint. The experience of musical sound (so long as it remains an experience of musical sound, of melos) permits us to pass out of the physical body. Then we instantly come back into it. In ascending pitch there is a continuous rising out of the physical body, an identification of the human being with the spiritual element. In music-eurythmy every ascending movement basically signifies *Ethos*. *Ethos* of the human being is a uniting of the soul with the spiritual weaving and essence. Ascending pitch: *Ethos*.

When, alternatively, pitch descends, and we are consequently obliged to follow, to make the movements lower in space (making each movement lower than the one preceding), we sink more deeply into the physical body with the astral body and ego. We are united more with the physical element. Descending pitch signifies a closer connection than normal with the physical element. This is *Pathos*. Ascending pitch: *Ethos*. Descending pitch: *Pathos*. 66

If you observe the unfolding of a piece of music with sound musical feeling, you will see that this is always the case. You will always experience *Ethos*, that is to say, a uniting with the spiritual element, when the pitch carries you upwards. You will always feel something of the nature of *Pathos* present in the music when the pitch causes you to descend. This can find expression in change of posture, and may indeed be specially clearly expressed by the movements of music-eurythmy.

Note values: note values are the feeling element as such. The faculty of feeling tends neither in the direction of the intellect nor in the direction of the will, but lives in its own element in note values. From what I have said about the way in which rests, for instance, or the pedal-point may be expressed in eurythmy, you will already have realised that feeling is active in note values. For it is indeed a fact that feeling is active to the greatest extent in note values. You need only recall in a feeling-way what you experience concerning a semibreve (whole-note), let us say, or a minim, crotchet or quaver (half-note, quarter-note or eighth-note). The shorter the length of the notes, the more your soul becomes inwardly filled, inwardly more formed and shaped. A vivid means of musical expression is made possible to a high degree by the contra-distinction between notes which are short and those of longer duration. Long, slow notes denote a certain indifferent emptiness of soul (to put things baldly), an indifferent emptiness of soul. And in this fullness in the soul or this emptiness in the soul, the second factor, the actual feeling element, is active. The feeling concerning long notes may be likened (there is a real resemblance here) to that of waiting for something which yet does not want to come. On the other hand, when someone continually seeks to stimulate us to activity, this is akin to the feeling-experience underlying short notes.

The head may be brought to our assistance when it is a question of experiencing note values; indeed, a certain use of the head in eurythmy now becomes necessary. But the question is: How may this be done?

You see, in pitch, the soul is purely concerned with itself. Consequently in pitch, the soul rises up to God or sinks down to the Devil, 67 living to the extreme completely within its own essence.

In note values a certain enjoyment and participation in the world outside, a contact with the world, exists. A relationship of the human being with the outer world is expressed in note values. For this reason an aesthetic and pleasing impression will be created when, in the case of short notes (beginning perhaps with minims, or half-notes, 68 and working up in ever-increased activity) you look in the direction of what you are doing with your arm, fingers or hand, looking at your own eurythmy, carefully following your own movements with your eyes.

When, alternatively, you have long semibreves (whole-notes), do not look towards but rather away from your movement, either straight in front of you or in some other direction. You will see that although this does not fully express the feeling involved here (this must be expressed through sustaining the note or through moving on), it will be accompanied in the right manner. There can be no doubt about the fact that in note values we have to do with the feelings. That is why the head may be brought to our aid. The head is not used here as a little interpreter; it simply expresses its participation in the feelings, and that looks quite pleasing.

The third element is dynamics. In the phrase, dynamics, the realm of feeling – which is always the source of the musical element –, are coloured towards the element of will. The will as such does not come into play in the musical element, for the musical element always remains in the sphere of feeling. But just as in pitch, where feeling tends to be coloured towards the intellectual element, so in dynamics, feeling tends to be coloured towards the will. Here it is somewhat different than with the head. In the head, that which is manifested in the arms as movement is brought to rest. The jaws can only move a little; they are at rest. Indeed the head is entirely at rest. On the other hand, the legs and feet do retain a certain similarity to the arms and hands, so the movements of the arms and hands might possibly be accompanied with parallel movements of the feet when expressing a certain emphasis, or a certain dynamic marking. If this were not so, there would be no dancing. Eurythmy should not become dancing, but there may be times when a tendency towards dancing may be a justifiable means of expression – when the dynamics demand that feeling be coloured through the element of will. In musical dynamics, the human being's relationship with the world is even more relevant. Only pitch remains entirely inward. Note values bring the human being into a certain connection with the outer world. Dynamics make this complete, for forte gains its strength from the will, whereas in piano the will-impulse is lacking. Here, then, the movements of hand and arm can be reinforced by corresponding leg movements. These movements, of course, have to be graceful in the highest sense of the word; they should not be awkward, but have to be similar in style to what the arms and hands do. You will feel then what the legs have to do.

Dynamics may be substantially supported if you are aware of the fact that increased dynamics is expressed by pointing the fingers, and a weakening of the sound makes the fingers rounded, so you can achieve something very expressive. Just think how much expression can be brought into the phrase which is already very expressive from a musical point of view. Think, in the first place, how we are able to express the phrase by emphasizing varied pitch in the way we have learned. This may be accompanied by bringing out note values by a use of the head, looking either at, or away from [the gestures]. The dynamics of the phrase may be lit up by a pointing or rounding of the fingers. This gives you the possibility of becoming a very expressive being within the phrase. You will be able to express much when you observe this variety in the phrase, in the continuation of the phrase, and so on.

There is another way of accompaniment which can increase your means of expression. You see, with certain very high notes (notes which ascend two octaves or more above middle C) 69 you may follow the movements with your eyes. Try, however, not to conjure up an active gesture of looking (looking gives an impression of note values), but let your eyes be swept up with the movement. And so when you would especially like to express very high notes, you will follow the movement with your eyes, too. You will try, though, not to produce the gesture of looking, but of being swept up with your eyes. Produce the gesture of being swept up with your eyes, as if they 70 would do this movement – and they should be swept up with the movement! In such a case the eyes do not look, but turn in the direction of the movement. Here we have still another means of expressing the things that are present in the phrase.

These things are initially bound up with the inner essence of the phrase, with the actual life of the phrase. And if you concern yourselves further with the phrase you will actually find, fundamentally, when you use these things, that you will be able to follow transforming and developing phrases.

I should just like to add the following. It is, of course, necessary that everything we have studied in these lectures (which have aimed at deepening eurythmy) should be developed with particular inner activity.

Let us now take the development of a phrase as it progresses through various musical sentences. Here we are able to differentiate whether it is developed in the form of repetition – so that the development signifies a certain intensification, a confirmation of the original phrase. In such a case, if other aspects do not indicate the contrary, much can be expressed by the treatment of the form.

Let us suppose that you have to carry out some form such as this (*Fig. 23a*) in a certain piece of music. Quite apart from what you express by means of your body, this form has to be carried out. If you follow your musical feelings you will be able to add, according to the progression of the phrase, certain steps backwards and forwards, still following the direction of the form (*b*).

If, however, the progression of the phrase is such that a second phrase follows the previous one similar to that between question and answer, it would be good if the progression of the form were treated in this way (*c*) – with a more complicated development introduced into the form.

Another means of expressing either a sequence or an answering phrase, the repetitive sequence or the contrast of phrases, is this. At specific points in the progression of a phrase, where the progression of the phrase is specially felt (where, let us say, a new metamorphosis of the phrase commences), the direction of the form can be directed towards the right (*b*). If another phrase is brought into conjunction with the first, at the point where this second

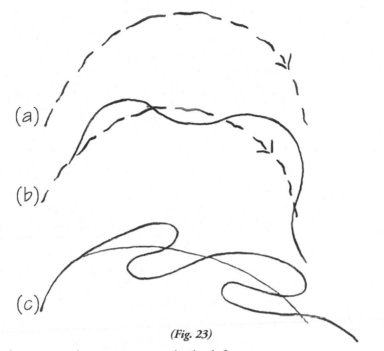

(Fig. 23)

phrase begins, make a turn towards the left.

Such things make the movements exceedingly expressive. And further, if you make the movements of this latter type stronger in a four-bar phrase, let's say, and bring out the eight-bar phrase (which has four main accents) by clearly showing the alternating direction of left-right, then you will succeed in expressing in eurythmy this plastically-formed development in the progression of the phrase.

When you come to apply the things we have been discussing, you will invariably reach a point where, in some way or other, the essential nature of the musical element is revealed in its onward progression. Here you actually pass out of the inner experience inherent in the soul of melos – as I'd like to put it – and you approach instead the life of melos. We can certainly differentiate between the soul and the life of melos. And the element which is less bound up with the soul and more with the life of melos is tempo, especially tempo changes. The human being, by living in time, has to live either at a quicker or slower pace. This is something which exerts a certain influence on his or her life from outside. A person certainly does not become someone else if circumstances compel him or her to do something in a shorter time than usual. It is not a question of becoming cleverer, or more stupid, but simply of becoming quicker. It is, then, the external element of time that causes increase of tempo.

Now it is a fact that in the musical element nearly everything depends upon changes, just as in movement generally everything depends upon changes. For this reason, change of tempo must be given special consideration in eurythmy. Let us suppose that we have an increase in tempo. An increase in tempo may not be shown simply by increased speed of movement, as this may be applied for pitch, for note values, and so on, but the body must make an abrupt movement (*Ruck*) towards the right. When you change to a retarded tempo, the body must be drawn (*Zug*) towards the left. Here you have a means of expressing change of tempo in such a way that the external element in it is given its adequate place in the moulding of the phrase.

You will say: "What a terrible amount there is to do!" But bring imagination to your aid and think how beautiful it will be when you carry out all this detail, how articulated and expressive a piece of music will become when interpreted in this way. A tempo remaining either quick or slow may be particularly well expressed when, with a quick tempo, the head is turned forwards to the right, and, with a slow tempo, backwards to the left. Naturally this cannot be intellectually proved, but, as with everything in art, has to be felt and experienced.

You will, then, have to do many different things simultaneously, and by means of this simultaneous devotion to one thing and another, it will be possible for you in the whole management of your body to go beyond yourself and to enter into the movement in such a way that you will succeed in giving a perfectly adequate revelation of the musical element.

Now, in doing all these things just feel how far we remove ourselves especially in music-eurythmy from anything of the nature of mime. Mime can have no place in music-eurythmy, and anything in the nature of dance is only permissible at most as a faint undercurrent. It is only with deep bass notes that the eurythmist may be tempted to add dance-like movements to colour his eurythmy. In this way eurythmy will really be kept in a sphere which justifies the name of "visible singing". Eurythmy is not dancing, not mime, but visible singing – a visible singing by means of which everything sounding in one way or another in instrumental music may be expressed. The feeling must never arise that we are dealing with anything other than visible singing. Here we come across something very instructive. With the means given here you will have no difficulty expressing anything that is purely musical. Certain difficulties will only appear when you have a musical phrase which you cannot bring to a conclusion. I am not going to rail against what is called "continuous melody", but you will invariably experience difficulty when you try to express this in eurythmy. As we saw yesterday, genuine cadences can be expressed in eurythmy. But what always wants to move on (and not to come to a close) will hold great difficulty in store for you when you try to find a means of expression for it. I will suggest, then, that you accompany the passage where a melody fades away, which just meanders on (as is frequently the case with Wagner's "continuous melodic phrases") [71] with some sort of movement, but this, when you pursue it eurythmically, will in fact appear extraordinary, will appear forced. In eurythmy it will appear laboured and artificial. It cannot be otherwise.

It may well be said that by its very nature, eurythmy will oblige people to return more and more to the pure musical element. When you come to apply all the means of expression of which I have been speaking, it will be necessary to engage your feeling for phrasing in music to the utmost. If you do not divide the separate phrases correctly, and are not clearly aware of how the notes should be grouped together, and then try to apply what I have discussed for a rest or a sustained note, it will appear ugly. Wrong phrasing, or a note falsely grouped and included wrongly in a phrase or allowed to remain isolated, will instantly be apparent. The very moment you phrase wrongly, the movement will become uncouth and clumsy. This is why it is of primary importance, when practising music-eurythmy, first to come to terms with the larger matters. As soon, then, as you have determined upon the phrasing and made up your mind about the progression of the music, the next step will be to discuss the phrasing with the person sitting at the instrument. [72] This simply belongs to the matter. When you are practising it will be necessary first to experiment and find your way into the experience of the music. Only then will you realise what the effect of this or that kind of movement will be. You will be filled with inner warmth or inner cold. This is what the inner life is. A eurythmist may often be able to feel how notes are grouped even better than the person sitting at the instrument. It is really necessary to come to an understanding with the musician so that the phrasing may be correspondingly carried out. Of course, people do generally phrase correctly, but in eurythmy it will be frequently noticeable that an accepted phrasing must be altered, owing to the very nature of eurythmy. You will discover that several matters need correction. [73]

Now, these are the things I wanted to give you in this course of lectures. In the first place it should be a stimulus to deepen music-eurythmy, and eurythmy in general. If in the near future it is shown that, through this, much in eurythmy (in music-eurythmy in particular) achieves a greater degree of perfection, and if it may be seen that speech-eurythmy too receives fresh life through what has been said, we will hold another course. In this way we shall be able to develop ever further what today is still only a beginning. But if, instead of the eight lectures, I had given fourteen, [74] I would have been concerned that the subject matter be properly assimilated. Then let us stay with what we have now received as a stimulus.

Herr Stuten: 75 *Dear Herr Doctor, I know that I speak for everyone when I express our heartfelt thanks to you at the close of these lectures. Once again you have thrown light on so many questions which we all carried within us, and given us much stimulus, that we see a great but completely unconstrained work before us. It is a great joy especially today to be allowed to express our thanks.*

Dr Steiner: Thank you very much. I have intentionally not asked for questions because I think the material needs to be worked through and in the course of time there will be many opportunities when the one or other question can be dealt with. Very little comes when questions are asked after the first hearing, and everything becomes hurried and mixed up.

Rudolf Steiner's personal lecture notes to "Eurythmy as Visible Singing"

(lecture course, Dornach 19-27 Feb. 1924)

A facsimile and transcription of R. Steiner's Notebook in German with a translation in English.

The facsimile should be consulted in conjunction with the letterpress because of the sketches, orientation of lines, more exact arrangement on the page, and so on. In the translation, musical notes are rendered in English (i.e. 'h' becomes 'b'), but the vowels remain as in the German original. Though it does not claim to be definitive, the translation does aim for accuracy, while seeking to retain the original character of a personal notebook.

For help in preparing the transcription I am especially grateful to Anne-Maidlin Vogel, and for help both in transcription and translation from Barbara Schneider-Serio, Dorothea Mier and Maren Stott.

A facsimile of Rudolf Steiner's own notebooks (mainly NB494) first appeared in the third German edition, editor Eva Froböse, who wrote "some drawings and text could not be included because of their aphoristic character".

NB494, now for the first time including the missing pages, is published here with kind permission of Rudolf Steiner-Nachlassverwaltung.

The facsimile © 1975 Rudolf Steiner-Nachlassverwaltung, Dornach, Switzerland. The transcription and translation © 1995 and © 1998 Alan Stott.

c' — as — f

g — es — c

f — des — b

c es g

Die Sprache ist die Zusammenfassung

der Wahrscheinlichkeiten —

a ∨ i ∨ x

c' - as - f
g - es - c
f - des - b
_____

c es g
===========

Die Sprache ist die Zusammenfassung
des Musikalischen –

⌒

a ⋀i | x

[Zum ersten Vortrag]   (1)

C' – Ab – F
G – Eb – C
F – Db – Bb
_____

C Eb G
===========

Speech is the synopsis of
the musical element —

⌒

a ⋀i | x

[To the first lecture]   (1)

Der Bericht entspringt aus dem Perripherie

der Ton im Centrum /

Accord =

Melodie :

c d e f g a h c'

Dur =

c d es f g as b c'   c e g

c es g

c e g

Der Laut ensteht an der Peripherie   c   d   e   f   g   a   h   c'
Der Ton im Centrum /

Accord: Dur: c e g

Melodie: c   d   es   f   g   as   b   c'

                                   c^0 c^2 e^2 g^2

[Zum ersten Vortrag]   (2)

---

speech sound is created on the periphery   C   D   E   F   G   A   B   C'
musical sound in the centre /

Chord: major: C E G

Melody: C   D   Eb   F   G   Ab   Bb   C'

                                   C^0 C^2 E^2 G^2

[To the first lecture]   (2)

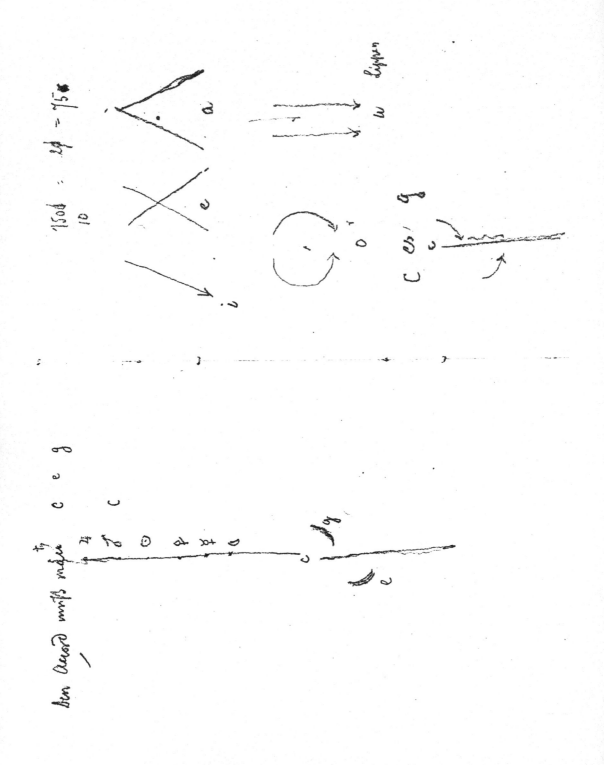

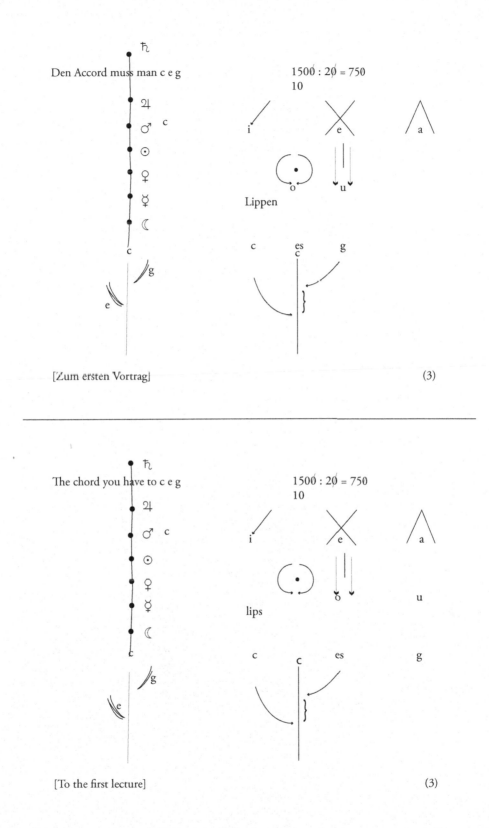

Den Accord muss man c e g

$$1500 : 20 = 750$$
10

ħ

2|

♂ c

☉

♀

☿

☾

c

g

e

i   e   a

o   u

Lippen

c   es/c   g

[Zum ersten Vortrag]   (3)

The chord you have to c e g

$$1500 : 20 = 750$$
10

ħ

2|

♂ c

☉

♀

☿

☾

c

g

e

i   e   a

o   u

lips

c   c   es   g

[To the first lecture]   (3)

Das Herz ist die Tonika Thematik

es müssen die melodischen Töne sich

in der Durstimmung hinauf – in der

Mollstimmung hinabbewegen –

links ist c e g

es fehlt einen Accord zusammen:

1.) Haltung

2.) zu von sich

3.) zu sich

Dur = Dreiklang
Im (~~Accord~~) Klingt zusammen

1.) bewegte Haltung = der Grundton

2.) die Bewegung selbst = der mittl. Ton —— rechts

3.) Die Gestaltung der Bewegung = der obere Ton. — links

Das Herz ist die Tonika
es mussen die melodischen Töne sich
in der Durstimmung hinauf – in der
Mollstimmung hinabbewegen –
links ist   c e g

es setzt einen Accord zusammen:
1.) Haltung
2.) von sich
3.) zu sich

Im Dur-Dreiklang klingt zusammen
l.) bewegte Haltung : der Grundton
2.) die Bewegung selbst : der mittl(ere) Ton — rechts
3.) Die Gestaltung der Bewegung : der obere Ton – links

[Zum ersten Vortrag]   (4)

The heart is the tonic
the melodic notes have to move
upwards in the major mood –
downwards in the minor mood –
left is   c e g

a chord consists of:
1.) position
2.) away from yourself
3.) towards yourself

In the major triad there sounds together
l.) moved position: the keynote
2.) the movement itself: the middle note — right
3.) the forming of the movement: the upper note – left

[To the lst lecture]   (4)

Jm Wirbel-Dreiklang:

1.) Haltung: es wird das Seelische zurückgeführt.

2.) es wird die Bewegung gehemmt

3.) es wird die Physische verhaftet.

Jm Dur-Dreiklang:

1.) Es wird das Physische unterschieden

2.) es wird die Bewegung entfaltet

3.) es wird das Seelische gestaltet.

es wird der Mensch in sich verborgen. =

c es g

reticierende Ekstase
gehaltene Bewegung und Zustan̄
(gehaltene Bewegung)

es wird der Mensch außer sich (vergeistigt)

geoffenbart

c e g

verwendete Ekstase
Bewegung nach außen ausgehalten
gehaltene Gestaltung (?)

Im Moll-Dreiklang:

1.) Haltung: es wird das Seelische
zurückgezogen
2.) es wird die Bewegung gehemmt
3.) es wird das Physische erkraftet

} es wird der Mensch in sich verborgen:

c eb g
rückwarts schreiten
links Bewegung nach Innen
Gestaltung drückend

Im Dur Dreiklang

1.) Es wird das Physische unterdrückt
2.) es wird die Bewegung entfaltet
3.) es wird die Bewegung gestaltet

} es wird der Mensch ausser sich
(nachgebildet)
geoffenbart

c   e   g
vorwärts schreiten
Bewegung nach aussen richtend
Gestaltung stossend

[Zum ersten Vortrag]   (5)

In the minor triad

1.) position: the soul element
is drawn back
2.) movement is restricted
3.) the physical element is
strengthened

} the human being is concealed within
himself:

c   eb   g
stepping backwards
movement to the left inwards
[the] forming pressing

In the major triad

1.) the physical element
2.) the movement unfolds
3.) the movement is formed

} is suppressed the human being is
(recreated) outside himself
revealed

c   e   g
stepping forwards
movement directed outwards
[the] forming pushing

[To the lst lecture]   (5)

Die reine Oktave: sie giebt den Menschen
sich selbst aus der Welt. Sie kommt im
im Grundton erregten Gehirn so entgegen,
daß sie diese Gehirn im Fühlen zur
Befriedigung bringt.

Die reine Quint: sie beschäftigt den
Grundton, indem sie ihn bis an die
Oberfläche des Menschen heraufführt.
Im Quintenintervall erlebt sich der
Mensch.

Die (grosse) Terz: sie trägt das innere
Erlebnis; im Tragen wird sie über den
Menschen hinaus. Er erlebt in ihr
seine Aktivität.

Die (kleine) Terz: sie trägt das innere
Erlebnis; im Tragen wird sie den
Menschen in sich hinein. Er erlebt seine

. Der Grundton ist immer die innere
Unruhe — Schreiten.

Sie sind ist immer die Beruhigung —
das Gehalten.

Ausser dem Gehalten liegt die Septime.

ganze Noten = o
punktierte Noten =
Viertelnote =
ein
übermässig: man
vermindert:

Die reine <u>Octave</u>: Sie giebt den
Menschen sich selbst aus der Welt. Sie
kommt der im Grundton erregten
Geberde so entgegen, dass sie diese
Geberde im Fühlen zur Befriedigung
bringt.

Die reine <u>Quint</u>: sie beschäftigt den
Grundton, indem sie ihn bis an die
Oberfläche des Menschen heranführt.
Im Quintenintervall erlebt sich der
Mensch.

Die (grosse) <u>Terz</u>: Sie trägt das innere
Erlebnis; im Tragen weist sie über den
Menschen hinaus. Er erlebt in ihr seine
Activität.

Die (kleine) <u>Terz</u>: sie trägt das innere
Erlebnis; im Tragen weist sie den
Menschen in sich hinein. Er erlebt seine
[Zum zweiten Vortrag]

➤ Passivität.

—————————

Der Grundton ist immer die innere
Unruhe – <u>Schreiten</u>.
Die Quint ist immer die Beruhigung
das Gestalten
Ausser dem Gestalten liegt die Septime.

—————————

Ganze Noten : durch die
halbe Noten : }
Viertelnote : }

rein:
übermässig: man
vermindert:

(6)

The perfect <u>octave</u>: it gives the human
being his very self out of the world. It
comes towards the gesture stimulated in
the keynote, so that this gesture is
brought in the feeling to fulfilment.

The perfect <u>fifth</u>: it engages the keynote
by leading it as far as the surface of the
human being. The human being
experiences himself in the interval of
the fifth.

The (major) <u>third</u>: it bears the inner
experience; in bearing it it points
beyond the human being. He
experiences in it his activity.

The (minor) <u>third</u>: it bears the inner
experience; in the bearing it points the
human being within himself. He
experiences his
[To the 2nd lecture]

➤ passivity.

—————————

The keynote is always inner
unrest — <u>stepping</u>.

The fifth is always the calming by
forming
The seventh lies outside the forming

—————————

semibreve (whole-note): through the
minim (half-note) : }
crotchet (quarter-note) : }

perfect:
augmented: you
diminished:

(6)

reine Intervalle = Prime . Quart .

unvollk. Konsonanz : Terz. Sext.

Differenzen = Secund. Sept.

Konsonanzen = Grosse Octave (grosse Terz)
Quint)
Secunde : Quart, kl.Terz. grosse kleine
Sext .

Gehende reine Octave: Schreiten zu.
gleich und Vorwärtsbewegen
der Armes — oder beider und
zurückziehen //
//
reine Quint : Schreiten mit blossem
weggezogenem
zurückziehen der (Arme)

Quintesverwandtschaft
be
c des

des f   c   e   g   h

as   e

Konsonanzen : (alle reinen Intervalle

unvollk. . grosse, kleine Terzen und
Sexten.

Differenzen Secunden Septimen.

RS's-NB–138

Quintterzverwandschaft
   h c
   c des

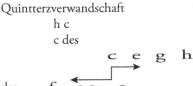

des   f a s c

reine Intervalle : Prim, Quart,
unvollk(ommen) Konsonanz : Terz,
Sext

Dissonanzen : Secund. Sept.

Konsonanzen : Prime Octave
QuintGrosse Terz.
dann : Quart, kl. Terz.grosse kleine
Sext.

Konsonanzen : vollk(ommen)
alle reinen Intervalle
unvollk(ommen) grosse, kleine
Terzen und Sexten.
Dissonanzen Secunden Septimen.

Geberde reine Octave. Schreiten
   zugleich mit Vorwärtsbewegen
   des Armes _ oder beider und
   zurückziehen //

reine Quint: Schreiten mit
   // blossem Umkehren der
   entgegengesetzten Hand.

[Zum zweiten Vortrag]
(7)

Fifth-third relationship
   b c
   c db

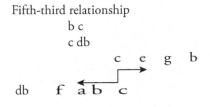

db   f a b c

perfect intervals : prime, fourth.
imperfect concords : third, sixth
third. sixth.

Discords : second, seventh.

Concords : prime octave fifth major third
then: fourth, min. third major minor
            sixth.

Concords : perfect all perfect intervals
imperfect major, minor thirds and
sixths.
Discords seconds sevenths.

Gesture perfect octave. Stepping
   at the same time with
   a forward movement of the
   arm — or of both arms and
   draw back //

Perfect fifth: stepping with a mere
   // turning around of the
   opposite hand.

[To the 2nd lecture]
(7)

Dies

Der Ton und der Laut = sie sind

Vorgänge im Ätherleib (Licht) und
Ich (Wärme) —
dabei geht die Seele so tief — und wieder
die Gebärde zielt "

(Die Spitzzeig im phys. Leibe
wieder —

Beim Singen und Sprechen ist der Ich
der Wille Herr außer des
Erlebnisses — in es ist der
Gefühle verlegt. —
Bei dem Gebärden ist der Gestalt
(central) der Verstandes —

reine Tanz = Schreiten = gleiche Hand

die gewisse andere Hand macht die
Bewegung so mit, dass sie

Man kann Darstellung conf. different —
mit (Schreiten breite Arme
machen.

Vierteltöne differenziren = man muss
beide Beine zu Hilfe nehmen
(Spricht)

Der Contonieren ist das zusammen als auf
dem Fortschreiten der Einen Beine

Der Differenziren durch den Beugen des
stehenden — oder das eine
Vierteltan beider Beine .

Die
Der Ton und der Laut : sie sind
Vorgänge im Astralleibe (Luft) und
                    Ich (Wärme) –
dabei geht die Seele in sich - und
bildet
Die Geberde giebt

      die Spiegelung im phys(ischen) Leibe
      wieder –

Beim Singen und Sprechen ist
das Ohr der stille Beobachter des
Erlebnisses – in es ist das Gefühl
verlegt.–
Bei der Geberde ist das Gefühl
(central) der Beobachter -

reine Terz : Schreiten : gleiche Hand
die jeweilig andere Hand macht
die Bewegung so mit, das sie

Man kann Dreiklänge cons(onantisch)
      disson(antisch) mit Schreiten beide
      Arme machen.

Vierklänge dissonirend : man muss beide
      Beine zu Hilfe nehmen (Sprung)

Das Consonieren ist auszudrücken
durch das Feststehen des Einen Beins

Das Dissonieren durch das Beugen
des stehenden – oder beimVierklang
beider Beine.

[Zum zweiten Vortrag]
(8)

The
The musical sound and the sound of speech :
they are occurrences in the astral body (air)
                    and ego (warmth) —
whereby the soul goes into itself - and forms
The Gesture reproducing —

      the reflection in the
      physical body

With singing and speaking the ear
      is the quiet observer of the
      experience –the feeling is put
      in it—
with the gesture the feeling
      (central) is the observer

Perfect third : stepping : the same hand
the other hand, respectively, joins in
the movement so that it

You can do triads as concords or
discords
with both arms while walking.
Four note chords, discordant :
You have to make use of both legs
(jump)

The concord is expressed
through standing firm on one leg

The discord through bending of this
standing leg or with a four-note chord,
both legs.

[To the 2nd lecture]
(8)

Die Drieut = die ich reich an Aufpreis
und verliert das den Mircklm
mirk — gebrught auch milk an
seine Grenze —

der Menph, der mig biß selbst
gefmallet.

Man kann sie nach mit der
Einen Hand, die man zum
gesprochen bringt, merken —

Mean hat bis zur beiut Orient
die Empfindlig des In - Sich -
seins —

Differenzen   Conformanzen —

RS's-NB-142

Die Quart : sie ist reich an Entfaltung
 und verlässt doch den Menschen
 nicht – gelangt auch nicht anseine
 Grenze /
 der Mensch, der nach sich selbst
 gestaltet.
 Man kann sie noch mit der
 Einen Hand, die man zum
 Gestalten bringt, machen –
Man hat bis zur Quart
die Empfindung des In-Sich-
Seins —   Dissonanzen Conzonanzen –

[Schluss des zweiten Vortrages]   (9)

The fourth : is rich in that it unfolds
 but it does not leave the human
 being — also it does not reach
 his border/
 the human being who forms
 himself as he is.
 You can do it still with one
 hand, which you bring to the
 formation —
Up to the fourth
you feel you are within yourself –   Discords Concords —

[End of 2nd lecture]   (9)

(Dur = Tonart:)

fac
e e g

Die Tonika — Es wird die
Tonart so gemacht, dass sie
dieselben Figuren zeigen, die
in verschiedenen Höfen liegen —
Die Tonika in der Mittellage
Die Unterdominante nach links
die Oberdominante nach rechts.

Ist die Tonika am Schluss, dann
Mittellage nach links =

(MollTonart:)

fa eg h
a c e

Die Tonika in der Mittellage in Mittel
Oberdominante links davon
Unterdominante rechts davon —

Man hat die Grundlage im Molldreiklang
denn die ersten Töne, die
wie die einzelnen Takten heraus,
kommen. —

(Dur:Tonart:)　　(Molltonart:)

fac　　ghd　　　　　dfa　　egh
　　ceg　　　　　　　　　ace

Die Tonika — Es wird die　　　　Die Tonika in der Mittellage im Mittel
Tonart so gemacht, dass sie　　　Oberdominante links oben
dieselben Figuren zeigen, die　　Unterdominante rechts unten –
in verschiedenen Höhen liegen –
Die Tonika in der Mittellage
Die Unterdominante nach links
Die Oberdominante nach rechts

Man hat die Grundlage im
Molldreiklang

Ist die Tonika am Schluss, dann　　dann die andern Töne, die wie die
Mittellage nach links :　　　　　einzelnen Taten heraus Kommen.–

[Zum siebenten Vortrag]　　　　　　　　　　　　　　　　(10)

(Major key)　　(Minor key)

fac　　gbd　　　　　dfa　　egb
　　ceg　　　　　　　　　ace

The tonic – the key is demonstrated　　The tonic in the middle region
in that it shows the same figures　　in the middle
which lie at different levels –　　　dominant above left [= from the left?]
The tonic in the middle region　　　subdominant below right [= from the right"?]
the subdominant to the left
the dominant to the right.

You have the basis in the minor triad,
then the other notes, which come out

If the tonic comes at the end　　　like the single deeds.—
then the middle region to the left:

[To the 7th lecture]　　　　　　　　　　　　　　　　　(10)

RS's-NB–145

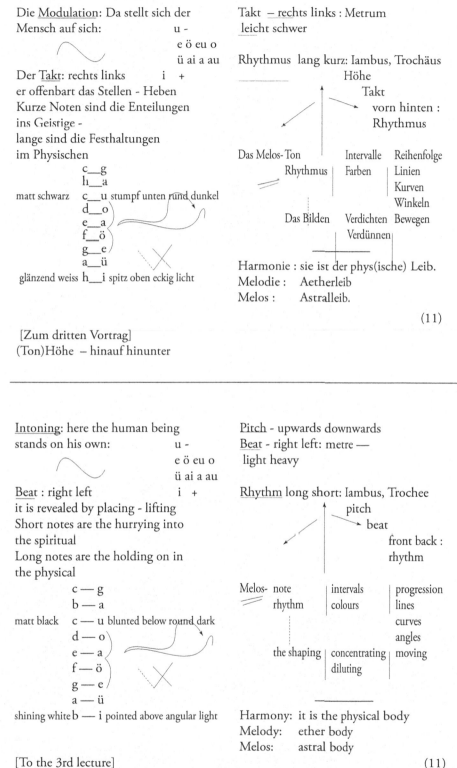

Die <u>Modulation</u>: Da stellt sich der
Mensch auf sich: u -
            e ö eu o
            ü ai a au
Der <u>Takt</u>: rechts links   i   +
er offenbart das Stellen - Heben
Kurze Noten sind die Enteilungen
ins Geistige -
lange sind die Festhaltungen
im Physischen
           c__g
           h__a
matt schwarz   c__u stumpf unten rund dunkel
           d__o
           e__a
           f__ö
           g__e
           a__ü
glänzend weiss h__i spitz oben eckig licht

Takt – rechts links : Metrum
 leicht schwer

Rhythmus lang kurz: Iambus, Trochäus
                 Höhe
                 Takt
                   vorn hinten :
                   Rhythmus

Das Melos-Ton   Intervalle   Reihenfolge
      Rhythmus | Farben | Linien
                     | Kurven
                     | Winkeln
Das Bilden   Verdichten Bewegen
          Verdünnen|

Harmonie : sie ist der phys(ische) Leib.
Melodie :   Aetherleib
Melos :   Astralleib.

                           (11)

[Zum dritten Vortrag]
(Ton)Höhe – hinauf hinunter

<u>Intoning</u>: here the human being
stands on his own: u -
            e ö eu o
            ü ai a au
<u>Beat</u> : right left   i   +
it is revealed by placing - lifting
Short notes are the hurrying into
the spiritual
Long notes are the holding on in
the physical
           c — g
           b — a
matt black   c — u blunted below round dark
           d — o
           e — a
           f — ö
           g — e
           a — ü
shining white b — i pointed above angular light

Pitch - upwards downwards
Beat - right left: metre —
 light heavy

<u>Rhythm</u> long short: Iambus, Trochee
                 pitch
                 beat
                   front back :
                   rhythm

Melos- note | intervals | progression
      rhythm | colours | lines
                     | curves
                     | angles
the shaping | concentrating | moving
          diluting

Harmony: it is the physical body
Melody: ether body
Melos: astral body

[To the 3rd lecture]   (11)

Die feste Form – die Umformung –
die Auflösung der Form ~

Fest = c
Flüssig = d
Luftf. = e
f
g Licht
a Chem.
h. Leben

Die Septime wird besonders wirksam, wenn sie zurück fällt in das Schreiten

Innere Bewegung = Schreiten
Bewegen Gestalten

Der Accord ist eurythm. nicht ganz durchzuführen ~

Die Melodie wird zum Melos.

Raum:

nach vorne: zum Harm. Materiellen Accord
nach rückwärts: zum Geistigen. Melodischen.

Heileurythmisch: Hand soll an derselben Stelle bleiben. – Belebung der Organe.

– Nachschreiten, so dass es aussieht, wie wenn man nachginge.

Die feste Form – die Umformung –
die Auflösung der Form -

Innere Bewegung : Schreiten
　　　　　　Bewegen Gestalten
Der Accord ist euryth(misch)
nicht ganz durchzuführen ~
Die Melodie wird zum Melos
　　　　　dann:
　　　Nach vorne : zum Materiellen
　　　　Harm(onisch) Accord
　nach rückwärts : zum Geistigen.

Melodischen.

———————

Fest : c
Flüssig : d
Luftig : e
f
g Licht
a Chem(ischer)
h Leben

Die Septime wird besonders wirksam,
wenn sie zurück fällt in das Schreiten-
Hand soll an derselben Stelle bleiben.
Nachschreiten, so dass es aussieht,
wie wenn man nachgienge.
heileurythmisch: Belebung der Organe

[Zum dritten Vortrag]

(12)

Firm form – re-forming –
dissolving of the form

Inner movement – stepping
　　　　　　moving forming
The chord cannot be carried
out completely in eurythmy ~
Melody becomes Melos
　　　　　then:
　　　Forwards: to the material [element]
　　　　　harm(onic) chord
　backwards: to the spiritual [element]
　　　　　[The] melodic.

———————

firm - c
fluid - d
airy - e
f
g light
a chem(ical)
b life

The seventh becomes especially effective
when it falls back into the stepping –
keeping the hand in the same place
step after it so that it looks as though
you are following it.
Therapeutic eurythmy:
enlivening of the organs.

[To the 3rd lecture]

(12)

Sexte heraufziehen

Quinte zurückziehen an den Körper
Hand wendet sich um

Quart : runden

Terz = ausreißen

Secund =

Sexte herausziehen
Quinte zurückziehen an den Körper
Hand : wendet sich um
Quart : runden
Terz : ausbreiten
Secund :

(13)

sixth pulling out
fifth pulling back
towards your body
the hand turns round
fourth : rounding
third : spreading out

(13)

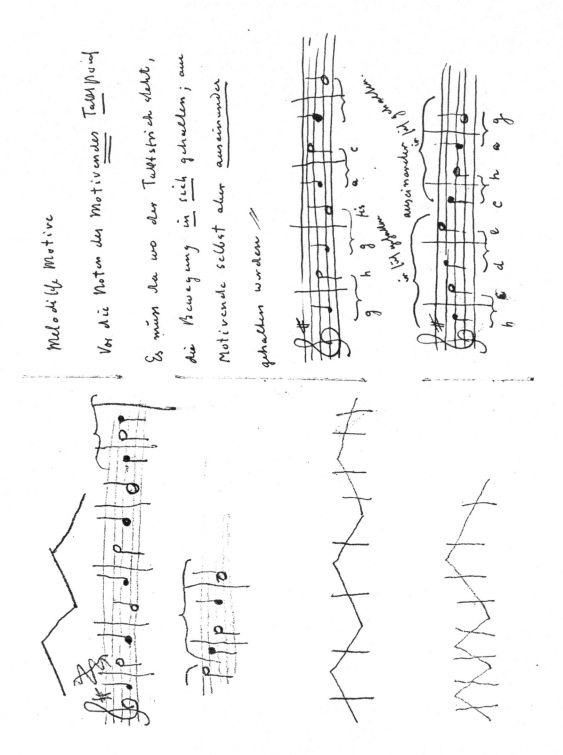

RS's-NB-152

Melodische Motive

Vor die Noten des Motiv<u>endes</u> <u>Tak</u>tstrich.

Es muss da wo der Taktstrich steht,
die Bewegung in <u>sich</u> gehalten; am
Motivende selbst aber <u>auseinander</u>
gehalten werden //

g h   g fis   a c

in sich gehalten auseinander in sich gehalten
h   c   d   c   h   a   g

[Zum vierten Vortrag]   (14)

Melodic motifs

Before the notes of the phrase-<u>ending</u>, <u>bar</u> line.

Where the bar line stands, the movement
has to be held <u>in itself</u>; at the end of
the motif itself, however, it has to be
<u>held-apart</u> //

g b   g f#   a c

held in itself held apart held in itself
b   c   d   e   c   b   g

[To the 4th lecture]   (14)

Intervalle die Dichterische —

Die Melodie nimmt den Geist auf;
der Mensch wird [sichtbar] bleibt im
Takt; er wird aufhört im
Rhythmus; und er voraus frei
ausdrücklich in der Melodie — in
der Sprache gibt die Melodie über
in der Worte

g h
e i

geschwind

Da zwar das Worte gehört natürlich
die Melodie — : die Folge ist, dass
im Gesange zu Tage tritt die
Nichtübereinstimmung des Tones mit dem
Worte — in der Recitation die
Vergrösserung des Musikalischen —
Es kann doch der Musikstoff
nicht in der Melodie frei =

Die Melodie nimmt den Geist auf;
der Mensch als sichtbarer bleibt im
Takt; er wird aetherisch im
Rhythmus: und er verrät sein
astralisches in der Melodie – in
der Sprache geht die Melodie über
in das Wort:

g   h
e   i

geschwind
=   =

[Zum vierten Vortag]

Intervalle die Diphtonge -

Der Sinn des Wortes zerstört natürlich
die Melodie – : die Folge ist, dass
im Gesange zu Tage tritt die
Nichtübereinstimmung des Tones mit
dem Worte – in der Recitation die
Vergewaltigungdes Musikalischen –
Musikalischen – Es kann daher das
Musikalische nicht in der Natur sein //

(15)

Melody takes up the spirit; the
human being as visible entity remains
in the beat; he becomes etheric in
rhythm: and he reveals his astral nature
in melody – in speech the melody
passes over into the word:

g   b
e   i
geschwind

=   =

[To the 4th lecture]

Intervals the Dipthongs -

The meaning of the word destroys
melody of course –:
the result is that in singing
there is revealed the non-agreement of
the notes with the words –
in recitation the violation of
the musical element –
Consequently the musical element
cannot be in nature.

———

(15)

Hat die Natur über den Menschen Gewalt,
so kann ihr Sprache der Mutterschoß

heilen ——

Die Sprache kann Takt und Rhythmus

haben ——

          gerophel —: h g –Tag.
          ir Rück –: i u – oclau

———— gerophel ——

         Hauf –× Tag–Arbeit
         auf – "

               e g=Tag
    balde   e g =Tag,–
Drü Tag. {
    wacht

ruhest du
c g c

Hat die Natur über den Menschen gesiegt,
so kann ihn, gerade des Musikalische
heilen // __
Die Sprache kann Takt und Rhythmus
haben –
    Gipfel –:h   g - moll Terz
    ist Ruh –:i   u - octav [siehe Vortrag, S.62]
    Gipfel –
      Hauch - moll Terz-Interval
        auch -   " ========
  Dur Terz. balde e g : Terz
     ===== { warte e g : Terz.-

          ruhest du
          c   g   e

[Zum vierten Vortrag]   (16)

If nature triumphs over the human being,
then it is just the musical element
which can heal him //–
Speech can possess beat and rhythm —

    Gipfel –:b g minor third
    ist Ruh –:i u octave [see lecture, p. 41]
    Gipfel –
    Hauch – interval of minor third
        auch –   " ========
  Major third   balde e g : third
     ===== { warte e g : third. -

          ruhest du
          c   g   e

[To the 4th lecture]   (16)

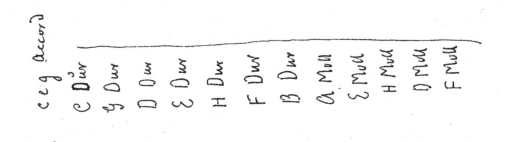

c e g Accord
C Dür
G Dur
D Dur
E Dur
H Dur
F Dur
B Dur
A Moll
E Moll
H Moll
D Moll
F Moll

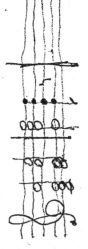

c e g Accord
C Dur
G Dur
D Dur
E Dur
H Dur
F Dur
B Dur
A Moll
E Moll
H Moll
D Moll
F Moll

(17)

c e g chord
C major
G major
D major
E major
B major
F major
B♭ major
A minor
E minor
B minor
D minor
F minor

(17)

von oben nach unten die Hände und
Stoffarbe nach Innen —
zusammenfassend)

von unten nach oben die Hände und Stoffarbe
nach außen ausbreitend.

tiefe Töne unten stumpf rund dunkel
sanft

immer zwischen die Rückwand der
Hand

hohe Töne oben spitz eckig, läßt ... gespannt

indem man hinaufsteigt, wird man größer

indem man hinuntersteigt, wird man runder.

Tiefe Töne unten stumpf rund dunkel
schwarz
moll

von oben mach unten die
Hände mit Hohlhand nach Innen –
zusammenfallend

immer zeigen die Rückwand der
Hand

von unten nach oben die Hände mit
Hohlhand nach aussen
deutend.

hohe Töne oben spitz eckig leicht weiss
glänzend

indem man hinaufgeht, wird man strahlend

indem man hinuntergeht, wird man rundend.

[Zum fünften Vortrag]

(18)

Deep notes below blunted round dark
black
minor

From above downwards the hands with
the palms inwards –
collapsing

always show the back of the
Hand

high notes above pointed angular light white
shining

from below upwards the hands with the
palms outside
pointing.

in going up you become raying

in going down you become rounded.

[To the 5th lecture]

(18)

Uebernehmen :
Motiv klingt an :
es wird bis zum Ende gehalten –
der nächste übernimmt es –
darauf wieder der nächste

C   Oberdominante
B   Tonika
A   Unterdom(inante)

A etc kann vermehrt werden _
Accorde stellen : dann die Motive
weiter schreiten lassen. –

[Zum fünften Vortrag]   (19)

Taking over :
the motif sounds :
it is held to the end —
the next person takes it over —
and then the next

C   dominant
B   tonic
A   subdom(inant)

A etc could be more people —
place the chords : then let the motifs
progress.—

[To the 5th lecture]   (19)

Die Tortilla — Unterton.
Oberton.
von Drei
oder mehreren —

Man kann sich nicht denken, dass
gleichzeitig die Motive wahrgenommen
werden —

Die Tonika —— Unterdom.
               Oberdom.
     von Drei
     oder mehreren –
Man kann sich nicht denken, daß

Stehend die Motive übernommen
werden–

<table>
<tr><td></td><td>a</td><td>o</td></tr>
<tr><td>h a</td><td>e</td><td>d</td></tr>
</table>

Deuten *

Accord
lang ausklingend

Melos das Ethische:
   Deuten *

<table>
<tr><td></td><td>a</td><td>o</td><td>g / f /</td><td>e / d /</td></tr>
<tr><td>h a</td><td>e</td><td>d</td><td>5 4</td><td>3 2</td></tr>
</table>

[Zum fünften Vortrag]

*[Siehe Anmerkung 46]   (20)

The tonic —— subdominant
           dominant
           from three [persons]
           or more –

one can't imagine that the motif be
taken over in standing.

Indicating [= distinctly (?)*]

<table>
<tr><td></td><td>a</td><td>o</td></tr>
<tr><td>b a</td><td>e</td><td>d</td></tr>
</table>

chord
long sustained

Melos to do with Ethos :

indicating [= distinctly (?)*]

<table>
<tr><td></td><td>a</td><td>o</td><td>g / f /</td><td>e / d /</td></tr>
<tr><td>b a</td><td>e</td><td>d</td><td>5 4</td><td>3 2</td></tr>
</table>

[To the fifth lecture]

*[See Endnote 46]   (20)

Tonika C dur
Dominante = g dur
Subdominante = F dur

f a c — c e g — g h d

die Modulation ≈ Übergang von einer
—————— Tonart in die andere. —

Tonika   C dur
Dominante: G dur
Subdominante: F dur

f a c – c e g — g h d

die Modulation - Übergang von einer
Tonart in die andere. –

(21)

Tonic   C major
Dominant: G major
Subdominant: F major

f a c – c e g — g b d

Modulation – transition from one key
into the other

(21)

Es handelt sich darum, nicht im Sinn
der Wörtlichkeit des Spruchs zu finden,
sondern im Melos der Sprache —
d. h. in der Auflösung in Bewegung —

Die Consonanten wollen entfaltigen
dass man die Vocale ein dann
Melos reint —

In den Vokalen verliert sich der
Mensch an die Welt =

In den Consonanten baut er sich
wieder sich auf
w a r t e
b e d

Der eurhyth. Sänger = er schöpft sein
Innenleben aus

Der eurhyth. Recitator = er erfasst die
Welt —

Im Musikalischen verschwindet die
Bewegung (Münodeshörung)
Ton = Eurythmie machen = Darstellung
der Weltdarstellung =

Laut = Eurythmie Weltdarstellung als
Menschendarstellung —

Der euryth[mische] Sänger : er dehnt
sein Innenleben aus

Der euryth(mische) Recitator : er erfasst
die Welt. –

Im Musikalischen verschwindet die
Bewegung (Ausdehnung)

Ton-Eurythmie Menschen-Darstellung
als Weltdarstellung :

Laut-Eurythmie Weltdarstellung als ⎫
Menschendarstellung –   ⎬

[Zum fünften Vortrag]

Es handelt sich darum, nicht im Sinn
das Wesentliche der Sprache zu finden,
sondern im Melos der Sprache –
d.h. in der Auflösung in Bewegung _

Die Consonanten müssen entschuldigen,
dass man die Vocale aus dem
Melos reisst –

In den Vokalen verliert sich der
Mensch an die Welt //

In den Consonanten baut er sich
    ausser sich auf
    w   r t
      a   e
    b   l d

(22)

The eurythmic singer : he stretches his
    inner life

The eurythmic reciter : he takes hold of
    the world —

In the musical element the
movement disappears (stretching)

Tone-eurythmy human presentation
as presentation of the world:

Speech-eurythmy   presentation of the ⎫
world as human presentation —   ⎬

[To the 5th lecture]

The main thing in speech is not to find
the most essential thing in the meaning
but in the Melos of speech —
i.e. in the dissolving into movement —

The consonants have to provide the excuse
that we tear the vowels out of Melos——

In the vowels the human being
is lost to the world //

In the consonants he
forms himself outside of himself

    w   rt
      a   e
    b   ld

(22)

motiv.
2

motiv.
1.

3

4

Während die Eine [ein] Motiv
euryth. Freiheit, bilden die
andern es so an, dann für
Abbild die Noten

1. Ton

2. Ton

3. Ton.

Accord

1.

2.

1. O

Ob

O
3

4. Ton.

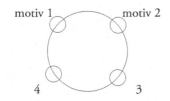 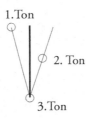

motiv 1   motiv 2   1.Ton

4   3   2. Ton

3.Ton

Während der Eine sein Motiv
euryth[misch] <u>schreitend</u>,
bilden die anderen es so aus,
dass sie <u>stehend</u> die Noten

Accord

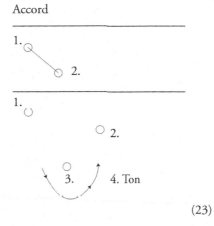

1.

2.

1.

2.

3.   4. Ton

[Zum fünften Vortrag]   (23)

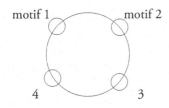 

motif 1   motif 2   1.Note

4   3   2. Note

3. Note

Whilst the first person <u>walks</u>
his phrase in eurythmy, the
others fashion it so that they
[carry out] the notes <u>in standing</u>

Chord

1.

2.

1.

2.

3.   4. Note

[To the 5th lecture]   (23)

Secunde = ist der erste Uebergang zum Leben:
die Hände fragend nach vorn –
Hohlhand nach unten – möglichst
weit nach unten. =

i – e Missbildung der phonetischen Phantasie.
h g

a o u –

Der Orgelpunkt: das Beharren.

Die Pause: Bewegung von dem
vorangehenden zum folgenden =

F dur Sonate Mozart:

Was drücken die Tongebilde des
Melos wirklich aus?

30

Secunde : ist der erste übergang zum leben:
    die Hände fragend nach vorn-
    Hohlhand nach unten - möglichst
    weit nach unten . //

Was drücken die Tongebilde des
Melos wirklich aus?

30
28
17[14 ?]

i - e Missbildung der phonetischen Phantasie
h / g
a o u -

Der Orgelpunkt: das Beharren

Die Pause : Bewegung von dem
vorausgehenden zum folgenden:

F dur Sonate Mozart

[Zum 6. und 7. Vortrag]

(24)

The second: is the first transition towards life:
    the hands questioning [turned] forwards-
    the palm facing downwards -
    as far down as possible.//

What do the tonal configurations
[i.e. notes] of Melos really express?

30
28
17[14 ?]

i - e distortion of the phonetic imagination
h / g
a o u -

The pedal-point: sustaining

The rest : movement from what
    has been to what follows:

F major Sonata Mozart

[To the 5th and 6th lectures]

(24)

c'

Man nennt die Bewegung (den Gestus) auf
spürt [sie in der Moglichus und

sie in der ... um sie dann im

Obersarm als das im unteren
zu ergreifen — [Vom Ausgebreiteten zum

(Man giebt (wie Ruhe (Starren) auf
nennt in die Bewegung hinein Oberarm
geht auf die Ebene über und Moment
zum Dirigieren des Fingers
(Vom ... Gefühlten geht
... Figur.]

Das

u
o
a ö
e ü

Tanz e

u
o
a
ö
e
ü

Moll.

c'
Man nimmt die Bewegung (des Geistes) auf
kommt zum Beruhigen der Finger
          b   as
spürt sie in der Hohlhand und ergreift
        g   f
sie in der ~~Elle~~Speiche, um sie dann im
es   <u>des</u>
Oberarm als die im Unteren ~~verschwinden~~
{ c
zu ergreifen - vom Ausgebreiteten zum
    { zusammengezogen[en]. }

Bewegung kommt von außen herein
und gelangt
im Innern zur Ruhe

Dür

Man giebt seine Ruhe (oben) Oberarm auf
kommt in die Bewegung hinein Oberarms
geht auf die ~~Speiche~~Elle über und kommt
zum Dirigieren der Finger:
    Vom <u>Z</u>usammen[gezogenen]
{ { Gehaltenen zur bewegten Figur. }

(25)

---

u
o
a
ö
e
ü

Minor:

c'
you take up the movement (of the spirit)
causing a calming of the fingers
        bb   ab
feeling it in the palm of the hand and lay hold
        g   f
of it in the ~~ulna~~radius, in order then in
eb   <u>db</u>
the upper arm as ~~the~~ in the under/inner [part]
~~to dissappear~~
{ c
to lay hold – from the opened-up
    { to the closed [figure].}

[The] movement comes from outside
and achieves tranquillity within [you].

Major:

You give up your tranquillity (upper arm)
enter into the movement of the upper arm
passing over to the ~~radius~~ulna and come
to directing the fingers:
    from [the] <u>closed</u> held [stance]
{ { to the figure in movement. }

(25)

Es läuft du untere Teil du Scala

am Oberarm — er ..... ist

Hand zu Terz (

am Oberarmschy Grössern — wird

am Oberarm zur Second und wird

zur Terz am Unterarmschy —

(grosse Terz Sperlz kleine Terz Elle)

dann ist Handauschy drängt ; die

(Finger)

Hand hebt Quint —

Finger bewegen Sext.

Die Ellenbogen ist entwickelt

grosse Terz

die Ellenbeuge kleine Terz

schleiftschben + läuft durch durch

$\dfrac{c}{d}$ | |

e

Es läuft der untere Teil der Scala
am Oberarm – er ~~wird in der~~ ist
~~Hand zur Terz (.~~
am Oberarmansatz
Grundton - wird am Oberarm zur
Secunde
und wird zur Terz am Unterarmansatz-
(grosse Terz Speiche kleine Terz
Elle) dann ist Handansatz Quart,
die Hand ~~selbst~~ (Finger) Quint -
Fingerbewegung Sext.

c
d|
e
/\ ↑↑

c

d
kl.T. gr.T

Quart

Quint

Der Ellenbogen ist ~~entweder~~
grosse Terz
Die Ellenbeuge Kleine Terz

Schlüsselbein
durch dieses läuft

bei der Quinte verliert
sich der Bewegungsimpuls
nach aussen –

Die kleine Terz As
Sext ist das Fortvibrieren
der Handbewegung
Septim (von aussen) in
der Speiche –

[Zum siebenten Vortrag] (26)

The lower part of the scale moves along
the upper arm — ~~becomes third in the~~
~~hand~~ the keynote is at the attachment
of the upper arm - and becomes
the second at the upper arm and third
at the beginning of the lower arm -
(major third radius, minor third ulna)
then the attachment of the hand fourth,
the hand itself (fingers) fifth –
finger movement sixth.

c
d
e |
↑↑ /\

c

d
min 3rd maj 3rd

fourth

fifth
sixth

seventh

the elbow is ~~either~~
major third
the inside of the elbow
minor third

collar bone
through this there moves

with the fifth the impulse
of movement loses itself
outwards

the minor third Ab
is the continued
vibration of the hand
movement (from outside) in
the radius –

[To the 7th lecture] (26)

Die Hand zum Begreifen

Schneidezahn = Vorstellen

[illegible] =

großes C

Subcontra C

kleine c

[illegible] C

Die Hand zum <u>Begreifen</u>
Schulterblatt : <u>Vorstellen</u>   grosses C
dazwischen musikalisches :   subcontra C

          c   kleines C

          d   ——————————

Speiche   e Elle Wadenbein Schienbein   geschstrichene[s] C

          f

          g   reine Prim   Terz klein

          a   reine Octave   gross

          h.   reine Quart   Sext klein

                           reine Quint   gross

[Zum siebenten Vortrag]   (27)

The hand for <u>understanding</u>
Shoulder-blade : <u>mental picturing</u>   the 8ve one octave below middle C
in between musical [activity]   the 8ve two octaves below middle C

          c   the 8ve beginning on middle C

          d   ——————————

radius   e ulna fibula tibia   the 8ve beginning one octave above

          f   (shin-bone)   middle C

          g

          a   perfect prime   minor third

          b   perfect octave   major

                           perfect fourth minor sixth

                           perfect fifth   major

[To the 7th lecture]   (27)

Das Erschaffen = Oberarmmuskel ×

Das „ = Oberarmen

Das „ Erschaffen Speiche

Das „ Erspeichen Hand wiegt ×

„ „ Oberspeich —

„ „ Unterspeich I

„ „ Unterbeugt —

nach oben =

Nun liegen ob die Hand

Trotz die Hand mit ihrer
bleiben.

Das Singen — es bleibt dort, wo
die Tonorgane mit dem
Knochengerüste von dem (Hand)
und Fuss (Bein) correspondiren —

Es sind die Gebärde wie dem Mund
fest gewordenen Bewegungsorgane —
Sprechen ~

RS's-NB-180

                                c
Nur legen   d   die Hand

Terz die Hand mit Kraft heben.

Das Singen - es bleibt dort, wo
    die Tonorgane mit dem
    Knochengerüste von Arm (Hand)
    und Fuss (Bein) correspondieren. –

Es sind die Gebilde um den Mund
fest gewordene Bewegungsorgane. -
Sprechen ~

[Zum siebenten Vortrag]

Das Erfühlen: Oberarmansatz x
Das   "   Oberarm
Das Erfühlen   Speiche
Das Erfühlen   Handwürzel x
   "   "   Oberhand
   "   "   Unterhand I
   "   "   Unterfinger -

              ~
_____

nach oben :

(28)

Only turn   c   the hand [*]
              d

third lift the hand [*] strongly

Singing – it remains where the
    organs of sound production
    correspond with the skeleton of
    arm (hand) and foot (leg).—

The structures around the mouth are
organs of movement which have
become firm –
speaking -

[* NB 'Hand' can also mean 'arm' in
Austrian dialect (Tr. note.)]

[To the 7th lecture]

The active feeling: beginning of upper arm x
The active feeling : upper arm
The active feeling: radius
The active feeling : wrist x
     "   upper part of hand
                      [metacarpus]
     "   base of fingers I
     "   finger ends -
                      [proximal & distal
                      phalanges]

                 ~
_____

upwards:

(28)

Kadenz = Harmoniewendung: Schluss unumstösslich

c e c e f g a h c d

man übergeht die Quint, geht zur Sext
d. i. man stellt einen Ton hin

der nicht anders sein kann.

Da muss die Bewegung nach
rechts
links gemacht werden bei
einer Dur-Kadenz

nach links bei einer Moll-Kadenz.

Kadenz : Harmoniewendung : Schluss unumstösslich
c d e f g a h c d

man übergeht die Quint, geht zur Sext d(ass) i(st)
man stellt einen Ton hin der nicht anders sein kann.

da muss die Bewegung nach
~~links~~ rechts gemacht werden bei
einer Dur-Kadenz
nach ~~rechts~~ links bei eine Moll-Kadenz.

[Zum siebenten Vortrag]   (29)

Cadence: harmonic progression: ending conclusively
c d e f g a b c d

you pass over the fifth, to the sixth, i.e. you
put a note there which cannot be different.

here the movement has to be made towards
the ~~left~~ right with a cadence in the major [= from the left?]
to the ~~right~~ left with a cadence in the minor [= from the right?].

[To the 7th lecture]   (29)

Das Schlüsselbein — so ist die
gründliche für die Brustlichtheit
der Armen:

Affen Rückenmuskel —

wenig ausgebildet: Katzen, Löwen
gar nicht: Pferde etc., die nur
laufen

Besonderes wirksame Kaum für die
Contra — und Subcardialsnes
deutlich mit dem Beinen zu verwählen
und Dabei Driepsben mit dem
Armen über wie umfallen:

Stoffspann nach Innen: Beugen

Das Schlüsselbein – es ist die
Grundlage für die Beweglichkeit
des Armes:
Affen Fledermäuse –

⁓

wenig ausgebildet: Katzen, Löwen
gar nicht: Pferde etc, die nur ⎱
        laufen ⎰

Besonders wirksam kann sein die
Contra- und Subcontratöne
deutlich mit den Beinen zu
versuchen und dabei dieselben
mit den Armen blos wie umhüllen:
Hohland nach Innen: Bogen

[Zum siebenten Vortrag]   (30)

The collar-bone — it is the basis
for the possibility of movement
of the arm:
monkeys bats —

⁓

less developed: cats, lions
not at all: horses, etc,
        which only walk/run ⎰

The notes two or more
octaves below middle C can
be especially effective, to
try distinctly with the legs
and at the same time merely to
envelop with the arms:
palm turned inwards: curve

[To the 7th lecture]   (30)

Der Tanz geht auf den Rhythmus
Pantomime

~

Freudigkeit in der Seele
gesteigerte Atemtätigkeit
natürlicher Antrieb zum Bewegen.

~

Je kürzer die Phrase,
um so ausdrucksmächtiger

Motive: in der Linie
Tonhöhe Tondauer Tonstärke.

es ist in dieser Richtung gegeben:
der Ausdruck.//

A
B Melodie   2 Schwerpunkte kleiner Satz
             4 oder mehr grosser Satz.

⎧ Wiederholung des Motivs:
⎨ Gegenübertreten 2 dem 1:
⎩ die Form geht fort -
  die Form biegt in sich ein -

Kadenz oder Fortsetzung?:

[Zum achten Vortrag]   (31)

The dance proceeds on the rhythm
mime

~

Joyfulness in the soul
increased breathing activity
natural impetus for movement

~

The shorter the phrase, the more
powerful the expression.

Phrases: in the line
pitch note-values dynamics

expression is given in this
direction.//

A
B Melody   2 strong emphases 4-bar phrase
            4 or more 8-bar phrase.

⎧ repetition of the motif:
⎨ placing 2 opposite 1:
⎩ the form continues –
  the form bends in itself –

Cadence or continuation?:

[To the 8th lecture]   (31)

Beim großen Satz = Andeutung des
Kleinen Satzes.

Zwerchfell: Verstand der Tänzer.

← beim Eurhythmisten:

die ..auf dem Telephon folgende
Note: starke. — K. —

Beim großen Satz: Andeutung des
kleinen Satzes.

⌣

Zwerchfell: Verstand des Tänzers.
_____

⌣ beim Eurythmisten:

die auf den Taktstricht folgende
Note: stark. - etc.-

(32)

With the large phrase: indication of the
short phrase.

⌣

Diaphragm: mind of the dancer
_____

⌣ with the eurythmist:

the note following the bar
line: strong – etc. –

(32)

bei ganzen Noten etc. den Kopf von
der Bewegung abwenden

$\frac{1}{2}$ $\frac{1}{4}$ etc. auf die Bewegung
hinüber — und dem
eigenen Körper folgen

keine hohen Noten und dem
Augen folgen; als ob sie
then, indem mit greifen
werden. =

Temperamenten: Blick und dem
Körper
gleichsam recht
vorwärts-äußern-Blick.

schnell: (Jähnlich) : Kopf rechts vom
dumpfem: (langsames) : Kopf linke
hinten

schwache Betonung = Finger spitzen =
starke Betonung: Finger einziehen =

RS's-NB-190

bei ganzen Noten etc den Kopf von
der Bewegung <u>abwenden</u>

½ ¼ etc auf die Bewegung
hinsehen - mit dem
~~Augen~~ Kopfe folgen
bei hohen Noten mit den
Augen folgen; nicht als ob
sie sehen, sondern mitgerissen
werden. //

Tempoänderungen: Ruck mit den
Körper
steigernd rechts
Schwache Betonung: Finger spitzen: verlangs(amt) - links.
Starke Betonung: Finger einziehen: schnell: (Interesse): Kopf rechts vorn
langsam: (Langmut): Kopf links hinten

[Zum achten Vortrag]   (33)

With semibreves (whole-notes) etc
<u>turn</u> the head away from the movement

minim (half-note), crotchet (quarter-
note) etc – look at the movement-
follow [the movement] with the
~~eyes~~ head

follow high notes with the eyes
not as though they see, but as
if carried along with them.//

Changes of tempo: jolt with the body
increasing right
slowing down – left.
weak emphasis : stretch the fingers:
strong emphasis : round the fingers
quick: (interest): head right forwards
slow: (disinterest): head left backwards

[To the 8th lecture]   (33)

Tonhöhe: es ist das Gefühl:

Sich auß dem Physklyin gehen:
Man geht hinauß: s° hij
kommen in Geiste

Sich in den Physkille versenken
Man geht hinunter: j m hij
kommen in Physklyin.

Erhören

Tonbauer = Entwicklhim u Leertein

                                    gegenüber des Einro enwelt-

Tonflächte : Maft us Ohnmacht
Sympachin enträngfin

Finger
form

gegründes hij fühlst. Geist

wenn das Gefühl in dem
Lopte hij außspricht ~

Gefühl im engen Sinne.

Wille — Gefühl im Willens. ~

Tonhöhe: es ist das Gefühl:

    Sich aus dem Physischen erheben   Ethos

    Man geht hinauf: zu sich   gegenüber sich selbst. Geist

    kommen im Geiste

    Sich in das Physische versenken   Pathos   wenn das Gefühl in dem

    Man geht hinunter: zu sich   Kopfe sich ausspricht –

    kommen im Physischen.

Tondauer : Erfülltsein – Leersein   Gefühl im engern Sinne.

hinsehen   gegenüber der Aussenwelt

nicht hinsehen }

Tonstärke : Macht und Ohnmacht

        Sympathie Antipathie   Wille   Gefühl im Willen./

Finger

Form

[Zum achten Vortrag]   (34)

Pitch: it is the feeling: Ethos

    You lift yourself out of the physical: in relation to yourself: Spirit

    You go up: coming to yourself

    into the spiritual

                        Pathos   when the feeling is expressed

    Sinking yourself in the physical   in the head

    You go down: coming to yourself

    in the physical

Note values: becoming filled – becoming empty   Feeling in the restricted sense

looking at it   in relation to the

not lookng at it }   outer world

Dynamics: strength and weakness

        sympathy antipathy   Will –   feeling in the will./

Finger

Form

[To the 8th lecture]   (34)

Musik = Die Bewegung des Atems =

Innere Bewegung ~ äussere Bewegung =

Die äussere folgt dem Willen, ~~die~~ sie ist das
~~innere~~
ergreifende, die Dinge umfassend nachahmende
im Aetherleibe ; die innere trägt das dadurch
geschaffene Bild —

Der Mensch ist die Octave =

Vor der Aufführg : Allg. Charakteristik.
    Das Wesentliche der eurythm. Gebärde.

In der Pause : Musik. Gebärden ; sie bilden
    den innern Menschen nach —
        Position — Bewegg — Gestaltg.
    Sprachl. Gebärden : sie bilden das
c d e f g a h c   Verhältnis des Menschen zur Welt nach
    Gestaltg variierend. immer ein
    Hinausgehen über die Quint.
    Es spricht eigentlich : c e g oder
      c a f.
    der Dur = oder Moll = Accord . =

Further notes to the lecture-course, from the 3rd German ed., pp. 136–143:

Musik - Die Bewegung des Atems -
Inner Bewegung - äussere Bewegung -
Die äussere folgt dem Willen, sie ist das
ergreifende, die Dinge umfassend nachahmende
im Aetherleibe; die innere trägt das dadurch
geschaffene Bild -
Der Mensch ist die Octave -

––

Vor der Aufführung (Ausführung[?]): Allg[emeine] Charakteristik.
     Das Wesentliche der eurythm[ischen] Gebärde.
In der Pause: Musik[alische] Gebärden; sie bilden
          den inneren Menschen nach -
             Position - Bewegung - Gestaltung.
          Sprachl[iche] Gebärden: sie bilden das
c d e f g a h c   Verhältnis des Menschen zur Welt nach.
          Gestaltung variierend. Immer ein
          Hinausgehen über die Quint.
          Es spricht eigentlich: c e g oder
             c a f

         der Dur- oder Moll-Accord. //

––

Music – the movement of the breath –
Inner movement - outer movement –
The outer movement follows the will, it is that which takes
hold, which embraces and imitates
in the ether body; the inner movement
carries the image thereby created –
The human being is the octave –

––

Before the performance (enactment[?]): general characterization
      The essential thing of eurythmic gesture.
In the rest: musical gestures; they recreate
         the inner human being –
           Position – movement - formation
         speech movements: they recreate the
         relationship of the human being to the world
c d e f g a b c   Varying formation. Always a going-beyond the fifth.
         It says actually: c e g or
           c a f

      the major or minor chord. //

Im Musikalischen wird der ~~Foo~~ räumliche Mensch
in den unräumlichen umgewandelt –
es liegt innerlich dem Musikalischen der geistige
Mensch zu Grunde. –
In der Sprache ist der Mensch aus dem Geistigen
herausgefuert. Es ist eigentlich das Geheime der
Sprache, das zu Grunde liegt – das dann in
die Bedeutung für das Sinnliche umgelegt wird.

    Dur – Festhalten gegenüber dem Verlieren }
    Moll –   "   "   dem Finden }

Skalenerlebnis =

Grosse Terz – Grundton ~~~~ Position /
        Terz   In sich bleibende Bewegg:
        Quinte   Gestaltung

Im Physischen Menschen: der ist im gegenw. Leben
    dazu gekommen: er schickt die innere äussere Bewegg
    in die Sprache, damit voriges Leben darin seine Bäume.
    Wille durch Gefühl in die Vorstellung.
Im aeth. Menschen: der kommt unmittelbar vor dem
    Erdenleben dazu: er schickt das geistige Erleben

Im Musikalischen wird der räumliche
Mensch in den unräumlichen
umgewandelt –
es liegt innerlich dem Musikalischen der
geistige Mensch zu Grunde. –
In der Sprache ist der Mensch aus dem
Geistigen herausgeholt. Es ist eigentlich
das Geheime der Sprache,
das zu Grunde liegt - das dann in
die Bedeutung für das Sinnliche
umgesetzt wird.

       Dur - Festhalten gegenüber dem Verlieren
       Moll - Festhalten gegenüber dem Finden
       Skalenerlebnis
Grosse Terz –   Grundton Position –
               Terz in sich bleibende Bewegung
               Quinte Gestaltung

Im Physischen Menschen: der ist im gegenw[ärtigen] Leben
dazugekommen: er schickt die äussere Bewegung
        in die Sprache, damit voriges Leben darin sein kann,
            Wille durch Gefühl in die Vorstellung.
Im äth[erischen] Menschen: der kommt unmittelbar vor dem
      Erdenleben dazu: er schickt das geistige Erleben.

In the musical element
the spatial human being is transformed
into the non-spatial human being -
the spiritual human being
is the inner origin of the musical element. -
In speech the human being is brought
forth out of the spiritual [realm]
It is actually that which is the secret
of speech that lies at its basis –
which then gets changed into meaning
for the sensory [realm].

       Major – holding your ground in the face of losing
       Minor – holding your ground in the face of finding
       Experience of the scale
Major third –   keynote position –
            third   movement remaining within itelf
            fifth   formation
In the physical human being: it has been added in the present life it sends the outer movement
into speech, so that the preceeding life can be in it,
           will through feeling in the imagination
In the etheric human being: it joins just before the
       earthly life: it sends the spiritual experience.

in die Musik –

Gefühl in Vorstellung.

Die Gebärde beim Musikhören:
sie bringt die innere Menschenform
zur äusseren Anschauung –

Die Gebärde beim Sprachlichen:
sie bringt die Weltenform, die
sich im Menschen abbildet
zur äusseren Anschauung.

Der Mensch ist etwas, was zur Welt
hinzukommt – die Welt wäre
ohne ihn nicht fertig /
Musik

Der Mensch ist ein Abbild der Welt –
die Welt ist in ihm noch einmal
vorhanden: /
Sprache.

In der Musik empfindet man
das Menschenwesen –

In der Sprache empfindet man
das Weltenwesen.
Vocalisch: Bild – Conf. den Bildner.

in die Musik –
    Gefühl in Vorstellung.
Die Gebärde beim Musikalischen:
  sie bringt die innere Menschenform
  zur äusseren Anschauung -
Die Gebärde beim Sprachlichen:
  sie bringt die Weltenform, die
  sich im Menschen abbildet
  zur ässeren Anschauung.
Der Mensch ist etwas, was zur Welt
  hinzukommt - die Welt wäre
  ohne ihn nicht fertig /
    Musik
Der Mensch ist ein Abbild der Welt –
  die Welt ist in ihm noch einmal
  vorhanden: /
     Sprache
In der Musik empfindet man
  das Menschenwesen –
In der Sprache empfindet man

  das Weltenwesen

  Vocalisch: Bild - Cons[onantisch:] den Bildner.

---

into music —
    feeling in the imagination
The gesture within music:
  it brings the inner human configuration
  into outer visibility –
The gesture within speech:
  it brings the configuration of the world,
  which is pictured in the human being,
  into outer visibility.
The human being is something which is added to the world –
  the world would not be complete without him: /
    Music
The human being is an image of the world –
  the world is once again present in him: /
    Speech
In music you feel man's being –
In speech you feel the world's being

  Vowel-like: image – consonantal: the shaper of the image.

In sich halten beim Taktstrich
Sich hinüberschwingen beim Übergang
von einem Motiv zum andern Motivmetamorphose

    Takt: phys. Mensch = wie schwer ein Mensch ist.

Rhythmus : — ᵕ — ᵕ : aeth. Mensch =

Melodie : astralische Mensch =

Sprache : Ich /

    Gesang : dem Melos nachgehen

<u>Goethes Gedicht</u> : über allen Gipfeln

    Gipfel Winkel h g   moll Terz   ist Ruhe h c Septime

Hauch auch

warte balde e g dur Terz   Hauch auch
            Terzen intervalle.

In sich halten beim Taktstrich
Sich hinüberschwingen beim übergang
von einem Motiv zur andern Motivmetamorphose

Takt: phys[ischer] Mensch - wie schwer ein Mensch ist

Rhythmus: —u —u: aeth[erischer] Mensch –
Melodie: astralische Mensch –
Sprache: Ich –
Gesang: dem Melos nachgehen –

Goethes Gedicht:
Über allen Gipfeln

Gipfel Wipfel	h g	Moll-Terz	
Hauch auch			ist Ruh h c Septim
Warte balde	e g	Dur-Terz Hauch auch	
		Terzenintervalle	

Remain within yourself with the bar-line
Swing yourself over in the transition
from one motif to another metamorphosis of the motif

Beat: physical human being – how heavy a person is

Rhythm: — u — u: etheric human being –
Melody: astral human being –
Speech: ego –
Singing: following the *Melos* –

Goethe's poem:
Über allen Gipfeln

Gipfel Wipfel	b g	minor third	
Hauch auch			ist Ruh b c seventh
Warte balde	e g	major third	Hauch auch
		intervals of thirds	

Index to the Lectures

Part II

A COMPANION
to
RUDOLF STEINER'S
EURYTHMY AS VISIBLE
SINGING

(GA 278)

Notes to the Lectures
with Appendices

compiled
by
Alan Stott

together with

JOSEF MATTHIAS HAUER
INTERPRETING MELOS

translated by
Alan Stott

Fig. 24:   Raphael, St Cecilia with St Paul, John the Evangelist, Augustine and Mary
Magdalen   c. 1516

Compiler's Preface

Eurythmy is practised world-wide today. It builds on the foundation of the original form of musical expression – singing – by making it visible. What wants to sing, the living movement in music, can be made visible by the human body, being itself a creation of what Rudolf Steiner calls the music of the spheres. Upon this premise, Steiner gave the lecture course *Eurythmy as Visible Singing* (GA 278; Collected Works No. 278) that represents his greatest contribution to *music*. Musical concepts are extended and new experience is opened up; it is not a new theory that is expounded. While inaugurating the new art of eurythmy, Steiner at the same time covers the most important essentials of the art of music itself. This is achieved through tracing the musical elements back to the human being. A pathway between naturalism and abstraction is indicated as a way for art to get beyond materialism. The middle way of Far-Eastern tradition is renewed in a modern context. Eurythmy is actually and historically neither an alternative nor a new-age phenomenon. The conviction, moreover, that eurythmy is not another form of the drama or the dance (whether sacred or secular) with its vocabulary of (spatial) movement of the limbs, but rather a new time art springing from a living renewal of the mysteries, has to be made, in the long run, by each person individually.

The study material comprising this companion volume to *Eurythmy as Visible Singing*, is offered to students by a fellow student. My aim is to assist the reader's approach to Steiner's meaning, mainly through his own words. I have chosen relevant passages from Steiner's other work (both the written books and the lectures), and have not hesitated to refer to the sacred and artistic links. Here I have followed Steiner's own hints, but also included suggestions from other researchers, thinkers and artists of the twentieth century and sometimes earlier. Whereas this selection is intended to be helpful for those with questions, it is clearly fragmentary and conditioned by the limited perceptions of the compiler.

The Appendices represent attempts to work out in detail specific obscure passages and crucial themes. Any attempt to approach the deeper nature of art will have to face questions about outer nature and inner experience, summed up in the question of personality, human and divine. My attempts still only represent a beginning in this field in the context of eurythmy. The many remaining questions for eurythmical research will not fail to strike the reader. It hardly needs mentioning that in our individual lives we all pursue our own path in scientific studies, artistic attempts and moral endeavour. My own path is practical and artistic. Yet there will be moments when we wish to relate generally and "compare notes" specifically. In this way, a fuller appreciation of what Steiner achieved in the field of renewing the art of music should emerge in due course. To Steiner, music and eurythmy are ultimately not separable; neither art is the personal property of any individual, of course. To such students who are willing to share notes, the following initial attempts are dedicated.

St Bernard of Clairvaux describes the situation in his time: "If then you are wise, you will show yourself rather as a reservoir than as a canal. A canal spreads abroad water as it receives it, but a reservoir waits until it is filled before overflowing and thus without loss to itself communicates its superabundant water. In the Church of the present day we have many canals but few reservoirs" (*Sermons on the Canticle*, XVIII. 2, 3). In our time the path to knowledge is perhaps more differentiated, and is not tied to ecclesiastical forms. It has to be based on *experience*; this leads to *results* that, in their turn, invite *interpretation*. These three stages are evident today in people's openness to change, in the achievements of analytical research, and in the attempts at constructive thinking. Steiner points to this process in his threefold differentiation of the soul: sentient-soul, intellectual-(or mind-)soul, and consciousness-(or spiritual-)soul. First in order comes experience; next, we begin to think about our experiences; finally, we creatively work over those thoughts. (For Steiner, it needs to be said, the last stage is not mere speculation but living experience. He did not use thinking perception as the occasion for delivering dogmatic pronouncements.) In my contributions, experience is assumed, the relevant thoughts are initially researched (clearing the channels) and some interpretations offered (the reservoirs identified).

Certain writers who are quoted, or whose work is listed, are chosen for their relationship to the path outlined by Steiner in such works as *The Philosophy of Spiritual Activity (Freedom): the Basis of a Modern World-Conception* (latest translation *Intuitive Thinking as a Spiritual Path: a Philosophy of Freedom*, tr. Michael Lipson. AP. 1995. "All real philosophers," Steiner writes in the Preface (1894), "have been artists in the realm of concepts" (emphases original), indicating that the bond between thinkers goes beyond any intellectual pigeon-holing. This artistic, basically human concern can, and I think must, be our guide as it was Steiner's. Thomas Meyer, for example, makes a start on our own pigeon-holing of Steiner by showing how *The Philosophy...* is "a modern T A O-book". Steiner himself calls this philosophy a Pauline theory of knowledge (R. Steiner. Lecture, Berlin. 8 May 1910). (Here I should add that Lorenzo Ravagli. *Das Evangelium der Bewusstseins-Seele*. Trithemius Verlag. Munich. 1995, has appeared too recently for me to make specific references.) I have assumed that readers are primarily interested in artistic, basically human questions, and are not over-concerned with concessions to the systematizing intellect. Today, the intellect that accepts the poetical work of such giants as Goethe and Coleridge, still tends to dismiss their scientific and philosophical work as amateurish. The terms "poet" and "philosopher" are by no means mutually exclusive. Some of the writers I quote are constructive or philosophic theologians. "Occult philosophy" is a term used for the central tradition that we now know inspired, for example, Shakespeare and Bach. The terms "traditionalist" and "metaphysician" are both applied to René Guénon, that independent thinker who did so much to research what he called the Primordial Tradition. Yet whatever terms are used to list the various disciplines and activities of the human spirit, it has to be admitted that the aim of all knowledge and experience is to manifest the truth about the human being and the unity of fully human realisation. In an essay mentioning Steiner, C.G. Jung wrote (1936), that "the West will produce its own yoga, and it will be on the basis laid down by Christianity" (see Appendix 3, Endnote 3, p. 365 below).

In the present studies, the bright quality of thinking, which may be described as Michaelic, is acknowledged wherever it appears to throw light on the creation and pursuit of eurythmy. (The archangel Michael, the countenance that Christ assumes for our age, began his present regency in 1879, a fact known to other groups besides anthroposophists.) This light-beam has been my guide throughout on the path that attempts to articulate artistic experience. Moreover, I see no need to apologise for naming the most wonderful event in human history, the Mystery of Golgotha, and for pointing to some great Michaelic teachers who interpret it to us. This interpretive action is neither exclusively intellectual nor exclusively theological, but points to the ultimate source of our human creativity and the unity of our experience. On this basis references to the New Testament are made. The growing point reappears wherever it will – it is not a different one that reappears in GA 278 (*cf.*, I Cor. 12:11).

Nowhere in these pages do I intend to convey any suggestion that art is a substitute for religion. Do we really need Arvo Pärt or John Tavener to remind us that all these activitiesare nearer *music* than is commonly believed? Neither philosophy, theology nor anthroposophy is "religion"; all these activities are nearer to *music* than is commonly believed. Surely the correct view is conveyed in the comprehensive vision of Archbishop William Temple, "truth is one… and each department in isolation is an abstraction". For, he adds elsewhere, "science and politics are the very arena wherein the divine purpose… is to be fulfilled" (W. Temple. *Nature, Man and God*. Macmillan. London. 1934. 506). This thinker cites the activities of the playwright and the composer as analogies to the activity of the Creator. Moreover if, as Michael Ramsey (the one hundredth Archbishop of Canterbury) reminds us, the centre of *worship* will be not the needs and feeling of men but the redeeming acts of God and the eternal truths which these acts reveal (A.M. Ramsey. *The Gospel and the Catholic Church*. SPCK. London. 1980), then in regaining its sacred heart, *artistic activity* may indeed aspire to a share in the movement of worship in the sense of John 4:23 and 24. "Religion is but the Godward aspect and end of all activities, consciously realised in one", writes O.C. Quick. (*The Ground of Faith and the Chaos of Modern Thought*. Nisbet. London. 1931. 136).

In this connection, it is interesting that Raphael's late painting of the patron saint of music, *St Cecilia* (1514-15), includes as well as Mary Magdalene, the figures of St Paul, St John and St Augustine. Augustine's ideal meaning of sacrifice (shared by F.D. Maurice, H. Scott Holland, and many others) can help musicians, too (NB salvation of the individual is *not* being proposed): "Sacrifice is every deed that is done to the end that we may cleave to God in fellowship in relation to that good end by which we might become blessed" (*De Civitate Dei*, X. Chap. vi). Despite the criticisms and misunderstandings provoked in our century, it is heartening to observe the courage as well as the scholarship and artistry of the spiritual witnesses from whom I have made my selection. Here I should add that although aware of the universal law of polarity before commencing the present work, I discovered the Lambda in Steiner before coming across Hans Kayser's great work *Orphikon* (Schwabe & Co. Basel/ Stuttgart. 1973) and consequently I have been able only briefly to allude to harmonical research in these pages.

Dr David Rycroft at an earlier stage kindly edited the Introduction (Part 1) and the Endnotes. Terry Boardman, an historian who has lived in Japan, helped with Appendices 4, 5 and 8. It would be difficult to list all the eurythmists, students and pupils who have indirectly helped, but I am nevertheless aware of their contribution and am extremely grateful for what they taught me. Dorothea Mier has been very supportive, and even if most of the others who have morally supported both the translation and the research work prefer to remain anonymous, they too receive my warmest thanks. Love for the work has created many lasting friendships – for what more could one ask?

Today, a would-be commentator of Steiner is faced above all with the example of the master of spiritual-scientific research, who, in connection with the future of the arts and of music in particular, points to "the Incarnation and the Hallelujah of Christ". But, Steiner – who is not alone here – points out that the work of salvation continues among us: it is not ours, but it is Christ's in us. Steiner's comprehensive experience, exemplary scholarship and creative personality must surely qualify him as the chief servant of Michael, whose name is less a statement than a challenge: "Who is like God?" Religious, artistic and scientific experience, and religious, artistic and scientific study all confirm that the answer for which Michael and the spiritual world is waiting, is "the human being".

Alan Stott, Stourbridge, 1995 (corrected 1998/2013)

Compiler's Notes

Note to the Corrected Edition (1998):

The facsimile of Rudolf Steiner's Notebook NB 494, was originally published in the third German edition in an edited form. Permission to include the missing sections here has been kindly granted by Rudolf Steiner Nachlassverwaltung, Dornach. I am very grateful to a colleague, Julian Clarke, for his suggested improvements to the translation that concerns the passage on the bar line in Lecture 4, and for his kind contribution of Endnote 25a, now 32. Werner Barfod most kindly and promptly contributed Endnote 52a, now 66. Regarding other comments made to me, three tendencies are worth mentioning: (i) Some practising eurythmists have wondered whether the study-material attempts to answer questions that are not being asked. Practice and theory, however, cannot be divorced. Research is an essential complement to eurythmy in practice. (ii) Others have wondered why at times firmer, clearer conclusions to some of the more speculative suggestions are not always drawn. In this area surely the danger of a dogmatic tendency has to be avoided? Putting it more positively, I believe informed suggestion may prove more fruitful. My own conviction in interpreting Steiner is that there is room for complementary approaches. (iii) There is a suggestion of over-emphasis.

To point (iii), the lecture-course "Eurythmy as Visible Speech", GA279, has first to be noted. Study of this (and "Eurythmy: Its Birth and Development". GA277a) provisionally completes the study of the origins of eurythmy, which study – like that of the human being – is actually never-ending. Here on earth we are forced to study things in order, but we should not forget that the human being is one. St Paul's "faith, hope and love" (three of the greatest words in human speech) are related by R. Steiner (lectures, Nuremberg. 2-3 Dec. 1911; E.T. *The Golden Blade*. RSP 1964) in the order "faith, love and hope" to the astral, etheric and physical bodies respectively. Yet he means the whole human being in each case, for we consist, as he says, of "members", not parts. Moreover, he tells the Waldorf teachers that the astral body that lives from "faith" (which involves the whole human being), simply "is music" (see Endnote 55, 2). We are all caught up in the details of daily concerns – including such activities as worship, family life, science, politics, economics, philosophy, education, sport, art, and music. These are all concerns of the Son of Man. My commentary arose out of the daily work and was directed by the subject in hand. Incidentally, comprehensive thoughts on "balance" are offered in the well-known and truly remarkable lectures, parts of which are well worth getting by heart (Dornach, 20-22 Nov. 1914. *The Balance in the World and Man*. N. Vancouver. 1977). In "striving to be conscious in the spiritual world" (17) our prejudices, assumptions and narrow specialisations fall away. All of them, yours and mine! Need it be added that I eagerly look forward to commentaries from, for example, Far-Eastern, Indian and African students of eurythmy. In the end, I believe that the links to the central western tradition presented in this commentary cannot be gainsaid. "No such thing as a profane domain really exists," René Guénon reminds us, "but only a profane point of view." Speaking precisely on musical studies, Steiner forsaw a union of art, science and religion ("*Fragebeantwortung* – Answers to questions". 30 Sept. 1920. GA 283. Germ. ed. 63).

Owen Barfield's kind words have greatly encouraged me. Other comments or possible reviews of which I could have made use for this revision, have unfortunately not come to my notice. It only remains to be said that, in addition to correcting typographical errors, some additions have been made to Endnotes 5 and 50; Endnotes 5, 32 , 37, and 66 are new. Some brief additions have been made to the study-material and to the book-lists. The lists and references are "Designed to captivate and charm/ More rather than to rouse alarm". They should assist (as "a Companion…") serious students to recognise (i) who their forerunners were, and (ii) who their true colleagues in today's world are. I believe that some evidence is thereby supplied that eurythmy, despite its low profile in some parts of the world, is nevertheless a strong "civilisation impulse". The future was ever prepared by a "remnant" in ways not always appreciated at the time. You may often feel isolated, but, along with many other spiritually-striving, humble (another word for truthful) people, you too are serving to advance the front line of humanity.

The omission of a line previously on p. 143, and incorrect book-title previously on p. 114, have been rectified. The painting '*Il Sposalizio*' (Raphael's "Marriage [Betrothal] of the Virgin") is recommended for study in the "Faculty Meeting". My references to Leonardo are now adjusted. No one is more aware of the remaining imperfections than myself, yet a re-working of the study-material is simply impractical at present. Appendix 7 is published as it first appeared, with all the guesswork. Steiner himself was subject to the creative powers of the universe, of which number is surely a main form of expression. Every single reference to number in GA 278 is important. The subject is still being researched. Finally, it was decided not to increase the size of the book. Those interested will find work is being published in the bi-annual *Newsletter* of the Section for the Performing Arts (Dornach), and in our own *Newsletter of the Association of Eurythmists in Great Britain and Ireland*. The essays "Character and Conduct in GA 278" (which attempts to trace a connection of the eight lectures with the Beatitudes and the Eightfold Path), a contribution on "The Meditation for Eurythmists" and a study on NB 494 will all appear in *A Further Companion for Eurythmists and Musicians* (forthcoming). Last but by no means least, my very grateful thanks to Tim Clement for his princely patience and technical help in preparing the disc for our most courteous printers.

Alan Stott, Stourbridge, Michaelmas 1998

NOTE to the revised and augmented edition (2013)

The Further Companion didn't materialise, but a number of articles and a website did (checklist after the Endnotes to the Lectures). Additions to the Endnotes, especially on the angle-gestures, several new illustrations, and eight new Endnotes on the Eightfold Path have increased the volume and hopefully also the usefulness of the Companion. All the Endnotes are renumbered (see Correlation, p. 324). I toiled to produce an Index. The Appendices, for all their faults, have to remain. They were the result of a bona fide approach to largely unchartered territory. Appendix 9 is new. Since the last revision, degree courses in eurythmy have sprung up. The critical stage with its "modes" can teach you clarity, but for creativity there is no substitute for concrete thinking (ouch!). Such pioneers as H. Pfrogner, H. Ruland and Chr. Peter have blazed a trail. These writers in German show how you can write sensibly about music; we are facing the task of wrestling for an adequate language for "visible singing". We shall achieve it with a comprehensive view of human creativity. Let the concert pianist Dennis Matthews inspire you: "To write about something is to get to know it better, and though I have always been a slow worker with words I have never regretted being obliged to find them" (*In Pursuit of Music*).

A. S., Christmas 2012

Endnotes to the Lectures

The following Endnotes are intended to suggest ways of following up selected aspects. This section claims to be neither exhaustive nor complete. Interpretation has largely been relegated to the Appendices, where the subject matter slightly overlaps, though some basic perspectives are discussed. Endnote ▨41▨ draws attention to the transition between the first half and the second half of the lecture-course. Endnotes ▨38▨, ▨39▨ (first sentence), ▨49▨ (first sentence), ▨53▨ and ▨62▨ (first sentence) derive from those of the German editor, Eva Fröböse. Endnote ▨32▨ was kindly supplied by Julian Clark, Endnote ▨65▨ by Werner Barfod.

Serious students will already possess Rudolf Steiner, *Das Wesen des Musikalischen*, GA 283 (the lectures but not the discussions are tr. in *The Inner Nature of Music*... AP. 1983; the Germ. ed. carries a comprehensive list of where and when Steiner spoke on music), and they will possess the other lecture-courses and writings mentioned in the Introduction. Essential reading for a more complete understanding of Steiner's thinking with regard to the present lecture-course is J.M. Hauer's *Deutung des Melos*, Tal & Co. Verlag. Leipzig/ Wien/ Zürich 1923. The Goetheanum Library carries a copy of the original, as does Rudolf Steiner Library, 35 Park Road, London NW1 6XT, U.K. <rsh-library@anth.org.uk>. An E.T., "Interpreting Melos", is included in the present volume. E. Zuccoli (see p. 218 below) provides an account of the early eurythmy work with which Steiner could assume his small audience was already familiar. "Tr. in MS" signifies a possible publication still awaiting funding. GA (*Gesamtausgabe*) = Bibliographic Survey numbers of Rudolf Steiner's works (1961), given for ease of reference. At the time of writing, a website exists offering the German texts for downloading in pdf-format: <http://fvn-rs.net/index>. Websites also exist offering certain texts by Steiner in English tr. for downloading, *e.g.*, <www.rsarchive.org>.) It is planned to collect the translations that appeared in *EA Newsletter* (the organ of the Association of Eurythmists in Great Britain and Ireland. Page numbers refer to the published E.T. where extant, otherwise to the German edition. The translations are frequently re-worked. I have been able only in a few instances to give bibliographical details of, for example, American editions. Many of the books cited are or were published outside as well as within the U.K., and the number of reprint editions is increasing. Certain texts in the public domain (out of copyright) are becoming available on internet libraries, *e.g.*, <www.archive.org>. For tracing books, too, our public library inter-loan service can be helpful; <www.bookfinder.com> is a good search-engine for the secondhand market.

The following works, in addition to those mentioned in the Introduction (in particular Kux, van der Pals, Husemann and Pfrogner), are also relevant:

Nachrichten der Rudolf Steiner-Nachlassverwaltung. Heft 26 (Dornach, 1969 reprinted 1980), is a special issue devoted to music. In the Introduction, Helmut von Wartburg surveys Steiner's relationship to music.

Rudolf Steiner. *"Das Goetheanum in seinen zehn Jahren"*. Essays 1923. In GA 36, and *Der Goetheanumgedanke*. Tb 635. Dornach 1982;

Rudolf Steiner, three introductions to eurythmy performances during the Christmas Foundation Meeting. Dornach 26-28 Dec. 1923. GA 277. 407-22 (tr. of II, R. Steiner. *An Introduction to Eurythmy*. AP 1984. 89-93); and the introduction at the founding of the General Anthroposophical Society. Dornach. 5 Jan. 1924. GA 277. 422-27 (tr. *EA Newsletter*, Spring 1996. Aberdeen).

Lea van der Pals. *The Human Being as Music*. Stourbridge. 1992. Tr. A.S. (distrib.: <eurythmywm@gmail.com>), is a useful introduction by a leading eurythmist.

Lea van der Pals and Annemarie Bäschlin. *Ton-Heileurythmie*. Dornach. 1991, contains useful summaries of the elements of eurythmy, including some early indications ("Music Eurythmy Therapy", tr. A.S., enquiries: <eurythmywm@gmail.com>).

Elena Zuccoli. *From the Tone Eurythmy Work at the first Eurythmy School in Stuttgart 1922-24*. Walter Keller Press. Dornach. 1981; an essential account of the early indications (page numbers refer to this edition). Expanded edition: E. Zuccoli. *Toneurythmie (1915-1924)*. W. Keller, Dornach. 1997 (rev. & augmented ed., not yet in E.T.).

Ursula-Ingrid Gillert. *Wege zum eurythmischen Gestalten*. Selbstverlag. 1993 (E.T. by A.S., "Ways to Eurythmical Interpretation"), is uncomplicated and offers much practical advice.

Christoph Peter. *Die Sprache der Musik in Mozarts "Zauberflöte"*. *Stuttgart. 1997* ("The Magic Flute": *Mozart's Language of Music*. E.T. forthcoming), is a truly Goethean, phenomenological study of music developed from Steiner's indications, and is as well the definitive study on *The Magic Flute*. A companion for the musical artist.

Hermann Beckh. *The Essence of Tonality*. Anastasi. 2001. Beckh expanded his thesis in *Die Sprache der Tonart*. Urachhaus. Stuttgart.

3rd ed. 1977/84 (E.T. "The Language of Tonality" in MS). Subsequent studies (Ruland, Peter) contain summaries.

Heiner Ruland. *Expanding Tonal Awareness*. RSP. 1992. A breakthrough in musical studies, with chapters on the development of tonal systems from Atlantis onwards, including future perspectives (a few inaccuracies of translation are mentioned in the review in *Anthroposophy Today*. No. 19. Spring 1993. RSP).

The young Ralph Kux relates his first meeting with Steiner:

> The most impressive thing for the newcomer was his expressive gestures. When speaking he placed intimate spiritual thoughts and feelings in the most wonderful way in the gesticulations of his arms and hands. The richly varied language of gesture was the most fruitful stimulus, especially for someone concerned with eurythmy. And so, if you did not want to miss the most intimate things, you could not lose sight of him while he was speaking. His deep, resonant voice was clearly audible everywhere, even when it had grown somewhat hoarse through delivering thousands of lectures (R. Kux. *Erringerungen an Rudolf Steiner*. Melinger. Stuttgart 1973. 8. E.T. by A.S.).

For a further account by W. J. Stein of R. Steiner as a lecturer, see Johannes Tautz. *Walter Johannes Stein*. Temple Lodge Press. London. 1990. 248-50. "A biolgraphical Sketch" by A. Heidenreich (in *Christianity as Mystical Fact...* R. Steiner Pub. Inc. New York. 1961. 15-33), is also valuable.

Since the last edition of this *Companion*, articles by the compiler have appeared in the *Newsletter of the Section for the Arts of Eurythmy, Specch and Music* (RB – *Rundbrief*), pub. bi-annually in Dornach; available online from RB 30 onwards, both English (RBe) and German (RBd) (contact <abo@dasgoetheanum.ch>), or download articles from my website <www.alansnotes.co.uk.> A check-list is to be found after the endnotes.

For the present edition, I have tidied up where I could, updated and augmented here and there and added some new Endnotes on what I take to be references to the noble Eightfold Path. The influence of this Path pervades these lectures; some initial observations were originally made in a longish article (RB 35, 36 & 37). The Endnotes are all renumbered; a correlation to previous editions is added at the end of the section. So many questions arise in study-groups with students, yet other priorities meant my desire to rewrite the whole *Companion* had to be curbed. Traces of "issues" certainly survive – they galvanised me in the first instance – and, oh dear, I am notoriously unsuccessful in "keeping cool". Let myself go, have I? To obstruct in any way has never been the intention. Please make no mistake, "evidence-based" criteria can be as specific as you like, but the phrase need not be narrowly interpreted today. In another field of enquiry, the "evidence of the rocks" is incontestable, but evolution cannot explain itself. So too with art. Though Steiner may certainly emphasise experience, he does not suggest we remain self-satisfied; he did his best to promote thinking. "A man's principles...", Coleridge points out (*The Friend*), "are the life of his life." My contribution, then, is just that, a contribution. I will say this: I do know we cannot fake relations to "what is", as the Psalmist with his "justify" knew of old. Blushing at the crudities, excesses and repetitions in what follows, I can only suggest the obvious: *Take only what could prove of value, kindly overlooking the imperfections and weaknesses.* What you have in your hands is the record of what moves an indolent English phlegmatic; it is a pioneer attempt. Paul speaks of having "run the race", no doubt a relay race, implying "take up the baton!" At the time of writing, a new publication of essays in German is in preparation. We can look forward to more fruitful developments supporting the young art, whose birth only 100 years ago we are celebrating world-wide.

Alan Stott, Christmas 2012

Note 2013

Meanwhile, "Right Balance between Heaven and Earth: Art as a WAY; the Way as ART" has been written and will appear in the companion, ed. Stefan Hassler (Dornach, forthcoming) in the German language. The English original, here Appendix 9, is also be available on my website: <www.alansnotes.co.uk>.

A.S. Epiphany 2013

Note on Steiner's Report

1 To achieve a "good style" in essay writing, Steiner advocates the chiastic form. Each sentence reflects around a central sentence, or pair of sentences. The final sentence has something to do with the first, the penultimate with the second, and so on.

> Only when [the essay-writer] comes to the middle of his essay can he allow himself to concentrate on one sentence alone. If an author has a true feeling for style in prose, he will have the whole essay before him as he writes (R. Steiner. Speech and Drama. Lecture 3. 7 Dec, 1924. GA 272. RSP. London. 1960. 68).

The chiastic form (from the Gk letter *chi*: X) is well known in biblical form-criticism. It has been found in the Psalms (Thomas Boys, ed. E.W. Bullinger. *A Key to the Psalms*. Eyre & Spottiswoode. London/ Young. New York. 1899), throughout the Bible (E.W. Bullinger. *The Companion Bible*. Oxford 1909–21. Kregel. Grand Rapids. 1990), and Shakespeare (Sylvia Eckersley. *Number and Geometry in Shakespeare's "Macbeth"*. Floris Books. Edinburgh. 2007). Steiner kept to his own advice throughout *all* his published *written* work; a seven-sentence, chiastic, musical rhythm has been discovered governing every section/ chapter (see Alan Stott in RB 44, 45 & 51).

The seven-sentence rhythm present throughout Steiner's writings supplies one answer to his indication (*The Gospel of St John*. GA 103. Lecture 1. Hamburg. 31 May 1908), given in connection with the Fourth Gospel, catharsis and initiation, to read the texts of spiritual science as "a pianist reads musical scores". The white notes of the keyboard picture the seven-note scale, the black piano-keys providing the other, chromatic notes. But, again, the indication includes *all* who live the 7-day week – the same yet always different –, which is a *human* rhythm.

The central sentences – of course, always check the original German – of Steiner's Report (the sentence structure is 7+12+7) are sentences 13 and 14:

> 13. Music eurythmy makes visible that which is invisible, but lives audibly, in music.

> 14. It is just here that we are in the gravest danger of becoming unmusical.

Much can be learnt from a study of the musical form of this Report. See Alan Stott. "'Ourselves our most severest critics…': Remarks on R. Steiner's Report on *Eurythmy as Visible Singing*" (see RB 55 and 56).

Fig. 25: Rudolf Steiner. (Photo, courtesy of R. Steiner Nachlassverwaltung, Dornach, Switzerland.)

Notes to Lecture 1

2 The word *Verständnis*, "understanding", is used five times at the beginning of this course of eight lectures: Eurythmy is complete when an audience is present; in portraying the sounds of speech and musical sound, the eurythmical gestures are to embody experience. The word "understanding" returns later in Lecture 1. 42. "Understanding" at the outset becomes a "laying-hold" at the end of Lecture 1 (47): without a knowledge of the "nature of the human being" and the capacity to pour yourself as a "whole human being" into the artistic event, you cannot achieve authenticity. *Right* or *Complete Understanding/ View/ Opinion* is the first step on the Eightfold Path, first given to the world by the Buddha, modernised and summarised by R. Steiner in *Knowledge of the Higher Worlds: How is it Achieved?* (GA 10. Chap. 5) in connection with the development of the 16-petalled lotus-flower, to which Steiner also links the Beatitudes (Matt. 5), (see R. Steiner. *A Spiritual Cosmogony*. Lecture, Paris. 6 June 1906. GA 94. Dornach. 1979). During the lecture-course, no imported "tradition" is explicitly mentioned; all the connections are intrinsic, awaiting discovery.

Adam Bittleston characterises the Eightfold Path as "relevant indeed to *all* the ways in which the astral body needs to be brought into a renewed right balance between heaven and earth" ("Traffic and Character". *The Golden Blade* 1968. 107-23, especially 116-21. Photocopies from <rsh-library@anth.org.uk>). The *Highway Code* provides a first step for road-users; similarly, the lecture-course offers *a guide to conduct*, a picture of the practical goal, that is, autonomous, creative artists.

Hitherto unnoticed, the Eightfold Path – down-to-earth and eminently helpful for artists – seems to inform each of the eight lectures of *Eurythmy as Visible Singing*, attaining specific mention through the lecturer's admonitions and "meaningful humorous asides". See below Endnotes **16**, **18**, **36**, **42**, **52**, **61**, **73**; which are based on Alan Stott. "Character and Conduct in GA 278". Parts 1, 2 & 3. RB 35, 36 & 37. Michaelmas 2001, Easter 2002, & Michaelmas 2002. See also the essay "A Right Balance between Heaven and Earth: Art as as WAY: the Way as ART", in German, in the compilation ed. Stefan Hassler (Dornach, forthcoming) and in English here as Appendix 9, and on my website <www.alansnotes.co.uk>.

Elena Zuccoli suggests a related eightfold overview; the lecture-course contains the principles of a path of practice with educational power:

If you survey the developing sequence of the eight lectures you can feel them like a scale from keynote to octave, but you can also use this sequence of the lectures as an ideal pattern for teaching music-eurythmy in the training. The artist finds in the given sequence of eurythmical laws a support for his/her imagination and rich suggestions for artistic ways of fashioning… *Everything in this lecture-course was completely new for us* (Elena Zuccoli. *Ton- und Lauteurythmie*. Walter Keller. Dornach. 1997. 39. Tr. A.S.).

Needless to say, the "ideal pattern" may help with making timetables and neat lesson-plans, yet far more concretely with the aim towards an actual artistic deepening that unites content and form, material and technique.

Further comments on the context of eight and three: On the path of gaining certainties, towards integrated personality, or T A O, the individual grows socially in the community and spiritually within humanity. This path is in essence traced in the lecture-course *Eurythmy as Visible Singing*, also in *The Philosophy of Freedom* (especially the last eight chapters), again as practical advice in the Eightfold Path and in the eightfold summary in 2 Peter 1:5 (for the latter, the exemplary and original exposition by "the blind seer of Scotland" George Matheson is probably essential: *Landmarks of New Testament Morality*. Nisbet: London 1888. 144-162; online <www.archive.org>). The gist in all this, that self-education and ethics are really one, is also confirmed in Schiller's *Aesthetic Letters* that together with his own *Philosophy of Freedom* Steiner recommended for eurythmy students (GA 277a. 143). Schiller and Steiner make explicit the poet's/ artist's philosophy of "what is". (Supplementary texts, some devotional and meditative, written in English are recommended in the following pages and in the companion to *Eurythmy as Visible Speech*.) Neither solely "rational" nor solely "moral" (to use the traditional words), the world, and life in it, is to become ever more *artistic* – this ideal perception, that humans are to become a work of art, combines *both* perspectives designated for present purposes here as "traditional".

Speaking of the arts in the future, Steiner (Torquay, 22 August 1924) points to *music*. A rigorous demand is made here, worth making explicit. The musical discipline is historical, educational and artistic at the same time. Let us attempt a "right understanding"! The intellect forever demonstrates it can only study one thing at a time. When the human being himself is the subject of enquiry, the approaches are certainly many, the traditions multiple. Inter-disciplinary studies attempt to overcome limitations. Musical and eurythmical studies, however, themselves *are already universal*: "I want to make clear to you the fact that in the musical element a real world is present, wherein we rediscover the impulses of the rest of the world" (R. Steiner. GA 278. Lecture 3. 62).

Hermann Pfrogner offers basic help for those aiming to act responsibly in the profession. His clear expositions of the musical system of humanity are the equivalent in musical studies to Steiner's fundamental work on the theory of knowledge (see Hermann Pfrogner. *Zeitwende der Musik*. Langen Müller: Munich & Vienna. 1986. E.T. by A.S. 'Music's turning point of time', forthcoming). *Music*, Pfrogner teaches, *as practised by the musically creative human being, arises from his inner being and from nowhere else besides, in conformity with a tonal arrangement disposed within him*. The natural overtones that feature in prevailing theories are a reflection but not a source of musicality – no heard interval would be recognised as such unless it were inherent in the listener. The three decisive categories in humanity's musical system are termed by Pfrogner (following Pythagoras' pupil Archytas) the diatonic, diatonic-chromatic, and enharmonic levels. With this insight, and with the concept of *Tonort* ("tonal position"), it is possible fully to appreciate, for example, Steiner's genial system of eurythmical angle-gestures (see Endnote 4). With this means, eurythmists are given the possibility to express the musical element, because the eurythmical instrument embodies the musical system of humanity. Thinking (the "rational" pole) and meaning (the "moral" pole) are experienced as precisely *one*, Apollonian-Dionysian. This middle way offers to heal the chaos caused by our unbalanced efforts and also our persistent arbitrarily tendencies. "It all depends on people," Steiner confirmed in Torquay, concluding his profound words about the future. Not merely to illustrate something temporary and stylistic but rather to point to fundamental tendencies, *three* composers are mentioned in the lecture-course *Eurythmy as Visible Singing*: *Hauer* and *Wagner*, who both receive qualified praise, and *Mozart*, who is actually quoted. The list of modern composers and players from Beethoven onwards who point to Mozart as a chief educational influence certainly adds weight to Steiner's indication that, it seems clear, concerns *method*. "My teachers," reveals Schönberg (to mention one musician), "were primarily Bach and Mozart, and secondarily Beethoven, Brahms and Wagner" (Arnold Schönberg. *Style and Idea*. London. 1975. 173). Imitation is obviously not the modern composer's aim, but to learn how, out of a supreme self-awareness, Mozart explores the richness of musical material. Ask orchestral musicians which composer they would choose to play all day, given the opportunity, and the answer is invariably "Mozart! There's so much going on." Christoph Peter explores in abundant detail the language of music through a study of this master's crowning masterpiece (bibliographical details, see p. 218 above). Not only the fairy-tale libretto, but the *music* of "*The Magic Flute*" is a comprehensive portrayal of the path to and goal of life, which, as Matheson puts it, is "generic humanity". The name "Tamino" contains T A O, yet, when his colleagues remind Sarastro that Tamino is a Prince, he replies: "Nay more – he is a human being."

3 "Choreography" is a term used by dancers; actors also speak about blocking their movements on the stage. *Eurythmieformen* (eurythmy-forms) reach beyond the category of space; they notate the movement in time, too. *Cf.*, Gurnemanz's words to Parsifal, concerning the transformation on their walk to the Grail Castle: "You see, my son,/ Time is here changed to space" (Wagner. *Parsifal*. Act I), Montsalvat representing "the centre of the world". René Guénon is one who questions the extent of Wagner's understanding of "esoteric" conceptions (*The Reign of Quantity*. Luzac. London 1953. 351/ Sophia Perennis 2001). The conception here does highlight the intention of eurythmical movement, which is *not* that of a spatial art that "illustrates" what is heard. Yet, far from denying space, through artistic imagination the eurythmist changes it (the physical body is taken "beyond physical laws"; GA 277a. 141). Compare:

> I have emphasised what doing eurythmy entails: it is work to raise (*heraufarbeiten*) the physical human being (which really only "sounds" in beat) to the etheric and the astral human being (GA 278. Lecture 5. 81).

The eurythmist *changes spatial qualities by creating new relationships while in the body*, in order that a new or renewed relationship to space become the vehicle for "that which is not heard" (Lecture 3), that is, "the musical element itself living in the movement of musical sound" (Lecture 6) that takes its course in the flow of time. Music as an earthly art never forgets its heavenly origin; eurythmy is to reveal its nature. Does music-eurythmy, then, attempt the contrary of Gurnemanz's statement? Musical "forms" (Steiner uses the term "rhythms" for the intervals – see Endnote 12 below) express in three-dimensional space "the tensions and resolutions" (Lecture 6) of the soul *creating* the music, that is, the inner constriction and release. The line on the paper serves only as a reminder. Perhaps it is helpful to get beyond an "either/or" thinking in questions to do with incarnation, where a reciprocal process is involved. The way "down" does not forget spiritual origins; the "return" does not forget the earth (see Endnote **7**). A transforming, Rosicrucian attitude penetrates into matter – here, the bones – in order spiritually to reach far beyond, ultimately releasing nature from its enchantment (R. Steiner. Lecture, Dornach. 12 Jan. 1924. GA 233. RSP 1982).

Ralph Kux (1903–65), the eurythmist-musician, describes how Steiner drew eurythmy forms:

> If time allowed, Steiner gave extra eurythmy forms before the dress rehearsal. For speech items he usually drew them at home or in his studio, whereas music forms were usually given in the presence of the artist who was to work on them. He sat calmly concentrating, with an empty page on his lap, taking the pencil easily between his fingers and letting it glide lightly and elastically over the page. As the musician played, he drew the piece in the most mysterious forms of movement on the page. His expressive hand and the pencil became as it were the rhythm of the music itself as he sat in inward calm. Then he took the paper with a loving look, as if admiring the wonderful fashioning of the world of life, and showed it to the artist. Everybody, a little awestruck, eagerly gathered round to look at this new creation. A part of the world had just come to birth, and in these forms we could reverently see into the concealed working of the world of music.
>
> If it was a piece to be presented by a group, he had it played several times, each time adding a further form to it. He drew uncomplicated pieces from the score, without having them played. In this way I experienced, for example, the *Minuet* by Bach for flute and piano [in C major]. I could stand beside him and admire how he drew each motif as a unique form. Once he had a form for a short Chopin *Prelude* moved on the stage straight away, to check its effect. However, since he saw the eurythmist could not manage it – the form was quite long –, he discarded the paper and immediately made a much easier form…
>
> On his death-bed in the studio, Steiner drew the last – and often quite complicated – forms from sheet music without anyone playing for him… Because he could not speak to the artist, he wrote that the forms could be varied in the manner of execution. In this way he always respected the artists' freedom in their own strivings and attempts (R. Kux, *Erringerungen an Rudolf Steiner*. Melinger. Stuttgart 1973. 14-15. Tr. A.S.; a shorter, similar account is given by A. Dubach-Donath. "Aus der eurythmischen Arbeit mit R. Steiner", in *Mitteilungen aus der anthroposophischen Arbeit in Deutschland*. Heft 97. 1971; reprinted in *Erinnerungen an R. Steiner*. Ed. E. Beltle and K. Vierl. Stuttgart 1979).

In his description of the first ten years of the Goetheanum, Steiner wrote:

> The artistic expression of eurythmy stems from sensory-supersensory insight into the expressive possibilities of movement of the human

body. For this insight only sparse accounts – so far as I am aware – are available from earlier times. In these times the human body was transparent, or more ethereal, for the soul and spirit elements than is the case today. These sparse accounts, which point to quite different things than are present in eurythmy, are of course used [today]. But they must be independently developed and transformed, and thereby completely changed, especially in art. Concerning the group-movement forms, I am unaware of any tradition… Art that grows from the same ground as the concepts of true anthroposophy can become real art. The soul-forces which form this conceptual content penetrate into the spirituality out of which artistic creativity originates. That which is formed into thoughts out of anthroposophical knowledge exists in its own right, and there is no need to express it symbolically in a quasi-art. On the contrary, through experiencing the realities contained in anthroposophy, an artistic need to experience this in form and colour is felt. These colours and forms exist in their own right too. They do not express ideas – as little or as much as a lily or a lion expresses ideas… Anthroposophy is life, a taking-hold of that which is universally human and of the world in and through the human being… Anthroposophy is the opposite of everything sectarian. It strives everywhere in freedom for the purely human element (R. Steiner. "Das Goetheanum in seinen zehn Jahren". Essay IV 1923, in GA 36, and *Der Goetheanumgedanke* Tb 635. Dornach 1982. 143-44 and 134-37; tr. A.S.).

Steiner's eurythmy forms (given 1920-25) for pieces of music from the 17th-20th centuries, with an introduction and notes by Eva Froböse, are published in a facsimile edition (R. Steiner. *Eurythmieformen*. Band IX. Dornach. 1989). Marie Savitch used the forms reproduced on pp. XXII and XXIII (drawn by another hand) with the audience on the opposite side, which would mean that they appear upside-down in the book.

Why no *Vortakt* and *Nachtakt* for music-eurythmy forms? An attempted answer: For speech items, these preludes and postludes in movement with chosen sounds given by Steiner, suggest a "musical" mood providing a "frame" for the respective piece in speech eurythmy. In music itself, consequently, anything more elaborate than, as it were, "bring the piece in with you" and "leave it in the air, before making your exit" would seem redundant.

4 THE ANGLE-GESTURES: The arm-gestures for the notes/ tones/ musical sounds were first given as angles of 180°, 90°, 60° and 30°; angles (and jumps) for the legs were also given. These gestures were designated with terms for degrees of the scale (23 Aug. 1915. GA 277a. 71 and 160f.). The gestures for the prime, second, third and so on, thus apply to *any diatonic (7-note) scale*, but they correspond with the archetypal scale of C major (see Fig. 26). The 30° angles are practised in the early stages of some eurythmy trainings. The basic diatonic scale is ideal for simple melodies.

The 7-note system soon developed differentiation. "After the end of the course we drew the notes/ musical sounds of C major with differentiated distances: for the semitones between E and F and between B and C a small angle of 15°, the same for the scale of A minor" (T. Kisseleff, *Eurythmie-Arbeit mit Rudolf Steiner.* Die Pforte, Basel 1982. 79, orig. pub. 1949; E.T. by A.S.). The gestures for the sharps and flats "followed immediately after". In the early years, simple pieces and songs were practised. Eurythmy forms only gradually developed during this period; pieces were carried out in standing, with the "swinging-over" movements between the motifs and phrases (Kisseleff. 79-80; and Zuccoli. 11).

The twelve divisions of the circle of 360° also includes the system of seven. This is a stroke of Steiner's genius. The angles create three double segments of 30° for the upper zone (major), and three correspond for the lower zone (minor). The fourth and fifth both occupy the horizontal position, that is, the threshold between the two tetrachords is shown, not through adjusting the angle, but by an *Umstülpung,* a "turning inside-out" – another stroke of Steiner's genius. The transition between the tetrachords is not shown, for example, in the educational gestures of Dalcroze-eurythmics (see Fig. 27). In the artistic system Steiner gave, the seventh and the second occupy the position 30° from the vertical; sixth and third 60°; the prime

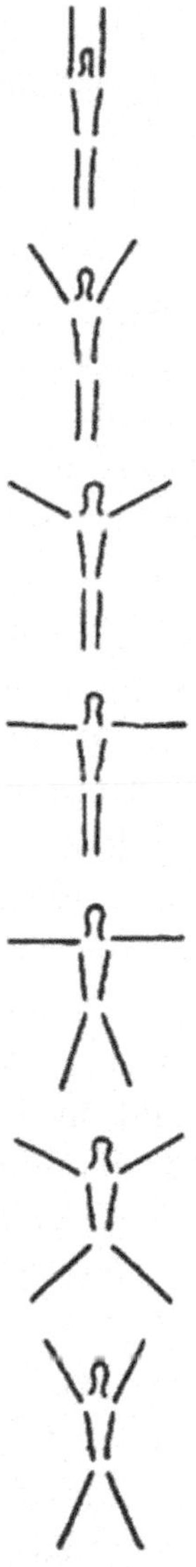

Fig. 26: The original angle-gestures, Prima, Secunda, Terza, etc. (after Zuccoli, and Kisseleff).

Fig. 27: *Arm-positions showing the degrees of the scale; an exercise inspired by Dalcroze-Eurhythmics (E. Findlay.* Rhythm and Movement: Applications of Dalcroze Eurhythmics. Van Nuys. CA: Summy-Birchard Inc. Dist.: Alfred Pub. Co., Inc. 1971. 52).

and octave occupy the vertical position. The angles for the legs for the fifth, sixth and seventh degrees of the scale (30°, 60° and 30° respectively) have been retained.

With these angles, students of astrology and astronomy will recognise a correspondence to some of the planetary alignments (opposition, square, sextile and semi-sextile).

The early eurythmists also report that, when asked about adjusting the angles to show semitones, Steiner answered, "*Meinetwegen*" – something like, "I have no objection", or "If you like". What was his precise meaning? The resulting angles incorporating the semitone steps more clearly differentiate the scales of our tonal system. The development of gestures for the flats and sharps (the 90° bending at the elbow, with a corresponding "lightening" and "darkening") apparently arose out of discussion. *By beginning with its own keynote, each scale now acquires an individual countenance.* The jumps on the 5th, 6th and 7th degrees of the basic scale remain for these specific notes; the basic scale is present underlying all the others. Unlike the system of modes, where each mode has its own pattern of tones and semitones, that of the basic scale in major is reproduced in all the other major scales, likewise the minor form/s. Of course, the upper tetrachord of any scale is felt as such, every time; this does not detract from the indisputable fact that, for example, horizontal arms and jump for the fifth degree marks a threshold, regardless of whichever note a particular scale begins, *e.g.* G major starts with three jumps on the first three degrees and on the octave degree; A major the first two and last two degrees, and so on. The suggestion of jumping on the 5th, 6th and 7th degrees of *every* scale is parochial; it makes nonsense of the system taken as a whole, that is, the whole circle of fifths. *With the adjusted angles, the artistic possibilities are vastly increased, in particular the process of modulation can be revealed.* The *diatonic* level (scale of seven notes) in the tonal system was first established with 30° angles; the adjustments allow a new level in the tonal system (the *diatonic/ chromatic* level of 12 notes) to be revealed.

The opinion that the adjusted angles are a limiting compromise made to please the musicians and eurythmist-musicians cannot be sustained. Steiner anticipated "a stream of development" (Lecture 8. 113). He acted on questions and suggestions (for example, the name "*Eurythmie*" was suggested by Marie Steiner; see GA 277a. 44. The word derives from architecture, was well-known and widely used at the time; the choice of name was no doubt influenced by Émile Sigogne's publication –

in Steiner's library – *Eurythmie. La Belgique artistique et littéraire.*
Bruxelles 1907), and he was also prepared to revoke early experiments
(two examples: the raised platform to show the octave levels was found
unnecessary, and eurythmy to singing was found to be superfluous –
see Lecture 7. 107 and Endnote **57**; Kisseleff. 81-2; Zuccoli. 33). Steiner
worked with specific artists in the creation of eurythmy forms. All this
suggests that for assessment, the subject of the angles demands *artistic*
criteria. Steiner included the artists in the creative process; though
decisive, he certainly did not behave like an oracle. Indeed, how else
could artists be encouraged to take responsibility for their art?

Steiner explained that it is "not the positions which represent the
audible notes. Rather they should be understood as *pathways of movement
between the notes*" (Zuccol. 8; emphases added). The numerical terms for
the degrees (*Stufen*, tr. "steps" in Zuccoli) of the scale seem to remind us
that eurythmy is primarily concerned with "that which lives between the
notes/ tones, and therefore you do not '*do* the notes/ tones'" (Zuccoli. 34).
The specific danger is that the audience sees arms instead of perceiving
singing gesture, differentiated movement, that is, *the music.*

Note-names may be convenient – we say "D", though there are as many
different "Ds" as there are scales: prime in D major/minor, second in C
major/minor, and so on. The system of note-names has sometimes been
compared to the efficiency of a modern filing-system – but that very
efficiency can be problematic for the unwary. The tonic-sol-fa system
is no doubt initially preferable. Again, it should not be overlooked that
numerical terms already imply music. When Steiner uses note-names,
he invariably means "degrees" of the scale (*cf.,* Steiner's comments
immediately after introducing Goethe's poem in Lecture 4: In saying
"C", he means "prime", and so on). In tonal music, notes never exist in
the abstract; they always carry a meaning as a degree of a scale, also as a
melodic interval – and in addition usually a harmonic interval, that is,
the interval from the fundamental note of the chord.

Of course, if the gestures are to sing the clarity of the angles is
presupposed as experienced reference points. Form is needed, but our
habits of language may have obscured Steiner's original intention; with
the degrees of the scale as numerical and geometrical designations, the
angle-gestures do not fall so easily into the danger of being treated as
representing either the physical sound, or as abstractions. But, respecting
the interval designations ("degrees of the scale" or "structural intervals")
means: *parallel arms for prime, horizontal arms for fourth and fifth, and
so on, regardless of how the key is named under the system of note-names.*

The "intervals" as degrees of the scale are already inherent in how the angles are formed, with corresponding nuances in the arm, different in each scale – consequently, not "notes/ tones" *or* "intervals" but notes/ tones *and* intervals. *Thereby the possibility of showing musical changes, notably modulation, is given.* Through the nuances in the arm – without changing the angle –, it can be shown how a note, for example, the second in the original key, changes function in a specific moment during a composition to become, let's say, the fourth in the relative minor; or, again, the sixth in the original key becomes second in the new, dominant key, and so on. The musical meaning can be revealed. In this way, the gestures in eurythmy offer a practical *method* artistically to research the cosmic picture, the "meditation for musicians", breaking down into 84 meditations = 7 degrees of the scale x 12 key-centres (actually 7 x 15 with the overlaps on the circle of fifths): R. Steiner. Lecture, Dornach. 2 Dec. 1922. *The Inner Nature of Music*... AP. Spring Valley. New York. 1983. 42f.

The connection of the zodiac to the circle of fifths further suggests that *the system of angle-gestures is a living, sounding solar image.* Here is another confirmation that eurythmy expresses universal life; solar images are to be found world-wide in ecclesiastical, agricultural, industrial, urban, commercial, and domestic architecture, fine art and folk art (see Alan Stott. "No more Tone Gestures in Eurythmy?" RB 37. Easter 2002. 48-53; and *The English Sunrise – Sonnenaufgänge.* Flash Books. New York. 1973/ Darmstadt. Melzer. 1975/ Mathews Miller Dunbar. London 1977; a collection of 78 full-colour photographs of solar designs).

The fact that the angles are not discussed in the present lecture-course implies that the developments were in order; this left Steiner free to bring new material. *One system was given for the angle-gestures corresponding to the world's one comprehensive tonal system; the angles received modifications at the time it was given in 1915, due to justified considerations concerning the semitones of the diatonic-chromatic level in the tonal system.* This conclusion opens the possibilities for showing *the nuances of aural and artistic experience.* The system of angle-gestures does not exclude any tonal experience: it can accommodate the future freedoms of what Pfrogner terms the final, third or "enharmonic" level in the tonal system. Further lecture-courses on eurythmy were planned, in which it is likely the subject would have been covered. No doubt, too, we meet here an example of Steiner's "educational stance"; the resolution of certain questions is left for the artists themselves. This freedom allows them to develop on their own responsibility upon the basis of understanding the early developments as attempts to reveal humankind's musical system (see further, Appendix 5; articles in RB 36, 37 & 39; and Maren Stott, "Eurythmy and the Musical System, with emphasis on the Diatonic Scale", online: <www.alansnotes.co.uk>).

Fig. 28: The Solar Logos, illustration by the Rosicrucian Robert Fludd.

5 In his studies on the alphabet, Ernst Moll remarks that the Viennese researcher Karl Faulmann connects the Greek name Alpha and the word *Elfen* (elves) and that Steiner points in the same direction. The Alpha or Aleph indicates the spiritual origin, the source of the etheric forces of the human being, or *the human being himself as this being of spiritual etheric forces*. This is presented in an elementary way in the lectures to the workers at the Goetheanum:

> Take… this letter… Aleph א (it was sketched on the blackboard). What does this Aleph signify for the sensory world? Well, here stands the human being. Here he stands, sending out his strength. That is this line (from below right to above left); he raises his right arm… that is this line; he stretches the other arm downwards… that is this line. In this way the first letter Aleph expresses the human being… The first letter for the human being was called by the Hebrews Aleph, by the Greeks Alpha, and they meant that which is moving spiritually in the human being, that which is spiritually behind the physical human being. But you also have an old German word… used when the human being has

special dreams; when a spiritual human being presses (*druckt*) him, then this is called a nightmare (*der Alpdruck, der Alp*). We say that something comes over the human being, possessing him. But out of this the *Elp* comes about, *Elp, Elf, der Elf, die Elfe* – these spiritual beings, the elves; the human being is but a consolidated elf. You can still recall this word *Elf* (elf) that leads back to *Alp*, in the Greek Alpha. You only need to leave out the A, then you have Alph (PH is the same as our F), elf; Aleph = a spiritual [entity]. Thereby, by substituting F, one says: the Aleph is the human being, the Alp in the human being. When, as is normal in Hebrew, you leave out the vowels, you get directly *Alph* = *Elf* for the first letter. People say "elf" for this spiritual being… The ancients said: "You only need to look at the human being himself, then you have the Alph, only the Alph is hidden in the body and is not a fine etheric entity, but a concentrated bodily entity in the human being." People, however, have long ago forgotten how to conceive the human being.

In spiritualistic sessions, Steiner continues, people look for an external manifestation of spirit. We need not become anxious, for

the table begins to dance because the subconscious forces affect it. What transpires is not something that wouldn't in a much higher sense transpire if the human being activated his own Alpha or Aleph in himself. People however have forgotten Aleph in the transition from the Greek to the Roman culture (R. Steiner. Lecture, Dornach. 8 Feb.1924. *Die Geschichte der Menschheit und die Weltanschauungen der Kultur Völker*. GA 353. Tr. A.S.).

Steiner is concerned to trace the alphabet to the human being.

Now if all the sounds of the alphabet were uttered from *A* to *Z* there would arise an etheric human being—only this etheric human being, born out of the human larynx and its neighbouring organs, would be imprinted into the air… Eurythmy… is a continuation of divine movement, of the divine creative forms in the human being (Rudolf Steiner. *Eurythmy as Visible Speech*, GA 279. Anastasi. 2005. 32f. & 37; see further on Aleph and the alphabet: R. Steiner. Lecture Dornach 18 Dec. 1921. GA 209; and Appendix 7 below).

In his study, Ernst Moll concludes by connecting water, the elves and the etheric realm:

Water is also an earthly image of that which is ever coming-into-being, of beginning, in living movement… In its continuous movement, water is the ever self-renewing entity and archetypal source of everything. Its unending transformation awakens ever anew our wonder, our astonishment. The soul is refreshed by the bubbling brook… Like water in the kingdoms of the visible realm, so the elves are the image of the movement, the ever-fresh coming-into-being in the etheric, invisible realm. Both belong together (Ernst Moll. *Die Sprache der Laute*. Freies Geistesleben. Stuttgart 1968. 50-5).

6 This description is not a relapse into primitive animism – Owen Barfield's "original participation"; see his masterpiece *Saving the Appearances*. Wesleyan. 1988. Steiner's philosophy, taking up the challenge of the modern "onlooker consciousness", shows how thinking can transcend this situation by uniting "I" and "world".

> The forces which are at work inside my body are the same as those which exist outside. Therefore "I" really am the things; not, however, "I" in so far as "I" am a percept of myself as subject, but "I" in so far as "I" am a part of the universal world-process. The percept of the tree belongs to the same whole as my "I". This universal world-process produces equally the percept of the tree out there and the percept of my "I" in here (R. Steiner, *The Philosophy...*, Chapter 6, tr. Wilson. 82; Stebbing. 70; Lipson. 98).

This is Barfield's "final participation". Abstractly stated, true knowledge is the coalescence of subject and object, of knower and known. Someone who sees eurythmy, Steiner explains,

> can say to himself, "Eurythmy enlightens me about the fir tree because the tree does not merely stand there in order to be what it is: the fir tree is a letter in which moves and blows the primeval, eternal, universal Word, as through the entire world. Eurythmy enlightens me as to how the fir tree speaks..., the spring..., the lightning, and so on" (R. Steiner. Intro. Dornach. 28 Dec. 1923. GA 277. 415, tr. A.S.; pub. tr. in R. Steiner. *An Introduction to Eurythmy*. 91. Cf. R. Steiner. *Eurythmy as Visible Speech*. Lecture 1. Dornach. 24 June 1924. 32).

This address occurred during the Christmas Foundation Meeting; students of mythology and the human mind will recognise the significance of the images. *Cf.*, for example: "The tree of life is mankind's most magnificent legend" (Holmberg. *Der Baum des Lebens*. 9). "We are not an earthly but a heavenly plant," Plato reminds us (*Timaeus* 90A). The answer to Christ's precept (Matt. 12:33) is to be found in John 15:5. Steiner's Notebook contains a sketch of the human tree, or macrocosmic man (NB 494. 4). Planetary signs are written along a vertical line. An explanation was not given in Lecture 1, but elsewhere Steiner explains to the musicians that the *Moon* provides the bodily basis; the *Sun* relates to the activity of the rhythmic system; *Saturn* to the central nervous system. *Jupiter* is related to the sense organs, particularly the eyes, *Mars* to the organs of speech and singing; *Venus* and *Mercury* to the sympathetic nervous system. Steiner concludes his explanation of "this ideal but very real musical instrument" within the human being:

> You only need to imagine the five [wandering] stars Saturn, Jupiter, Mars, Venus and Mercury – not the ancient planets described in *Occult Science*, but those in the present-day heavens – descend on to the human tree. They stretch lyre-strings on him, so that he becomes a musical instrument. There hovers over the whole, descending out of the spiritual universe, the tuner of this instrument, the phoenix bird, the immortal human soul (R. Steiner. Zweites Schlußwort, Dornach 7 Feb. 1921, GA 283. Dornach 1975. 99, E.T. in *EA Newsletter*. Aberdeen. Spring 1998 – NB Fig. 1 should be inverted; see also A. Stott. "The Scale in GA 278". RB 28 & 29. Dornach. 1998).

See *inter alia*, R. Steiner. Lecture Berlin, 17 Dec. 1906, in *The Festivals and their Meaning*. RSP 1981. 37-9 contains a discussion on the Christmas Tree; R. Guénon, *Symbolism of the Cross*. Luzac. London 1958/ Sophia Perennis. Ghent 2001. Chapter 9, "The Tree in the midst". 46-53; C.G. Jung, "The Philosophical Tree" (1945/54) in *Collected Works*. Vol. 13. Routledge. London; Alan Stott. "*The Philosophy of Freedom* as a Musical Composition: The seven-sentence rhythm of love" Parts 1, 2. RB 44 & 45 and "Why Chapter 15 of *The Philosophy of Freedom*?" RB 51.

> The human being, in his movements, is really an intermediary between cosmic letters, cosmic sounds, and that which we employ in the sounds and letters of our poetry. A new art will emerge in eurythmy. It is an art for everyone (R. Steiner. Lecture, Dornach. 7 Oct. 1914. GA 277a. 65).

The poet William Wordsworth already speaks of "eye-music" in recapturing an experience of unity – which is the work of the imagination:

> A soft eye-music of slow-waving boughs,
> Powerful almost as vocal harmony
> To stay the wanderer's steps and soothe his thoughts.

> "Airey Force Valley" (composed? pub. 1842)

"A soft eye-music of slow-waving boughs" creates, and is the symbol of, the dream unity. It also describes what happens when watching eurythmy: the eyes are invited to subordinate their objective coolness and engage sympathetically, as the ears do. Then felt gesture, issuing out of the imagination, can speak. We conclude: The person engaged in eurythmy is to "speak" and "sing" – not "illustrate" through acting or dancing – the letters of the creative Word, originating from the Tree of Life at the centre of the world.

"*Ex uno verbo omnia et unum loquunter Omnia*", wrote Thomas à Kempis – "From one Word proceed all things: and one is that which is spoken by all things", and he continues, "and this is the Beginning, which also speaks to us." John 1:1; 8:28, Vulgate. *The Imitation of Christ*, also called *The Ecclesiastical Music*, I, iii. This little book, recommended by Rudolf Steiner in his *Knowledge of the Higher Worlds – how is it attained?*, is a philosophical tract, in the form of an inner soliloquy, *i.e.*, philosophy as meditation.

7 The passage about the relationship of speech-eurythmy and music-eurythmy is crucial. How is the spatial language to be understood? The following considerations may help to bring out Steiner's clarity:

(i) The researcher of the spirit engages in a struggle with language. Modern languages have become weighted by materialism, rendering the use of similes necessary when speaking of higher worlds (R. Steiner. *Theosophy.* RSP 1973. 72-3). Literal, quantitative thinking is simply out of place in interpreting the present lecture-course. Following Goethe, Steiner characterises the major and minor moods as movement, flow and direction. These are attempts to describe *soul-and spirit-experience of the personality*, which can be artistically shown in free, ensouled movement. A paraphrase of the passage here would read: "From the point of view of *speech*, I am leaving the sense-world for the soul-world; from the point of view of *music*, I am entering my spiritual being" (NB Steiner's exact language – "my spiritual being" not "the spiritual world" itself. The two, of course, are related; illusions might be avoided by a correct reading here).

Steiner reports, "In the spiritual world everything is in continuous mobile activity, ceaselessly creating". In addition to spiritual sight, there is spiritual hearing, "The observer feels as if he were in an ocean of musical sound" (R. Steiner. *Theosophy*. Chap. 3. 92f.). In the Introduction to a eurythmy performance during the Christmas Conference, Steiner pictures the dry land as the world of speech, "in the musical element you live as in a weaving spirit-ocean", and he characterises the shoreline between sea and land (Dornach. 28 Dec. 1923; quoted in Endnote 65 below).

Gottfried Richter (following Emil Bock) uses the imaginative language of simile to depict "the path of the Sun God from the sea to the solid land", as the "innermost secret of the history of mankind from Egypt to Greece". It is also "the way of Christ", who in significant events actually lived the path from "water on to the land, into the house and [then] on to the mountain" of the Ascension (Gottfried Richter. *Art and Human Consciousness*. Floris Books, Edinburgh/AP 1985. 107-108).

(ii) The individual today experiences the world "outside" as the sense-world: the description "entering my spiritual being" through music – specifically, the major mood – consequently has to be recognised as a simile. But it conveys the true state of affairs: *musical creation is a concern of the human being as a being of soul and spirit to him-/herself*. A few paragraphs later Steiner adds a general observation on the basis of feeling the connection between the world and the human being. Speaking of speech and music, he says, "the gestures of music[-eurythmy]... have to flow back into the human being". A paraphrase would read: "The world of music does not relate to the outer world, but is the relationship of the human being as a being of soul and spirit to him- or herself." The *eurythmist* (like any performer) is concerned to "sing out"; for the *audience*, the gestures of themselves relate (or "flow back" as a counter-stream) to this centre, as do the angle-gestures. All and every living process is reciprocal; confusion, however, may arise from mistaking the modality.

The system is neither pantheistic nor mechanical. A mechanical conception of countermovement suggests a gross misunderstanding. In reality, this countermovement results from a living exchange of personal movement. Steiner's phrases may not be reduced to a physical-spatial meaning: "the human being" is clearly not merely synonymous with corporeal modality. Here *the etheric human being* is initially meant; this is described as the cross of movement (Lecture 3) with its central region of freedom. The ego, diving into the astral body (our musical world), takes up this cross of movement as the means of expressing our art of music (see Endnote 28). In Lecture 4, Steiner says: "The eurythmist is really obliged to study the way in which the human being streams out, as it were, into the musical element [melody, rhythm and beat]." *The human being "streams out" because he or she is centred, and this is established at the beginning of Lecture 1*; the counter-stream of gesture flows back of itself; the universe comes to the focus of self-consciousness, the basis of all social/artistic intercourse

> ... in the very world, which is the world
> Of all of us, – the place where in the end
> We find our happiness, or not at all.

> (W. Wordsworth. *The Prelude*. Bk. XI.)

(iii) Steiner expresses hope for the future of eurythmy:

> Eurythmy will present in the finest movements and revelations everything of the human being that is revealed in soul and spirit, and is received by the inwardness of soul and spirit [of the viewer]. It calls up soul and spirit *in most complete concentration*, to be beheld by the audience. And that is basically the highest ideal of all the arts... What the human being brings to revelation and what eurythmy appeals to [is] that which is most completely, totally interested in what is human, in so far as this is an expression in a microcosm, a revelation of the great world, of the macrocosm (R. Steiner. Introduction 18 Feb. 1923. GA 277. 320).

What is crudely simple is absent from these lectures. For instance, the word "empty" (a concept drawn from the physical world) is not used in the present context (the phrase "an emptiness of soul" is used *only* in Lecture 8 to characterise the feeling-experience of long notes, where the contrast is between "interest" and "disinterest").

(iv) The puzzling passages, if taken out of context and quantitatively interpreted, may even lead to a confusion of spiritualities, indeed the presence of "inverted spirituality" (R. Guénon's phrase in *The Reign of Quantity*... Luzac. London 1953; Penguin. Baltimore, Md. 1972; Sophia Perennis, Ghent 2001). In the brief Chapter XXVI of *The Course of my Life*, GA 28, Steiner records the central experience of his life (in the last sentence of this chapter, biographers recognise a reference to his Damascus-experience; see Introduction, Endnote 18). It is precisely in this chapter that reference is also made to Ahrimanic beings, for whom "it is an absolute truth that the world must be a machine. They live in a world which touches directly upon the sense-world" (GA 28. 275).

Steiner demands the bringing of "human personality as soul into the musical element"; making the audible the vehicle for the inaudible is precisely the task of the eurythmist (Lecture 3). The body is not a prison but the organ of the soul. Hauer might speak of "subduing the personality" and of "dissolution of the individual". But personality is always social; the loneliness of a personality single and sundered is a condition that of necessity does not belong to life. The content of personality is the necessary standard by which the human being judges all things, human or divine. The central perception is Gal 2:20; John 5:20 forms a significant comment; both phrases are but comments on John 17:23-26.

On ecstasy, mystical experience and the ego, see R. Steiner. *Macrocosm and Microcosm*. Lecture, Vienna. 21 Mar. 1910. RSP 1968; compare "the art of the dance is sweeping, ecstatic gesture", R. Steiner. GA 276. 97. See also Introduction, Endnote 23; Endnotes 20 & 25 below; Steiner's Notebook entry concerning transformation, or "overcoming", quoted at the end of "A Note on the Bar Line", Appendix 4, iv, below; and the two missions of Michael outlined on p. 404f. Today, the later mission is sometimes confused with the former mission, or indeed denied. Humanity without personality is a contradiction in terms. By striving to avoid subjectivism we fall into it, because no criterion remains. But the Michaelic path is the path of spiritualisation through incarnation (see, for example, R. Steiner. Introduction, Dornach. 8 July 1923. GA 277. 368-69; tr. *An Introduction to Eurythmy*. 78-79). According to Emil Brunner, the decline of personalism in modern history is due to immenentism, individualism and spiritualism-materialism (Emil Brunner. *Christianity and Civilization*. Nisbet. London 1948). The individual becomes a cipher when unqualified and abstracted from the conspiration of local and national influences "without which or divided from which his Being cannot even be thought" (Coleridge).

(v) In the initial stages of the lecture-course, how far, then, is spatial language *imagery*? The context of Lecture 1 provides a further, perhaps conclusive, consideration. The lecture-cycle presents a process of manifesting ensouled movement: *spatial precision does not arrive until Lecture 3*; melodic movement in Lecture 4; and choral eurythmy is first introduced in Lecture 5, and so on. The language of fourteenth-century mysticism may help here solely to suggest the correct context for Lectures 1 and 2, where the subject of movement is inward (that is, a manifesting of *time-processes*):

> So take care not to interpret physically what is intended spiritually, even
> though material expressions are used, like "up, down, in, out, below,
> before, this side, that side…" For, spiritually, heaven is as near down as
> up, up as down, behind as before, before as behind, on one side as on that
> (Anon. *The Cloud of Unknowing*. Tr. Clifton Wolters. Penguin Books.
> Harmondsworth 1961. Chapters 61 & 60. 128 & 126).

The words of this passage are clear, but to avoid the nebulous here a spiritual centre has to be understood. The question for the artist is: In what way can healthy mystical-musical experience become manifested as a shared experience that is socially fruitful? The clarification of one technical matter might help. Expressions like "major direction" and "minor direction" that are sometimes used today in a spatially-extended sense, can become confused with the indications for "dominant" and "subdominant" (Lecture 5). The gestures for the major and minor triads belong to the right and left sides of the eurythmist's *instrument*, and any specific "direction" can only apply to in-streaming and out-streaming soul-movement. This provides further evidence that in Lecture 1, Steiner establishes the eurythmical centre with its reciprocal dual activity of respiratory life (the pole of time). This is the creative centre itself. Alpha–Aleph, representing the spiritual human being, Steiner suggests, can be rendered as "he who feels his own breathing" (R. Steiner. Lecture Dornach. 18 Dec. 1921. GA 209). Recognition of the creative centre is the essential first step in trying to lead the feeling-life evident in mysticism ("the experience of the Holy Spirit" – R.C. Moberly. *Atonement and Personality*. 312) into a modern expressive and social art (*cf.* John 20:23).

"Something artistic can only endure when the whole human being has poured himself into it" (Lecture 1). This can be read as more than a platitude. Paul uses the Greek work *kenosis* (emptying, pouring Himself out – both the prepositions "out" and "in" are applicable, depending upon the point of view in describing the action) to describe the self-limitation of Christ (see Endnote 41). The language used in Lecture 1 draws attention to Steiner's act of renewing the great mystic tradition of John and Paul (*cf.*, O.C. Quick. *The Gospel of Divine Action*. Nisbet, London 1933. Chap. 3). The fourteenth-century mystic's experience (see quotation p. 240 above) is not contradicted when the centre is nevertheless localised here. Steiner indicates that the experience of *time* is the basis of apprehending God as Unity, and the experience of *space* the basis of apprehending God as Triune.

> Experience of the three dimensions was much more intensive in the ancient world, especially with the Hebrews. For the Rabbis, one of the names of God was "space" (*Raum*); space and God are the same [entity]" (R. Steiner. Lecture, Dornach. 20 Sept. 1918 in GA 184, E.T. Z.362, R. Steiner Library, London; on *hammaquom*, see p. 449 below).

Modern civilisation and art (the drama, music, poetry, and so on) developed from the dawn of general human personality (the consciousness-soul) in English and European civilisation of the fourteenth century. By means of a certain recapitulation that (we suggest) includes that stage of personality, Steiner is inviting his listeners to recognise and to enter – artistically, therapeutically and educationally – the nature of transformed space *from the first lecture onwards*. The imbuing of art with "human personality" (the positive energies of reason, will, love and so on) is Steiner's most likely fundamental intention (see Endnote 28 and Appendix 7).

(vi) Time; space; the creative/transforming centre – these all belong to the unity: EURYTHMY. Lectures 1 and 2, devoted to releasing something of the *Regsamkeit... Entstehen... Werden* – "constant activity... becoming" (38), point to time-processes. Here the nature of the three dimensions and the phenomenon of death, introduced in Lecture 3, should be mentioned for the sake of completeness. George MacDonald (1824-1905, novelist, translator of Novalis, writer of modern fairy-tales and "fantasy novels"), draws attention to the historical revelation of the finished, completed Incarnation-process of transforming space, which is at the same time *the precise moment of its re-birth or restoration*:

> Of the peace that followed that cry [Mark 15:34, quoting Psalm 22, which ends in confident faith], the peace of a perfect soul, large as the universe, pure as light, ardent as life, victorious for God and his brethren, he himself alone can ever know *the breadth and length, and depth and height*....Without this last trial of all, the temptation of our Master had not been so full as the human cup could hold (George MacDonald, "The Eloi". *Unspoken Sermons (Series One)*. 163-79. A. Strahan, London 1867/ Johanneson Printing and Publishing, California 1977, italics added).

MacDonald, echoing Paul, is probably drawing on the same experience of Christian cabbala; compare too, Paul's phrase "the firstborn among many brethren" (Rom. 8:29, also James 1:18 and Gal. 3:28): unity is re-found in the renewed purpose of creation. Steiner foretold that many people from the first third of the twentieth century onwards would experience what Paul did; *cf.*, Acts 9:5 and Eph. 3:16-19.

The deepest darkness at the heart of the world is now changed into radiant, eternal light by the divine fire and heart of Love. In Lecture 5, love of the visible world is mentioned five times. This does not refer to the enjoyment of natural scenery – including beautiful bodies – but the human personality is to continue the work of the Incarnation of the Word, where now the flesh must become spirit (R. Steiner. Dornach. 22 Nov. 1919. GA 194, see p. 404f. below). The Word (language and music), is neither abstract nor (merely) natural. It is perceived ever present, ever sounding sacramentally in our human world. It can be "made visible" by the human instrument, that is the whole human being, that reveals "your soul and spirit" *in the relationship with the audience* who inwardly participate, personally, here and now. In so far as the nascent body of glory is glimpsed, the shining is *backward in the dimension of time* (see Endnote 8, below). The Cartesian division of matter and spirit can be transcended, and in ways congruent with our age that follows that of the scientific revolution. This calls on the forces, not of revival, but of redemption.

8 The eurythmy exercise "Behold yourself, behold the world" shows the basic breathing of all eurythmy. The entire range of ensouled gesture is included here ("All organic movements are manifested through diastole and systole [expansion and contraction]" – Goethe, "Sketch for a Theory of Music", see Endnote 9). In Lecture 1, "outer world" and "self" are contrasted. This dichotomy (in Coleridge's words) is "a fact of our nature, not a conclusion of our judgment" (Steiner discusses, and bridges, this dichotomy in his *The Philosophy of Freedom*). For the individual, *the threshold* is not simply identical with his/her skin, but is to be found between the act of thinking and its product, thought. Yet this "fact of our nature" stands behind the creation of two different points of departure for eurythmical activity (speech and music). Speech-eurythmy is able to release "the spirit enchanted in nature", for only to our daytime consciousness do we appear "separated" from her. The poetic element is the forming of the world of imagination (*Vorstellung*); the musical element is the forming of the world of feeling (R. Steiner. GA 277. 415). Outer nature may correspond to the human being, yet not completely, for the musical world "belongs only to man" (Lecture 4). The musical world is truly *the inner human world*; we enter it at night (lecture, Berlin. 12 Nov. 1906, quoted in the Introduction, Endnote 6). The gestures of music-eurythmy all relate to that world; our music is a world of "feeling", related to the "tension and relaxation" of dreaming (Lecture 6). The artist receives in order to release into singing, whether in music-making, or in "a singing eurythmy" which is "the expression of instrumental music" (Lecture 6). For the eurythmist, the point of departure between the shoulder-blades (see Endnote 55) is the point on the instrument where the impulse is received. In this region an inversion, or transition, occurs, enabling the artist to transform "music into movement" from the collar-bone and through the arms in "visible singing" (Lecture 7; see also Armin Husemann. *The Harmony of the Human Body*. Floris Books. Edinburgh. 1994. Section 31; van der Pals and Bäschlin. 1991. 29f.). Our persistent mechanical preconceptions may lead to a confused reading of the present lecture-course. A reconciliation of apparent contradictions is attempted in Endnote 7, above.

In the two paragraphs (p. 42), Steiner sums up his characterisation of speech-eurythmy and music-eurythmy. The summary starts from "the whole human being", who has to pour him-/herself into art (see Endnote 41 on *kenosis*). The polarity of the relationships involved in speech-eurythmy ("the outer world") and music-eurythmy ("the human being") is comprehensive (see "Note", p. 449 below).

We recall that all the arts (including speech-eurythmy) are to become "more and more musical"; the old sculptural, architectural impulse is to be transformed (see Introduction, Endnote 1, p. 25 above). Spatial knowledge is to be spiritualised if Michael's mission is to be accomplished (R. Steiner. Lecture, Dornach. 13 June 1914. GA 219; quoted in van der Pals 1992, endnote 42). This strongly suggests that the basic polarity of space and time is addressed here (no doubt the caduceus, which portrays dual reciprocal movement, is a helpful symbol):

(i) The realm of speech-eurythmy "brings us into a relationship to the outer world".

(ii) The words *zurücklaufende Gebärde*, the gestures of music[-eurythmy], which "lead back (*hineingehen*) into the human being" predominantly suggest *time processes*. The spiritually-transformed human being, for *us* a future possibility (hence the gestures "flow back" in *time*) has already been achieved by the Son of Man (John 16:33; see also Endnote 41), and His forces may be invoked (John 16:17, 24) at any moment since the first Pentecost/ Whitsun event (Matt. 28:20). Compare Austin Farrer's summary of Paul's doctrine of the Body:

> The full gift of the Spirit is only possible in and with that of the body. That body is its home, as the sun is the home of the sunlight: yet it can shine abroad – *outward in the dimensions of space*, from our Lord's Glorified Body to our mortal bodies; *backward in the dimension of time*, from our true and ultimate being to what we now are. These two participations – in what Our Lord already is, and in what we ourselves are to become – are themselves complementary and inseparable (A. Farrer, "Eucharist and Church in the NT" in *The Parish Communion*, ed. A.G. Hebert. SPCK London 1957. 79. Italics added).

Steiner did say "visible word" for speech-eurythmy (Report. 31f.). *Cf.* Augustine: "It is when the Word is added to the element that the sacrament results as if itself also a kind of visible word" (Augustine. *On the Gospel of John.* Trac. 80.3). The Creator-Word nourishes human beings through art, too.

9 By describing the experience of major and minor moods as a fundamental breathing process, Steiner explains the riddle they present to theoreticians. For example:

> Why the hardly-worth-mentioning distance between minor and major third qualifies for such an exceptional psychological effect, is now as it ever was, an unsolved riddle (Paul Hindemith. *The Craft of Musical Composition*. Schott. London 1945).

For the connection between experience of major and minor and the lungs, see A. Husemann. *The Harmony of the Human Body.* Floris Books. Edinburgh. 1994. Part 4. Steiner is enlarging on observations made nearly two hundred years ago by Goethe. In a letter to Schlosser, 15 May 1815, Goethe described the "primal contrast" of the major and the minor: "the major mood arises through ascent... the minor mood arises through descent." Goethe saw "the exposition of this antithesis as the foundation of all music" (see van der Pals. 66-7; Kux; and *Resonanz* 9. Spring 1989. Kooperative Dürnau, is devoted to Goetheanism and Goethe's short "Entwurf einer Tonlehre" – "Sketch for a theory of music"; see also *Goethes Gedanken über Musik.* Insel Tb800. Frankfurt am Main. 1985). An Am. tr. "Theory of Tone [A Schematic Fragment]" is included in *Goethe, Scientific Studies*, ed. and tr. by Douglas Miller. Suhrkamp Publishers. New York. 1988. 299-302).

In their comments, Goethe and Steiner reach beyond the localised phenomenon of chordal analysis, and music of the past based on classical theories of harmony. The experience of "major" and "minor" is redefined "in the most comprehensive sense" as fundamental moods of "the entire tonal configuration" of music that also embraces possible future developments. Experience of the whole scale and the whole melodic phrase is implied. Thus all ascending intervals and passages partake of "major"; all descending intervals and passages of "minor", either joining the respective "out-streaming" or "in-streaming", or striving against it. The major and minor triads are a true polarity, for each contains something of its opposite (for example, the C major triad contains a minor third E-G; the minor triad a major third E♭-G).

The "major" and "minor" streams are the basis of all ensouled movement. The former streams along the outer part of the arm to the back of the hand, the latter "towards you" along the palm and the inner part of the hand (Lecture 7). The right, out-going side of the human body is involved in expressing the major triad, the left, in-streaming side for the minor triad. Originally, the major angle-gestures were confined to the upper zone (above the horizontal) and the minor angle-gestures to the lower zone (below the horizontal) "as pushed forward and together, as if forced into the three-dimensional space of gravity" (see Zuccoli. 8, 13ff. See also Ruland's comments in Endnote 22).

Fig. 29: Apollo and Marsyas – panel of a sarcophagus (The Louvre, Paris).

Notes to Lecture 2

10 The opening sentence presents one artistic pathway: *experience* leads to gesture. The opposite pathway – starting from the *gesture* – is recommended in Lecture 1, and also later in Lecture 2 (p. 54); for both pathways: "It is only through practising that you really get into it. Then you will see that this is precisely the method of music-eurythmy" (Lecture 7, p. 106).

The historical beginnings of religion, which include the beginnings of music, speech and the dance, is described in Chapter V "The Lemurian Race" in R. Steiner. *Cosmic Memory.* Garber Communications Inc., Blauvelt, New York 1987. 81f.; also in GA 277a. Anastasi. 2002. 15.

11 See R. Steiner. "The Ear". Lecture, Stuttgart 9 Dec. 1922. GA 218. E.T. *The Golden Blade.* RSP 1970; a section is translated in Lea van der Pals. 1992. 58-60. Musical sound is already etheric experience. "Properly speaking, it is not the physical but the ether-body that is the real organ of perception" (R. Steiner. Lecture, Dornach. 20 Nov. 1914. *The Balance in the World and Man.* GA 158. Steiner Book Centre. N. Vancouver 1977. 5). Compare:

> The ear is that organ which first separates the air element from the note before we actually hear it, so that we receive the note in our experience as a resonance, or a reflection. The ear is actually that organ which throws back the airborne note into man's inner being in such a way that it separates out the air element; then, in that we hear it, the note lives in the etheric element. In other words, the ear is actually there (if I may put it like this) to overcome the resounding of the note in the air and to throw back the pure etheric experience of the note into our inner being (R. Steiner. Lecture, Stuttgart. 7 Mar. 1923. GA 283. Tr. A.S.; pub. tr. 48-9).

The following two paragraphs summarise Ernst Lehrs on the activity of listening: The ear does not perceive like the eye. One half corresponds to the activity of the "eye"; the other half is "larynx". "In order to come consciously to a perception of sight, we must 'listen' to the 'deeds and sufferings' (Goethe) of light, while at the same time we meet them with the help of the 'speaking' of our inner light. Something similar holds good for hearing." *Hearing is always accompanied by an activity of the larynx, even though a silent one.* The activity of nerve and blood is reversed in eye and ear. The eye is primarily nerve, the ear blood. The receptive part of the ear belongs to the limb-organisation, the responsive part is the nerve-organisation. Outer acoustic movement is transferred to the fluid of the inner ear, thence to the fluids of the body, and lastly the muscular system. What we hear directly works on the will, which connects to the limbs. Eye-impressions cause us to think, ear-impressions to dance. The muscles are always altering their length and elastic tension; they change their vibration, or inner sounding. In bodily movement the muscles are sound-producers, in acoustic perception they are sound-receivers.

The nerves damp down the compulsive limb movements, so that we can perceive the astral, musical element invading the muscles. In seeing, the blood counteracts the pain produced by perceiving light. In hearing, lack of equilibrium would produce ecstasy. The nerve-system damps down the potential ecstasy of limb movement, enabling us to perceive the astral, musical processes. "Optical impressions are accompanied by dim sensations of sound, and aural impressions by dim sensations of colour" (Ernst Lehrs. *Man or Matter*. RSP 1985. 350 & 438-40. See also Lea van der Pals. 1992. Endnote 8).

12 Steiner spoke of the full experience of the octave as a development belonging to the future: "People will feel 'I have found my "I" anew; I am uplifted in my humanity by the feeling of the octave." This musical experience

> will become for the human being proof of the existence of God, because he or she will experience the "I" twice: once as physical, inner "I" (prime), the second time as spiritual outer "I"... directly experienced, in that we arrive at the next higher octave (R. Steiner, lecture Stuttgart 7 Mar. 1923, in GA 283, tr. in *The Inner Nature of Music*.... 48, 54, 56-7).

Steiner here contrasts the musical experience of the far past (Atlantis), the present, and the far future (57).

Hermann Pfrogner suggests that the octave is the alpha and omega of music. Every age has divided the octave in its own characteristic way to form its tonal system. How did it first come about?

> As we know from Steiner [*The Four Sacrifices of Christ*, Basel. 1 June 1914 (AP. 1944/81); additional perspectives in *The Pre-earthly Deeds of Christ*. Lecture, Pforzheim. 7 March 1914. RSP. 1947; both GA 152], that being penetrated by Christ (later called Apollo by the Greeks) at that time [last period of Atlantis] once again harmonised the relationships of thinking, feeling and will of humanity, which otherwise were moving towards disorder. We may assume (in reference to what Steiner described elsewhere [*Wonders of the World...*, Lecture, 23 August 1911. GA 129. RSP. 1963] concerning the nature of Dionysos and his followers, sileni and satyrs, that the musical element in its beginnings on Atlantis was more or

less exclusively determined by the Dionysian principle. It was only later, at the end of the Atlantean epoch, that the influence of the illuminated Apollonian principle, from the Christ, began to be felt. And what else could this influence have been, this heavenly, harmonising Christ-filled force from the Sun-sphere, than the gift of the "archetypal concord", the octave experience? (H. Pfrogner. *Zeitwende*. Langen Müller. München/ Wien. 1986. 299-300.)

Eurythmy-forms for the intervals were given by Steiner in a lecture to musicians, Stuttgart 8 March 1923. GA 283. All music "forms" are actually three-dimensional. Those for the intervals of the sixth and the seventh, for example, do not exhibit a crossing, but a passing-over as the movement proceeds on and up. Is the term "form" a misnomer in English? Steiner goes on here to speak of "rhythm into the will... *that which passes from the interval into rhythm*" (GA 283. 72). "Rhythm" comes from the Greek *rhuthmos* related to *rhein*, "to flow". Consequently, the term "interval-rhythms" is preferred by some eurythmists. For further insights into the intervals, see Kux; van der Pals 1992; Chr. Peter, *Die Sprache der Musik in Mozarts "Die Zauberflöte"*; and H. Pfrogner, *Lebendige Tonwelt*. Langen Müller. München/ Wien. 1981.

A practical question in any given musical passage, especially of piano music, is whether a real octave experience is present. For example, the degree of the scale may be more evident; again, passages of doubling at the octave, or a repeat an octave higher (as if, say, given to the flute) may rather be for changes in tone-colour than clear *melodic* octave-experience. This consideration suggests a sparing use of the gesture for the octave.

13 Heiner Ruland explains that the natural seventh ⁷⁄₄ formed the basis of the Atlantean pentatonic scale, which is formed – as all scales are – by octave transposition, or displacement, of a series of notes derived from a single basic interval. (See H. Ruland. *Expanding Tonal Awareness*. RSP. London. 1992. Chapter XXVI.) This explanation casts doubt on a phenomenal interpretation of Steiner's words, *e.g.*, Husemann. 1994. 161f. When Steiner speaks of the preference for larger intervals during long epochs in the far past, he is speaking of the forming interval existing in the etheric level of the tonal system (scale-formation). At the phenomenal level (music-making) the different pentatonic scales came about. Then, as the forming intervals became progressively smaller expressing the changes in the incarnation of humankind (the make-up of human beings), the results are heard in the systems of 7-note modes and eventually our major-minor system. Pfrogner & Ruland look forward to developments away from our present situation of equal temperament (equal semitones), that is, a variable tuning expressing felt nuances.

14 Here and in Lecture 7, Steiner uses the conventional German musical terms for the intervals of the third: *grosse Terz* and *kleine Terz*, (literally, "large third" and "small third"). This bears on the question of ascending and descending thirds. The passage in Lecture 4 (p. 75) has *Dur-Terz* and *Moll-Terz*, where musicians would speak of an ascending minor third and a descending major third (incidentally, *Dur* and *Moll* derive from the Latin, meaning "hard" and "soft"). Steiner's definition of "major" and "minor" concerns "out-streaming" and "in-streaming" movement (see Endnotes 9 & 59). For Goethe "the minor scale extended upwards would have to become major" (Suhrkamp edition. 302).

15 The Greek legendary figure MARSYAS discovered the aulos created by Athena. After mastering it, he challenged Apollo, who played the kithara (lyre), to a contest. The Muses, who were the judges, awarded the prize to Apollo, who tied Marsyas to a stake and flayed him ("Why do you tear me from myself?" Ovid. *Metamorphoses*. VI. 385). Ruland explains this legend (1992. 104, also 99ff, 110, & 159; and Pfrogner. *Lebendige Tonwelt*. 93-94). Two types of experience based on two types of scale are pictured here: (i) the Dionysian nature-bound realm of life-forces that gets "under the skin", and (ii) the realm of Apollonian beauty with its "protective skin" of beauty. Marsyas, Steiner explains, is already skinless by nature. Speaking of the eurythmy-forms ("rhythms") for the intervals, he directly relates experience of the intervals to higher stages of consciousness:

> Someone who experiences sevenths – if he survives this experience – knows what Intuition is. What I mean is that in the experience of the seventh, the form of the state of soul is the same as clairvoyantly with Intuition. The form of the state of soul during the experience of the sixth is that of Inspiration during clairvoyance. And the experience of the fifth is a real Imaginative experience. The state of soul needs but to be filled with vision. Such a state of soul is definitely present with the musical element. That is why you hear everywhere that in the older mystery schools and remaining traditions clairvoyant knowledge is also called musical knowledge, a spiritual-musical knowledge (R. Steiner. GA 283. 2nd ed. Dornach. 1975. 145, tr. A.S.; pub. tr. 73).

See also Edgar Wind, *Pagan Mysteries of the Renaissance*, Chapter XI "The Flaying of Marsyas" (Faber. London 1967; OUP 1980). For ORPHEUS

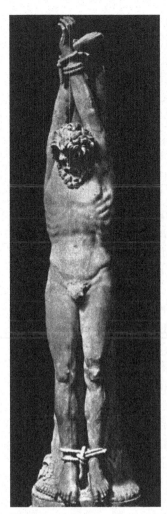

(mentioned in Lecture 5), see R. Steiner. Lecture, Berlin. 25 Oct. 1909 in *The Christ Impulse*. GA 116. AP. 1976; R. Steiner. Lecture Berlin. 16 Jan. 1911, in *Background to the Gospel of St Mark*. GA 124. RSP & AP. 1968; H. Pfrogner, "Der zerrissene Orpheus" in *Zeitwende*, and especially the chapter "Griechenland" in *Lebendige Tonwelt*. The Orpheus myth is retold as a poetic drama in O. Barfield, *Orpheus*. Lindisfarne Press. West Stockbridge. 1983. For a mention of Bach's use of the Orpheus myth, see Wilfrid Mellers. *Bach and the Dance of God*. Faber. London and Boston. 1980. 118ff.

16 This joke about a "tired" eurythmist being "a caricature" could be a hint at the second stage on the Eightfold Path (see Endnote 2) made in Lecture 2: *Right Thought* or *Decision/ Judgement* – decide on meaningful actions. Two is the number of division but also of productive polarity. Steiner's joke raises the question: When is an artist not an artist? – that is, not specifically, or professionally in creative mode: he "cannot always be at it". When, for example, away from the canvas or the instrument, when not moving on the boards in private life, perhaps tidying the place, cooking, out shopping, or driving – surely these activities, too, can all become artistic? It seems to be a matter of degree, of controlling energy; ultimately, through a homeopathic principle ("a little and often") and the grace of God, the whole of life is to become an art.

Fig. 30: Marsyas about to be flayed. Antique sculpture (Conservatori Museum, Rome). See Fig. 29 on p. 246

This introduces deeper considerations, hinging on the concept of *paradox* (a word emphasised by Steiner here), of duality, or division. Lecture 2 is full of productive polar activity; dual conceptions are also mentioned. Pain and suffering as well as joy are necessities, the lecturer maintains, out of which human expression arises in the first place. Here Steiner answers the age-long question about the origin of music; from its very beginnings, music expresses *inner* experience. The second step of Christian initiation is the schooling in how to meet pain: the Master did not conceal an escape route. In eurythmy "the whole human being is to become a sense organ", to "become in some respects a new human being". "Poor me", or even "wonderful me", is left behind; a new existential inner life undermining our complexes is begun.

17 WAGNER, Richard (1813–83): It is important here to attribute equal weight to both of Steiner's statements concerning this controversial artist. Three points emerge: Wagner's work is (a) music, (b) "unmusical music", tending towards speech, *i.e.*, illustrating something extra-musical, (c) justified. The present lectures express two reservations about musical style: (a) the "thematic" content (with Wagner, no doubt the *Leitmotiv*) (Lecture 3); and (b) "Wagner's continuous melody" (Lecture 8). At the beginning of his anthroposophical work, Steiner spoke several times about Wagner's creations. The renewal of the *Gesamtkunstwerk* ("unified work of art") and the re-enlivening of Teutonic mythology, he regarded as

Fig. 31:   Richard Wagner
(1813–1883)

especially significant. Steiner's lectures on Wagner are not all published in translation, though typescript trs. can be loaned from R. Steiner Lib. <rsh-library@anth.org.uk>.

The controversy between "pure music" and the "barbarism" of "music as expression" (Brahms's followers v. Wagner's followers) was a social phenomenon in Steiner's youth. He came to understand Wagner's work as something that "humanly, obviously was a significant cultural phenomenon" (R. Steiner. *The Course of my Life*. GA 28. Chapter IV). Pfrogner suggests that this basically Apollonian and Dionysian struggle heralded the split of music into tonality and atonality (*Zeitwende*. 355). Compare the comments of Steiner here with those of Hauer (to whom Wagner was wholly "decadent"), and Furtwängler, the famous conductor, who in 1937 said: "Wagner is a poet who pursues his poetic dreams with the aid of music. But he is in a category by himself" (*Concerning Music*. Boosey and Hawkes. London. 1953. 32). On the other hand D.F. Tovey (1875–1940), the famous English musician and musicologist – Casals called Tovey one of the greatest musicians of all time (Corredor. 104 –

see Intro. Endnote 9, p. 27) – testifies that his own attempt at writing an opera revealed to him "the paramount greatness of Wagner as a musical composer". D.F. Tovey, "Musical Form and Matter" (1934), in *Essays and Lectures on Music.* Oxford. OUP 1949.

Wagner, Steiner says, "was immersed in the nature of true mysticism" (4 Dec. 1906. GA 68). His artistic creations are concerned with a "deep understanding of Christianity. He knew that Christianity can best come to manifestation in musical form" (16 Jan. 1907. GA 97). The intention was there, Steiner remarks, to found a new mystery art with *Parsifal*, but Wagner does not quite attain his ideal in music; he falls into symbolism – the Communion and the Dove are symbolically represented (29 July 1906 in GA 97, and 22 Aug. 1924 in GA 243). People have compared the attempt at Bayreuth with that at Dornach. Steiner declared:

> Anthroposophy would take the path to the spirit in the plastic arts too. That was our intention in building the Goetheanum at Dornach, that work of art wrested from us [by arson, New Year's night 1922/3]. And we must do it [take the path to the spirit] in the new art of eurythmy. And in recitation and declamation (R. Steiner. GA 276. Pub. tr. 116).

Wagner's whole output is surveyed from the aspect of his mastery of tonality by H. Beckh, *Die Sprache der Tonart*, op. cit.; and from religion in "Wagner and Christianity", *The Christian Community Journal* 1933 (copies from Floris Books, Edinburgh). Beckh's *Das Parsifal Christus-Erlebnis* (Die Christengemeinschaft, Stuttgart. 1932; tr. in MS "The Parsifal Christ-experience") was a pioneer work. F. Oberkogler, *Vom Ring zum Graal* ("From Ring to Grail") (Stuttgart. 1978), wrote a comprehensive musical study; F.E. Winkler, *For Freedom Destined* (Waldorf Press. New York. 1974) describes ("mysteries of man's evolution in the mythology of *The Ring* and *Parsifal*".) See also the chapter ("The occult in the life and work of Wagner" in E. Schuré: *The Genesis of Tragedy.* Rudolf Steiner Pub. Co. London. 1936). 84-110; also the remarkable essay by E. Bock, "Götterdämmerung und Auferstehung, Richard Wagners mythische Weisheit" in *Die Christengemeinschaft*, March 1928 (tr. in MS, "Twilight of the gods and resurrection"); and R. Frieling, "King Ludwig II von Bavaria" (*Die Christengemeinschaft*. June 1956. E.T. in MS).

Wagner is also mentioned at the end of Endnote 48 below. A note by Ilona Schubert "Ein wichtige Bemerkung Rudolf Steiners" in *Was in der Anthroposophischen Gesellschaft Vorgeht* (Dornach 19 Feb. 1975, 52. Jg. Nr. 10), reports that after a rehearsal of Lenau's poem "Merlin", Steiner, in answering questions, confirmed that Merlin was an earlier incarnation of Wagner: "You can feel it in his music." (Another comment made during Steiner's visit to Tintagel is reported by E. C. Merry, *Life Story: an autobiographical Experience of Destiny.* Mercury Art Pub. London. 1987.) See also F. Oberkogler. *Merlin – Richard Wagner: Eine karmische Betrachtung.* Selbstverlag. 1974, for a study on the entelechy of this individual; and "Merlin", a poem by Edwin Muir. *Collected Poems.* Faber. London. 1952. 51f.:

Merlin

O Merlin in our crystal cave
Deep in the diamond of the day,
Will there ever be a singer
Whose music will smooth away
The furrow drawn by Adam's finger
Across the meadow and the wave?
Or a runner who'll outrun
Man's long shadow driving on,
Break through the gate of memory
And hang the apple on the tree?
Will your magic ever show
The sleeping bride shut in her bower,
The day wreathed in its mound of snow
And Time locked in his tower?

Notes to Lecture 3

18 *Right Speech* or *Communication* is the third step on the Eightfold Path (*cf.,* Endnote **2**). Formative speech can help in the present dire situation. The third Beatitude promises that "the meek" – not the materialist – "will inherit the earth" (Ps. 37:11 refers to Palestine; Matthew means "the Kingdom"). The word "meek" has changed its meaning over the centuries; "patient" and "long-suffering" are alternative translations. The meek are the non-self-assertive; "He who says 'I' in me" can *speak* with them. Moses and Jesus were meek (Num. 23:3, Matt. 11:29). Gerald Heard (*Training for the Life of the Spirit.* Cassell. London. 1941. 6) suggests the Greek work for "the meek" really means "the trained", the training being the life of the spirit. Right Speech respects the spirit, which is divine action.

Coming to terms with materialism is a main concern of Lecture 3, where death is encountered. Spirit continually brings "life to the lifeless", especially potent with the musical descending seventh. The raising of the sensory element to etheric experience results from finding the middle way between naturalism and abstraction. Finding the "melody in the single note" between memory and expectation is proposed, one of several triads in Lecture 3. Speech is a human faculty (p. 72); its origin is divine. Christoph Rau discusses Luke 8: 1-9:50 which includes the Parable of the Sower [of the Word]. (Christoph Rau. "The Eightfold Path in Luke". *Perspectives.* Mar.-May 2002–Nov./Dec. 2003. Floris Books. Edinburgh. Tr. A.S. from: *Die Christengemeinschaft.* Jan–Mai 1990. 14-18; 66-71; 130-35; 189-94; 222-27. Stuttgart. See also Chr. Rau. "Das Rätsel des Lukas" in *Das Goetheanum.* Nr. 50. 15. Dez. 1991. Dornach. Tr. A.S. in MS.)

In lecture 3 the three planes are introduced with the three-dimensional cross. We are "to enter" and "make use" of it; the verbs in the gospels are "take up" and "follow" (Matt. 16:24; Mk. 8:34; Luke 9:23 adds "daily"; John 12:26 adds "serve").

19 If we compare the expression "noise" with the use Hauer makes of it, it is clear that Steiner is not primarily commenting on the musical life of 1924. Steiner has more to say to Hauer's sweep of history, where he traces the path from spiritual, live melos to acoustic, dead noise. Steiner comments on naturalism in art. "Materialism had to happen," he declares (GA 276. 111). "We must will to penetrate spiritually into this material world... not by developing dry symbolism or allegory... [which] are inartistic. The starting point for a new life of art can come only by direct stimulation from the source whence springs all anthroposophical ideas." In the eurythmy lecture-course he takes up, for instance, the major and minor chords (to Hauer, these are acoustic "noise"), and shows how by releasing the common chord (to Steiner: "the burial of melody"), melos regains life in gesture.

20 Compare this exercise concerning inner experience with that of Hauer:

> You slowly play all the twelve notes within one octave (actually a major seventh)... let it resound within... What is experienced between the notes, between the intervals, as it were outside of space, of material, of the senses, that is pure movement, movement itself, intuition, the archetypal musical experience... The intuitive human being, the "musician", dismisses the "world" and space – of course, only apparently –; he feels within the cosmos and lives in the temporal, in the juxtaposition, in organic growth (J.M. Hauer. *Deutung des Melos.* 22. E.T., 504f.).

Hauer's exercise leads to repose, a "dismissal of the world"; Steiner's leads to artistic expression. The abstract and the concrete face each other. Perhaps Steiner's insistence on the experience of the keynote (which appears several times in these lectures) is a reminder that eurythmy is a spiritually centred musical path: "The scale is the human being" (Lecture 3). Pfrogner sums up the sevenfold scale as "the sounding image of the human being, pure and simple". Pfrogner, following Steiner, argues that the diatonic system has a future, if inner listening in connection with the scales pioneered by Bartok and Schlesinger develops beyond tempered tuning. Steiner's suggested solution to the problem of the romantic ego is evidently not Hauer's solution. Hauer claimed absolute objectivity ultimately demands "the subduing of the personality" (J.M. Hauer. *Vom Wesen des Musikalischen.* 40), and "Intuition demands a blossoming (*Aufgehen*) of the individual into something greater, namely into that of the primal element of everything existing which possesses a forming capacity" (J.M. Hauer. *Deutung...* 26. E.T. 506). See, too, Philip Barford's masterly article "Tonality". *Music Review.* XXIV (1963). With Hauer we meet "the East/West tension" in a particular form. In 1922, Steiner said that "the question is: whether all the Asiatic features that Europe had to overcome have in fact been overcome, so that after finding itself Europe can now, from the centre of the world's development, also reach an understanding with the East". R. Steiner. *The Tension between East and*

West. GA 23. AP 1983. 147. See also A. Steffen, *Der Künstler zwischen Westen und Osten*. Grethlin. Zürich/ Leipzig 1925; and Appendix 2, below.

21 The connecting thread in Steiner's thought is something like this: naturalism results above all from a misuse of chordal harmony, which was originally made possible by polyphony. Obviously, at the back of his mind is the unmusicality of the eye. The story of the Arab is taken from Hauer (*Deutung*. 34. E.T. 510). Polyphony in particular is generally regarded as the contribution of European music, for example, Hans Mersmann: "The one paramount revolution in the history of music is the advent of polyphony. Polyphony really decided the destiny of music in the West and clearly distinguished it from all other cultures. Through polyphony music rises from mere melodic existence to the heights of contrapuntal architecture and dives into the depths of harmonic colour and associations." "Through developing the element of harmony," Schumann wrote, "passion attained to more refined levels of expression, and through this music was placed amongst the highest organs for art, those which use writing and symbol for all conditions of soul" (quoted in Chr. Peter. *Die Sprache der Musik...*, tr. A.S.). Polyphony and harmony is certainly absent in the East, but is indigenous and widespread in Africa (see *inter alia*, G. Kubik & D. Rycroft: "African Arts: Music". *Encyclopaedia Britannica*. Vol. xiii. 1988). Hauer claims:

> The overtone series, its structure, the physiological element in it became – as spatial image – the point of departure for part-writing... Polyphonic music is not music, only noise organised into several voices! (Hauer. *Deutung*. 34 E.T. 510, below).

Steiner is at pains to point out that music does not originate from *a* single note with its acoustic overtone chord (a materialistic view), but in the future music will be composed from inner experience of *der einzelne Ton*, (*the* single note, that is, from the supersensory experience of inner listening – see Endnote 22). Music at *all* times has arisen from inner listening (*cf.*, p. 50). The overtone series, as Pfrogner never tires of explaining, is a *reflection* in nature corresponding to the musicality inherent in the human being. An interval "out there" in the overtones would never be recognised as such if it were not inherent in our listening.

22 The subject of "the melody in the single note" (according to Steiner a completely inner experience, outside "time") has presented a riddle for musicians. Steiner appears to be acting educationally in leaving the riddle for his followers to resolve. In GA 276, Steiner speaks of

the necessity of getting beyond materialism in art. In this connection, he mentions the three-dimensional space of the sculptor, the two-dimensional plane of the painter, and "with the musical element we enter man's inner world". He introduces a sketch of musical history and from a characterisation through certain intervals (seventh, fifth and third) discusses the need for "spiritualisation... a recognition of the special character of the individual note". The expression seems to relate music to the single dimension:

> Music is linear-like, one-dimensional; is experienced one-dimensionally in the line of time. In music the human being experiences the world as his own. The soul... experiences something which lives and vibrates here and now, on earth, in its soul and spirit nature (R. Steiner. GA 276. 36-7).

See R. Steiner's lecture Oslo, 20 May 1923. GA 276. 106: "If we immerse ourselves in the note it reveals three, five or more notes; the single note expands into a melody and harmony leading straight into the world of spirit"; and especially the answers to questions, Dornach 29 Sept. 1920. GA 283, and 5 Jan. 1922. GA 303; and the lecture 8 Mar. 1923, where, after mentioning "musical differentiation within the single note", Steiner goes on to describe the intervals and eurythmy, in GA 283. Eurythmy, we might say, is only possible because of "the melody in the single note". An archetypal instance is practised, for example, in the opening exercise "seventh, prime, third" – the musical correspondence to the original "I, U, A (*ee, oo, ah*)" exercise, given during the Faculty Meeting of 30 April 1924. GA 277a. This exercise is the musical version relating to one half – "Behold thyself" – of the exercise "Behold thyself, behold the world". In the seventh-prime-third exercise, the prime is approached by a descending seventh, and relinquished through an ascending third. Here the prime, a single note, becomes the turning point between the two melodic intervals ("past" and "future"), and manifests the eternal "present". In other words, one possible melody as etheric movement appearing in the C is carried out in time for the purpose of an exercise. *The eurythmist has continuously to create this "present" through etheric, ensouled movement.*

This thought of "the eternal present" suggests Janus, the god of Initiation, and "master of threefold time". *When we rise above the transitory, the present contains all reality* (see Alan Stott, "The melody in the single note" in RB 33. Michaelmas 2000).

The question is also discussed in Pfrogner, *Zeitwende* and Ruland 1992, Chapter XXXVI (166), and especially H. Ruland's article in *Die Neugeburt der Musik aus dem Wesen des Menschen* (Schaffhausen. 1987.

67), where the three notes are related to the three soul-forces: will-like expectation turns outward (major) and feeling-imbued recollection desires to descend melodically (minor) – *cf.*, Endnote 9 above. After detailed illustration, Hilde Raske concludes that the task of laying hold of the musical experience of the single note as melody was fulfilled in the First Goetheanum: "throughout all the individual forms of the capitals, each form relates to the previous one and to the following one" (Carl Kemper. *Der Bau.* Stuttgart 1984. 95); see Fig. 51 on p. 378 below.

A summary of the main conclusions and implications of recent musical research could also be attempted: The various arrangements of seven dividing the octave represent the etheric human being within the tonal system. Steiner described Schlesinger's discovery as an "archetypal" musical fact. This original scale forms the "key" to the tonal systems of all epochs of the age of music from Atlantis onwards. We begin to appreciate the measure of Steiner's time-scale. *He surveys the entire musical field.* From detailed research already published, it is already possible to anticipate possible future developments in the tonal system – not, of course, unwritten compositions. The etheric body develops, as we know, through penetration by the ego-forces. This calls for application and patience, hence Steiner's educational stance. The current enthusiasm for microtonality could be penetrated by the forces of inner listening, but – through the computer – it could alternatively be a preparation for the unleashing of an atavistic flood of aural delights which threatens to wipe out mankind's future ego-development. The sacrifices of Christ mitigated chaotic situations in the past, including the conspiracy of Jundi-Shapur (Arabian hybrid-third – see Ruland. 1992) to abort the birth of the consciousness-soul, and consequently of all possibility of any spiritual development. Will further sacrifice be needed? Here the musical artist too is given a means to contribute through preparatory work for the future. (The above paragraph is based on the researches of Pfrogner and Ruland. See also Appendix 3.)

23 Steiner is indicating an etheric level of musical experience. *Cf.*:

The simplest tune requires a knowledge of form. The physical ear can hear only one sound, or a vertical group of sounds, at a time; the rest is a question of memory, co-ordination, and anticipation. When the first note passes on to the second, the hearer must not only keep the first note in memory, but co-ordinate it with the second, and so on to the third; and occasionally he has to anticipate what is to come... if we did not have these powers, the simplest tune would be meaningless. To appreciate [Beethoven's] "Hammerklavier" Sonata or the Ninth

Symphony requires exactly the same qualities as the appreciation of the simplest tune – such as "The Bluebell of Scotland", which any child can learn – only to a greater degree (R. Vaughan Williams. "The Making of Music" 2 in *Nationalism in Music and other Essays*. Ed. M. Kennedy. Oxford. OUP 1987. 211).

24 Steiner's definition of music highlights the reality that is often instinctively assumed by musicians. This "unheard", yet experienced element is investigated in such eurythmical studies as Kux (especially with regard to the intervals) and Chr. Peter. *Rests and Repetition in Music*. Stourbridge 1992, and Peter. *Die Sprache der Musik... E. Kurth's Grundlagen des linearen Kontrapunkts*. Bern. 1917, was a pioneer work: The melodic line possesses "energy" not "in" but "between the single notes of a progression" (9), the expression of "strength of movement between the notes", which appears "not as something additional, but as the entity that carries it". E. Kurth. *Musikpsychologie*. Bern. 2nd ed. 1947. 76. See Dolores Menstell Hsu: "Ernst Kurth and his concept of music as motion". *Journal of Music Theory*. X. 1966. See also, "Melody as movement" in Kux 1976). Performers who practice awareness of "that which lives between the notes give life to their re-creations". Diran Alexanian wrote of Pablo Casals: "When he plays, each note is a prophecy or a recollection; this magician induces in us the presentiment of what is to come, as well as the remembrance of what has been" (quoted in J. Ma. Corredor. *Conversations with Casals*. Duddon. New York. 1956. U.-I. Gillert prefaces her book:

> Steiner suggests we feel that in eurythmy we have to seek for the inaudible element. Consequently this can in no way mean that the person engaged in eurythmy should concern him- or herself to make visible in movement that which is audible, or the notation, to the audience. For sure, some of my readers will indignantly say that nobody wants to do this. My many years experience have shown me something different (U.-I. Gillert. 1993. 8. The author attempts to give advice about how to overcome this situation).

25 The word "personality" is linked historically to the activities of the theatre and of Christian meditation. The English word "personality" and the German *Persönlichkeit* were created by the mystics of the fourteenth century (Hans Rheinfelder. *Das Wort Persona*. Halle. 1928). The German *Person* comes from the Latin *persona* (mask) – as does the English "person" via Old French *persone* and French *personne* – perhaps connected with *personare*, "to sound through"; the large-mouthed mask

of the actor was named from the voice sounding aloud through it. The theatrical meanings in both German and English are covered by recent loan-words *Maske* (mask) and *Rolle* (rôle). *Person* (person) remained in use with the philosophers, lawyers and theologians. Boethius gave the standard definition of the Middle Ages: "*Persona est natura rationabilis individua substantia* – the individual subsistence of a rational nature" (*Contra Eutzychen et Nestorius*. c. 3). The distinction of being in the Godhead expressed as the three Persons of the Holy Trinity, is the most philosophical attempt to conceive of God as Personal. In the most important practical statement in the New Testament, Paul expresses the complete unity of the divine activity: "*Through* Christ we have our access *in* one Spirit *unto* the Father" (Eph. 2:18). The most ancient form of the doxology is "Glory be to the Father, through the Son, in Holy Spirit" (Evelyn Underhill. *Worship*. Nisbet. London. 1936. 64; Fontana/ Collins. 1962. 73.) The phrase "the personality of God" is unknown to Christian theology until about two hundred years ago. Steiner speaks of personality in the theological tradition (see, for example, Introduction, Endnote 23, p. 28). In a remarkable triune expression, he refers to [the wholeness of] "personality" in connection with the eurythmist's "humanity", at the very beginning of the speech-eurythmy lecture-course:

> For the eurythmist, that which above all is necessary in every area, is that in the art of eurythmy he can live in the eurythmical activity with his personality, with his humanity, so that eurythmy will become an expression of life. This cannot be attained without penetrating into the spirit of eurythmy as a visible speech (R. Steiner. *Eurythmy as Visible Speech*. GA 279. Lecture, Dornach. 24 June 1924. Anastasi[Ltd] 2005. 28).

In this lecture, Steiner characterises "the Word", and speaks of the entire alphabet and "the whole human being". He links to the tradition of the Logos-doctrine: "To primeval human understanding the idea, the conception, 'the Word' comprised *the whole human being as an etheric creation*... The etheric human being is the Word which contains within it the entire alphabet" (24 & 27). The Logos doctrine combined Hebrew revelation and prophecy ("the Word of Yahweh", which was understood as God's ceaseless, creative activity, with a strong affinity to the "wisdom" passages in the poetic books, too) with the "reason" of Greek philosophy. The writer of the Fourth Gospel proclaims the crucial event, that "the Word *became* flesh" (not a visit), which "in scientific language... introduced a new species into the world... communicating His vital energy by a spiritual process to subsequent generations of men" (J.R. Illingworth, in *Lux Mundi*. John Murray.

London. 1889/1904. 151f.); seconded by C.F.D. Moule: "The Incarnation is something absolute and final because of its unique quality: an act of creation only comparable to God's initial creation" (C.F.D. Moule. *The Sacrifice of Christ.* Hodder & Stoughton. London. 1956. 29); see Appendix 7 below, and Endnote 7 above). The Biblical reference and Steiner's subsequent discussion (indeed, the whole lecture-course), clearly produce the impression: *eurythmical activity is a sacred art.* This conclusion, that we are dealing with supreme creativity (or, in Blake's words, "the Human Form Divine"), would seem initially to preclude from Steiner's meaning of the word "personality" (i) a limited, everyday, subjective meaning (which had already begun with Descartes), and (ii) the definitions of recent schools of psychology (a science, moreover, still undergoing development in 1924). Steiner, moreover, avoids such words as "illustration" and "symbol" in discussions on art, forcibly dismissing them (respectively) as naturalistic and abstract. The challenge consists in this: *the eurythmist, a unit of personality in the process of becoming, is both instrument and voice.* Compare:

> It is no bad figure which symbolises personality by a melody, in which each note is continuous with the rest and exhibits a tone-colour and value dependent on the whole, the melody meanwhile perpetually building itself up in successive notes which in turn subtly reflect the entire musical conception... We must speak not only of a continuity of being but of a continuous becoming. It is no defect in finite personality that it should have this character; it is simply its nature (H.R. Mackintosh. *The Doctrine of the Person of Jesus Christ.* T. & T. Clark. Edinburgh. 1913. 496).

For Steiner, such a musical conception is more than a metaphor, and far more comprehensive. Music is the art that "contains the laws of the ego" (GA 275), that is, the personality. He lays down the basis for an inner musical history of the race in the present lecture-course (see Appendix 8). The details have been researched (H. Ruland. 1992). A basis for a musical understanding of the Incarnation is given by H. Beckh, *Der kosmische Rhythmus im Markus-Evangelium* (Verlag Freies Geistesleben. Stuttgart. 1960); and his version of the tone-zodiac (see Fig. 42 on p. 351 below). Bach's esoteric plan for *WTC II* was suggested by Hans Nissen and further researched by H. Kluge-Kahn (see p. 286, entry (3), and Appendix 7, p. 415 below).

A related meaning to the word "personality" is found in the English "parson". This denotes a person who fulfils a dual rôle (R.C. Moberly. *Ministerial Priesthood.* SPCK. London. 1969. 260). He/she represents the *persona* of the community and mediates the world of grace, "Godward for man" and "manward for God". In the eucharist the dual activity of proclamation of the Word and the giving of thanks is also clearly enacted at the left and right sides of the altar of The Christian Community (see R. Frieling. *Sacrament and Ritual.* Floris Books. Edinburgh. 1988. Chapter 14, "Right and Left". 35-38). The Christian life is perhaps even summed up in the dual, creative call to "watch and pray" (in the "little apocalypses" of Mark 13:33 and Luke 21:36; in Gethsemane Mark 14:38, Matt. 26:41; also Heb. 13:17-18 and 1 Peter 4:7). *Cf.,* "activity" and "life" of the Meditation for Eurythmists (Endnote 63); also, Jachin and Boaz in Solomon's Temple; the pillars of Judgement and Mercy of the Tree of Life; and the Lambda discussed in Appendix 7.

Studies by theologians, philosophers and psychologists (some of exceptional literary grace) may help artists, teachers and therapists to deepen their creative endeavours. One work to stand alongside Steiner's *Philosophy of Freedom* is Wilfrid Richmond. *An Essay on Personality as a Philosophical Principle.* London. Edward Arnold. 1900/ Kessinger 2007; and the short introduction *Experience: A Chapter of Prolegomena.* London. 1896. Online: <www.archive.org>. Other works include: J.R. Illingworth. *Personality Human and Divine.* Macmillan. London. 1894: "The freedom of the human spirit through union with God became… a familiar thought… It had previously been an esoteric doctrine. Luther proclaimed it from the housetop; and in so doing dignified and deepened the whole sense of personality in man"; in many ways, Luther's comments on Gal. 2:19 & 20 remain unsurpassed (see Martin Luther. *A Commentary on St Paul's Epistle to the Galatians.* James Clarke. London. 1953. 158-80; Kregel, Grand Rapids, Mi. 1979); the first two chapters are famous of Friedrich von Hugel's masterpiece *The Mystical Element of Religion.* Dent. London. 1908/23; J. Clarke. London. 1961: Christianity, "the revelation of personality and depth", forms a triad with Hellenism and Science – see also Joseph Whelan. *The Spirituality of Friedrich von Hügel.* Collins. London. 1971; C.C.J. Webb. *God and Personality.* London & New York. 1918; and *Divine Personality in Human Life.* 1920; John Macmurray. *The Self as Agent* Faber. London. 1957 and *Persons in Relation.* 1961; R.C. Moberly, *Atonement and Personality.* London. 1901; William Temple. *The Nature of Personality.* London. 1911; and *Christus Veritas* (Am. title *Christ the Truth.* London/ New York. 1924, the recognised constructive Christian philosopher working in English, who (for A.M. Ramsey) was yet *par excellence* the born theologian; Ramsey also recognised H. Scott Holland as a theologian of genius: the latter's sermon "Christ, the Justification of a Suffering World" in *Logic and Life.* London. 1883. 81-98 "is among the greatest of all time" (A.M. Ramsey. *From Gore to Temple.* London. 1960. 45) which comment surely applies to the four following sermons on sacrifice, too; Phillips Brooks, who delivered his remarkable 1879 lectures, *The Influence of Jesus.* London. 1880; he defines the sermon as "truth through personality" in *Lectures on Preaching,* held 1877; John Oman. *Grace and Personality.* CUP. 1931/ Fontana 1960, is a classic – Oman's triadic sentences reveal an almost constitutional understanding of polarity and triune activity; J.K.

(i) Proclamation of the Gospel
(ii) Offertory
(iii) Consecration
(iv) Communion

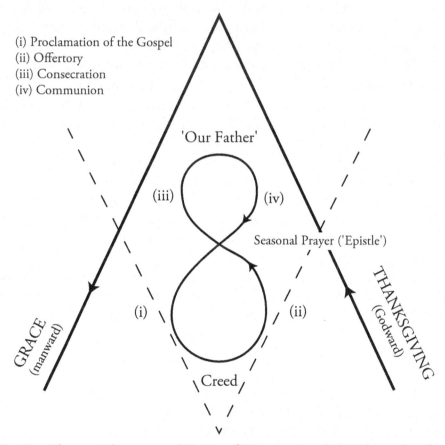

Fig. 32: The musical structure of The Act of Consecration of Man (the modern form of the Western rite) of The Christian Community. The fourfold lemniscate pattern depicting the movement of the liturgical book (the word and the action at the altar) is a Tree of Life. In the full celebration, seasonally appropriate music is played and sung at the crossing point, which is also the beginning and ending of the ritual, and instrumental music is also played after the insertions (the Creed and the Lord's Prayer). The crossing point depicts the eternal present; it is the point of departure. 'The Epistles' are a new development in the history of liturgy. The lambda —— = experience of the congregation; the inverted lambda – – – = 'onlooker' consciousness, superseded in and by communion (A. Stott, 1976/95/98).

Mozley's "Grace and Freedom" in *Essays Catholic and Critical.* London. 1929/Books for Libraries Press. Freeport, New York. 1971. 224-45; Emil Brunner. *God and Man.* London. 1936, and *The Divine-Human Encounter.* London. 1944: when God meets man, Christian truth comes into being; H.H. Farmer, *The World and God.* London. 1935/1963, and *God and Men.* London. 1948/ Abingdon Press. Naschville, Tenn. 1961, discusses man's experience of God as personal. Whatever else the Godhead is, at the very least the fellowship of the self-conscious and self-determining Creator with His/Her creatures is spoken of today as "personal" (*cf.* the frequency of the first person pronoun in Psalm 23). That fellowship is creatively unlimited (*cf.*, John 10:30) for:

> the Person of Christ is all that God can be to man, all that man should be to God. Nor can there be any Gospel which possesses the character of real good news save one that emphasises the reality, the value, and the permanence of personality both in God and in man; nor can we rightly speak of redemption unless it be redemption not from, but of and to personality (J.K. Mozley. *The Heart of the Gospel.* London. 1925. 174f.).

The way of mastery has been revealed in the body (2 Cor. 4:10), for

> The body of Christ was not merely the instrument of His intercourse with men… it was more than that; an integral element of His life and work. He controls its appetites under temptation; He goes about when weary doing good; he forsees yet faces suffering; He masters pain to speak words of kindness; He accepts death by crucifixion. And these things do not merely show, they actually make His human character. The stress and strain of them fashions and forms it… the bodily organism, so far from being a hindrance, is an essential ingredient in the progressive development of holy personality (J.R. Illingworth. *Divine Immanence.* London. 1898/1913. 133f.).

Austin Farrer (1904–68), who was altogether remarkable, also makes similar observations.

> In Christ never was there a man whose words and actions were more utterly his own. The spontaneity of his compassion moves us to tears, the blaze of his indignation shocks us: his speech is an unforced poetry, the coinage of his heart; the sacrifice on which he spent his blood was a decision personally made in agonies of sweat. If any man made his own life, Jesus did; yet what was the impression he left on his friends? That his whole life was the pure and simple act of God. What Jesus did was simply what God did to save us all… it is the most serious established conviction of twenty centuries, that if the action of God is anywhere to be seen it is in the free, the human life of Jesus Christ. The more human it is, the

more it is divine; the freer it is, the more it is the will of God (Austin Farrer. *A Celebration of Faith*. London. 1970. 147f.).

The point summarised in the last sentence, for example, is not to add items of belief; it challenges the eurythmical artist to achieve *the right and complete attention to artistic detail*.

See also H. Wheeler Robinson. *The Christian Experience of the Holy Spirit*. London. 1928/ 1962. Chapter 12; *The Christian Doctrine of Man*. Edinburgh. 1926. 275-88; and *Redemption and Revelation*. London. 1932, Chapters 8, 3 & 14; also W.R. Matthews. *God in Christian Experience*. London. 1939: "The artist, *qua* artist, would wish always to be creating. And we may suppose that the creative activity of God likewise is without limit or desire of cessation" (216. See also 87 on the highest anthropomorphism). J.C. Smuts coined the term "holism" as "the fundamental factor operative towards the making or creation of wholes in the universe" in *Holism and Evolution*. London. 1926; Chapters 10 and 11 are devoted to personality, "the most holistic entity in the universe". Holism, and Lloyd Morgan's "emergent evolution", reached a new height in the work of Teilhard de Chardin. Steiner, already in the 1880's, had drawn attention to Goethe's pioneer work in science, today hailed as "holistic"; and in 1932 Owen Barfield delivered his Dornach lecture on "The Philosophy of Samuel Taylor Coleridge" (in *Romanticism Comes of Age*. Wesleyan. 1966) on the poet's important "Theory of Life" – see p. 331 below).

A far-reaching, non-technical introduction to the concept of personality is provided by C.G. Jung, for whom personality is also an expression of the wholeness of the human being; an adult ideal whose conscious realisation through individuation is the aim of human development in the second half of life; the individual is faced with making moral decisions to discover "a new way to greater certainty". See C.G. Jung, "The Development of Personality" (lecture, Vienna. 1932. Pub. 1934; E.T. 1939/40, reissued in *The Development of Personality*. *Collected Works*, Vol. 17. London. 1954/91. 167-86; Jung's observations appear to parallel Steiner's, not least in a shared admiration of Schiller's *Aesthetic Letters* and a shared recognition of T A O: "Personality is T A O", Jung concludes (186). See also C.G. Jung. *Aeon: Researches into the Phenomenology of the Self. Collected Works*. Vol. 9 Part II. London. 1968/91. See also Endnote 41 below.

26 One approach to Steiner's view of what today is called "audience participation" might include a comparison with his description of a

human meeting, of "perceiving another's personality (perceiving the ego)": "I have really perceived another person's thinking." R. Steiner, *The Philosophy...*, Appendix to rev. ed. 1918 (tr. Wilson. 224ff.; Stebbing. 170; Lindeman. 248f., Lipson. 245). This is described as an oscillation of "sympathy and antipathy, not in the feeling life but of *what takes place in perception when you confront somebody*". (R. Steiner. *Study of Man*. Lecture 8. Stuttgart 5 Sept. 1919. RSP. 1966. 118). The relevance to the perceptive activity of an audience is clear. Steiner probably spoke of the etheric body of the spectator joining in the eurythmy that is perceived (source untraced). Compare:

> In a manner of speaking you are always engaged in the speaker's talk with your organs of speech, and the ether-body always speaks, too, always does eurythmy whilst listening. The movements conform absolutely to the movements of eurythmy, but usually you are unaware of this unless you have learnt eurythmy (R. Steiner. From *Orientierungskurs*. GA 339. Lectures Dornach 11-16 Oct. 1912, reprinted in R. Steiner & M. Steiner-von Sivers. *Creative Speech*. RSP. 1978. 215).

Pfrogner's description of musical performance (relevant for eurythmy, too) involves composer, performer and audience:

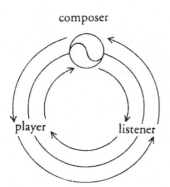

Fig. 33:   The artistic event, after H. Pfrogner, Zeitwende..., op. cit., p. 234. In the context of eurythmy, player = player and eurythmist; listener = listener and viewer.

Art comprises two parties risking a creative encounter in freedom... It is the sign of complete musical reality that the circuit of inner listening closes from composer via player and listener and once again to composer. Music achieves from person to person its highest and ultimate presence if the circuit of inner listening is closed (H. Pfrogner. "Musik und Elektronik" 1960, pub. 1962, repub. in *Zeitwende*. Chapter 13. 223-42).

Pfrogner argues that the case is quite different with electronics. Steiner's phrase concerning "annulling" the eurythmical movement emphasises the fact that (i) it is alive, (ii) a "threshold" exists between physical space and the eurythmical transformation of space into the flow of time. Clearly, Steiner is keen on vitality, articulation and differentiation in artistic matters.

27 Dr Armin Husemann. *The Harmony of the Human Body*. Floris Books. Edinburgh. 1994, points out that

three octaves proceed from the seventh-region of the throat: the sculptural octave of the head, the musical octave of the collar-bone and shoulder-blades, and the speech octave of the word".

See also "The human form mirrored in the intervals", in Kux 1976). "The larynx is absolutely a stunted head; a head which cannot become completely head and therefore lives out its head nature in human speech." R. Steiner. *Study of Man*. Lecture 14. Stuttgart 5 Sept. 1919. RSP. 1966. 185.

28 The description of the three-dimensional cross with its six directions combines the vertical cross with the horizontal cross (see Fig. 34b; depicts this same cross as three planes; *cf.* Dante, *Divina Commedia, Paradiso* XXVII, 106-107 and XXXIII, 115-120). The six cardinal points with the centre form the septenary. The cabbala speaks of the "Holy Palace" or "Inward Palace". The Logos manifests at the centre of all things

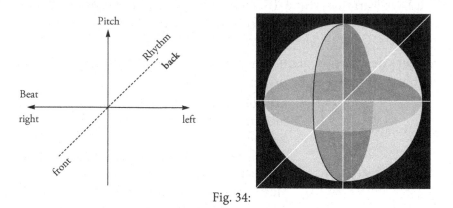

Fig. 34:

in the primordial point, the "motionless mover" (*Ching-Ying*, the "Invariable Middle", where the "Activity of Heaven" is directly manifested), of which all extent is merely the expansion and development. René Guénon points out that it is the centre of space and of time, and indeed of all the worlds. (This is portrayed in the central figure of Leonardo's painting "The Last Supper".) Steiner describes the central "free space":

> You will find the intervening regions... between the onsets from before and behind and from above and below... where Yahweh created the human being, as it were in the form of a cube, so filled with his own being, with his magic breath (*Zauberhauch*), that the effect spreads into the regions of Lucifer and Ahriman. Here in the midst, bounded by right and left, above and below, before and behind, is an intervening space where the breath of Yahweh enters directly into the spatial, physical human being (R. Steiner. Lecture, Dornach 21 Nov. 1914 in *The Balance*

in the World and Man, GA 158. Steiner Book Centre. N. Vancouver. 1977. 30f. Tr. rev. A.S. See also Endnotes **7** and **37**). The four Hebrew consonants of the Tetragrammaton [YHWH] etymologically represents a slight modification of the Hebrew verb "to be", which also signifies "to breathe").

"From God, Heart of the Universe," said Clement of Alexandria, "issue all the six directions of space… in Him the six phases of time are accomplished…; herein resides the secret of the number seven." The three-dimensional cross comprises the seven solar rays of Vedic tradition; the six directions also correspond to the lower part of the Sephirotic tree of the cabbala. The cross symbolises the realisation of Universal Man, Primordial Man, Adam-Cadmon of the cabbala, King (王 *Wang*, this ideogram of the Great Triad presents the human being as a cross between "heaven" and "earth") of Far-Eastern tradition (*TAO-te-Ching*. XXV; some translators, without an explanation, read here the lambda-like ideogram, 人 "the human being"), and is alluded to by Paul, who prayed:

> May HE grant you, out of the wealth of HIS light-glory, that the higher power may take hold of you which through HIS Spirit brings to birth the Inner Man in you. This happens when the Christ dwells in your hearts through your faith, and when you are firmly rooted and grounded in love. Then you will also have the power, together with all who have a share in the salvation, to grasp what is the secret of length and of breadth, of height and of depth; you will comprehend the love of Christ which is greater than all comprehension, and you will be filled with all the fullness of the highest God (Ephesians 3:16-19; *The New Testament*, a rendering by Jon Madsen. Floris Books. Edinburgh 1994; the translator here explains in his Foreword that HE and HIS refer to the Father, and Spirit with a capital S refers to the Holy Spirit. The six directions of the cross are implied in this passage, which can be seen as evidence of an emerging Christian cabbala).

John Wesley writes on v. 18: "*Ye may comprehend* — So far as a human mind is capable. *What is the breadth of the love of God* — Embracing all mankind. *And length* — From everlasting to everlasting. *And depth* — Not to be fathomed by any creature. *And height* — Not to be reached by any enemy." John Wesley. *Explanatory Notes upon the New Testament*. Epworth. London. 1950. 711. The nature of God's Word or utterance (the Logos) is self-manifestation. He appeared to Moses "in the midst" of "a bush" (Ex. 3:2); and later "in the midst" of the disciples themselves (John 20:19). In heaven, he appears "in the midst of the throne and the four living creatures, and... of the elders" (Rev. 5:6). The cross, God's throne, is the key to – because the heart of – everything in human existence.

By insisting that the human being "enter" and "make use of" the six dimensions, Steiner's immediate comments in the present lecture point to *a way of love that redeems materialism*. Mythologically speaking, the Cross is the Tree in the midst (see Endnote 6). After thoughts on "the corpse" and that "melody dies in the chord", the present description (which follows indications on etheric experience in music) is of etheric man himself "that which can manifest in space as movement". Compare the cross-gesture of the central figure in a portrayal of the complete penetration of the etheric body, "The Transfiguration" by Fra Angelico in San Marco, Florence. Fig. 35. Through eurythmy "the etheric body makes its effect directly... on the physical plane". The comprehensive categories of music are applied to this cross: "The astral body becomes what the etheric body is otherwise, going over into the ego-organisation, so that we have the human being standing already in a higher world." (R. Steiner, "Faculty Meeting", Stuttgart 30 April 1924. GA 277a. 141).

> The etheric body, which is in perpetual movement, is continually giving expression to the human being's thinking, feeling and will... In the physical body form and strength (*Kraft*) are the essentials, in the etheric body, movement and life, in the astral body, consciousness (awake and asleep)... We can go on to study still higher regions of human life ("duty" and "right"; "fire of self-love" of Lucifer, and "cool calmness" of Ahriman) (R. Steiner. *The Balance*... Lecture Dornach. 22 Nov. 1914. 33 & 40-4).

The etheric body "gives expression" to the three soul-forces; that which is "higher" needs the existence of that which is "lower" in order that it might manifest itself. This is the principle of sacramentalism, the climax of William Temple's philosophy: see Appendix 1. Perhaps the most advanced physical scientists today would agree with the metaphysician René Guénon, that "the whole of nature amounts to no more than a symbol of the transcendent realities" (Guenon. *Symbolism*... 14). Steiner relates the instructions of a Rosicrucian teacher of the Middle Ages:

> Your physical body is of profound spirituality... You are human only in your physical body. In your etheric body you are still animal, but an animal enspirited by the second hierarchy... And by weaving in the aeriform element you do not belong to the earth but to... the third hierarchy (R. Steiner. *The Christmas Conference*. 31 Dec. 1923 in the evening. AP. 1990. 235-38).

Steiner describes the mission of the Earth and the cross in nature; Plato (in the *Timaeus* 35-37) had described the world-soul crucified on

Fig. 35:   Fra Angelico *The Transfiguration* (San Marco, Florence).

the cross of the world-body. R. Steiner. *Universe, Earth and Man.* GA 105. Lecture 8. RSP. 1987. (NB The diagram on p. 115 should be rotated clockwise through 90 degrees; it is correctly given in the earlier edition RSP. 1955, 118). Christ has given the impulse of love whereby man may transform the earth "drawing along with him the lower creations... Christ as the spiritual Sun has given the impulse towards the re-uniting at some future time in one body of the sun and the earth" (114). Coleridge expands on this basic cross in his "Theory of Life". See also Appendix 5. 404f. For a summary, with comments, on Plato's account in *Timaeus*, see R. Steiner. *Christianity as Mystical Fact.* GA 8. RSP. 1972. Chapter 4. 55-7; the release of this crucified soul "had to be enacted in man... if he was to be qualified for the Osiris existence" (85). Steiner elsewhere mentions "the cross of knowledge" of spiritual science; he mentions sacrifice, and names the resurrection forces in art. There is "only one way" to get beyond the desert of abstract concepts. (a) To begin with spiritual science "must be a field of corpses". (b) "As a follower of Christ, who carried the Cross to 'the place of the skull' [Golgotha] and passed through death", we too "pass as through death in spiritual science itself". (c) From His inner presence, a person "transforms his living, inner soul"; this life is "a living source of those new impulses in art which can turn… (the mysteries of spiritual science) into reality" (R. Steiner. *The Temple is – Man!* Lecture Berlin, 12 Dec. 1911. GA 286. RSP. 1951. 29-30. Tr. rev. A.S. See also lectures, Dornach 20/21 Sept. 1918. GA 184. E.T. Rudolf Steiner Library Z.362).

The cross is mankind's most ancient symbol for himself. "Music", which is "the whole human being" ("the spiritual human being" – see Notebook 494. p. 197 above), can be "expressed" through the three-dimensional cross; music itself can portray "the Incarnation and Hallelujah of Christ" (see Appendix 4, iii. below). R. Steiner, lecture Dornach 30 Dec. 1914 in GA 275, points to the path of initiation and music of the future; René Guénon. *The Symbolism of the Cross* (Sophia Perennis. 2001), especially Chapter IV, "The directions of space"; and R. Guénon, *The Great Triad* (Quinta Essentia. Cambridge. 1991), especially Chapter 17, "Wang: The King-Pontiff"; O. Barfield, *What Coleridge Thought* (Wesleyan. 1971), Chapters 3 and 4; geometry is alluded to in "An esoteric intermezzo". 116ff. below; see Matt 10:38 and Lk 14:27, and the true cross of light in the gnostic "Acts of John". E. Hennecke. *New Testament Apocrypha.* Vol. 2. J. Clarke. 1991. 232; also mentioned by D. Fideler. *Jesus Christ, Sun of God.* Quest Books. Wheaton. 1993. 280; E. Francis, "The Sign of the Cross". *The Christian Community Journal* 1948. 37-39; K. Bittleston. "The Three Crosses in Space" in *The Christian Community Journal* 1954. 75-77 (copies from Floris Books. Edinburgh); Charles Williams explains "the Cross was He and He the Cross" in the symposium, *What the Cross means to me.* Ed. J. Brierley. J. Clarke. 1943. 168-177, reprinted in Chas. Williams. *Selected Writings* chosen by Anne Ridler. Oxford: OUP 1960. 94-105; F. Temple speaks of "The Three Crosses" on Golgotha in *Thoughts on Divine Love.* SPCK. London. 1910. 39-47:

> All Christians have, in their degree, to bear the Cross of Christ… yet… The true Cross of Holiness He alone could bear; but between the Cross of Penitence and the Cross of Condemnation it is still ours to choose.

The "blind seer" G. Matheson comments on Simon of Cyrene, who was "compelled… to carry His cross" (Mk 15:21):

> The fate of Simon is not merely historical; it is typical… The choice is not between taking the cross of Christ or leaving it; we *must* take it. The choice is, shall we be compelled to bear it or *im*pelled to bear it; shall it be thrust upon us by law or shall it be appropriated by love? (George

Matheson. *Studies of the Portrait of Christ*. Vol. II. London. 1900. 292 (online: <www.archive.org>).

Matheson explains:

> His Cross was made, not of wood, but of *love*. The cause of His suffering was the source of His individual rest. He had become oblivious of all personal pain, because love had given Him a pain that was impersonal; the throbbing of the pulse of humanity stilled His own (G. Matheson. *Landmarks in New Testament Morality*. Nisbet. London. 1888. 244).

Phillips Brooks speaks on three trees in the Bible, in "The Tree of Life". *Seeking Life*. New York/ London. 1904. 161-77: "The story of the tree of life and the story of the prodigal son are the same story."

29 See Endnote **11**.

30 This correspondence of vowels with the scale also appears in Hauer:

> Pure melos presents the spiritual connection between all these things, as also the connection between the single notes creating the melody. The meaning of a word, a "melody" with vowels and consonants, lies in its melos. The vowels are fixed notes with particular tone-colours which move within the range of an octave (u, o, a ö, e ü, i) and whose absolute pitch depends on the vocal organs; diphthongs correspond to the intervals, and so on (J.M. Hauer. *Interpreting Melos*. Tr. A.S. See 501 below).

Singers, too, speak of "whispered vowels"; it is unclear whence the tradition originates. Steiner gave consonantal correspondences for U (*oo*) – W (*v*), A (*ah*) – R and I (*ee*) – L. Lea van der Pals researched further from the eurythmical connections and presents a completed series in her *Ton-Heileurythmie*, where the series "note – interval – vowel – consonant", involving the change from music to speech, is carefully described.

```
C – prime   – U  (oo) – W  (v)
D – second  – O  (o) – B
E – third   – A  (ah) – R
F – fourth  – Ö  (ir) – G
G – fifth   – E – (a) – S
A – sixth   – Ü – (eu) – F
B – seventh – I – (ee) – L
C – octave  – U  (oo) – W  (v)
```

The authors add a reminder that the point of departure for the eurythmical gestures for the notes and intervals lies between the shoulder-blades (see Endnote 55). The gestures and movements manifest through the human being in music (R. Steiner. Lecture, Dornach. 23 Aug. 1915. GA2 77a. 68. See van der Pals and Bäschlin. 1991. 26-31).

Notes to Lecture 4

31 *MOTIV* – The terms for melodic form are not unanimously employed by scholars. The unit or figure, motif, phrase, sentence or period and section are used differently by different authorities. R.O. Morris (*The Structure of Music*. OUP 1935) has sensible things to say. Murray Brown records general practice in Britain when he says, "it is simplest to refer to all subdivisions of sentences as phrases" (*A Handbook of Musical Knowledge*. Part 2. London. 1967). Steiner mostly employs *Motiv*, occasionally *Satz* and *Phrasierung*. The translation chiefly uses "motif", and "phrase" where the context suggests it; *Satz* is translated with "musical sentence". *Kleiner Satz* probably implies "four-bar sentence", and *grosser Satz*, "eight-bar sentence" in NB 494. 31.

Steiner emphasises the study of phrasing in the Faculty Meeting, 30 April 1924, and he also mentions

> beat, harmony, melos… Bach, Mozart and Beethoven as composers… All the students should learn to improvise on the piano… Explain the form of the sonata, how the sonata is the whole human being" (R. Steiner. GA 277a. 142).

For an investigation of Steiner and the piano, see Robert Kolben *Klavierunterricht – rechtzeitig?* in *Erziehungskunst*, 56. Jg. Heft 8. Stuttgart Aug. 1992; author's tr. with R. Steiner Lib. London, e-mail address: <rsh-library@anth.org.uk>. See also Endnote **72** below.

32 DEAD INTERVAL: This is the expression popularised by Hugo Riemann, for example in the Introduction to his *System der musikalischen Rhythmik und Metrik*. (Breitkopf und Härtel. Leipzig. 1903. 14). Riemann gives a usable description of the melodic interval between successive notes *within* a phrase, emphasising that it is not merely a relationship between two points but rather "a real journey through the intervening space" (*wirkliches Durchlaufen der betreffenden Strecke*), an "actual *movement* in the realm of pitch" (*ein geschehende Tonbewegung*). He rightly points out that the relationship between successive notes belonging to *different* phrases is different. Steiner is understandably unhappy with the term "*dead* interval" for this different relationship; in the course of these two paragraphs he is not arguing against the comparison of music with speech, and indeed he underlines the similar importance of the inaudible in the two media. It was the generally-felt validity of this comparison that led to the "period" in the realm of music. Riemann's "dead interval" between two musical phrases should of course be compared to the relationship between two spoken *phrases*, in contrast to the relationship between spoken words *within* a phrase (Note by Julian Clarke).

33 The BAR LINE: Note values began to be notated in the tenth century, necessitated by the development of polyphony. The earliest use of bar lines (1448) were casual, an aid to correlate music and text. Bar lines were used in the 16th and 17th centuries in keyboard and lute works (tablature) to mark arithmetical units. Solo parts and part-books of compositions by Palestrina, Byrd and others, were originally published without bar lines. Bar lines to precede the main accent, became customary only after the mid-17th century. This led to irregular barring – the classic example is Stravinsky's *Rite of Spring* (1913). Frank Berger, "Stravinsky's *Rite of Spring* and the birth of eurythmy" in *EA Newsletter* (Aberdeen 1995), traces an astonishing relationship.

Historically, we can follow the gradual union of melos and rhythm with the element of beat, which as Dionysian element lived in the dance throughout the period sketched above, its own living rhythms becoming progressively forced into beat.

Wrong barring can be found in some hymn-books. Some composers, it is (mostly impudently) claimed, are guilty of wrong barring too. Some of Steward Macpherson's examples (*Form in Music*. Joseph Williams. London. 1930) are pieces to which Steiner drew eurythmy forms. Should Chopin's *Nocturne* in E♭ (op. 9, no. 2) be written in 6/8, thus creating nice 4-bar phrases (40); or should the bar line be moved to the half-bar, producing an upbeat consisting of two beats (Percy Scholes. *Oxford Companion to Music*. OUP 1970. 610)? Should the bar line be similarly moved in Mozart's *Andante grazioso*, K. 331? Musicians confirm that musically Mozart's text is definitely correct; moreover, the only upbeats in the phrasing to come into question occur in bars 7, 15 and 17. The Chopin example remains a question.

Beat is shown in "the overcoming of the forces of the earth" (R. Steiner, Notebook entry, Prague, 2 May 1924. GA 277. 436). All dance is based on beat, but eurythmy alone shows the bar line. In this sense, Steiner is the first to draw attention to the bar line, and to relate it to the human being. The bar line is complemented with the *Hinüberschwingen* or *Motivschwung*, the "swinging-over"; both are examples to show how "melody receives the actual spirit and carries it on". With the bar line you are "pushed together"; you become "stuck in the form"; it is "a holding-on to yourself" (*In-sich-Halten*. The Notebook reads *in sich gehalten* which has to be translated "held in itself". This detail of translation is another reminder that the eurythmist is to *become* the music (p. 74). To Lea van der Pals, the bar line is

> an act of freedom... that gives the new first beat of the next bar its energy to begin afresh. It is an increasingly short sleep out of which we awake strengthened every time (Lea van der Pals. 1992. 21).

The term "sleep" here is confusing – is it a momentary loss of consciousness? Elsewhere she states that the bar line demands "presence of mind, ego-activity" (van der Pals and Bäschlin, *Ton-Heileurythmie*. Dornach 1991. 65). Steiner reminds us that during sleep the ego and astral body work more powerfully into our physical organisation than is possible during the day. Lea van der Pals describes the carrying-out of beat: "we allow ego-consciousness, as if from outside, to penetrate the skeleton which we use as an instrument" (79). Presumably "as if", because the decision is not spatially locatable.

In the challenge of carrying out the bar line in eurythmy, is the experience to be filled or is it of emptiness, or does an alternative possibility exist? See "(iv) A Note on the Bar line" on p. 392.

34 It is well known that Steiner invariably approaches a subject from various points of view in order to achieve a fuller picture and to avoid dogmatic schemes. Notebook 494 to the present lecture-course (2, p. 129) suggests a basic polarity of speech and music (outer world and inner world). Steiner gave *three orders of the arts*, which differ because of the point of view:

(1) In a lecture of 1909, the order of the arts arises out of their deeper spiritual background: the dance, mime, sculpture, architecture, painting, music and poetry (R. Steiner. Lecture "The Being of the Arts". Berlin. 28 Oct. 1909. GA 271. Tr. A. Bittleston. *The Golden Blade* 1979. RSP; reprinted: *The Nature and Origin of the Arts*. Mercury Press. New York. 1992).

> Behind the three arts of the dance, mime and sculpture, the human figure appears in *space*. Behind the three arts of painting, music and poetry the human soul appears in *time*. Eurythmy as the new art in human existence, embraces both realms (Ralph Kux. 1973. 162).

(2) In the lecture of 29 Dec. 1914, the order of the arts proceeds from the members of the human being: architecture, sculpture, painting, music, poetry, eurythmy and an unnamed (social?) art yet to be born. Music ("the art of inwardness") "contains the laws of our ego, though

not as they are manifested in ordinary, everyday life, but pressed down into the subconscious, into the astral body; the ego/"I", dives, as it were, beneath the surface of the astral body, there to flow and stream within the organisation of the astral body" (R. Steiner. *Art as seen in the Light of Mystery Wisdom.* GA 275. RSP. 1984. 37. See Kux for a fuller discussion).

(3) In the lectures in Munich of 5 & 6 May 1918, GA 271, another sequence of the arts is elaborated from experience relating to pre-birth, to that summarising incarnation, to that preparing for after-death: architecture and sculpture, experience of colour, poetry and music (see Fig. 40 on p. 340 Appendix 1, below).

35 Goethe's poem "The Wayfarer's Night Song II" is discussed from another point of view in R. Steiner. *Eurythmy as Visible Speech.* GA 279. Lecture 8. Dornach, 3 July 1924. Anastasi. 2005. Trs. by Henry W. Nevinson and David Luke are given (97). Longfellow translates it:

> O'er all the hill tops
> Is quiet now;
> In all the tree tops
> Hearest thou
> Hardly a breath;
> The birds are asleep in the trees
> Wait, soon like these
> Thou too shalt rest.

See also Introduction. Dornach. 11 Feb. 1923. GA 277. 311f.

36 Music is "the self-creating [power] in the human being" (p. 79). The fourth step on the Eightfold Path (see Endnote 2) is *Right Action* or *Deed*. The down-to-earth reference in Lecture 4 is the appeal to the difference between "two eurythmists, one of whom is an intellectual... virtuoso", the other "an artist". What is Right Deed for the artist? Mediocrity in not implied in either executant – mastery is assumed – neither is Steiner condemning a certain specialisation. Rather, as a criterion for human art he is contrasting *the integrity of the artist* with *the fragmentation of the virtuoso* – wholeness and harmony *versus* estrangement and disintegration brought about through a dry symbolism that in art ultimately leads to meaninglessness.

The appeal in Lecture 4 is uncompromisingly expressed:

> You see, the presentation of eurythmy quite especially reveals that the melody takes up the actual spirit and carries it on. Fundamentally

speaking, everything else does not add the spirit of the musical element, being at all events a more or less illustrative element.

In Lecture 4, too, artistic method is described. We already heard how through eurythmical gesture "I become the tree" (40; see sketch of macrocosmic man NB 494. 3; also Endnote 6). In lecture 4, rather than a tendency musically to *imitate* "Rustling Forests" and so on (76), we are introduced to the Tree of Knowledge and Life. The eurythmist *unites* through the musical categories with the three-dimensional, etheric cross of movement:

> It is really true to say: "As physical human being marking the *beat*; as etheric human being expressing the *rhythm*; as astral human being evolving the *melos*; it is thus that I appear before the world" (In the original German, the word *ich*, "I", occurs once).

In Christian initiation, "Bearing the Cross" is the fourth stage. The cross is God's throne, His "chariot" (*e.g.*, I Chron. 28:18; Ezek. 1; Sirach 49:9; Psalms 80:1; 104:3; 68:17). It is also the Tree of Life (Gen. 2:9) in the midst of heaven (Rev./Apoc. 4 and 5:6). The central sanctuary of the Hebrew nation, the Hekal (the "Holy of Holies") was a cube room, the sides of which, when extended, form the three-dimensional cross. It *was* heaven. It pictures the upper chest region of the human being, exempt from the attacks of the adverse powers. Moses heard "the voice of one speaking unto him… between" the wings of "the two cherubims" (Num. 7:89), that is, between the shoulder-blades "Yahweh's magic breath enters directly into the spatial, physical human being" (R. Steiner. *The Balance in the World and Man*. GA 158. Lecture, Dornach. 21 Nov. 1914. Steiner Book Centre: N. Vancouver. 1977). We recognise the point of departure for singing gesture. The Debir (the "Holy") was the Garden of Eden (see: Margaret Barker. *The Gate of Heaven*. SPCK. London. 1991. Margaret Barker. *The Revelation of Jesus Christ*. T & T Clark. Edinburgh. 2000).

37 The description of some speech sounds here recalls Plato's *Cratylus*, the first recorded theory of language. Cratylus is an important personality; see Ita Wegman "A Fragment from the History of the Mysteries", lecture Michaelmas 1928, in Ita Wegman. *The Mysteries*. Temple Lodge. London 1995. 54-74. For Plato's dialogue: The Loeb Classical Library. *Plato* Vol. VI. Tr. H. N. Fowler. Harward, Cambridge Mass./ London. 1926.

38 R. Steiner. *The Course of my Life*. GA 28. Chapter 3. AP. 1951, reprinted 1986.

39 *"Waldesrauschen"* ("Forest-Rustling") by Franz Liszt and *"Bächlein im März"* ("Brook in March") by Jan Stuten were performed in eurythmy on 26 Dec. 1923 in Dornach. Steiner's point is clear and unequivocal: The musical element does not require extra-musical images for its interpretation, and naturalism is no source for musical composition (nor of art in general: see GA 276. See also Appendix 1, below). U.-I. Gillert advises:

> Especially in music we are dealing with a completely inner process. We are always inclined to bring in pictures from nature in order to facilitate explaining to ourselves the musical process. We should certainly avoid this as far as possible, especially when teaching. Nevertheless, we often can't do otherwise than call on pictures as a help. We should then do it consciously, by saying, for example, "like flowing water, upon which rays of light fall". This is a help to show that we are employing imaginative perception as a comparison, and do not mean that the music in actual fact *is* the image (U.-I. Gillert. 1993. 40-1. Tr. A.S.).

40 The Old Testament speaks of the "covenant of salt", *e.g.*, Lev 2:13. "Salt is the emblem of perpetuity, and especially of friendliness perpetually preserved" (E.W. Bullinger. *A Critical Lexicon & Concordance*. London. 1895. 658). All the New-Testament sayings about "salt" refer to discipleship. "The connotation of 'salt' in rabbinic metaphorical language is mainly 'wisdom' and this is indicated by the fact that the basic meaning of the verb *moranthe* ("has lost its taste", RSV) is also "to be foolish'" (K. Stendahl, in *Peake's Commentary of the Bible*. Nelson, London. 1962. 776). Comparing Lk 14:34-35, Mk 9:50 and Matt 5:13, W. Manson finds that salt means "the capacity or willingness to make sacrifice" for the sake of Jesus and the gospel, influencing society "by a principle of eternal worth" (W. Manson. *The Way of the Cross*. Hodder & Stoughton. London. 1958. 47). J.D.M. Derrett concludes that salt is a spiritual preservative in this life and the life to come (*Studies in the NT*. Vol. 1. Brill, Leiden. 1977. 25-29).

In Hermetism, the triad "spirit, soul, body" corresponds to the triad of the alchemical principles "Sulphur, Mercury, Salt". The action of Sulphur (spirit, masculine, active) on Mercury (soul, feminine, passive) is "crystallisation", that is, "Salt", which creates a common boundary, or neutral zone, between inward and outward.

Salt, represented as a cube, is also a symbol of stability. It represents the body if viewed from one perspective... In a less restricted application Salt will correspond to the individuality as a whole.

(FN) From this point of view the transformation of the "rough-hewn stone" (or "rough ashlar") into the "cubical stone" (or "perfect ashlar") will present the development that ordinary individuality must undergo if it is to become capable of serving as a support or basis for initiatic realisation..." (R. Guénon. *The Great Triad*. Quinta Essentia. Cambridge. 1991. Chapter 12. 86).

See R. Steiner. *From Jesus to Christ*. Lecture 8. Karlsruhe. 12 Oct. 1911. RSP. 1973. 144; the nature of the body of light, "the Phantom", is revealed, and the meaning of the Gospel saying of Christ: "You are the salt of the earth." R. Steiner. *An Occult Physiology*. GA 128. Lectures, Prague 26, 27 & 28 Mar. 1911. RSP. 1983, speaks of the connection between salt-processes, the bones and conscious human life; the forming quality of salt crystalisation (cubic), and the future goal of earth evolution. The Heavenly Jerusalem ("Jupiter"-embodiment of the Earth in Steiner's terminology) is described as a radiant, perfect cube in Rev. 21:16-17; final equilibrium is attained for the cycle in question (see R. Guénon, *The Reign of Quantity...* Chapter 20 and pp. 194-95). Steiner defines the

bone-nerve element, and indeed... the material-mineral element as a whole... The dead physical element is permeable for the spirit, whereas the living-organic element is impermeable for the spirit (R. Steiner. *Study of Man*. Tr. Harwood. RSP. 1966. 176.

See also R. Steiner. *Exoteric and Esoteric Christianity*. GA 211. Lecture, Dornach. 2 April 1922; the 7th Apocalpytic seal, in GA 284). The foundation of alchemy is described in the lecture in Neuchâtel, 28 Sept. 1911. S. Prokofieff sees the three alchemical stages renewed in the Foundation-Stone Meditation (1994. Chapter 6); see also Endnote 28, and Appendix 5 below. See also C.G. Jung. *Psychology and Alchemy. Collected Works*. Vol. 12 (Routledge. London. 1968), and Jung's last great work *Mysterium Coniunctiones*, an inquiry into the separation and synthesis of psychic opposites in alchemy (*Collected Works*. Vol. 14. Princeton Univ. Press. Princeton, N.J./ Routledge. London. 1970).

The question of *which* salt is highlighted by the persistent, international mass-medication campaign that promotes fluoridisation of the water supply with the poisonous waste-products of the aluminium industry. In addition to the attack on the immune system and the impairment of the mental faculties (the evidence of experiments with animals even suggests a long-term experiment in population control), will the long-term effects of *preserving* the teeth and bones for the eventual goal of dragooning the human spirit, be mitigated by the long-term effects of sacramental *transformation* of the whole body "to consecrate as an offering to God the earth itself and all that is in it" (O.C. Quick on salt of the earth, in *The Gospel of the New World*. Nisbet. London. 1944. 114)? See Marcia Dodwell. "The Bread of Life" in *The Christian Community Journal* 1947. 84f. on silica and light-processes in wheat.

41 A Coleridgean "landing place" (*The Friend*) seems demanded at the end of Lecture 4, the mid-point of the lecture-cycle. Here, natural processes are banished, and eurythmy therapy is indicated, that is, healing processes. In the dramatic transition between these two activities, transformation is implied. This fact allows the lecturer's fundamental intention to indicate help to shine through. The expression "Out you go!", addressed to unmusical [decadent] nature in man, ultimately derives from the permanent, continuing presence of the Mystery of Golgotha (the expression "second coming" does not occur in the New Testament; He *has* come) "at the turning point of time".

The practical concept here is the *kenosis* of Christ, who "emptied himself (= poured himself out)… humbled himself, becoming obedient to death" (Philipp. 2:7, 8; based on Is. 53:12). The term comes from Paul's well-known appeal to the Philippians to pursue true unity by participation in the Spirit. H. Wheeler Robinson suggests that the *kenosis* (the emptying) was properly that of the Crucifixion, though naturally involving the Incarnation (*The Cross in the Old Testament*. SCM. London. 1955. 105). As the death was whole and complete (Matt. 26:38), *i.e.* more than physical, so was the restoration and exaltation into glory, *i.e.* more than spiritual (O. Quick. *Doctrines of the Creed. Nisbet. London. 1938/ Fontana. 1963*). "The Servant-Son of Man is confessed as Lord, a perfected humanity is combined with the majesty of Yahweh. The universe gives glory to God and thereby attains the goal of its creation and redemption", concludes G.R. Beasley-Murray. *Peake's Commentary on the Bible*. Nelson. London 1962. 987. "The Death… is the lowest point of the descent… but it is also the beginning of the ascent", writes F.J.A. Hort. *The Way the Truth the Life*. Macmillan. London. 1894. 151, in one of the few outstanding books (others include Oman's *Grace and Personality*, and Rittelmeyer's meditative works on St John) that reveal the inner side of religious truth.

The cry of dereliction on the Cross, "'My God, my God, why hast thou forsaken me?" (Mk. 15:34; Matt. 27:46) writes Hort's disciple C.E. Raven, is

> at once the utterance of total loneliness, of the surrender to the ultimate assurance of the divine presence; and thereby the means to and the endorcement of the final triumph. Here is fulfilled the paradox of life lost and gained (C.E. Raven. *St Paul and the Gospel of Jesus*. SCM. London. 1961. 45).

And C.G. Jung:

> Here his human nature attains divinity; at that moment God experiences what it means to be a mortal man and drinks to the dregs what he made his faithful servant Job suffer... the divine myth is present in full force. And both mean one and the same thing (C.G. Jung. *Answer to Job*. Chap. 7. *Collected Works*. Vol. 9; and Ark Paperbacks. London 1984. 74).

On Philippians, see also the commentaries of Lightfoot (1868/79, reissued), 110ff.; F.W. Beare. A. & C. Black. London 1969; R.P. Martin. Eerdmans. Grand Rapids. Mich. 1980; G.D. Fee. Eerdmans. 1995.

Kenosis, self-giving, is demanded of the artist, Steiner points out in Lecture 1 – see Endnote **7**, iv. If the *kenosis* of Christ is more than a metaphor, and continues in His followers, and if the artistic, evolutionary form of the present lecture-course is taken into consideration (a concrete, artistic example of how ontogenesis recapitulates phylogenesis; see Appendix 8), then it is likely that "Out you go!" (after the remarks about "salt processes", see Endnote **40**) corresponds to the central, critical turning-point. Ultimately, it relates to the Mystery of Golgotha, and the death in us of the first Adam (1 Cor. 15:22 & 45) by the inclusion of our death to sin in His death that slew death itself by taking the life entire *through death, cf.* Rev. 3:1 (see "To the Old Adam", a poem by O. Barfield. *The Golden Blade*. RSP. 1950). A further stage, moreover, is taken in the next lecture which deals with the challenge of transforming space, and, touching on the problems of the body, offers the T A O-exercise as "a wonderful means of making *your inner bodily nature* flexible, inwardly supple, and able to be artistically fashioned for eurythmy". This appears to refer to the body of exaltation (Paul's "spiritual body"), universally available upon our experiencing the initiatic secret of "dying to live" (the opposite of a living death). Just as "the first Adam" brought consequences for the human race by descent, so Paul's "second Adam" represents the human race by the spiritual link of corporate personality (Rom. 5:15; I Cor. 15:45-47). If, as Paul proclaims, "God was in Christ, reconciling the world unto himself, not reckoning unto them their trespasses"

(II Cor. 5:19), we may not reckon unto us our virtues, but join Paul's further confession in Gal. 2:20 (where the word "me" is unique in the New Testament). A – possibly perfect – religious explanation of sickness and restoration which corresponds to the aims of eurythmy therapy, is provided in a sermon, "The Law of Forgiveness III", in H. Scott Holland. *Creed and Character*. London. 1897. 219-232: "God's forgiveness issues out of Heaven in the shape of a Man, wearing human flesh... Christ, the Forgiveness, becomes the one forgiven Man." "Christ," Moberly sums up, "is God – not generically but identically just as He is Man – not generically but inclusively" (R.C. Moberly. *Atonement and Personality*. London. 1901. P. xx); see also Moberly. *Sorrow, Sin, and Beauty*. London. 1889, especially 102-04.

This implies that salvation is not for the individual but for the new corporate personality (*koinonia*, the common life, fellowship, participation; in Latin, the *ecclesia*, the assembly), the redeemed community, ultimately the family of mankind itself. The redeemed community is His Body, not ours, but:

> "Just as the life of Christ in the days of his ministry permeated, vitalised and integrated every cell of His earthly body, so thenceforward the existence of the Church depends similarly upon the extent to which the life of Christ is its life... [I]t is impossible to identify [the Church with] any of the existing societies... [; it] is and can only be the Communion of Saints," affirms C.E. Raven. *Lessons of the Prince of Peace*. London. 1942. 57f.

The redeemed community, or Church, as Hort defines it, "is mankind knowing and fulfilling its destiny" (1894. 219). And that is the way to unity and wholeness (John 17:23-26). These considerations on the final self-revelation of divine Love and Life (Forsyth provides a particularly helpful key-word: the power of "self-concentration") also describe the essential and specific processes in which human artistic creation and interpretive practice partake; here, for example, the "burial of melody" in the chord and its subsequent release into the life of movement; the bar line (see Endnote 35, and Appendix 4, iv); furthermore, it enables the transition from solo to choral eurythmy to occur at this half-way stage between Lectures 4 and 5. See also "the cross of knowledge" (lecture Berlin 12 Dec. 1911, Endnote 28 above) and the "spiritualising of bodily activity" in eurythmical activity (R. Steiner. *Study of Man*; see Endnote 64 below). For a further meditative exercise involving "light" and "weight", see R. Steiner. *Rosicrucianism and Modern Initiation*. Lecture, Dornach.

12 Jan. 1924. GA 233. RSP. 1982; the student may meditatively follow the initiatic, dual process of incarnation.

An "'emptiness' into which the Christ-impulse can penetrate" characterises eurythmical movements, as Owen Barfield points out (*The Golden Blade*. London 1954. 60), though to avoid misunderstandings Barfield's exclusive claim for eurythmy as a Christian art should be related to what Steiner terms the musical element and the artistic future (lecture, Torquay 20 August. 1924; see Appendix 4, ii). Barfield's masterpiece on the development of human consciousness, *Saving the Appearances* (Faber. London. 1957/ Wesleyan Univ. Press. Hannover, New Hampshire. 1988) fuses science, poetic imagination and religion in pointing a way forward for mankind in the sense of Hort's definition (see p. 284 above); Georg Kühlewind. *Becoming Aware of the Logos*. Lindisfarne Press. Great Barrington Ma. U.S.A. 1985, an original, deeply Johannine thinker, attempts something similar in the cognitive realm.

Kenotic mysticism is present in Meister Eckhart: "the Father begats me as his Son, and the same Son, without distinction" (R.B. Blakney's translation. Harper. New York and London. 1941. 181; the begetting is timeless, of course. See also Rudolf Otto. *Mysticism East and West*. Collier Books. New York. 1962. 187-206. In Russian spirituality, *kenosis* is involved in the whole divine conflict with evil, in the very act of creation, and even in the life of the Trinity. See G.P. Fedotov. *A Treasury of Russian Spirituality*. Sheed & Ward. London. 1950, reprinted; and *The Russian Religious Mind*. Harvard Univ. Press. Cambridge. Mass. 1946. Chap. iv, "Russian Kenoticism"; also N. Gorodetzky. *The Humiliated Christ in Modern Russian Thought*. AMS Press. New York. 1938/79 and forthcoming: Christ is still humbling Himself and waiting for the decision of man's freedom (171). The beautiful story of St Seraphim by Iulia de Beausobre. *Flame in the Snow*. Constable, London. 1945/Fount-Collins. Glasgow. 1979, could only have been written out of a spiritual sublimation of suffering (see her *Creative Suffering*. SLG Press. Oxford. 1984; and her remarkable autobiography *The Woman who Could not Die*. Chatto & Windus. London/Macmillan. Toronto. 1938, and Constance Babington Smith's biography, *Iulia de Beausobre*. Darton, Longman and Todd. London. 1983). Hegel worked it out philosophically: spirit, the true actuality of the world, is the kenotic process of negativity, "it is absolute distinction from itself, is pure process of becoming its other" (*Phenomenology of Spirit*. OUP 1977. English kenotic theologians include Frank Weston. *The One Christ*. Longmans, Green. London. 1907; and P.T. Forsyth. "The Divine Self-emptying" in *God the Holy Father*.

Independent Press. London. 1957, and especially *The Person and Place of Jesus Christ*. 1909/Independent Press. London. 1955: Christ's *kenosis* is followed by his *plerosis* [self-fulfilment]); see also W. Wheeler Robinson. *Redemption and Revelation*. Nisbet. London. 1942. 259 and Chapter 14. D.M. Baillie's *God was in Christ*. Faber. London. 1948/61 records objections to some forms of the theory (94-98); E.L. Mascall. *Christ, the Christian and the Church*. Longmans, Green. London. 1946, a study of the Incarnation and its consequences, contains a valuable critique of modern exponents of kenoticism. In the place of Hauer's term "subduing the personality", we may suggest substituting "kenotic experience" or rather "kenotic mastery", or simply "Love (*Agape*) at work", to describe the artist's work of self-abnegation. Or, remembering *plerosis*, is it "Self-affirmation"? "In essence," writes R.E.C. Browne, "humility is exposing oneself by a wholehearted attempt to express deep feelings and beliefs in a manner neither uncontrolled nor self-conscious" (*A Dictionary of Christian Ethics*. Ed. J. Macquarrie. SCM. London. 1967. 159); *cf*. I Cor. 2:10-16. In which case, a flood of light is also shed on *the concept of "late work"*. In this light, consider artistic/mythological portrayal and kenotic mastery in the entire careers of, for example:

(1) Shakespeare: see Ted Hughes. *Shakespeare and the Goddess of Complete Being*. Faber. London. 1993.

(2) Blake: see Thomas J. J. Altizer. *The New Apocalypse; the radical Christian Vision of William Blake*. Michigan State University Press 1967; and Kathleen Raine. *Blake and Tradition*. New York. 1968/ London. 1969.

(3) Bach: see Wilfrid Mellers. *Bach and the Dance of God*. Faber. London and Boston. 1980; and H. Kluge-Kahn. *Die verschlüsselten theologischen Aussagen in seinem Spätwerk*. Möseler. Wolfenbüttel and Zürich. 1985. E.T. by A.S. in MS); and Helga Thoene on the works for solo violin <www.helgathoene.de> which helped inspire the eurythmical interpretation of Bach's Chaconne (see "Johann Sebastian Bach & the Dance of Heaven and Earth". Anastasi [Ltd] 2003, also available (enlarged ed.) as an e-book Anastasi [Ltd] 2012 ISBN 978-1-909124-08-0.

(4) Beethoven, who kept a mystical saying framed on his desk: "I am that which is. I am all that was, that is, and that shall be." The late Piano Sonata, op. 110, sums up the essence of kenotic mastery to an exceptional degree. See Philip Barford. "The Piano Music II" in *The Beethoven Companion*. Ed. Dennis Arnold & Nigel Fortune. Faber. London. 1971/3; Anthony Hopkins. *Talking about Music*. Pan. London.

1977. Chap. XXVIII; and Wilfrid Mellers. *Beethoven and the Voice of God*. Faber. London. 1983.

(5) Wagner: see the remarkable essays by Beckh and Bock, Endnote 17 above).

(6 & 7) Carroll and MacDonald: see John Docherty. *The Literary Products of the Lewis Carroll-George MacDonald Friendship*. Edwin Mellin Press. Lewiston/ Queenston/ Lampeter. 1998.

(8) R. Steiner: see Sergei Prokofieff. *Rudolf Steiner and the Founding of the New Mysteries*. Temple Lodge. London. 1994.

Notes to Lecture 5

42 "... the concerted working of a number of persons":

Lectures 1–4 have for the most part addressed the experience of the individual. A single step is taken with the gestures for both the major and the minor triads (Lecture 1); breaths between phrases has been introduced with the bar line (Lecture 4). The first real mention of moving with others comes at the beginning of Lecture 5; the fifth step on the Eightfold Path is *Right Livelihood* or *Profession*. Rather than take matters "schematically", the lecturer says, eurythmy colleagues – actual human being – open up further artistic possibilities. We are not shown a philosophy, theology or ethics different from the systematic schools, but the great deliverance from them; the human essence is brought into play. As members of humanity in the present fifth post-Atlantean epoch, we may join to effect all transforming work that – like "the metamorphosis of salt", mentioned at the heart of the lecture-course (46) – concentrates the whole of human endeavour. The effort to "raise the physical human being" (70) is arduous, but it leads to "power to become the sons of God" (John 1:12).

"Five," Steiner says, confirming the negative symbolism, "is the number of evil" (R. Steiner. Lecture Stuttgart. 15 Sept. 1907. GA 101. Anthroposophic Press: New York 1972. 32f.). The reference in Lecture 5 to the obstinate fact of "bodily hindrances and impediments" (55) recognises the presence of sickness and evil, or Sin and Death, in their true form (in Christian initiation, "Descent into Hell"). Sin is "lawlessness" (I John 3:4): chaos, rebellion, apostasy. Steiner criticises neither the perishing human race, nor the atonal concept that proposes release; he offers practical help. Can we "love the visible world"? No other verb will suffice. The word "love" is used five times in lecture 5, to counter "hate" also used five times. Redemptive love begins with the consciousness-soul; Christian initiation speaks of "Mystic Death". Words spoken to Nathaniel (John 1:47) really mean, "You belong to the fifth grade of the Mysteries and have overcome all deception of the sensory world" – including naturalism *of* sensory sound and theoretical abstraction *about* it, that, as Luther put it, would throw the baby out with the bath-water. Expressions in Lecture 5, such as "freedom to carry out the movements beautifully" (53) and "true human dignity" (55) indicate a growing responsibility. This indicates love of the resurrection body is meant, lovingly and scientifically described in detail especially in Lecture 7. A freedom from constraints exist, it is true, as well as a freedom *for* spontaneity.

In the two texts Steiner recommends for eurythmy students (GA 277a. 143), the middle way of artistic risk aims to achieve a new naivety – music-critic Alfred Einstein calls this "a re-born innocence", re-born because fully aware. The goal of both recommended texts is integrated personalities living in civic freedom. Schiller (*Aesthetic Letters*) claims human beings exercising the "play-drive" are to become a work of art, Steiner's "ethical individualism" (*The Philosophy of Freedom*) born of vision, is neither idiosyncratic nor dictatorial but social, enabling contributions in productive living. Is not most talk of "freedom" sentimental moonshine and/or adolescent growing pains?

Precisely in Lecture 5, the T A O-exercise is given to people living and working in the fifth post-Atlantean epoch. It is one of Steiner's greatest eurythmical attempts to assist the Spirit's slow healing of mankind's congenital sickness, termed in theology "original sin". This exercise concerning "the *body* as instrument" is for "inner strength… to carry over into all your eurythmy" (54ff.) leading to inner suppleness and a deepest awareness of the point of departure for singing gesture itself in the physical body. Alignment to that centre counteracts the Fall of Man. The unified, perfected human being who "surrenders to T A O… renew[s] creation" (Marin Buber. "The teaching of the T A O". 1910. *Pointing the Way: Collected Essays*. Humanity Books. New York. 1999. 31-58. Quote, 54). As in the Grimms' fairy-tale, known variously as "Sleeping Beauty/ Little Briar Rose/ Hawthorn Blossom", Nature's enchantment can be lifted. To live in harmony with both nature and spirit is *Right Livelihood*.

43 HAUER, Josef Matthias (1883–1959), developed his twelve-note conception independently of (some claim a little before) Arnold Schönberg (1874–1951), and by a different route. His theoretical writings include *Vom Wesen des Musikalischen* (Leipzig/Vienna. 1922) ["On the nature of the musical element"]; *Deutung des Melos* (Leipzig/ Wien/ Zürich. 1923), "Interpreting Melos"; *Vom Melos zur Pauke* (Vienna. 1925), "From Melos to the drum"; and *Zwölftontechnik* (Vienna. 1925) "Twelve-note technique". Otto Stoessl wrote a novel dedicated to Hauer, depicting his life until the discovery of the 12-note system (*Sonnenmelodie. Eine Lebensgeschichte*. Stuttgart: Deutsche Verlags-Anstalt 1923). Hauer's music seems relatively harmless today, and is even treated as a

historical style. Steiner suggests there is much more to learn here. We meet the East/West tension in a particular form (see Appendices 2 and 3).

The word "atonal" historically derives from journalism; initially "*a-tonal*" meant "non-sounding". This is how Hauer uses it in his 1923-manifesto, *Interpreting Melos*, and also how Steiner comments on it in lecture 5 of *Eurythmy as Visible Singing* (GA 278) of 1924. A translation of Hauer's text is included in this volume for two reasons. (a) Steiner in indebted to Hauer for many things, especially the latter's rather devastating diagnosis of the modern situation with his references to the effects of materialism. (b) Steiner's sympathy, nevertheless, should not blind the reader to the fact that the lecturer also faces the fundamental challenge of "the atonal conception". *Steiner's answers this abstraction with the creation of music eurythmy.*

Fig. 36: J. M. Hauer.

The illuminating explanations by Hermann Pfrogner (1911-1988) on modern developments can be recommended, here especially the chapter "Arnold Schönberg und Josef Hauer" in *Die Zwölfordnung der Töne*. Amalthea-Verlag. Zürich-Leipzig-Wien. 1953. 184-232; reprinted in *Zeitwende der Musik*. Langen Müller. München-Wien. 1986. 93-135. The twelve tones were known in ancient China as the 12 liu, though only five were used (pentatonic). The twelve tonal realms are indeed spiritual; musicians who identify them with the twelve well-tempered keyboard notes/ tones prematurely "fix" the realms; they inevitably become abstract when treated indifferently. In the last resort, Pfrogner declares, atonality is not an empirical material phenomenon (connected to equal temperament) but a living, musical phenomenon. Pfrogner created the term *Tonorte*, "tonal positions, realms", for these 12 tones. This term, he claims, helps to dispel a possible confusion of thinking. Each tonal realm contains at least two notes, for example, $F^\#$ and G^b, as well as E^x. Consequently, Pfrogner prefers the term "enharmonic" for this level in the tonal system. With variable tuning all actual scales can be accommodated, with each specific answer to question of the division of the octave. The musical system, Pfrogner teaches, is three-layered: diatonic, chromatic, and enharmonic, corresponding *in the musical system* to the etheric, astral, spiritual levels of existence. Incidentally, this theorist points out, the chromatic "scale" is a misnomer – the chromatic notes added to any seven-note scale, "fill out" a given musical passage. The keyboard has certain advantages, but its easy accessibility – as Hindemith also remarks – facilitates over-hasty connections. For example, what about E# and B#, also Cb and Fb? A chromatic sequence carried out as a eurythmy exercise includes these notes. For the ascending sequence, each note is sharpened; for the descending sequence each note is flattened. The chromatic "scale" of equal semitones, consequently, is incomplete.

"Inaudible melos", as spiritual listening, points to the musical element lying between the notes. However, by divorcing audible sound and regarding it as sensory noise, the atonal conception is left high and dry as a "reaching for the stars". By concentrating exclusively on this level in the tonal system, the diatonic (7-note) level is ignored. This seems obvious, but it took an inspired music theorist to point it out! The 12-note conception cannot quite succeed; we hear, for example, a fifth as such and not seven semitones. In fact, Pfrogner says, we would never hear a fifth and the other intervals, did it not correspond to our experience, based on our make-up. (Despite the theory, it has to be admitted that much 12-note composition is basically ultra-romantic.) The scale is no mere convention; the musical system is a reflection of how we are created, as Steiner affirms, "The scale is the human being" (GA 278. Lecture 3). Since it underwent modifications over the ages, the development of the scale also presents the inner story of human consciousness. Pfrogner's researches (*Lebendige Tonwelt.* Langen Müller. München-Wien 1981) are further pursued by Heiner Ruland (*Expanding Tonal Awareness.* Rudolf Steiner Press. London. 1992).

Steiner, too, despite his sympathy for Hauer's sensitive diagnosis, also regards Hauer's "atonal concept" as abstract (*cf.* such phrases as "the astral body in repose". GA 278. Lecture 5). Steiner reports he "could never take Hauer's atonal melos as a basis for the gestures of eurythmy" (GA 278. Lecture 5). The 12-note of conception of Hauer and Schönberg attempts to abolish the diatonic level in the tonal system. The creation of the eurythmical gestures, based on the seven-note, diatonic scale (*Eurythmy: Its Birth and Development.* GA 277a. 71) given at the very beginning of music eurythmy is thus also Steiner's answer to Hauer's atonal theorizing. The gestures reveal the two tetrachords and the crucial turning-inside-out (*Umstülpung*), or threshold between them; the two zones for the major and minor modes was also given. By treating "any note as keynote" the same patterns of the major and minor scales can unfold, revealing "the character of each individual key" (GA 278. Lecture 5) of the circle of fifths. This is the practical way of carrying out the meditation given to musicians, or actually 7 x 12 meditations (strictly speaking even 7 x 15 with F$^\#$ and G^b and the overlaps on the circle of fifths of C$^\#$ and C^b) and the variations of the degrees in the minor mode (R. Steiner. Lecture, Dornach. 2 Dec. 1922, in *The Inner Nature of Music…* Anthroposophic Press, Spring Valley. 1983. GA 283). The angles of the degrees of the primal scale are experienced together with the degrees of whichever scale is practised (that is, there is not *one* D, or second degree, since D is second in C major, third in B^b major, and so on).

Eurythmists are offered endless opportunity to enter into the nuances of musical expression revealed in the eurythmical gestures. Yet for this revelation of musical experience, eurythmists cannot be simplistic: the process involves notes/ tones *and* intervals/ degrees – not notes/ tones *or* intervals/ degrees! In the far future, says Pfrogner, the twelve primes will come into their own. Since we know the mathematics, the scales of the future are already known, but we do not yet possess authentic compositions – we are citizens of the *fifth* post-Atlantean epoch, not yet of the sixth and seventh epoch. Ego-development cannot be forced – yet, Pfrogner adds, as with all development, preparation has to take place in advance.

Pfrogner points out that the atonal conception need not have happened the way it did, with its denial, or implied denial of sensory existence. Steiner stresses that eurythmy retains and expresses the full human connection – we are called not to "hate" but to "love" (both words are used 5 times in lecture 5. GA 278) the sensory world that includes the manifestations of art. Through devotion, art raises the phenomenal world to express the reality of soul and spirit experience. The physical world is never "merely" matter; the arts exist to cleanse what Blake called "the doors of perception", in order to experience "what is" – that is, the world as a whole, available to musicians and eurythmists in the circle of fifths, and described in cosmic terms in the lecture of 1922, cited above.

44 Steiner wrote of the close association of the First Goetheanum with eurythmy:

> How do the smaller forms of our double-cupola building emerge from the larger ones?… if someone were to try to dance the forms of the large structure according to eurythmical laws, the forms of the small structure would come about… the [concept of] the twelve columns and the cupola

would emerge of themselves. And I hope that something else will dance eurythmically in the building, something invisible: The Word. That will provide a good acoustic experience (R. Steiner. Lecture. Dornach. 7 Oct. 1914. Dornach. GA 277a. 65).

Building and eurythmical movement should coalesce... the audience should feel in the building itself a companion in understanding the words and musical sounds that are heard... Perhaps eurythmy could not have been found without the work on the building; before the thought of the building, [eurythmy] only existed in its first beginnings (R. Steiner, "Das Goetheanum in seinen zehn Jahren" [1924], in *Der Goetheanumgedanke*. GA 36, and Tb 635. 144-5; Tr. A.S.).

In the progression from oriental to Greek architecture, a significant descent to the earth can be seen. Gottfried Richter describes "the centre of gravity" of Chinese buildings is not inside, but outside and above "like vessels held open to receive what comes toward them from heaven and the spiritual world" (Richter 1985. 4). Greek art exhibits a harmony of above and below, of heaven and earth, inner and outer; the Greek "wants to stay 'outside', confronting, free" (76), and only the priest enters the temple. The First Goetheanum unites the music of heavenly proportions and the exercise of human freedom; the architectural relationships function together with the interaction between stage-area and audience during artistic activity (the primal movement is a lemniscate). The scene of activity has become interior, but the doors are open to humanity (see A.J. Husemann. *Das Wort Baut.* Stuttgart. 1988; Endnote **51** and Figs. 44-46, below).

45 The German text has "*der Charakter jeder einzelnen Tonart –* the character of each individual key". From the discourse, the reader might expect "chord", or "harmony". In the choral exercise an "invisible element wends its way". But does "the invisible element... of the musical element which is becoming progressively unmusical, and that eurythmy may make musical once again" (88), here still refer to chords, "the burial of melody" (Lecture 3)? Could it not rather refer to a broader experience of music as "the invisible element", and at the deepest level of listening, the "enharmonic arrangement" of twelve? This suggests that Lecture 5 contains an answer to the challenge in J.M. Hauer's *Interpreting Melos* (see Appendix 3).

46 "T A O is ever inactive, and yet there is nothing that it does not do" (Lao-tze, *TAO Te Ching* XXXVII). Steiner mentions the T A O (not strictly-speaking a "word") in the speech-eurythmy lecture-course. An accurate translation of the passage would read:

> This T A O, "t", is actually something we can imagine as presenting the most important, and just the creative thing, that which rays distinctly (*deutend strahlt*), especially from heaven to the earth. It is this important raying. We can say, this "t": significant streaming from above downwards... it has burst in upon me (R. Steiner. Lecture, Dornach. 25 June 1924. GA 279).

The I A O is a related exercise. It embodies the first indications for the sounds of speech (Munich, beginning September 1912; see GA 277a. 23). See also R. Steiner, lecture 22 April 1924 concerning the mysteries of Greece and the name Yahweh; lecture 18 Dec. 1921 (GA 209) for cosmic connections and the name IOANNES, both quoted in Hilde Raske, "I A O – the cosmic image of man", in *The Language of Colour in the First Goetheanum*. Walter Keller Verlag. Dornach. 1987. 117-22. For the T A O in connection with the laying of the foundations of both Goetheanums; see Hilde Raske in Carl Kemper. *Der Bau*. Stuttgart. 1984. 264. The "I" ("*ee*") can be felt as an inner answer to the inward-streaming of the "*t*". The TIAOAIT exercise includes the sounds of both T A O and I A O, explained in Annemarie Dubach. *The Basic Principles of Eurythmy*. Mercury Press. Spring Valley. 1990. 236ff. (NB The diagram on p. 236 contain an error, also the detail p. 239, above. The direction of the arrows should be reversed for this section of the form; similarly for one half of the harmonious-eight figures on pp. 46 & 47. The diagram on p. 107 is printed upside-down).

The T A O-impulse originates with the Sun-oracle in Atlantis, and is connected to "the Great Spirit of the World", to the creation of the human ego.

> The Atlantean did not raise himself to his God through the concepts of reason, but he felt the fundamental chord of the Godhead in nature; he as it were breathed in and breathed out his God. If he wanted to express what he heard, he summarised this in a sound similar to the Chinese T A O (R. Steiner. Lecture 16 Nov. 1905. GA 54; tr. A.S.; see also R. Steiner. *The Festivals and their Meaning*. RSP. 1981. 40).

The musical experience of the Atlanteans, of our present age, and of the future, is sketched in the lecture Stuttgart, 7 Mar. 1923 in *The Inner Nature of Music...* (see also Endnote 42 above, and Appendix 4 below).

The eminent philosopher Martin Buber (1878–1965) writes (1910):

> The perfect revelation of T A O... is not the man who goes his way without alteration, but the man who combines the maximum of change with the

purest unity… [T]he unity of the world is only the reflection of his unity; for the world is nothing alien, but one with the unified man… [T]he unified man is for the T A O-teaching the creating man; for all creating, from the point of view of this teaching, means nothing other than to call forth the T A O of the world, the T A O of things, to make the latent unity living and manifest… Only the perfect man possesses eternity. The spirit wanders through things until it blooms to eternity in the perfected man… [T]o purify one's own soul means to purify the world, to collect oneself means to be helpful, to surrender oneself to T A O means to renew creation (Martin Buber. *Pointing the Way*. Humanity Books. New York. 1999. 47. 48. 49. 50. 54).

47 See Endnote 16, end.

Notes to Lecture 6

48 ARABESQUE is a style of decoration characterised by intertwining plants and abstract curvilinear motifs. As adapted by Muslim artisans about AD 1000, it became a highly formalised, essential

Fig. 37: Wagner being given the 'thumbs down' by music critic Eduard Hanslick*

* Silhouettes by Otto Böhler, Courtesy of Nationalarchiv der Richard Wagner Stiftung, Bayreuth.

part of the decorative tradition of Islamic cultures. The earliest Western models inspiring the early Renaissance derive from ancient Roman stucci, plaster models found in Roman tombs. Compare Eduard Hanslick (1825–1904):

> The content and the actuality of music are simply and solely mobile forms in sound. In what way music can convey beautiful forms to us without the content of a specific passion, is pertinently shown by a branch of decorative design in pictorial art, the arabesque. We behold sweeping lines, here gently sloping downwards, there boldly striving upwards, meeting each other and letting go, corresponding to shorter and larger curves, apparently incommensurable, yet always well proportioned, everywhere meeting a contrasting or contributory piece, a collection of small details and yet a whole. Now imagine an arabesque, not dead and immobile, but continuously forming itself before our eyes. How the strong and fine lines follow each other, raising themselves from small curves to splendid intensity, then sinking again, expanding themselves, drawing together and in sensory change from calm and tension always surprising the eyes afresh! Here the image becomes indeed more elevated,

Fig. 38: Hanslick being cut down to size

more noble. Imagine finally this living arabesque as active outpouring of an artistic spirit, which unremittingly pours the whole abundance of its imagination into the veins of this movement; does not this impression approach very closely to the musical element? (Eduard Hanslick. *Vom Musikalisch-Schönen*. 1854. Tr. A.S.; pub. tr. Eduard Hanslick, *The Beautiful in Music*. Bobbs-Merrill. Indianapolis 1957).

This book by Hanslick (a prominent opponent of Wagner), Steiner says,

may become an historic memorial of recent times. Hanslick was a straggler, a reactionary of the fourth cultural epoch... which is now passed... We must reconcile ourselves to the fact that the musical element, as Hanslick understands it, is expanding into something altogether new.

Wagner is

a personality of great artistic gifts" who "interprets spiritual mysteries... down to the very details of his art. One day, he will have to be regarded as a representative of our fifth cultural epoch, of those who felt the urge to express that which lives in musical sound, the impetus towards the spiritual world, who looked upon a work of art as the outer language of the spiritual world (R. Steiner. *Occult History*. Lecture 29 Dec. 1910. RSP. 1982. 54-5).

For another comment on Wagner and Hanslick, see R. Steiner. *Study of Man*. Lecture 5. GA 293. RSP. 1966. 80-81. For Steiner, music is not a decorative art. It does not have a subject that exists in the outer world, as is the case with painting (R. Steiner. GA 283. 120; Am. tr. 47).

The essential content of music is the melodic element... a kind of temporal sculpture... People recognise the real origin of musical themes so little because what is expressed in the musical themes they experience in the time between falling asleep and awakening... This unconscious element operating in the dream we have to get hold of in the art of teaching, in order that we get beyond materialism through the art of teaching... Few people realise that a sentence consisting of a subject, verb and object is really a melody in the unconscious... The child writes his essay – a triad, a common chord, is experienced in our innermost depths (R. Steiner. *The Renewal of Education*. GA 301. Lecture, Dornach. 16 May 1920. Rudolf Steiner Schools Fellowship. Forest Row. 1981. The full passage is included in van der Pals. *The Human Being as Music*. Endnote 3. 48-9).

49 A reference to *"Der Geruchsorgel"*, a humorous poem by Christian Morgenstern, in the collection entitled *Palmström*. Behind the joke, however, are the facts of Ancient Saturn-evolution. See R. Steiner. *Occult/Esoteric Science*. GA 13, tr. Monges. 129-130; tr. Adams. 125; tr. Creeger. 148.

50 Attempts have been made to write music in the way described in this paragraph. For his *"Saturn Auftakt"* Josef Gunzinger used the lecture-cycle R. Steiner. *The Inner Realities of Evolution.* Berlin 31 Oct.–5 Dec. 1911. GA 132. RSP. 1953. In northern and western Europe, the previously much stronger capacity for experience of nature is reduced today by our intellectuality. The unpretentious descriptions of occult science are to awaken intense feelings: that of Ancient *Saturn* "consonant with the mood of spring"; that of Ancient *Sun* "analogous to the emotion of exultation once experienced on Midsummer night"; that of Ancient *Moon* "the mood of autumn"; that of *Earth*-evolution "a mood similar to the approaching winter-solstice and an indication is given of the central experience connected with the mood of Christmas" (R. Steiner. Lecture, Vienna. 23 March 1910, in *Macrocosm and Microcosm.* GA 131. RSP. 1968. 58-9).

Further artistic hints are given concerning R. Steiner's *Occult Science*, Chapter 4:

> An architectural mood underlies the description of the Saturn evolution, a sculptural mood... the Sun, and a pictorial mood... the Moon... To submerge the ego in the astral body in the right way is to enter into the divine world, and this is the passage through initiation. A picture of this is given to us in the processes we perceive in musical compositions (R. Steiner. Lecture, Dornach. 30 Dec. 1914. GA 275. 53-7).

Christoph Peter, "*Die Sprache der Musik...*", demonstrates some initiatic details in Mozart's musical language.

51 Steiner uses the image of a cake-mould and cake, to point to what is important about the Goetheanum:

> What you go into when you enter the building, what you stand within and cannot see but can only feel – that is the thing that matters... within the walls will be the feeling and thoughts of the people who are in the building. These will develop aright if those who are in the building turn their eyes to its boundary, feel the forms and then fill these forms with forms of thought. What is inside the building will be like the cake, and what we build is the mould that holds and shapes the cake. And the mould has to be of such a kind that it leads to the development of right thoughts and right feelings... In the art of olden times, the essential thing was what is outside in space; but in the new art... the essential thing cannot be created by the artist at all, it is what is within (R. Steiner. Lecture, Dornach. 21 Nov. 1914, in *The Balance in the World and Man.* 30f.).

The ultimate dwelling is the Temple; the Psalmist aspires to make the Temple his home. Ps. 24 declares that he may stand in the temple "who has clean hands and a pure heart"; vv. 1-6 contain all three images of the passage in Lecture 6: "face", "waters" and "his holy place", or the house of the Lord. Early in his gospel, John associates this Temple with "the temple of his body" (Jn. 2:21) in and through which the Mystery of Golgotha was accomplished. The sixth "Word from the Cross" is "It is finished" (Jn. 19:30), that is, "accomplished/ completed/ fulfilled", signifying total victory. The creator acted to create man; it needed His suffering to re-create man (*cf.* Heb. 3:6; Matt. 7:24-27; II Cor. 5:1-4; Eph. 2:21-22).

52 Here, with a concrete example of painting a picture of "a house", a reference to the sixth step on the Eightfold Path (see Endnote 2) is indicated: *Right Effort* or *Striving*. The activity of drawing – no doubt justified as a technical explanation of visual subjects – from the hands of a master will even supersede a technical category. Steiner's drastic language, taken in the context of his examples, suggests that the drawn line is an *artistic* lie. The sixth Beatitude concerns ultimate seeing (Matt. 5:8). Pursuing the theme, we note that Steiner, scrupulous in his use of terminology, speaks of "*Kunsterkenntnis*—knowledge/ appreciation of art", never (to my knowledge) "theory". *For the productive artist there is no division between theory and practice.* There is "no such thing as drawing", neither an acoustic science to interest the artist *qua* artist (Lecture 8), nor, consequently, in music is there a "music theory". Of course, the subject presents an educational challenge; rudiments need to be explained – but how? The Waldorf-School class-teacher, too, is to introduce the alphabet, mathematics, and indeed *all* subjects with as much imagination as he can summon. Explanations and attempts at musical appreciation exist which are extremely helpful, inasmuch as appeal is made to musical processes and experience. Did not the author of *The Philosophy of Freedom*, mentioning the principles of musical composition, claim: "All true philosophers were *artists in the realm of concepts (Begriffskünstler)*" (Foreword to 1894 ed. rev. Emphases original). Where would we be without sympathetic and inspiring musicians and musicologists—indeed, of Steiner's own examples in the lecture-courses on eurythmy?

Meditative consciousness ("awake dreaming") is described in Lecture 6, with the suggestion of putting *Occult/Esoteric Science—an Outline* (GA 13) into music. This "outline" summarises the mind of the Creator-Logos. Steiner's suggestion, with its far-reaching relationship between art, anthroposophy and the Christ-Impulse, is directly made to creative artists. The Goetheanum revealed the human, cosmic laws, hence it "was musical, it was eurythmical"; it was a "House of the Word". The First Goetheanum was as the cake-mould is to the cake; the cake being "the right feelings and right thoughts" of those within the building (see Endnote 51). The sixth degree of Christian initiation is "Entombment", or "Burial": becoming united to the earth. The earth becoming a new Sun: Resurrection.

53 "*Fisches Nachtgesang*" ("Fish's Night-Song') from Christian Morgenstern's *Galgenliedern*. (Bilingual ed. *The Gallows Songs*. Univ. of California Press. 1992.)

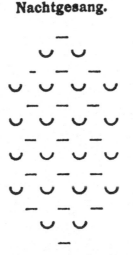

**Fisches
Nachtgesang.**

Christian Morgenstern, Phonetic poem
Fig. 39:

Notes to Lecture 7

54 For a detailed discussion of the important physiological details in this lecture, see Armin Husemann. *The Harmony of the Human Body*. Floris Books. Edinburgh. 1994, Part 4, especially 189-93. Here, too, we find an explanation of *"beim auftreten"*, rendered "with the first step", and the crucial "transition" (*Übergang*, or *Umstülpung*: a "turning-inside-out") between the musical construction of the organism and music translated into movement. From feet to head the body corresponds to the musical progression of prime to octave. In the region of the throat (seventh), besides the construction of the head, two other octaves present themselves: (i) the octave of speech as such, and (ii) the whole scale once more presented in the whole construction of shoulder-girdle, arm and hand. The eurythmical point of departure for the musical prime, consequently, is as it were already raised an "octave" above the organic basis, that is, already working towards allowing the resurrection body to be glimpsed. Dr Husemann presents an accessible way to justify eurythmical art.

55 *ANSATZ*: This is the normal German word for the place where musical sound is initiated: in England "embouchure" is usually employed by wind players, and "attack" is another term; string players "articulate" with their bows. The translation has used "point of departure" as the nearest English equivalent in the context of eurythmy. Steiner speaks of the collar-bone as the crystallisation of the musical element in the human instrument. In the same year that these lectures were given, Steiner spoke in some detail of how the human skeleton is born out of the cosmic, astral world. The musical point of departure for the singing movement is the point between the shoulder-blades – doctors suggest the sixth thoracic vertebra, between the shoulder-blades. This fact completes what is said in the present lecture. Cosmic rhythm is *incorporated* in the human astral nature that has formed the bodily instrument. The artist awakens to the cosmic Word, which "becomes the human ego-organisation" that plays upon this instrument (GA 308; see 2 below, also van der Pals. 17). Musical sound originates in the inner world ("centre"; see Notebook. 2); the spiritual ocean of music is perceived as the resounding backspace (see Endnote 65). Below are five important passages taken from other lectures of 1924:

1. If you consider that part of the human organism beginning from the shoulder-blades and proceeding to the arms, this is a result of the prime, the keynote, living in the human being; coming to the second, this lies in the upper arm. The facts are shown in eurythmy (R. Steiner. *The Roots of Education*. Lecture. Bern. 15 April 1924. GA 309. RSP. 1982).

2. The astral body is not natural history, natural science or physics; it is music. So true is this that it is possible to trace how the music of the astral body in its formative activity builds up and fashions the human organism. From here formative activity streams out, first into the tonic of the scale; flowing onwards into the second, it builds the upper arm, into the third the lower arm. When we come to the third we have the difference between the major and the minor and we find two bones in the lower arm, not only one. The radius and ulna represent the minor and the major... (R. Steiner. *The Essentials of Education*. Lecture, Stuttgart. 10 April 1924 a.m. GA 308. RSP. 1968).

3. Approaching from within, Steiner describes the shoulder-blades as "the octave... We can observe this, how the octave proceeds backwards from the shoulder-blades and along the bones [of the arm], and that the formation of the bones in the arms cannot be understood from the aspect of mechanical dynamics, but they can when you approach with a musical understanding. Here we find the prime from the shoulder-blades as far as the point of departure of the bones of the upper arm..." (R. Steiner. *Pastoral Medicine*. Lecture Dornach. 9 Sept. 1924. GA 318. Tr. A.S.; the pub. version. AP. 1987. 15).

4. The prime is situated behind at the point of departure on the collar-bone and shoulder-blade. It shoots out of the astral body into form. The second, major and minor thirds then follow... (R. Steiner. "Faculty Meeting at the Eurythmeum, Stuttgart, 30 April 1924". GA 277a. 140).

5. That which is situated at the back of the human being, where the shoulder-blades come together, beginning from here and flowing from here in a formative capacity into the whole human being, are those human forms which are fashioned out of the prime (quoted by Albert Steffen in "The human being as music", in A. Steffen, *Dante und die Gegenwart* ["Dante and the present day". Dornach. 59]).

Werner Barfod studies the three points of departure for eurythmy: (i) the "spiritual point of departure" of light, behind and above the head, as the source for the intention of eurythmical movement (predominant for speech-eurythmy); (ii) the "etheric point of departure" in the region of the solar plexus gives the basis for eurythmical movement ("allowing the movement to appear out of the spatial element and into the flow of time"); and (iii) the "point of departure of the soul" between the shoulder-blades at the level of the heart (for both speech-eurythmy and music-eurythmy, but predominant for music-eurythmy). See Werner Barfod. *Ich denke die Rede...* ("I think speech..."). Verlag am Goetheanum. Dornach 1993. See further, Appendix 7, iii; and Alan Stott. "The Point of Departure" in RB 27. Dornach. January 1997. 26-29.

56 The stenographic report (which was unrevised by the lecturer) has *Speiche* ("radius"), and this was reproduced in the first German edition. The discussion on p. 103 and the drawing suggest it must be *Elle* ("ulna"). The same applies to p. 108, lines 2 & 3 from below, where the first edition similarly exchanged *Speiche* and *Elle*. (Further details can be found in Husemann. 1994.) Some people question the correctness of the exchange. An entry from the Notebook 494, corrected in Steiner's hand (25) suggests that the correction to the text is indeed justified.

57 In an introduction to a performance during the Christmas Conference (28 Dec. 1923), Steiner said:

> If you do eurythmy to singing, you merely illustrate the musical content of the song. But this is decidedly inartistic. If people want to place eurythmy next to singing – or if you like, the singing accompanied by an instrument –, it will have to be something quite different from both our musical and speech-eurythmy today... Music-eurythmy is singing in movement, is already a singing – let's say, to the one or other instrument, or even the orchestra – and does not require that we sing twice! That is the point (R. Steiner, in GA 277. 417, pub. tr. in R. Steiner. *An Introduction to Eurythmy.* AP. 1988. 92f.; the circumstances are told in Zuccoli. 33).

Speaking to the actors, Steiner explains:

> Eurythmy gives what cannot come to expression in music alone or in recitation alone; it takes them further, continues them. No one could feel it to be true eurythmy if done to the accompaniment of singing. In singing, music has flowed over into speech. The eurythmy would merely disturb the singing, and the singing the eurythmy. Eurythmy can be accompanied by recitation, which itself has nothing to do with bodily movement; for in recitation gesture has become inward. Eurythmy can also be accompanied by instrumental music. But not by singing, if one wants to let eurythmy work in a way that corresponds with its true ideal (R. Steiner. Lecture, Dornach. 15 Sept. 1924, *Speech and Drama.* GA 282. RSP. 1960. 252f.).

The exception is recorded in Lecture 5: it seems (unless we assume a slip here) that it is permissible to sing the T A O, as well as to declaim the speech sounds. Research into the question of doing eurythmy to someone-else's singing, would concern the nature of both language and music, and the composer's intention with the chosen art-form. Steiner insists on the polarity of spirit-world and sense-world, and on observing a clear threshold between them. The musical element is a "flowing spirit-ocean"; the speech-element is "the shoreline between water and earth"; and eurythmy reveals the spiritual element in the outer world. Steiner often points to the "hidden eurythmy" in the art of speech. This art concentrates on "the musical content, not the prose content" of meaning.

We can initially say that a composer sets the words of the poet, creating out of his aural imagination. The content of the song needs no further "illustrating"; the art of the song is complete. "Certainly," Steiner adds, "the arts can combine" – no doubt, for instance, in the music-drama, and in the art of song – but "the point is to be quite clear that music-eurythmy is singing in movement." In other words, Steiner did not aim for a *Gesamtkunstwerk* ("unified work of art") by combining existing arts, but by creating a new art. Instrumental music is free from the element of speech, yet instruments in their specialised form (strings, woodwind, brass and keyboard instruments) all "sing"; they all possess a "voice". The instrumentalist's soul is releasing the music of the listener's "Apollo's lyre" (see R. Steiner, in van der Pals, Endnote 8). The eurythmist's concern is with "inaudible experience" (see Endnote 24), that is, the musical content (melos, the intervals, and so on). Eurythmy does not "illustrate". It portrays the "weaving spiritual ocean" that the composer has managed to evoke in his score, which is a

> true reflection of the spiritual world… the soul's home… Unconsciously the musician has received the musical prototype from the spiritual world, which he then transposes into physical sounds (R. Steiner. Lecture, Cologne. 3 Dec. 1906. GA 283).

58 The direction culminating in the scientific views of Helmholz and Riemann at the end of the nineteenth century, and Hauer's expositions on vibrations of sound, and so on, is no doubt referred to here.

59 The eurythmy figures were made from sketches by Steiner for the speech sounds, with the designations "movement, feeling, character":
Eurythmy
1. Movement which carries qualities of soul – imagination (*Vorstellung*);
2. Feeling – perceived on the outer world – feeling;
3. Character – it is revealed from within outwards – will; [these things are] that which comes into consideration in an art, which you can

express through its means (R. Steiner. Notebook entry. Dornach. 4 August 1922. GA 277. 284).

The figures were first shown at the education conference at Oxford in 1922 (see R. Steiner. *The Spiritual Ground of Education.* Garber Communications, Inc. New York 1989. Lecture 8. 116ff.). There are only two figures for musical sounds: the major and the minor triads, or rather cadences (see pp. 36-7). Here the designations are "melos, rhythm, beat" for the dress (movement), veil (feeling) and muscular tension (character). On the reverse of the figure for the major triad is written C E G, and the musical notation. On the reverse of the minor figure C A♭ F is written. Steiner's Notebook entry (see p. 197) reads: "It says actually C E G or / C A F / the major or minor chord"; and again, though not in connection with the triad, "the minor third A flat" in NB 494. 179). U.-I. Gillert questions whether the original designation was in fact a mistake; it raises the question about Steiner's descriptions of the ascending third and descending third. Frau Gillert suggests that after studying Lecture 4, eurythmists will have to decide for themselves individually what he really meant. M. Proskauer suggests that the description C A♭ F is "a concession to the usual way of describing it", and that our feeling for the ascending and descending melodic movement explains the respective gestures for the major or the minor third (RB 22. Dornach January 1992; tr. *EA Newsletter.* Aberdeen. Summer 1994). The gestures for what we term the "major third" seem to apply to *both* ascending thirds, and the gesture for the "minor third" for *both* descending thirds. No doubt here as elsewhere "dogmatism" should be avoided, and "artistic feeling" be followed in the individual case (see also Endnotes 9 and 14).

60 The additional subjects discussed in the Faculty Meeting held in the Eurythmeum, Stuttgart, 30 April 1924 are:
1. prosody, poetics, which then leads over into aesthetics;
2. beat, harmony and rhythm;
3. geometry;
4. anthropology

["Whole science of man; physiological & psychological science of man; study of man as an animal." *Concise Oxford Dictionary.* Oxford. 1964];
5. singing and recitation;
6. basic education;
7. basic anthroposophy (from: R. Steiner. GA 277a. 141).

61 The seventh step on the Eightfold Path (see Endnote **2**) *Right Mindfulness*, summed up as *Right Memory* or *Remembrance*—learn as much as possible from life, in its wholeness—is pointed to with the phrase "esoteric realm" in connection with instrumental awakening of the eurythmist. "Seven is the number of perfection," Steiner confirms. *Occult Signs and Symbols*. Lecture, Stuttgart. 15 Sept. 1907. GA 101. 43. Eurythmy can claim to be sacramental, in the sense Steiner already outlines in his earliest writings and to which he remained true throughout his life.

> *Becoming aware of the idea within reality is the true communion of the human being.* Thinking in relationship to ideas signifies the same as the eye for light, the ear for sound. *It is an organ of perception.* (R. Steiner. Goethean Science. GA 1. Mercury Press. Spring Valley. New York. 1988. 91. Emphases original.)

This perceptive, active thinking is eurythmy: firstly, speaking of the instrument – "intuitive vision" directed to the limbs is a thinking with the whole body; and secondly as an expressive art – "the ear for sound", both speech sound and musical sound. Living sound itself expresses the human being; it is portrayed in eurythmy by the whole human being. Inner life and manifestation, reflection and action are unified; intention and motive coincide. When this superseding of dualism occurs, action is at once moral (meaningful) and spontaneous, and consequently free.

Notes to Lecture 8

62 *Tonhöhe, Tondauer, Tonstärke, Tempowecksel*: the translation uses the terms in use today. These terms are musical designations, as distinct from acoustic phenomena. *Cf.,* "Acoustics has no significance, except for physics" and "Acoustics only exists for [physical] sounds (*Klänge*); a science of acoustics for musical sounds (*Töne*) does not exist" (R. Steiner, lectures Stuttgart. 8 & 7 Mar. 1923. GA 283. 142 & 120. The pub. tr. of the second quotation is unclear). This distinction probably prompted Pfrogner to analyse musical sound into the categories *Tonkern* and *Klanghülle* (*Zeitwende*. 212). Later he added a third category, *Schallhülle* (*Lebendige Tonwelt*. 194). These refer to the spirit, soul and body of musical sound, and could be rendered: (i) musical essence; (ii) mantle of sound (or resonance); (iii) acoustic reverberation. The first category lives in the domain of inner listening and is clearly the musical material for eurythmy (in Lecture 3 Steiner distinguishes the spiritual element between the notes from the sensory manifestation of the notes themselves). For Pfrogner, there is in the world today (i) an art of *music*, (ii) an art of *sound*, and (iii) a bare-faced art of *noise*. These categories cut right across the conventional ones (classic, pop, *etc.*), which do not adequately explain the musical phenomena of the twentieth century at the level that Pfrogner's categories do, expanding on Hauer's and Steiner's thought. Music, once a threefold being, has been torn apart into three directions in the twentieth century: atonality, tonality and electronics (H. Pfrogner. "Der zerrissene Orpheus", in *Zeitwende*). One of the tasks of eurythmy is to help the art of music to develop. To do so demands an understanding of the musical material, and a perception whether that material has left the musical realm of melos, thereby relinquishing the possibility of being revealed in free and expressive artistic movement.

63 The lecture-course on speech-eurythmy was held 24 June–12 July 1924 in Dornach; Rudolf Steiner. *Eurythmy as Visible Speech*. Anastasi. 2005. Steiner's death in 1925 prevented any further courses in speech-eurythmy and music-eurythmy from being held.

The rather wistful note in the phrase "perhaps an attempted beginning", ultimately demands a recognition of the true beginning, or source. It has been observed that Steiner's earlier utterances (just prior the birth of eurythmy) on the re-appearance of Christ in the twentieth century passed over into what he had to say about eurythmy (see Michael

Debus, "The Being of Eurythmy" in RB 55, Michaelmas 2011, 6–12, and subsequent discission RB 56, Easter 2012). This recognition inevitably connects to the Mystery of Golgotha. This source is also hidden in the "Meditation for Eurythmists" (given in *Eurythmy as Visible Speech*. GA 279. Lecture 14. 152f.), which speaks of "activity" and "life" in the "the thinking of my head", "the word of my feet" and "the singing of my hands" (the entire limb is no doubt implied; Steiner used some Austrian expressions like "hand" = arm; "foot" = leg). These three activities are related to three manifestations, "the heavenly power of light", "the earthly forces of weight" and "the forming might of the air". Heaven, earth, and the human being are linked in a comprehensive, reciprocal, sacramental activity. Here the Great Triad of Far-Eastern tradition is renewed, too.

Yet are the heart and the lungs and their rhythmic activities omitted, or are they somehow *present in the formulations*? Do we not, in fact, breathe the air of the Resurrection appearances? Everything in this Meditation is related to creative activity, manifesting through the "I" in human movement. It starts from the unity of personality (1 line), passes through polarity (2 lines) to a trinity of activities in communion with the world in two series of dual expressions (3 x 3 lines), and ends with self and world in a purified, creative harmony that expresses participation in the fellowship of the three-in-one (2 lines). (See A. Stott. "The Meditation for Eurythmists" in RB 30. Dornach. Easter 1999.)

NB *wie* (l. 13) should be translated "how" (not "so"). The German construction may not be immediately understandable when retained in English: the pronoun *es* ("it") of ll. 4, 7 and 10 stands for the nominative phrase making up the line that follows (for example, ll. 4-5 could be expressed more prosaically: "the heavy weight of earth tells me..."). The given construction in German, on the other hand, does allow more subtle and rhythmic meanings to be felt. The three "tells me" of the verse culminate in the concluding "How the world in the human being..."

> *Ich suche im Innern*
> *Der schaffenden Kräfte Wirken,*
> *Der schaffenden Mächte Leben.*
> *Es sagt mir*
> *Der Erde Schweremacht*
> *Durch meiner Füße Wort,*
> *Es sagt mir*
> *Der Lüfte Formgewalt*
> *Durch meiner Hände Singen,*

Es sagt mir
Des Himmels Lichteskraft
Durch meines Hauptes Sinnen,
Wie die Welt im Menschen
                    Spricht, singt, sinnt.

I seek within [myself]
the activity of creative powers,
the life of creative forces.
The earthly force of weight
speaks to me
through the word of my feet;
the forming might of the air
speaks to me
through the singing of my hands;
the power of heavenly light
speaks to me
through the thinking of my head,
how the world in the human being
                    speaks, sings, thinks.

(tr. A.S.)

64 Steiner's comments about the "intellectual" physicist are initially directed against the materialistic conceptions of acoustics of his – and our own – day taking over in artistic matters. The censure bears on the relationship of scientific enquiry and the endeavours of the artist.

A different science of sound altogether, that of *harmonic*, or *harmonical research*, is based on measure and value. This discipline is concerned with restoring ancient wisdom (particularly Pythagorean), and it involves philosophical mysticism and metaphysics. The Lambda, developed into the Lamboda, provides the key. Introductions to harmonical theory include Rudolf Haase. "Harmonics and Sacred Tradition, in *Cosmic Music*. Joscelyn Godwin (ed.). Inner Traditions. Rochester, Vermont. 1989; and Hans Kayser. *Akroasis: the Theory of World Harmonics*. Plowshare Press. Boston, Mass. 1970. Both books contain booklists. See especially, Hans Kayser. *Orphikon*. Schwabe & Co. Basel/ Stuttgart. 1973. Hindemith was interested in Kayser's researches.

Students of both anthroposophy and harmonics, or harmonical theory might mutually learn much; the intention towards renewal is a shared aim. A mutual danger of jumping to premature and facile conclusions may also exist. In the present context, we may suggest that art (beauty) is to be developed and deepened, not invaded, by science (truth). Steiner insists on the supersensory nature of art and of musical sound: "The musical element is that which you do not hear! That which you hear is never musical" (Lecture 3; cf., Pfrogner's analysis of musical sound, Endnote 61). Steiner's artistic definition is also scientifically accurate. Moreover, it includes the listener. In simple terms, eurythmy is *not* simple "visible listening" (a moving to that which is heard); it does, though, demand enhanced activity from all those concerned, including the audience. In one of his important characterisations of eurythmy, Steiner mentions pro-*active* listening.

> The "I" always participates in eurythmy, and what eurythmy puts before us through the physical body is nothing other than listening made visible. You always do eurythmy when you listen, and when you actually perform eurythmy you are just making visible what remains invisible when you listen. The manifestation of the activity of the listening human being is, in fact, eurythmy. It is not something arbitrary, but rather the revelation of the activity of the listening human being... People cannot listen and will become increasingly less able to do so in our age, unless the power of [pro-active] listening can be re-awakened by eurythmy (R. Steiner. 25 Aug. 1919. *Practical Advice to Teachers*. AP. 2000. 57).

The challenge is highlighted in the contrast of the [physical] overtone chord, and the [etheric] melody in the single note (see Endnote 22). "The Michael-age demands that that which lives in human beings alone... in time, in the supersensory, [be carried] once more into space. Spatial knowledge has to be spiritualised" (R. Steiner. Lecture, Dornach. 17 June 1914. GA 219. AP 1963; the paragraph is quoted in van der Pals. Endnote 42). It is not scientific method, but the rampant materialistic conception of musical sound that challenges every individual artist and music-lover today. The Christian position – more accurately, movement and life! – has been stated; it is the principle of self-knowledge – see I, Introduction, Endnote 20; Endnote 23, above; and compare Moberly's classic chapter on the relation of inward and outward: "The real meaning of bodily life is its spiritual meaning, and conversely man's spiritual being has no evidence, no expression, no method other than the body; in so much that, if he is not spiritual in and through the body, he cannot be spiritual at all" (R.C. Moberly. *Ministerial Priesthood*. SPCK. London. 1969. 39f.).

65 The verb used here is *denken*; here the English continuous tense gives the correct translation. Compare: "Such elementary movements... must become second nature so it is no longer necessary to think about them, any more than it is necessary to think about the letters of a word that is spoken" (Lecture 2). For Steiner, thinking is never intellectual speculation, but spiritual activity. "All true philosophers were *artists in the realm of concepts*" (R. Steiner. *The Philosophy*. Foreword to first edition 1894. Emphases original). Steiner's written works, including *The Philosophy*, are to be read "like musical scores" (see Intro. Endnote 6, and *cf.* Lecture 6 on conscious dreaming). "If we turn towards thinking in its essence, we find in it both feeling and will, and these in the depths of their reality," Steiner adds (in the Author's additions, 1918 to Chapter 8 of *The Philosophy*).

The art of eurythmy is not an activity of the head that concentrates on meanings of words and illustration of music. *Music-eurythmy* in particular essentially releases the activity of the central, chest region, that is the rhythmic system, seat of the feeling soul. *Speech-eurythmy* portrays the poetic imagination at work, which perception reveals the spirit in nature:

> The musical element relates to human feeling; the poetic element relates to human imagination (*Vorstellung*)... The day before yesterday I said eurythmy is sculpture in movement, and today I will add that the musical element lives completely within the human being. The musical element is the artistic fashioning of the world of feeling (a flowing sea of spirit). The poetic element lives more towards the periphery of the human being. This is the fashioning of the world of imagination through speech (on the shoreline between water and earth). Beyond the world of imagination, going beyond yourself, you live in perception. Whatever is not sensory in perception, but spiritually experienced (the spirit in outer nature), is portrayed in eurythmy (made present on the human being). For this reason, by perceiving the movement of the eurythmist, you actually sense (*wittern* – "perceive, sniff") nature everywhere. When you sense nature everywhere (the spirit in nature), you perceive eurythmy in the right way... Nature is intensively and qualitatively rich, not merely extensively and quantitatively rich (R. Steiner. Introduction. Dornach 28 Dec. 1923. GA 277. 414f.; phrases in brackets are inserted from his previous paragraph).

This description of consciousness in the eurythmist and in nature recalls the classical statement of the doctrine of non-duality *advaita*:

> Where there is duality, one smells another, one sees another, one hears another, one speaks to another, one perceives another, one knows

another, but when everything has become the Self, by what and whom should one smell and see and hear and speak to and perceive and know another? By what should one know that by which all this is known? How should one know the knower? (*Brihadaranyaka Upanishad* 2: 4: 13.).

For Hindu tradition, the knowledge of Self is the ultimate form of knowledge. In this experience, the mind knows itself intuitively; the knower, the known and the act of knowing are one. This is also the goal reached by western philosophy, the development of which Steiner chose to expound in his *Riddles of Philosophy*. GA 18. AP. 1973. Steiner's own philosophical contribution links to the monistic philosophy that culminates in Hegel, whilst at the same time it makes explicit that of Goethe. In this monistic philosophy, both east and west meet.

Regarded as an art of movement, eurythmy stands midway in a triad with mime and the dance. Today, just as you sit "in a railway carriage", Steiner explains, so

> your soul sits in your head, which calmly allows itself to be carried forwards by the limbs… The head brings to rest in you what the limbs perform in the world by way of movement… All true dancing has arisen from imitating in the limbs the movement carried out by the planets, by other heavenly bodies or by the earth itself… *A reflecting back of the world from within outwards – such is the nature of the musical arts…* With respect to our head we are descended from the animal world. There is no denying it – the head is only a further evolved animal… Your head is not merely the lazy-bones on your shoulders, it is that which would really like to maintain you in animality… *Eurythmy, external activity permeated with purpose, is a spiritualising of bodily activity,* and the arousing of interest in your teaching (provided it is genuine) is literally a bringing of life and blood into the work of the intellect (R. Steiner. *Study of Man.* GA 293. Lectures 10 & 12. RSP. 1966. 144, 145, 146, 162 & 181; Am. tr. *The Foundations of Human Experience.* AP. 1996).

Armin Husemann (1993. Germ. 3rd ed. 264-65) speaks of the metamorphosis of the chewing function of the teeth into sense-perception and analytical thinking. His example of an overcoming of this animal inheritance is a "plastic-pictorial thinking" shown by Goethe with his discovery of the archetypal plant. This is Michaelic thinking, for Michael "is able to unfold his activity in the human being who lays hold of and utilizes thoughts according to their living, cosmic origin".

> [Gradually we see] the cosmic sun-nature, lost through Lucifer, rises in our feeling and will, how it rises again through Christ in our feeling and will, and how from there it can take hold of our intellect. That is the way all spiritual understanding of the world has to take in the future…

Gradually the Mystery of Golgotha in its depths finds its way into the whole course of humanity's evolution,… [it] will fill out the human being with an inner, a second human being (R. Steiner. Lecture Dornach. 1 Aug. 1915. GA 162). *Cf.* "It is from feeling and the experience of the impulse towards action that all eurythmy has to proceed" (R. Steiner. GA 278, Lecture 7).

When thinking and action unite in artistic feeling, living thinking can result:

Music is nothing other than the laws of pure thinking, nevertheless transferred to the level of pure artistic feeling. The ego accomplishes this thinking while not fully conscious, but is submerged in the unconsciousness of the astral body (R. Steiner. GA 275. 37)… In order to become music, thinking has to be finished, as does all thought-content that has to be led over into pure thinking. But the leading over of one thought-form to another as continuous stream of thinking or sequence of thinking is quite possible for music… The intellect must die beforehand and be resurrected as pure thinking, in order itself to become music, or even to lay hold of music (H. Ruland. "Musik und Denken" in *Resonanz* 9, Dürnau. 1989. Tr. A.S.).

Steiner describes the polarity between "the universe from within – light; from without – thoughts. The head from within – thoughts; from outside – light" in a lecture on "Thought and Will as Light and Darkness", Dornach 5 Dec. 1920, in R. Steiner. *Colour*. RSP. 1992. For comments on *sinnen*, "thinking", of the eurythmy meditation (NB not "*denken*"), see R. Savoldelli, "Eurythmy as a spiritual-scientific impulse" in *EA Newsletter*. Summer 1996; original in *Was in der Anthroposophischen Gesellschaft Vorgeht*. No. 43. Dornach. 24 Oct. 1993). See also Savoldelli. *Bedingungen eurythmischer Kultur*. Stuttgart. 1989.

66 Put briefly, *Ethos* means an affirmed, moral attitude and way of thinking, which is as much as to say: light-filled and spiritual. *Pathos* means being taken hold of by suffering, which is as much as to say: passionate and sensual (see Hauer. *Interpreting Melos*. "Melos culture").

Pitch is mentioned in Lectures 3 & 5 (66 & 88). Here in Lecture 8, the subject is developed a stage further: pitch is "entirely inward… the soul is purely concerned with itself". Steiner introduces pitch through the feeling element, which on the one hand rises up to the head, and on the other hand falls down to the limbs. It rises to the intellect, yet remains feeling; with the astral body and "I", it falls into the physical body.

When melos rises into the spiritual element, soul and "I" are identified with the light of the circumference, bringing about *ethos*.

Melos, falling into the physical and becoming, condenses into warmth, brings about *pathos*. Ethos fills the soul with light, pathos with warmth and suffering. For Beethoven, melos becomes the striving into the light and the wrestling with his own darkness, which he has to overcome—a conflict in life's struggle with the problems met in our earthly, material existence (*cf.*, "Thy heavens has me by the hair, Thy earth drags me into hell ..." Clemens Brentano. "Nachklänge Beethovenscher Musik" (2). *The Penguin Book of German Verse*. 1959. 306). In the inner constitution of music (a stage where the soul identifies even more strongly with the musical categories), ethos – pathos is precisely the wrestling for the middle. (Based on explanations kindly supplied by Werner Barfod.)

The middle way, termed T A O in the Far East, is created out of the very tensions of polar opposites. The Meditation for Eurythmists speaks of "activity" and "life" of the creative process. On the level of earthly incarnation, we meet the problems of suffering, evil, illusion, love, the divine, and so on: Steiner mentions "God" and "the Devil" in connection with "the soul" (116). In his last *Piano Sonata*, op. 111, Beethoven portrays the very essence of the creative process. The two poles inspiring sonata form itself are revealed in the work's two contrasting movements; amongst other things, *pathos* and *ethos* are strongly evident. The final pages include a portrayal of initiation itself, including a consummation (see R. Kolben. "Three, four, seven: Beethoven's use of number". Rudolf Steiner Lib. London). Phillips Brooks clearly describes the overcoming of opposites through creation, and the alternative:

> *Compromise* leaves out the essence and strength of two truths and then makes a barren union of the colourless remainders. *Comprehension* unites the spiritual substance of both with a larger truth than either, and then lets the new unity create its new form with perfect freedom (Phillips Brooks. *The Battle of Life*. Dutton. New York. 1893. 281; see also Appendix 1, below).

67 Are "God" and "Devil" here theological or moral terms? The context suggests a psychological meaning of personal energies, which would be recognised as such by artists like Liszt, Berlioz, Goethe and Blake (*cf.*, Brentano's poem, Endnote 66 above). "Without Contraries is no progression. Attraction and Repulsion, Reason and Energy, Love and Hate, are necessary to Human existence." William Blake. *The Marriage of Heaven and Hell* (1790–93). Blake's "Lamb" and "Tiger" from *Songs of Innocence and Experience* (1789-94) are justly famous poems. In *The Secret of the Golden Flower* (E.T. by Cary F. Baynes. RKP. London.

1962), Richard Wilhelm explains the polarity of human nature (*hsing*) and consciousness (*hui*) – the yang pole of intensity – and life (*ming*) – the yin pole of extensity. He also speaks the Chinese concepts of the Creative and the Receptive (*Chien* and *Kun*) that originate in the *I Ching*, symbolised by heaven and earth. (*Cf.*, the Johannine "light" and "life". John 1:4.)

See René Guénon. *Symbolism of the Cross*. Chapters 3 and 4, on the vertical axis, and compare Steiner: "The Above and Below is the line from infinity to infinity or from the conscious to the unconscious... the mysterious relation to the spiritual and material worlds... at the same time a participation in cosmic intelligence" (R. Steiner. Lectures, Dornach. 20-21 Sept. 1918. GA 184. Typescript tr. Z.362. R. St. Lib. London). "Satan and God are the extremes, between which stands man. The devil is the negating, God the creating power," said Novalis (*Pollen and Fragments*, New Fragments No. 291, tr. Arthur Versluis. Phanes Press. Grand Rapids. 1988).

Emil Bock speaks of the autumn festival of Michaelmas:

> The Archangel, holding the Scales, intervenes between Virgo and Scorpio, between the Woman and the Dragon. The Michael power of balance prevails in the battle of angels and demons. A conscious crossing of the threshold of autumn every year makes us partakers of the drama which the Apocalypse depicts in the twelfth Chapter (Emil Bock. *The Apocalpyse*. Floris Books. Edinburgh. 1986. 101-2).

68 The terms for note values in the lecture are consistent and follow Notebook 494 (33): *halben Noten* ("half-notes"/ minims). There is a simple practical question here. Since the basic pulse of most music is notated as quarter-notes/ crotchets, Steiner may be taking "whole note" to mean "whole beat". Of course, note values are relative, depending on the tempo.

69 The text has *viergestrichene Noten*. If this means the notes of the *viergestrichene Oktave*, then the notes three octaves and more above middle C would be meant. These notes are written above the fifth leger line above the treble clef, *i.e.*, they are extremely high. In Lecture 7, the *Kontra* and *Subkontra* notes are described. These are written below the second leger line below the bass clef, that is, below the cello C string. If these passages correspond, Steiner could be referring to the notes beyond the extreme range of the normal human voice, that is, beyond the four octaves between the second leger line below the bass clef to the second leger line above the treble clef. This interpretation has been adopted in the translation.

70 The German text has *Sie* (upper case) = you. This would translate: "let your eyes be swept up with the movement… produce the gesture of being swept up with your eyes, as if you would do this movement – and you should be swept up with the movement!" But since the word was spoken, it could be *sie* (lower case) = they, meaning "your eyes". The translation adopts this second reading: "let your eyes be swept up with the movement… produce the gesture of being swept up with your eyes, as if they would do this movement – and they should be swept up with the movement!" This reading agrees with R. Steiner's Notebook (NB 494. 33).

71 The criticism not only concerns Wagner's style (since eurythmy is not practised with singers; see Endnote **57**). It may also contain a warning concerning a one-time popular image of "floating eurythmists". These hypothetical creatures apparently never attempt a bar line, their "swinging over" is indistinguishable from the singing movement, and they never stoop to include an abrupt movement including erasures of discords, not to mention the "annulling of the movement" at the end of a piece. Their heels seldom touch the earth, and they presumably prefer to "fade out" like most popular or light "music" that betrays a decadent, certainly a sentimental tendency. Surely this tendency of "soul without spirit" (Bock) is not cultivated anywhere today? Steiner wrote:

> A person, or a group of people, can carry out movements which present the musical element and the speech element in the visible realm, just as the organs for speaking and singing do so in the audible realm. The whole human being (or groups of people) becomes a "larynx"; the movements speak and sing as the larynx produces the sounds of music and speech. Eurythmy is based on something arbitrary as little as is speech or singing. It makes just as little sense to prefer spontaneous movement to eurythmy as it is to say that arbitrary sounds and notes are better than the ordered sounds and notes of the creations of speech and music. Eurythmy is not to be mistaken for the dance. You can carry out in eurythmy music that is played at the same time. It is not dancing to music, but making visible that which "sings" (R. Steiner, "The Goetheanum: ten years in retrospect" 1923. GA 36 and Tb 635. 142-43. Tr. A.S.).

U.-I. Gillert writes on improvisation in eurythmy:

> With time we can bring order to initially completely unordered movement; but without deepening yourself in the music it is difficult to

arrive at a real interpretation... For many eurythmists "improvisation" is an important stage of practising, and no objections should be brought against it. Quite a different way can be, first to enter into the composition, initially without our "head" (without "knowing" anything) but purely the listening experience, the experiencing-listening. In a short time a progressive path for work results... In order to get away from a pure improvised, random movement and to get away from a dictionary-style translation of music into movement, we have to apply a lot of work (U.-I. Gillert. 1993. 25 & 15).

It is often observed that eurythmy is not an art of "improvisation"; the element of spontaneity, however, is not lacking. "Improvisation" in music has always been a combination of music to conventional, set patterns and "freely" invented passage-work and ornamentation (virtuosity). This appears formally in classical music (cadenza). There is also an art of extemporisation, reflected in written Preludes, Toccatas and Fantasies. Some especially gifted musicians are even capable of improvising on the keyboard strict fugues of several voices. "Improvisation" lies at the root of traditional folk-music, and is one of the sources of western music as well as jazz.

Nobody claims the composer of "Dumbarton Oaks Concerto" (1938) was a prude, and Stravinsky (1882-1971) said of jazz:

The percussion and bass... function as a central-heating system. They must keep the temperature "cool", not cool. It is a kind of masturbation that never arrives anywhere (of course) but which supplies the "artificial" genesis the art requires. The point of interest is instrumental virtuosity, instrumental personality, not melody, not harmony, and certainly not rhythm. Rhythm doesn't exist really because no rhythmic proportion or relaxation exists. Instead of rhythm there is "beat" (*Stravinsky in Conversation with Robert Craft*. Penguin. Harmondsworth. 1962. 129).

Performers are aware of two types of spontaneity: (1) an initial, instinctive kind, and (2) a regained kind, the transformed result of study and practice. It is this second kind, which passes beyond a death-point to a re-creation, that is artistically cultivated in eurythmy. Steiner points to this crucial death-point when speaking of the transformation of true dance to inner singing (*i.e.*, eurythmy):

All true dancing has arisen from imitating in the limbs the movement carried out by the planets, by other heavenly bodies or by the earth itself... The movements we perform in the world are stemmed or stopped, as it were, in the head and in the chest... The head (lazy fellow) rests on the shoulders and does not let the movements reach the soul... The soul begins to reflect from within itself the dancing movements of the limbs.

When the limbs execute irregular movements, the soul begins to *mumble*; when the limbs perform regular movements it begins to *whisper*: when the limbs carry out the harmonious cosmic movements of the universe, it even begins to *sing*. In this way the outward dancing movement is changed into singing and into inner music (R. Steiner. *Study of Man*. GA 293. RSP. 1969. Tr. Harwood. 144; Am. tr. *The Foundations of Human Experience*. Tr. R. Lathe & N.P. Whittaker. AP. 1996. 167, is inaccurate here: the verbs *brummen, lispeln* here are "mumble, whisper", not "growl, murmur"; in the last phrase "outwardly" qualifies the dancing, not the singing. The resulting inner music, the soul's own expression, is the source of music-eurythmy).

72 "The person sitting at the instrument" is normally a *pianist*; Steiner obviously means the *musician*, whichever instrument he/she plays. Some people even today question the suitability of the piano for eurythmy. Empiricists claim that the piano (and indeed the harpsichord, harp, lyre, guitar and so on) cannot produce a legato, because the sound is produced by hammers, or by plucking strings. "This is the fallacy of confusing cause with effect," writes D.F. Tovey. The empiricist's view, thus expressed, is only a half-truth that does not take into account all the empirical facts. Some people, he goes on, confuse the mechanics of sound-production with the evidence of their own ears: "The ear knows nothing as to the mechanical cause of this mode of vibration." For Steiner, too, the science of acoustics has nothing to do with the art of music (see Endnote 61). Of course, Tovey continues,

> many players exult in their capacity to bring the whole weight of their muscular apparatus on to every note. Their beautiful tone then reduces all melody to a series of bugles, and gives rise to the conviction that Mozart, Beethoven and Brahms were all ridiculously mistaken in imagining that the pianoforte could combine with other instruments at all... The earliest pianoforte composers regarded the instrument as entirely a vehicle for cantabile; and Mozart is not afraid to make it play a sustained theme that has just been given out by the clarinet... Clearly, then, the classical art of pianoforte playing was always an art of suggestion; and it makes no difference to the power of suggestion that the half-period of the pianoforte strings [referring to the decay of the physical sound] was far shorter a century ago than it is now (D.F. Tovey. Preface to *Beethoven: Sonatas for Piano*. Associated Board. London. 1931. 55-56 – Edwin Fisher referred to this "great book").

Further help for the player is offered by Ralph Kirkpatrick (1911–84), the harpsichordist:

If a harpsichord or any other instrument has to be made to "sing" it is because the notes have been put into a context that makes them sound as if they really were being sung. What passes for a singing tone is the relationship of that tone with other tones and the rightness and meaningfulness of its context. With considerable bitterness, I think of time wasted in my youth being concerned about a singing tone, when I would have done better to examine questions of articulation and phrasing. It is not the notes themselves but the intervals between them that constitute a melody... Great playing plays the right notes, but it also plays what connects those notes, what gives those notes meaning...

Kirkpatrick points to "the inner ear", where the eurythmist has to expand to "inner feeling for movement and gesture":

The player's aim might well be to hear with the ear of the composer... It is continually necessary for the performer to check the inner ear with the outer ear... The inner ear is the repository of what one has captured in one's best moments, and a fund of insurance to help salvage one's worst. It is, in short, the storehouse of inspiration (Ralph Kirkpatrick. *Interpreting Bach's Well-tempered Clavier*. Yale University. New Haven and London. 1984. 61, 109, 111).

Steiner points to the one important fact about the piano: it offers a unique possibility of transformation. His example is Bruckner. "In playing Bruckner on the piano, the piano seems to disappear from the room! You forget the piano and think you are hearing other instruments" (R. Steiner. Lecture, Stuttgart, 8 March 1923. GA 283; E.T. *The Inner Nature of Music*. 75, slightly amended A.S.). See also Endnote **31**.

Steiner wrote in 1924:

Our musicians who place their artistic gifts in the service of eurythmy are bringing music forward in a quite special direction, I am convinced, through the way in which they do this and through the great enthusiasm which ensouls them in their work with eurythmy. I do believe that the musical sense which lives in them finds its true *liberation* when placed in this connection. In this case, in the work of our musicians within the framework of eurythmical activity there is a deeply satisfying expansion of the musical into the general sphere of art. And its fruitfulness is shown again in the way its works back so beautifully on music as such (R. Steiner, in *Nachrichtenblatt*. 8 June 1924, in GA 279. Anastasi 2005. 188).

Here a new collaboration between the arts is sketched, which has implications for the future. Development "all depends on people" (R. Steiner. GA 243. Torquay. 22 August 1924).

73 The final words of Lecture 7, "in retrospect complement our studies", point to the final step on the Eightfold Path (see Endnote **2**)— *Right Concentration*: "gently taking counsel with ourselves, shaping and testing our basic principles of life", and, quite practically here, discussing the music with "the person sitting at the instrument". We are reminded, that "on the esoteric path, we must be aware that what matters in not 'good intentions', but what we actually do" (R. Steiner. *Knowledge of the Higher Worlds—how is it achieved*? RSP. 124. AP. 141). Harmony of our thoughts and words with the events in the outer world helps the gift of clairvoyance, of deep insight – the development of the sixteen-petalled lotus-flower.

> The eighth exercise of the path, which in a sense includes all the others, calls for an inner life that leads to genuine self-knowledge. This can seldom be achieved directly, simply by looking at ourselves; objective standards, and a lively understanding of our environment, are needed first. From these, we can glance back towards ourselves (Adam Bittleston. "Traffic and Character". *The Golden Blade* 1968. RSP. 121).

Discussing phrasing with the player – "It simply belongs to the matter" – is a comment on the artistic profession; for Steiner music and eurythmy are not separable. Playing for eurythmy is a new branch of the profession, not quite the same as the work of a *répétiteur*. The "matters" that "need correction" rightly refer to the practising artists themselves. Steiner's comment to discuss phrasing is far removed from advocating "being nice" to your pianist, which can be patronising. Musicians are forgiving, but there are limits to what is bearable.

Artists practise *method*, never such a creature as "theory". Steiner's mission – to track thoughts to their origin – was likewise essentially creative. He did it by researching normal thinking *activity* as distinct from its product "thought". Eurythmy, moreover, is neither separable from life, for everyone – including the audience – is engaged on the inner path whether they know it or not. Aware of the inner path, I may yet be under some grand illusions of my progress. The circuit from *composer*, via the *interpreter/s*, via the *audience* and back to the composer has to be complete for a spontaneous artistic event to take place (Pfrogner. Fig. 33, above). Artists are servants from the first note to the last. In other words, the activity of persons in relation – practical ethics – that includes a study-of-man as its spiritual-scientific basis, turns out to be the really essential thing. Eurythmy is not only "visible singing" and "visible speech" but also "visible karma".

74 Steiner finally speaks of "fourteen" lectures. If the *eight* that were given relate to the 16-petalled lotus flower in the region of the larynx (eight petals are given; eight are to be developed), the *six* unspoken lectures may have related to the 12-petalled lotus flower of the heart (six petals are given; six are to be developed). Feeling "inner warmth or inner cold" when practising "is what inner life is"; it characterises the 12-petalled lotus flower. With this link, Steiner may have enlarged on the divine-human system of angle-gestures; here number becomes geometry. This comprehensive solar system of angles, with its stroke of genius combining the 12 and the 7, reveals the musical system of humankind. The angle-gestures (see Endnote **4**) give the possibility of portraying both the clarity and the expressive nuances of musical experience for which, like study of the human being, there is no foreseeable end.

75 Jan Stuten (1890–1948) was a gifted musician, actor and stage-designer, who worked at the Goetheanum from 1913. His compositions for the drama (including Goethe's *Faust*) and for eurythmy are still performed. Stuten mentions some suggestions of Steiner's for musical composition, and records his respect for Steiner's musicianship. While Steiner was suggesting improvements to a composition, Stuten was

> surprised to see how quickly he could find his way in a manuscript which even a professional musician could hardly be expected to decipher… Ever and again we experienced in [Steiner's] work that (as he himself said) artistic working has to be drawn out of direct experience. Afterwards you can become conscious of what you did. Not the other way round, that out of conceptual life (*Vorstellungsleben*) art can be developed which should be alive. This fundamental error, which unfortunately we meet repeatedly, Steiner was forever trying to get out of people's heads. We can develop consciousness in the creative process and can penetrate this afterwards with thinking, but not the other way round, create real creations out of theories (J. Stuten, from the *Nachrichtenblatt* Nr. 40. 29 Sept. 1929 of *Das Goetheanum*, reprinted in RB 21. Dornach. 1991. 22. Tr. A.S.).

Correlation of Endnote numbering:

[the present rev. ed. 2013] and (corrected ed. 1998)

1	(–)	Steiner's Report; chiasm
2	(–)	The Eightfold Path; Right Understanding
3	(1)	Choreography
4	(2)	The angle-gestures
5	(2a)	Alphabet, Aleph
6	(3)	The tree; macrocosmic man
7	(4)	Speech eurythmy and music eurythmy; space & time
8	(5)	Gestures "lead back"; inner & outer polarity
9	(6)	Major and minor
10	(7)	Eurythmical method; origin of speech and singing
11	(8)	The ear
12	(9)	The octave
13	(10)	The Atlantean scale
14	(11)	Musical thirds
15	(12)	Marsyas
16	(–)	Right Thought
17	(13)	Richard Wagner
18	(–)	Right Speech
19	(14)	Noise
20	(15)	Challenge of the abstract (Hauer) v. tonal
21	(16)	Polyphony
22	(17)	"Melody in the single note"
23	(18)	"Recollection and expectation"
24	(19)	Definition of music
25	(20)	Personality
26	(21)	The artistic event
27	(22)	Three octaves
28	(23)	The three-dimensional cross
29	(–)	(redirection)
30	(24)	Vowel-scale correspondence
31	(25)	Motive, phrase
32	(25a)	"Dead interval"
33	(–)	Right Action
34	(26)	Bar line
35	(27)	Three "orders of the arts"
36	(28)	Goethe's poem *Über allen Gipfel*
37	(28a)	Plato's *Cratylus*
38	(29)	Ref. to Steiner's autobiography
39	(30)	Pictures from nature
40	(31)	Salt
41	(32)	A "landing place": *Kenosis*
42	(–)	Right Livelihood
43	(33)	Josef Matthias Hauer

Collected Articles (1997–2012): a checklist

by Alan Stott, pub. in the *Newsletter from the Section for the Arts of Eurythmy, Speech and Music* (Dornach, Switzerland), with responses, in English and German, also available online: contact <abo@dasgoetheanum.ch>, or download my articles from my website <www.alansnotes.co.uk>.

(1) The Point of Departure (RB 27. Jan. 1997) + *Owen Barfield*: Concerning Speech Formation and the English Language (RB 27. Jan. 1997).

(2) The Scale in *Eurythmy as Visible Singing* (GA 278) – Part 1 (RB 28. Jan. 1998).
The Scale in GA 278, Part 2 (RB 29. Summer 1998).

(3) The Mediation for Eurythmists (RB 30. Easter 1999).

(4) The "Melody in the Single Note" and the second mission of Michael (RB 33. Michaelmas 2000).

(5) Hallelujah (RB 32. Easter 2000).

(6) Character and Conduct in GA 278. Criteria for Art (Part 1) (RB 35. Michaelmas 2001).
Character and Conduct in GA 278. Criteria for Art (Part 2) (RB 36. Easter 2002).
Character and Conduct in GA 278. Criteria for Art (Conclusion) (RB 37. Michaelmas 2002).

(7) No more Tone-Gestures in Eurythmy? (RB 36. Easter 2002).
The Sun Sings. A glance at contemporary practice (RB 37. Michaelmas 2002).

(8) *Reinhard Wedemeier*: What's up with the "Gestures for Music"? (RB 39. Michaelmas 2003).
Maren & Alan Stott: Falling Asleep while Staying Awake: in answer to Reinhard Wedemeier (RB 39. Michaelmas 2003).
Hans-Ulrich Kretschmer: Absolute Tone-Gestures or not? (RB 39. Michaelmas 2003).

(9) *Bevis Stevens*: The Angle-Gestures: a confirmation of Eurythmy as Visible Singing (RB 41. Michaelmas 2004).
Julian Clarke: Fréderic Chopin, 24 Préludes pour le pianoforte (RB 41. Michaelmas 2004).

(10) Reader's letter (RB 42. Easter 2005).
The Angle-Gestures revisited (RB 42. Easter 2005).

(11) Chopin's Homage to BACH. Part 1: Implications for several Doctor-Forms (RB 38. Easter 2003).
Chopin's Homage to BACH. Part 2: Towards a "second chapter in eurythmy" (RB 39. Michaelmas 2003).

(12) *Robert Kolben*: 24 Préludes pour le pianoforte dédies a son ami J.C. Keßler par F. Chopin (RB 40. Easter 2004).

"The area of the fifth": in answer to Robert Kolben (RB 40. Easter 2004).
Robert Kolben (1929–2005) (RB 43. Michaelmas 2005).

(13) "One-for-one" in Eurythmy: Slavery or Marriage? (RB 43. Michaelmas 2005).
(14) *The Philosophy of Freedom* as a Musical Composition: the seven-sentence rhythm of love – Part 1 (RB 44. Easter 2006).
The Philosophy of Freedom as a Musical Composition: the seven-sentence rhythm of love – Conclusion (RB 45. Michaelmas 2006).
(15) Shakespeare: Who Held the Pen? (RB 47. Michaelmas 2007).

(16) *Hugh O'Connor*: For the Price of a new Shirt (RB 32. Easter 2000).
Christopher Cooper: R. Steiner "Eurythmy as Visible Speech" (RB 44. Easter 2006).

(17) Why Chapter 15 of *The Philosophy of Freedom?* (RB 51. Michaelmas 2009).
(18) Round Pegs in Square Holes? Debussy and Eurythmy 100 years on (RB 54. Easter 2011).

(19) "In the technique": Remarks on Steiner's Report on *Eurythmy as Visible Speech.* (RB 55. Michaelmas 2011).
(20) "Ourselves our most severest critics…": Remarks on R. Steiner's Report on *Eurythmy as Visible Singing.* (RB 56. Easter 2012).
(21) "Something cannot be. Only it is": Beyond the Murder of Gonzago. Unpublished. See my web-site, <www.alansnotes.co.uk>. A shorter version was pub. in *Das Goetheanum* weekly, "Wer was Shakespeare?" 28. Jan. 2012. Nr. 4 (pp. 4-7).
(22) "A Right Balance between Heaven and Earth: Art as a WAY: the Way as ART", Eng. original available to download from <www.alansnotes.co.uk> it forms Appendix 9 below. Germ. version pub. in a commentary on GA 278, a compilation ed. Stefan Hasler (Dornach forthcoming); it forms Appendix 9 below..

Errata and Corrigena to the articles:

(4) *The Melody in the Single Note.* P. 4, sub-section "The Heart". The second indented quotation ends "physical human being." A new paragraph begins "From this central area…"
(5) *Hallelujah.* Sub-section "Hallelujah in eurythmy". (iv), l. 3 for "sould 'l'", read "sound 'l'.
(6) *Character and Conduct. Part 1.* l. 5 from end: for "anthesis" read "antithesis".

Endnote 37, l. 5: after "first para." add "RSP p. 144".
Character and Conduct. Part 2. penultimate para, l. 2. The "sixth planetary embodiment of the Earth" takes Mars/Mercury as two counts. Strictly speaking, "New Jerusalem" – in Steiner's terminology Jupiter embodiment – is the fifth planetary embodiment.
Character and Conduct. Part 3. The 3-line paragraph immediately preceding the sub-section "Artistic Criteria" should be an indented quotation.

(7) *No more Tone Gestures in Eurythmy?* In the caption to the illustrations: for "ecclestical", read "ecclesiastical".
Sub-section "Something Crucial". Third and second lines towards the end: for "the singing and into inner music", delete "the".

(11) *Chopin's Homage to BACH. Part 1.* The caption to the penultimate musical example and diagram for Prelude 23 is missing. Add: "The BACH-motif appears in both voices in a reflected form; *cf.*, the two fishes in the zodiacal sign for Pisces; in Hermann Beckh's arrangement, F major belongs to the Fishes, the twelfth position. In bar 4 the form of a cube can be discovered (read two-dimensionally), a well-known symbol signifying the conclusion of a cycle (see R. Guénon)."
Chopin's Homage to BACH. Part 2. Sub-section "The Mission of the Musical Arts". The indented quotation translates "*Bild*" as "picture". In speaking of music perhaps the word should be "audition".

Appendix 1
Nature and Art

The One Life, Within us and Abroad.

S. T. Coleridge

The higher philosophy deals with
the marriage of nature and spirit.

Novalis

A musician might defend the whole question of programme music, opera, and extra-musical stimuli – literature, art, biographical events, and so on. These stimuli are more or less incidental, for as soon as the musician starts composing, he enters on musical problems and the "scenery" he creates is purely musical. "Music does not merely reflect the events of life, is not merely occasioned by them… it is self-sufficient", Furtwängler claimed (86), which agrees with Steiner. Beethoven's *"Pastoral" Symphony, No. 6*, for example, is not about the countryside, but as the composer writes in the score, the first movement evokes "the awakening of cheerful feelings on arriving in the country", and so on. But since Beethoven, as Hauer complains, the tendency towards programme music in "absolute music" grew, and this no doubt was both symptom and cause for the confusion about the musical element itself. Steiner, consistent in his distinction, points out that in the last movement of his *Ninth Symphony*, Beethoven leaves the purely symphonic realm by introducing a sung text (lecture, Torquay 22 Aug. 1924. GA 243). D.F. Tovey (1875–1940), applying Andrew Bradley's artistic philosophy, claims that there is no theoretical or practical impossibility in "reconciling the claims of absolute music with those of the intelligent and intelligible setting of words" (see D.F. Tovey, "Beethoven, Ninth Symphony in D minor, op.125 – its place in musical art", in *Essays in Musical Analysis*. Vol. 2. OUP 1935, reissued in *Symphonies and other Orchestral Works*. OUP 1989. 3; also D.F. Tovey. *A Musician Speaks, 2. Musical Textures*. OUP 1941). Beethoven's conception of the human voice in the Choral Symphony appears more "instrumental" than "vocal", more a rediscovery of the ultimate musical instrument – the human voice.

This gave the precedent for Wagner's mature style. In *The Mastersingers* (1862-7), a middle period work, "the thread of melody runs, not in the voices, but in the orchestra... diametrically opposed to that used by all the older masters" (C. Osborne. *The Complete Operas of Wagner*. Gollancz. London. 1992. 163). To Steiner, Wagner's music "has its justification in our age"; Steiner's aim for absolute symphonic music is an attempt to indicate the essential musical pathway for the future. Eurythmy does not attempt to unite drama and music. Not the linguistic and visionary elements, but "musical experience is to be expressed in gesture... the actual music, the progression of notes" and the experience of the intervals (Lecture 2).

At first glance it might be thought that Steiner would censure Debussy's "impressionism". Yet Debussy (1862-1918) did not approve of the term "impressionist" applied to himself. The titles for Debussy's *Preludes*, for example, are printed after the music, with plenty of dots... as though to indicate that their rôle is merely to set the aural imagination working. To Steiner, Debussy is one composer "who lives in the single note, who experiences the single note" (R. Steiner. Discussion. Stuttgart 14 June 1921 evening. GA 342. 261; see also GA 283. Dornach 1969. 85). Clearly, then, Steiner is not against "impressionism" but its caricature, materialistic naturalism (Lecture 4), and a materialistic concept of musical sound. He was open to any conscientious artistic attempt, as can be seen from the variety of musical "styles" represented in the numerous eurythmy forms he created.

In the present lecture, Steiner makes a distinction between "the human realm" and "nature". He tried to avoid confusion in his work by sometimes adding "phrases prepared for translation". He gives the example of adding the phrase "the sensory world" where the normal word would be "nature"; "for that is roughly the meaning *Natur* has assumed in today's German" (lecture 5 Jan. 1922 in R. Steiner. *Soul Economy and Waldorf Education*. RSP/AP 1986. GA 303). How does this tally with Goethes claim for nature: "She is the unique artist" (in the prose fragment *"Natur"*), to which Steiner attached such importance? (Translations by G. Adams in *Anthroposophy*. 1932; and by Douglas Miller, see below; Steiner's essay (1892) on this work is reprinted in GA 30, and *Goethe-Studien* Tb 634. Dornach 1982. Steiner was fond, too, of quoting Goethe's "Prose Aphorisms" especially Nos. 310 and 311 (*Sprüche in Prosa*, ed. and with commentaries by R. Steiner. Stuttgart. 1967, for example, in the essay "Das Goetheanum in seinen zehn Jahren", in GA 36 and *Der Goetheanumgedanke*. Tb635. Dornach 1982. 136.

The two Munich lectures mentioned above set out to justify Goethe's Aphorism No. 310: "He, to whom Nature begins to reveal her open secrets, feels an irresistible longing for her most worthy exponent, Art."

Two considerations are essential here; (i) the concept of the evolution of consciousness, and (ii) research into the changing meaning of the word "nature" (see, for example, lecture 20 Aug. 1911 in R. Steiner, *Wonders of the World...* RSP. 1963. Here one of Coleridge's "fruitful distinctions" is basic. Coleridge (1772-1834), like Goethe (1749-1832), anticipated Steiner; as a knower, Goethe was primarily interested in the world around him, whereas Coleridge was primarily interested in the activity of mind. These thinkers are mutually complementary. Coleridge's "whole system of *thought* resembled in character the organic *world* which Goethe revealed in his natural scientific writings'; he "was able to know nature by mentally re-creating her" (O. Barfield. *Romanticism comes of Age.* Wesleyan. 1967. 146 & 161). For Goethe, the two principal concepts concerning nature are "polarity" and "intensification" (an outstanding example taken from the *Theory of Colour* is the intensification of yellow, via orange, to red, and of blue, via violet, to red – a mere mixing of pigment produces green). Coleridge takes up the scholastic view that nature manifests in two ways: *natura naturans* ("nature naturing"), or life, is Perdita's "great creating nature" (Shakespeare, *The Winter's Tale.* IV:iv, 89); *natura naturata* ("nature natured") is the material world. The former is not a metaphor for the human (subconscious) mind, but is itself identical with it. In other words, the Word is not only the life; it is also the light of men (John 1:4). Nature out there has gradually lost the creative spirit. Steiner calls it *"Räderwerke—*clockwork" (*The Philosophy...*, for example: Chapter 15); elsewhere he calls it "finished work" (R. Steiner. *The Michael Mystery*; see bibliography, p. 336 below). The present lecture seems to refer to sensory nature.

Human (self-)consciousness, on the other hand, continually grows and blossoms. "Great creating nature" has entered human consciousness. *In the human being, nature achieves its highest goal: self-consciousness.* "In Man the centripetal and individualizing tendency of all Nature is itself concentred and individualised – he is a revelation of Nature!... He who stands the most on himself, and stands the firmest, is the truest, because the most individual, Man. In social and political life this acme is inter-dependence; in moral life it is independence; in intellectual life it is genius" (S.T. Coleridge. "Towards a more Comprehensive Theory of Life" in *Collected Works.* Vol. 11. Ed. H.J. Jackson & J.R. de J. Jackson. Routledge/ Princeton 1995. 485-557; *Selected Poetry and Prose of Samuel Taylor Coleridge*. Ed. D. Stauffer. Random House. New York 1951. 601). In this context, Steiner respects scientific consciousness as the greatest achievement of human development because of the freedom it necessitates, and he praises the appropriateness of Goethe's holistic scientific methods. But if Nature is an artist, our approach to understand nature adequately must be artistic at the same time. Steiner completed Goethe's work by making explicit the latter's theory of knowledge, and went on to extend the area of research beyond all arbitrary "boundaries to knowledge". On the basis of moral responsibility, the human being may enter into research and inter-communion with *natura naturans*, or with "the spiritual world" (see R. Steiner. *Occult/Esoteric Science*. Chapter 1. This important chapter fully argues Steiner's claim for a spiritual science, since "today science has only an earthly meaning; its purpose is to help human beings to become free here on earth" and he adds, "but the gods cannot use this [natural] science for the continued cosmic creation" R. Steiner. GA 276. 67). On the suggested path objectivity is retained; science overcomes one-sided emphases; art and religion gain greater universality. Today, we are "to find the path that could lead to an inner harmony" of science, art and religion, and "once again to see and hear the supersensory together with the sense world" (GA 283, E.T. 90). Creation now takes place within and through the human being, but, as Shakespeare's Polixenes claimed, "The art itself is nature" (*Winter's Tale*. IV:iv. 97). "A development of the higher organs is not unnatural; for in the higher sense all that man accomplishes also belongs to nature… All education… also develops further the work of nature" (R. Steiner. *Theosophy*. RSP. 1973. 70).

Steiner describes outer "nature" as a residue, or deposit, from a previous all-embracing spiritual existence. This latter remains the abode of the archangel Michael. He distinguishes between external nature as a "mirror of higher spirituality" free from the Dragon's power, and "nature in the human being" as the seat of the Dragon with which the soul has to struggle through devotion to Michael's power. The human being participates in the coming to birth and the dying away in the course of the year (see also Endnote 67, last quotation).

> Spring and summer are the seasons of nature-consciousness of the human soul; autumn and winter are the seasons of the realisation of self-consciousness… Goethe felt that nature is neither essence nor covering; she is both together. For nature, death is necessary for life; the human being can also experience (can live) death. Thereby he penetrates deeper into the "inner" side of nature… to the strengthening of his own spiritual

nature… With art, the spirit sends a shoot into the sensory world which only appears unreal because its origin is "in another world" (R. Steiner. GA 36/ Tb 635. 168-175; tr. A.S.).

Goethe claimed that "the dignity of art appears with music perhaps most eminently, because there is no material that has to be reckoned with. It is all form and content, raising and ennobling everything that it expresses" (Goethe. *Sprüche in Prosa*. No. 342). But, Steiner comments, this aim can apply to every art. He begins with the polarity of sensory world and the unconscious (which are breached by the human sense-organisation). The former initially shows an *enchanted nature*; the latter a pathologically compulsive *visionary* tendency. In art, the first tendency merely "copies" the appearances, whereas the second fixes the vision with "symbols of straw and wooden allegory" by its "pedantic thoughts". True art, he continues, arises when both poles livingly interweave: (1) impressions from the outer world restrain the subconscious vision and bring it into form; (2) the surging subconscious "kills" the prosaic details and ('with humour') releases the spirit enchanted in outer nature, completing it. Art continues the activity of Perdita's "great creating nature" with the "higher, supersensory life" of Intuitions (R. Steiner. Lectures Munich, 15 and 17 Feb. 1918. GA 271; see Fig. 40 on p. 340 below).

The universal law of polarity is basic to Steiner's thinking. He applies it practically, too, for example in exercises described in R. Steiner, *Knowledge of the Higher Worlds, how is it achieved?* GA 10, and the exercises for painters (sunrise, sunset, and so on). "Everything in the world is formed as a polarity – *Alles ist in der Welt polarisch gestaltet*", he declares (Dornach. 9 June 1923. GA 276. 79; tr. rev. A.S.). The Far-Eastern doctrine of heaven and earth, light and dark with the "middle way" is reborn in the West. It was Plato who clearly restated the principle of the triad: "it is impossible that two things only should be joined together without a third. There must be some bond in between both to bring them together" (Plato. *Timaeus*. 31b-c). A basic example of Steiner's teaching is the soul-forces of thinking and will, mediated by feeling. We understand the real meaning of these polar faculties when the concept of metamorphosis is applied. With reference to the present theme: a hardening tendency (head) opposes the surging instincts (trunk), rendered artistically as Ahriman and Lucifer in the wooden statue, the Group (lecture, 17 Feb. 1918); he explains impressionism and expressionism, labels of modern art (lecture, 15 Dec. 1918); there are "two human types", the Apollonian and Dionysian (R. Steiner. *Friedrich Nietzsche, Fighter for Freedom*. GA 5. Sections 27-29. Garber Communications. New York. 1985. 111-120.

Polarity is seen as a key to the world-situation of art in A. Steffen. *Der Künstler zwischen Westen und Osten.* Grethlein. Zürich-Leipzig 1925. Steffen points to the ultimate unity:

> The real goal is shown when Dionysos spiritualises into light, and Apollo incarnates in love, and when light and love unite to prepare the deed of redemption, resurrection from death. This is proclaimed in Steiner's Christology (A. Steffen. Chapter 3. 82; tr. A.S.).

And this Christology confirms the view of such artists and thinkers as Steffen and Coleridge who see "the one voluntary origin of *natura naturans* itself became manifest as *natura naturata* in the body of a single human being" (O. Barfield. *What Coleridge Thought.* 157).

The polarity in nature of "life" and "death", shown as "summer-will" and "winter-will" in the human being, "will interest eurythmists" (R. Steiner. Lecture, 25 Nov. 1923). The seer describes the relationship of the arts to "pre-birth" and "after-death" experiences (R. Steiner. Lecture, 15 Feb. 1918). Architecture and sculpture render into form (in space and time) that which is carried over from pre-birth existence. Poetry and music already prepare for the conditions after death. Between the two poles lives the experience of colour. Painting brings the experiences undergone between sleeping and waking on to the canvas (R. Steiner. Lectures, Dornach. 12 Sept. 1920 and 9 April 1921. GA 271). And eurythmy attempts to embrace the whole artistic spectrum.

> As Schiller regarded Goethe, he said: only through the dawn of beauty can you penetrate to the land of knowledge. In other words: only through artistic life of the full human soul can you endeavour to reach the spheres to which knowledge strives (R. Steiner. Lecture, Dornach. 9 April 1921).

The "two sources of art" (lecture, 17 Feb. 1918. GA 271) unite in the silent language of eurythmy:

> The categories of the musical element (harmony, melody) are not directly suited to express the full, inner human experience. The musical element resists especially strongly the expressionistic, visionary element. Something unsound enters the musical element when it wants to incline towards the visionary pole.

Expressionistic painters "have not found the means to express what they inwardly experience..." and neither can

> impressions from nature be artistically copied. But [in eurythmy] the human being is a higher instrument, making visible the inner experience (which does not come to spoken language, to the inartistic element of thought) by taking what can be observed, the movements of the human being. The viewer not only receives the direct impression; expression too

is certainly achieved in eurythmy (R. Steiner. Lecture Dornach. 14 Feb. 1920 in GA 277 & Tb 642. 75-6).

Eurythmy involves

> that which is taken from the earthly life, the physical material: the instrument for eurythmy is the human being himself. That which is inwardly studied in a sensory-supersensory manner (which has formed the larynx and the organs for speech), is allowed to appear on the human being. This is passed over to the limbs, to that which prefigures the life after death. The fashioning and movement of the human organism in eurythmy is a direct external demonstration for the participation of the human being in the supersensory world. In doing eurythmy the human being links directly with the supersensory world (R. Steiner. Lecture, Dornach. 12 Sept. 1920. GA 271).

After mentioning some results of polar logic, one of Coleridge's definitions should also be given. Coleridge, as J.S. Mill claimed, possessed a seminal mind; his "dynamic philosophy" is indebted to, but not derived from, Fichte and Hegel ("*Sein, Nicht-Sein*, and *Werden*"; and "thesis, antithesis and synthesis"), and Schelling. The importance, for instance, of Coleridge's "Theory of Life" has been argued by Owen Barfield and Craig W. Miller. Coleridge spoke of

> the tendency at once to individuate and to connect, to detach, but so as either to retain or to reproduce attachment... Polarity, or the essential dualism of Nature, arising out of its productive unity, and still tending to reaffirm it, either as equilibrium, indifference, or identity (Coleridge. "Theory of Life", in D. Stauffer. 578).

We meet Steiner's version of Coleridge's productive unity or separative projection in a triune sentence during the account of Ancient Moon evolution. Unity, being productive, strives to reproduce itself and yet in the same act and moment to overcome that individuation, thus maintaining the unity. An event at that time shows:

> The whole of evolution depends first upon the severance of independent being from surrounding life; the environment then imprints itself upon this severed being as though by reflection, and then this separated entity develops further independently (R. Steiner, *Occult Science*, Chapter 4. Tr. Monges 151, consistently the most accurate; tr. Adams 141; tr. Creeger 170).

Perhaps it was Schiller's grasp of the creative process and what Henry James called "the civic use of imagination" (developing "play-drive" through transcending polar opposites) that underlies Steiner recommending (during the Faculty Meeting) Schiller's, *On the Aesthetic Education of Man*.

Schiller sets himself the question: How is it possible to rise above slavery to duty and attain to love of duty? Of course, he does not use the expressions "Lucifer" and "Ahriman", because he does not see the question in its cosmic aspect. Nevertheless, these wonderful *Letters* of Schiller... are directly translatable into spiritual science (R. Steiner. *The Balance in the World and Man.* Lecture, Dornach. 22 Dec. 1914. 43. Tr. slightly edited A.S.).

Steiner also mentions *The Philosophy of Spiritual Activity – a Philosophy of Freedom:*

It would be good if you develop how the first part could be understood if you could work out a eurythmical-consonantal study; where the [second] part goes on to moral imagination you arrive at the vowel element. Lead everything to eurythmy (R. Steiner. Faculty Meeting. Stuttgart 30 April. 1924. GA 277a. 143).

This hint of an inner pathway is also alluded to in the text itself: the thinker begins from the "periphery" and finally (Chapter 15, sentences 63-65 - for tr. see p. 451 below) arrives at the centre (see A. Stott, final reference below).

Steiner spoke about the origin and sequence of the arts from two further aspects (see Endnote 35 *). See also:*

R. Steiner, The Michael Mystery. *GA 26. St George Pub. New York 1984. Especially Letter XIV (28 Dec. 1924). R. Steiner.* A Theory of Knowledge. *GA 2. Chaps II & XXI. AP 1968;*

Friedrich Schiller. On the Aesthetic Education of Man. *Ed. and tr. with an Introduction, Commentary and Glossary of terms by E. M. Wilkinson and L. A. Willoughby. OUP 1983/9 – the definitive edition; see p. li on Schiller's pattern of three: 9 x 3 = 27 Letters. See also:*

Elizabeth M. Wilkinson. "Reflections after translating Schiller's Letters", in Schiller, Bicentenary Lectures, *ed. F. Norman. University of London 1960.*

Further on Schiller (1759–1805):

R. Steiner. The Course of my Life, *Chapter 3;*

R. Steiner. The Riddles of Philosophy. *AP 1973. 131-141;*

R. Steiner. The New Spirituality and the Christ-experience of the Twentieth Century. *GA 200. Lecture, 24 Oct. 1920. RSP;*

R. Steiner. "A turning-point in modern history". Lecture 24 Jan. 1919 in The Golden Blade *1977. RSP;*

R. Steiner. Lecture 4 May. 1905 in GA 53. Dornach (apparently not translated).

C.G. Jung. *"Schiller's Ideas on the Type Problem in Psychological Types"*, Collected Works. *Vol. 6. Chapter 2 (Chapter 4 discusses Nietzsche's ideas), presents Schiller as the "introverted thinking type". A highly instructive psychological perspective, but Wilkinson cannot take it as final (see E. M. Wilkinson. 76).*

E. Jenaro. *"Impressionism and Expressionism: The Two Sources of Eurythmy"*, in EA Newsletter. *Aberdeen. Spring 1993. 6-9;*

R. Savoldelli, *on summer-will and winter will in "Eurythmy as an impulse of spiritual science" in* EA Newsletter. *Summer 1996.*

O. Barfield. What Coleridge Thought. *Wesleyan Univ. Press. Hannover, New Hampshire. 1971;*

O. Barfield. Saving the Appearances. *Wesleyan. 1988. One of Steiner's foremost interpreters provides essential insights into man's relation to nature and God in the age of physical science;*

O. Barfield. Romanticism Comes of Age. *Wesleyan. 1967;*

Craig W. Miller. *"Coleridge's Concept of Nature"*, in the New York Journal of the History of Ideas. *January-March 1964;*

Alice D. Snyder. *"The Critical Principle of the Reconciliation of Opposites as Employed by Coleridge"*, Contributions to Rhetorical Theory IX, ed. *Fred Newton Scott. Ann Arbor. 1918;*

Kathleen Coburn. *"The Interpenetration of Man and Nature"* in Proceedings of the British Academy. *Vol. 49. 1963. 95-113;*

R. Modiano. Coleridge and the Concept of Nature. *London. 1985.*

M.A. Perkins. Coleridge's Philosophy: the Logos as Unifying Principle. *Oxford. 1994; a link to Teilard is suggested in Appendix 2.*

The central scientific text of Teilhard de Chardin (1881–1955) is The Phenomenon of Man. *Collins 1965;* Le Milieu Divin. *Collins. 1960 is remarkable – the French title was kept because no English equivalent for mileau (which implies both centre and environment or setting) could be found. See also* The Future of Man. *Collins. 1964;* Man's Place in Nature. *Collins. 1966;* A Hymn to the Universe. *Collins. 1965; introductions to this convinced monist, with a flair for synthesis, include two biographies:*

Robert Speaight. Teilhard de Chardin. *Collins. London. 1967;*

Claude Cuénot. Teilhard de Chardin. *Helicon. Baltimore Md. 1965;*

B. Delfgaauw. Evolution, the Theory of Teilhard de Chardin. *Fontana/ Collins. 1969;*

N.M. Wildiers. An Introduction to Teilhard de Chardin. *Collins 1968;*

C.E. Raven. Teilhard de Chardin, Scientist and Seer. *Collins. 1962, links to the "emergent evolution" of Lloyd Morgan, Smuts, and to other contemporary thinkers (Oman, Temple).*

Teilhard's work was posthumously published; his powerful synthesis of science and religion could surely unite the otherworldly tendency of theology (for example, L. Thornton. The Incarnate Lord. *Macmillan, London 1928 and those who insist that God is also revealed in nature (see C.E. Raven.* Natural Religion and Christian Theology. *Cambridge 1953. Paul was a strong inspiration for Teilhard. This thinker's version of an emergent evolution with its concepts of "complexification" and "convergence" to the "Omega point" and the concept of the "noossphere" (the collectivity of human knowledge and humanistic attitudes, especialy love) has impressed many readers. Barfield claims that the tripartite division of* The Phenomenon... *is incomplete; the super-individual stage of speech should be included: matter, life, speech, mind (O. Barfield.* The Rediscovery of Meaning. *Wesleyan. Middletown Co. 1977. 168f.).* Goethe, Scientific Studies. *Ed. and tr. by Douglas Miller. Suhrkamp. New York. 1988, contains the* Theory of Colour *and the* Theory of Music;

Henri Bortoft. Goethe's Scientific Consciousness. *Institute for Cultural Research. Tunbridge Wells. 1986, is a comprehensive introduction; now superseded by H. Bortoft.* The Wholeness of Nature: Goethe's Way of Science. *Floris Books. 1996;*

Ernst Lehrs. Man or Matter. *RSP. 1985 is a pioneer work on Goethean science.*

Olive Whicher. Projective Geometry: Creative Polarities in Space and Time. *RSP. 1971, is an introduction to the concepts of polarity and movement.*

Anders Nygren. Agape and Eros. *SPCK. London. 1982, a study of two fundemental motifs, has been influential;*

R.G. Collingwood. The Idea of Nature. *Galaxy Books. OUP 1965, approaches the subject historically;*

John F. Danby. Shakespeare's Doctrine of Nature: a Study of King Lear. *Faber. London. 1961, describes two views at a time of changing consciousness, and Shakespeare's indication of a third view;*

John Oman. The Natural and the Supernatural. *Cambridge. 1931, argues in the tradition of Schleiermacher for the apprehension of the supernatural in and through the natural.*

René Guénon. The Great Triad. *Quinta Essentia. Cambridge. 1991, a penetrating focus on Far-Eastern tradition and its relevance today;*

Alan W. Watts. The Two Hands of God: the Myths of Polarity. *Braziller. New York. 1963, is stimulating;*

Rupert Sheldrake. The Rebirth of Nature. *Rider. London. 1990, suggests a synthesis of traditional wisdom, scientific insight and personal experience.*

William Temple. Nature, Man and God. *Macmillan. London. 1934, culminates in a philosophy of a sacramental universe (the gist is contained in an earlier article "The Sacramental Principle" in* Pilgrim 1. *January 1925. 218-27); see also A. Stott. "William Temple and Rudolf Steiner – Fighters for the Spirit", in* Perspectives. *Oct./Nov. 1994. 6-9 and Dec. 1994/Jan. 1995. 4-6. Floris Books. Edinburgh.*

H. Wheeler Robinson. Inspiration and Revelation in the Old Testament. *OUP 1962, introduces the Hebrew conception of nature.*

G. *Matheson.* The Psalmist and the Scientist. *Blackwod. Edinburgh & London 1887, a discussion that is still relevant; his* Aids to the Study of German Theology. *T. & T. Clark. Edinburgh 1874, is a brilliant, concise introduction to the thought of Kant, Schleiermacher, Fichte, Hegel, Schelling, etc.*

Alan Stott. "The Philosophy of Freedom *as a Musical Composition: The seven-sentence rhythm of love" Parts 1, 2. RB 44 & 45 and "Why Chapter 15 of* The Philosophy of Freedom. *RB 51. Demonstrates a chiastic, seven-sentence pattern discernable in* all *Steiner's written texts.*

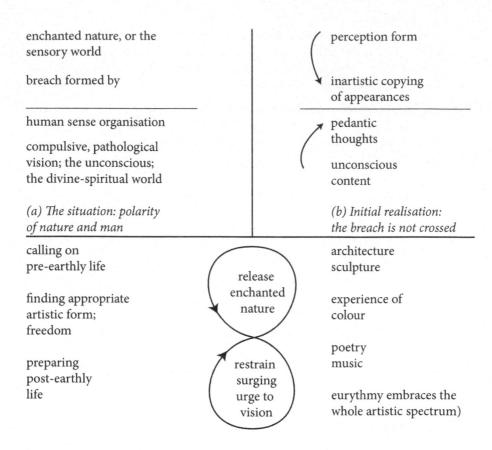

enchanted nature, or the sensory world	perception form
breach formed by	inartistic copying of appearances
human sense organisation	pedantic thoughts
compulsive, pathological vision; the unconscious; the divine-spiritual world	unconscious content
(a) The situation: polarity of nature and man	*(b) Initial realisation: the breach is not crossed*

calling on pre-earthly life	release enchanted nature	architecture sculpture
finding appropriate artistic form; freedom		experience of colour
preparing post-earthly life	restrain surging urge to vision	poetry music
		eurythmy embraces the whole artistic spectrum)

(c) Artistic interweaving leads to true, living art (both creation and enjoyment); artistic activity crosses the breach initiating a harmony.

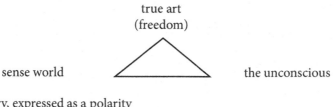

true art
(freedom)

sense world   the unconscious

(d) Summary, expressed as a polarity

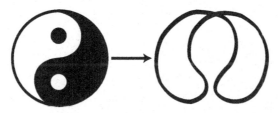

(e) A metamorphosis of the yin-yang symbol into the "harmonious eight"-figure is also suggested (see also Appendix 4). (A. S.)

Fig. 40:   A summary of the origin of the artistic element, after R. Steiner, lectures Munich 15 and 17 Feb. 1918, and Dornach 12 Sept. 1920. GA 271. (A.S. 1995)

(*Note*: A diagram can only assist apprehension, especially of the law of polarity which is the very law that governs the relation between nature and spirit. For Steiner, in bridging over the antithesis of "I" and "world", "lies ultimately the whole spiritual striving of mankind" (R. Steiner. *The Philosophy of Freedom*. Chapter 2. Tr. Wilson. 14).

Appendix 2
The artist between East and West

Oh, East is East, and West is West, and never the twain shall meet,
Till Earth and Sky stand presently at God's great Judgement Seat;
For there is neither East nor West, Order, nor Breed, nor Birth,
When two strong men stand face to face tho' they come from the
ends of the earth!

R. Kipling, refrain from "Ballad of East and West" (1889).

The earth and heaven, so little known,
Are measured outwards from my breast.
I am the midst of every zone
And justify the East and West;

G. M. Hopkins

J.M. Hauer's view of the world (see Lecture 5) is dualistic: the Orient is musical, spiritual, inspired by melos, "pure movement", "the T A O"; the Occident is linguistic-conceptual, material, emotional and personal. The transition was accomplished by the Greeks who brought everything "into the theatre", that is, into space and outer effect. To Hauer there was an "either-or"; he turned his back on western development.

Steiner's view of the world is monistic; the spiritual and phenomenal worlds are two aspects of the same world. "A healthy human thinking keeps to this world. It does not bother about any other. But at the same time, it spiritualises this world. It sees in concepts and ideas realities of this world just as much as in the things and events perceptible through the senses" (R. Steiner. *Goethean Science*. GA 1. Mercury Press. Spring Valley. New York. 1988. 256. See also R. Steiner. *The Philosophy...*). Barfield sums it up: "Consciousness is not a tiny bit of the world stuck to the rest of it. It is the inside of the whole world" (O. Barfield. *History, Guilt, and Habit*. Wesleyan. 1979. 18). True individuality was born with the Christ-event, which ultimately unites all polarities. The possibility is there for the individual to apprehend reality: "*Becoming aware of the idea within reality is the true communion of the human being*" (R. Steiner. *Goethean Science*. 91. Italics original). This language implies a sacramental view of the universe. Out of this source, art – and especially the musical element – can now develop, and consequently the art of eurythmy, too. The creation of eurythmy is Steiner's answer to Hauer's claims that we stand "at the turning point of culture", that "modern music is experiencing its complete breakdown", and that "the noise-producing chord" forming "the greatest mistake of all the centuries" can only be "mitigated" through a return to "listening" to atonal melos (Hauer. *Deutung*. 36. E.T. 511 below). In overstating his case, Hauer totally ignores what happened in Judea during the reign of Tiberius Caesar, between the Orient and the Occident, at "the turning point of time".

When Steiner remarks, "The point is whether we can also *love* the visible realm" (see p. 83), he touches on what is perhaps the central theme of the romantic movement (M.H. Abrams. *Natural Supernaturalism*. Norton. New York. 1971, is the definitive literary study). A philosophy of redemption is implied in Coleridges oft-quoted lines ("Dejection, an ode"):

> ...we receive but what we give,
> And in our life alone does nature live.

Steiner lives fully in this tradition of "wedding Nature to us". The call is neither (i) to "put nature on the rack" to torture her secrets from her (attrib. Francis Bacon, a founder of modern technological science); nor (ii) to return to a "natural state", of "the natural man" (J.-J. Rousseau), for by the end of Lecture 4 "natural processes" have been dismissed from the "human organism"; but (iii) to "love the visible realm". Steiner here uses the word "love" five times, contrasting with "hate", used five times to characterise Hauer's attitude. This love is that *transforming love* of the consciousness-soul, also called the "spiritual-soul", that ultimately renders the human being "a nature humanised" (Coleridge's phrase, used in describing his favourite example of "genius", Shakespeare); this is also the content of the "Meditation for Eurythmists". See, further, R. Steiner, *Calendar of the Soul*, for the living interplay between "self" and "world" – for example No. 33, which speaks of a new creation and is the only verse to use the word 'death' (see also D.E. Faulkner Jones. *The English Spirit*. RSP, 1982, especially Chapter 2; O. Barfield. *Romanticism Comes of Age*. Wesleyan. 1967).

In Steiner's philosophy, our knowledge of reality is distorted by our organisation. We initially perceive the sense world as incomplete, but are able to restore it to complete reality by our own inner effort. Steiner calls his theory of knowledge "a Pauline epistemology" (R. Steiner. *The Karma of Materialism*. Lecture 6. 1917. GA 176. RSP & AP 1985; and Lecture. Berlin. 8 May 1910, in *The Christ Impulse*. GA 116. AP. 1976). The first

Adam comes to experience the world as it really is through Christ (the second Adam). Nature has suffered the fall, brought about by mankind, and is in that sense innocent and helpless. "For the creation waits with eager longing for the revealing of the children of God", wrote Paul (Rom. 8:19). Anthroposophy "will lead over to the genuinely artistic element without losing any of its cognitional character… The human being is on earth because the gods need him… If, in sacrifice and art, the human being gives back what the gods gave him – he co-operates in building the cosmos. He is connected in soul with cosmic evolution" (R. Steiner. GA 276. 42 & 66-7).

In the musical realm, Pfrogner pointed out the limitation inherent in both Schönberg's and Hauer's abstract conceptions of the twelve notes, which deny the diatonic system of seven. He suggests that the twelve-note system is a shadow cast by the light of the "enharmonic arrangement", the third and deepest level of aural awareness (after the diatonic and chromatic levels), the full possibilities of which would be a possible direction for the development of music. Perhaps this abstract conception of the note-material, spurning the phenomenal world and the "subjective ego", is the reason why Steiner suggests that Hauer's atonal melos does not lend itself to eurythmical interpretation (which is based upon diatonic experience). If twelve-note music is attempted in eurythmy, we should realise that we are interpreting it diatonically, or in a diatonic-chromatic manner (see Appendix 3).

Steiner responds to Hauer's mentioning the T A O (*Interpreting Melos,* see 524 & 526 below), and introduces the T A O-meditation ("an esoteric intermezzo"). In ancient China, it was believed that a person who can integrate the yin-yang polarity may eventually regain the T A O, the undivided great One. Steiner, like Schiller before him, showed that a "middle way" between extremes (for Schiller the "aesthetic state" between Reason and Instinct, or the necessity of Spirit and the necessity of Nature) does exist in its own right. The middle way between the tension of polar opposites has to be created through human effort. Art, says Steiner, "forms the bridge opening out before the human being in religion and cognition"; it draws from spiritual sources and adds by means of its creations "which originate from human nature", something that hitherto was not present in the world (GA 276. 45, 87). In the present lecture-course, Steiner indicates the path between *naturalism* and repose of the astral body (that is, *abstraction*) in artistic conception, both of which need the corrective influence of eurythmy. The three composers named in GA 278 – Wagner, Hauer and Mozart – also seem largely to represent the tendencies mentioned here. Mozart is perhaps supremely qualified to represent the middle way (see p. 394 below). "The great secrets of the world and of life which must be revealed out of anthroposophical research", Steiner claims, "will prove to be artistic; will culminate in art" (GA 276. 25). Art is the path of 'beauty' and lives in 'freedom'.

Already in 1888, Steiner said that the artist raises the world into the sphere of the divine (see Introduction, Endnote 7). In other words:

Fig. 41: M o z a r t , unfinished portrait (1791), by Josef Lange *(Mozart Museum, Salzburg).*

The movements in space through which the human being endeavours to imitate the movements of his heavenly archetype constitute eurythmy. And so it is not just mimicry, nor mere dancing, but stands midway between (R. Steiner. GA 276. 97).

Once again, "midway between" does not mean an amalgam but an anterior "productive unity" (Coleridge) on another level:

> Through eurythmy… the movements of the etheric body appear instead of the physical body, so that the laws of the physical cease, and the etheric body makes its effect directly in the physical world on the physical plane… the etheric body moves so that it is in the physical world. The astral body becomes what the etheric body is otherwise, going over into the ego-organisation so that we have the human being standing already in a higher world… When the human being moves in the super-human sphere, the laws of the world are not decisive any longer (R. Steiner. Faculty Meeting. Stuttgart 30 April 1924. GA 277a. 141-142).

During the Faculty Meeting, Steiner recommends as excellently suited for eurythmists the study of Schiller's, *On the Aesthetic Education of Man.* E.M. Wilkinson claims: "It stands in the grand tradition of doctrines for the attaining of true wisdom and the realisation of the psyche… of both East and West… What Schiller has to say in Letters XIII-XV about the birth of the play-drive is, structurally speaking, exactly analogous to the opening of the 'Third Eye' in Zen Buddhism." (The "third eye" is surely more an Indian notion?) The book traces the process "from unawareness towards self-awareness"; it stands "alongside *Faust*" and "it is high time it was reckoned among the great books of the world" (E.M. Wilkinson 1960. 78-80 & 82. See Appendix 1 for further details of Steiner's comments on Schiller.)

Etheric movement raises, amongst other things, the subjects of (true) rhythm and repetition, but also counter-movement and a dynamic conception (imagination) of spatial direction and relationships, "imaginations that are both subjective and objective – wherein idea and operative law become one in human being" (O. Barfield. *What Coleridge Thought*. 143). In the soul-element "we can approach nature's creating in the artistic, plastic formative-forces, if we sympathetically and devotedly lay hold of them as they live in metamorphosis…" In order to enter more deeply into the nature of the three soul-capacities, how they mutually metamorphose, we have to "link ourselves in soul with the essence of the soul-element…" Thinking then becomes "spirit-enlivened,… is metamorphosed into vision… and becomes free of the body… We overcome ourselves through this vision of metamorphosis of that which is alive. We enliven our own thinking" (R. Steiner. "Goethe und Goetheanum". Essay in GA 36 and Tb 635. 126. R. Savoldelli suggests that living thinking is the basis of eurythmy in *Bedingungen eurythmischer Kultur*. Stuttgart 1989).

It emerges that, following Schiller, Steiner conceives the contemporary artist (wherever he lives, and however humble his endeavours) as a contributor to an evolving third culture that could transcend the existing geographical-spiritual East-West tension. An environment of freedom will encourage artists to renew ancient traditions which they are bound to discover in their endeavours. It is precisely eurythmy that may herald the "yoga of the West" that C.G. Jung recognised (1936) "the West will produce… on the basis laid down by Christianity" (C.G. Jung. *Psychology and the East*. Ark Paperback. London 1991. 85; see also Appendix 4, where an initial connection to the very beginnings of cultural activity is made, in the light of the renewal which occurred when the T A O eurythmy-exercise was given).

Owen Barfield sums up:

> I would suggest that the East will only understand its own "path" in the terms demanded by our own time, if it learns to link to its own tradition all that the West has been developing as history; and conversely I hold it equally true that the West will only understand its own history – its own child, as it were – by learning to interpret it in terms of a "progress", somewhat resembling the Eastern "path" of the individual soul from terrestrial to divine (O. Barfield. "The 'Son of God' and the 'Son of Man'" in *Rediscovery of Meaning*. Wesleyan. Middletown, Conneticut. 1977. 259).

Appendix 3
"The character of each individual key" (Lecture 5)

There are twelve different pictures of every single human ego, and only after contemplating it from twelve different standpoints do we acquire a complete picture.

Rudolf Steiner. Lecture. Vienna, 29 March 1910,
in Macrocosm and Microcosm *(RSP 1968)*

A careful reading of Lecture 5 suggests a vast canvas. The warning about "taking things schematically" mentioned at the outset may even be seen as a main reason for this lecture; certainly, Steiner is not complaining about the artist's preparation in harmonic analysis! [1] With the warning, *artistic help* is offered. Steiner is concerned with "tackling the most predominant element of all artistic endeavour". This is what he calls "making... spirit and soul manifest". Steiner's advice is uncomplicated, more far-reaching than appears at first glance, and in delivering it he faces his own challenge to keep "within the musical element". He vindicates tonality as a pathway to "real humanity" (89).

In two places in Lecture 5, Steiner mentions "atonal music" (82, 86). It seems clear here that "music" = "musical conception", or "musical system" (not "pieces"). In her synopsis of the lecture, Marie Steiner took atonal music to mean "inaudible melody, non-sounding music". This is not an incorrect designation of Hauer's later career. It is, nevertheless, far too simple an interpretation of Lecture 5, which deserves a fuller discussion. It is also misleading simply to state that eurythmy "translates the audible into the visible" (*Eurythmy as Visible Song.* 1932. xvi). "Eurythmy", writes M. Proskauer, "does not make visible, and thereby illustrate, that which is audibly heard. What is heard is transformed in practising to an inner, inaudible singing. This singing unites with the feeling which comes towards the soul upon the waves of the air" (*RB* 22. Dornach. January 1992, tr. in *EA Newsletter.* Aberdeen. Summer 1994). Moreover, from the point of departure onwards, the eurythmist and the musician seek together for the musical element; otherwise the eurythmist is forever "late", and merely "illustrates" the audible sounds. (This means, of course, that the musician has to extend awareness into the eurythmical space, just as an accompanist inwardly sings with the singer or the instrumentalist.) In attempting to discover Steiner's meaning, light may be shed on the question of eurythmy and twentieth-century music, one that is apparently not directly discussed. I believe that in this lecture Steiner gives to contemporary artists the most helpful, practical hints for a way forwards in freedom.

The atonal conception

The dictionary definition today of "atonal" is "not in any key", *i.e.*, lacking a tonal centre, or keynote (compare, "the heart is the tonic". NB 494. 4). The attempt of atonality to "reach for the stars" caused a split with tonality on the *musical* level. Atonality identified the twelve "tonal realms", or "tonal regions" (Pfrogner's "*Tonorte*") with the twelve tempered, semitone-spaced notes of the keyboard which exist on the *empirical* level (C to B in tonal notation). These notes were then made absolute in a thoroughly abstract manner. This decision means that a new notation should have been found, but the attempts never caught on. Atonal music is *not* "music like any other music", as is often claimed. It denies the diatonic arrangement of seven, and consequently also the harmonic realm based on it. But the fact remains that when the interval C-G sounds, we all hear a "fifth" and not "seven semitones"! The diatonic arrangement is demonstrably inherent in our listening. Ruland regards the atonal step as an historically necessary "death", which ushered the experience of twelve, initially separate, primes. "We remain captives of the Kali Yuga [the age of darkness which began 3101 BC and ended in AD 1899] until the tyranny of the system of twelve has been overcome" (Ruland. 1992. 164).

From the point of view of Steiner's "educational stance", the phrase "character of each individual key" might be compared with his phrase "melody in the single note" (see Endnote 17); in other words, we are invited to do some thinking. With the latter we have a "window" into etheric experience. Other intervals, too, can become "windows" into the spiritual world – when we "become" them (see Lecture. 1 Jan. 1915 in GA 275. RSP. 1984. 100ff.). According to Pfrogner and Ruland, experience of melody in "the single note" leads us to the arrangement of seven, the etheric level in the tonal system. Here in Lecture 5, the sentence after the one mentioning "each individual key" speaks of "the difference between major and minor keys". This is an important hint. In Lecture 8 we learn that what forms the difference is the polarity of "receptive feeling" and "active will", which we recognise the dark (feminine) spirit and the light (masculine) spirit of the yin-yang polarity (see also Kux. 1973. 60). It is from the soul-experience of "feeling" and "action" that "all eurythmy has to proceed" – consequently, Steiner adds, "you must not be thinking!" (see Endnote 65) while engaged in eurythmy. This, of course, is no prohibition to research, which would seem to be demanded as well.

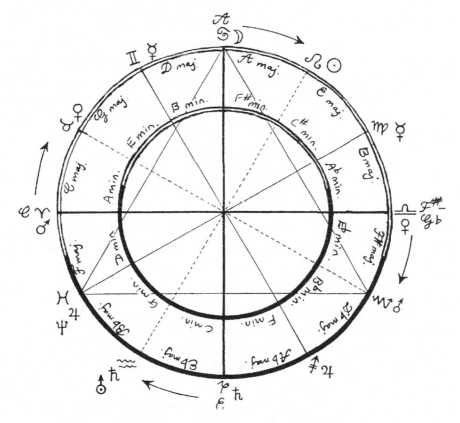

Fig. 42:   Beckh's Tone-Zodiac (H.Beckh, op. cit.) first published in 1925, showing lighter keys (above) and darker keys (below) and three 'crosses of keys' .

The diatonic system

Since c.1685 the use of *musica ficta* and the advent of harmony (Monteverdi (1567–1643) had already resolved the dominant seventh chord to the tonic), contributed to reduce the musical system of eight (some scholars number more) primarily monophonic modes to two standardised modes, the major and minor scales. The enhanced experience of the tonic as centre shows that "music" incarnated further into the human being, creating at the same time the dominant and subdominant directions (which are not part of monophonic, modal music). Just as the concept "human being" is split into the two sexes, so these two scales are united in a higher concept, too. Steiner's "each individual key" becomes *the one fundamental key in dual form* that became prominent after the Renaissance. (Perhaps this is the most likely reason why Steiner identifies the degrees of the scale of C major with the intervals, *appearing* to confuse note and interval. In other words, C is the archetypal prime, and so on.) From approximately the time of the voyages of discovery in the physical world, this "individual key" began its exploration of the circle of fifths, sounding now from one, now from another of the twelve directions of the inner, or cosmic, world (Steiner's "invisible element") which stands in the background. This background is Beckh's "spiritual unity of twelve", and Pfrogner's "enharmonic arrangement of twelve". (Pfrogner revives the terms diatonic, chromatic and enharmonic for the "realms of the etheric, astral and ego *in the tonal system*".) It is this background which manifests "the character of each individual key" *in musical compositions*. This character derives from the inner listening of the composer. (Beckh's pioneer work on the keys – see Fig. 42 on p. 351 above – is uncontested by anthroposophical musicians, such as Ruland, Peter, and Oberkogler.) This inherent aspect of the enharmonic arrangement of twelve is to be heard through (or put another way, released in our inner listening by) the "standard" diatonic major or minor key, or the arrangement of seven. (Below, some practical ways of working are reported, p. 354f.)

The twelve tonal realms, then, are likely to be the spiritual reality that may allow the "possible corrective influence of eurythmy *in this direction too*"; that is, in addition to the "naturalism" mentioned in previous lectures, we now face the *abstract, atonal conception* to which "we approach very near", but from which "it is not possible to come to the movements of eurythmy" (82). The long list of twentieth-century composers who found new things to say with diatonic music (the arrangement of seven against the background of the enharmonic arrangement of twelve) is proof enough that the diatonic system is not out-dated. Yet, as has been claimed, tonality did suffer a "death" after the turn of the nineteenth century, though it was not destroyed. (See Karl H. Wörner. *Die Musik in der Geistesgeschichte: Studien zur Situation der Jahre um 1910. Abhandlungen zur Kunst-, Musik- und Literaturgeschichte.* Band 92. Bonn 1970; usefully summarised in Frank Berger. *Gustav Mahler: Vision und Mythos.* Stuttgart 1993. 100ff.) Consider a few events: Mahler's death (1911); Schönberg arrived at atonality with his op. 11 (1908), his "method of composition with twelve notes" with opp. 23 and 24 (1923); Hauer's first twelve-note piece, *Nomos*, (1919); Stravinsky's ballet music *Rite of Spring* (1911-13) – for parallels here see F. Berger, "Stravinsky's 'Rite of Spring' and the birth of eurythmy" in *EA Newsletter*. Aberdeen. 1995); Berg's *Wozzek* (1914-20) – also, Kandinsky's abstract pictures; Einstein's theory of relativity; social upheaval; individual and national independence; the First World War; and anthroposophy itself! Charles William's phrase concerning poetry after the death of Hopkins – "unredeemed tradition plunged into one of its recurrently ghastly pits, and redeemed tradition underwent one of its periodical phoenix-changes" – can be applied here too, but not everything can be so neatly summarised. A "threshold situation" existed when eurythmy was born, a fact fully appreciated by Steiner. Eurythmy is an art that stands on the threshold, revealing the invisible element that has to be experienced and created at every moment.

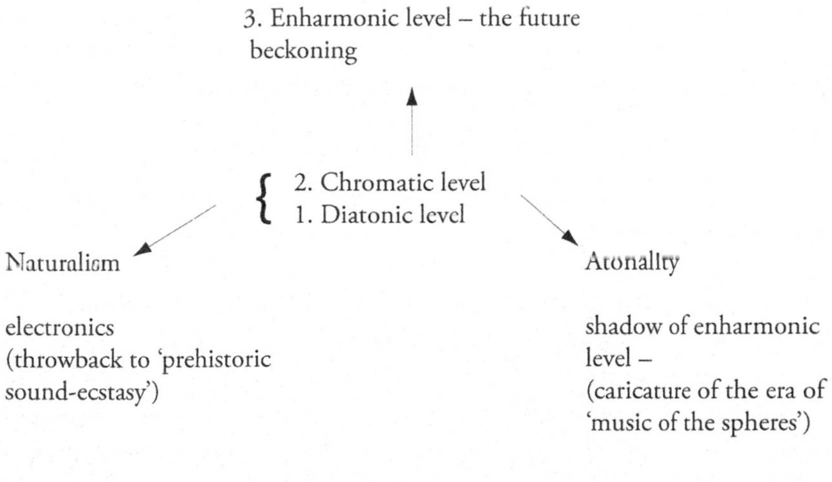

3. Enharmonic level – the future
beginning

↑

{ 2. Chromatic level
{ 1. Diatonic level

Naturalism ↖   ↘ Atonality

electronics   shadow of enharmonic
(throwback to 'prehistoric   level –
sound-ecstasy')   (caricature of the era of
                               'music of the spheres')

Fig. 43:   A survey of twentieth-century developments in music: The diatonic-chromatic levels of the tonal system, growing into the enharmonic level, and the main deviations – after H. Pfrogner, "Orpheus Dismembered" (1957) in *Zeitwende*. (A.S.)

The harmonic element

The harmonic significance of chords, often metaphorically described by musicians as "directions", becomes actual visual directions of eurythmical space. Since "musical sound appears through the whole human being" (whereas "the spoken word appears on the human being". R. Steiner. Lecture. Dornach. 23 Aug. 1915, in GA 277a. 68), the human being can "fill up" these directions and reveal the way musical harmony behaves. This activity adds a social dimension ("quite another aspect"), and develops a "choral eurythmy".

Now the twelve zodiacal positions in eurythmy (introduced in the "*Eurythmy as Visible Speech*". GA 279. Lecture, Dornach. 7 July 1924) are another matter. They are *Stellungen*, "postures". The musical realm is the astral realm of *Melos*, not that of the "ego-organisation" of speech, mentioned again at the outset of Lecture 5. Yet the "astral human being" is not to "remain stuck" in this astral (= "starry") realm of light. The artistic path is meant to overcome "the astral body in repose" that does not want to manifest melos. In Steiner's psychology it is the head that is "at rest" (like a spectator "calmly sitting in a railway carriage… carried forwards by the limbs" – R. Steiner. *Study of Man*. Lecture X. RSP. 1966. 143). Steiner does not lapse into slogans in this lecture, but "abstraction" is clearly meant. Steiner saw it as his mission to tackle abstraction. Beginning with his philosophical works, he 'wished to rescue knowledge out of this destructive element" (op. cit. 54).

Tonality as a path forward

Music-eurythmy is not concerned with illustrating the "moods" of the keys. It has nothing to do with illustration. Through showing the "tensions and relaxations" (Lecture 6) in musical sound, eurythmist and musician together create the moods. A concrete means is provided through ensouling the angle-gestures. U.-I. Gillert describes the combining of the feeling for intervals with the angle-gestures (1993. 16ff.). A further stage is the practising of awareness in the arms of the degrees of the scale of the key in question, together with its relation to the archetypal key (C major). Take F major as an example: the gesture of width (which approaches from below the threshold between lower and upper tetrachords of C major) becomes prime in F major. E as the seventh, contains something of the character of E as the third of C major. B, the striving seventh of C major, is flattened to become the relaxed fourth degree of F major, and so on. These phenomena (amongst others) contribute to the traditional pastoral, religious and even jovial character of F major, which, when felt in the arms, is portrayed in the eurythmy gestures. This way of working characterises solo and group work in eurythmy. Choral eurythmy can enhance that which a solo performer can accomplish through the possibility of showing the detailed changes in the composer's harmony, and in particular modulation to other keys.

Here we should pause to consider the relationship of the subject (harmony) with that of "major and minor". Steiner takes up Hauer's limited view ("acoustic noise") and redeems the triad by relating the terms major and minor to the two fundamental streams of all ensouled movement, and furthermore relates these to the human organism (see Endnote 9). The gestures for the triads are used in eurythmy interpretations, though it *can* be claimed that they were given as exercises

Fig. 44:   A Chinese Temple (from G. Richter, Art and Human Consciousness, reproduced by courtesy of Floris Books, Edinburgh).

to show a primal polarity in all music. Like the movements for the triads, movements expressing harmony are also artistically shown on stage. Are we to conclude that "harmony" is limited to music's classical epoch? Is something beyond a traditional harmony exercise also implied for choral eurythmy in Lecture 5?

At the end of the present lecture-course, Steiner describes eurythmy as "a beginning, perhaps only an attempted beginning", and furthermore, the simplicity of the musical example in Lecture 4 is recognised as "somewhat home-spun". At the same time, such concepts as "major and minor" and "tonic, dominant and subdominant" go further than Hauer's remarks about "acoustic noise". ("Every chord in itself is a noise, as long as it is not dispersed into a melody by the musical human being. A chord

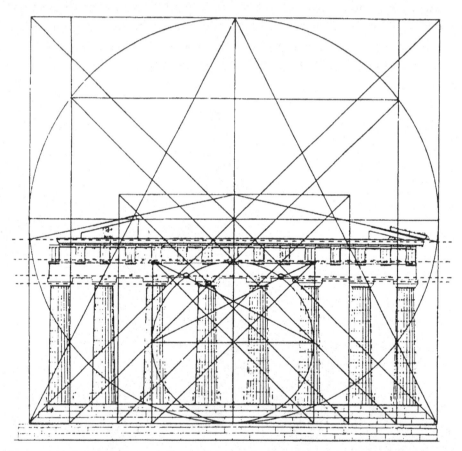

Fig. 45:   In this geometric analysis of the Parthenon by Tons Brunés from his book The Secrets of Ancient Geometry, it can be seen that the architecture is governed by the relationship between side and diagonal in a series of squares. Each of the squares is in relationship to the larger square enclosing it in the ratio of 1 to 1.25; therefore the whole proportional system is based on the functional relationship of 2 to 1 to 1.25 (or 5/4). From R. Lawlor, Sacred Geometry (Thomas and Hudson 1982).

is... a sensory crudifying of melody." Hauer. *Interpretation*...; see 503 below). Steiner treats all the subjects of the lecture-course as simply and basically as possible, to allow "a living stream of development". By taking the static chord and showing the inherent movement in it, Steiner is acknowledging that music has arrived on the earth and that it expresses the human personality. (This situation is the pre-condition for the birth of eurythmy as an art.) The ability to express the principle of transformation, he implies, will herald a re-won, cosmic future. No technical matter of art, and no mystical wish will guarantee this. "It all depends on people", that is, on artistic personalities who accept the challenge *to re-learn*, and thereby transform, their artistic material into *representative human expression*. However unassuming the attempt, this will be "soul and spirit" made manifest.

In this way, it could be imagined that Steiner's indications regarding "tonic, dominant and subdominant" in the context of choral eurythmy may expand beyond their classical definitions. These directions are available to express the lightening of the dominant and the darkening of the subdominant realms of experience in musical form, and in particular the changes between the two. This experience continues in modern tonal composers, who (as Pfrogner observes) are approaching the freedom of the enharmonic arrangement in the tonal system. (A detailed discussion of the present musical situation is presented in Ruland 1992, especially Chapters XXXV and XXXVI. Ruland describes how a complete reversal of the subjective Dionysian (radial) and cosmic Apollonian (cyclic) principles took place at the beginning of the twentieth century. The crisis has been to find a way "for permitting the Dionysian streams, carrying the inward life of the human soul, to flow into the realms of objective, cosmic law... The creative, cosmic archetype of the twelve can begin to illuminate the inner world of the human soul" (151 & 157). Ruland concludes by pointing to a uniting of the polarities of centre and periphery, of cosmic and earthly in the cyclic forces of twelve primes and the radially-tuned scale of seconds, as a musical pathway forward.)

Steiner insists that the development of eurythmy will depend on research into the musical element as "inaudible element", and that its "social aspect" involving "transitions" as a central concept will enrich the endeavour. Perhaps the development of tonal composition in the twentieth century can be met in the interpretations of choral eurythmy. Many composers have found a musical pathway beyond the limitations of the romantic ego, without denying personality or splitting the human being. Eurythmy, it is suggested, can develop to reveal these explorations. Unity has to be achieved, not simply maintained, in both arts. The eurythmical aim, Steiner adds, is to render "the whole musical element in a visual image" (Lecture 5). [2]

The question of the third

We may conclude that Steiner's lecture upholds the artistic path of tonality, and inspires the recognition that the "age of the third" (GA 283, lecture 7 March 1923) has not yet run its complete course. This age began in the Middle Ages when

Fig. 46: The capitals and architrave of the large cupola of the First Goetheanum, drawn by Friedrich Bergamann (from A. Husemann, Der Bau Spricht, reproduced by courtesy of Verlag Freies Geistesleben, Stuttgart).

the human being unites his own feeling for destiny in normal life, with the musical element... the major and minor moods, this peculiar connection with human subjectivity, the active inner life of feeling, in so far as the life of feeling is bound to the earthly corporeality (R. Steiner. GA 283. 125. Pub. tr. 52).

Ruland reveals that the third brought about

the first true musical marriage of radial and cyclic powers... The earlier, classical marriage was accomplished by the cadence, in which both the old, cyclic system based on fifths and fourths, and the radial system of thirds or triads, played a part. In their new union, the cyclic forces rule the twelve-note system of primes while the radial forces rule the seven-membered scale of seconds.

He insists that "our contemporary, third-oriented consciousness is just the right soil for a fruitful development of the two contrasting forces of the future that are embodied in the prime and second. And here they can develop side by side, in harmony" (Ruland. 1992. 165-6).

Human subjectivity caused Hauer to revolt. Yet in this subjectivity lies the seed of freedom which leads the soul to grow beyond itself. The

T A O eurythmy-exercise introduced in Lecture 5 is a means of helping the individual "to overcome *bodily* hindrances". It must be recognised that this tackles the congenital human sickness, which is detachment, apostasy, or in theological terms "original sin" (colloquially, "the perishing human race"!). The notes of the T A O eurythmy-meditation come from four corners of the twelvefold cosmic (not physical) space (see Pfrogner's study, mentioned at the end of Appendix 4. There also appears to be a link to Plato's "World-soul"). The chosen intervals descend in an incarnating gesture. It is a means *"to make your body inwardly supple… for eurythmy"* (89). Personality does not "dissolve" into the cosmos, but is to become a vessel (see Introduction, Endnote 23). The eurythmist, we recall, is "all sense organ" (Lecture 2), an "artist" who today should "feel his real humanity within himself" (Lecture 5), and not an "intellectual virtuoso" (Lecture 4). He or she is "to become a new being" (Lecture 2), and "bring the human personality as soul into the musical element… as the vehicle for the inaudible" (Lecture 3).

The temple of humanity

"The Great Spirit of the world" of the T A O-philosophy has already been creative on the earth. Architecture (a spatial art) is Steiner's example: *Oriental* architecture is "music in space… [it] contains a great deal of eurythmy"; *Greek* architecture, however, is "dreadfully symmetrical"; but the *Goetheanum* "was musical, was eurythmical" (see p. 83, 90 and Figs. 42-44). (The word "eurythmy" itself is taken from architecture: "beautiful proportion", hence "beautiful, harmonious movement". *Oxford English Dictionary*.)

"Over in Greece everything strives forwards… [there is a] freezing into form, a hardening into form… Our building is there… in order to dissolve the forms… It overcomes its own boundaries… and leads out further into cosmic spaces" (R. Steiner. Lecture 31 July 1915, GA 162; see also GA 276. 20-22). (Steiner wrote the following words to the sketch for the south window of the Goetheanum: *"Ich schaue den Bau. Und der Bau wird Mensch. Die Welt baut.* – I behold the building. And the building becomes human being. The world builds." The figure of Orpheus carries a lyre, a musical instrument.) After describing the "mutual relationship of the resting forms of the interior architecture and the sculpture… The building and eurythmical movement should grow together to a whole". Steiner declares that "the forms of the building that I fashioned in feeling originate from the same condition of soul out of which the pictures of eurythmy originate… Probably eurythmy would not have been found without the work on the building… A unity of architecture, and word or music was attempted" (R. Steiner in 1924. GA 36 & Tb 635. 144-145). Surely there is a link to the painting of a picture of "a house", in Lecture 6? After speaking of erasure, and "passing over into the spiritual", we reach "the point where the arts should be… The house will come about. That's what art has to work for" (p. 98).

East and West meet in Steiner's conception of creativity; the "Great Spirit" can be reborn in the human soul. As C.G. Jung puts it: "In the

Christ-symbol the deepest religious experiences of the West and of the East confront each other." Paul expresses the central thought, for example, I Cor. 3:16, 17, and 6:19. [3]

"It is not for nothing that people in ancient times felt the body as the temple of the soul. This indicates how architecture is related to the relationship of balance between the whole body and the whole cosmos" (R. Steiner. Lecture, 5 May 1918. GA 271). The language used is that of melos. In renewing the T A O-impulse, Steiner points to a renewal of tonality as well. "The scale is the human being" (Lecture 3), that is, the etheric human being. In *moving* the concepts of harmony (= "sounding together", or a social counterpoint), there is included the cosmic dimension of "many mansions" or "dwelling places" of John 12:2 (this, of course, is one interpretation of John; the reference is to the Temple), which together form the "holy city" with its twelve named gates (Rev. 21:12). The "heavenly Jerusalem" pictures fulfilled humanity, or in Steiner's terminology "Jupiter" existence. (To René Guénon it is "both 'the Centre of the World' and a symbolic image of the Universe in both

Melos:
the "self-creating musical element in the human being"
"conscious dreaming"
Eurythmy:
the feeling soul expressed in artistic movement
T A O:
"real humanity".

Naturalism		Abstraction
"illustrative"		"schematic"
"(linguistic) thematic"		"astral body in
"from outside"		repose" within.
"the film"		Hauer's "12-note game"

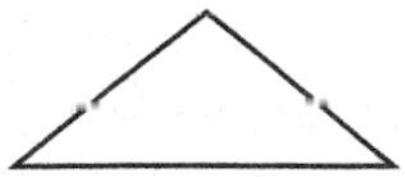

(The triangle is a visual aid, offering an initial – and not exclusive – suggestion towards picturing dynamic relationships.)

Fig. 47:   Eurythmy as ensouled movement between tendencies in art to deviate from the musical element – after Steiner GA 278 (A.S.).

a spatial and a temporal sense" R. Guénon, *The Great Triad*. 115). This interpretation of art is neither "schematic" abstraction, nor symbolism but "the manifesting of soul and spirit... through the human being" centred here on earth, in ensouled movement. The "inaudible element" enables us to "bring the human personality as soul into the musical element" (Lecture 3). "It is really possible today that all the musical elements may be included in eurythmy" (Lecture 7).

In this connection, an extraordinary statement by Steiner about the carved wooden statue that was to stand in the First Goetheanum is illuminating:

> A figure of archetypal man will be set up, which we can also speak of as Christ, and which will have Lucifer on the one side and Ahriman on the other. What is concentrated in Christ we extract and divide up again between Lucifer and Ahriman – in so far as it can be divided up. What is welded into one figure, we perform musically, in that we make it into a kind of melody: Christ-Lucifer-Ahriman. Our building really is formed according to this principle: Christ-Lucifer-Ahriman. Our building... bears the special basic imprint in itself of bringing the sculptural forms into musical movement (R. Steiner. *Der Baum des Lebens und der Baum der Erkenntnis des Guten und Bosen.* "The tree of life and the tree of knowledge of good and evil." Lecture, Dornach. 31 July 1915. GA 162. This quotation immediately follows the passage reproduced as Endnote 1, Introduction.

In the light of this insight, a further interpretation opens up. It is not a question of labelling, but of understanding a polar tension and a resulting "unity of opposites" which transcends both polar opposites. Polar opposites are not logical opposites producing a static balance as a third value. Each value contains something of its opposite, a relationship which can only be imagined. Barfield pictures "two nations at total war, each with a network of spies and a resistance movement, distributed throughout the whole of the other's territory – and each with a secret underground passage into the citadel in the heart of the enemy's metropolis". Barfield points out that such a picture can only help the imagination, indeed, 'the apprehension of polarity is itself the basic act of imagination" (O. Barfield. *What Coleridge Thought.* Wesleyan. 1971. 36). In the triad Christ-Lucifer-Ahriman, Steiner reveals a basic triad of human life and human art. The conception that spurns matter is "Luciferic"; that which is confined to matter is "Ahrimanic". But inasmuch as the former is abstractly systematised, it manifests as "Ahrimanic" in the human unconscious. Inasmuch as the latter limitation is taken for reality, it produces "Luciferic" illusion in the human unconscious (R. Steiner. Lecture Dornach 22 Sept. 1918). Lucifer and Ahriman have been described respectively as "soul without spirit" and "spirit without soul" (Emil Bock. *The Apocalypse.* Floris Books. Edinburgh. 1986. Chapter VII). The underlying triad of the present lecture-course might be expressed as follows, where the apex stands for the dynamic principle of transformation itself.

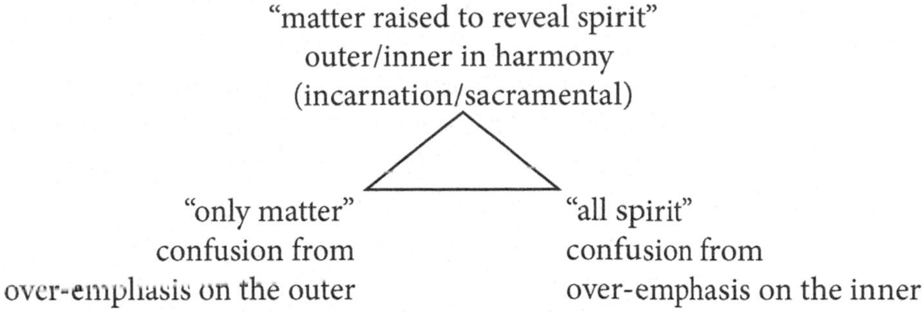

"matter raised to reveal spirit"
outer/inner in harmony
(incarnation/sacramental)

"only matter"   "all spirit"
confusion from   confusion from
over-emphasis on the outer   over-emphasis on the inner

Fig. 48:   Underlying triad of *Eurythmy as Visible Singing* (A.S.)

(The art of eurythmy can artistically reveal the nature of all three values in this triad. Indeed, eurythmy was first publicly introduced in Steiner's third mystery drama, where Luciferic and Ahrimanic beings were portrayed.) For providing resistance, Ahriman actually deserves more than ours thanks:

> By the coming of Ahriman into the world, the human ether-body has become so hardened that it cannot develop eurythmy as a natural gift… In music, in singing, and even in speaking… [it] can express [eurythmical movements] through one channel only – in the lungs and larynx, when it forces the air through these organs… The ego, through desiring to eurythmise completely the ether-body, is obliged to content itself, in singing and speech, with a part instead of the whole of the human being (R. Steiner. Lecture 9 Jan. 1915 in GA 161; tr. Z.69, R. Steiner Lib. London).

Now we recall that "the musical element belongs only to man, not to nature" (end of Lecture 4), and "anything based on the musical element may be expressed in music-eurythmy" (Lecture 7). The human soul is at home in the musical element, where the inner and outer are in harmony; the soul can *breathe*. Out of this law of breathing, there arise the basic streams of ensouled movement, that is, the extended meaning of the moods of the vowels and of the major and minor moods of tonal music. It is "from *feeling* and the experience of the impulse towards *action (Tat)* that all eurythmy has to proceed" (Lecture 7). The spiritual background, the "higher unity" uniting *both* kinds of eurythmy, is the speaking-singing, singing-speaking (a phrase borrowed from lecture of 2 Dec. 1922, in GA 273), or the creative cosmic music of the hierarchies (the zodiac). Since the Mystery of Golgotha, this reality is summed up in the phrase "cosmic Christ", whose work is the transformation of the earth through human beings (see also Introduction endnotes 18 and 20, on p. 28 and Appendix 5).

The creation of eurythmy and of the First Goetheanum are artistic gifts from Rudolf Steiner's life. Only the *light* of the Christ-Sun active in the astral body of the initiate could keep Lucifer in his power, and only the *life* of the Christ-Sun active in his etheric body could keep Ahriman in his power. See further: S.O. Prokofieff. *The Occult Significance of Forgiveness*. Temple Lodge Press. London 1992.

---

[1] *A clear exposition of tonality and key-relationships is given by D.F. Tovey in* Musical Articles from the Encyclopaedia Britannica, *and* Beethoven *(both OUP 1944), and more briefly in his great* A Companion to Beethoven's Pianoforte Sonatas *(The Associated Board. London 1948). Charles Rosen.* The Classical Style *(London. Faber. 1976) follows in the same critical tradition.*

[2] *For an introduction to gesture in Leonardo's "The Last Supper", see A. Bittleston, "The Twelve",* The Christian Community Journal *1948. 39-43; reprinted in Perspectives, June-Aug. 2003. 5-9 (copies from Floris Books, Edinburgh); reprinted in Kenneth Gibson. Adam Bittleston: His Life, Work and Thought. Floris Books. Edinburgh 2010. 222-227. Andrew Wolpert (seminars in Emerson College, 1990s) finds Bittleston's zodiacal designations problematic; he sees, probably correctly, the zodiacal sequence beginning from the disciple on the far left of the picture (Bartholomew) with Aries (Bittleston designates Taurus), and proceeding through to Pisces. Important comments on this painting by Steiner about "the Sun-existence concealed within the Earth" and that which "radiates from the colouring of this picture" appear in, R. Steiner.* Inner Realities of Evolution. *Lecture 2. RSP. 1953. 35f., and Lecture 3. 51f. Leonardo was able to express "the highest and most significant thing". The "inhabitant of Mars" (mentioned by Steiner) who could learn "the meaning of the earth" is likely to refer to the Buddha. This being inhabits the Mars-sphere; his teaching of compassion became historical reality in Christ's sacrificial deed: "the "Wisdom of Love" became the "Power of Love"" (R. Steiner.* The Gospel of St Luke. *GA 114. Lecture 9. Basel. 23 Sept. 1909. RSP. 1964. See also R. Steiner.* Between Death and Rebirth. *GA 141. Lectures 5 and 8. Berlin 22 Dec. and 11 Feb. 1912. RSP. 1975). Steiner explains that Buddha shone down into the astral body of Jesus of Luke's Gospel. R. Steiner.* The Gospel of St Matthew. *RSP. 1965). Christoph Rau discovered the eightfold path renewed by Christ in the mealtimes recorded in St Luke's Gospel:* Die Christengemeinschaft, *Stuttgart, Jan.– Mai 1990; ET in Perspectives 2002. Floris Books, Edinburgh; see also Chr. Rau. "Das Rätsel des Lukas" in Das Goetheanum. 15 Dec. 1991. Dornach). The Nathan-soul is directly connected to the origin of St Luke's Gospel: see S. Prokofieff. Rudolf Steiner and the Founding of the New Mysteries. Chapter 3); Prokofieff also gathers evidence for his continued activity in connection with the building of the First Goetheanum and the creation of eurythmy; see also Appendix 4 (ii) "An esoteric intermezzo", below.*

Leonardo collaborated with a leading mathematician Lucus Paciolo, Divina Propotione *(Venice. 1509), with designs of the Platonic solids. "The Last Supper" is based on relations of 12:6:4:3, which are musical proportions (3:4 the fourth; 4:6 the fifth; 6:12 the* octave). *Leonardo wrote: "Proportion is found not only in numbers and measurements but also in sounds, landscapes, times and places, and in any form of power at all" (K.49r). On the geometry of "The Last Supper", see Martin Kemp.* The Science of Art *(Yale, New Haven/ London 1990) and Leonardo da Vinci:* The Marvellous Works of Nature and Man. *London/ Cambridge, Mass. 1981. 190-99; D. Marini.* An Analysis of Leonardo da Vincis Last Supper. *Harvard Univ. Graduates School of Design. 1982; P. Steadman in* Leonardo da Vinci *ex. cat., Hayward Gallery, London. 1989; F. Nauman. "The construzione legittima: in the reconstruction of Leonardo de Vincis Last Supper",* Arte Lombard *LII, 1979. 63-9; Giovanni Degl'Innocenti, in C. Padretti.* Leonardo Architect. *London. 1986. 283ff.*

[3] *Here we may mention again Jung's warning concerning the West's simple imitation of Oriental yoga. The changed psychological conditions demand that we know who we are and how we are constituted. But "the West will produce its own yoga", he concludes, "and it will be on the basis laid down by Christianity". C.G. Jung, "Yoga and the West" (1936) in Collected Works, Vol. 11. Routledge. London. 1969; also in C.G. Jung. Psychology and the East. Ark Paperbacks. Routledge. 1991. 77-86. Steiner adds that the bodily conditions, too, have changed. R. Steiner. Dornach. 3 Oct. 1920 in GA 322; see also "Yoga in East and West", Lectures V & VI in R. Steiner.* An Esoteric Cosmology. *Lectures, Paris. 25 May to 14 June 1906. St George Publications. New York 1978. Had Jung looked deeper into anthroposophy, he surely would have recognised how it fulfils that for which he looked, and not only for the West. And he may also have agreed with Steiner's claim that eurythmy is "an art for everyone" (R. Steiner. Lecture, Dornach. 7 Oct. 1914; quoted in GA 277a, 65. See short quote, Endnote* 6 *, p. 236 above).*

Appendix 4
T A O

The great TAO comes forth from the centre.
Do not seek the primordial seed outside!

from the Hui Ming Ching

You would not seek Me if you had not already found Me.

Pascal. Pensées. *VII. 553.*

(i) The Tradition

Steiner speaks but little on the T A O. His lecture "The seed of wisdom in the religions" is important here:

T A O is translated as "the goal", or "the way". But we do not get a clear idea of the essence of this religion [more accurately "philosophical, or metaphysical tradition" – Tr. note.] with this translation. T A O expresses – and for the greater part of humanity already for millennia has expressed – the highest to which humanity could aspire. It is the highest that the human being carries as a seed, which one day will blossom fully out of innermost human nature. T A O signifies both a deep, hidden fundament of the soul and an exalted future. It was not only with reticent reverence that the T A O was spoken and thought of by those who knew what was involved. The T A O-religion rests on the principle of development, and it avows: "What today surrounds me is a stage which will be overcome. I have to be clear that this development in which I find myself has an exalted goal towards which I can develop, and that a power lives in me which motivates me to reach that great goal. When I feel this great power, and feel that all beings are moving with me towards that goal, then this force becomes the directed power of movement that sounds to me out of the wind's blast and out of the stone, flashes out of the lightning, sounds out of the thunder and sends its light from the sun. In the plant it appears as the force of growth, in the animal as feeling and perception. It is the force which ever and again brings about form upon form, through which I recognise that I am one with all nature, which streams in and out with my every breath. It is the symbol of the highest self-developed spirit which I experience as life.

I feel this power as T A O." Initially in this religion a god beyond was not referred to, but instead something through which power could be found for humanity's advance.

The stages of humanity's religious development since Atlantis are summarised in this lecture. The word "religion" means to "re-connect", or "re-bind", the inner and outer realms originally experienced as one. Steiner concludes by pointing to the Trinities: Father, Son and Holy Spirit; Isis, Osiris, Horus; Atma, Buddhi, Manas. Trinities are named where the human being felt

> there sounds a corresponding primal sound, which was heard quite clearly in the past, as the primal ground out of which humanity proceeded. This developed to what it is today, and strives towards the future out of the midpoint of his self. The earlier spiritual investigators felt this as the Trinity in the human being... *Theosophy* means "wisdom and truth"; *theology* means "the teaching of wisdom and truth". Theology came from spiritual science, and it has to return to spiritual science (R. Steiner. *Die Welträtsel und die Anthroposophie.* GA 54. Lecture, 16 Nov. 1905. 173 & 175; tr. A.S.).

Albert Steffen suggests that "the Druid culture, Lao-tze, and the teaching of the Logos, when rightly taught, were nothing other than pre-Christian Christianity... in the characters of Chinese writing, the runes of the Teutonic tribes and the numbers of Pythagoras" (A. Steffen. *Der Künstler und die Erfühlung der Mysterien.* 232 – the T A O is described on p. 246ff.).[1]

Richard Wilhelm writes: "The fundamental idea is that the T A O, though motionless, is the means of all movement and gives it law. Out of the T A O, and the *T'ai-chi*, there develop the principles of reality, the one pole being the light (*yang*) and the other the dark, or the shadowy (*yin*)... the characters refer to phenomena in nature", and are the active and passive principles. Chinese thought, however, is monistic, not

---

1   *Sinology has considerably developed since Steiner's day. Instructive introductions to Chinese spirituality include Arthur Waley,* The Way and its Power: A Study of Tao Te Ching and its Place in Chinese Thought *(Allen & Unwin, London 1934; repr. Mandala Ed. 1977; Houghton Mifflin Co., New York 1935). Perhaps the best translations of* Tao Te Ching *are by Ch'u Ta-Kao (Unwin Paperbacks, London 1972); Richard Wilhelm (E.T. by H. G. Ostwald),* Tao Te Ching *(Arkana, London 1989) contains a useful commentary and notes;* Tao te Ching, *tr. by Victor H. Mair (Bantam Books 1990) incorporates details from recently discovered manuscripts. Another important Taoist text is R. Wilhelm and C.G. Jung,* The Secret of the Golden Flower, *tr. Cary F. Bayes (RKP, London 1962). See also Ben Willis,* The Tao of Art *(Century Hutchinson, London 1987); Alan Watts,* Tao: The Watercourse Way *(Pantheon Books, New York 1975; Arkana, London 1992); and especially René Guenon,* The Great Triad *(op. cit.), which is centred on* T A O-*philosophy and shows the triad 'Heaven, Earth and Man' as an inescapable feature of all spirituality. Chr. Peter,* Mozart's "The Magic Flute"... *(forthcoming) is a clear exposition of the language of music as an expression of poplar forces.*

dualistic. "It is quite clear that a metaphysical dualism is not the basis of these ideas. Less abstract than *yin* and *yang* are the concepts of the Creative and the Receptive (*Ch'ien* and *K'un*) that originate in the *Book of Changes [I Ching]*, and are symbolised by heaven and earth. Through the union of heaven and earth, and through the efficacy of the dual primal forces within the field of activity (governed by the one primal law, the T A O), there develop the "ten thousand things", that is, the outer world' (R. Wilhelm. 11-12). Wilhelm's well-known translation of the *I Ching, or Book of Changes,* is rendered into English by Cary F. Baynes (Arkana, London 1989); see also *I Ching*, tr. by John Blofeld (Mandala 1984).

C.G. Jung (1875–1961) characterises the T A O as "to go consciously, or the conscious way... by which to unite what is separated... The unity of... life and consciousness is the T A O, whose symbol would be the central white light" (Wilhelm and Jung. 97-8, 103). In his commentaries, Jung pays respect to eastern thought, while – like Steiner – insisting that science and scholarship be retained (as a means, not as an end in itself). He also emphasises the danger of facile western "imitation" (specifically the practice of yoga; see Appendix 3, Endnote 3. p. 365). Steiner comments on the breathing exercises of yoga, higher stages of consciousness, and *The Philosophy of Freedom*:

> This book was meant as a schooling for the soul, to show what western people can do in order to enter the spiritual world itself. In place of these the Westerner must put perception and thinking. Where the Oriental speaks of the development of physical breathing, we in the West say: development of a breathing of the soul and spirit within the cognitional process through perception and thinking (R. Steiner. *The Boundaries of Natural Science.* GA 322. AP. 1983. 121).

T.H. Meyer. *Clairvoyance and Consciousness: the T A O Impulse in Evolution.* Temple Lodge. London. 1991, refers to Steiner's *Philosophy of Freedom* as a modern path to experience the T A O. Sense-free thinking is spiritual activity, and already today contains "the pearl of clairvoyance" as distinct from caricatures of clairvoyance which do not include thinking.

The anti-western polemic of some writers is not only unnecessary but also misleading. The West is not all intellectualism, materialism and destruction – nor for that matter is the East all exoticism, opium and moral turpitude! Watts, for instance, betrays the old Nominalist view of thinking (42). Steiner's philosophy supersedes abstraction. And the point about universal claims of T A O-thought is that they are neither localised nor limited to a particular historical time. René Guénon

(1886-1951), in his suggestive study of traditional triads (*The Great Triad*), centres on Taoist philosophy. A penetrating study of progressive thought in the West might investigate the reappearance of Oriental thought and attitude (in thinkers often unaware of the connection) in the Neoplatonic stream: for instance, in Schiller, Goethe, Hegel and the German Idealists of the early nineteenth century which culminate in Steiner (see R. Steiner. *Riddles of Philosophy*), and (in our own country) in the creations of that lonely genius Blake (1757–1827), and also the largely unsung Scottish saint George Matheson (1842–1906), whose thought, both theological and devotional, is consistently profound and genial. We have pointed to the importance of Coleridge (1772–1834) as philosopher, scientist and theologian (whose expositions, though often fragmentary, were coherently conceived).

The principle of "separative projection" and "unification of opposites" is to be found everywhere, Coleridge claimed, from the creativity of the Trinity to the workings of nature, as well as in society and in individual consciousness: "Every power in nature and in spirit must evolve an opposite as the sole means and condition of its manifestation; and all opposition is a tendency to re-union" (S.T. Coleridge. *The Friend*. I). Outstanding synthetic thinkers in the twentieth century include the scrupulous scientists Jung and Teilhard; the original and bold Scottish theologian John Oman (1866–1939). See in particular *Grace and Personality* (Cambridge. 1917, 4th ed. 1931; Collins. 1960); in *The Natural and the Supernatural* (Cambridge. 1931), Oman argues for the apprehension of the supernatural in and through the natural; O. Quick (1885–1944), *The Christian Sacraments* (Nisbet. London. 1927/ Fontana. 1964) and *The Gospel of Divine Action* (Nisbet. London. 1933); and above all William Temple (1881–1944), theologian and social prophet, whose *Nature, Man and God* (Macmillan. London. 1934), a study in constructive dialectic, argues for a "sacramental universe". The formula *Deus, Homo, Natura* derives from the Middle Ages, but Temple's lectures form another "modern T A O book" (to borrow T.H. Meyer's designation of Steiner's *The Philosophy...*). The crucial point about Steiner is (1) his demonstration that ordinary thinking already contains the intuitive, spiritual element and this can be strengthened, and (2) in eurythmy (and the other arts) the body – or the mode belonging to nature – can become a vehicle for the spirit (T A O). Steiner's philosophy is not "mystical", but a Christian sacramental monism, which relates to S.T. Coleridge's "dynamic philosophy", William Temple's "dialectical realism", and Austin Farrer's "metaphysical personalism".

The implications are that within much western art and thinking, Taoist philosophy is reborn; it also manifests in the complementary categories of eurythmy (*e.g*, speech/ music; the details in music: major/ minor streams; ethos/ pathos; sustained note/ rest; swinging-over/ bar line; the up-down, forwards-backwards, right-left; straight lines/ curves, and so on). The intertwining, interpenetrating yin-yang symbol metamorphoses into the continuous "harmonious-eight" figure. Here, the introduction of a crossing also creates a *third* space within the dual spatial form, an inner space that yet remains open. The "harmonious eight" retains the harmony of the older symbol (as "World-Egg", its two halves have not yet separated to become Heaven and Earth) and develops it. The creative tension is also perceived as the complementary dynamic of the inner and outer curves (see Fig. 40 on p. 340; R. Guénon. *The Great Triad*, especially 33-5; and R. Guénon, *The Symbolism of the Cross*. Chapter XXII).

Polarity also manifests in

(1) *physiology*: A primary example is head/ limbs (rounded/ linear). The collar-bone (mentioned in Lecture 7) with its rounded end and open end is seen as the archetypal bone (for a detailed study, see Husemann. 1994. Part 4). At the next level (the etheric), this polarity becomes reversed as "thoughts" (linear forces) and "will-substance" (rounded gesture); compare Steiner's Notebook 494. 18;

(2) the *human soul* (thinking/ will): *Feeling*, as the middle term, is the realm of art, whose new impulse, "the musical element", began a development since the Renaissance (see Introduction, Endnote 3). This already involves:

(3) the principle of *spirit*: "Ego-consciousness" forms the "crossing point" between the polarity of outer and inner aspects of reality; the lower human members are gradually transformed into higher members, for the sake of the whole earth. The adjective "cosmic" becomes synonymous for "inner"; Steiner's "spiritual world" is the inner, collective unconscious objectively researched and described. *Within* "the human personality as soul" (Lecture 3), cosmic realities are rediscovered, humanised, on earth. In a monistic philosophy, the whole of nature (macrocosm) *corresponds* to something in the human being (microcosm). A marriage of "spirit" and "nature", pre-figured in the Incarnation, becomes the artistic aim (see Appendix 1 above; Endnote 63 and Alan Stott, "The Meditation for Eurythmists" in RB 30. Easter 1999).

A. von Thimus (1806–78), the pioneer polymathic researcher into ancient harmonic theory, quotes Li-si-tschai on *TAO Te Ching*, Chap. 52:

> The T A O is like a tree, whose light is the roots, and whose rays of light are the branches. These branches ray out and bring about in human beings the capacity to see, to hear, to feel and to perceive. The T A O streams from the roots into the branches. Human striving for wisdom begins from the branches in order to seek the roots. For this reason Lao-tze says: "When the human being turns to the glorious rays of the T A O in order to return to its light then it is said of him, that he will be eternally illuminated" (Albert von Thimus. *Die harmonicale Symbolik der Altertums*. 2 vols. Cologne 1868/76. Reprinted G. Olms. Hildesheim & New York. 1972; I. 335. Tr. A.S.).

René Guénon concludes his study with Lao Tze, too:

> "The way which is a way (which can be travelled) is not the (absolute) Way" (*T A O Te Ching*, Chapter 1), because for the being who has become effectively established at the total, universal centre, it is this unique point and this point alone that is the true "Way" – apart from which there is nothing (R. Guénon. *The Great Triad*. 171).

For Coleridge, see p. 331f. above.

S.T. Coleridge. Biographia Literaria. Ed. James Engell and W. Jackson Bate *(Princeton. New Jersey. 1993) is the definitive edition. Everyman edition (ed. G. Watson) is a readily available text with translations of all quotations from ancient and foreign sources (Dent. London. 1956). For the "Theory of Life", see p. 313f. above.*

C.M. Wallace. The Design of Biographia Literaria *(Allen & Unwin. London. 1983) is concise, lucid and very helpful;*

O. Barfield. What Coleridge Thought *(Wesleyan. 1971) is a comprehensive introduction;*

J.H. Muirhead. Coleridge as Philosopher *(Allen & Unwin. London. 1930; Thoemmes, Bristol 1992) still holds its own for usefulness;*

M.A. Perkins. Coleridge's Philosophy: the Logos as unifying principle *(Oxford. OUP 1994);*

J. Robert Barth. Coleridge and Christian Doctrine *(Harvard University Press. Cambridge, Mass. 1969);*

J.D. Boulger. Coleridge as Religious Thinker *(New Haven, Conn. 1961).*

I.A. Richards. Coleridge on Imagination *(Routledge & Kegan Paul. London. 1950).*

(ii) "An Esoteric Intermezzo"

> Looking deeply into the human heart, we can only say: The most important point in the evolution of earthly humanity is that at which people learn to know that there is a power in the Christ-Impulse through which, if they make it their own, they can overcome the forces of death within themselves (Rudolf Steiner. *Exoteric and Esoteric Christianity*. Lecture, Dornach. 2 April 1922. RSP. 1948. 15).

> A faculty destined for development in the whole human race must, initially, be fully evolved in a single person... That which in pre-Christian times could only draw near to man through the mysteries, can, since the Christ-Event, become to some extent a common attribute of human nature, and this possibility will increase (R. Steiner. *The Gospel of St Matthew*. Lecture 7. Berne 7 Sept. 1910. RSP 1946. 104).

Greek culture is frequently referred to in the account of the early developments (GA 277a) and in *Eurythmy as Visible Speech* (GA 279). Greek temple dance is renewed, and the etheric archetype of the human being is to be found in the alphabet as an entirety, and so on. The Greek language is also touched on in the present course (Lecture 1). In Lecture 5, Steiner looks again at Greece, and is in agreement with the musician, Hauer, who complained that the Greeks ruined music by bringing "everything that is related to art into the theatre, thus pouring everything that is audible into visibility". The main point for Steiner is "whether we can love the visible realm". He uses the word "love" five times (linking to a romantic philosophy of redemption; see Appendix 1).

With music, Steiner links to a culture that flourished earlier than ancient Greece, or even ancient India. "Oriental architecture was really music in space; it has within it a great deal of eurythmy" (Lecture 5). The T A O eurythmy-exercise links to ancient China. "We must go very far back, back to the ancient civilisation of China, if we are to find our way into this meditation in eurythmy." We quote on p. 367 above, a long passage from Steiner's lecture on the T A O-experience of the Atlanteans, which was carried over into the Chinese civilisation. Steiner connects to the very beginnings of religion. Religion, he affirms, began when the dichotomy of "I" and "world" began; it has always sought to "re-connect" the human being to the divine world. Steiner's T A O-eurythmy-exercise not only links to the beginnings of human culture; the implied transformation brought about by "love of the visible world", which begins with the development of the consciousness-soul, or spiritual-soul, points to the goal of human evolution.

H. Pfrogner, *T A O – ein Vermächtnis* (Novalis Verlag. ND; tr. in MS, "T A O – a legacy"), is a study but not an exhaustive explanation of Steiner's "four-note sequence". Pfrogner's musical explanation of Plato's account in *Timaeus* of the creation of the "soul of the world" which most likely derives from Pythagorean sources (*Lebendige Tonwelt*. 1981. 107-10), could, however, be even more relevant. Plato's combined arithmetical and geometrical sequences ("two interwoven tetractys, the first produced out of the proportions of the octave 1:2:4:8" – 1, 2, 2^2 and 2^3 –, "and the second out of the twelfth 1:3:9:27" – 1, 3, 3^2 and 3^3 –, and the addition of "two new terms" explained by Plato, produces the "framework of the world-soul". After the initial unity, the two sequences thus begin with 2 and 3 (*cf.*, Matt. 18:20). Pfrogner regards his explanation of the musical series to be in the Dorian mode.

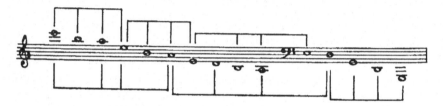

Fig. 49:   The musical framework for Plato's world-soul (after Pfrogner. 1981)

The notes (and their sequence) which Steiner gives for the T A O, occur twice consecutively (indeed, barring one note, it appears three times) within the four octaves plus a sixth. According to Pfrogner's study *T A O...*, we perform the equivalent of the religious act of "crossing ourselves" with the T A O- exercise; if the T A O-exercise relates to Plato's account of creation, then the individual may also attune him/herself to the "soul of the world", and assist "the cosmic process" of its release (see Steiner's summary of Plato's account. Some translations of, and commentaries on, Plato's *Timaeus* are listed below). This attuning strives for the reconciliation of opposites, the harmonising of heaven and earth, and the result is *productivity*.

In the Faculty Meeting (GA 277a), Steiner speaks of "a plastic-musical anthropology", which is surely relevant here. After mentioning the intervals, he continues "in addition to this the human being is constructed out of music. You come to this when you see how he is formed on the left and on the right. He is formed on the ratio of two to three. The lungs are formed on the right according to the number three, to the left according to the number two. This is an inner musical fact. In the relationship of the lobes of the lung you have the fifth". He continues with the proportions for the intervals (which he terms *Töne).* "The whole human being is a fifth up to the surface [of the skin], but he is also inwardly formed according to it" (R. Steiner. Stuttgart 30 May 1924. GA 277a. 141). See also R. Steiner. *Occult Physiology.* Lecture 24 Feb. 1911. RSP. 1983 on the skin; Husemann. 1994, for more details on the fifth; even in external facts, in stepping, the statistical relationship between the time the foot rests on the ground and the time it is in the air also results in 3:2 (Germ. 2nd ed. 207).

"Plato's sculptural-musical path" (Husemann. 1995, Germ. 2nd ed. 77-8) is one of the sections omitted from the English edition. The author sees a "spiritual-historical stream in western civilisation" linking Plato's sculptural account of the world-body and the musical account of the world-soul in *Timaeus,* with "the sculptural-musical-speech work of 1924 which was given for "the urgent necessities of this century". We offer below some initial observations to Steiner's T A O-eurythmy-exercise, a subject still awaiting a major study. (If a link between Plato's world-soul and Steiner's T A O-exercise for eurythmists has already been made, more specifically than Husemann's general link to Plato, the present writer is unaware of the fact.)

Initial observations and suggestions concerning Steiner's T A O-exercise:

(1) unites the world of speech and music, yet retains the distinction;

(2) brings together consonant and vowel, note and interval; the speech sequence suggests "spiritual impact", "minor", and "major" pointing to the essence of the musical world and a modern "middle way" (see Bindl. 383; Ruland. 82). The cosmic connections of the sounds T, A and O in eurythmy are Leo (heart), Venus, Jupiter; Pfrogner discovered a cross from the cosmic connections of the musical notes in his study *TAO*....;

(3) relates the more mobile intervals (seventh, sixth, third and second) to the modern keynote (C) which does not sound. This suggests that the framework of the perfect intervals (prime, fourth, fifth and octave), which are the more formed intervals, has to be inwardly experienced by the individual meditant (without Steiner's decisive description, the note-sequence would easily be heard in D, as Pfrogner heard his musical version of Plato's mathematics). The four notes, it could be argued, are pentatonic – yet by using interval terms, Steiner implies C as keynote, thus relating to "European civilisation" (Lecture 5). The four notes, or degrees of the scale, become the inner two degrees of both upper and lower tetrachords, ending with the second "the gateway of the musical

realm" (Lecture 7). In carrying out the exercise, there are four notes, but three "moments".

(4) In Plato, the worlds from the non-dimensional to the three dimensions are traversed in the mathematics (the four stages may be taken as an esoteric shorthand for the four elemental worlds of fire, air, water and earth – see Fideler. 234). A further human orientation involves the numbers two and three themselves (left and right side, lung formation and the fifth). With the musical system of seven, Steiner's sequence becomes a meditative act that is prepared with the (not-sounding) octave ("Higher-Self", see Endnote [12]), begins with the entry of spirit (sounding 7th-6th), proceeds past the threshold between upper and lower tetrachord (not-sounding 5th-4th), to the realms of "feeling" (3rd) and "will" (2nd) (compare here the Goethean threefold picture: hand, lower arm, upper arm correlates with thinking, feeling and will. The vowels of the T A O correspond with the minor and major streams of music, flowing along the inner and outer sides of the arm, as well as left and right sides of the body). A dynamic (fast to slow) is shown in the overall allargando ("the final note sustained for a long time"). The implied (not-sounding) prime (the "Unplucked String" of the ancients) might be experienced as the reawakened centre within the incarnated individual. In Far-Eastern tradition this is the "Invariable Middle", the place of perfect equilibrium, and the point where the "Activity of Heaven" is directly manifested.

The exercise is "a wonderful means of making your inner bodily nature inwardly supple, and able to be artistically fashioned in eurythmy" (Lecture 5). Husemann explains that the "sculptural" octave of the body becomes the musical octave of the collar-bone, taken as "prime" in eurythmy (1994. 192). Perhaps this octave/ prime fact can become transformed into a prime/ octave experience in this exercise, as the light of consciousness penetrating the whole physical instrument releases a counter-movement in the sense Steiner explains with the "inside of the bones" (lecture Dornach 12 Jan. 1924. GA 233; see p. 407 below). For the initiate, the incarnation of the soul means a progressive uniting with the macrocosm. "We become at one with Him, as He becomes incarnate in us," C.E. Raven concludes (*Jesus and the Gospel of Love*. Hodder & Stoughton. London. 1931/49. 447). The same can be expressed in humanist terms. Leonardo's famous Vitruvian drawing of one figure in two positions within a square and a circle, shows his awareness of both facets; the human being on earth can, at any moment, enter the heavenly state (see Fig. 50). Steiner adds meditative words ("I think speech", and so on) to Agrippa's Vitruvian figures.

In the tonal sequence T A O, perhaps the prime, fourth, fifth and octave can be felt as the complete counter-movement, or better, "given" circumstance; they do not need to be played or carried out with the arms. To Pfrogner "they give the most fundamental orientation that a person needs in order to cope as an ego-being both in relationship to himself and in relationship to the world" (*Lebendige Tonwelt.* 251; see Fig. 55 on p. 382, below). In any case, even without the suggested involvement of these intervals, the exercise becomes self-renewing. See Appendix 5; compare Endnote 41; and "A Note on the Bar Line", Appendix 4 "(iv)").

The T A O-eurythmy-exercise also:

(5) relates the individual to the archetypal pattern of creation, or the "universal law of polarity", which at the same time unites opposites by an act of centring, and so offers a way to overcome dichotomy. Moreover, in Chinese philosophy, 2 and 3 are the numerals of earth and heaven

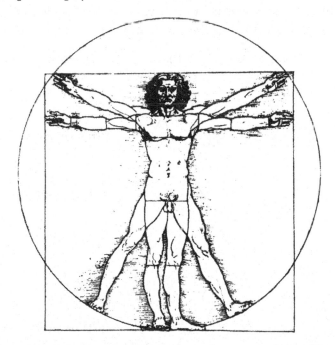

Fig. 50:   Leonardo da Vinci's proportions of man according to Vitruvius.

respectively. These aspects would suggest a renewal of "the middle way", indeed of the Great Triad itself. The West, however, developed dichotomy which began long before the Cartesian division. Steiner often points to the disastrous effect towards materialism produced by the decision the Eighth Ecumenical Council of AD 869, that the human being consists no longer of body, soul and spirit, but only of body and soul – the latter *unam animam rationabilem et intellectualem* – "one rational and intellectual soul" (see, for example, R. Steiner. *Study of Man*. Lecture X. Tr. Harwood. 146f.; A.P. Shepherd. *The Battle for the Spirit*. Anastasi. Stourbridge. 1994). The meditative T A O-eurythmy-exercise points a way to heal this dichotomy. Renewed eastern tradition and restored western tradition meet in a form suitable for our fifth post-Atlantean epoch;

(6) opens to something higher that is yet related to the individual. By uniting with every gesture the "language of the cosmic Word" is given a chance to live in the eurythmic interaction of people (eurythmist; audience, patient, pupil). The meditation is regarded as something the individual carries out; "you will gain an inner strength which you will be able to carry over into all your eurythmy" (Lecture 5). Like the grain of mustard seed of the Gospels, the meditation contains the essence of the activity ("A" and "O" contain the Alpha and Omega of music and of speech); from the introductory words in Lecture 5, its effect is clearly intended to be "sacramental" (following Steiner's language in GA 1, see p. 343, and

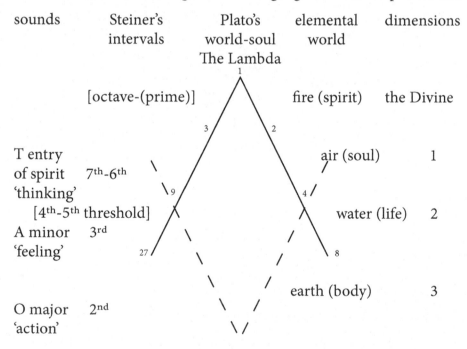

Fig. 51:   A suggested correlation between Plato's World-soul and Steiner's meditative T A O-exercise for eurythmists. Inverted lambda ------ = subjective perception; lambda —— = divine gesture; both should coincide (A. Stott. 1994/98).

Temple's definition, see p. 338). The arrival at the "prime" immediately becomes "octave" upon repeating the sequence. From the point of view of the spirit, the process is incarnation; from the point of view of the individual, the process is spiritual offering. The two aspects belong to *one activity* (compare here the macrocosmic and microcosmic Lord's Prayer, described, for example, in S. Prokofieff. *Rudolf Steiner and the Founding of the New Mysteries*. Temple Lodge Press. London. 1994. Chapter 3). Both movements make up the Incarnation, as St John describes it. "The divine glory" and "the Word became flesh" are two facets of one journey, *one* Christ: "one; not by conversion of the Godhead

Fig. 52:   The figure of Arithmetic between Boethius and Pythagoras, with the generative, geometric progressions written on her thighs. The two series (the Lambda) are used by Plato in *Timaeus* to describe the creation of the world-soul (16th century woodcut).

into flesh: but by taking the Manhood into God" (from the *Quicunque Vult*, the so-called "Athanasian Creed").

Fig. 51, an attempt to summarise processes as a diagram, carries all the reservations of such abstractions – correlations may not be simply "read off" horizontally as equivalents. The diagram is intended to accompany experience of the exercise, and in no way to "explain it away". Rather like a photograph, a static diagram can only suggest movement: here, what is essential in any category is the *movement* (a) of manifestation "out" ("down" in the diagram), or (b) of realisation or "returning" (up in the diagram). Eurythmists bring to life on their instrument the sounds and intervals (was it originally carried out only with angle-gestures?) – "It

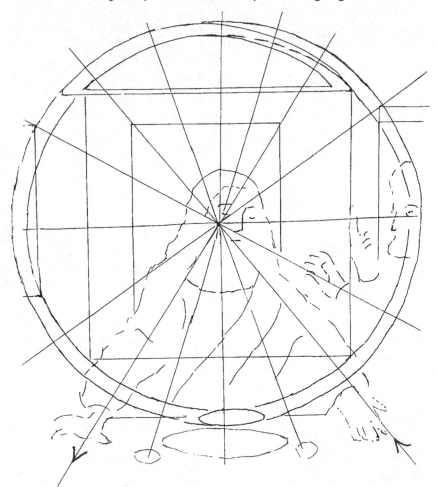

Fig. 53:   A freehand sketch of Leonardo's mural The Last Supper (1495-1497) (detail) in Santa Maria dell Grazie, Cenacolo, indicating some of the geometry. The lines (angles approximate here) continue in the picture (construction of the roof and floor, wall coverings, and so on). An ouroborus, sun disk, lambda, chi-rho and axis-mundi can all be discerned (A.S.).

will become apparent through doing it" (Lecture 5). Afterwards they may care to reflect on the historical and spiritual-scientific background. Further research into the four worlds of tradition will note the modern re-expression in R. Steiner. *Supersensible Man*. Lectures The Hague. 13-18 Nov. 1923. RSP. 1961. 44; and the important lecture Dornach. 9 Jan.1 1915 in GA 161 (typescript tr. Z.69, R. Steiner Lib. London), where Steiner expects "hundreds, indeed thousands" of diagrams arising out of work on the lecture-courses, "for in this way we progress". *Cf*, too, René Guénon. *The Reign of Quantity*.... 63-4, and Fig. 64, below.

"We must go very far back, back to the ancient civilisation of China, if we are to find our way into this meditation in eurythmy" (Lecture 5). Mystery tradition has also come to us via ancient Greece. Compare here: "In this *streaming and receiving* (of the Exusiai) the world-processes are incorporated that appear outwardly to man as natural phenomena" (R. Steiner. Lecture Stuttgart 9 March 1923. GA 283. E.T. 81, emphases added). The Greek Lambda, written on the thighs of the figure "Arithmetic" in an early woodcut as symbol of generation (Fig. 50), is now found in eurythmy also transferred to the arms, and connected to the future organ of generation, the larynx. This may cause us to view afresh the central figure of Leonardo's *The Last Supper*, with the arm-gestures of giving and receiving that portray expansion and contraction, action and non-action (musically, major and minor) that stand behind all creation (*cf.* Fig. 56: "The geometry of Creation"). The geometry of the room-perspective reveals a Chi-cross (X). The central figure's arms, when their

Fig. 54:   Leonardo da Vinci, The Last Supper (detail).

direction is imagined as extended behind, also reveals a cross – the axis-mundi. In this mural, there is one central vanishing-point; it is situated in Christ's right cheek. The square and circle (upon which J. Michell reveals the plan of Stonehenge and Glastonbury) as symbol of the New Jerusalem, or the Temple restored, is also to be found around the central figure in Leonardo's picture. The art of "squaring the circle" requires a triangle; this too is present with the arms of Christ (*cf.*, "of all triangles the largest and most conspicuous in the world are the four sides of the Great Pyramid…" whose "original function… to promote the union of cosmic and terrestrial forces… is clearly stated in the symbolism of its geometry, for the Pyramid is above all a monument to the art of squaring the circle" (J. Michell. 1972. 60). According to Steiner, Leonardo has depicted "the highest and most significant" thing. We still await a full eurythmical study of the T A O, I A O, and the lambda-figure in connection with the gestures and geometry in Leonardo's mural (see also bibliography, end of Appendix 3). (With the connection to the arms, is it a coincidence that Steiner specifically points out that there are 27 bones in the hand and wrist (Lecture 7, p. 107)?

(7) A movement of incarnation can be traced historically in mankind's history. Ontogenesis and phylogenesis are familiar concepts: the history of the individual recapitulates the history of the race. A suggested correlation does not mean the eurythmist "acts out" an imagination of past-present-future (7th-6th: pre-Christian cultures; 3rd: "age of the

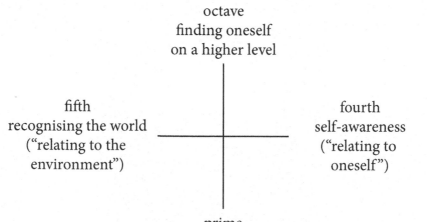

Fig. 55:   "The cross of orientation" (after Pfrogner); contains both "I and Thou" and "you and me".

third"; 2nd: anticipation of the sixth epoch). The meditative act is neither symbol nor historical memorial (just as celebrating Christmas, let's say, or celebrating The Act of Consecration of Man, or the Eucharist, is not merely a memorial to an historical event), but a sharing of present life and a creative movement allowing the future to flow in, here and now. The given link to the beginning of culture is transformed to the goal, because the approach is now reversed (see "the two missions of Michael", lecture Dornach. 22 Nov. 1919, in R. Steiner. *The Mission of the Archangel Michael*. GA 194. AP. 1961; and the description of the "Sun hero" as re-won rhythm and regularity, in R. Steiner. *The Festivals and their Meaning*. RSP. 1981. 36-7). One significant detail emerges: the 5th-4th threshold is silently crossed (the Mystery of Golgotha occurred for us all). Since "the purport of [Christ's esoteric teachings] was that the Cross on Golgotha must not be regarded as an expression of earthly conditions but is of significance for the whole cosmos" (R. Steiner. *Exoteric and Esoteric Christianity*. Lecture, Dornach. 2 April 1922. RSP 1948. 17), we are individually invited during and also between each repetition of the exercise, inwardly to pass the 4th-5th threshold as a counter-move on our own initiative, on the way to the octave (Higher Self at one with the world). Pfrogner (*Lebendige Tonwelt*. 251) depicts these degrees of the scale as a diagram – see Fig. 55 on p. 382. In eurythmy, these degrees actually correspond with the angle-gestures in the archetypal scale of C major:

In the feeling realm of music, the suggested octave-prime, prime-octave context is taken as a calling on the "Higher Self" (see Endnote 12). This "Self" is not an object, of course, but is approached through the whole process that lives between the polarity of "I" and "world". The Higher Self is neither "I" nor "world" alone, but may be experienced in and between both poles. Through the T A O-eurythmy-exercise, each individual person may evoke (1) the creative movement towards incarnation (interval sequence up the arm of the person engaged in eurythmy). This ends on the second degree ("a question to the world"). The question can be answered, but only by penetrating to (2) the inner answer of a counter-movement from "within the bones" towards the world (see p. 407 below). The suggested correlation of the eurythmist's movements and the lambda-figure clearly points to a counter-movement (down the arm of the diagram). This depicts a synthesis: a step towards the union and fulfilment of humanity, and the possibility of the instrument during this fifth post-Atlantean epoch becoming a bearer or representative of "real humanity within yourself" (Lecture 5).

The Pythagorean declared that creation began with One (pre-existent unity) divided by Two (all manifestation requires polarity). Musically, this is the octave. The suggested implication of the T A O-eurythmy-exercise points to a future re-union: the musical experience of the octave, according to Steiner, (R. Steiner. Lecture. Stuttgart 7 March 1923. *The Inner Nature of Music*. 56) "will become for the human being proof of the existence of God, because he or she will experience the 'I' twice: once as physical, living, inner 'I' ("prime", p. 54), the second time as spiritual outer 'I'... directly experienced, in that we arrive at the next higher octave". The spiritual "I", however, is experienced as cosmic communion. The carrying out of the T A O-exercise, and eurythmy in general, is the very opposite of an isolated occupation.

Plato's cryptic account of creation has inspired much profound thought and speculation; see, in addition to Pfrogner:

R. Steiner. Christianity as Mystical Fact. *GA 8. RSP. 1972, Chapter 4 "Plato as mystic". 55-7 and 85, summarises Plato and his significance.*

Translations and commentaries include:

The Works of Plato. Tr. and with commentary by Thomas Taylor. Vol. II (London 1804). 438-45; 595-657 convey the views of the fifth-century commentator Proclus; re-issued The Writings of Plato II (The Thomas Taylor Series X). The Prometheus Trust. Frome. Somerset 1996.

R.G. Bury. Plato. Vol. IX in the Loeb Classical Library. Harvard University Press. Cambridge, Mass. & London 1929, reprinted) gives text, tr. and comments;

A.E. Taylor. A Commentary on Plato's Timaeus. *Oxford. 1928. Tr. and commentary;*

F.M. Cornford. Plato's Cosmology. *Kegan Paul, Trench, Trubner. London; Harcourt, Brace. New York. 1937), tr. and commentary;*

Plato. Timaeus. *Tr. with an intro. by H.D.P. Lee. Penguin. Harmondsworth 1965; contains very brief summaries of A.E. Taylor and Cornford.*

Mathematical commentators include:

Ernst Bindel. Die Zahlengrundlagen der Musik. *Stuttgart. 1985. Chapter 9;.*

Heiner Ruland. Expanding Tonal Awareness. *RSP. 1992. 81-2, summarises Bindl and points to a major/minor polarity in the arithmetic and harmonic division;*

Robert Lawlor. Sacred Geometry. *Thames & Hudson. London. 1982, reproduces illustrations, p. 7; Chap. VIII and explores "Geometry becomes Music", mentioning the tradition of male/female with odd/even numbers: "as Platonists we remember that Two symbolises the power of multiplicity, the octave, the female, mutable receptacle, while Three symbolises the male, specifying, fixing, immutable pattern-giver whose multiplication table gives the entirety of music. This was the 'music of the spheres', the*

universal harmonies played out between these two primal male and female symbols"
(83);

John Michell. City of Revelation. *Garnstone Press. London. 1972, presents much that is supremely informative and suggestive. Plato's gematria in revealed in Chapter 8, "1746, the number of fusion". He shows that Plato's cross of creation of the "same" and the "different" (or "same" and "other"; Timaeus 35), is not + but X; that "the first stage in the creative process is the birth of the Son", and that the third stage forms the* vesica piscis. *"Creation comes about through the union of two forces, positive and negative, corresponding to the symbolic [solar and lunar] numbers 666 and 1080... The gematria of Plato's phrases relates [the geometry of the number seven] to the ideal city, described in* Laws, *which is also the city of New Jerusalem, the lost and promised Kingdom" (86-7). Michell's interpretation of Plato's account of creation remains the most convincing;*

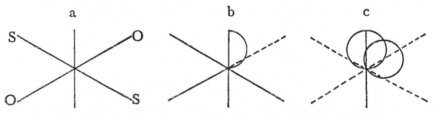

Fig. 56:   Plato's geometry of Creation (after J. Michell. 1972).

John Michell. The Dimensions of Paradise. *Thames and Hudson. London. 1988, is a revised, expanded edition of, but not a substitute for, his earlier book (see above); Chapter 4 is devoted to "The cities of Plato" (107-67);*

Ernest G. McClain. The Pythagorean Plato: Prelude to the Song itself. *Nicolas-Hays. York Beach, Maine. 1978), a complete guide to Plato's musical-mathematical formulations;*

Keith Critchlow, "The Platonic Tradition on the Nature of Proportion", in Rediscovering Sacred Science. *Ed. and intro, by Christopher Bamford (Lindisfarne Press/ Floris Books. Edinburgh. 1994) 133-68, is helpful;*

Joscelyn Godwin. Cosmic Music, op. cit., *includes several references to the Lambda (and Lambdoma, as developed by von Thimus);*

Joscelyn Godwin. Harmonies of Heaven and Earth *(Thames & Hudson. London. 1987) concludes with a section on "The Lambdoma and the Pythagorean Table" (190-3), mentioning von Thimus, Hans Kayser and Plato's* Republic, *and quotes R. Guénon. The "Pythagorean Table" on p. 191 (from Levarie and Levy,* Musical Morphology. *Kent State U.P. 1983. 230) images the universe. "Whenever the two forces of contraction and expansion meet and are held in some proportional balance, a being arises – and a tone is sounded. Every being is both number and tone; both quantity and quality; both existence and value." We may add here that such numerical information may suggest a therapeutic application; in the hands of unscrupulous sonic experts it has produced unbelievable weapons of destruction. See also:*

Hans Kayser. Akroasis. *Ploughshare Press. Boston. 1970; an introduction to harmonical theory;*

C.G. Jung. "A Psychological Approach to the Trinity, III Greece" in Psychology and Western Religion. *Ark Paperbacks. Routledge. London. 1988. 13-24, and;*

David Fideler, Jesus Christ, Sun of God: Ancient Cosmology and Early Christian Symbolism. *Quest Books. Wheaton, Ill. Madras & London. 1993. 220-23 and 234-35, for additional insights.*

P.T. Forsyth. The Person and Place of Jesus Christ. *1909/ London. 1955; describes the* kenosis *and* plerosis *as mutually related movements. See also* The Work of Christ. *1910/ London. 1952, by this master.*

Chr. Peter. Die Sprache der Musik in Mozarts 'Zauberflöte' *traces polarities in all the categories of music (e.g., abundant "life", constricting "form" or again "inner space", "inner time") and the transition between them ("inner centring").*

René Guénon's work on spiritual traditions and their relevance today is outstanding; his approach is metaphysical and he does not proselytise.

C.G. Jung, Psychological Types *(149ff.) draws attention to the affinities of Schiller's* Aesthetic Letters *with eastern thought. His commentaries on eastern texts are included in* "Psychology and Religion: West and East", *Collected Works. Vol. 11. Routledge. London & Princeton, New Jersey; also readily available as C.G. Jung.* Psychology and the East. *Ark Paperbacks. 1986.*

Hertha Kluge-Kahn. Johann Sebastian Bach: Die verschlüsselten theologischen Aussagen in seinem Spätwerk. *Möseler. Wolfenbüttel & Zürich 1985 (tr. in MS), gives a detailed revelation of Bach's creative use of the magic of numbers in the cycles of his last twelve years, demonstrating his use of cabbalistic, pythagorean and other traditions; Kees van Houten and Marinus Kasberger.* Bach en het getal *(De Walburg Pers. Zutphan. Holland. 1985) is apparently a similar study, and includes the Passions.*

Martin Buber. I and Thou. *T. & T. Clark. Edinburgh. 1959; Scribner. New York 1958; first appeared in 1923 in German. Sections of this modern classic on relationships can be read as a suggestive commentary* inter alia *on the mystery of the octave. The translation by W. Kaufmann contains notes, but the tr. is disappointing. Scribner. New York. 1970.*

(iii) R. Steiner, Torquay, 22 August 1924

The Divine Father-Principle has always been associated, and rightly so, with the transition from the supersensory to the material, and through the Divine Son the transition is brought about from the sensory and material to the supersensory (R. Steiner. Lecture, Basel. 26 Dec. 1921 in *The Festivals and their Meaning.* GA 209. RSP. 103).

Thoughts and experiences arising from the lectures *Eurythmy as Visible Singing* and in particular concerning Steiner's T A O-meditation for eurythmists, may help an approach to the enigmatic passage at the end of the lecture-cycle held in Torquay. [1] Music is given a future possibility to manifest "the Christ-Impulse in its true form". There are accounts that the expected musicians were not present at the lectures, and that Steiner had to be content merely to hint at this subject. A lecture-course for musicians – as well as further courses for eurythmists – was planned, in which Steiner may have expanded on the theme, but his death prevented this from taking place.

It is perhaps not without significance that the subject was raised in England, the westernmost Eurasian counter-pole to the Mongoloid Far East. Both the musical subject of the Torquay lecture and the T A O-exercise for eurythmists concern incarnation, and the transformation that is required for a new beginning. After the rejection by the Allies of the German peace initiative of 1916 to end the War, Steiner lectured in Basel, 21 Dec. 1916 on "Christmas at a time of grievous destiny". [2] A link, indeed a message, to some of the descendants of the Ingaevones seems to be intended; the Anglii are specifically mentioned, and the divinity "Ing". The Anglo-Saxon rune is translated: "Ing was first seen among the East Danes. Later he went towards the East. He walked on the waves, followed by his chariot." The northern mysteries decayed, but the Nertus-Ing symbol was fulfilled in the birth recorded in St Luke. We see how "people in the north developed a particularly intense feeling for Jesus" (68). The intention of the builders of Solomon's Temple is also described: "The Temple was like a star whose light enabled spiritual beings to guide the souls into bodies which would be capable of understanding its meaning. *It was the central star of the earth*, shining out with special brightness into the spiritual heights" (58-9). Solomon's Temple is the central symbol of Freemasonry, that form of occultism that has spread from Britain throughout the world. The physical temple lost its significance when Christ entered earth-evolution. Understanding of that Event is not widespread, and the crucifixion continues. "A time must come when the second part of the Christmas proclamation becomes reality: 'Peace to the men on earth who are of good-will'," Steiner proclaimed. (72)

The following clues may prove helpful towards finding a way of working with the musical passage of the lecture at Torquay, which many people while not claiming to understand the whole content, yet, with its reference to "the highest summit of earth evolution", feel that it points to some ultimate secrets.

Two movements seem to be characterised:

(a) the Incarnation (minor stream);

(b) the response of "the human being yearning towards the cosmos" (major stream). These movements correspond to, and develop now on a cosmic basis, Goethe's designations of "ascending" and "descending" movement, with its accompanying "expansion" and "contraction" upon which polarity Steiner develops music-eurythmy.

Further points: (1) "The third in the major" which is brought "inwardly as far as a mystical feeling... totally enclosed musically within the human being" may epitomise most of our "age of the third".

(2) The musical interval of the fifth is a *perfect interval* (that is, there is no major-minor differentiation). The *diminished* fifth (for example, C to F#) forms the exact physical middle or threshold that halves the octave (C to C') into two tritones. The note occupying the dividing position (F#), however, does not sound in the major scale (C major), being the new note of the next scale (G major) on the sharp side of the circle of fifths. The fourth (F) approaches the threshold from below; the perfect fifth from C (G), forms the first degree of the upper tetrachord, and marks the threshold within the sevenfold scale. Some musicians think the phrase "area of the fifth in major", which "as a protective mantle" forms the "boundary between the human and the cosmic realm", refers to the whole system of the circle of fifths, and moreover in a progressive movement in the "sharp" direction (with the sun, or clockwise, in Beckh's diagrams). This is a reflection of the cosmic twelve within the human soul. Music "lives and vibrates here and now, on earth" (GA 276. 36-7).

Steiner beautifully and scientifically describes how from the fourth post-Atlantean epoch onwards "the human being unites his own feeling for destiny in normal life, with the musical element... the major and minor moods, this peculiar connection with human subjectivity, the active inner life of feeling, in so far as the life of feeling is bound to the earthly corporeality". [3] This seems to be summarised here as "the area of the third". The "area of the fifth" (taken to mean our tonal system) forms the "boundary" where the human being "yearns out towards the cosmos".

(3) The cosmic side of the picture is described as commencing with "discords of the seventh". Composers, as Steiner puts it, "never make use of a discord unintentionally" simply as unpleasant noises; they provide "inner movement" (Lecture 6) and stimulate consciousness. The seventh directly represents the stage of Intuition in spiritual consciousness (GA 283. 145; E.T. 73), that is, the third and highest stage (beyond "seeing" and "hearing" of Imagination and Inspiration) to a

higher "life" that unites with spiritual beings. It is a turning-inside-out, a Marsyas-experience (see Endnote 15). These discords express human experience "on the way to the various regions of the spirit" (not, to be exact, "of the soul"). This points to initiation experience beyond, or better behind, the circle of fifths of earthly music. (For all its richness, this circle anticipates a further spiritualisation from further penetration in musical development.) May we not reasonably assume that the beings of the zodiac ("regions") are meant (mentioned in the "meditation for musicians")? [4] As these sevenths "vanish" they become "'a musical firmament' to the musical experience". This cosmic background implies something even more sublime than our art of music has so far produced. The creative forces of the zodiac are already present in the background (Pfrogner's "enharmonic level", or "the spiritual level in the tonal system") of the circle of fifths; perhaps the passage in question points to a more direct manifestation of "the enharmonic level" in the future, as Pfrogner suggests (*Zeitwende*. 89).

The discords seem to be produced by "the subtle intimation of a minor experience" (Incarnation) "in the major experience" ("storming out with yearning"). A simultaneous movement and counter-movement is described. Then, we are to "find our way back… in an intense minor mood from the discords of the seventh… into the realm of the fifth in the minor" permeating it "with the area of the minor third". We "let the octave stand behind the firmament, but only approximately". Steiner's language is an attempt at describing "feeling experience". In the eurythmy-lectures, he describes how "the octave simply falls into the keynote… [it] comes to meet you from the world in order to calm the prime within itself. That which was unfinished to begin with is now complete" (Lecture 2). Once again, this describes movement and counter-movement (or response). Steiner points out elsewhere that the complete experience of the octave will only mature after thousands of years. This feeling-experience relates, as we have seen, to the divine (Lecture 7. March 1923. GA 283. 128; E.T. 57-8). It appears that we are to unite in feeling with the life of the cosmic Christ, which we meet "on the way to the various regions of spirit", for He not only sums up the entire zodiac but the entire sevenfold scale as well. In the Incarnation, God became Man. From that achievement, Christ leads the way back to God from within humanity. [5]

These thoughts do not exhaust the meaning of what Steiner alluded to in Torquay. Further details result from considering the planetary spheres, which relate to the descriptions in *Theosophy*. [6] The musician, we recall, is encouraged to research the life between death and a new birth (see, *e.g.*, Introduction, p. 20f.; "you could make a symphony" of the cycle GA 153). "The area of the fifth" could refer to the Sun-sphere, to which the Mystery of Golgotha is connected (GA 141. 183); this Deed ensouled earthly culture. The Sun-Sphere marks the boundary between the soul-world (inner planets) and the spirit-world (outer planets). The path of incarnation described in Torquay, proceeding from the divine world (octave), through the "discords of the seventh" (zodiac) and outer planets, brings what evolved on Ancient Moon. "The death on Golgotha… was the birth of the Earth-Soul, and everything that can be brought to the Earth from cosmic expanses, even from beyond the Saturn sphere, is related to the Earth-Sphere as the Earth-Body is related to the Earth-Soul" (GA 141. 186). The inner planets (Moon, Mercury and Venus) comprise the soul-world. "The sentient soul relates to the minor third, the sentient [or astral] body to the major third… The facts of human evolution are expressed in musical development more exactly than anywhere else" (R. Steiner. Lecture Stuttgart, 8 March 1923. GA 283. E.T. 70. In this lecture, Steiner, using interval terms, describes how he wrote *Theosophy*; he also gives the eurythmy forms for the intervals. In the tradition of mystery wisdom, he sees musical knowledge and spiritual knowledge as correlative).

As an initial summary, we would underline two points:

(1) In the "concord of the third in the *minor* there lies the possibility to represent the Incarnation as something musical";

(2) when you go back (counter-movement, or response) in the *major* in this region, the "Hallelujah" of Christ will be allowed "to sound in a purely musical way out of the formation of the musical sounds".

The Incarnation historically occurred; "it all depends on people" to take up the inspiration of "anthroposophical spiritual-science" and unite with Christ's Impulse of love, for humanity to join His "Hallelujah". This musical, and simultaneously human, path

(a) cannot be forced on anybody from outside. But it is precisely because music "appeals to the human being's earth-dwelling soul-spirit nature" (GA 276. Lecture 2 June 1923. 37) that "in the artistic sphere, the musical element belongs to the future of humanity";

(b) cannot be crudely systematised; it is to be musically created.

In his vision of future symphonic music, Steiner mentions three composers. (a) In his *Ninth Symphony*, Beethoven strayed from the realm of absolute music, and set a text (but see Appendix 1 above).

(b) In *Parsifal*, Wagner was content with stage symbolism (the Dove, Communion, and so on). His attempt at a mystery art did not fully succeed. [7] Music "inspired by spiritual science…", however, "will reveal purely artistically and intuitively how the Christ-Impulse in the cosmos and the earth can be awakened symphonically in musical sounds". (c) Bruckner was hampered "by the narrowness of traditional limitations". [8]

The lecture-excerpt from Torquay is unlikely to present direct material as "exercises for eurythmists" (though simple experiments may stimulate experience), but it certainly illuminates much that has been given. "The way to the heart is through the head," as Steiner explains in *The Philosophy*, Chapter 1, and the language of the heart is "the musical element". The way to mankind's future "Hallelujah" (which, we note, has already been achieved by Christ) implies the other stream, the continued suffering of the Incarnation. The mystic death of pre-Christian initiation, Steiner explained in 1905, has been superseded because Christ "suffered for everyone" by undergoing the Mystery of Golgotha. The past tense is correct, yet His suffering continues. His atoning death is the gateway for his followers, who, in pursuing Christian initiation (the deepest source of the creative life), may earn the right to participate in the resurrection body of light. This may synthesise both streams mentioned above (Christ's suffering and our yearning), and also leads to the *secret of the octave*, 1:2. Here we may compare the High-Priestly Prayer: "that they may be one even as we are one, I in them and you in me, that they may become completely one, so that the world may know that you have sent me and have loved them even as you have loved me" (John 17; 22-3).

Steiner concludes his elucidation of the concept of the atonement: "Through Christianity much that is of a communal nature has been brought about, which previously was not communal. The active power of this substitution is expressed in the fact that through inner vision, through true mysticism, community with Christ is possible." [9]

[1] *R. Steiner,* True and False Paths of Spiritual Investigation, *GA 243. RSP 1985. The passage on music, the last third of the last lecture of 22 Aug. 1924, is inaccurate in all three published editions of this lecture-course. An accurate translation, slightly abridged, appears in Lea van der Pals,* The Human Being as Music. *Stourbridge. 1992. Endnote 40. Distrib. <eurythmywm@gmail.com> and Anastasi Ltd.*

[2] *R. Steiner.* The Festivals and their Meaning. *RSP. 1981.*

[3] *R. Steiner. Lecture, Stuttgart. 7 March 1923. GA 283. 125, pub. tr. 52. Ruland (1992. 18) arranges the seven modes in a sequence of fifths from the Lydian [F] to the Locrian [B];*

the former is the most "major" and the latter most "minor" in our modern terminology. Since the age of the consciousness-soul, the major and minor keys (deriving from the Ionian and Aeolian modes) became paramount, though in folk-music and ancient chants of church music the modes live on to this day.

[4] *See R. Steiner, lecture Dornach, 2 Dec. 1922 in GA 283. 113-14; E.T. 42-3.*

[5] *See, for example, R. Steiner. "The birth of Christ within us". Lecture, Berlin. 27 Dec. 1914.* The Festivals and their Meaning. *GA 209. RSP. 1981.*

[6] *See R. Steiner.* Between Death and Rebirth. *Lecture, Berlin 1 April 1913. GA 141. RSP. 1975.*

[7] *See nevertheless, Hermann Beckh,* Das Parsifal Christus-Erlebnis *(Die Christengemeinschaft. Stuttgart. 1930), where Wagner's theme is fairly closely related note for note, interval for interval, to Steiner's account in Torquay (FNs. 3, 5 & 9).*

[8] *Beckh comments on Bruckner's Ninth Symphony as a "threshold symphony" in* Die Sprache der Tonart. *Stuttgart. 1977. 256-61. See also M. Seyfert-Landgraf. "Anton Bruckner", in* Anthroposophical Quarterly. *Vol. 19, 3. Autumn 1974. This writer, following a remark of Karl König, proposes that seven composer-initiates – Bach, Haydn, Mozart, Beethoven, Wagner, Bruckner and Mahler – kept alive awareness of the spiritual world during the onslaught of materialism in the nineteenth century, in "Ludwig van Beethoven, Part II".* Anthroposophical Quarterly. *Vol. 16, No. 2. Summer 1971. Seyfert-Landgraf. "Gustav Mahler and his spiritual relationship to Rudolf Steiner" in* Anthroposophical Quarterly. *Vol. 18, 1. Spring 1973, sketches an incarnation-and-excarnation pattern in the symphonies, a concept worked out in detail by Frank Berger.* Gustav Mahler. *Stuttgart. 1993.*

[9] *R. Steiner. Lecture, Berlin. 27 Aug. 1905.* Foundations of Esotericism. *RSP. 1983. 14. See also R. Steiner. Lecture, Cologne. 8 May 1912. GA 143. E.T. in* Anthroposophical Quarterly. *Vol. 18, 1. Spring 1973. An error in translation occurs on p. 10. The sentence beginning on line 13 should read: "When after long contemplation of the Christ-idea as conceived by spiritual science, an attempt is made to present the figure of Christ, the countenance will be found to contain something that all the arts can, but also must and will make great exertions [to portray]".*

(iv) A Note on the Bar line

In carrying out the T A O eurythmy-exercise, the polarity is present out of which the whole musical and human world emanates: T – spiritual impact; A – "minor" stream; O – "major" stream. In carrying out beat, the T A O eurythmy-exercise stands in the background; the bar line provides the impetus, and counter-stream movement is implied in the "right-left". In this sense, the T A O-exercise not only stands behind the "right – left" of beat, but also the "forwards – backwards" (awake, dream and the *Ruck* or change between) of rhythm, and the "up – down" of pitch (being bound, being freed and the transition in consciousness between them).

Christoph Peter shows that the "separation of the bars promotes consciousness, wakefulness. The power of uprightness dominates. Ties over the bar line form a contrast to this... We dive into the world of the unconscious, where the will-forces are slumbering". [1] Peter's description of how Mozart evokes the naive world of Papageno, but also the fearful world of the Queen of the Night and her vassals, includes the treatment of bar lines (slurs and ties over the bar line). The progress of the opera's princely protagonist, Tamino, is from dependence on the instinctive nocturnal world, to initiation into the radiant world of wisdom.

The artist, says Steiner, must "dream consciously" (Lecture 6); he or she must "livingly anticipate the future" (Goethe). But we experience the bar line as *"a source of light"* (van der Pals and Bäschlin. 44), a momentary awakening when spirit is active. The equivalent spiritual moment in the etheric level of musical sound is the distinct change of consciousness (*Ruck*) between short and long in the life of *rhythm*; in the astral level it is the transition between being bound (deep register) and being released (high register) in the breathing of *melody* (like the silent '*ee*' in the change of direction between major and minor streams); all three require a definite grip. "Awareness of the Now" is described by Georgiades: [2]

> Awareness of the Now, and thus of the action, becomes visible as fire and power that scorches and blasts everything. It is like a flash of lightning which reveals Substance itself, with the sudden illumination that Meaning, as it were Eternity, is manifested as the Now, as unique moment.

Imaginatively speaking, a "bar line" occurred in world-history between 1 BC and AD 1. [3] During the life that began "at the turning point of time" (a phrase from the "Foundation-Stone Meditation") other "bar lines" occurred: (i) the Baptism, (ii) the Transfiguration, (iii) the Death. [4] Christ achieved the unprecedented in fulfilling the Mystery of Golgotha: by uniting with every cell of the body, the physical form was completely reconstituted. [5] "The light does not merely shine upon the gloom and so dispel it; it is the gloom itself transformed into light," writes W. Temple. [6] "At first sight the bleeding body may seem funereal to us. Is it not from the night that it shines forth?" asks Teilhard de Chardin. [7] Steiner reveals that the Body on the Cross actually began to shine and turn into light.

"The Cross of Golgotha is the Mystery cult of antiquity condensed into a fact... a fact that would be valid for the whole of humanity." [8]

In its musical images, Steiner declares, music anticipates "what the soul consciously experiences in the life of initiation". [9] This would seem to confirm that the challenge of the bar line is not to emphasise *der Leichnam*, the untenanted, material corpse which we leave behind at death, but *die Körpergestalt*, the bodily form… "a holding-on to yourself", that is, the spirit-filled body of light (*cf.*, "It is finished/ fulfilled", John 19:30). Steiner surely hoped his listeners would realise the difference between *der Leichnam* and *der Phantom*, "the prototype of the physical body… the real human physical force-body"? He is at pains to emphasise that the resurrection body was physical (yet not material). It is not simply the etheric body, either. "For the first time it is possible to describe how an individual, through the requisite exercises of feeling in the course of Christian initiation, makes him/herself ripe to receive the *Phantom* which rose from the grave of Golgotha." [10]

In carrying out the bar line, our experience since the Mystery of Golgotha (Gal. 2:20, the whole verse) of the vertical axis may relate to "the axis of the world". In Far-Eastern tradition, the *Wang Tao* ("Royal Way") or *T'ien Tao* ("Way of Heaven"), are one and the same. The *Wang*, the "King-Pontiff", "true man" or even "transcendent man", himself becomes the "channel" or "Middle Way" between Earth and Heaven; [11] (*cf.*, Rev. 1:6). [12] Perhaps it is not a coincidence that the name "Tamino" contains the sounds of T A O. The goal of Mozart's *The Magic Flute* is "the right union of the Papageno world or our natural origins, with the world of Tamino, our striving spirit". [13] Chr. Peter discusses the polarity of growth and form in music, and the lightning power creating dynamic balance. [14] For eurythmy, it is clear that the inherited "Papageno/ Papagena" natural (talent, vitality and beauty of the eurythmist and his/her natural environment) only provides the instrumental basis for a transforming art expressing "real humanity within themselves" (Lecture 5). Entering into beat with the forces of the upright posture, the transition (bar line) gives the artist the only possibility of freedom to rise above the pull of weight "in the overcoming (*Überwinden*) of the forces of the earth".

In "visible singing":

> Gesture is the original element –
> It expresses the stimulation which an outer thing or
> occurrence inspires in the feelings.

Beat	in the overcoming of the forces of the earth.
Rhythm	in the overcoming of the rhythms of the environment. Forces of the periphery.
Melos	in the overcoming of the characteristics of things and events. – Forces of the heights. – [15]

---

[1] *Christoph Peter.* Die Sprache der Musik in Mozarts "Zauberflöte"; *section on "Beat".*

[2] *Thrasybulos Georgiades,* Musik und Sprache, *Springer-Verlag. Berlin/ Heidelberg/ New York. 1974. 120, tr. A.S. E.T.* Music and Language. CUP. *1982. Tr. by Marie Louise Göllner. Quotation 113f.*

[3] *O. Edwards.* The Time of Christ. *Floris Books. Edinburgh. 1986, demonstrates that the traditional date (3ʳᵈ April, AD 33) is correct; this is also confirmed by Steiner. The birth of Jesus is beautifully described in the apocryphal Book of James, or Protevangelium, XVIII, 2, beginning "Now I Joseph was walking, and I walked not" (*The Apocryphal New Testament, *translated by M.R. James. Oxford. OUP 1924. 46; rev. ed. J.K. Elliott (Ed.). Oxford OUP 1993. See also* New Testament Apocrypha, *rev. ed. Wilhelm Schneemelkler, E.T. ed. by R. McL. Wilson (James Clarke. Westminster/ John Knox Press. 1991). The passage referred to inspired N. Nicholson's poem "A Turn for the Better", in* Selected Poems of Norman Nicholson. Faber. London. 1966. 44. *&* Norman Nicholson. Collected Poems. Faber. London 2008. *235f.*

[4] *Friedrich Rittelmeyer links the threefold manifestation of spirit (spiritual seeing, inner hearing, and higher life) to be found in the three stages of the Christ's Incarnation into the astral, etheric and physical bodies of Jesus. See F. Rittelmeyer.* Christus. Stuttgart. *1936. Chapter 1 (E.T. in MS).*

R.H. Lightfoot points out that in Mark's gospel (the first to be written) the Greek word for "to rend" occurs twice: (i) the heavens are rent asunder at the Baptism (1, 10) and (ii) the curtain of the Temple at the death (15, 38). In the former event "heaven and earth were joined in an irrevocable, unbreakable union"; in the latter "the at-one-ment between God and man" is described. "In Him earth has now been raised to heaven" the "partial relations... of the old covenant... now attain their completion or fulfilment". The title beloved, or only, Son of God occurs in the account of the Baptism, Transfiguration and the centurion's confession; "the only three occasions in Mark when the divine Sonship is directly ascribed to the Lord". God is revealed (R.H. Lightfoot. The Gospel Message of St Mark. Oxford. OUP 1950/2. *56f.).*

[5] *Compare Mark 1:10-11 with Mark 15:33-4, and Steiner's comments in R. Steiner.* The Gospel of St Matthew. *Lecture XII. Berne. 12 Oct. 1910. RSP. 1965. GA 123; this lecture-course describes the microscomic and macrocosmic directions of initiation.*

[6] *William Temple.* Mens Creatrix. Macmillan. London. 1917. *322.*

[7] *Teilhard de Chardin.* Le Milieu Divin. *Fontana/ Collins. 1964. 104. See also the poem "He is the lonely greatness" by Madeleine Caron Rock, No. 279 in the collection* Come Hither *by Walter de la Mare. Constable. London/ A. Knopf. New York. 1923/28/57; Puffin Books. Harmondsworth. 1973; Avernal Books/ New York. 1990.*

[8] *R. Steiner.* Christianity as Mystical Fact. *RSP. 1972. 143.*

[9] *R. Steiner.* Art as seen in the Light of Mystery Wisdom. *Lecture, Dornach. 30 Dec. 1914. RSP. 1984. GA 275.*

[10] *R. Steiner.* From Jesus to Christ. *Lecture X. Karlsruhe. 14 Oct. 1911. RSP. 1973. 169. Cf., The resurrection of the body is "the same body, glorified... the same body though not of the same dead matter." G. MacDonald.* Unspoken Sermons. First Series. *Johanneson. Ca.. 1997. 240f.*

[11] *R. Guénon.* The Great Triad. *Quinta Essentia. Cambridge. 1991. Chapter 17.*

[12] *Translations vary, reflecting an improvement in the Greek text. Scholars regard "kings" ("kings and priests". AV) as defective, preferring "kingdom": "a kingdom of priests" (GNB and J.B. Phillips), "a kingdom and priests" (NIV), "a kingdom, priests" (NRSV), "line of kings, priests to serve his God and Father" (JB), "a royal house to serve as the priests" (REB). James Denney explains: "The dignity conferred on us is not that of sovereignty, but of citizenship... in virtue of His action we are constituted a worshipping people of God; on the ground of it we have access to the Father." James Denney.* The Death of Christ. *London. 1911. 176f.*

[13] *Chr. Peter,* Die Sprache der Musik in Mozarts "Zauberflöte" *(E.T. forthcoming); a T A O-companion for the musical artist.*

[14] *Chr. Peter. Die Sprache der Musik... Stuttgart 1997; see also* Rests and Repetition. *Stourbridge 1992. 42f. Distrib.: <eurythmywm@gmail.com>.*

[15] *R. Steiner, from Notebook entry. Prague. 2 May 1924. GA 277. 436. Cf.: "The human being, standing there within the sphere of gravity, overcomes this force by means of his or her own soul-forces... with every gesture he seems to assert: 'I carry a heavenly human being within my earthly humanity...' The human soul engaged in eurythmy appears to us to pour itself into the transient human form out of the eternal [wellspring of] human nature." R. Steiner.* Introduction. *Dornach. 8 July 1923. GA 277. 368-9; tr.* An Introduction to Eurythmy. *AP. 1984. 78-9 (slightly amended A.S.).*

Fig. 57: Raphael: The Marriage (Betrothal) of the Virgin
Note the vanishing-point where heaven and earth meet (+); the lambda
and its inversion (gaze of Mary and Joseph); the sacred Marriage 11 (= 6
+5 figures, meeting on the 11th tesselation); the ring about to be placed in
the vertical axis. From this union issues God's utterance or WORD.

Appendix 5
The Angle-gestures

What the intellect perceives in the physical world as law, as
Idea, is revealed to the spiritual ear as a spiritual music.

Rudolf Steiner. Theosophy. Chapter III. 3
The Spirit-land. RSP. 1973. 93.

Art is eternal; its forms change.

Rudolf Steiner. Lecture, Dornach. 9 June 1923. GA 276.

(The following study develops from Endnote 4.)
E. Zuccoli includes two sketches: the first symbolically represents the
creative forces of the zodiac on the growing embryo (1981. 6), and
another shows the angles of the sevenfold archetypal scale against this
background of the twelve (7). Lea van der Pals and A.-M. Bäschlin also
mention the music of the spheres in connection with the embryo and
the backbone. They give further sketches (1991. 10f.). The sketch for the
note — interval — vowel — consonant series (29) portrays the world
of *music* (inspired from the "back space", passing through the "centre"
of the point of departure) and the world of *speech* (involving "forward
space" of the "periphery", or the surroundings). The first indications for
the notes belong to the time when eurythmy was "in its infancy" (see
Endnote 4); the accounts mentioned above show that Steiner follows
the Goethean method of initially presenting a picture of the whole, and
that "the world of music is revealed out of and through the human being
himself" (Goethe. *Theory of Music.* See Endnote 9). The human and
cosmic worlds meet here in a beautiful harmony: the system of *seven*
(Pfrogner's "resounding image of the human being, pure and simple")
and the cosmic system of *twelve* standing in the background are initially
presented as a complete (if undeveloped) entity.

Cosmic considerations for eurythmy inspired many of the early forms
and indications (see GA 277a). These initial attempts draw on the tradition
of sacred geometry and sacred symbols, many of which inspired sacred
art and architecture throughout civilised times. That which existed as
sacred tradition (compare, for example, the Great Pyramid, Stonehenge
and Chartre Cathedral as models of the universe) also relates to the

dimensions of the human body, on the basis of the correspondence of microcosm and macrocosm. (Solomon's Temple, too, "was like a star whose light enabled [higher beings] to guide souls into bodies which would be capable of understanding its meaning. It was the central star of the earth, shining out with special brightness into the spiritual heights" (R. Steiner. Lecture. Basel. 21 Dec. 1916. *The Festivals and their Meaning*. 58-9; see A. von Baravalle. "Salomonischer Tempel — Goetheanum". Carl Kemper. *Der Bau*. Stuttgart. 1984. 201-2. See also Tons Brunés. *The Secret of Ancient Geometry*; Fred Gettings. *The Secret Zodiac*. Arkana. London. 1989: an account of San Miniato al Monte, Florence, "probably the last surviving church to have been designed by initiates"; also György Doczi. *The Power of Limits*. Shambhala. Boston. 2005) The manifestation of eternal cosmic verities has never been "fixed" during any cultural epoch, but has been creatively varied to suit humanity's development. Some symbols, however, increase in importance at specific times, for example, the pentagram during the fifth post-Atlantean epoch. (For a survey of architectural development, see R. Steiner. *The Temple is — Man!* Lecture, Berlin. 12 Dec. 1911. RSP. 1951, where an ego-development is pictorially described; also R. Steiner. *Universe, Earth and Man*. Lecture 1. Stuttgart. 4 Aug. 1908. RSP. 1987. During the Faculty Meeting, Stuttgart 30 April 1924. GA 277a. 140, Steiner recommends the study of geometry in Raphael's "The Marriage (Betrothal) of the Virgin"; also the human organism in relation to the golden section; the pentagram; and the figures of Agrippa. From his school-days onwards, Steiner found in geometry a spiritual discipline — see R. Steiner. *The Course of my Life*. GA 28. Chapter 2. We return to the subject of geometry below.)

The tonal system and meditation

The question of the development of the tonal system surely affects eurythmical development. We know that any instrument capable of variable tuning can produce the notes of any scale (past, present or future) that has first been inwardly heard by the player. The string-player's finger-board, for example, enables the players to exercise their technique and sense of intonation in order to express their musicality. In a similar way, eurythmists directly tune their instrument. In the case of the eurythmist in particular, a divorce of technique from experience is unthinkable. This is one reason why research into scales could be fruitfully based on such exercises as U.-I. Gillert describes (1993. Chapter 1). For the musician and eurythmist, the concern is not precision alone (Pfrogner once called this "intonation antics"), but artistic research, that is, concrete experience of the worlds of soul and spirit. The inherent nuances of the scales likely to be used in future epochs (involving different-sized seconds, and so on; for details see Ruland. 1992) may one day be shown on the eurythmist's three-dimensional "finger-board" (if the point of departure can be so described — see Endnote 55). But the way to these nuances will be through realising those of the scales in use during the present epoch.

A practical pathway is indicated to realise Steiner's meditation for musicians of 12 (or even 15 including the overlaps on the circle of fifths) scales of 7 notes = 84 (or 105) actual meditations, not including the minor scales for the moment (see Introduction, Endnote 18; and Appendix). Eurythmists practise each note of the scale with a subtle awareness in the collar-bone and arms of the interval (the degree of the scale). Prime coincides with the first note of C major (called 'C' for short); C becomes second in B^b major, third in A^b major, and so on for all the scales in which it appears, yet retaining its "archetypal" prime quality (the angle) at the same time; and all the other notes similarly. (Eurythmy possesses the artistic possibility of showing three types of interval experience: the degree of the scale, the melodic ["horizontal"] interval, and sometimes the harmonic ["vertical"] interval as well.) The exercise alluded to above points to a realisation of Steiner's meditations for musicians in a practical, musical way in the expressive arm-gestures of eurythmy. The meditations are not simply imagined linguistically or pictorially, or felt in some other way. In doing them, the quality of "the twelve" will be shown through the whole diatonic scale (in the "transitions". Lecture 5) just as they are heard (that is, in the background) as the deepest level of listening. This is Pfrogner's third ("enharmonic") level in the tonal system. "Illustration" is avoided; the exercises remain in the musical element.

On the subject of meditation for eurythmists, Willi Kux relates:

> The undertaking of a path of schooling and the world of eurythmy are both inwardly related... A eurythmist told me... she had screwed up her courage to ask the revered teacher if he would not also give a meditative exercise for her personal use. To her astonishment Steiner answered that he had a long time ago given her such an exercise. As she shook her head in denial, he said to her full of seriousness: 'But you have already received from me the exercises for eurythmy.' Then she realised all of a sudden the concealed side of this artistic activity" (Ralph Kux and Willi Kux. *Erinnerungen an Rudolf Steiner*. Melinger Verlag. Stuttgart. 1976. 26-7; tr. A.S. See also Endnote 63 regarding the eurythmy meditation).

The Creative WORD

These observations suggest that the eurythmist is given the task to realise *a new cosmological centre* directly within his or her instrument (the body as temple). In this connection, the architectural relationships of the First Goetheanum are instructive. In earlier domed buildings, for example, St Peter's, Rome, and St Paul's, London, the continuation of the sweep of the single dome is far above the head of someone standing under it. In the First Goetheanum, figures on the stage were seen to move under the painted dome depicting the world of initiation through the ages; lecturers on spiritual science, proclaiming the Word, stood at the point of intersection of the two domes (corresponding to the larynx—the lectern, too, was shaped like a larynx; see Fig. 58, & Fig. 66, p. 428. Compare, too, the Taurus imagery in the church of San Miniato al Monte, Florence, and the part of the preacher plays by providing an actual throat to complete the imagery of the pulpit; Fred Gettings. *The Secret Zodiac*. Arkana. London. 1989).

> The building and the movements of eurythmy were intended to grow together to a whole... And when the architectural forms of the stage received the fashioning of eurythmy, as it were, as something belonging to them, so did those forms in the auditorium receive the recitation or declamation appearing parallel with the eurythmy... Such a unity of building-form and word or music was striven for... A kind of orchestral co-operation of the spoken and visible presentation of the words would appear to have been achieved (R. Steiner. *Das Goetheanum in seinen zehn Jahre*. GA 36. Dornach. 1962; also Tb 635. Dornach 1982. 144, 143).

The positioning on the plan of the columns and indeed the whole stage area and the auditorium, was related dynamically through a lemniscate movement. The intersection of the lemniscate occurred at the "larynx" point.

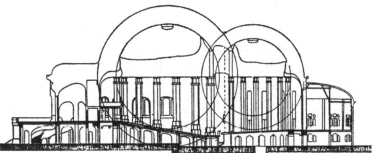

Fig. 58: The First Goetheanum (southern elevation). From Kemper, Der Bau, (reproduced by courtesy of Verlag Freies Geistesleben, Stuttgart).

An artistic means exists for individuals to take up the real challenge of overcoming the Copernican world-view, described by Steiner as the last great Ahrimanic deception of humanity (that is, to view the outer appearances, "Maya" or semblance, as "reality"). "As far as the spiritual influences are concerned, the Earth and not the Sun stands at the centre of the cosmic system" (R. Steiner. *The Spiritual Hierarchies...*, lecture 15 April 1909. AP. 1970. 78). In this sense, eurythmy is an artistic, practical path of self-knowledge which is at the same time a path to knowledge of the world. The angles for the note-gestures are objectively present as a system; the "visible singing" of the trained artist, however, does not show a system nor does it imitate external reality. It is a creation born of artistic freedom. Such a creation cannot be arbitrary; it is a taking-hold of the world of appearances and transforming it. The audience in the First Goetheanum saw human beings freely moving on the earth (stage) under the dome of heaven (cupola). The harmony of the Great Triad of Far-Eastern tradition (heaven, earth and the human being between) was made visible and renewed. "Real strength cannot be felt in the artist who impresses the observer with the true imitation of [outer] reality, but the artist who compels us to go along with him when he creatively continues the cosmic process in his work" (R. Steiner. *Goethe as Father of a new Science of Aesthetics*. The first lecture: Vienna. 9 Nov. 1888. Endnote 2nd ed. Dornach. 1919). The eurythmist may become representative of a creative world-view that transcends the merely arbitrary and the spatially fixed.

With the question of *artistic truth*, we could compare Steiner's answer to the prevailing theory of art. In his first lecture (*ibid.*), he cites Schelling, for whom "the highest human activity is the perception of the eternal archetypes of things... All sensory beauty is merely a weak reflection of that endless Beauty which we can never perceive with our senses". On this view art and science is the same, since they both adopt as a basis "eternal Truth", which is also "Beautiful". This illustrating of concepts that rightly belong to science, is, for Steiner, "a false theory". Steiner sketches an "aesthetics of the future", as fathered by Goethe: Art does not stand "for the embodiment of the super-sensory, but for the transformation of the physical and the actual..." Beauty is "not the Idea in the form of a phenomenon", but "is an appearance... a sensory reality appearing as though it were Idea" (*ibid.*). The latter inverts the former view. Here Steiner is emphasising the crucial direction of artistic activity; he is not denying science.

In anthroposophy, spiritual-scientific knowledge, artistic activity and religious inwardness are sought from a single source... I pointed out how, in the Goetheanum, art is drawn from the same spirituality which, when anthroposophy appears in the form of knowledge, seeks to be revealed in ideas (R. Steiner. *Der Goetheanumgedanke.* GA 36 and Tb 635. Dornach. 1982. 133-4).

The eurythmical instrument and the system of seven

If the provisional conclusions sketched above are accepted, there is a practical way towards a deeper understanding of the 1915 angles, and the later development in general use (basically 18 degrees per semitone, and 36 degrees per whole tone). A provisional perspective has been established to view the matter as an artistic creation of Steiner's. This perspective incorporates the responsibility and the direction noted in the previous paragraph. To sum up: In eurythmy, the instrument is recognised as made out of music (in embryological development). Individually, we have left the womb. As members of a civilisation, we no longer visit either standing stones under the naked dome of the heavens (compare the two circles at Penmaenmawr and the intersecting cupolas of the First Goetheanum), nor the inner seclusion of mystery temples of Egypt and Greece to receive formative cosmic music. Both streams, the northern and the Egyptian (R. Steiner. *The Gospel of St Matthew.* Lecture VII. Berne. 7 Sept. 1910) are united since the Christ-Event, and may unite in music as an autonomous art (see Endnote 50; Introduction, 20, and 24f.). Music has developed only recently in humanity's development, but its contribution is crucial to all further artistic development. In essence, the musical element is the rebirth within, or an internalisation, of the creative forces, experienced formerly as approaching humanity. Today, music stands at a crisis to retain its autonomy and its character as a true image of the supersensory world—that is, some people are seeking for its rôle as a mystery art. The help that eurythmy can offer here has not been widely recognised, either by eurythmists, musicians or music-lovers (Chr. Peter. *Die Sprache der Musik...* is a pioneer study in this respect).

Here we should refer to Steiner's tremendous revelation of the two missions of Michael. The first mission prepared for the Mystery of Golgotha and is expressed in the opening words of St John's Gospel ("In ancient times the Word lived in a spiritual form, but the Word became flesh and dwelt among us"). The second Michael mission came into effect especially from 1879, and proclaims: "And human flesh must again become permeated by the spirit so that it may become capable of dwelling in the kingdom of the Word in order to behold the divine secrets." Thus "the Word become flesh is the first revelation of Michael, and the second revelation of Michael must be the flesh become spirit" (R. Steiner. Lecture. Dornach. 20 Nov. 1919. *The Mission of the Archangel Michael*. GA 194. AP. 1961). These words contain "the profoundest mystery of the human physical body and its future connection with the Michael-Christ Impulse" (S. Prokofieff. *Rudolf Steiner and the Founding of the New Mysteries*. Temple Lodge Press. London 1994. 105). For "flesh to become spirit", the spirit has to penetrate right to the deepest, mineral element. We learn that the organic, living element "does not let the spirit and soul through", but "the bone-nerve element, and indeed… the material-mineral element as a whole,… the dead physical element, is permeable for the spirit" (R. Steiner. *Study of Man*. RSP. 176). Steiner also explains:

> The only body on the earth that has ever acquired control over the force by which cartilage and bone substance are held together was that of Jesus of Nazareth through its "Intuition" by the Christ. Through this control over the bones a force entered the world which is actually able to overcome death in physical matter… The Christ [-Impulse] is the living force that is capable of transforming the bones again, that is to say, of leading [people] gradually towards spirituality. [Moreover:] Through having assimilated the Spirit of Christ, the earth will once again be united with the sun… the coming of Christ is not only of importance to mankind, but a matter of consequence for the evolution of the comsos itself (R. Steiner. *Universe, Earth and Man*. 150, 152-3).

Armin Husemann. *The Harmony of the Human Body*. Floris Books. Edinburgh. 1994. Section 31, describes how technically, too, an inversion, or rather a turning-inside-out (corresponding to the internalisation mentioned above) has to form the basis of the art of eurythmy, which is meant to reveal the creative forces at work. This is situated within the instrument (collar-bone and shoulder-blades), necessary for whatever system is adopted for the angles. This not only incorporates the spiritual law of "death in life", but appeals to and reveals the forces of awakening which reach as far as the bones themselves. The system of angles archetypally pictures the harmony of both the system of seven *and* the arrangement of twelve. The modifications of the angles retain the harmony of seven and twelve; the adjustments reveal even more clearly the details and richness of our tonal system. Either way, eurythmy enables the human being experiencing music "here and now on earth" (GA 276. 37) to begin to "speak to the stars" (a phrase from Steiner's meditation given to Marie Steiner, Christmas 1922. See also R. Steiner. *Love and its Meaning in the World*. Lecture, Zürich. 17 Dec. 1912. RSP. 1960. This artistic pathway promotes a dialogue between "earth" and "heaven", that is, between day-consciousness and night-consciousness, for those experiencing eurythmy. From this, eurythmy derives its claim to be a mystery art, or an art of the threshold. As we saw, the complete artistic portrayal of eurythmy occurred for the audience experiencing the events on the stage situated under the small cupola of the First Goetheanum. Eurythmy survived the physical destruction of the Goetheanum, and the positive task is to realise that wherever it takes place, eurythmy may help to create and reveal the supersensory Goetheanum.

With the angle-gestures, or note-gestures, the artist takes hold of the densest part of the body (the bones) and attempts the long task of re-tuning the human instrument, so that it "sing a new song" (Rev. 14:3). At the same time, the attempt to transform the bones is one that seeks to reveal *the inner, human light* (R. Steiner. *From Jesus to Christ*. Lecture VI. Karlsruhe. 10 Oct. 1911. RSP. 1973).[2] One interpretation is: with parallel arms the light is narrow; with the first opening the light between the arms grows, and continues until the horizontal is reached. Then, over the threshold between the two tetrachords, the light penetrates the horizontal through the body (the fifth, which is "the human being", enlivens the legs, too); the light enters the lower half of the sphere. The arms draw the light with them from below the horizontal, back via the sixth and seventh degrees to the parallel arms of the octave. The circle, or rather sphere, of light is completed. (A representation is conveyed by Grünewald's painting of the resurrection in the Isenheimer altarpiece, Colmar, France.)

This leads to our conclusion that the angle-gestures are a solar image, expressing a universal truth of humanity, which Goethe expresses in his poetic work *Faust*. The Archangel Raphael speaks, opening the "Prologue in Heaven" (tr. Shelley):

---

2   The approach here is from hearing to seeing. Descriptions of the spirit usually begin with seeing, but Steiner significantly adds: in spirit-land "the archetypes that are perceived are heard as well" (R. Steiner. *Theosophy*, 73). Is "the reference to spiritual music… omitted for the sake of simplicity" here a concession to "the despotism of the eye" (Coleridge)? If so, this implies that eurythmy calls on that enhanced sense of sight, described in *Theosophy*, that sees with but also beyond the physical phenomena. Because of the word "with" in the last sentence, we can call this a "redeemed" perception of participation.

The sun makes music as of old
Amid the rival spheres of Heaven,
On its predestined circle rolled
With thunder speed: the Angels even
Draw strength from gazing on its glance,
Though none its meaning fathom may:–
The world's unwithered countenance
Is bright as at Creation's day.

The system of angle-gestures is the mobile, dynamically expressive, artistic manifestation of a universal image to be found world-wide in ecclesiastical, agricultural, industrial, urban, commercial, and domestic architecture, fine art and folk art (see Alan Stott. "No more Tone Gestures in Eurythmy?" RB 36. Easter 2002. 48-53; and *The English Sunrise – Sonnenaufgänge*. Flash Books. New York. 1973/ Darmstadt. Melzer. 1975/ Mathews Miller Dunbar. London 1977; a collection of 78 full-colour photographs of solar designs).

World-geometry

In a lecture delivered in Dornach 12 Jan. 1924, Steiner speaks of the six-pointed star ("Solomon's Key" or "Seal"), pointing out that "you only come to the real meaning of such symbols when you find them in the essence of your own human organism... like fables, legends and fairy-tales... you should identify with them". This meditative exercise is often carried out in eurythmical connections, and is one of the forms to be found metamorphosed in the First Goetheanum (see Carl Kemper. *Der Bau*. Stuttgart. 1984. 95). Steiner speaks of "weight bearing downwards" and "light streaming upwards"; also of "matter" and "form"; the bones and spinal-marrow, and he quotes the verse:

Behold the man of bone
And you behold Death
Behold within the bones
And you behold the Awakener.

Thinking is experienced through the inner recognition, through the inner feeling of the structure of your bones. You just do not think with your brain. With sharply-defined lines of thoughts, you think in reality with your skeleton. When thinking becomes concrete, as in *The Philosophy of Freedom*, then thinking goes over into the whole human being... When the pupil [of a certain Rosicrucian group of the early nineteenth century] acquired knowledge of the inside of his skeleton, and thereby in reality the authentic world-geometry (*Weltgeometrie*), learning to know the way in which the forces have been inscribed into the world by the gods, then his understanding grew of how form influences entities... minerals... plants... animals... and human beings (R. Steiner. Lecture, Dornach. 12 Jan. 1924. GA 233. Dornach. 1980. 70ff., tr. A.S.; pub. tr. *Rosicrucianism and Modern Initiation*. RSP. 1982. 70ff.).

"God geometrises constantly," Plato reminds us (Plutarch. *Table Talks*), and Steiner echoes the thought: "God engages in eurythmy, and the result of His eurythmy is the beautiful human form" (Lecture Dornach. 24 June 1924. *Eurythmy as Visible Speech*. Anastasi. 2005. 37). Armin Husemann found a link between Plato's world-soul and the sculptural, musical and speech work of 1924 (Husemann. Germ. 2nd ed. 78). The further suggestion of a link between Plato's *Timaeus* and Steiner's T A O eurythmy-exercise is made in Appendix 4 above. The reference above to "world-geometry", the "structure of the bones", and "thinking" that involves "the whole human being", points to the musical world of number, proportion and rhythm (form) at work throughout the kingdoms of mineral, plant, animal and man. Steiner calls this "the earthly projection of the music of the spheres", and he also says:

> The human skeleton can be understood figuratively as if someone were playing a sonata and preserving it through some sort of spiritual process of crystalisation; if we were to do this we come upon the principle forms, the arrangement of forms of the human skeleton (R. Steiner. Lecture, Stuttgart. 16 Sept. 1920. *Meditatively acquired Knowledge of Man*. GA 302a. Rudolf Steiner Schools Fellowship 1982; see also van de Pals. 1992. 53).

In the lecture of 13 Jan. 1924 (GA 233, see above) Michael's gaze is characterised, for which the individual may learn whether his offering to the gods is accepted or rejected. Steiner's own example is his work on Haeckel's *Anthropogenesis*. The resulting transformation of natural science is "what is related about evolution in my *Occult Science*". Acquiring spiritual knowledge through study of this book, and *Theosophy*, which are musically structured, "permeates the human soul and spirit with the forces that conquer death" (R. Steiner, lecture Dornach. 10 July 1921. GA 205. Dornach. 1967. 187).

The arrangement of twelve

Eurythmy was born during the second decade of the twentieth century when music, originally a threefold being, split into tonality and atonality (another split, into electronics, occurred in the 1950's; see Pfrogner, "Der zerrissene Orpheus", in *Zeitwende*). Pfrogner describes the atonal twelve-note system (which dispenses with the seven-note system of scales) as an abstract shadow cast by the light of the approaching reality of the "enharmonic arrangement of twelve" (*Zeitwende*. 88f.). One day in the far future (seventh post-Atlantean epoch), the experiences of the (twelve) prime(s) will have matured. The "cosmic twelve" are already heard behind the twelve keys of diatonic music (see Beckh's pioneer work), and even more directly in some twentieth-century developments. (The number twelve [4 x 3] is related to space, and seven [4 + 3] to time, as everyone knows. "The twelve" is not as graspable in the eurythmical world of *music* as it is in that of *speech*: music-eurythmy is not a spatial art.)

The crucial criteria is whether the substance of music itself is artistic sound created out of the human "middle", or whether we are dealing with abstract or material (even sub-material) aberrations (for further discussion, see Appendices 3 & 6). Only through appreciation of the spiritual-scientific basis of eurythmy, can support be found for Steiner's claim that eurythmy may become "a corrective influence" on art in general. In Torquay, 24 Aug. 1922, commenting on the future of music, Steiner said (see Introduction, Endnote 1): "It all depends on people" – not, we might add, on any sign, symbol, or system, which are all projections to help us find and express our human personality.

We may conclude by noting that Steiner's teaching, giving details on the meaning of earth-evolution, also confirms the account highlighted at the beginning, middle and end of the Bible. The light created at the beginning of the world (Gen. 1:3) came to the darkened earth, became man (John 8:12), died, and was re-born in human hearts. As the power of love, the light proceeding from the Body at the Mystery of Golgotha is an "impulse" that the individual must recognise and allow to shine for other people. It will eventually transform the earth to its ultimate destiny, which is to shine again as a star. After the cycles of seven in the Book of Revelation, John describes it "coming down out of heaven... radiant... clear as crystal", with its "twelve gates, and at the gates twelve angels..., twelve names..., twelve foundations..., the tree of life with its twelve kinds of fruit" (Rev. 21:22). This cosmic vision at the end of the Bible of the New Jerusalem in the form of a radiant cube (the shape of a salt-crystal; see Endnote 40) may carry a musical meaning too, and relate to one of the deepest aspects of music-eurythmy—the angle-gestures. These angles of the arms are filled with the light of consciousness. The living forces which became the symbols of the axis-mundi and the Celtic cross are invoked by the individual artist. Eurythmists are given a direct, spiritual discipline to "think with the whole body".

8. Kilaghtee (Donegal). The cross is contained in the sun disc.
9. St Kevin's Cross, Glendalough. The freely shaped cross carries the sun in it.
10. Aghowle (Wicklow). The sun disc dominates.
11. National Museum, Dublin. The sun nucleus (Christ) is surrounded by the three solar year emblems, carried in the cross.
12. Nurney (Carlow). Here the cross predominates with the sun nucleus (Christ) centre. The sun disc retreats.
13. Eustace East, Kildare. Another variation of penetration of the sun disc and cross.
14. Reefert Church, Glendalough. The sun disc is formed as an unbroken ring.
15. East side of Kilree (Kilkenny). Sun disc with Christ-centre inside, sun aura ring outside carried by a dominating cross.
16. Southern Cross, Ahenny (Kilkenny). Cross with sun ring in harmonious balance. In the

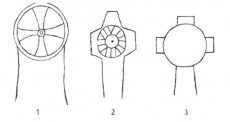
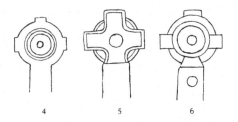
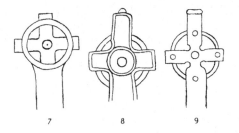

Fig. 59:   Basic types of early Christian crosses (from Jakob Streit, Sun and Cross [Floris Books, Edinburgh 1984])

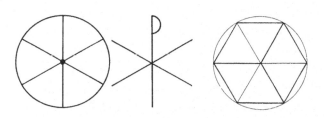

Fig. 60:   The axis-mundi and four rivers of Eden; Chi-rho; and cube as hexagon.

Appendix 6
Live music, recorded sound and eurythmy

What Steiner has achieved in these lectures will be appreciated by all those people – eurythmists, musicians, artists, and the many lovers of art – who wish to take responsible steps to care for a human future. Positive action is the best antidote to the illusory and degrading effects of recorded sound, which feeds into the soul via the ear. [1] It is necessary to affirm this now that the forces of technology and finance, under the guise of offering "help" for inner work from recordings, have finally invaded the very heart of eurythmy practice. Marie Steiner (in her Foreword to the 1927 edition of *Eurythmy as Visible Speech*) took a stance to the invention of the gramophone. Since then, the situation has become more critical.

Fig. 61: Chartres Cathedral, south rose window, c. 1227 (exterior). The radial supporting masonry could suggest a correspondence to the geometry of the angle-gestures of eurythmy. The masonry supports the glass that provides the experience of light and colour with the chosen images. In eurythmy, the instrument itself (the bones) also participates in the light which is created between the eurythmist and the viewer.

Six months before delivering the present lectures, Steiner was in England, where he spoke about recordings and the cinema. [2] The subject is also mentioned in Lecture 6, above, two days after the T A O-eurythmy-exercise was introduced. In the same year, 1924, he returned to England and spoke about the future of music, concluding:

> The musical element is capable of placing before the world this Christ-impulse in music, in formed, ensouled and spiritually permeated sounds. If music allows itself to be inspired by anthroposophical spiritual science, it will find the way in the purely artistic sphere to resolve with feeling the riddle of how to bring to life in symphonic sound what lives as the Christ-impulse in the universe and the earth. [3]

Bruno Walter (1876–1962), the famous conductor and near contemporary of Steiner, who acknowledged his debt to the latter with courage and certainty in his *On Music and Music-Making*, [4] also intended his description of the mission of music to be taken literally: "Music's wordless gospel proclaims in a universal language what the thirsting soul of man is seeking beyond this life." Referring to the unlimited possibilities of the film camera, Walter wrote (1944): [5]

> But will the reproduction by an apparatus, no matter how perfect, ever be able to achieve the blissful and elevating effect of spontaneous interpretative art produced by living people? Will the time come when mechanically contrived proceedings no longer taste as if they had come out of a tin? The answers to these questions will be furnished by the highly gifted people at work upon the discovery and development of the film style of tomorrow.

Today, almost seventy years on, people who are seeking that "wordless gospel" are called upon individually to answer these questions. Music is complete in every individual, though awareness may be slumbering. And it is vital that this is awakened in the individual. Steiner, in all his dealings with art, uses the words *empfinden, erfühlen* and *erleben* ("sense", "feel" and "experience"). This was his way of taking precautions. For the future of music depends upon people sensing, feeling and experiencing, and not upon the technology of reproducing sensory images. In all art, these three inner experiences penetrate the outer manifestation (catgut, wood, horse-hair, metal and so on); the sensory element cannot be spurned. Living art transmutes the sensory element. The art of eurythmy is directly concerned with this essential human activity. It "is neither indicative nor sweeping, but is expressive gesture... expressive visible gesture". [6] Let us not delude ourselves! How, then, can technology claim any part in this process?

Let us follow up one line of thought about the origin of "the musical element" and the challenge of recordings and the film. The gist is already encapsulated in a passage in *The Philosophy of Freedom*. Steiner faces an objection that "observing thinking" is an "illusion... just as when in an illumination by means of a rapid succession of electric sparks we believe that we are seeing a continuous movement" (that is, the film, or movie). But, Steiner writes, [7] this is to forget that

> it is the "I" itself which, from its standpoint inside the thinking, observes its own activity. The "I" would have to stand outside its thinking in order to suffer the sort of deception which is caused by an illumination with a rapid succession of electric sparks.

It follows that whatever "feelings" are stimulated (our reactions are actually determined by the soundtrack), the art of the film is not in the same sense an "art of the ego". Hence Steiner calls lovers of the film "unmusical" (Lecture 6).

> Now that naturalism has followed the grand road from naturalistic stage productions to the films – neither philistine nor pedant in this regard, I know how to value something for which I do not care too much –, we must find the way back to presentation of the spiritual, the genuine, the real; must re-find the divine-human element in art by re-finding the divine-spiritual. [8]

---

[1] *See GA 278. Lecture 6, also GA 227, Lecture 11 on recordings. For a discussion of recorded sound as a spiritual pathway see* Resonanz 1 and 2 (1985) *and articles in* Novalis *Jan. 1991 by Prof. Balan, M. Frensch and H. Ruland ("The Reversal of Aesthetics" takes Steiner's first lecture of 1888 as a starting point. See Introduction,* Endnote 7. *1-28). These writers set out opposing views on a common theme: musicosophia as a direct opponent of anthroposophy. In his standard books, Pfrogner offers a complete analysis of musical sound, and the nature of electronic sound and of recordings. He demonstrates that the creative risk, essential for art, is present only in the former.*

[2] *Steiner speaks of the damaging effects of driving and other activities in the technical, mechanical realm. These can be healed and balanced out by the individual. "The matter is different... with the gramophone. With the gramophone, humanity wants to force art into the mechanical realm. If humanity acquires a passionate preference for such things – where that which comes down as shadow-image of the spiritual world would become mechanised –, if humanity would show enthusiasm for such a thing for which the gramophone is an expression, then it would no longer be able to help itself. Here the gods would have to help" (R. Steiner. The Evolution of Consciousness. Lecture, Penmaenmawr. 29 Aug. 1923. GA 227). Does anyone imagine, along with Prof. Balan, that the intervention of "the gods" would be a pleasant affair?*

[3] *R. Steiner.* True and False Paths in Spiritual Investigation. *GA 243. RSP. 1985. An accurate translation of the last part of the final lecture of 24 Aug. 1922 appears in*

Lea van der Pals. 1992. Cf.: "The basic mood of the new world-conception [since the Mystery of Golgotha] is musical, whereas the basic mood of the old world was sculptural. The basic mood of the new age is really musical, and the world will become ever more musical. In order to continue rightly on the path of human evolution, we must know the importance of striving towards a musical element and not repeating the old sculptural one" (R. Steiner. Der Baum des Lebens and der Baum der Erkenntnis des Guten und Bosen ['The tree of life and the tree of knowledge of good and evil']. Lecture, Dornach 31 July. 1915. GA 162).

[4] *Bruno Walter.* On Music and Music-Making. *Faber. London. 1957. 212. The passage quoted also appears in the article "Bruno Walter and Emil Bock" in* The Christian Community Journal. *Floris Books. Edinburgh. 1962. 71-5; see also 51-52.*

[5] *Bruno Walter.* Theme and Variations. *Hamish Hamilton. London. 1947. 309; previous quotation 380.*

[6] R. Steiner. The Arts and Their Mission. *Lecture, Dornach. 27 May 1923. GA 276. AP. 1964.*

[7] *R. Steiner.* The Philosophy of Spiritual Activity, a Philosophy of Freedom. *RSP. 1992, author's addition to Chapter 3, 1918 (final italics added).*

[8] *R. Steiner. Lecture, Dornach. 20 May 1923. GA 276. 115.*

Appendix 7:
'ALP-Elf'

We say "ah". The Greek language was the last to say "alpha". Go back to the Hebrew – "aleph". The sound as such had a name then; the sound was something real. The further back we go in language, the more essentially real we find the sounds. When we name the first letter in the Greek alphabet, alpha, and trace back the significance of this word alpha (it is a word which really encompasses the sound), we find that even in the German language many words still exist closely related to what lies in the sound alpha or aleph — as, for instance, when we say *Alp, Alpen* (Alp, Alps). And this leads us back to *Alp–Elf* ([the] Alp, [the] elf) — to a being in a state of constant activity, of becoming, of coming-into-being, of lively movement. The "ah" sound has completely lost all this because we no longer say "alpha" or "aleph"... The spine is really the starting point for the development of such a being as an aleph (Rudolf Steiner. GA 278. Lecture 1).

It is just in re-finding that you obtain the right orientation to the wisdom that has survived from olden times (R. Steiner. Lecture, Dornach. 12 Jan. 1924. GA 233. *World History...* RSP. 1977).

IMPORTANT DISCLAIMER NOTE to the revised edition, 1998: *Since the original publication of these studies, a passage from one of Steiner's lectures to the workers at the Goetheanum has shown that my suggestion that* Elf *(elf) be taken as* elf *(eleven) has, technically speaking, started a false trail to discover Steiner's original meaning (see Endnote* [5]*). I know I should, yet I am reluctant to withdraw Appendix 7. Although fragmentary, as far as I am aware the discoveries and speculations are not dogmatically presented. Moreover, Appendix 7 may not only be interesting in itself (if only to show my credulity); parts of it may still be relevant.*

Steiner's main indication that the letter Aleph pictures the spiritual human being is, after all, the traditional mystical wisdom: the whole alphabet, he points out, is to be taken as presenting the whole human being. This tradition, which we meet in the cabbala, no doubt points back to the unpublished spiritual science of Aristotle that Steiner so frequently mentions (for instance, when introducing the exercise "Light streams upwards...", 12 Jan. 1924. GA 233). Alexander the Great carried Aristotelian spiritual science to Asia; western Europe met the tradition through Arab and Hebrew science and mystical science. In Marie Steiner: her Place in World Karma. Temple Lodge. London. 1995, Hans Peter van Manen throws a new light on Aristotle and his followers, linking what happened to Theophrastus and Aristotle's estate with Marie Steiner and R. Steiner's literary estate, the Nachlass. Historical awareness is extremely relevant to artists today, who shall forever be grateful to Marie Steiner for her work in the arts. As far as Appendix 7 is concerned, the imperfect presentation is retained here; my re-writing could hardly do justice to such an important subject. The reader is in the position to adjust certain speculations and develop that which may be of value for him/ herself —A.S. 1998/2011.

(i) Esoteric Tradition

In the above quotation, the meaning of *Alp* – *Elf* – "[the] Alp, [the] elf" – does not seem entirely satisfactory. We can question whether Steiner intended something more with this hint at the outset of the lecture-course on music-eurythmy. The context of both Greek and Hebrew suggests gematria, or the number-alphabet (for a full exposition, see *Encyclopaedia Judaica*. Keter. 1972). This is further indicated by the word which is given in the German text as *Elf*, but which could be written *elf*, meaning "eleven". In the gematraic system, where each letter carries a numerical equivalent) ALP (a Hebrew word for "unity". W. Parfitt. 1991. 52) is A = 1, L = 30 and P = 80, totalling 111. Following these suggestions, the literal meaning now becomes "unity, eleven", with a hidden meaning of "one hundred and eleven", *i.e.*, 1, 11, 111.

René Guénon points to the positive symbolism of 11. As 6 + 5 (which is [2 x 3] + [2 + 3]), it symbolises the central union of "Heaven" and "Earth", of terrestrial and celestial man, of soul and body (*The Great Triad*. 63; see also *Symbolism of the Cross*. FN2. 124f.). This is geometrically explained by John Michell and Christine Rhone; their diagram uniting of pentagonal and hexagonal figures "is a symbol of the esoteric philosophy which constituted the wisdom of Solomon" (J. Michell & C. Rhone. *Twelve-Tribe Nations*. 179. The authors explain the geometry and relate it to the plan and function of ancient Jerusalem, which itself geographically extends the function of the Temple. Concerning the pentagonal and hexagonal figures, compare the transforming relationships of the Foundation Stone Meditation in eurythmy). Guénon's explanation of the number 11 as incorporating the "hierogamic" exchange, or "sacred marriage", is no doubt the most profound view of the positive significance of this number. The Lambda (the 11th Greek letter) picturing the union of the Pythagorean "male and female" numbers (mentioned in Appendix 4, above) is summarised in Matt. 18:20. Guénon claims that the most diverse of traditional doctrines are in complete agreement: eleven is "the number that establishes the perfection (*ch'eng*) of the Ways of Heaven and Earth (*ch'en Han-chu*)".

Guénon explains the number 111, too: it "represents unity in the three worlds, which is a perfectly apt way of describing the very function of the pole". The pole, he goes on, is a designation of "all the traditions" indicating "the highest spiritual power active in the world" (R. Guénon, *Fundamental Symbols*. Quinta Essentia. Cambridge. 1995. 79f.). Furthermore, the Hebrew spelling of "aleph" can also be read as "eleph" (a thousand) — which may hint at the mystery of "the one and the many", but probably is a fourfold insistence (unit, ten, hundred and thousand) on the concept of unity. Principial unity is the beginning of all beginnings. Divine Love is never idle, as the mystics maintain; hence Steiner's description *Regsamkeit*—"constant activity". (*Cf.*, Augustine's phrase about the nature of Almighty God, "*semper agens, semper quietus* – always active, yet always at rest".)

Does Steiner intend that the birth of eurythmy be seen as issuing from this marriage of heaven and earth? What is its relation to this imagery that, as we know, is perhaps the most profound in the New Testament (*e.g.*, Rev. 21:2)? The rest of this section offers some initial circumstantial evidence. To begin the enquiry (whether Steiner is alluding to this type of mysticism), we might ask what a cabbalist would understand by the reference *ALP-elf*. In the attempt, we include reference to one of the greatest of all musicians, J.S. Bach, and the traditions that he took up, and also some suggestive findings of recent writers. It is clear that by linking with the esoteric tradition, Steiner is drawing attention to the point of departure. This subject is more than a technical matter. The Logos-teaching of St John's Gospel is connected here, too, especially when we bear in mind Steiner's question to Margarita Woloschin after his lecture in Hamburg, 8 April 1908, on the Prologue: "Could you dance that?" (GA 277a. 15), and the reference to the Prologue in Lecture 1 of *Eurythmy as Visible Speech*; see section iii, below. Logos and Lambda, discussed below, begin with the same letter, of course. (For a geometrical representation of Being that includes an extended gloss on the concepts of point and circumference, see R. Guénon. *Symbolism of the Cross*. Sophia Perennis. Hilssdale, NY. 2002, and its sequel *The Multiple States of Being*. Sophia Perennis. Hillsdale, NY. 2002.

The legacy of Judaism

Brian Lancaster points out that A, the timeless source of the spiritual dimension, starts with a silent aspirate (a breath). The breath, "as carrier of pure sound is our most direct contact with the divine process of becoming itself" (139), and is probably implied, too, in Steiner's words concerning "becoming" and "constant activity". L, meaning "learn" (as does A, too), is associated with spiritual teaching; P meaning mouth is associated with language, and gives expression to the insight of O (Ayin), or "eye" that perceives unity in diversity. The connection to eurythmy is clear ("visible Word"—Augustine's term for the sacrament is used by Steiner for eurythmy: see p. 31, and the quote, end of Endnote 8, p. 244 above. True art nourishes through presence of the Creator-Word). Lancaster ends his introduction to Judaism with an exposition on the divine name, concluding with aleph, which is

> the principle of balance... In its symbolism, aleph is mirrored by the six-pointed Star of David which comprises two triangles. The upwards-pointing triangle symbolises the impulses from below which elicits the higher impulse symbolised by the downward-pointing triangle. The fire of human spiritual endeavour is answered by the rain of divine influence... a harmonious alignment of heavenly and earthly powers (Lancaster. 1993. 140).

In her studies on the first Temple and its mythology through biblical and rabbinical texts, Margaret Barker describes how the imagery (Garden of Eden) and ritual practice was designed to create a place on earth that would promote the harmony of heaven and earth. John Michell and Christine Rhone use the word "alchemical" to describe the effect of the ceremonies and festivals which brought harmony to the people and fertility to the land (compare GA 277a. 31). Temple imagery of the early writers, including the Book of Enoch, has been taken over without interruption by Christian writers from the New Testament onwards. Donald Strachan gives perhaps a unique musical interpretation of the Jewish calendar with a solution to the problem of the "Pythagorean comma" solved by the Jubilee year; he also suggests a musical interpretation of the proportions of Solomon's Temple. The cubic Holy of Holies (prime 1:1) resounded to the pulse of creation itself: Yahweh came and dwelt in his house when music was raised (1 Chron. 25) by a particular number of musicians and singers. In his Bible marginalia, Bach wrote: "This chapter is the true foundation of all acred music acceptable to God." To 2 Chron. 5:13, Bach wrote, "with devotional music God with his mercy is present at any time"; to I Chron. 28 (29):21, Bach wrote "... music too was ordered from the spirit of God through David" (Kluge-Kahn. 25-7).

Some words from the worship of the Temple have come down to us. "The religious lyric," writes H. Wheeler Robinson (*The Psalmists*. D.C. Simpson (Ed.). OUP 1926. 45), "is the one great artistic achievement of ancient Israel, and the Book of Psalms is the chief literary monument of that achievement." "In the Psalter," writes Athanasius, "you learn about *yourself*" (*Letter to Marcellinus*). The Psalter is the most quoted book of the New Testament. Psalm 1 describes the person who "delights in the Law of Yahweh" (or "the Lord") in terms of the Tree of Life: "He is like a tree that is planted/ by water streams,/ yielding its fruit in season, its leaves never fading;/ success attends all he does" (v. 3).

Psalm 11 contains the words:

> Yahweh is in his holy Temple,
> Yahweh whose throne is in heaven;
> his eyes look down at the world,
> his searching gaze scans all mankind...
> Yahweh is righteous, he loves virtue,
> upright men will contemplate his face. (vv. 4, 7)

Psalm 111 (and the 111th in the Vulgate, *i.e.*, our 112th Psalm) is an acrostic psalm composed of 22 lines, each beginning with a letter of the Hebrew alphabet from aleph to tav. The other acrostic psalms are Psalms 9-10, 25, 34, 37, the great 119 – in praise of the divine law –, and 145. Psalm 111 is the first of seven that begin with "Hallelujah" (the Jewish church called them "the grand Hallelujah"). The word "Hallelujah" was the first to be carried out in eurythmy (for a study, see RB 32, Easter 2000). The Psalm begins: "I will give thanks to Yahweh with all my heart." It ends with the well-known passage declaring that "the fear of Yahweh is the beginning of wisdom", or "The zenith of wisdom is the fear of Yahweh" (v. 10), a favourite saying from the Wisdom literature. A.M. Ramsey expresses the long-held recognition that "In Christ the praise of God, the wonder before God, the thirst for God, the zeal for God's righteousness, which fill the pages of the Psalter, find pure and flawless utterance... It is the voice of the Israel [= a Prince of God] of God... It is the prayer book of Christ [= the Anointed One] Himself" (A.M. Ramsey. *The Glory of God and the Transfiguration of Christ*. Longmans. 1949/1967. 93, 96f.). The apocalyptic Christ uses Temple imagery: the culminating sixth and seventh promises "to him who overcomes" are "I make a pillar in the temple of my God", and "I grant to sit with me in my throne" (Rev. 3, 12 and 21). The Psalter is not the exclusive property of any group today. It conveys something of the speech (if no longer the music, though Esther Lamandier is one musician who claims to have reconstructed it) of the worship in the Temple, and some even of Solomon's Temple. Science, art and religion still operated as a unity in this mystery centre. Today, the Psalms may command renewed respect when the sacred roots that have led to the modern art of eurythmy (speech and music) are studied. Incidentally, in Hebrew "the sweet psalmist of Israel" (2 Sam 23:1) refers to *musical execution* not authorship; the old histories dwell on David's musical skill and how he *danced "with all his might"* before the ark as it was brought up with joy to Jerusalem (2 Sam 6:5, 14).

The oldest cabbalistic text (said to originate from Abraham) is the *Sepher Yetzirah: The Book of Creation* (or *Formation*). The meditative and contemplative functions described are designed to uncover the inner forms of things. The sephirot are the roots of the framework that

THE PENTAD OF OPERATIVE CHRISTIANITY.

———•———

Prothesis
Christ, the Word.

Thesis	*Mesothesis*, or the Indifference,	*Antithesis*
The Scriptures.	The Holy Spirit.	The Church.

Synthesis
The Preacher.

The Scriptures, the Spirit, and the Church, are co-ordinate; the indispensable conditions and the working causes of the perpetuity, and continued renascence and spiritual life of Christ still militant. The Eternal Word, Christ from everlasting, is the *Prothesis*, or identity;—the Scriptures and the Church are the two poles, or *Thesis* and *Antithesis*, and the Preacher in direct line under the Spirit but likewise the point of junction of the Written Word and the Church, is the *Synthesis*.
This is God's Hand in the World.

Fig. 62:   (i) Coleridge's 'Pentad of Operative Christianity' (prefacing his Confessions of an Inquiring Spirit [London 1840, third edition 1853; reprinted Adam & Charles Black, London 1956]. Its importance has been pointed out by commentators (for example, O. Barfield, and M. A. Perkins); its relationship to the tetractys suggests a parallel creative-evolutionary interpretation.Christ, the Word

	Christ, the Word	
Texts and musical scores	The Holy Spirit	The School of Spiritual Science: Section for the Performing Arts
	The artist/s and participating audience	

(ii) An application of Coleridge's 'Pentad' attempting to indicate the sacred core of the performing arts. Art relates to, but is not a substitute for, religion. Neither science, art nor religion is exclusive. Not institutionalism, but the principle of self-knowledge is the seed of a new humanity. This principle links the activities represented in the diagrams, that portray the movements of ∧ and ∨ as well as that of the cross + (A.S. 1995).

shapes our world; they are the "depths" of beginning, end, good, evil, and the six directions, but they themselves transcend all these dimensions. They are interrelated by twenty-two paths. In this account, God creates the world by uttering the sounds of the alphabet. Ten sephirot and twenty-two paths make thirty-two, the gematria for "lev", *heart*. For Jewish mysticism, the sephirot tree is the very heart of creation. Perhaps Steiner's *elf* is also a reference to the eleventh sephirah, *Daat* (knowledge) situated at the larynx, our instrument for speech and song. *Daat* is "the rainbow bridge" at the confluence of wisdom and understanding, "the gateway to the 'hidden' tree". See Parfitt. 131; and R. Steiner. Lectures, Dornach 20-22 Sept. 1918. GA 184 (MS tr. Z.362, R. Steiner Library, London).

Steiner's lecture Dornach 9 Jan. 1915 on what we may call "ten-fold man" (GA 161, typescript translation Z.69) is particularly important. The Pythagorean tetractys is easily recognised in the accompanying diagram (see Fig. 64). The cosmic future appears diagrammatically here as the inversion of the initial tetractys. It shares the same base, thus creating sixteen members in seven lines that represent the seven planetary embodiments. The eleventh member represents the cosmological stage that crosses over into spiritual existence (Jupiter evolution). This can already be prepared by individuals and especially new group activity that may be described as sacramental in the sense touched on in this book, and which may approach Steiner's description of the inverted cult. The future stages (the second tetractys) could well be described as "the Tree behind the Tree", and the eleventh stage, "the rainbow bridge" (microcosmically situated on the Tree of Life at the throat, or larynx). The larynx is to become the organ of human creativity that continues the divine work (compare John 10:34-6). Eurythmy today may contribute to the sum of sacramental work of transformation that cumulatively prepares for the eleventh member (belonging to the fifth planetary embodiment) where humanity is to achieve angelic status (Rev 21:17).

A comment of Gareth Knight is revealing: "In Christian language *Daat* is the sphere of the Upper Room at the descent of the Pentecostal flames. In pre-Christian times it was the sphere of the Creative Fire in the realm of the Mind" (Gareth Knight. *A Practical Guide to Quabalistic Symbolism*. Vol. 1. Kahn and Averill. 1986. 103). Study of the cabbala was a major force in the middle ages, and there is a Christian development. In this connection, the recent manuscript discoveries (the Byrom collection) which include the original plans for the Globe theatre which suggest (similar to several cathedrals and churches) that it, too, was a "model of the universe", may also help solve the riddle of Shakespeare's creative methods and possibly even of his contested identity.

Bach and the esoteric tradition

H. Kluge-Kahn has shown that Bach used the structure of the Tree of Life as the basis for *The Goldberg Variations*, because he wished to create after God's own example a hymn in praise to the Holy Spirit. In the following extended excerpt on the 11th Variation (*Veränderung*, "transformation"), she throws some light on how the number eleven was experienced by a great (perhaps the greatest) musician. (Bruckner was another musician who was fascinated by number.) Such testimony is worth more than groundless or subjective speculation about the creative process, and is likely to contribute clues to Steiner's meaning, too. (For information: the eleventh letter of the Hebrew alphabet is "kaf", meaning "palm" with significant association of "weighing in hand": the tenth letter "yod" means "hand", with significant association of "hands that mould the clay; direction").

> The sign "lambda" occupies the eleventh position in the Greek alphabet (see Fig. 62a). A transformation occurs when this sign is placed together with its inversion (b), forming a rhombus (c). When the two signs, mirroring each other, meet at their points, then "chi" appears, which occupies the twenty-second position in the Greek alphabet as the sign of the cross (d). Bach made it visible in a crosswise disposition of notes as the transverse cross and sign of the suffering and death of Jesus. This is generally known. But it is not known that Bach visually transferred the form of the rhombus as well as the cross in his notational idiom, relying on ancient Hebraic-Hellenistic interpretation.

> According to Jewish exegesis, in connection with the Pythagorean's philosophic theory of numbers and their harmony, an emblem for God

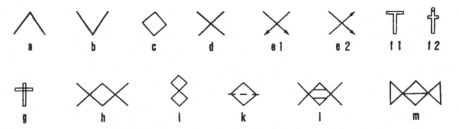

Fig. 63:   Signs and figures (after Kluge-Kahn). Compare NB 494. 3.

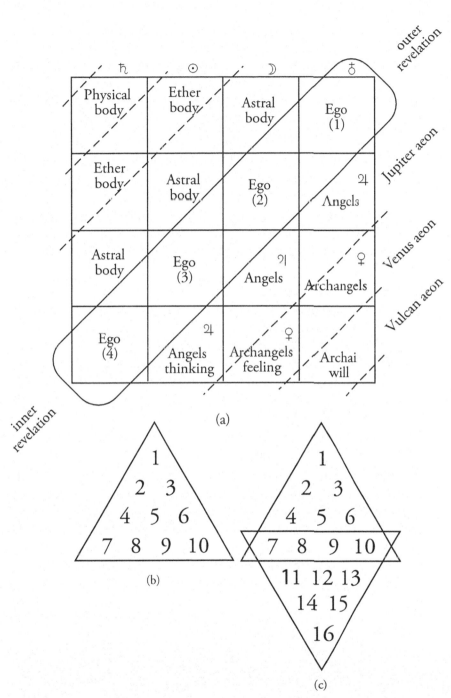

Fig. 64: (a) R. Steiner's diagram, lecture Dornach 9. Jan. 19 15 (see p. 437 below); (b) Pythagorean tetractys (sometimes the numbering runs from right to left); (c) Steiner's diagram restated numerically (A. Stott, 1995). The succession of planetary embodiments starts from unity, develops to multiplicity, and progresses to final unity. The human being 'comes to himself' (Luke 15:17) during the earthly embodiment. Precisely here, creative possibility begins (egos 2 & 3; explanation, p. 437 below). The earthly journey, implying the entirety (1-16), is often portrayed in cyclic literary and musical forms.

was seen in the "telos" sign of the cross, and in the *Sepher Yetzirah* the crossing of two arrows is described as "arrow-cross" (e1 and e2). It is supposed to have originated from the primeval cross sign of the twenty-second Hebrew letter "tav", whose graphic signs (f1 and f2) and the one for "aleph" (= 1), are the first Hebrew letters. People saw in them the unity of beginning, middle and end.

Sayings concerning the above signs from the oldest Jewish account of creation are rendered by von Thimus (p. 93): "Unite the end with the beginning; as a flame is connected to the coal" (f2). And further: "God made the letter 'aleph' (= 1) king in a breath, and put on it the crown. Rev. 1:8: *Ego sum Alpha et Omega*." The certainty grows that Bach must have known this oldest account of creation and the telos sign; for he made this cross sign (e1 and e2) visible in the theme of the eleventh Variation.

Linking on to the saying in Revelation about beginning and end, and on him "who was, and is, and is to come", the ancients saw in the crossing of the heavenly equator and the ecliptic in the form of a cross, the "throne", the "temple" of God. Here the spiritual birth of Christ occurred ("this day have I begotten thee" Ps. 2:7, Heb. 1:5). Proceeding from this region of the heavens, heaven and earth, sun, moon and stars, the four elements, all things in the universe were created in geometrical figures through the breath of the divine voice. The earthly cross (g) became the sign of Jesus' death. But after Christ's resurrection and his return to the throne of God and after his elevation and coronation, it is the heavenly sign of victory. The theme of Var. 11 shows how Bach, the earthly master builder, "inscribed/geometrised"…

If we observe the unusual disposition of the notes of Var. 11, there is revealed that the words of Psalm 11 fit the divine sign of the "arrow cross" and the rhombus: "The Lord is in his holy temple, the Lord's throne is in heaven." In this region, the spiritual birth of the Son of God occurred. Psalm 2:7 speaks of it initially with the prophecy of Christ's kingdom: "I will declare the decree: the Lord hath said unto me, Thou art my Son; this day have I begotten thee" (Hertha Kluge-Kahn 1985. 93f.; tr. A.S.).

Fig. 65: The opening of the 11th Variation for double-manual harpsichord, from J. S. Bach, *Goldberg Variations*.

The creation of eurythmy

The above extract of a detail of recent scholarship, while omitting much, does establish something of Bach's method of working with the esoteric tradition. Hertha Kluge-Kahn's study traces how, for Bach, the magic of number, theology and music were aspects of the same creative process. Like Shakespeare (whose use of number, as exhibited in the First Folio of 1623, was researched by Sylvia Eckersley. *Number and Geometry in Shakespeare's* Macbeth. Floris Books. 2007), Bach's creative example stands at a transition in music's development. Steiner's relationship to this tradition seems more a concern with renewing the tradition itself. The ancient mysteries, as we know, were concerned with maintaining the harmony of heaven and earth. "The mystical code of number... was at the root of all ancient arts and sciences, particularly in connection with the measurements of prehistoric temples and monuments," John Michell reminds us. *The New View over Atlantis*. Thames and Hudson. London. 1983. 7).

The founding of the new mysteries is accomplished precisely as a deed that we, on our part, are free to recognise. Steiner, too, stands at an important juncture: the opening decades of the Michael age, and the transition of music at the end of the romantic age. Eurythmy and anthroposophy, or spiritual science, link to the occult philosophy of the Elizabethans in more ways than simply a taking up Agrippa's Vitruvian figures. In anthroposophy, there is no intention of reinstating gnosticism, mysticism or any ancient tradition, but of developing science into a truly comprehensive activity. Steiner's definition of science is undertaken in *Occult Science*, Chapter 1. This account at the same time establishes a modern basis for other meaningful human activities (art and religion); these include a scientific side just as science includes an artistic and religious side (pioneered, for example, by Goethean science). Charges of dogmatism and arbitrariness are met. Anthroposophy is a scientific path that transforms the spirituality in all valid traditions, by tracing them back to their source in the human being. Primordial man, or "the Son of man", is "the measure of all things", more than Protagoras knew (*cf.*, 1 Cor. 15), for this includes the human being's divine origin and divine destiny. "Primordial man" is Adam-Cadmon, called by Steiner the "Nathan-Jesus". He is the radiant aura of Christ himself, the archetype of "the one who receives the Christ' (R. Steiner. Lecture, Dornach. 21 April 1924. GA 233). We may conclude that the Lambda (the eleventh Greek letter) that points to the mystery of creation and the mystery of the number 11, probably stands behind the expression *ALP-elf* (but NB the "*Important disclaimer...*", at the outset!). It points to the creative activity of the personality, or true ego, to which philosophers and theologians point as an intuitive experience. Coleridge's definition is perhaps the most famous (*Biographia Literaria*, Chapter 13, see bibliography below. For further study on the Lambda, see Hans Kayser. *Orphikon*. Schwabe & Co. Basel/ Stuttgart. 1973).

A study of the origins of eurythmy that reaches beyond documentation seems demanded. Nevertheless, near the close of these initial studies, we may conclude that Steiner is alluding to the western esoteric tradition at the outset of the lecture-course on music (termed "[the] self-creative power in the human being" in Lecture 4), that is, to that world of Inspiration where mathematics and music co-habitate. Rather than discuss the merits and demerits of a tradition (with all the side issues of irrationality, magic, and so on), he leaves a hint for students, and concentrates on artistic, specifically musical, renewal. A training in traditional mystical studies becomes transformed today into artistic activity. Steiner names Abraham as the inaugurator of arithmetic (*The Gospel of St Matthew*. Lecture 3 Sept. 1910. RSP. 1965). Perhaps Bach had something to do with helping to lead the activity of reckoning back to creative, spiritual concerns. However that may be, the artistic wonder is not that Bach cleverly hides esoteric symbolism and thinks numerically (which is a wonder of technique); the artistic wonder is the inspiration that lives in his music. The wonder of eurythmy, too, is not, for example, the fact that geometric forms are moved, and that the axis mundi, the Celtic cross, and so on, can be recognised in the angle-gestures, but that it is now possible artistically to free and reveal the composer's and the musician's creative source. This raising of symbolism and mysticism – that threatens to run solely into intellectual, speculative paths – through the recreating of music is the artistically conscious, potentially fuller and legitimate path of the art of eurythmy, offered as nourishment for the potential benefit of all humanity.

Addenda:

Further significance of the number 11 should still be mentioned. (i) In this concept, eleven is taken as the penultimate number to the completion of twelve. A relevant example is the genealogy in Luke's gospel. The first advent occupies the 11 x 7th place (Austin Farrer: "Note: The Genealogies of Christ" concluding "On Dispensing with Q" in D.E. Nineham (ed.).

Studies in the Gospels. Blackwell. Oxford. 1955. 87f. Farrer cites I Enoch 93 as a precedent for grouping generations in "weeks" or sevens. In New Testament terms, we are living in the time before "the perfect period at which the Son of Man" returns. Luke narrates the birth of the Nathan-Jesus, to which the genealogy refers. According to Steiner, this spiritual being inspired Luke's writing. According to Sergei Prokofieff's research, this being inspired Steiner's artistic creating, too (Prokofieff 1994). The Adam-soul, the true Christopher, received the Logos itself. The creation of the art of eurythmy witnesses to the return of the Logos as the Son of Man (see also, Emil Bock. "The Son of Man". *The Christian Community Journal* 1947. 99-102 and 121-125. Floris Books. Edinburgh.

(ii) A further example of the position of the number 11 is offered by K.F. Althoff, who writes: "Eleven stands between 10 and 12, and like the Communion [of The Act of Consecration of Man] links the knowledge of earthly man (10) with the spirit in the universe as expression of heavenly man (12). We can say: the number 11 appears in the light of the Communion; it is the number which strives to knowledge. The eleventh line of the Lord's Prayer – the doxology – is like a communion hymn" (K.F. Althoff. *Das Vaterunser*. Urachhaus. Stuttgart. 1978. 248).

The interpretations of ALP-elf offered in Appendix 7 are not necessarily mutually exclusive. The intention, at least, that underlies Steiner's attempt at renewal, is quite clear: Sacred, mystical tradition is to be transformed into a new art of the future. Such awareness on the part of the artist would seem to be crucial for the further development of eurythmy: only true esotericism can renew art. A reasonable summary would suggest that Steiner wished to point beyond tradition to the ultimate source of eurythmy. This is a spiritual being, traditionally called both primordial man and the Son of Man (the son of humankind). The earnest message can perhaps be expressed in simple words: Those who wish to continue this act of creation that, with his death in 1925, Steiner left as a task for the eurythmists to develop, should learn to approach this spiritual being.

A note on magic: In *Eurythmy as Visible Speech* (GA 279), lecture 12, Steiner forbids "the least trace of what might be called magic... suggestiveness" (131) in the art of education, specifically the "I and You" exercise. The words "magic" and "magical" are sometimes used journalistically in connection with musical performances. If this concept is divested of arbitrary and mechanical interpretation and "make-believe", it may serve as a description of an aspect of sacramental and artisic life. In that case, the "magic" is controlled respectively by the presiding priest or minister and the performing artist, with the co-operation of those taking part. However, the use of the word "magic" today seems inadequate, because it suggests something sensational. Theologians, for example, prefer to speak of faith-union with Christ and his redemptive work. In artistic performance and experience, expressions like expectation, participation and of "the willing suspension of disbelief" (Coleridge) are used. In all this we are dealing with legitimate functions of the will. "Magic" as a term for depicting a change to the better, that is, transformation and not mere ritualism, is the very heart of Mozart's most profound opera, *The Magic Flute*, and embraces his use of the musical elements.

Today, on the one hand, mechanically produced illusion (CDs, videos, virtual reality, and now holographs) provide widespread counter-phenomena; users are noted to betray in varying degrees symptoms

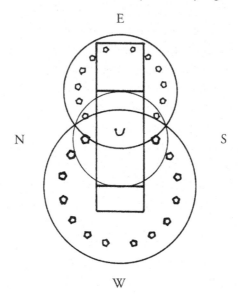

Fig. 66: The outline plan of Solomon's Temple (rectangle) superimposed on that of the First Goetheanum (from Kemper, *Der Bau*, reproduced by courtesy of Verlag Freies Geistesleben, Stuttgart).

of addiction. On the other hand, the divine creative activity that is described in *Sepher Yetzirah* is also at work: Steiner refers to "Yahweh's magic breath" (see Endnote 28) in connection with creative human activity. Eurythmy may contribute to the enhanced responsibility of the human being to follow the Creator's own example. In this sense we might be entitled to speak of "magic" in our experience of eurythmy and of art in general. Music, in its prehistoric beginnings, was certainly magical.

Today, then, we can witness both uncontrolled and mechanically-fixed "throwbacks" as well as conscious attempts to enhance perception in the pursuit of true freedom. Perhaps John Oman sums it up: "Our concern with God's will now," he writes, "and the personal insight and personal consecration it requires, gives us hope that all the truth, beauty and goodness realised in this world will follow us, because what we will have won of true freedom will be our true selves" (John Oman. *The Natural and the Supernatural.* Cambridge. 1931/49. 466).

Rudolf Steiner. The Gospel of St Matthew. *RSP. 1965, presents an account of how Christ inaugurated initiation of the ego.*

R. Steiner. The Temple Legend. *Lectures, Berlin between 23 April 1904 and 2 Jan 1906. RSP. 1985. For Steiner on mathematics, see the* Übersichtsbände, *Vol. 2. Dornach. 1980.*

Sepher Yetzirah. The Book of Creation. *Tr. by A. Kaplan. S. Weiser. York Beach, Maine. 1990.*

G. Scholem. On the Kabbalah and its Symbolism. *Schocken Books. New York. 1965;*

G. Scholem. Origins of the Kabbalah. *Princeton. 1987. This scholar is the achnowledged authority on the subject of Jewish mysticism.*

Dion Fortune. The Mystical Qabalah. *Aquarian/Thorsons. London 1935/1987; a classic introduction to this subject;*

Will Parfitt. The Qabalah. *Element Books. Shaftsbury. 1991;*

Brian Lancaster. The Elements of Judaism. *Element. Shaftesbury. 1993; a distinquished introduction.*

Margaret Barker. The Older Testament. *SPCK. London. 1987; the survival of themes from the ancient royal cult in sectarian Judaism and early Christianity;*

Margaret Barker. The Lost Prophet. *SPCK. London. 1988; the Book of Enoch and its influence on Christianity;*

Margaret Barker. The Gate of Heaven. *SPCK. London. 1991; history and symbolism of the Temple in Jerusalem; scholarly and readable; stimulating studies of Judaeo-Christian traditions;*

Margaret Barker. The Great Angel: Israel's Second God. *SPCK. London. 1992, a study of Yahweh-Christ, the "great angel";*

Margaret Barker. As in Heaven, so on Earth. *T. & T. Clark. Edinburgh 1995; Temple symbolism in the New Testament;*

Margaret Barker. The Risen Lord. *Edinburgh. 1996; the Jesus of history as the Christ of faith.*

Owen Barfield. Saving the Appearances. *Wesleyan 1988. is indispensable; 'The Psalms of David" in* The Rediscovery of Meaning. *Wesleyan. 1977. 237-48 should not be missed.*

H. Wheeler Robinson, 'The Hebrew Conception of Corporate Personality' in Beihefte zur Zeitschrift fur die alttestamentische Wissenschaft. 66. 1936. 49ff., reprinted in Corporate Personality in Ancient Isreal (Fortress Press. Philadelphia/ T. & T. Clark. Edinburgh. 1981), which contains an appreciation of this scholar, all of whose work repays study. This second edition contains an introduction by Cyril S. Rodd that takes account of criticisms of this widely-influential theory, for example that of J.W. Rogerson in Journal of Theological Studies (1970). 1-16. For a guide to inner experience, see H. Wheeler Robinson. Inspiration and Revelation in the Old Testament. OUP 1946. Reprinted).

Frances A. Yates. The Occult Philosophy. Routledge. London. 1979/ Ark. 1983; on Renaissance thought and literature, is a valuable introduction to her other works on these subjects.

Hertha Kluge-Kahn. Johann Sebastian Bach: die Verschlüsselten theologischen Aussagen in seinem Spätwerk. Möseler. Wolfenbüttel u. Zürich. 1985; a detailed study of Bach's thought in the instrumental cycles from his last twelve years; MS tr. by A.S. The author began her research by substantially confirming Hans Nissen's thesis (Bachjahrbuch 1951/2) that in his WTC II, Bach combined the two fundamental major/minor streams with his artistic plan to portray the Biblical account of salvation: pieces in major keys (God's plan), pieces in minor keys (the human condition, or humanity's need). Bach portrays how God takes on and transmutes mankind's suffering in the second (New Testament) half of this cycle.

Joy Hancox. The Byrom Collection. Johnathan Cape. London. 1992; discusses the recently-discovered original plans of the Globe Theatre and the esoteric background. Representations of the cube room, the Tree of Life, and other sacred geometrical figures abound in the collection. The diagram Fig. 67 on p. 437 below (geometrical illustration of Robert Fludd's summary of traditional wisdom concerning God) is, I believe, relevant to the angle-gestures of eurythmy. The axis-mundi and the cube as hexagon are clearly visible in the context of the Platonic triangular surface, which begins at the apex with the tetractys.

On the mystery art of Shakespeare, E. Schuré. The Genesis of Tragedy. Rudolf Steiner Pub. Co. London. 1936/ Kessinger Pub., reprint edition, is still relevant; see also Sylvia Eckersley. Number and Geometry in Shakespeare's "Macbeth". Investigation of the First Folio texts shows each scene, act and play is symmetrically constructed. A similar symmetrical candlestick pattern has been found in each section and each chapter of Steiner's written work (see Endnote 1 for references).

John Michell and Christine Rhone. Twelve-Tribe Nations. Thames and Hudson, London 1991; the chapter on the Temple at Jerusalem forms the climax to this popular-scholarly survey of the cosmic ordering of society. 164-183.

Leo Schaya. "The Meaning of the Temple" in The Sword of Gnosis. Jacob Needleman, Ed. Arkana. London/ Boston and Henley. 1986. 359-365; links the outer court, the Holy and the Holy of Holies with the three traditional stages of the mystic path.

A.G. Hebert. The Throne of David. Faber. London. 1949; a study of the fulfilment of the Old Testament in Jesus Christ and the Church.

Sergei Prokofieff. Rudolf Steiner and the Founding of the New Mysteries. *Temple Lodge Press. London. 1994; includes an investigation of the continued activity of the Nathan-Jesus.*

Gordon Strachan. Christ and the Cosmos. *Dunbar. 1985; a sympathetic survey of increasing spiritual awareness today of our responsibility to the earth.*

Albert v. Thimus. Die harmonicale Symbolik des Altertums. Bd. 1. Cologne. 1868. *Reprinted G. Olms. Hildesheim and New York. 1972; a poineer work still apparently untranslated.*

Keith Critchlow. "The Platonic Tradition on the Nature of Proportion" in Rediscovering Sacred Science. *Ed. and intro. by Christopher Bamford. Floris Books. Edinburgh. 1994; an introduction to Greek cosmology, and Plato in particular (see also bibliography, end of Appendix 4).*

Hans Kayser. Orphikon. *Schwabe & Co. Basel/ Stuttgart. 1973; an impressive symbolic-mythical study, featuring the Lambda and Lambdoma.*

S.E. Gillingham. The Poems and Psalms of the Hebrew Bible. *Oxford. OUP 1994; an introduction that points out musical qualities from the very first page; contains a useful bibliography.*

Edgar Jones. The Cross in the Psalms. *Independent Press. London. 1963; a short, valuable study.*

Helmer Ringgren. The Faith of the Psalmists. *SCM. London. 1963; an introduction to modern studies. Modern commentators on the Psalms include those of Gunkel. Fortress. Philadelphia. 1967; Mowinckel. Abingdon. New York. 1962; and Weiser. SCM. London. 1962.*

Alexander Maclaren. The Psalms. *The Expositor's Bible; London. 1892-4; Eerdmans. 1956; Klock & Klock. Minneapolis. Minnesota 55411, is still a valuable commentary.*

Rudolf Frieling. Hidden Treasure in the Psalms. *Floris Books. 1967; studies and appreciations of 21 representative prayers and praises.*

G.D. Carleton. The English Psalter. *Mowbray. London. 1953; a devotional commentary.*

(ii) "A remarkable tradition"

> Here it would perhaps be well to remind ourselves of a remarkable tradition which today is little understood, and of which you find some indication when you take the beginning of St John's Gospel: "In the beginning was the Word, and the Word was God, and a God was the Word" (R. Steiner. GA 279. Lecture, Dornach. 24 June 1924).

> The concrete historical facts... are, themselves, the manifestations of the universal Personality... The fact abides transfigured by the Divine Immanence. The personal Will of man closes with the personal Will of

God through the permanent fact which embodies God's intention and releases His purpose (H. Scott Holland. *The Philosophy of Faith and The Fourth Gospel*. Murray. London. 1920. 158; also published separately as *The Fourth Gospel*. 1923. 71).

Lecture 1 of *Eurythmy as Visible Singing* (Dornach, 19 Feb. 1924) should be compared with lecture 1 of *Eurythmy as Visible Speech* (Dornach, 24 June 1924. GA 279. Anastasi. 2005; page-numbers below refer to this edition) for an amplified account of the point of departure for eurythmy. Three performing arts are compared. Imitation characterises the art of *mime*, which "emphasises speech"; the art of *dancing* involves "an outpouring of the emotions, of the will, into movements of the human body". Both of these arts add to the possibilities present "on the physical plane". The art of *eurythmy*, however, is "a creation out of the spirit… [it] makes use of his human form in the physical world; the human being in movement serves as the means of expression" (R. Steiner. GA 279. 29). The antithesis of physical and spiritual, of the temporal and eternal, the natural and the human worlds, seems unequivocal here. The difference is crucial for an appreciation of the point of departure of eurythmy, yet it is still incompletely grasped today. In the lecture-course on speech-eurythmy, Steiner does not dwell on the sister arts, but proceeds to renew what he terms "a remarkable tradition".

Steiner begins with the larynx: "The whole human being must become a kind of larynx" (29). "The entire alphabet" ("primeval Word") expresses "the entire etheric human being". Here "out of the etheric" (*aus dem Ätherischen*, Germ. 4th ed. 51) does not refer to etheric forces of the natural world, but to *the entire human being* "created out of cosmic depths" which later "received form as a being of air" then "fluid form, and later still, solid physical form". "Lightning is in continual movement; lightning is in continual flow. The etheric body is in continual motion, in continual activity" (30; compare the raying image of "a flash of lightning" for "t", or T A O. 43). Steiner points to the activity of the *transformed* human ether (that is, the chemical ether) and ultimately to the future spiritual member of the human being (Life-Spirit), rather than the natural etheric of the sleeping vegetable kingdom and phenomena of the watery world.

Near the outset (as in GA 278), Steiner fulfils a law that esoteric development requires a link to esoteric tradition. The "remarkable tradition which is little understood today" and which is indicated in the Prologue to the Fourth Gospel, is unlikely in the first place to derive from the Logos doctrine of the Alexandrians, but the Hebraic "word of the Yahweh" (often translated "word of the Lord"). F.D. Maurice (1856),

H. Drummond (1903) and H. Scott Holland (1920), for example, tried to retain a perspective.

"'The Word became Flesh.' Would it ever have been conceivable that an Alexandrian Platonist could have arrived at such a phrase, and not given some signal of the surprise, of the shock, or the recoil that it would cause?" asks H.Scott Holland (*The Fourth Gospel*. Murray. London. 1923. 81). "It would have appeared an inversion of all values, whether religious or metaphysical," adds H.A.A. Kennedy (*Philo's Contribution to Religion*. Hodder & Stoughton. London 1919. 177). Theologians agree in denying the impact of Hellenistic thought in the Prologue: "Logos never has the sense of reason in the New Testament... The theological use of the term appears to be derived from the Palestinian *Memra*, and not from the Alexandrine Logos" (B.F. Westcott. *The Gospel according to St John*. Murray. London. 1898. 2-3). Rendel Harris. *The Origin of the Prologue to St John's Gospel* (1917) remarshals evidence of the Jewish origin of the Logos doctrine. That the evangelist *thought* in Aramaic may be regarded as established. He appears to have chosen a term between Jews and Greeks as the expression of a uniting faith. "The special suitability of the term Logos lay in its power to express both the thought behind the word and the uttered word itself" (H. Wheeler Robinson, in *The Bible in its Ancient and English Versions*. H. Wheeler Robinson, ed. Oxford. OUP 1940. 285). See also the commentaries of J.H. Bernard (1929), E.C. Hoskyns (1940) especially 152-164 (2nd ed. 1947. 154-163), W. Temple (1945), R.H. Lightfoot (1956), J. Marsh (1968), C.K. Barrett (1978), also Margaret Barker (1992) on theological fashion regarding *Memra*; for comments on Johannine Inspiration and Intuition, and the synoptic Imagination referred to in the Lucan "eye-witnesses and servants of the Word" (Luke 1:2), see R. Steiner, *The Gospel of St Luke*. Lecture, Basel. 15 Sept. 1909. RSP. 1964. The Johannine motifs of light life, and love (designating the three stages of higher consciousness) substantiate Steiner's explanation of the Word as "the whole human being as an etheric creation" (29). His phrase here directly links the ancient mysteries and modern spiritual science. Steiner echoes Biblical language, too: out of the creative movement of the gods "the dust of the earth forms itself and the human form eventually arises" (36). It can be seen that much of the subject matter of the baffling *Book of Creation (Sepher Yetzirah)*, the creative power of the alphabet, the planets, the zodiac, and so on, reappears in an artistic form in GA 279. This all suggests that *Sepher Yetzirah* could represent that "remarkable tradition" mentioned at the outset. *Cf.* Ps. 33:6:

By the WORD of YAHWEH were the heavens made
their starry host by the BREATH/ SPIRIT of his mouth.

Further evidence that Steiner is referring to this sacred and magical tradition (and for *Eurythmy as Visible Singing*, for additional reasons mentioned above), is initially supported by the following remarks:

(1) The gods' primordial movement lies behind eurythmy. "God eurythmises, and... there arises the human form... in the beginning, God created the beautiful human form out of movement" (37). The Johannine Creator-Word, the agent of creation and the supreme and final manifestation of the Divine Name, links to Israel's Creator-God, Yahweh (*cf.*, the phrase "Yahweh's magic breath". Endnote ▨, above), himself a Son of God or manifestation of the unmanifest *El Elyon*, "God Most High" (see Margaret Barker 1992). *The Book of Creation* opens with a recital of the ten names of God. Man, created in God's image, a microcosm attuned to the great world, may attain a pure and sacred knowledge of the secret names of all things.

(2) "To primeval human understanding, the idea, the conception 'the Word' comprised the whole human being as an etheric creation" (29). "The etheric man is the Word, which contains within it the entire alphabet" (31; the acrostic Psalms may acquire a new significance in this light).[3] "The entire human etheric body is there, proceeding out of the larynx, out of the womb" (35). The larynx is in "a continual state of creation... a continuous becoming... Every time we speak we transpose ourselves into the cosmic evolution of man as it was in primeval ages" (33). Humanity's "primeval intuitive knowledge" is acknowledged. Biblical tradition ("the Word of Yahweh") seems implied, and the mystery terms "Son of Man" and 'Son of Yahweh', too.

(3) "That... to which we give the name 'tree', is a part of ourselves, a part of our own etheric being" (32). This may include a reference to the Tree of Life. Such a suggestion may seem far-fetched, but a reference here does support the main point that the human being "utters *himself* and consequently the entire universe" if the whole alphabet were uttered in a particular way from beginning to end (32. See also Endnote ▨, above). The letters are the signatures of all creation. It is also worthwhile noting that scholars maintain that from one fundamental alphabet "of the Syro-Palestinian Semites... have descended all past and present alphabets" (D. Diringer. *The Alphabet*. London. 1947. 216f.).

---

3   The artifice of acrostic "symbolizes the setting in order of the moral chaos wherein humanity
     was fallen" (R.M. Benson).

(4) During the lecture that introduces the Hallelujah exercises (GA 279. Lecture 13. Dornach. 10 July 1924), Steiner refers to "certain Mystery Centres where an art of movement existed such as we are endeavouring to renew in eurythmy" (143). Poetry then, he says, arose out of a preceeding "eurythmical movements and gestures". The eurythmist has to be able to feel: "Was the poet himself a eurythmist?" (143). This reference is likely to include Hebrew religious poetry; the lecture ends by referring to the gesture for devotion. (Note that the sounds used in the creation account of Genesis are discussed in R. Steiner, *Genesis*. Lectures, Munich 17-26 Aug. 1910. GA 122. RSP. 1959, reprinted.)

The Hebrew and Greek languages (the languages of the Old and New Testaments) are mentioned with the example of the sound A (*'ah'*). The Bible contains the story of the creation, fall and redemption of the human race. It has been termed the text-book of the human ego; St John's Gospel is singled out as "the book of the mystery of the ego" by Friednrich Rittelmeyer (*Letters on St John's Gospel*. Typescript with Floris Books, Edinburgh). It is within the context of the Hebrew and Greek traditions which meet in Christianity (and significantly in the word Logos—"Word" and "Reason"), that we are to understand the attempted renewal of the creation of eurythmy. Other ancient mystery traditions are mentioned (for example, western Asia [the Hebrews?], southern Asia (India) and Africa (Egypt) in connection with the sound "F". Lecture 2. 43f.). The alphabet points to the "collective word" (32), and the existence of different languages points back to one primeval language ("there is no doubt that such a language did exist". 46).

In the Hebrew aleph, "wonder" (Biblical "fear of the Lord") is specified; in the Greek alpha it is "love of wisdom" (philosophy). These two polar streams which manifested historically in Hebrew and Greek thought, continue in human consciousness (religion/ philosophy, will/ reason, revelation/ illumination, image/ symbol, instrument/ sign, ear/ eye, and so on). The universal law of polarity is also manifest in creative human relationships; famous examples include Goethe/ Schiller, and Wordsworth/ Coleridge. The concept of polarity produces the two forms of eurythmy (speech and music); polarity is fundamental to GA 278, too. This discovery leads to a fuller understanding of the T A O eurythmy-meditation, and also the enigmatic passage on music that concludes the lecture Steiner held in Torquay 22 Aug. 1924 (see Appendix 4, iii).

The alphabet (as well as self-knowledge and artistic creation itself) begins with the sound A (*'ah'*), corresponding to "man filled with wonder at his own true being... man in his highest, most ideal culmination...

We actually only have the human being before us when we perceive the full measure of that which is divine within him" (34). "Self-knowledge… this self-observation begins with the sound 'ah'… it requires great effort, great activity, to attain to such knowledge of the human being." The phrase "the divine within" is not an invitation to indulge pious sentiments. The context shows the attempt to formulate an accurate description of the creative source, as well as of the ultimate fulfilment of the human being. This process is summed up as "self-knowledge". The I AM, an *act* that identifies subject and object, is the absolute ground of all knowledge (see R. Steiner. *The Philosophy of Freedom*; and René Guénon. *Symbolism of the Cross*. Chapter 17).

> Christ the Lord by the pressure of His own Personality forces up our personalities into activity, into prominence. He intensifies our self-knowledge, self-criticism,. self-disclosure… He draws us into speech, into self-realisation… We, made to be a Word of God's own, we live in His utterance, we live in His light… By self-knowledge, self-searching, self-control, self-discipline, self-understanding, self-direction, we work out our career and verify our qualification for an existence beyond death in the Kingdom (H. Scott Holland, "Consciousness, Subconsciousness, and Superconsciousness", a sermon on John 1:1, dated 1907, in *The Philosophy of Faith and the Fourth Gospel*. 98, 101).

The concept of Incarnation

> Jesus, knowing that the Father had given all things into his hands, and that he had come from God and was going to God… (John 13:3).

> The Prologue is an account of the life of Jesus under the form of a description of the eternal Logos in its relations with the world and with man, and the rest of the gospel [is] an account of the Logos under the form of a record of the life of Jesus; and the proposition "and the Word, flesh it became" binds the two together, being at the same time the final expression of the relation of the Logos to man and his world, and a summary of the significance of the life of Jesus (C.H. Dodd. *The Interpretation of the Fourth Gospel*. Cambridge Univ. Press. 1953. 285).

> The Incarnation of the Word of God… carries with it the guarantee that our human nature is not alien to God in itself, and that there is sufficient kinship between the human and the divine for the human to utter and express the divine (H. Wheeler Robinson. "The Bible as the Word of God" in *The Bible in its Ancient and English Versions*. H. Wheeler Robinson. Ed. OUP 1940. 286).

"The divine" initially relates to the last and highest category employed in the lecture under discussion, 24 June 1924 ("physical, etheric, astral and ego"). In an important lecture, Dornach 9 Jan. 1915 (Z.69. R. Steiner Library, London) "the ego" is described in its four manifestations. The ego is perceptible:

(1) outside (in another human being)
(2) in speaking and singing
(3) in the creative imagination
(4) in inner experience.

In both these lectures (24 June 1924 and 9 Jan.1 1915), it has to be recognised that the Incarnation of the World-Ego, the Creator-God

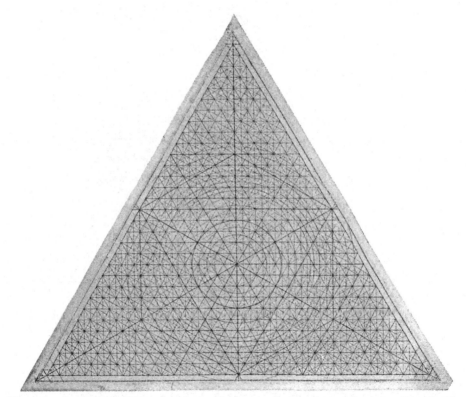

Fig. 67: A geometrical study of a surface composed of triangles (after Plato). The 30x30x30 triangles begins at the apex following the pattern of the Pythagorean tetractys (1+2+3+4). The emphasised lines clearly show the axis-mindi, the cube as a hexagon, and the eurythmy angle-gestures. This study (early C17th) was used as a basis for several architectural plans (Westminster Abbey; King's College Chapel, Cambridge; London theatres, including the Globe Theatre) (from Joy Hancox, *The Byrom Collection* [Johnathan Cape, London 1992]).

himself, is implied. It forms the conclusion to the Prologue quoted by Steiner: "and the Word became flesh" (John 1:15). The evangelist essentially does two things: firstly, points to the very beginning "before" creation (as Genesis itself cannot be held to do), and secondly, that in the life, death and resurrection of Jesus Christ, the Creator not only called a new people or a new humanity to himself, but began a new creation (see E.C. Hoskyns, "Genesis I-III and St John's Gospel", *JTS* XXI. 210-18). Patristic thought recognised that the Incarnation continues in humanity: for example, Irenaeus, "He became what we are in order that He might make us become what He is" (*Adv. Haer.*, v. Pref.), and Athanasius, "He became human that we might become divine" (*De Incarn.* 54, 3). The union of God and man in Christ is the subject of L. Thornton's profound study *The Incarnate Lord.* Longmans,

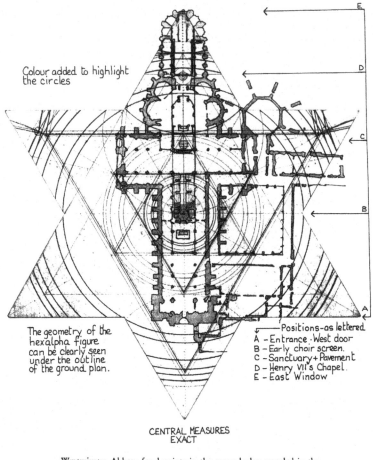

Westminster Abbey: focal points in the ground plan revealed in the geometry.

Fig. 68:

Green. London. 1928. The union is dynamically described by P.T. Forsyth (*The Person and Place of Jesus Christ.* Independent Press.

London. 1909/55, Lectures XI and XII) as two reciprocal and mutually involved movements (that is, not states) of a personal character from God to man and from man to God. "The diminuendo of the *kenosis* went on parallel with the crescendo of a vaster *plerosis*. He died to live" (308). "In finding the sheep that were lost he gradually finds the self, the mode of self, that consciousness, he had renounced" (311). Forsyth sees *kenosis* as "concentration... self-reduction, or self-retraction". "Man," he says, "attains the kingdom by the constant act of faith which integrates him into the act of grace. Life, history, at its highest may be figured as a wire traversed in opposite directions by these two great spiritual currents, movements or acts" (340).

The Byrom Collection

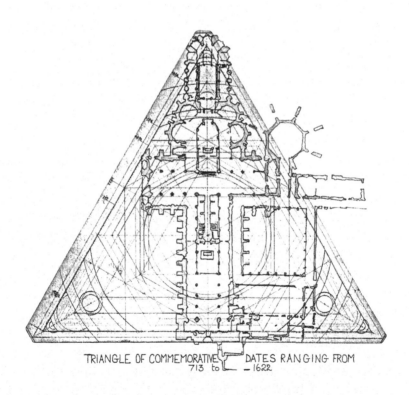

TRIANGLE OF COMMEMORATIVE DATES RANGING FROM 713 to 1622

History expressed in number and geometry, the ground plan of Westminster Abbey superimposed. The two dates 1051 and 1154 draw the eye towards the intersection in the Chapel of the Confessor. The other main intersection at the entrance to the choir leads to the date 1622. Thus number links with geometry to demonstrate concepts to be found in the Abbey – sanctity, destiny, harmony and continuity.

Fig. 69:

Dual reciprocal movement is a concept frequently elaborated by Steiner, often in detail and in various connections. In particular, it is to be perceived underlying his attempts to describe musical processes. Music is eminently suited "to portray the Incarnation and Hallelujah of Christ" (see Appendix 4, iii). Steiner emphasises process (the reciprocal movement, or act), for example, the "constant activity" of the etheric human being (which has nothing whatever to do with hyper-activity but, as we have seen, refers to creative activity). The concept of Incarnation appears to be the key to Steiner's most profound meaning; it is the primal picture of continuous creativity itself, meditatively studied in the T A O-exercise for eurythmists (see Appendix 4).

Sonata form portrays the deeper meaning of duality and its overcoming (two initial tonal centres become one). This provides one interpretation of the advice to "show how the sonata is the whole human being...' (R. Steiner. GA 277a. 142). Beethoven's last piano sonata in two movements, op. 111, is one artistic revelation of the archetypal polarity of action (tragedy/energy) and contemplation (fulfilment/ peace), or "this world" and "the world to come" (Edwin Fischer). Furthermore, the familiar U-shaped pattern of evolution is frequently to be discovered in artistic forms – in single works and in larger designs (see Schwebsch. E. Schwebsch. *J. S. Bach und Die Kunst der Fuge*. Stuttgart. 1988.). Robert Kolben discovered the candlestick pattern in Beethoven's *'Diabelli' Variations*, op. 120 and Chopin's *Preludes*, op. 28 (articles in R. Steiner Library, London). A similar artistic pattern, the cyclic form, is discussed by M.H. Abrams. *Natural Supernaturalism*. Norton. New York. 1971. Perhaps the form is archetypally shown in the parable of the Prodigal Son (Luke 15), a story of Everyman that also includes imagery of "music and dancing" (v. 25). We might add here that the thinking in some scores and texts, and particularly the Johannine writings, suggest the spiralling and mounting of an eagle. This may be presented as a lemniscate movement that includes a crossing point in the process, enabling the inner curve/ space to become outer curve/ space, and vice versa.

The simpler U-shaped pattern may stand behind the entire output of a creative artist, too. The conventional divisions into early, middle and late works can be further differentiated in the works of creative artists, for example, Shakespeare, Beethoven, Wagner and Mahler. The U-shaped pattern of evolution may be recognised in the plan of GA 278 (as outlined in Appendix 8, below). The ultimate example (as Steiner confirms) includes the Creator's deed of Redemption that promises and enables the fulfilment of earthly evolution, the goal of forming a tenth hierarchy. "In eurythmy… the human being to a certain extent ascends to a kind of angelic existence, out of which in the course of evolution he has descended during cosmic evolution" (R. Steiner. Stuttgart. 30 April 1924, in GA 277a. 141).

In GA 279, too, this pictured fulfilment is based on an activist view of human nature, and of the divine being: "The human being only really exists before us when we perceive the full measure of that which is divine (*Göttliches*) within him/her." We are led to the tremendous conclusion that eurythmy "is a continuation of divine movement, of the divine-creative forms in the human being" (37). The universal and spiritual character of eurythmy, consequently, does suggest the possibility of its practitioners contributing to a universal Whitsun. This festival of the spirit renews the earlier one celebrating the revelation on Mount Sinai; the first Whitsun event (Acts 2) also reversed the confusion of the one universal language that resulted from the building of the tower of Babel (Gen. 11).

The obvious anthropomorphism of the conception of Yahweh (both of the Old Testament prophets and of the theophanies of the Enochic tradition) is our direct antecedent; this anthropomorphism is our only valuable line of thought concerning God, whom we know by the highest in ourselves. The "highest anthropomorphism" of "the prophets and Messianic consciousness of Jesus is counterbalanced by theomorphism in the doctrine of man. 'Let us make man in our image'; the Son of Man the express image of the invisible God: upon these two conceptions turn the Christian doctrine and experience of God," concludes W.R. Matthews (*God in Christian Thought and Experience*. Nisbet. 1939. 87); "We are intended to make man the interpretation of God," claims Scott Holland in his powerful defence of the supernatural in view of modern critical methods (*Christ or Ecclesiastes*. Longmans, Green. London 1894). Prophets, theologians and philosophers attempt to approach the nature of creative activity with their chosen terms. Artists may prefer the word "imagination". For Coleridge, this was "a repetition in the finite mind of the eternal act of creation in the infinite I AM" (S.T. Coleridge, *Biographia Literaria*. Chapter 13). And so, for finite human personality, the historic deed of imagination (Coleridge's "prime agent of all human perception" is not exclusively limited to artistic re-creation) leads, in the words of W.E. Hocking, "to a knowledge that this act of mine which I now utter is to succeed and hold its place in history' (*The Meaning of God in Human Experience*. Yale Univ. Press. New Haven/ Oxford. OUP 1912. 484, 503).

(iii) The point of departure – a note for artists

What is spatial in [the human being] does not belong to eurythmy. But what can manifest in space as movement; that is what belongs to eurythmy (Rudolf Steiner. GA 278, Lecture 3; I. 31).

[The] astral body contains the real musical element... After death we discard our astral body: then – pardon the banal expression – everything musical in us switches over (*schnappt hinauf*) into the music of the spheres. Thus in music and poetry we have an antecedent (*Vorleben*) of what our world, our existence, is after death (R. Steiner. Lecture, Dornach. 12 Sept. 1920. GA 271. Tr. A.S.).

The allotted function of art is not, as is often assumed, to put across ideas, to propagate thoughts, to serve as example. The aim of art is to prepare a person for death, to plough and harrow his soul, rendering it capable of turning to good (André Tarkovsky. *Sculpting in Time*. Faber. London 1986. 43).

We are slow to learn that truth is never that which we choose to believe, but always that which we are under a necessity to believe. In proportion to the earnestness of the pursuit, we discover that we needs must be servants when we thought to be masters. A life devoted to truth is a life of vanities abased and ambitions forsworn. We have to advance far in the willing servitude before we recognise that it is creating for us a new and another freedom (F.J.A. Hort, *The Way The Truth The Life*. Macmillan, London. 1893. 93f.).

The question of the survival of the early indications for eurythmy deeply concerns many people. If, as performers, we start from the question of the creative challenges in the twenty-first century, can we unite the concern for survival with the search for development? Challenges posed by the performing arts; problems of what the public expect or what they can accept; the capabilities of eurythmists today; experiments undertaken, and so on, are all well-known phenomena. Are all the judgements and claims made in the name of eurythmy clearly thought through? Attitudes, opinions and criticisms abound. Can we find the one comprehensive question that can lead to the heart of the matter, whose solution will unite all the deep concerns? If the architectural and other links discussed earlier are taken seriously, then the subject of Steiner's initiation (see Introduction, Endnote 18) becomes more than a pious phrase. The practical artistic path he indicated will inevitably provoke the demons of fear, mockery and despair within ourselves, but also the strength to overcome them within ourselves. The source of our problems lies neither in the world, nor in the audience, neither in our colleagues nor in our musicians, neither in problems of workspace nor money nor electro-acoustic sound-producers. The source of initiatic realisation that will resolve our problems lies in you and me.

The most likely single, comprehensive question is that of *Ansatz*, which is translated in the Lectures as the "point of departure". Lea van der Pals and Annemarie Bäschlin write with clarity and precision, summarizing the technical side of the point of departure given by Steiner (see Endnote 55). In the section "The C-major scale and vowel correspondence" (*Ton-Heileurythmie.* 29-31) they describe the note-interval-vowel-consonant series. Cosmic music and its relation to the human being is mentioned. For the angle-gestures: "the place where the astral body rays in, the point of departure is between the shoulder-blades (sixth thorasic vertebra), from where the arms are raised into the gestures (the jumps, too, must start from here)."

Armin Husemann (see Endnote 54) describes the "turning-inside-out" at the region of the collar-bone as the physiological justification of the art of music-eurythmy which predominantly employs the arms as its musical instrument. The comprehensive art of music enables the human soul to respond creatively to the Father; it is pre-eminently suited to portray "the Incarnation and Hallelujah of Christ" (R. Steiner. Torquay 22 August 1924), a phrase that points to the ultimate creative path for human beings. The physiological fact (emphasised by Dr Husemann), gives the human being the possibility through eurythmy to call on the ever-present redeeming activity of Christ, alluded to by Steiner. In other words, art may become a vehicle for the forces of regeneration, but only through a living sacrifice to the spiritual world (the Father) like the sacrifice of Christ, of the unity of self, soul and body. Steiner would agree with H.A. Williams' claim that "We are invited to share in it, to make our individual contributions to Christ's redeeming work" (H.A. Williams. *God's Wisdom in Christ's Cross.* Mowbray. London. 1960. 26).

The last two paragraphs above summarise that to which Steiner points concerning the point of departure. However, the phenomenon of what amounts to a pragmatic and often confused search for other points of departure (for example, the finger-tips, the feet, "from everywhere", not to mention unconscious mannerisms), suggests a more thorough investigation is required. Some observations on the possibility of uniting permanence and progression, are offered here in the current search for a way forward, which many people recognise as a general crisis:

(1) Conceptions like "the limbs shoot in" (R. Steiner. *Study of Man*) belong to the subject of embryology. Applied to eurythmy, they raise

questions concerning the psychology of the will. In art, a dominance of individual psychology that is permitted to overstep its domain threatens to obscure the clarity of spiritual-scientific conceptions, and above all the point of departure in the artist for "visible singing". Moreover, the sacredness of the ear is an ancient conception (for example, with the Hebrew people). What relationship does that deep tradition assume today (see Endnote 11) when the sacredness of the larynx is the new conception that is to be developed? Steiner did not describe eurythmy as a simple visible listening; does this imply a check to our possible reactionary or illustrative tendencies that veer towards the art of the dance (see *Study of Man,* quoted in Endnote 65)? We clearly need both ear and larynx; perhaps a threshold situation is indicated here: We learn that musical movement is not a relationship to the world (Lecture 1), and nowhere in the lecture-course or elsewhere is an appeal made to the control of other beings, natural or supernatural. "'Out you go!'"... for the musical element belongs only to man, not to nature"; it is the "self-creating force in the human being" (Lecture 4) demanding the conscious control of the artist throughout (see Endnote 7, also Endnote 71 regarding "jazz").

Research into the connection to the spiritual forces behind the physical world (the spiritual-physical being of the Father) confirms the spiritual ground of the bodily instrument. This spiritual concept is as fundamental for the early stages of child education, as it is for the monotheistic religions. Responsibility in human creativity does not deny the world of the Father by asserting that God has a Son who incarnated into a human body precisely in order to recreate it. The body is acknowledged to be "a musical scale" (Lecture 3), that is, an instrument. Pfrogner describes the two contrary spiritualities as the way of "universal concord" and the way of "ego concord" (Introduction, Endnote 22). The latter way is that of sonship (Gal. 4:6).

(2) Observers sometimes experience an egoistical interpretation of the point of departure in the collar-bone. Some eurythmists are even unaware of the point of departure between the shoulder-blades. Both these phenomena can hardly be merely technical, especially when the ethical aspect is voiced. Following Steiner's lead, perhaps the fact of the Incarnation can cast light on this matter and may lead beyond reactionary responses. It is generally recognised that fear or even denial of the Christ-event in the sub-conscious manifests as a problem amongst certain sections of humanity, not least amongst the followers of the monotheistic religions. The present question, certainly, concerns the

phenomenon of artistic egoism, but this problem is in no way isolated from the East-West tension. The source of that tension (like all others) is to be found in the battleground of the individual heart (Matt. 15:18 & 19). The problems in society are but our own magnified; this means that we are all involved, and especially so with the subject of music. To what do the phenomena point? Can eurythmists and their colleagues also contribute to world peace by facing the problems at home? Questions of the threshold may not always manifest as an either-or, black-or-white choice: here, for example, the charge of egoism may indeed be just, if the viewer is uncomfortably aware of the individual performer rather than the art of free and expressive movement. But is an unrecognised egotistical element present in such value-judgements, as well? (Steiner frequently warns his pupils against the tremendous reality of our unconscious, overbearing egotism.) Is the crucial distinction once again between individualism and personality (see Endnote 25)? The potential enormous benefit from solving eurythmical problems may help towards solving universal problems and not merely those of the individual.

(3) Metaphorical, spatial language is potentially confusing if followed too literally, or pressed too far (see Endnote 7). This is especially apparent when the point of departure is neglected. For example, the conception of the notes flowing "in" along the arms followed by a sudden flowing "out" along the arms in singing gesture, seems to contradict the descriptions contained in Endnote 55. The confusion of in-flowing tonal gesture with the minor in-streaming is one obvious danger. In investigating this conception, it will be expedient to apply the principle that aspects of the whole truth may be contained in opposing views: What may be learnt here?

(i) Is the view that seeks to re-create the angles (as it were, from outside) actually necessary? If the angles already exist, they only require to be sounded (just as the violinist does not tune-up, nor the flautist re-bore the holes of his flute, between every note of a tune); (ii) if the question (like all others in eurythmy) is not merely technical, then the pragmatic answer is not satisfactory, either. The shifting sands of individually-varied points of departure that occasionally "works" hardly offers a lasting solution or basis for building an edifice that will serve for a lifetime and more; (iii) if conceptions of cosmic music are involved, then the earlier statement (included in the Introduction, Endnote 18) would suggest that the cosmic realm is being confused here with the empirical realm (that is, it is not an outer but an inner question); the astral music that formed the body is being confused with the singing soul that uses the body as its instrument: "as astral human being I [not the bodily instrument] am the evolver of melos" (Lecture 3); (iv) if individual psychology plays a part, then any distrust of Steiner's recommendation has to be justified when questioned.

(4) The relationship of the pupil on the spiritual path to the subject of sin and sacrifice (for F.D. Maurice, "the eternal polarity"), is summed up in Steiner's words on egoism at the end of *Knowledge of the Higher Worlds – how is it achieved?* (Chapter 11). As far as artists are concerned, there is unfortunately no guarantee that if we imagine the zodiac, or "cosmic music" pouring in from all sides (flowing along the angle-gestures of the arms) we will dissolve our egoism. On the contrary, such a conception is likely to put us firmly into the centre of egotism, which is the true wilderness. (Self-assertion, as we are all-too-well aware, can also masquerade as an over-sensitivity to ourselves.) Abstracting personality from the artist (the tragedy of Hauer and his "twelve-note melos") leads to what is expressed in Hebrew in one unit, וְלֹא־אִישׁ a "no-man" (Psalm 22:6), just as abstracting the sense of personality from the concept of God leads to a "no-god" (compare Isaiah 44:9-20, and Barfield's study on idolatry, *Saving the Appearances*, also Appendix 3 above). A revival of "original participation" or "universal concord" will not save us.

However, Steiner's definition of music (see Endnote 24), points to the essential experience necessary to finding the way beyond materialism in music. This materialism is predominantly a fixation with "that which is heard" leading to a consequent crudity of gesture and movement. Even here, let it be added, the great mystics and those who have suffered testify with the Psalmist, that God is to be found even in the Hell of isolation. But the abstracting tendency, briefly characterised above, implies "inverted spirituality" according to R. Guénon (*The Reign of Quantity*). Both Guénon and Steiner use the strongest counter-name (Antichrist), a term which they define exactly. Both teachers are perfectly aware of the struggle at the end of the century, that, in a word, is actually ourselves. These studies would be incomplete if no mention were made of it. Surely Steiner, Michael's foremost servant, foresaw our need?

(5) By appreciating what the creator of eurythmy indicated, perhaps all our problems may be confidently met. For, precisely from the centre of the Cross on which our selfhood is nailed, that specific null-point that can be entered at any moment and anywhere, do we not have access to the whole spiritual world (Col. 1:16)? The first verse of *The Calendar of the Soul* ends:

then streaming out from selfhood's sheath
go thoughts into the distant skies
and dimly bind
man's inmost nature to the spirit's being.

(From 'Easter mood', Verse 1 of R. Steiner, "The Soul's Calendar", a translation by Julian Pook that retains the original rhythms. Regarding "selfhood's sheath" compare 2 Peter 2:24 and Philipp. 3:21. For Steiner, thoughts are the product of spiritual activity, that is, light radiating from a living, personal source; compare also I Cor. 15:42-29 and the Johannine concept of the "glory" of the Incarnation in connection with the Father, for example, John 1:14, 14:13, 17:1.)

According to the degree of our artistic preparation, which is an *offering* (see R. Steiner. Lecture, Dornach. 8 June 1923. GA 276. 66f.), the content of the spirit can be personally revealed, flowing towards humanity, towards a particular audience. This offering is one way to practice the maxim "whoever shall lose his life shall preserve it" (Luke 17:23). The Jewish interpreter C.G. Montefiore comments:

> Here again we have what is practically a new conception. Self-denial was not unknown before Christ; but the clear conception of it and the ideal which it suggests *were*, I think, new, and they in their turn have exercised an immense influence upon men's thoughts, aspirations and actions. More restricted, but not less intense, has been the effect of the next words "let him... take up his cross and follow me" [Matt. 16:24, six days before the Transfiguration; also Mark 8:34; Luke 9:23 adds the word "daily"]. The true follower of the Master, in proportion to the perfection of his discipleship, must endure and renounce, suffer and die (*The Synoptic Gospels*, I. Macmillan. London. Rev. ed. 1936. 211. See also à Kempis, *The Imitation of Christ* II, xi and xii).

The Buddhistic ideal of self-renunciation is different: the supreme ideal is not Love but Renunciation of all personal existence. In its original form this is not religion but ethical discipline. The last two sentences may be historically correct, yet they are not intended to exhaust the significance of the Buddha nor of Buddhism (see R. Steiner. *From Buddha to Christ*. Five lectures given in various cities 1908-12. AP. 1978; R. Steiner. *Spiritual Foundations of Morality*. Three lectures 28th-30th May 1912. Norrköping, Sweden. RSP. 1996; see also Appendix 3, Endnote 2). Christ's cross, however, finally and completely answers *all* forms of extinguishing renunciation, including Hauer's problem of "sacrifice of the ego" and "dissolution of the personality". Jesus didn't kill anything. He died. And to die is not to kill. He died by giving Himself (see Endnote 41). Surrendering to God is to give ourselves to the source of our being, to unconditional love, to ourselves as we really are and in time shall become (I John 3:2). We are given no comforting fantasies but challenges to new adventures and understanding; transformation is essential. The phrases Steiner uses concerning the three-dimensional cross of movement show the exemplary tact and discretion of a great teacher of humanity in respect of the sanctity of the human personality: "to enter, in some way or other, these three different directions", and "to find some way of making use of these three directions" (Lecture 3); the Gospels (as cited above) use the verbs "take up" and "follow".

(6) In music, does the physical localising of imaginative images drawn from the natural world (including astronomical images) tend to fix and thus degrade them? All such images here are "models"; does a confusion of the modality involved permit idiosyncrasy that unbeknown invites the possibility of artistic caricature, crudity and insincerity? The present studies describe phenomena and name tendencies solely as a means to establish eurythmic principles. The discussion has touched on the question of apostasy, the proper name for "detachment", or in its less popular Christian terminology, "original sin", or "the sickness of sin". The gain from recognizing a problem lies not only in suggesting its technical solution. The healing of a family sickness benefits all the family of humankind. No deeper aspect, level or solution is possible for human beings who are to become creators. Steiner confirms the Hermetic theory of correspondence:

> The human being, compared to the macrocosm (the great world), is a microcosm (a small world). Observing artistic activity in general, it is a small creation compared to the great creation, and in the most eminent sense, by carrying it out through the instrument in which all the secrets and laws of the divine-spiritual universe are concentrated, we do carry out a small creation: that is the human being (R. Steiner. Intro. Dornach. 22 April 1924. GA 277. 453).

The crossing point, or the threshold, where the macrocosm becomes the microscosm (and vice versa: compare *schnappt hinauf* of GA 271, in the second quotation heading this section, p. 442 above; compare, too, St Paul's "twinkling of an eye", I Cor. 15:52), is the inner crux for human beings (see Appendix 1). An initial conclusion suggests that the way of love and understanding will prove a more lasting solution than pragmatism and any attempted elevation of irrationality as an artistic method. For the pragmatists, "the show must go on" whatever the human cost, and it is certainly remarkable what life produces despite and even because of our shortcomings. Eurythmical life, certainly, has to decide what part compromise may play, but also how that relates to the New Testament commentary (especially the Johannine writings and St Paul's epistles). The "God-concept", psychologists and others claim, provides the necessary solution to problems that require Him. The present problem qualifies in this respect, as Steiner indicates. In these studies, it should be clear that religious concepts are employed quite concretely with the intent of pointing to Steiner's meaning. "In primeval times…," Steiner affirms, "the human being could receive religious instruction by being taught music" (R. Steiner. Lecture, Stuttgart. 7 March 1923. GA 283. E.T. 55. See also his vision of the union of knowledge, art and religion: Lecture, Stuttgart. 9 March 1923. 89f.). Clearly, the human being is not a cipher, but without the reality of spiritual transformation he may indeed become one. "Abstract thoughts are the ultimate abstraction, the corpse of the spirit-world" (R. Steiner. GA 276. 67). By demanding the development of personality in art (GA 278. Lecture 3, and GA 279. Lecture 1), Steiner indicates the human path forward. This we may summarise: The only way to develop free and ensouled movement, and the only redemptive way beyond the danger of illustration and that of insistent individual psychology in the present context, is to realise creatively the personal point of departure indicated by Steiner. Each person has to do it for him/herself (Lk. 9:23, 14:27).

On several occasions, Steiner sketched the three-dimensional cross. On one occasion he points to the experience of the unity of God:

> The basis of monotheism lies in the ancient experience of time: the basis for perceiving the Trinity lies in the ancient experience of space… One of the names for God among the Rabbis is "space"; space and God denote the same [entity] (R. Steiner. Lecture, Dornach 20 Sept. 1918. GA 194, Z.362, R. Steiner Library, London).

Perhaps "omnipresence" is the name to which allusion is made; in Rabbinical Hebrew, God is often spoken of as "the Place", *hammaquom* (Greek equivalent *ho topos*, known to Philo) (Schürer. *Jahrb. für prot. Theol.* 1876. 166ff.). See also R. Steiner. Lectures, Dornach 24 & 25 Oct. 1914, and 17 March 1921 on arm movements and walking). The eurythmical point of departure is the centre of the three-dimensional Cross (Fig. 3) which is at the same time the apex of the Lambda (Fig. 1: Note that "the spine is really the starting point for the development of such a being as an aleph". Lecture 1), united and consecrated through the Mystery of Golgotha by Christ for humankind, that is, every person on earth (for "every eye will see him, every one who pierced him". Rev.

1:7). The way of love and understanding will recognise its ethical and artistic source; in the words of A.M. Ramsey, echoing F.D. Maurice: "Christ's death is the death of you and me" (see also Endnote 41). The mediating link uniting all humankind in fellowship and at the same time linking humankind to the divine world in communion, has been achieved (1 Tim. 2:5, Eph. 2:18); there is no other. Human arms opened wide (see Fig. 1) and united their centre (the focus or burning-point), with the centre of the Cross (see Fig. 3). From now on, both TIME (*cf.*: "a being in constant activity". Lecture 1) and SPACE are consecrated. The settlement has been made. The ultimate powers of sickness and death (the spectres of irrationality and destruction) have indeed been finally overcome, however insistent the powers of illusion may and do threaten: human-divine, divine-human, here is the eternal Heart of the World.

(7) In this light, is it to be wondered at that all attempts in eurythmy practice to find alternative points of departure than that given by Steiner both 'outside' the instrument and elsewhere on the instrument (together with all flirtation with the dance- and theatrical-world) appear to many people as irrelevant antics? To other people, this question will sound arrogant, righteously indignant and exclusive, especially when ripped out of its context. Nevertheless, the artistic criterion has been left with us; our fate is in our own hands. If divisions are occurring in the world of eurythmy, all artists who feel responsible for the future will feel duty-bound to understand each other and face the issues together. The widespread crisis in eurythmy is to be welcomed, for any progress whatsoever comes from growth *and* crisis. All our unacknowledged fears and unrest in art and in life are surely the prelude to eventual confidence and freedom, which (according to P.T. Forsyth) are other names for divine peace.

It will be retorted: Do not other movement artists also achieve etheric movement? But, it appears, natural etheric movement is not enough, for "you are animal-like in the etheric realm" while yet "belonging to the spirits of the second hierarchy" (R. Steiner. *The Christmas Conference*, 31 Dec. 1923 p.m. RSP. 1990. 237; fuller quotation given in Endnote 28). Comparative study of the arts really is altogether another question. In the present perspective, so much may be said: no human and artistic lesson is excluded; on the contrary, they are all included in the death-point of you and me (*cf.*, 1 Cor. 1:21-4), because the Representative of Humanity has united the ethical, artistic and physical points of departure for evermore. "The essential novelty of Christianity, when viewed from the side of human history, was its presentation of a new life, in which creed and conduct were intimately, indissolubly, necessarily one" (J.R. Illingworth. *University and Cathedral Sermons.* Macmillan. London 1893. 5f. The work of this eloquent writer, who contributed to the epoch-making study *Lux Mundi*, is still relevant today).

In Steiner's *The Philosophy...*, which is "founded on the Christ-impulse in the human being" (R. Steiner. GA 74. Lecture, Dornach. 24 May 1920), the reader finally arrives at this personal centre in the culminating Chapter 15 (that contains the word "reality" with its derivatives and pronouns over forty times in 102 sentences) in sentences 63-65 around the golden section:

> Every human being, in his thinking, takes hold of the universal primordial Being which penetrates every person. To live in reality, filled with the content of thought, is at the same time to live in God. A merely inferred Beyond that cannot be experienced, is based on a misunderstanding by those who believe that this world does not contain within itself the meaning of its existence (R. Steiner. *The Philosophy of Freedom.* GA 4. Tr. A.S.; pub. tr. R. Stebbing. 162, M. Wilson. 215, M. Lipson. 236, W. Lindeman. 238).

This book, following the movement "from the periphery to the centre", is, in T. Meyer's phrase, "a modern T A O-book" (see further R. Guénon. *Symbolism of the Cross, passim*: "Universal Man... has passed from the circumference to the centre", Chapter 16. 123); this counteracts the Fall of Man (see p. 462, below).

(8) There is no occasion here for exclusive claims either for a specific art, a group of artists, or any individual artist: All artistic and human endeavour (including eurythmy) only contributes to human evolution when it originates from the light of "the Incarnation and Hallelujah of Christ". This last oft-cited phrase, originates from the lecture held in Torquay, England, where it is used in a purely artistic and practical context. To employ the term "mystical" here – as also to the writer of the Fourth Gospel with his Logos doctrine – would be misleading (see Appendix 4, iii). Artistic endeavour does not primarily depend upon intelligence, education or knowledge – an exclusive, purist attitude cannot be justly levied against Steiner as an artist. The phrase that sums up his contribution is not "purist", but the most thorough and truly helpful *integrity*. The challenge for all his pupils is, how can we transform our pragmatism into the integrity that unites heaven and earth, here and now?

(9) One important research subject should also be mentioned: the decades-long diversity of those who think "either notes *or* intervals"

and those who think "not only notes but *also* intervals". For Steiner, the angle-gestures are "pathways between the notes" (Endnote 2), and the intervals are the inaudible experience "between the notes, that is, music in reality, for that is the spiritual element of the matter, whereas the other [that which is audible] is the sensory manifestation of it" (Lecture 3). Steiner's account is clear and complete; the artistic issues today seem to focus on questions of our naivety, both straight-forward and confused.

The step towards inartistic materialism potentially present in the "either/or" view seems confirmed when exercises are practised that introduce an unauthorised *Ruck* ("jolt", or "sudden movement") between notes and intervals. Remarkable as it may sound, is there lurking here a fear of recognising the spiritual nature of the human astral (= 'starry') body here on earth, *i.e.*, notes are "pure" and intervals somehow "fallen"? The point is, do additions to the theory given by Steiner introduce, or do they in fact preclude, musicality and its refinement in the practice? The question is far from being academic, as the investigation of Hauer's position in Appendix 3 should have made clear. A perceptible hint is present of the mysticism of Swedenborg – which harks back to Plotinus – that, like Hauer's mysticism, spurns bodily existence as impure and problematic. The subject is not irrelevant to music: the Swedenborgian novel *Seraphita* made a lifelong impression on Schönberg (see Pfrogner, Introduction Endnote 11). The subject is crucial to eurythmical artists, whether or not they have heard of Hauer's interests in the spirituality of China, or of Arnold Schönberg's interest in Swedenborg.

Schönberg speaks (lecture, Los Angeles. 26 March 1941) of the "principle of unity of the musical space" in which "as in Swedenborg's heaven (described in Balzac's *Seraphita*) there is no absolute down, right and left, forward and backward", where the "imagination and creative faculty" of the composer sees before it the "row" in every conceivable level simultaneously and proceeds therewith (A. Schönberg in *Style and Idea* Leonard Stein (Ed.). Faber. London and Boston. 1975. 223). Pfrogner points out that the "imagination" here is abstract and not to be confused with our concrete terms like $B^\sharp$ and C. He shows how atonality abolishes the system of seven (that has been developed since the giving of the octave: see Endnote 12) and "reaches for the stars" by making the system of twelve absolute. (Following Pfrogner, H. Ruland. *Die Neugeburt der Musik*…. Schaffhausen. 1987. 12, characterises the step to atonality as music's "crossing the threshold", a deed that cannot be reversed, however much people may wish the contrary.) It is precisely the consequences of the crisis of recognition of what Steiner calls "bodily impediments and hindrances" (Lecture 5) that lies behind this unprecedented split of the art of music into tonality and atonality. Steiner tackles the problem of the body precisely in Lecture 5, by introducing help in the form of the T A O-eurythmy-meditation "to make your inner bodily nature supple for eurythmy".

The evidence seems unequivocal: we are to understand that eurythmy is born of the Michael-Logos tradition (GA 279. Lecture 1) which knows no absolute antithesis between spirit and body. In R.C. Moberly's phrase, "neither is body without spirit, nor spirit without body" (*Atonement and Personality*. 89). Eurythmy can claim to be "an art for everyone" (R. Steiner. Lecture, Dornach. 7 Oct. 1914. Dornach. 1935) because it refuses a Cartesian split of the human being. By keeping human nature entire, eurythmy aims to spiritualise this entirety (GA 279, Lecture 1). Steiner proclaims the two missions of Michael: (1) the Word became flesh in order that (2) the flesh may become spirit (GA 194, Lecture 20 Nov. 1919). For the artist, this means (i) ever further presence of mind and penetration into the life of musical gesture in the moment of creation; involving (ii) a recognition on the path of self-knowledge of the presence of possible mystical tendencies that are inadequate to the question of the body. These tendencies are to be transformed into expressive art. (iii) The ages are past when artistic naivety might have been allowed.

Speaking of artistic necessity (that is "no infringement of freedom"), Steiner suggests: "What always remains is the freedom to carry out each individual movements beautifully" (Lecture 5. 87). Is it possible to express in fewer words the nature of true freedom, that has to be discovered afresh by each rising generation? Furthermore, such demonstration is essential if musicians and others who question the justification for eurythmy are to recognise "visible singing"' The alternative possibility is that these critics may be confronted by mere claims and possibly a movement-spectacle of idiosyncratic floor-travel that might unfortunately serve to confirm their forebodings.

(10) Steiner, following Schiller, renews the middle way beyond the extremes of reason and instinct. The way of art that restores the unity of knowledge and feeling, may overcome the naivety of both a one-sided emphasis on technique (a tendency towards the dance) and a one-sided emphasis on individual mysticism: both emphases fail to overcome materialism.

> In the older mystery schools and remaining mystery traditions clairvoyant cognition is also called a musical cognition... The mysteries refer to... ordinary bodily, intellectual cognition and

spiritual cognition, which is in fact a musical cognition, a cognition of the musical element (R. Steiner. Lecture, Stuttgart. 8 March 1923. GA 283. E.T. 73).

The outstanding pioneer music theorist of our century is H. Pfrogner (see Introduction), who contributes essential insights from a renewal of mystery wisdom (to which his own thinking demonstrably evolved). Above all, the study the musical-spiritual laws of metamorphosis, form, and so on, is directly involved when reading Steiner's written work as "musical scores" (see Introduction, p. 20), that is, the author transforms intellectual forms of knowledge into exact, disciplined, mystical texts (the correlative to the new, exact clairvoyance). The researcher's discoveries awake in the reader through his/her own activity of musical awareness and analysis; these discoveries are demonstrable, repeatable and thus scientific at the same time.

In the above suggestion for eurythmy-research (9, para. 1), does a confused instinct for locating the threshold need clarifying, too? The path of initiation that combines freedom and discipline in art and in life, recognises the need for clear distinctions of "self" and "world". This path acknowledges the threshold. It is the path of self-knowledge, explored by Steiner in *The Philosophy of Freedom* and artistically presented in the 52 verses of *The Calendar of the Soul*. This path attempting to realise the spirit in the present moment counters the premature, Ahrimanic tendency to judge both ourselves and others absolutely, and also the Luciferic tendency to idealise the wonderful past (that is, both individual and racial throwbacks). The human personality is a developing being (see Endnote 25); when recognised, this concept will steer human beings away from fixed notions leading to the tragedy of divisions and lead instead towards understanding, fellowship and eventual fulfilment.

To summarise: A sufficient realisation of the initiatic centre should adjust any one-sided caricature resulting from possible pragmatic approaches that may exist between the extremes of

(1) an over-emphasis on the instrument, producing charges of individualism; and

(2) an over-emphasis on the periphery, producing charges of false mysticism and de-personalisation.

The details that cause confusion include:

(i) a linguistic confusion of everyday usage and Steiner's use of such words as "self", "person", "personality", "ego" (see Endnote 25);

(ii) insufficient differentiation of the point of departure for speech-eurythmy and music-eurythmy (see Endnote 7);

(iii) an over-emphasis on imaginative aids (for example, the finger-tips, the feet, the stars, the earth, and so on), that only achieve eurythmic significance in connection with the personal point of departure for singing gesture;

Fig. 70: A mid-14th Century depiction of the Crucifixion, 3rd April, 33 AD. The Redeemer's open arms reverse the Lambda: ∧ becomes ∨ (Greek: λογοζ - Logos or Word, becomes Latin: Verbum - Word) on earth, initiating the re-creation of humanity from within heavenwards. The human heart at the centre of the world is (i) the place of intersection of the cross-beams of 'the Tree of Life in the midst', (ii) the issuing centre of the Lambda=Logos/Verbum, and (iii) the centre of an X-cross (the World-Axis) uniting the Sun – St John and the Moon – St Mary, a human group initiating the new human relationships of the Ecclesia (*Chapel, Castel Tirolo, Museo Provinciale per la storia e l'archeologie, Tirolo, Italy*).

(iv) an inability to distinguish the spirituality of the bodily instrument from the spirituality of the singing soul. The question "which spirituality?" is supremely crucial, not only for the future of eurythmy (see Endnotes 28, 41 and 65);

(v) questions of pantheist tendencies, and of abstraction; the influence of the dance, and partially-digested and misapplied knowledge; our failings arising from fears that stem from insufficient transformation – no scientist, artist or citizen is free from these issues; the admission that such is the case of our own heart may be the first step to finding a solution which would also benefit the world.

In the present studies, several details have been mentioned and a few have been explored showing in what way eurythmy, as personal, representative human movement, may be an art of the threshold. For the artist, the ultimate Michaelic challenge/ realisation can be expressed in these words: "I am related to the creative 'Being in constant activity' who finally and completely revealed Himself in the Mystery of Golgotha, and whose mission was not self-glory but to glorify the Father. The more I am permitted to unite with that Deed of Life and Death, the more I myself am the threshold." If Acts 9:5 & 6 applies to us all, and if "the city" is mythologically as well as literally interpreted, we are given a vista as far as Jupiter and beyond, which is the fulfilment of the Kingdom of God — not a state of mind but a society.

Art is neither science nor religion; it exists as a third, middle category or 'way'. Yet (as James Denney reminds us) a fact without a theory lacks meaning. If the essential pursuit of art involves the secret of our humanity (as Schiller, Steiner and other artists maintain), then artists wishing to deepen their art and at the same time wishing to justify it, will not only live but seek to define that secret heart or way. The subject is the very life of eurythmy, and for that reason theory and practice can hardly be separated, and will directly relate to the spiritual path towards "true humanity" (Lecture 5).

See Endnote 6 for references to René Guénon and C.G. Jung on the cross; also Appendix 4. Roger Cook, The Tree of Life (Thames & Hudson, London 1974) explores this 'symbol of the centre'. From the side of religion and ethics, some great writers on the atonement ("at-one-ment", enabling reconciliation), have made lasting contributions: J. McLeod Campbell, The Nature of the Atonement (1856/1996); R.C. Moberly, Atonement and Personality, op. cit. (1901); John Scott Lidgett, The Spiritual Principle of the Atonement (London 1897); J. Denney, The Death of Christ (1903; ed. Tasker, London 1951), and The Christian Doctrine of Reconciliation (London 1917); Hastings Rashdall, The Idea of Atonement in Christian Theology (London 1919); G. Aulén, Christus Victor (London 1931); Emil Brunner, The Mediator (London 1934); Vincent Taylor, Jesus and his Sacrifice (London 1937), The Atonement in New Testament Teaching (London 1940/45), Forgivness and Reconciliation (London 1941/46). Insights and guidance on the subject are also to be found in: J.K. Mozley, The Doctrine of the Atonement *(London 1915); essays in* Foundations *(London 1912);* V. Taylor, The Cross of Christ *(London 1956), an accessible introduction that surveys the modern theories;* J.W.C. Wand, The Atonement *(London 1963) a lucid and comprehensive introduction: 'The atonement... is... the permanent action of the reconciling love of God... a witness to the redeemability of man's culture, his art, his language, his science, his industry — everything in fact which now shows the contamination of his sin' (p. 84f.);* F.R. Barry, The Atonement *(London 1968); and* Paul Avis 'The Atonement' *in* Keeping the Faith, Essays to mark the Centenary of 'Lux Mundi', *ed.* G. Wainwright *(London 1989).* J.M. Creed, The Divinity of Jesus Christ *(CUP 1938/Fontana 1964) is a short, masterly study of Christian doctrine since Kant;* R.S. Franks, The Work of Christ *(London 1962), a remarkable deomonstration of theological progress. 'Our thinking about atonement, to be real, must be our own'; insists* H.R. Mackintosh, The Christian Experience of Forgiveness *(London 1917/Fontana 1961), Chapter 9 'The Atonement'. The change from revenge (racial suicide) to forgiveness (restored community) is vividly portrayed by Shakespeare in the movement from* Hamlet *(1603) to* Measure for Measure *(1604); see* John Vyvian, The Shakespearean Ethic *(London 1959); responsibility for our karma is a practical concern, see* S.O. Prokofieff, The Occult Significance of Forgiveness *(Temple Lodge, London 1992).*

Endnote *25 of the Introduction, p. 29, may initiate a study of Steiner on the atonement: for him the subject is more than a doctrine; it is a Person who is present as an Impulse in human lives. The concepts of spiritual science, given by the first scientific initiate, do provide the means to understand the Mystery of Golgotha. These concepts, however, do not explain it away; it still remains a Mystery, that which reveals the secret and invisible power of God.* M. Barker's *fresh approach to Christian origins is quite indispensable, see* The Risen Lord *(Edinburgh 1996). Two popular studies on the atonement contain insights that Steiner had already made public (e.g. what happened in Gethsemane and at the Ascension):* W. Russell Maltby, Christ and His Cross *(London 1948/1963);* L.D. Weatherhead, A Plain Man looks at the Cross *(London 1945); and the poetic masterpiece of the blind seer* G. Matheson, Studies of the Portrait of Christ, II *(Hodder & Stoughton, London 1900).*

For passion, vitality and profundity, the following writers may still be unsurpassed: F.D. Maurice, 'The Atonement' *in* Theological Essays *(1853/London 1957) and* The Doctrine of Sacrifice *(London 1854);* H. Scott Holland, Logic and Life *(London 1882/5), Sermons 5-9, and* Creed and Character *(London 1887), Sermons 13-15 — Holland, recognised as a theolgian of genius, also possessed remarkable artistic genius;* B.F. Westcott, The Victory of the Cross *(London 1888) emphasises Heb. 5, 8;* P.T. Forsyth, The Person and Place of Jesus Christ *and* The Cruciality of the Cross *(both 1909) (London 1955), and* The Work of Christ *(1910) (London 1952) —* K. Barth *was one who recognised Forsyth's genius.* A. Farrer's *homily 'Atoning Death' throws light on the 'Meditation for Eurythmists', in* Said or Sung *(London 1960), U.S.A. title,* A Faith of Our Own *(New York 1960).* Evelyn Underhill, Worship *(1936) (Fontana, London 1962) is a famous, sympathetic study of the practical aspect of religion; her* The Mystery of Sacrifice, a Meditation on the Liturgy *(London 1938) is a useful introduction.*

Appendix 8
GA278 as an esoteric document

It is, of course, exceedingly difficult today to speak to people about the things which spiritual science has to impart...[With] world-evolution... what really is essential, is the inner movement which is described... [Ancient] Saturn is very well suited to musical expression, to composing... For me it all depends on how the movements of a dream take place – then the dream really is a piece of music, because you could write it down in no other way than in musical notation (R. Steiner. GA 278. Lecture 6).

The practical indication here, linked to others cited in the Introduction, confirms that Steiner hoped his followers would work in a creative way with the accounts of spiritual science. He referred to a "cookbook" mentality that only seeks for information, but also to the reading of spiritual-scientific literature (specifically *The Philosophy of Freedom* and *Occult Science*) as "musical scores". The former approach cannot initially be avoided: the Index to the Lectures has been compiled in this way, as an aid to the memory of the student. But it is also possible to apply the advice of attempting a "musical" appreciation of the present lecture-course, which is concerned with the subject of music itself. (Appendices 7 & 8, relying on whatever scholarship could be summoned in the previous studies, are not intended to stand alone.)

The initial suggestions made here represent an intermediate stage in the progression from the recipes of a "cookbook" attitude to one that is creatively artistic. "Musical" is taken here to mean an awareness of such things as process, transition and form. Such awareness is part of the creative process, which, for a composition to come to birth, involves notation. The writing-down of music involves shaping and balancing musical ideas, deciding what to develop and what to leave undeveloped, counting bars, planning sections, and so on. The form of a successful work of art matches the content (works of the great masters repeatedly illustrate the original touch of genius that appears "inevitable" once recognised). Steiner points out that musical composition is "an external picture of what the soul unconsciously experiences in the life of initiation" (GA 275, see Introduction, Endnote 5). Works of art (musical scores in particular) and accounts of spiritual science, are not merely analogous, he claims, but can be directly related.

Lecture 7 ends with a comment that the eighth lecture will "in retrospect complement our studies". A felt sevenfold structure (7 + 1) is here confirmed (similar to the diatonic scale, the structure of the lecture course can also be taken as 4 + 4); eight transcends the natural world. An interesting comment from *The Philokalia* suggests:

> The number eight signifies that He is the Creator of intelligible realities, for intelligible realities come into being outside the cycle that is measured by time... The number eight, understood mystically, denotes the intelligible nature of incorporeal beings, which understood in terms of spiritual knowledge it denotes the supreme wisdom of theology (St Maximos the Confessor (580-662 CE) in *The Philokalia*. Vol. 2. Faber. London. 1981. 130f.).

For *eight* signifying resurrection in the NT, see 1 Pet 3:20-21; 2 Pet 2:5. It is possible to read the lectures with directed feeling derived from the study of the musical intervals (the degrees of the scale: prime to octave), the cultural epochs, and the descriptions of planetary evolution. (Regarding the order of appearance of the kingdoms of nature, compare the lecture to the workmen, Dornach, 30 June 1924 in R. Steiner. *The Evolution of the Earth and Man*. AP & RSP. 1987. GA 354). These subjects correlate. The claim made here has doubtless been made before: the knowledge of *when and how* Steiner brought a subject leads to a deeper appreciation of what he said.

The following initial aphoristic suggestions are offered to encourage further research. Though we may not be able to write symphonies, we can put down our observations and allow them to speak. Steiner's remarks at the start and at the end of each lecture frequently give clues to his deeper meaning. We can also trace through the lecture-course how the descriptions of movement itself progresses from a more stationary, individual (but inner, and comprehensive) basis, to group movement in space, together with articulated feeling for movement in specific bones of the arm. This is accompanied by a developing revelation of "what lives between", that is, the nature of the various transitions within the musical categories.

A relationship to John's Gospel (the Word – life – light – love – freedom) runs through this lecture-course (suggested especially by a meditative application of the seven "I am" sayings, in the order presented in the Gospel); both deeply musical documents are concerned with Christian initiation (*cf.*, too, the seven promises to "him who overcomes" in Rev. 1-3). The practical Eightfold Path seems to be indicated in the eight asides and admonitions of the eight lectures (see Appendix 9).

Lecture 1: Steiner begins with the Word (compare John 1:1), specifically the vowels and the initial '*ah*' (alpha, aleph; see Appendix 7 concerning *ALP-Elf*: in the Hermetic and cabbalistic traditions 11 [= 5 + 6] is the synthesis, or marriage, of the microcosm and the macrocosm). An allusion to the Trinity may also be contained in the word ALP. The experience of God as unity is based on experience of TIME (lecture, 20 Sept. 1918). The paradisal images of mountain and tree (in connection with '*ah*' and '*o*') are – mythologically speaking – to be found at the centre of the world. The two movements major and minor, or inner movements outwards and inwards, suggest the world-egg (in other connections known as yin/ yang, action/ non-action, active/ passive. (Compare Leonardo's portrayal of the disciples to right and left of the central figure in "The Last Supper". The arms of Christ portray the two streams of giving/ receiving, major/ minor, A and O or Alpha and Omega of speech, music, and indeed of all existence.) The major and minor triads are described as a polarity: the first steps ("outwards" and "inwards" — see the sketches) are taken. The initial description of the moods of the triads, and flow of movement carried "throughout music's entire tonal configuration", contains as a seed all that is developed in the lectures that follow. The mood of Ancient Saturn (correlating with Ancient India) is invoked (even the tree — if taken as a "fir tree"; see Endnote 6 — is a Saturn tree).

Lecture 2: The polarity of "active" and "passive" is developed. (*C.f.*: 'polarity in nature (*i.e.*, manifestation)… [is] the fundamental law." R. Steiner. Lecture, Dornach, 22 Sept. 1918). "An experience of the ear or larynx only, now has to become an experience of the whole human being." "The soul must engage" in the gesture; "the body does not come to the assistance of the eurythmist". The subject of the origin of music – expression of pleasure and pain; on this subject, recent thought (Anthony Storr) suggests that motherhood is an archetypal experience – implies that the human being is divided. He yearns to develop by transcending opposites (the animal world is also mentioned). Polarities of self and world; poetry and prose; concord and discord are contrasted. The flow of movement becomes more differentiated: the intervals (beginning with "a wholeness", the parameter of prime-octave) concentrate on the polarity of seventh and third ("going-out-of-yourself" and "inwardness"), with the fifth as balance ("boundary"). "The fifth is the human being" in the midst of the scale, and "the experience of the fourth [is] of particular interest" (*cf.*, Lecture 7: after the fourth, the scale "opens out"). There is an implied threshold between the upper and lower tetrachords. The dichotomy which began during Ancient Sun (correlative, Ancient Persia) is evident.

Lecture 3: The human being enters upon movement in space, but "what belongs to eurythmy is not spatial". Death, too, has a mission: the phenomenon of death (a threshold is implied), and etheric experience of music (for example, descending intervals; an after-death experience – see van der Pals. 1992) are described; "melody in the single note" as a Janus-experience which transcends as the "eternal present"; and "the scale is the human being"). The etheric cross of movement (the "tree in the midst" – see Endnotes 6 and 28, and R. Guénon, *The Reign of Quantity...*, Chapter 23. 195: movement towards the centre, that is, realisation, counteracts the Fall of Man) links the taking-up of the physical world (the cross of three dimensions, six directions) and the revealing of the musical element (melos, rhythm and beat) that embraces "the whole human being" (as an individual personality). The experience of the three dimensions of space is the basis for experience of the Holy Trinity (lecture 20 Sept. 1918). The question of 'noise' today; the musical element is "what you do not hear", it is not material; music is "the human being". "Human personality as soul" is encouraged. The vowels and the scale are related. The picture-consciousness of Ancient Moon, and aspects of Ancient Egypt, are recapitulated.

A note on the (verbal) musical triads: In Lecture 4, the eurythmist reveals that which is inaudible (swinging-over, the bar line, and so on). The *spirit*, lighting up within the soul-experience, is expressed through the bodily instrument. The context of that instrument (astral, etheric and physical bodies of the eurythmist) reveals the musical triad: *melos, rhythm & beat*. Does this perhaps provide a clue to elucidating the question of the musical triad of *melos, harmony & rhythm*, given to the musicians in connection with "experience of the musical element" (lecture, Stuttgart. 8 March 1923. GA 283)? A contradiction need not necessarily be assumed. The two triads, taken together, can even enliven our conceptions; living conceptions can be exact without becoming fixed. For example, *harmony* used in its original sense of "a joining, an agreeable combination", can manifest in the *rhythmical* life of manifold smaller and larger musical forms – here, once again, our technical definitions of music need to be extended. A further musical triad is given in Lecture 8: *pitch, note values & dynamics*. These tonal terms of actual musical production, point at the same time to differentiated soul-experience. All three triads highlight a particular description of the threefold human being (who remains a unity, of course); each triad, moreover, is comprehensive within its context. Labelling them might prove more confusing than helpful (for they all involve creation, experience and expression); a progression, nevertheless, seems to be apparent.

Lecture 4: To "understand lectures on spiritual science", you "have to listen between... and in the words... [for] what lies behind them". "The spirit" is now named as the essential eurythmical element ("everything else... is more or less an illustrative element"). Art needs Lucifer (literally: "light bearer"), but also the light itself (the *Schwung* flashing between phrases, and the bar line). Naturalism is static; "Melos is the musical element". A further correspondence to musical speech explained (intervals); recitation has to be musical. By the end of Lecture 4, the climax of the first half of the lecture-course is reached: "natural processes" (St Paul's "first Adam") are completely banished from the human being – only the image of the cubic salt crystal (six sides) for "what is human" remains. The cube (an image of fulfilled Earth-existence) occupies the middle point of the cross of six-dimensions. Steiner has indicated a path beyond material nature (outer appearances) as the artistic lesson, but also the human lesson of the whole Earth embodiment (initially a concern of the consciousness-soul, or spiritual-soul). The Divine Sun-being of Love became the World-soul by entering Earth evolution during the fourth post-Atlantean epoch, at the 'turning point of time' (see Endnote 193 in GA 342. 261). From this central planetary embodiment, He (St Paul's "second Adam") leads humanity to reconstitution from within: *kenosis* leads to *plerosis*.

A threshold between Lectures 4 & 5 is crossed (see Endnote **41**). In the second half of the lecture-cycle, the themes of transformation, movement of more than one person engaged in eurythmy ("choral eurythmy"), and forms in [transformed] space are developed. Paradisal images (Lecture 1) give way to architecture (pointing to the "temple" image of New Jerusalem, itself a "city"); both are situated at the centre of the world. The stages of initiation mentioned below, are described in R. Steiner, *Occult Science*, Chapter 5.

Lecture 5: Transformation of the historical past, and of the individual, is the presented task. The human being has to "raise him/herself through work" to get beyond abstraction. "Love the visible world" is emphasised: this is the activity of the consciousness-soul. Transformation requires the process of time (the image is architectural development: oriental, Greek, the Goetheanum). East and West appear at the centre of this lecture-course, as in the Foundation-Stone Meditation. "Choral eurythmy" is introduced. The T A O-eurythmy-exercise (a renewal carried out in the fifth post-Atlantean epoch) is revealed in Lecture 5 as the meditative source for productivity, linking to the Divine and to all creation, too. Living and mobile "awake picture-consciousness" (to be developed as the second stage of initiation in our age) that comes into its own in the future planetary embodiment (Jupiter), is carefully indicated within a musical context. The fifth is a "real Imaginative experience" (GA 283; see Endnote 15); here the circle of fifths may be implied (see Appendix 3).

Lecture 6: "The fifth is the human being", but now in a social context (*cf.,* Lecture 2). The word *Ruck* ("jolt", "impetus"), employed in connection with "everything that lies between the notes", occurs in this lecture that advocates "awake dreaming" and meditation (anticipating the sixth cultural epoch, and the Venus stage of consciousness). Naturalism has led to the film: "stimulus from outside." Dreaming, rests and erasure inaugurate a peripheral consciousness. The musical element is also to be sought ("a kind of meditation") outside the musical sphere (musical and unmusical vowels). The theme of transformation continues: *Occult Science* can be made into music. The human face is mentioned, and the architectural image continues: "the house will come about" through shading the surrounding area (not through "drawing" – *cf.,* Steiner's "cake and cake-mould" image for the Goetheanum, Endnote 51): spiritual activity is that which carries substantial truth. The interval of the second is "a musical question". Its inclusion here *appears* to be due to an oversight, linking back to Lecture 2; it also leads to Lecture 7 (why is the ascending sixth absent, as it were, the "second" of the upper tetrachord?). The musical level ("Inspiration"), the third stage of initiation (of "reading the occult script") is sounded in this lecture.

Lecture 7: For the artistic justification of eurythmy, Armin Husemann (1994) discusses the transition (*Umstülpung* – a "turning-inside-out") at "the seventh region of the throat", outlined at the beginning of the lecture. The interval of the seventh ("Intuition". GA 273, see Endnote 12) leads to the point of departure in the organism (see Endnote 22). "Thinking with the bones" (12 Jan. 1924 in GA 233) concerning inner light, is developed ("And the house becomes the human being" can already be applied to Lecture 6). The universal stage is reached (pointing to the seventh post-Atlantean epoch, and the far-off planetary embodiment Vulcan).

As consciousness penetrates the bones, nature begins to be redeemed from within (animals are characterised in relation to eurythmy). The fourth stage of initiation is "living into the spiritual environment". The "light of consciousness" (or, the creative forces) is available since the resurrection (or, more accurately, Pentecost); here the practical study of "developing the consciousness" in the point of departure and in the bones of the arm "may lead over into the esoteric realm". The "Universal Man" of light (the actual subject of all the lectures) enables the possibility of "a singing eurythmy", a "singing through movement". "Feeling" – specifically, interest and love – for gesture and movement of specific bones is emphasised. Cosmic music produced the bones before they hardened: two bones for the lower arm "because there are two thirds"; from the fifth "the scale expands" and is "reproduced" in the hands. "Eurythmy has been drawn out of the organism of the human being" in every detail; it is completely human. Eurythmy therapy is mentioned (linking to Lectures 3 & 4); the streams of major and minor, "action" and "feeling", "giving" and "receiving" (a link to Lectures 1 & 2).

Lecture 8: The opening reference to "feeling" and "the heart" is to the centre of freedom within each individual. (In the Bible, the "heart" is synonymous for the centre of the personality or the personality as a whole. Emil Brunner. *Revelation and Reason*. 427); it is "the sharp dividing line between our mortal and our immortal part" (John Oman). This "heart" is not isolated but open, providing the human material for artistic work (we could say that the heart becomes an altar; Heb. 13:10): a further ensouling of the three planes (Lecture 3) is described. The term "the heart" characterises the centre of all the worlds; the "heart of the world" (the "octave stage") is reached from which another cycle (or "scale") of lectures could potentially evolve ("fourteen", 7 x 2 is also 8 + 6, of course, is mentioned at the very end). *Eurythmy as Visible Singing* inaugurated the art of expressive movement which is to grow into a "living stream of development" towards further articulation, differentiation and expression. "Pitch, note values and dynamics" are musical activities relating to thinking, feeling and will; the sentient soul, mind-soul, and consciousness-soul come into effect (van der Pals. 1992. 19f.). Details of differentiation of phrasing are sketched, and working with musicians is encouraged. Musicians may open their eyes, and eurythmists may open their ears; both may discuss the music. This could renew artistic endeavour out of the new mysteries, founded within the centre (the heart) of each individual, and cultivated in freedom. "The feeling must never arise that we are dealing with anything other than visible singing" (86). The Johannine virtues of "life, light and love" (terms for higher consciousness) are cumulative. Inasmuch as a modest beginning is made, the practice of art in future will be *social*, and may contribute to what the alchemists termed "the Great Work", which is the furtherance of the whole of creation.

In conclusion, we can say that the initiatic, musical-eurythmical process is: initial centring and manifestation of the process of TIME (Lecture 1); transformation of the natural instrument (Lectures 1-4); transformation of SPACE through a social art with further penetration of the instrument, that is, the complete human being (Lectures 5-8). Here, the way of the Christ-Sun to overcome Lucifer and Ahriman is demonstrated (see Prokofieff. 103). The final image of the arts collaborating gives a glimpse of the life and re-found unity within the New Mysteries. A triune path of relationships in this lecture-cycle is traced from the realm of the Father, through that of the Son, towards that of the Spirit. This reflection of the eternal activity of the Holy Trinity is the path of creative, redeeming, inexhaustible Love that was revealed to us fully and finally when it walked the earth, singing-speaking with a human tongue and human larynx, and accomplished the Deed which enables us all to live.

The Waldorf-School teacher Rudolf Treicher relates an incident with which we may suitably conclude the present studies:

> I especially remember a visit of Rudolf Steiner to my classroom that left a deep impression on my heart. It was during an English lesson, and we were working (as I repeatedly did later on) on the Lord's Prayer. I had begun to teach it to the children. Rudolf Steiner entered the room just as we were speaking the concluding words "for thine is the kingdom, the power and the glory, for ever and ever". When we had finished, Steiner went to the blackboard, picked up a chalk and said to the children: "You have just spoken the beautiful concluding words of the Lord's Prayer in English, and you know, of course, the German words for it. Now, each kingdom has a certain circumference, a certain size." With these words

he drew a circle. "And the power of this kingdom; where now is this situated?" "In the middle," came the answer. "Yes, in the middle." He put in the middle point of the circle and the rays of light surrounding it. Then he continued: "Well, how does all this look now?" After a short hesitation, from all sides came the call: "Like the sun!" "Yes, that is the sun," Rudolf Steiner said, visibly satisfied, and he went out. We left his sketch on the blackboard for a long time, like a living greeting from him to the class (Rudolf Treicher, Wege und Umwege zu Rudolf Steiner. Tr. A.S., quoted in GA 342. Endnote 193. Dornach. 1993. 261).

Appendix 9
"A Right Balance between Heaven and Earth
Art as a WAY: the Way as ART"

"Eurythmy as Visible Singing" is frequently consulted for help with specific musical-eurythmical questions. Taking the lecture-course as a whole, can we today establish a context *for these questions, first intuited by Elena Zuccoli (1901–96)? To this early eurythmist, the lectures unfold like the scale, suggesting an artistically educational pattern.*[1]

Imagine a young eurythmist who experiences Rudolf Steiner's lectures on music eurythmy. Shall we name her 'Anna'? 'Anna' writes a daily diary. After each entry, we could a few sentences (in italics) to summarise. This seems a suitable method to start recognising when and how the lecturer brings his material. Does this teaching add up to a consistent training for the artist? The phenomena should speak for themselves. (Enjoy walking the path, yet not imagining one should necessarily consume eight days' provisions in one sitting!) 'Anna's' diary might open as follows:

It's a brisk February. We meet in the Glasshouse near the Goetheanum – eurythmists, musicians, the Executive Council – expecting Herr Doktor. How does he do it? Sometimes four lectures a day, to experts: physicians, scientists, farmers, priests, teachers… Well, we eurythmists are hardly experts! I play the piano a little, and sing for enjoyment, that's about it. In music eurythmy we have practised only the angle-gestures for the basic scale in the major and minor zones,[2] applied them to little pieces, moving breaths between phrases. After seeing Frau Hollenbach's[3] children's choir perform in eurythmy the songs they had sung, we were inspired to take up eurythmy and develop it.

Lecture 1:

Dr Steiner began by pointing out how people often prefer our primitive music eurythmy to our more developed speech eurythmy. We need to *understand* eurythmy properly! He said it *five* or *six* times.[4] Later he emphasised it *three* more times, twice more in conclusion.[5]

---

1   Elena Zuccoli. *Ton- und Lauteurythmie.* Verlag Walter Keller: Dornach. 1997. 39.
2   GA 277a. 68; and Elena Zuccoli. 1997. Chapter 1.
3   GA 277a. 119-121; and Zuccoli 1997. 21f.
4   GA 278. *Eurythmy as Visible Singing.* Eight Lectures. Dornach. 19–27 Feb. 1924. Anastasi. Tr. with commentary by Alan Stott. Page references to 1998 edition/ 2013 edition: 5/37.
5   10/43, 14/47.

Unless *such understanding* is acquired, we shall never be able to stand with our whole being within the realm of art... Something artistic can only endure when the whole human being has poured himself into it.

Invertebrate and vertebrate animals are mentioned, and the importance of the backbone. The soul expresses itself in a differentiated manner in the sequence of vowels. For example, with "*o*", I encircle something: "I become one with the tree because I make this gesture."[6] Gestures in music eurythmy "flow back"[7] from the future into the here and now: I go out to "my spiritual being"[8] (major mood), or, alternatively, laying hold of my instrument (minor mood). This whole experience of the vowels and the major and minor moods runs "throughout" music's "entire tonal configuration".[9]

People go to any conceivable length to avoid thinking. The lecture-course begins decisively. The lecturer knows no doubts, pulls no punches. A Right Understanding – no "theory"! – means dedicating the whole of me, all my experience: head, heart and limbs; thinking, feeling and doing. T.S. Eliot ("Four Quartets") perceived it as the

> condition of complete simplicity
> (Costing not less than everything).

Like the Beatitudes (Matt. 5) that employ parody of the Tanakh, *the Hebrew Bible, rather than the* world *being turned upside down, is it rather* we *who are being put on our feet at last? Is the upright, the "tree", to show us our bearings? Perhaps, as an athlete conducts his or her physical life, are we aspiring artists being invited to join an inner way of conducting life – perhaps even an* interiorised assault course for artists?

Lecture 2:

Today we heard and saw the intervals for the first time! We already practice the degrees of the scale and now we can draw out their relationship to the keynote, by expanding down the arms as the angles open out, finally embracing a complete surrounding circle of shining awareness. Dr Steiner introduced the intervals mostly in pairs. He pointed out that our life generally is like that: we are split – for example, "a painter can't always be at it!"[10] And we eurythmists, too, actually do

---

6   8/40.
7   10/42.
8   9/41.
9   14/47.
10   20/54.

little other than rehearse, somehow fitting our jobs into the day. We had to laugh at the idea of the "impossible sight of a tired eurythmist",[11] but isn't it true? life is full of paradoxes. Wagner – who has dramatically split the musical public – tells wonderful stories in music. But music can tell its *own* story through its progressions. Music illustrating some event certainly whips up my emotions; the picture-house [cinema/ movies] without the piano-player would be a dull show!

Artists stand in the actual world that is full of logical contradictions. Polar opposites are different (each pole contains something of its opposite) – they produce creative tension. Joy contrasting with pain are necessities out of which human expression arises in the first place. Here Steiner answers the age-long question about the origin of music. "The human being cries out into the world as a result of pleasure or pain,"[12] no doubt the origin of everything from lullabies to laments. The universal law of polarity is the law of life: "Everything in the world is formed as a polarity."[13] Such a busy and interesting situation continually demands Right Decisions. While acknowledging polarity as essential to artistic method, is the aim of performance also to supersede dualism? In the process are there stages, degrees – perhaps what we call the "intervals" in music? Is it now really possible to trace and fashion metamorphosis between stages?

Lecture 3:

Dr Steiner spoke about the present sorry state of our speech; recitation and acting today are rather histrionic. Speech has to be authentic, that is, shaped, filled with imagination. *Right Speech* contains a "hidden eurythmy".[14] So as eurythmists we reciprocate by uniting with the musicality of the trained speaker, not illustrate the prose meaning. Following in the footsteps of the genius of language we co-create the meaning: the sound creates the sense. This takes up, almost word for word, a tradition as old as the first known theory of language in Plato's "*Cratylus.*"[15] In eurythmy I'm wonderfully carried on Frau Doktor's speech. Slowly the corrective influence of true musicality will bring a change to our materialistic age. Music doesn't represent 'Rustling Forests' – the title of a piano-piece recently[16] performed in eurythmy.

---

11   21/55.
12   18/52.
13   GA 276. *The Arts and their Mission*. Lecture, Dornach. 9 June 1923. AP: Spring Valley, New York. 79. Tr. rev. A.S.
14   26/60.
15   Plato. *Cratylus*. 426C–427D.
16   Franz Liszt. 'Waldesrauschen.' Dornach, 26 Dec. 1923. *Cf.* p. 28/62 and p. 45/79.

Dr Steiner said we should practise an inner listening at the piano out of an inner stillness, and then move what we pro-actively hear.[17] From keynote to octave – following the scale, not with twelve abstract notes[18] – we reproduce the whole human being! In the first two lectures we were reminded (1.) of "the whole human being", *i.e.*, unity, then (2.) "paradoxes", *i.e.*, duality. In these eight lectures themselves, are we being led from foot to head as a scale?[19] Is the lecturer weaving in other parallels linked by number? Let's see…

Today, in Lecture 3, he mentioned the fact of death. I know death inspired an elaborate cult during the *third* post-Atlantean epoch, with its pyramidal society and architecture. Mummification must have reminded the soul – during that age naturally rather dreamy – that the earthly life *was*, and consequently still *is*, significant for the future. Dr Steiner spoke of the triad: even here, in this solid chord of *three* notes, a melody is buried. He introduced several other *triads*: search for the melody in the single note "between recollection and expectation as adjacent notes".[20] So, in inner consciousness, we ride on the wave of the musical flow, leaving the old, ever reaching for the new – Goethe's "livingly anticipate the future", what, I think, is called the "eternal present". In music we continually transform the spatial (= three-dimensional) element, especially that which has coagulated into chords and harmony. The musical element is "what you do not hear"[21] but you certainly experience – the time element, melos, the *melodic line*.

And this experience can be shown before and with people's eyes as if they were ears: "There are *three* things we can say about the human being"[22] (it looks as if that *is* the theme today!). The rise and fall of pitch is experienced in the vertical dimension, *up-down*; the pulsing rhythm of wake and sleep in the *forward-backward*; and the supporting beat or metre in the *right-left*. The complete experience is expressed through the three-dimensional cross, and *each* of the three categories of music is the product of creative polarity. We are "to enter" and "make use"[23] of the three-dimensional cross; the verbs in the first three gospels are "take up" and "follow"; Luke adds "daily", John adds "where I am, there shall my

---

17 *Cf.*, GA 294. Stuttgart, 25. August 1919. RSP. P. 64f./ AP. P. 56f.
18 *Cf.*, J.M. Hauer. *Deutung des Melos*. E.P. Tal: Leipzig, Wien, Zurich. 1923. 22f.
19 *Cf.*, Elena Zuccoli. 1997. 39.
20 29/63.
21 29/64.
22 30-31/65.
23 31/66.

servant be".[24] Music doesn't represent 'Rustling Forests'; it is the singing Tree of Life itself!

Right *('proper' as opposed to 'false')* Communication *arises out of polar tension as a third factor, a decidedly human creation. My authentic experience repeatedly creates the human middle in all sorts of situations. Poets speak of the voice heard* "in the stillness/ Between two waves of the sea" *(T.S. Eliot); heard* "between the thumpings of the blood" *(Norman Nicholson).*

Fig. 71: *A medallion from the C15ᵗʰ showing Christ as Janus [IHS = Jesus Hominem Salvator: Jesus Saviour of Humankind]. The middle, third head – the present between past and future – cannot be presented in a visual image. There is a danger of fixing the living element, seen in Methusa's head of snakes that turned the onlooker into stone.*

Lecture 4:

Within the flow in time there are breaths between phrases and breaks, and what the musicologist Riemann calls a "dead interval", notated as bar lines [Am. bars]. But the in-between, Dr Steiner insists, is where the *living* spirit manifests: in the transitions. The Doktor brought a little "homespun" eight-bar ditty, analysing the metamorphoses in respect of motif, "swinging-onwards" (what we call the "breath") and "restraining-ourselves" (bar-line). A complicated exercise! Eurythmy, he said, reveals the melody, the actual spirit, and carries it on. Everything else is "a more

---

24   Matt. 16:24, Mk. 8:34, Luke 9:23, John 12:26.

or less illustrative element"[25] – uncompromising words! Is this *Right Action* for my personal, artistic path?

Not self-presentation, then, but: "As physical human being marking the *beat*; as etheric human being expressing the *rhythm*; as astral human being evolving the *melos*: it is thus that I appear before the world".[26]

I have to choose between either presenting what I have learned, leading to virtuosity and ultimately fragmentation, or presenting "a knowledge derived from feeling-experience", that is, "develop a real art"[27] that is socially fruitful. An outer show does not reveal the inner events.

The Doktor told of some personal experiences with dialect as a boy in his village and with theories of language as a student, and then he came to the main point: naturalism is not musical. "Music is the self-creating [power] in the human being, and imitating nature is an aberration of the musical path."[28]

The centre of the three-dimensional cross is a cube. During the fourth post-Atlantean cultural epoch, he once explained,[29] the "central star on earth", Solomon's Temple, was a focus for science, art and religion. Its heart was a cube room. Here "between the two Cherubim"[30] statues, between the shoulder-blades, "Yahweh's magic breath" (YHVH = "He who causes to be") was once heard and still manifests in the physical-spatial body today.[31] It is our point of departure for melos, for singing gesture (localised in the 6th thoracic vertebra[32]).

The "dissolving of salt and the metamorphosis of salt" is mentioned. I recall the fairy-story of the youngest Princess who loved her father "like salt" (*e.g.*, 'Cap o' Rushes' in Joseph Jacobs' "*English Fairy Tales*" [www.archive.org], and in the Grimms' 'The Goosegirl by the Spring'); "I love your Majesty/ According to my bond", says the true Cordelia in Shakespeare's *King Lear* (I, i). "You are the salt of the earth" from the Sermon on the Mount[33] images those accomplished trainees who get their act together. Insipid brine is cast out, but salt as a condiment to humanity's self-dedication (to art) points to the Creator, now internalised as Head Chef. Salt was once used in pacts of amity, of perpetual

25 39/73.
26 40/74. This translation retains the single appearance in the original German sentence of the personal pronoun, the word *ich* (Eng. "I").
27 43/77.
28 45/79.
29 GA 173. Basel, 21 Sept. 1916.
30 Num. 7: 89
31 GA 158, Dornach. 21 Nov. 1914.
32 Lea van der Pals u. Annemarie Bäschlin. *Ton-Heileurythmie*. Dornach: Verlag am Goetheamun. 1991. 12.
33 Luke 14:34, Mark 9:49-50, Matt. 5:13.

friendship. Salt preserves for this world and for the next. The salt crystal is cubic, symbol for the earth itself. According to Shakespeare's Prospero, the earth and all human achievement "shall dissolve",[34] echoing 2 Peter 3:10-11. Dr Steiner mentioned here the therapeutic effects of music eurythmy. On this *Friday* (22nd February) – the day of Freya (Venus), the goddess of love, and the day of the Crucifixion –, he spoke final words to natural processes in the human being: "'Out you go!' – for these movements are solely human and have nothing of nature about them. The musical element belongs only to man, not to nature."[35]

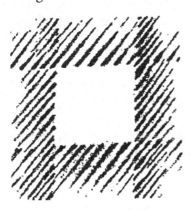

Fig. 72:   *From Rudolf Steiner's lecture, Dornach, 21. Nov. 1914.*

Right Deed *is creative because it is based on nothing else than personal, individual testimony, i.e., it centralises. The Voice of the divine "I AM", however, won't and can't be conjured, "to appear here and not elsewhere, now and not some other time, thus and not otherwise".[36] Composers daily practising their craft take about ten years, so it is said, to find their own voice (music "contains the laws of our 'I'"[37]). The full waste-paper baskets testify of the work to get there – yet* much more *do the inner suffering and loneliness of the creative artist.[38] Composers, poets and critics have so far only explained and described circumstances, not yet the elusive moment of inspiration itself. Bach wrote in his Calov-Bible to II Chron. 5:13 (when music sounds, God enters the Temple): "NB. With a devotional music God in His glory is present at all times."[39]*

We have now reached the halfway point of eight lectures, between the 22nd and 23rd February. It corresponds to the critical moment between the two tetrachords in the scale (4 + 4). Inner experience has been progressively followed, natural man has been dismissed and now we stand there as awakened individuals.

34   Shakespeare. The Tempest. IV, i.
35   46/80.
36   Martin Buber. *Kingship of God.* London: Geo. Allen & Unwin. 1967. 106.
37   GA 275. *Art as seen in the Light of Mystery Wisdom.* Dornach 29 Dec. 1914. RSP: London. 1984. 37.
38   GA 275. Dornach, 30. Dec. 1914. RSP. 56.
39   Hertha Kluge-Kahn. *Johann Sebastian Bach: Die verschlüsselten theologischen Aussagen in seinen Spätwerk.* Wolfenbüttel und Zürich: Möseler Verlag. 1985. 26.

Except for the point, the still point,
There would be no dance, and there is only the dance.

(T.S. Eliot. Four Quartets.*)*

In the lecture-course, as in the historical turning-point of time, the 'turning inside out' comes at precisely the right moment – halfway through the whole. I submit that the imagery and themes – "the dissolving and metamorphosis of salt" (the mineral element), love, sacrifice and healing – all point to the mystery of the atonement and the reconstitution of the human being. Here is the intimate link between lectures 4 and 5 and therewith between both halves of the lecture-course, as well as the musical and human parallels mentioned in this essay and all the others for which there is no space to mention. The one secure basis that unites science, art and religion is present. For Tennyson's poetic vision:

Closer is He than breathing, nearer than hands and feet.[40]

"Only an I has access to another I";[41] consequently, the communication is indubitable. Let us now resume the 'diary' as long as 'Anna' can usefully relate the events.

Lecture 5:

Immediately Dr Steiner recommends choral eurythmy, "the concerted working of a number of persons"; moreover, we are not merely to take these things "schematically" but "work together".[42] Is that the next theme: the question of *Right Livelihood*, of finding and working with colleagues in artistic presentation? The astral ("starry") organisation is the fundamental basis, but we are not to remain in a state of repose – with closed eyes, I suppose, enjoying the music. *No!* We can manifest what our soul and spirit nature is experiencing, take *aural* music further, since manifesting is "the most predominant element of all artistic endeavour". "*Heraufarbeiten*" – it's a *lifetime's work* to "raise the physical human being",[43] to unfreeze the music in the instrument, clear the sand out of the flute.

The story of the composer J.M. Hauer was most sympathetically told, from his "*Interpreting Melos*" that appeared last year (1923). But Hauer doesn't like "manifesting"; in fact, he is altogether disinterested in the phenomenal, visual world. A sensitive musician indeed! Does

40 Alfred Tennyson (1809–92). From 'The Higher Pantheism'. *Tennyson: Poems and Plays.* Oxford: OUP 1953/65. 222f.
41 GA 13. Tr. Creeger. 88. Tr. Monges. 74. Tr. Adams, 82.
42 47/81.
43 47/81.

Hauer with his atonal concept succumb to the "schematic" threat? Is Dr Steiner answering Hauer's radical stand? Lecture 5, the *fifth* post-Atlantean cultural epoch – that's *now*. Hauer recognises the twelve tonal centres of the circle of *fifths* – that is, the cosmic, universal level.[44] Hauer reaches for the stars. But to be contemporary are we obliged to follow his example and dismiss the 7-note scale, our down-to-earth diatonic level? What a loss – throwing out the baby with the bathwater! The "gestures of eurythmy could not be found" out of Hauer's atonal concept.[45]

Today the Doktor gave a method in choral eurythmy to fill out the transitions, and manifest "the character of each individual key".[46] Dr Steiner used the word "love" *five* times in lecture 5; this counteracts the word "hate" he also used *five* times.[47] With the circle of *fifths* as the musician's *Imagination* of the whole human being,[48] tonality triumphs in the face of an abstract atonal concept.

An "esoteric intermezzo" is introduced to make our *physical* instrument "inner bodily nature flexible, inwardly supple",[49] that is, change from within. *What's that?* My eurythmical instrument, a piece of box-wood, might yet rival a violin made by Stradivarius? Power of the imagination! Power of redemption!! T A O appeals to the Great Spirit. Like Hauer, Dr Steiner glances back to China, to the very beginnings of cultural history. Is there a continuous, spiritual-musical thread throughout the cultures, inwardly linked to the creative Voice, or Melos? That Voice guided the Emperor of China in bygone ages; his pictogram 王 shows him (a cross) uniting heaven and earth (horizontal lines above and below). Perhaps today we are each to rule our own kingdoms.

The Doktor also mentioned the musician Orpheus,[50] the mythical founder of the Greek civilisation, whose music could move nature. He created a eurythmy-form for Marie Savitch (6 Aug. 1922) for Shakespeare's Song from *King Henry VIII*:[51]

---

44 See Hermann Pfrogner. 'Arnold Schönberg und Josef Matthias Hauer' (in: *Zwölfordnung der Töne*. Amalthea-Verlag. Zürich–Leipzig–Wien: 1953. Pp. 184-232, on Hauer pp. 210-232); reprinted in H. Pfrogner. *Zeitwende der Musik*. Langen Müller. München–Wien: 1986. Pp. 93-135 (on Hauer, pp. 116-135).
45 48/82.
46 53/87.
47 49/83, 56/90 and 48f./82f.
48 18/52, 64/98.
49 55/89.
50 56/90.
51 Shakespeare. King Henry VIII. III i.

SONG

Orpheus with his lute made trees,
And the mountain tops that freeze,
    Bow themselves when he did sing;

To his music plants and flowers
Ever sprung, as sun and showers
    There had made a lasting spring.
Every thing that hears him play,
Even the billows of the sea,
    Hung their heads and then lay by.
In sweet music is such art,
Killing care and grief of heart
    Fall asleep or hearing die.

It feels as if we are joining to *a pathway that was always there.* Dr Steiner does not name the historical tradition advocating the Path. He must be leaving it up to us to discover the Eightfold Path as a universally-human, artistic "training in living". It seems the theme of freedom, indeed crisis as such, belongs particularly to this fifth stage.[52] Today for the first time the lecturer divulged the whole secret: "freedom to carry out each individual movement beautifully."[53] Surely Dr Steiner, who advocates "ethical individualism", is a "knowing doer" of "*The Philosophy of Freedom*" (Chap. 1)? I need not be shy of using the traditional names about something universal; here with the Path are no membership clauses, neither copyright nor visa restrictions, neither sell-by date nor small print.

A devoted working with and for others develops relationships which ultimately ray out to benefit the environment. "Personality is T A O", concludes C.G. Jung.[54] *The unified, perfected human being who "surrenders" to T A O "renews creation", as Martin Buber*[55] *puts it. Grimms' traditional fairy-tale 'Dornröschen', is widely known – variously translated as 'Sleeping Beauty/ Little Briar-Rose/ Hawthorn Blossom'.*

---

52   GA 101. Stuttgart. 15 Sept. 1907. *Occult Signs and Symbols.* AP. New York 1972.
53   53/87.
54   C.G. Jung. The Development of Personality. Collected Works. Vol. 17. London: Routledge/ Princeton: Princeton Univ. Press. 1954. 186.
55   Martin Buber. 'The Teaching of the T A O' (1910) in *Pointing the Way: Collected Essays.* Humanity Books: New York. 1999. 31-58. Quotation, p. 54.

Nature's enchantment can be lifted through love. To live in harmony with both nature and spirit is Right Livelihood.

Lecture 6:

Today the lecturer asked, "What is music meant to express?"[56] He has already rejected naturalism, and has redeemed the abstract atonal concept through the creation of eurythmy. Now he can say that music-critic Eduard Hanslick's view of music as abstract patterns, arabesques, "is utter nonsense".[57] Music is not stimulus from outside, but how *you* move from note to note. Dr Steiner also encourages us to recognise the musical element as it lives beyond acoustic music in the narrow sense. In speech, the vowels "*ah*" and "*o*" are musical. The poet, the artist, he said, must be able to dream yet keep awake, that is, to meditate.

Then Dr Steiner revealed to *us* practising artists the important thing about accounts of spiritual science. The facts have to be correct, he admitted, but the important thing comes out in the style of the accounts. This expresses the inner tensions and relaxations, the inner movement that mainly suggests *rhythms*. These can "only be written down in musical notation".[58] That must mean groups of notes, note values, time signatures, *etc.*, – all these can be summed up as numerical relationships. No wonder this came during Lecture 6; the musical sixth is the first interval expanding beyond the halfway threshold in the scale into the world of *Inspiration*.[59]

Our teacher cited four bars from a sonata movement by Mozart – perhaps an exemplary composer who, standing between Wagner and Hauer, balances out the demands of the material world and mental world? He spoke of articulation, the melodic climax (in this musical example) on the sixth degree is reached over the threshold of the fifth, beyond, too, a rest and a bar line.

With discords, too, you "pass over into the spiritual".[60] He elaborated on this passing-over. In drawing, the line amounts to an artistic lie – it isn't there in life. Shapes arise through shading or out of colour. The horizon between sea and sky isn't 'there'. When painting a picture of a house, the lecturer continued, approach it from the surrounding air:

---

56   57/91.
57   57/91.
58   60/94.
59   GA 283. Stuttgart 8 March 1923. *The Inner Nature of Music...* AP. Spring Valley. 1983. P. 83.
60   62/97.

"the house will come about. That's what art has to work for!"[61] This all sounds very much like *Right Effort*, or *Right Striving*.

In lecture 5, Steiner claimed the [First] Goetheanum, the "House of the Word", "was musical... was eurythmical".[62] It housed the right feeling and right thoughts of those within.[63] These researches embrace the whole creation. Inner and outer mutually interact – the cosmic word is heard "between" and "behind"[64] the human word. Lecture 6 expands on Right Speech of Lecture 3.

Perhaps at this juncture we can say goodbye to 'Anna's' diary-convention. It has served to reflect the fact that the oral teaching is personal and educative. Coming up to date, as the Path winds further in in order to reach further out – the double principle of incarnation –, for the concluding two lectures we'll simply continue summarising the teaching, now that the mutual connection of musical experience, meditation and universal processes has been made in Lecture 6.

The names of the stages of the Eightfold Path sum up advice in lifestyle; like the Beatitudes,[65] Psalm 119 with its 8 complete alphabets and 22 paths[66] celebrated by Bach in his "Goldberg Variations",[67] or the Path as it appears in 2 Peter 1:5-7,[68] the application is universal. The aim, in Adam Bittleston's words, is "to achieve a right balance between heaven and earth" (pictured, for example, in Solomon's Seal ✡). I submit that the whole exercise, eminently suited to artists wishing to deepen their art, is the basic assumption of the lecture-course.

Steiner gives indications, not judgments – carrot, not stick. The lecturer did not deem it necessary to name any tradition of The Way, excepting the very early T A O-philosophy. Add to this what is well known, that both

---

61   63/98.

62   49/83.

63   GA 158. *The Balance in the World and Man*. Lecture, Dornach. 21 Nov. 1914. Steiner Book Centre. N. Vancouver. 28f.

64   38/72.

65   J. Duncan M. Derrett. *The Ascetic Discourse*. Ko'amar: Eilsbrunn 1989; *The Sermon on the Mount*. Pilkington Press: Northampton 1994, are outstanding. The SM, "the great ascetic discourse", this historian, lawyer and independent scholar shows, is a practical manual for living.

66   The two (different) commentaries of R.M. Benson occupy a place of their own. *The Way of Holiness*. Methuen: London 1901/Kessinger 2007 (on Ps. 119) <www. archive-org>; *The War-Songs of the Prince of Peace*. 2 vols. John Murray: London 1901 (on the Psalter as a continuous epic). <www.bookfinder.com>.

67   Kluge-Kahn 1985. Chap 8. Pp. 80-105 (FN 39 above).

68   On 2 Pet. 1:5-7 see George Matheson. *Landmarks in New Testament Morality*. Nisbet: London 1888/Cambridge Scholars Pub. 2010. 143-162. An original exposition (www. archive.org).

Buddhism and Christianity[69] *began as ethical pathways. We recognise "a Buddha or the Evangelists did not utter their own revelations but those which flowed into them from the inmost being of all things".*[70] *In bona-fide work there is no umbilical chord to any "system", so attempts to fix things are redundant. Nowhere, moreover, do I meet commonplace moralising. On The Way I am honoured to shake hands with Freya, Orpheus, Lauzi (or Lau Tzu), Plato, Moses, Solomon, the Buddha and Jesus as 'primary sources'; happy, too, to read signposts labelled 'Wagner', 'Hauer', 'Mozart' – and 'Hanslick' – instead of some abstract nouns. Shakespeare, Bach, Goethe, T.S. Eliot, Tennyson, Norman Nicholson, C.G. Jung and Martin Buber have all earned their right as fellow traveller-trainees to share a few words on The Path, or Way. Luke built his gospel on it, around the eight mealtimes.*[71] *And, in no way to be omitted, by relating the Path to our everyday driving, Adam Bittleston*[72] *in his genial way has shown how practical the whole thing is.*

Lecture 7:

In Greece the practical directions for 'Inland' and 'Abroad' on post-boxes/ mailboxes appear as εσωτερικός (= 'Esoteric') and εξωτερικός (= 'Exoteric'). The penultimate sentence of Lecture VII describes "learning eurythmy" as an "awakening of the eurythmy that is within you" through "deep insight... leading into the esoteric [= 'inland'] realm".[73] This is the *practical, instrumental awakening of the eurythmist* – "transferring the inner impulse of feeling" into the limbs, which themselves are "an outer, concave image" or metamorphosis of the inner organs.[74] The seventh step on the Eightfold Path, *Right Mindfulness*, summed up as *Right Memory/ Remembrance*, is where we are to learn as much as possible from life, in its wholeness. Traditionally, seven is the number of perfection: it is the number of Life. "In the experience of the seventh the form of the soul's constitution is the same as clairvoyantly [= "exceptional

---

69 *Cf.*, Acts 11: 26.
70 GA 10. *Knowledge of the Higher Worlds...* Tr. Metaxa rev. Monges, AP 170. Tr. Metaxa rev. Osmond & Davey, RSP. 146.
71 Christoph Rau. 'The Eightfold Path in Luke.' *Perspectives.* Mar./May 2002 – Sept./Nov. 2003. Floris Books. Edinburgh. Tr. A.S. from: *Die Christengemeinschaft.* Jan–Mai 1990. 14-18; 66-71; 130-35; 189-94; 222-27. Stuttgart. See also Chr. Rau. 'Das Rätsel des Lukas' in *Das Goetheanum.* Nr. 50. 15. Dez. 1991. Dornach. Tr. A.S. in MS.
72 Adam Bittleston. 'Traffic and Character.' *The Golden Blade* 1968. 107-23 (esp. 116-21). Emphasis original. Photocopies from <rsh-library@anth.org.uk>.
73 77/111.
74 77/111.

insight"[75]] with *Intuition*."[76] Intuition confirms the right to *think*, and to think purposefully. Animals are mentioned (link to lecture 1) in order to compare, not the size of their brains, but the length of their collar-bones, which enables dexterity and freedom of movement of the upper limbs. Here is to be found the seat of their movement-intelligence.

And so, in this comprehensive context, eurythmy can claim to be sacramental in the sense Steiner already mentions in an early preface to Goethe's scientific writings[77] and to which he ever remained true.

Perceptive, active thinking is eurythmy:
1. speaking of the *instrument* – "*intuitive* vision"[78] directed to the limbs is a thinking with, that is, an awakening of, the whole body –; and
2. eurythmy as an *expressive art*, both speech sound and musical sound (linking to the opening of Lecture 1[79]).

Living sound itself expresses the human being; it is portrayed in eurythmy by the whole human being. The intervals are described from within – the creation-metamorphosis follows the scale, initially given in Lecture 2. Inner life and manifestation, reflection and action are unified; intention and motif coincide. The theme of "paradox" or rather of *polarity* throughout music's "entire tonal configuration" of lectures 1 and 2 is overcome through the antecedent unity – the total human being. When this superseding of dualism occurs, action is at once moral (meaningful) and spontaneous, and consequently free.

With Right Mindfulness we research the whole body as a musical formation, tuned to cosmic, universal laws, in order to reveal 'what is'.

Lecture 8:

The final words of Lecture 7, "in retrospect complement our studies",[80] point to the final step on the Eightfold Path – *Right Concentration*: gently taking counsel with ourselves, shaping and testing our basic principles of life, and, quite practically in Lecture 8, discussing the music with the player. In *Knowledge of the Higher Worlds: How is it Achieved?* we read:[81] "On the esoteric path, we must be aware that what matters is not 'good intentions', but what we actually do." Harmony of our thoughts and words with the events in the outer world helps the gift of awake

75 Mid-C-19th. *The New Shorter Oxford English Dictionary*. Oxford 1993.
76 GA 283. Lecture, Stuttgart 8 March 1923. Spring Valley: AP. 73.
77 GA 1. Chap. VI. 'Goethe's way of knowledge.' Spring Valley: Mercury Press. 1988. 91. (Reprinted from Kürschner's prestigious "Deutsche National-Literatur", ed. R. Steiner. 4 vols. 1883–97.)
78 67/101.
79 5/37.
80 77/111.
81 GA 10. *Higher Worlds*. AP. 141/ RSP. 124.

clairvoyance (that is, with and through our human sense organs), the development of the sixteen-petal lotus flower. Bittleston[82] comments:

> The eighth exercise of the path, which in a sense includes all the others, calls for an inner life that leads to genuine self-knowledge. This can seldom be achieved directly, simply by looking at ourselves; objective standards, and a lively understanding of our environment, are needed first. From these, we can glance back towards ourselves.

Discussing the phrasing with the player is a comment on the artistic profession; for Steiner music and eurythmy are not separable. The "matters" that "need correction"[83] rightly refer to us practising artists. The right intensity of the musical and eurythmical intentions can only be achieved through the indication to discuss phrasing with the musician – "It simply belongs to the matter... this is what the inner life is".[84]

Artists practise *method*, never such a creature as 'theory'. Spiritual research – to track thoughts to their origin – is likewise essentially artistic. As a creative activity, eurythmy, too, is not separable from life, for everyone – including the audience – is engaged on the inner path whether they know it or not. Aware of the inner path, I may yet be under some grand illusions of my progress. Artists are servants from the first note to the last. In other words, the activity of persons in relation – practical ethics – with an anthropology or 'study-of-man' as its spiritual-scientific basis, turns out to be the really essential thing. Eurythmy is not only "visible singing" and "visible speech", but also "Visible Deed". This may be the reason why Schiller's "*Aesthetic Letters*" and Steiner's own "*Philosophy of Freedom*" are recommended for eurythmy students.[85] Composers are served by the rules of composition. Likewise: "All real philosophers are *artists in the realm of concepts*."[86] Thinking, then, is an art comparable to composing. The human being himself is to become a socially productive work of art. This discussion with the musician mentioned in Lecture 8 is the fulfilment of *Right* or *Complete Understanding* of Lecture 1. It is more than a pow-wow; "this is what the inner life is" – a foretaste of heavenly citizenship of the whole upcoming post-Atlantean epochs.

The lecture-course carries its own conviction that the eternal act of creation finds its continuation in the finite personality. A developed language of incarnate gesture leads to a knowledge that these acts of

---

82   Bittleston. 1968. 121.
83   87/121.
84   87/121.
85   GA 277a. 142.
86   GA 4. *Philosophy of Freedom*. Preface to first edition, 1884; rev. 1918. 270.

communication – my own included – will hold their place in history. One can consequently say, the mathematical symbol for eternity ∞ (= horizontal 8) portrays the actual process of the mutual give-and-take of the performing arts between stage and audience. These two areas are embraced by this symbol in a living, breathing movement that brings the inner-side outside and the outer-side inside as those involved move in perceptive consciousness through the crossing point, the threshold. (This movement is also contained in the eurythmical gesture for the octave interval.) Such a musical-*architectural* relationship between stage and audience in both plan and elevation – that is, three-dimensional – was achieved in the First Goetheanum.[87]

This pattern can be perceived in the lecture-course itself; it has also been our thread here: correspondence of lectures (as 4 + 4: 1–8, 2–7, 3–6, 4–5; further correspondences rest on the fact that the scale is also 7 + 1, that is, 1–7, 2–6, 3–5, 4, + 8); parallels with the cultural epochs; initial investigation of number-rhythms presented as phenomena (it might initially appear as listing 'facts') clearly corresponding to the degrees of the scale, first suggested by Elena Zuccoli as seminal for the training.[88] The attempt has also been made here to point out the transitions between the lectures themselves. The 'turning-inside-out' has been quasi-dramatized by creating 'Anna' who 88 years on couldn't quite keep up. As Zuccoli says: "Everything in this lecture-course was completely new for us." *This Steiner knew:* "I think the material needs to be worked through."[89] *In other words, there is no trace of 'theory' here. Alongside the founders of civilisation mentioned by Steiner and the most significant reformers that have ever lived, I have mentioned a few links to outstanding personalities and events in world-culture – no contemplating navels here!*

Right Concentration practises a free interaction in a becoming-one with the living environment. The Sower of the Word (in Luke, in the section on *Right Speech*) reckoned with 25% success (Lk. 8:15/ Matt. 13:8), which is not negligible and could be improved with husbandry (Matt. 9:37-8, 13:30).

Unspoken lectures

Steiner finally mentioned "fourteen" lectures.[90] If the *eight* that were given relate to the 16-petalled lotus flower in the region of the larynx

---

87   Carl Kemper. *Der Bau.* Freies Geistesleben: Stuttgart. 1966/2007.
88   Elena Zuccoli. 1997. 39. Emphases original.
89   88/122.
90   87/121.

(eight petals are given; eight are to be developed) to which Steiner[91] relates the Eightfold Path, then the *six* unspoken lectures may have related to the 12-petalled lotus flower of the heart (six petals are given; six are to be developed). Feeling "inner warmth or inner cold" when practising "is what inner life is";[92] it characterises the 12-petalled lotus flower. With this link, Steiner may have enlarged on the divine-human system of angle-gestures; here number becomes geometry. This all-embracing solar angle-system, with its stroke of genius combining the 12 and the 7, reveals the musical system of humankind. Out of *inner silence, the still-point* calming the limbs that would be taken up with an instinctive dancing, the reborn, autonomous musical arts – poetry, music, eurythmy[93] – reflect from within a true balance of heaven and earth:[94]

> The soul... in silence... begins to reflect from within itself the dancing movements of the limbs. When the limbs execute irregular movements, the soul begins to *mumble*; when the limbs perform regular movements it begins to *whisper*: when the limbs carry out the harmonious cosmic movements of the universe, it even begins to *sing*. In this way the outward dancing movement is changed into singing and into inner music.

Anna has sent a message:

"'Mumble..., whisper..., sing' – precisely!

Now I get the italics, which is only fair! I just wanted to say, it's fine you didn't need me for the last part. It's true, we did take Dr Steiner's revelations lying down. We also didn't realise how fierce the atonal-tonal conflict would wage in the twentieth century, so, at the time, we didn't quite get the struggle between musical world-views referred to in Lecture 5. But in case you form the wrong picture, we were not SO slow *we couldn't tell the keyboard from the music!*

I mean, the keyboard pictures the tonal-system, but the musician sings the tune. The keyboard is the same, but the piano sounds differently if I play a tune or whether Rachmaninoff, Rubinstein or Richter does. Obviously! But isn't it the same in eurythmy? We all 'mumble' and 'whisper' at first, until we find our way on the keyboard/ fret board, or finger-board – our 'fret board' for the arms, if you will. What a brainwave *of Dr Steiner to unite the 7 and the 12! The solar angle-gestures are 'there', representing the whole tonal system of humanity; they are* our *means of singing in gesture.*

---

91 GA 10. *Higher Worlds....* Chap. 5. "The fact that these conditions [of development] correspond with certain teachings of the Buddha is no reason for not finding them true in themselves." (Tr. Metaxa, rev. Monges. AP: New York. 1947. 146/ Tr. Metaxa, rev. Osmond & Davey. RSP: London. 1969. 128.)

92 87/121.

93 GA 271. *Kunst und Kunsterkenntnis.* Dornach, 12. September 1920.

94 GA 293. *Study of Man.* Lecture, Stuttgart, 1 Sept. 1919. RSP 1966. 144.

You find solar motifs in ecclesiastical, agricultural, commercial, domestic and folk-art venues and contexts the world over. Eurythmy lets them all sound – what's 'specialist' here? In eurythmy – "this art is for everyone"[95] *– all the arts are present.*

Of course, you can give cosmic names to the 7 and 12. Rudolf Steiner did so,[96] *and what he left are our marching orders for work: 7 x 12 meditations (7 x 15 with the overlaps) of the circle of fifths, is practical, intensive work for eurythmists.*

So – just for the record – do remind people we did *practice* Tonansatz, *the point-of-departure, the embouchure for singing between the shoulder-blades, described in detail in 1924 to the teachers and doctors.*[97] *We worked with* Tonansatz *all the time! The lecturer assumed this, just as he assumed the angle-gestures were known – perhaps, also, he didn't mention these things in these lectures because you don't always stare at the sun, do you? And, as noted, he was most probably going to speak about it next, but his death prevented this from happening. We undoubtedly* did *know that the music was not the positions but 'pathways of movement between the tones'.*[98] *Each 'pathway' is unique – not only tones but also intervals (degrees)!*

I am glad you have shown more clearly the training of the personality, not the disappointing mask ('little me') in front but the living personal Voice *heard* with *and* through *it. For the 'between' is that which enables us "in the most eminent sense to bring the human personality, the human personality as soul, into the musical element'.*[99] *The 'how'! You can't do without it, melos, and there is no end to it! For sure, name and study the stages; but also be aware of metamorphosis – the changes between. These can't be named so quickly, as Lao Tzu*[100] *warns! All three kinds of 'intervals' (melodic, harmonic and degrees of the scale), as all numbers in music and in the lecture-course itself, are 'rhythms'*[101] *– not, for example, 'things'. Not 'only' tones but also intervals (degrees!), but gently, carefully... There lies the human element and that is the music. William Blake knew, 'If the sun and moon should doubt,/ They'd immediately go out.'*

Thank you all, from the heart. I wish you all Good Luck! Enjoy practising, while you have the chance!—'Anna'."

---

95   GA 277a. Dornach, 7 October 1914. 65.

96   GA 283. Dornach, 2 Dec. 1922.

97   GA 308. Stuttgart, 10 April 1924; GA 309. Bern 15 April 1924; GA 277a. Stuttgart, 30 April 1924; GA 318. Dornach, 9 Sept. 1924; Albert Steffen. *Dante und die Gegenwart*. Dornach. 59.

98   Elena Zuccoli. *From the Tone Eurythmy Work*. Walter Keller Press: Dornach 1981. 8.

99   30/64.

100 Lao Tzu. *Tao Teh Ching*. I.

101 GA 283. Stuttgart, 8. March 1923. 144.

Fig. 73: Some solar motifs in the vicinity – UK–Stourbrdge, York, Stoud, and CH–
Dornach.

Part III

JOSEF MATTHIAS HAUER

INTERPRETING MELOS:

A question to the artists and thinkers of our time

Translated from the German

by

Alan Stott

from

DEUTUNG DES MELOS:

Eine Frage an die Künstler und Denker unserer Zeit

E.P. Tal & Co. Verlag. Leipzig, Wien, Zürich. 1923

Translator's Note

J. M. Hauer (1883–1959) is credited with the discovery of 12-note

Fig. 74:   Josef Matthias Hauer (1883–1959)

technique – today called "atonal music" – even a year or two before Arnold Schönberg (1874-1951). The word "atonal" historically derives from journalism; initially "*a-tonal*" meant "non-sounding". This is how Hauer uses it in his 1923-manifesto, *Interpreting Melos,* and also how Steiner comments on it in lecture 5 of *Eurythmy as Visible Singing* (GA 278) of 1924. A translation of Hauer's text is included here for two reasons. Steiner is indebted to Hauer for many things, especially the latter's rather devastating diagnosis of the modern situation with his references to the effects of materialism. Steiner's sympathy, however, should not blind the reader to the fact that the lecturer also faces the fundamental challenge of "the atonal conception". Steiner's answer to this abstraction is the creation of music eurythmy.

The illuminating explanations by Hermann Pfrogner (1911-1988) on modern developments can be recommended, here especially the chapter "Arnold Schönberg und Josef Hauer" in *Die Zwölfordnung der Töne*. Amalthea-Verlag. Zürich-Leipzig-Wien. 1953. 184-232; reprinted in *Zeitwende der Musik*. Langen Müller. München-Wien. 1986. 93-135. The twelve tones were known in ancient China as the 12 liuh, though only five were used (pentatonic). The twelve tonal realms are indeed spiritual; musicians who identify them with the twelve well-tempered keyboard notes/ tones prematurely "fix" the realms; they inevitably become abstract when treated indifferently. In the last resort, Pfrogner declares, atonality is not an empirical material phenomenon (connected to equal temperament) but a living, musical phenomenon. Pfrogner created the term *Tonorte*, "tonal positions, realms", for these 12 tones. This term, he claims, helps to dispel a possible confusion of thinking. Each tonal realm contains at least two notes, for example, $F^\#$ and G^b, as well as E^X. Consequently, Pfrogner prefers the term "enharmonic" for this level in the tonal system. With variable tuning all actual scales can be accommodated, with each specific answer to question of the division of the octave. The musical system, Pfrogner teaches, is three-layered: diatonic, chromatic, and enharmonic, corresponding *in the musical system* to the etheric, astral, spiritual levels of existence. Incidentally, this theorist points out, the chromatic "scale" is a misnomer – the chromatic notes added to any seven-note scale, "fill out" a given musical passage. The keyboard has certain advantages, but its easy accessibility – as Hindemith also remarks – facilitates over-hasty connections. For example, what about $E^\#$ and $B^\#$, also C^b and F^b? A chromatic sequence carried out as a eurythmy exercise includes these notes. For the ascending sequence, each note is sharpened; for the descending sequence they are flattened.

metaphor

"Inaudible melos" as spiritual listening points to the musical element lying between the notes. However, by divorcing audible sound and treating it as sensory noise, the atonal conception is left high and dry as a "reaching for the stars". By concentrating exclusively on this level in the tonal system, the diatonic (7-note) level is ignored. This seems obvious, but it took an inspired music theorist to point it out! The 12-note conception cannot quite succeed; we hear, for example, a fifth as such and not seven semitones. In fact, Pfrogner says, we would never hear a fifth and the other intervals, did it not correspond to our experience. (Despite the theory, it has to be admitted that much 12-note composition is basically ultra-romantic.) The scale is no mere convention; the musical system is a reflection of how we are created, as Steiner affirms, "The scale is the human being" (GA 278. Lecture 3). Since it underwent modifications over the ages, the development of the scale also presents the inner story of human consciousness. Pfrogner's researches (*Lebendige Tonwelt*. Langen Müller. München-Wien 1981) are further pursued by Heiner Ruland (*Expanding Tonal Awareness*. Rudolf Steiner Press. London. 1992).

Steiner, too, despite his sympathy for Hauer's sensitive diagnosis, also regards Hauer's "atonal concept" as abstract (*cf.*, the phrase "the astral body in repose". GA 278. Lecture 5). Steiner reports he "could never take Hauer's atonal melos as a basis for the gestures of eurythmy" (GA 278. Lecture 5). The 12-note of conception of Hauer and Schönberg attempts to abolish the diatonic level in the tonal system. The creation of the eurythmical gestures, based on the seven-note, diatonic scale (*Eurythmy: Its Birth and Development*. GA 277a. 71) given at the very beginning of music eurythmy is thus also Steiner's answer to Hauer's atonal theorizing. The gestures reveal the two tetrachords and the crucial turning-inside-out (*Umstülpung*), or threshold between them; the two zones for the major and minor modes was also given. By treating "any note as keynote" the same patterns of the major and minor scales can unfold, revealing "the character of each individual key" (GA 278. Lecture 5) of the circle of fifths. This is the practical way of carrying out the meditation given to musicians, or actually 7 x 12 meditations (strictly speaking even 7 x 15 with F# and G♭ and the overlaps on the circle of fifths of C# and C♭) and the variations of the degrees in the minor mode (R. Steiner. Lecture, Dornach. 2 Dec. 1922, in *The Inner Nature of Music…* Anthroposophic Press, Spring Valley. 1983. GA 283). The angles of the degrees of the primal scale are experienced together with the degrees of whichever scale is practised (that is, there is not *one* D, or second degree, since D is second in C major, third in B♭ major, and so on). Eurythmists are offered endless opportunity to enter into the nuances of musical expression revealed in the eurythmical gestures. Yet for this revelation of musical experience, eurythmists cannot be simplistic: the process involves notes/ tones *and* intervals/ degrees – not notes/ tones *or* intervals/ degrees! In the far future, says Pfrogner, the twelve primes will come into their own. Since we know the mathematics, the scales of the future are already known, but we do not yet possess authentic compositions – we are citizens of the *fifth* post-Atlantean epoch, not yet of the sixth and seventh epoch. Ego-development cannot be forced – yet, Pfrogner adds, as with all development, preparation has to be made in advance.

Pfrogner points out that the atonal conception need not have happened the way it did, with its denial, or implied denial of sensory existence. Steiner stresses that eurythmy retains and expresses the full human connection – we are called not to "hate" but to "love" (both words are used 6 times in lecture 5. GA 278) the sensory world that includes the manifestations of art. Through devotion, art raises the phenomenal world to express the reality of soul and spirit experience. The physical world is never "merely" matter; the arts exist to cleanse what Blake called "the doors of perception", in order to experience "what is" – that is, the world as a whole, available to musicians and eurythmists in the circle of fifths, and described in cosmic terms in the lecture of 1922, cited above.

In the translation, capitals are used for "Intuition" and "Idealism" as technical terms of philosophy. "Atonal", as "a-tonal", originally meant "not sounding", though Hauer seems initially to have made a compromise, since he speaks of "atonal instruments" (piano, harmonium, celeste), which are normally tuned to equal temperament. Later the word "atonal" became synonymous for "music without a keynote" or "composition using 12 equal-tempered semitones", or simply "twelve-note/tone music"—A.S.

"Wikipedia" helped with these terms:
Affekte (Germ.): The doctrine of the affections, or known as the *doctrine of affects*, was a theory in musical aesthetics popular in the Baroque era (c. 1600–1750). It derived from ancient theories of rhetoric, and was widely accepted by late-Baroque theorists and composers. The essential idea is that just one unified and "rationalised" *Affekt* should be aimed at by any single piece or movement of music, and that to attempt more was to risk confusion and disorder.

Why we need musicology

According to the "doctrine of the affections" there are three pairs of opposing emotions that make six "affects" all together: love/hate, joy/sorrow, wonder/desire.

Nomos: The nouns *nómos* and *nomós* both derive from the verb νέμω, *némō*, to dispense or to allot, with *nomós* being the *result* of allotment and *nómos* being the *manner* of allotment or dispensing (justice).

Ethos: (Gk ἦθος) meaning "character" that is used to describe the guiding beliefs or ideals that characterise a community, nation, or ideology. The Greeks also used this word to refer to the power of music to influence its hearer's emotions, behaviours, and even morals. Early Greek stories of Orpheus exhibit this idea in a compelling way. The word's use in rhetoric is closely based on the Greek terminology used by Aristotle in his concept of the three artistic proofs.

Pathos: (Gk: πάθος, for "suffering" or "experience;" adjectival form: "pathetic" from παθητικός) represents an appeal to the audience›s emotions. Pathos is a communication technique used most often in rhetoric (where it is considered one of the three modes of persuasion, alongside ethos and logos), and in literature, film and other narrative art.

Emotional appeal can be accomplished in a multitude of ways:

by a metaphor or story telling, common as a hook,

by a general passion in the delivery and an overall emotion and sympathies of the speech or writing as determined by the audience. The pathos of a speech or writing is only ultimately determined by the hearers.

Pathos is often associated with emotions, but it is more complex than simply emotions. A better equivalent might be appeal to the audience's sympathies and imagination. An appeal to pathos causes an audience not just to respond emotionally but to identify with the writer's point of view – to feel what the writer feels. So, when used in tragedy, pathos evokes a meaning implicit in the verb "to suffer" – to feel pain imaginatively or vicariously. Pathos is often employed with tragedies and this is why pathos often carries this negative emotional connotation. Perhaps the most common way of conveying a pathetic appeal is through narrative or story, which can turn the abstractions of logic into something palpable and present. The values, beliefs, and understandings of the writer are implicit in the story and conveyed imaginatively to the reader. Pathos thus refers to both the emotional and the imaginative impact of the message on an audience, the power with which the writer's message moves the audience to decision or action.

Josef Matthias HAUER

Interpreting Melos:
A question to the artists and thinkers of our time

How as a small boy I learned the fundamentals of European composition

In his joyless youth, my father often took refuge in music. As someone self-taught, under the guidance of a village musician he also gained the knowledge, which helped him later as a part-time zither teacher. My parents lived in Vienna-Neustadt in an old monastic building that at this time also housed a junior school. At the age of five I wanted to go to school. With screams and tears I begged my mother to send me at last to school, I was already big and clever enough. My mother did not know what to do, but my father who wanted to channel my creative energies decided to give me zither lessons. I received some lessons in which I learned the necessary fingerings despite the smallness of my hands. I was soon able to tune the zither and in this way learned the circle of fifths and fourths, the keys and key-signatures. Writing and reading music was not difficult for me, so that I was already able to write music and play the zither before I entered school. In a few years I had learned the songs and dances commonly played on the zither. My father himself composed a few pieces, and if somebody sang a song for him he was able to arrange it skilfully for the zither. This art tremendously impressed me then, and one day I tried to arrange a piece for the zither that I had heard on a barrel-organ. On this occasion I learnt from my father about eight-bar sentences because I had not taken into account the upbeat crotchet in the division into bars. Writing down the bass line and melodic accompaniment on the fingerboard proved intractable. My father played a series of chords for me, which he stated was to be found in this way in nearly every piece. Later this sequence was revealed to me as the cadential chords. My father did not know the names of chords, inversions and the cadential 6/4 chord; he just played for me all the cadences which he knew in the different keys and time-signatures. Now when I heard a song or a dance somewhere, I was able to write down what I had heard or to play it straightaway. Through this I achieved a certain respect from people; this skill I practised in entertaining little parties.

One hindrance had still to be overcome. For double stopping and two-part settings I was initially helped by means of a pattern that has helped every European from the path of the purely musical, melodic element into the element of organised noise: parallel sixths and thirds, the faburden.[1] Anyone who knows the fingerings of an instrument tuned in fifths knows that minor and major sixths can be comfortably played on it because the fingers only need to be placed side by side. But thirds and double stoppings are more uncomfortable as they demand a twisting of the hand. But here, too, native cunning found a way out. The zither has an extra G-string on the fingerboard which is a fourth from the D, on the side of the player. Through this major and minor thirds can be comfortably played through the adjacent placing of the fingers. My joy in playing thirds and sixths faburdens did not last long – which, by the way, forms the foundation of counterpoint – for I soon realised that melodies in thirds or sixths did not always work out. My father could also help me out of this dilemma. He showed me on the zither with songs and dances the secrets of polyphonic setting, but only with the advice, "You see, you do it like this, and here like that". The horn fifths which became popular in Vienna through Bruckner – which are allowed even in strict writing –, suspensions and syncopation, the avoidance of the tritone, passing notes in the accompaniment, modulating to other keys with a satisfactory cadence, in short all the practical elements of polyphonic setting were taken for granted by my father (without his being aware of it). We often played together in two parts without written music and the pleasure consisted in this, that the one had spontaneously to "give way" to the other, that is, the one started a melody and the other immediately accompanied it, by which imitation, variation and canonical forms came about by themselves. This way of music-making was great fun and I could not have imagined then that this – only more complicated and mixed with extra-musical elements – is the length and breadth of European music, upon which I completely turned my back in my life.

From my tenth year I received "higher" and the "highest" teaching in music. Through this the zither became discredited. In the course of my studies I assimilated the works of the famous composers, where at every step in their musical works I repeatedly met "old acquaintances". In

---

1   Faburden, *Fauxbourdon*, *Falsoburdone*: false bass or drone; the habit of doubling or tripling voices by permitting them to run parallel in certain intervals.

recent years I also arrived at the purely musical element in atonal melos – in other words, movement itself in its primal form. Consequently, I formed the conviction that I had actually received everything that you could learn in Europe about music between my fifth and tenth year from my father.

I place this description of a musical biography – its like is no rare thing in Austria – at the beginning of this book in order to draw the reader's attention right from the beginning that in the human being the musical element is the purely spiritual one, with its possible musical knowledge and abilities having nothing to do with talent. For this reason it is possible even for a child to have at his disposal an understanding of European music up to now, which only reaches the level of impetus and instinct.

Musical training

Although the art of "music" is supposed to be the spiritual leader of all the others, in Europe it is this art that has sunk the deepest and of all arts is pursued most "bestially". This lies in its nature. If it errs from the purely spiritual, from melos, from melody, then nothing remains with it but notes, noise. In language, for example, the "meaning" of words can never be completely denied and for this reason besides the emotion it produces, a certain spirituality always has to be present. Music on the other hand can easily avoid this hindrance to the point of its complete degeneration. In this way it can sink down to a purely conventional affair. In the proper recognition of this fact, composers since Beethoven have increasingly taken refuge in a programme, in the dramatic element, in tone-poems, not realising that by doing this they imitate once again the worst aspects of the other arts. Polyphonic tonal music, drama and genre painting were from the very beginning compromises to the instinct of the masses and the spiritual and anti-artistic withdrawal from pure movement, from melos.

Since Beethoven music in the first place has consequently become a social affair to whose production appliances, organisation and training is necessary. The "professionals" distinguish between theatre, church, concert, chamber music and music-making at home and even see in it a certain measure of value. They distinguish the more "humble" from the "more demanding", the "large scale" from the "smaller" forms, and demand (God forgive them) that in our time it should be as after the Thirty Years War when the best music was in actual fact cared for in family circles. This view completely and utterly also does homage to the authoritative factors of the different musical institutes (musical politicians) and correspondingly sets up the whole musical business and musical education of the youth. Every musician receives his subject, his repertoire, which presents a compromise between inclination, abilities and the demands of the audience. In the shortest time the cinema organist will be the ideal, as the one musical training most worth striving for, because he so to speak has to master the whole repertoire (beginning with the Funeral March from [Beethoven's] "Eroica" Symphony, down to obscenity); correspondingly he may demand his wages.[2] Nevertheless, a danger also lies in store that the use of the sound track, which at one go could make all cinema musicians redundant.

But what will become of music as an art? The question for a musical person is probably easily answered. He knows that he has music in himself – there is only one music, and that is melody – that he can "hear" only this music he himself produces, or reproduces. He has long known that going to the opera and to concerts only distracts him, but not in the way that he can really "hear" music. He rather listens to music in complete tranquillity and alone without the social diversions, without unmusical additions – libretto, programme, sound effects, and so on. He "reads" music – as you read a poem or a story – and for this you do not need a social event, no organised noise. Printed music of good musical works are still the cheapest. A piano, a small harmonium or a simple celeste probably stands at home, and when its playing does not demand any virtuoso technique – as is and should remain with all real music –, then a musical person can satisfy his own purely musical needs without a professional training, without the years of drill, also without a lot of fuss.

Two paths of musical training exist which lead to different goals. The outer musical training is pursued in conservatoires and similar institutions through a spirit-killing drill lasting several years. It produces performers, virtuosos, choirmasters, conductors, tone-poets and tone-painters, also refined "appreciators". The inner musical culture is pursued through an intuitive listening to melody; it produces knowledge of the musical element, it produces musicians. In our age both paths are completely separate; a compromise to unite them would be unthinkable. Consequently, a musical person today avoids the official music business.

---

2   This was written in 1920, in the days of silent movies/films, when shows were accompanied on an organ, or in smaller picture-houses on a piano. The musician provided some emotion-jerking music, improvised, or partly improvised, to accompany the "action". It has always been known that a sound-track is essential for the success of a movie [Tr. note.]

Because all the appearances of the world can be spiritually derived from pure melos, the musical person is really the "cultivated" one. Next to musical training in the true sense everything else is adaptation, habit, practice, drill, and is directed towards the animal instinct, towards the physiological part of the human being, towards experience. The primal cause of everything, its motivation, can really only be grasped spiritually in melos. The listening human being, consequently, is from the beginning the spiritual person, in contrast to the person only speaking, seeing, and understanding. "Hearing", perceiving (reason) is the human spiritual act, the listening to the unchanging non-touchable, *inconceivable*, unchangeable, eternal—of melos. Only he who hears also recognises, interprets, thinks, speaks, lays hold of, grasps. With the realisation, the making clear, intensifying of melos to melody, the connection with the sensory world is accomplished, which through this receives its "sense", or meaning. The rhythm of melody, the articulation (*BeTONung*) leads to the sound (*Ton*), to the vowel, to noise of sound (*Tongeräusch*), to the consonants; the intervals correspond to the colours, proportions; the sequence of notes (*Töne*) of the melody with its rhythm, the lines, curves and angles. The sound producer, sound body, brings structure, weight, the solidity of the material "to sound", "to resonate" ("*Tönen*", "*Erklingen*"), leads it therefore nearer to the spiritual, the audible, towards melos, to the possibility of its being understood through the human being who can only interpret it rightly from melos. Pure melos presents the spiritual connection between all these things, as also the connection between the single notes creating the melody. The meaning of a word, a "melody" with vowels and consonants, lies in its melos. The vowels are fixed notes with particular tone-colours which move within the range of an octave (*u, o, a, ö, e, ü, i*) and whose absolute pitch depends on the vocal organs; diphthongs correspond to the intervals, and so on. The human being always sings when he speaks, and vice versa he hears the melody out of speech, the "tone" ("*Ton*") of the speaking. In short, the whole universe, the cosmos is spiritualised into melos and if somebody seriously claims to be educated, then he has to be able to establish the connection between melos and the cosmos. There can be no talk of a different education.

Melody or noise?

A full-blooded Wagnerian, forced into a corner and asked what he imagined the word "music" meant, answered, "Whatever is acoustically pleasing is music". This saying of a contemporary European "enthusiast" about art is so typical that we will take it as our starting point for the following observations.

What is acoustically pleasing? Where are the limits of what is unpleasant? One person finds the sound of the wind pleasant, in another person it awakens unpleasant feelings. Let us, however, go to meet the opera enthusiast as far as possible and keep to a well-known physical and physiological law: When a body vibrates irregularly, a noise arises (the unpleasant sound), with regular vibrations a note (the pleasant sound). Out of the sound of a note – out of its overtone series – we hear the major triad. Now, people exist (and they are and were naturally always in the majority) who in listening to music find nothing else important than to allow these pleasant and unpleasant feelings to come about in richer and more varied alternation. They present an "ideal" of the pleasant feeling in the major and minor triads and called it a concord, all other chords, however, they term discords and moreover differentiate degrees of further or nearer proximity to this concord. The more complicated this interchange of pleasant and unpleasant was, the stronger the contrasts and the greater the sensory sensations were which they released, all the more "developed" they called the whole piece of music. Ever-new intensifications are thought out, the contrasts are formed increasingly cleverly and more surprising, and in this way in the course of development the intensification came to a certain climax. This was so exceptionally complicated that it took the whole thing back to what it originally was, namely noise. Out of the overtone series of the note/tone (*Tons*), out of the primitive imitation of nature of the vibrating body, *tonal* music slowly evolved till it led in modern music to absurdity. Once again ended at its point of departure, the complicated noise of vibrating material, the noise of notes. Most people view music from the standpoint of feeling of the pleasurable and non-pleasurable, of the effects of concords and discords from the stronger and weaker contrasts. This consequently turned into a drug – with all the effects of such. They do not think at all of asking of music more than acoustic, in other words purely physiological aural sensations, each according to time and circumstances.

Every natural music inclines more to the moment of noise, to what is crudely rhythmical. Consequently, tonal music in Europe for ages followed the national speech and dance forms, which likewise originate out of the natural, physiological and emotional elements of a folk. *Rhythm* suppressed the *melos*, the actual musical element. Polyphony of tonal music originates in the same way according to its natural noise character, the imitation of the note with its overtone chord. Chords actually only exist for unmusical people, which they treat as the noise of some sort of sensory quality, using their ears only as an organ of touch. The musical human being, however, possesses the capacity and the need to disperse a chord, to transform it into a melody, by which it first gains musical significance. We can say that every chord in itself is a noise, as long as it is not dispersed into a melody by the musical human being. Since we can extract from, and invest, a chord with many melodies, it is – seen from the purely musical point of view –, everything else being equal, a sensory crudifying of melody, of the musical element. Consequently polyphony from the beginning becomes problematic.[3]

Music, which is closer to noise than to the purely musical element, to melody, becomes by itself tone-painting and as such requires an object. This does not always need to be an outer one, it can arise out of the things in music itself, out of moments of noise – concords and discords, the pleasant and unpleasant, more melodic and more elementary, simple and compound, in instrumental technique, and so on. All these purely physiological moments of music which build its inner object, but which are also explicable psychologically ("physio-pathologically") are especially suited to accompany a dramatic action, of the typically Idealistic art-form of speech. Even symphonic form of seemingly absolute music is a re-creation of Greek tragedy – themes as active characters, development as tragic conflict, finale the solution, and so on. With the fugue form, image and spatial experience play a role as well. But as soon as music completely sinks to the level of noise – by the above-described detour –, it is inconceivable without an outer object, without a programme.

In its purely musical form, tonal music, as single-voice melody in its great variety, came out of the Orient to Greece. From the beginning it was misunderstood, reappearing later as what is called Gregorian chant and later on as sacred and secular song. Through counterpoint and instrumental technique it approached the frontier of noise, until in the end in the diatonic major and minor system it received the above-mentioned baroque degeneration with the theory of concord and discord. With the classical composers, this musically experienced its utmost possibilities and in modern music its breakdown.

Only after the chaotic dissolution of tonal music does the actual musical element begin in Europe in the pure melos of atonal melody.

---

3   Atonal music, which does not possess concords and discords, can only be homophonic, unless it should make a similar impression as reading several poems at the same time. (This is so obvious it should not need mentioning!)

It is very difficult to make someone understand what atonal music is who thinks and feels in a linguistic-conceptual way. The name says only this much: that it is not tonal, not built on the laws of frequencies of the notes. We could also say quite briefly that atonal music is pure music, music as such. Tonal music on the other hand is imitation of nature, more or less complicated, with physiological, intoxicating, crude sensory effects, which once again stem from the personal feeling and linguistic-conceptual images of the composer. Atonal melody, however, originates in the musical Intuition of human beings, in other words in that sphere of imagination which once again becomes completely tangible only in atonal melody.

Perhaps I can help a musical European to an experience of Intuition by enumerating everything which does not belong to intuition, what hinders the experience of Intuition, when I give what is the physiological prerequisites. To make Intuition possible it is initially required to extinguish everything of the senses, of the emotions – comfortable clothing which is not too tight anywhere allowing the blood to circulate freely, easily digestible, sparsely spiced food, bodily position such that you are not aware of yourself, all muscles relaxed, head straight (Eastern peoples have already worked out the bodily position) – absolute stillness in the room (remember Intuition is above all an experience in time, initially there exists but one *musical* Intuition) – calm, medium light, moderate temperature, everything removed which could disturb inner balance – it works, even if a busy European can hardly imagine it. Now you choose a good atonal instrument (piano, harmonium, or celeste). Why precisely one of these? Because this in return gives most easily the physiological prerequisites to make Intuition possible. Through equal-tempered notes and intervals everything of a crude sensory nature in music – the beaten track of the leading-note, different sounds of the individual notes, and so on – are excluded as far as possible.

In this condition of complete calmness and under the above-mentioned prerequisites, as it were in a thought and feeling vacuum, you seat yourself at the instrument and play in the middle register, mf, slowly, first of all two notes one after the other, then a third, and so on until all the twelve notes within one octave (actually a major seventh) are played. Now you make a short pause during which you allow what you have just heard to resound within. Then you repeat the same sequence of notes with somewhat more expression with the agogic and dynamic shadings which you become aware of – as it has resounded within you in the stillness. In the meantime the purely (atonal) melos has already become atonal melody through the rhythmic divisions. And now you may repeat as often as you like and listen inwardly till you have the firm conviction that the melody just played can only be conceived thus and not otherwise. But what is experienced between the notes, between the intervals, as it were outside of space, of material, of the senses, that is pure movement, movement itself, intuition, the archetypal musical experience. Everything harsh, contradictory, anything producing effects, moods, things of the senses, eroticism, have to be excluded in order to make intuition possible. The intuitive human being, the "musician", dismisses the "world" and space – of course, only apparently –, he feels within the cosmos and lives in the temporal, one after another, in organic growth.

Intuition and Idealism in Antiquity

Very little is recorded of the earliest musical culture of antiquity. But it is undeniable that with the purely intuitive culture of Mesopotamia and Egypt, music – which still stands closest to intuition – must also have achieved a high degree of development. I believe music was not written down at all for the knowledge that every proportion, colour, curve, every angle, in other words every "interval" contains its moment of movement, its melos which once again through the melody itself can be musically manifested. In music-making something was always produced, something new was created, and what we mean by learning pieces of music probably did not exist at all. For these peoples everything was movement, melody, music. We can conclude by inference from recorded documents on the visual arts, that to the ancient oriental at least everything physical-mathematical, the "anatomy" of music was known in detail, which later was transmitted by the Pythagoreans. I am firmly convinced that the ancients even knew of equal temperament, that is atonal music. Is not intuition in the first place an experience of progression, and the atonal melody the direct incorporation, manifestation of this experience, intuition in its purest form? We can imagine to ourselves quite well that atonal instruments could have been produced of small range as string instruments, glockenspiel-like instruments and flutes, as occurs even today in China. The irrational numerical relationships of the proportions of their monuments that agree with the tempered intervals, which – with their associated symbolism once again is only completely understandable for a musical person – led me to the thought that all the civilisation of Egypt and Mesopotamia, indeed of the whole Orient, signifies a music-making in the spiritual sense. The oriental

translates the feeling for melody into lines, colours, surfaces, bodies –
that is, into space. His language of syllables with the many possibilities
of emphasis also approximates to the melodic element. Oriental writings
are as it were written music, which, read musically, have to be musically
decoded. The oriental engages himself when observing a work of art as
though listening to a melody. He is inwardly moved ("sings") with it and
in this way his "gestures", not understood by us Europeans, come into
being. All branches of knowledge are for him penetrated with music,
with melody. He experiences everything in listening, in the movement,
and it is also possible for him in every smallest, insignificant thing to see
a "world", to penetrate into the "essence". Confucius describes music as
the highest of all the arts and testifies that musical intuition is the point
of departure of oriental culture. In the Orient the first and most rigorous
test for the spirituality of a person is musicality. An unmusical person as
a spiritual dignitary would be unthinkable in the Orient.

The large-scale "music-culture" of Egypt and Mesopotamia in pre-
Christian times arrives with the little crowd of Greeks and experienced
there its transformation, which the whole of Europe was to carry until
the Great War. The Greek philosophers, Plato above all the others,
struck out on a new path. They certainly took over some of the secret
doctrines of the Egyptian priests and the cultural patterns based on
them. They tested them, however, in a biased way for their suitability
and usefulness for the conceptual life of the senses of the individual and
the race. Intuition demands a blossoming (*Aufgehen*) of the individual
into something greater, namely into that of the primal element of
everything existing which possesses a forming capacity. But when from
the beginning this spiritualised view of life is made so sensual and
conceptual that the usefulness to the individual is placed as a contrary
ideal, then contradictions, subjective opinions, personal interpretations
will arise. The Greek philosophers foundered on this rock. They were
forced to compare, to standardise, to generalise, and in order to save
something spiritual, the ideal of the personality came about on the one
hand, chance, the tragic destiny on the other hand, in short Idealism as
cultural form. This, beginning with the Greeks "lives on" even to our
time in continuous friction, disintegration, inner struggles, dissension
in the individual as well as in society. This of necessity had to lead to
a complete sensualising, to the expediency of technology, to the set
concepts and phrases, to the cult of the personality, to – a complete
lack of culture. Out of the intuitive culture of "listening" the conceptual
culture of vision, conceiving, comparing, on the place of the primal

experience in the essence of being of the most insignificant things there appeared the widespread visible, sensory, conventional ideal of beauty. In place of "melody", the "theme" appeared.

I do not want to go into details on the development of the Idealistic culture of Europe beginning with the Greeks, neither do I want to list the many martyrs of intuition in Europe, who as magicians, magi, sorcerers, cabbalists, geomancers, alchemists, astrologers, fortune-tellers, miracle doctors, spiritualists and hypnotists were maligned, scorned, martyred and killed, nor do I want to deny the real value of Idealism which lies in the social sphere, in mass suggestion, organisation and discipline of the masses. I only want to show with music how the misunderstanding of the intuitive, purely cultural element was fulfilled by the Greeks.

Only tonal music, nevertheless in its purest musical form as homophonic melody in individual groups, came from the Orient to the Greeks. But how was it taken up and used in the beginning? Employed for its usefulness, that is, according to its physiological, sensory effect! The Greek philosophers and statesmen looking on music as the means of education for the youth, only allowed the use of certain keys. In Sparta, for example, the Dorian mode (on E) was introduced. That had its evil purpose. Those who know the character of the Dorian mood will agree with me. But who in Europe knows or knew it? I will describe the character of the Dorian key in a few words, in defiance of the unmusical and therefore uneducable European music teachers and even with the danger of being branded by them as a dilettante with unimportant subjective arbitrary statements. It is wild, rough, stimulating, fluctuating, highly active like the bright red colour of the blood, of fire. With it, the youth of Sparta was educated to conduct wars, stirred up to fight, hardened, similar to how a bull is stirred up when you hold a red rag in front of it. This was the "ethos" of music with the Greeks! Even Plato did not know differently when, for the education of the somewhat finer and more noble youth of Athens, he allowed the Lydian, Phrygian and Aeolian modes, with whose intoxicating sensuality and enlivening freshness he might not have speculated in vain. That the Greeks strictly knew how to fend away any further good musical and truly artistic influence of the Orient, the following case gives enough evidence. A decree of the Ephorii of Sparta still exists, in which a certain Timotheus from Milet was threatened with banishment from the town unless he cut off five strings from his twelve-string lyre. The motivation for this ban is explained by the decree that young people would be made too soft through the over great variety of his music. That this concerns, with this twelve string lyre, the introduction of the five enharmonic notes (F#, A♭, B♭, D♭, E♭) of the tonal scale, concerning the *temperament* (which must have been already known in the Orient!), is even accepted by the painstaking collector Albert von Thimus, in his work *Die harmonikale Symbolik des Altertums*, although, as an incarnate Idealist, he does not divine the value and musical meaning of temperament and fights it in his book. Later in the time of decadence, temperament was nevertheless introduced by the Greeks, but only for purely sensual (chromatic) use. It was consequently already then regarded as an "emergency", and as a "compromise", misused and musically misunderstood.

Gothic and Baroque in Music

A characteristic phenomenon of Greek Idealism in Europe is polyphonic music. It originates from the original tendency of Idealism, of deviation from Intuition into the sensory realm, called forth by the will for power, the greed of the individual and the race. Intuition leads to melos, to the most inner experience and feeling of the *essence* of things, to the *form* in and for itself. Idealism however already proceeds from that which is formed; for it the Intuitive recognition of the idea became the Ideal, the visible, that which can be grasped. Idealism turns away from melody; it carries out tests using its sensory, conceivable, physiological *effects* on the individual, on the masses. Intuition is consequently the actual bearer of culture, whereas the (Greek) Idealism causes (European) civilisation. Both these spiritual movements in man's life, the Intuitive and the Idealistic, penetrate each other in the most varied ways in the smallest and greatest intervals of time, in the individual's life as well as that of whole peoples and races. The one leads to the highest recognition of the individual self in becoming conscious and in self-contemplation (understanding yourself), the other is effective and shines out in the deed and the will.

Viewed on their own, some of these waves result in that phenomenon in Europe which we describe as Gothic and Baroque. We can however also use the expressions Gothic and Baroque in the most extended sense for all cultural phenomena. Gothic is the movement from chaos to form, Baroque that from the formed to diversity. The Gothic is turned towards the greatness and the condition of confusion, of disintegration, of sensuousness (which is indeed expressed in the "falling", in the "gravity" of material), the Baroque proceeds from the respectively achieved form of the Gothic and organises the diversity of material. Gothic and Baroque are inseparably bound to each other. They are only to be differentiated by the stronger predominance of the one or the other movement. They determine each other. European Idealism would not be conceivable without the previous oriental Intuition, civilisation not without culture, a manifestation not without knowledge, a practice of music not without inner listening. And vice versa, terrible wars preceded the exceptionally highly intuitive Chinese culture. In retrospect, on the external form there can be measured in retrospect the height and intensity of knowledge, the rising can be measured on the descent.

I have repeatedly pointed out that melody is the real musical element; everything that distances itself from it, belongs to the noise-frontier of music. The Gothic, Intuitive movement in music leads to melody, to the experience in melos, to the highest form. The Baroque, Idealistic life-movement belongs to the performing of melody, its realisation, its effect on the senses. Since a chaos of some kind of assault always precedes the Gothic experience, and since the reverse – the once achieved form of Gothic experience, melody, shows again the structure of the material from which it originally grew – then we have to be able to recognise, as original chaos, the noise of sound in tonal melody (with its overtone structure, the overtone intervals) and noise as such for atonal melody (all the endlessly many intervals, the "structure" of *totality*). For music the noise of the material is what for the builder is the heaviness, strength and texture of the building material. The form lies in the way of overcoming these moments.

We have to look in the Orient for the great Intuitive ascent of tonal music. Tonal melody in its complete form already came to Greece. At the beginning of the Middle Ages it still remained in single-voice tonal melody in the various keys. But later the decay went so far that people did not understand them as melody (could not grasp its *melos* any more) but only perceived the sensory effect of its succession of notes (with their overtones, that is, the series of overtone *chords* of the notes). The *faburden*! This was the chaos of polyphonic music, its sensory assumption! That it went so far in Europe, lies in our Idealistic leaning (always turning away from Intuition), to misunderstand the musical element (in which only the moment of movement in the interval, melos, that which follows one after the other, plays a role) and profanes it to pure sensory effects, to noise, to the material element, to juxtaposition, to the "conceivable". It does not remain with the faburden, with this pronounced parallelism. In time the joke would be too simple. Moreover, avoiding parallel octaves, fifths and fourths and retaining faburdens of thirds and sixths, there came later contrary movement of voices, counterpoint, which finds its model – completely corresponding to the once begun direction – in the laws of space of the visual arts. The overtone series, its structure, the physiological element in it became – as spatial image – the point of departure for part-writing. In this way a music for the eyes came about, which naturally in the first instance has to be conceived spatially. Once again corresponding completely, melody sank down to theme (*cantus firmus, dux, comes*), interludes, to imitation, variation, to spatial concepts like diminution and augmentation and to the absolutely unmusical, pictorial-like inversion of themes. A thousand handholds, partially taken from the visual arts, which tiresome experience and tradition ("trade secrets"), the feeling for concord and discord, pleasant and unpleasant [sounds], satisfying and unsatisfying (that is, things which with pure music may not play for a moment even the slightest role!), in short, the purely sensory, physiological nature of listening with which the ears are misused merely as an organ of touch, to "grasp", during the course of centuries set up that chaos up to which the Intuitive musician repeatedly has to face, in order out of the turmoil of some rules and a hundred exceptions, to make "music". With each new musician the exceptions increased, till finally in our time only exceptions exist and actually everything is allowed. What a crude misunderstanding of the musical element! I have to say to European humanity, to its face, that there is no polyphonic music, only noise organised into several voices! This reminds me of the story of the Arab for whom a professor of music wanted to play on the piano a busy fugal prelude. "Stop! Slow down! We have time! One song at a time please," said the Arab. Of course the European smiled, proud of his "musical" superiority.

I see some Pharisees approaching me with the question, "Now what do you say then about our classical composers, eh?" My answer is, the masters, despite counterpoint, theory of harmony, *according to the chaos* with which they had to deal, for their time wrote the best possible music and consequently were also ignored or despised by their contemporaries. During the course of my life and during my thorough studies I became acquainted with all their stations of suffering, lived through them and have arrived at the realisation that it does not so very much depend on what they have actually written in their miserable existence, but with them upon that which can be read between the notes, between the lines – and this is with all proper musicians, with all genuine artists always the interpretation of melos.

Do I have now to tell of the smaller hills and dales of the Gothic and Baroque waves, from the first musical highest achievement within the tonal realm of the use of scales, of Palestrina, from the ever stronger emphasis of Baroque degeneration, of the major and minor system with its prominent sensory and unmusical non-entities of concord and discord, from the last great Gothic upsurge within this, of the *Well-tempered Clavier*, the form-giving importance for the Baroque masters of the symphony, Haydn and Mozart? Do I have to describe that after the appearance of the *Well-tempered Clavier*, that is, after the perfection of form which ended tonal music, the Kapellmeister Josef Fux wrote his *Gradus ad Parnassum*, in which he ignores the *Well-tempered Clavier*, once again warming up the coals of counterpoint so that this textbook later on was revised by a certain Bellermann and is still used in music schools today, although in the meantime Hugo Riemann has written a quite excellent *Analysis of the Well-tempered Clavier* which mostly points to the musical matters. Or if I should speak of opera at all, that unique example of comedy and noise, in which now and then out of sheer "desire to squander beauty" the masters (to which I do not by the way count Wagner and those decadents) have contributed by mistake a couple of genuine melodies? Do I have to report on romanticism, on Beethoven, on modern music that today is experiencing its complete breakdown, or, to conclude, should I mention those smallest waves of Gothic and Baroque creating that can be recognised within the creations of the individual or indeed within a single work?

In spite of everything, the modern, mundane "music-malaise" of the noise-producing chord forms the greatest mistake of all the centuries, the terrible chaos of the times, which can only be mitigated through *"listening"* to atonal melody.

Melos-culture

Even when one single atonal melody was formed, it already showed its own particular laws which allow neither linguistic nor any other principles to influence it in the slightest. In its formed state it becomes the utmost perfection itself, the concept of everything cultural. It contains *Ethos* (this time, however, in the true sense of the word, the opposite of *Pathos*), the element liberating from all incidental, sensory, emotional, and pathological factors; it takes up the challenge of totality, of the strongest, most mighty chaos. Its variety is remarkable. Imagine a musical person is able to distinguish one single atonal melody as pure musical form from 500,000,000 possibilities. Similar to the steel that is magnetised, is the musical person, the gifted person – that means, one who is equipped with a comprehensive capacity to conceptualise, a strong imagination, but also a well-organised brain. The force certainly is present in him, but only Intuition, knowledge, illumination by the atonal melody orders the molecular forces to the poles of Idealistic effectiveness. In any art, what the actual creative, spiritual, formal principle is, lies in the musical element, in the melody, that is, in the moment of movement. Everything else in the arts is unfruitful and is like the material noise in music. Every atonal melody is a "world" in itself, a closed form, but which allows itself as an organic part to be included in other, greater forms. The point of departure of atonal melody is (pure) melos, the respective juxtaposition of well-tempered intervals. In melos, rhythm is already present, that is, each of the possible combinations possesses its very own connecting emphases – must possess, or should they all be sung in the same tempo, with the same agogic and dynamic shading? Whoever once in his or her life has interpreted an atonal melody – and certainly everyone who wants completely to enter into the contents of this book must have done this – will become aware of the frankly cunning laws of intuition, of the purely musical element; dead matter acquires life, the resting side by side in space acquires movement in the succession of time. Atonal melody sings the life of speech, the visual arts, but also that of nature – the universe. It is the purest, clearest source of recognition and of knowledge, of form and movement itself.

In creating atonal melody the Intuitive (Gothic) is expressed in the laying hold of melos as an organic whole, as a unity. The rhythmic division of this unity of form is already the Idealistic (Baroque) tendency, which practices its effects on the senses, that is, "beautiful" in the customary sense. In atonal melody the most extreme pole of our spiritual life is incorporated: from highest knowledge to the most comprehensive manifestation; from Intuition to Idealism; Gothic vital movement to Baroque vital movement; and the apparition of madness to crime. Only in music is it possible so to unite both poles that it has one form directly understandable by everybody on the earth, only in atonal melody are Intuition and Idealism completely able to be held in balance. And this lies in the nature of Intuition, which is only possible when everything material is shut out – spatial considerations, dead things, restrictions, the sensory world, and emotional states. Music is the least "weighted down" by matter, its sounds (noises) permit themselves through equal temperament to be put down in unreal schemes (dots) which say nothing in themselves, so that from the beginning there remain only the intervals, the moment of movement of melos. With the other arts, Intuition is only possible in a transferred sense – through the agency of melody, the musical element –, because it is too strongly subject to the Idealistic, already formed, conceptual element, of objects, but mainly to the spatial, to matter, and consequently does not allow to thrive the moment of movement, the musical Intuition – and only one such exists. In the Orient everything cultural is musically conceived and consequently there exists a more heartfelt connection of the cultural life with Intuition, the musical element. In Europe the purely musical element has been missing all along; consequently also no Intuitive culture has existed – and this actually means no culture at all.

Intuition, the specifically musical faculty in man, can only find its expression as perfected form, generally comprehensible, in atonal melody. Whereas the ascending, Intuitive, Gothic tendency to highest knowledge of form in melos is only possible in music; the descending, Idealistic, Baroque tendency is towards rhythm, towards emphasis (*BeTONung*), to sound (*Ton*), noise, to variety of material. On this path atonal melody with its immeasurable richness of possibilities meets the other arts, but also the European forms of culture. It would be impossible, for example, to conceive an atonal melody out of a European linguistic work of art, that is, to set it atonally. But it is quite conceivable that an already formed atonal melody fructifies the linguistic and pictorial realm, that the melody is "poetised", painted, chiselled, built. The elements of the other arts (colours, vowels, consonants, proportions, angles, curves, structure of material) are absolutely to be found in melody. They are *anchored* in the melodic element, *in the movement itself* (through its moment of movement!); melos is its "meaning".

This is the decisive thing between the Intuitive and the Idealistic conceptions. The musical, absolutely gifted person conceives out of melos; the unmusical, constrained, limited person, conceives from the rhythmical element, moments of noise, by matter, by spatial concepts, by the sensory, erotic, emotional aspects, by intellectual and conceptual considerations, be he musician, poet, philosopher, painter, sculptor or architect. Melos is the purely spiritual element; rhythm already approaches the material sphere. The rhythm of atonal melody, however, is so varied – because it comes from melos! –, that the possibilities of all the arts find a place in it. For this reason atonal music cannot adapt itself to any other art; a whole cannot become subject to its parts, the mobile and vital to the resting and "dead", strength and cause to the effect. The Chinese artist – whether poet or painter – in the first place conceives the melody and then "poetizes" it with his melodic language of syllables, paints it with his Intuitive writing. Every oriental artist, philosopher, is quite certainly in the first place a musician, a "follower of the muses", a melodist, whereas in Europe itself the "musician" was in the first place a producer of rhythms, of noise, that is, a tone-poet, a tone-painter.

Through the discovery of atonal melody the purely musical, Intuitive principle has given Europe a perspective which of necessity must manifest in some sort of fruitful, purifying way on everything purely cultural. From this, no artist, no thinker can exclude himself. We shall not proceed a step further with the rigid, instinctive art of emotional effects, with concepts in thinking which ignore the spiritual element – the atonal melody. It has to do now only with how atonal melody – in its realisation already a new concept, the Ideal – could be built into our cultural life. Without doubt a time will come when for the artist nothing will remain but to conceive purely musically, Intuitively, from melos. Atonal melody demands nothing technical, drilled, complicated, to do with craft, in short, nothing but the musical element. Indeed, it makes it impossible for unmusical "musicians" to make a business out of it. Everyone can easily judge from atonal melody whether he is really musical, that means, whether he is a spiritual human being. Atonal melody does not tolerate empty activity, and – heaven be praised – it soon become too insipidly boring for the unmusical person proceeding from the unmusical, intoxicating effects and crude sensory delights proceeding from polyphonic, organised noise. He decides against it, and this is the most sensible thing that he can do. In this consists our cultural emptiness and mendacity, that we want continually to make compromises. No, here we have to do with a once-and-for-all either-or.

The culture of music today, the entire culture of Europe has now become an art of *interpretation*, the conveying of the purely spiritual, of "*writing*" in the truest sense. The variety of atonal melos is an inexhaustible spring for musicians, poets and thinkers, for the visual arts. Since atonal melody, for itself alone, is intelligible to all the spiritual – and that is musical – people of the earth, it can consequently serve as the "universal language", as a mutual means of understanding, as the basis for the other arts, which through it are able to move more freely, relying less on the limitations of both the conceptual approach and of things, objects.

Goethe's Theory of Colours

The sciences of experience have all along rejected Goethe's *Theory of Colours* and what we call the spiritual sciences have never known how rightly to deal with it. Goethe himself is supposed to have said that his *Theory of Colours* was his best work. Besides this, a few literary people talk foolishly about the *Theory of Colours*. In this way hitherto the "people of the poets and thinkers" are faced by the favourite work of one of its greatest spirits – powerless and without comprehension!

The honest investigator of nature becomes conscientiously engaged with a subject and everything that he cannot "comprehend" he prudently leaves to one side. He is the craftsman at work, the thorough professional on whom we can rely, but who will also abandon us when it concerns new ways. He works out of his instincts, without actual spiritual control and his importance lies in whether he can or cannot confirm out of his experience something conceived purely spiritually.

Goethe gave this ponderous science of experience which is subject to the laws of matter a tremendous "push" forwards, and has drawn its attention and its ability to differentiate towards those points which contributed essentially towards its own existence. We can think about Goethe's observations and physical experiments as we like, can reject his hypotheses or ridicule them; one thing they certainly have offered – the stimulus towards new methods of research. I have to cite my own case as an example.[4] Acoustics knows no more of tone-colour (*Klangfarbe*) than that it is decided by the number and pitch of the overtones. This can be found in any book on physics and with this people are satisfied. Now as a musician, I arrive with the interval, the melos, and explain the sound with its overtone-series simply as noise, of some kind of sensory quantity and quality. But *tone*-colour (*KLANGfarbe*) – if we can talk at all about such a thing in physics – I place in the intervals. A more strongly prominent, or the highest strongest perceptible overtone, forms a series with its keynote, because only this interval can be laid hold of purely musically. Without intervals, without melos there would be no music, but only a (rhythmical) noise. Consequently, physics may either not speak of *tone*-colour (*KLANGfarbe*) but only of noise, of tone-noise, or my assumption of the more strongly prominent overtone with its intervallic relationship to the keynote is correct. So far perhaps the empiricist can follow me, for he knows that the sounds of the instruments show different complexes of vibrations, which form the basis for an interpretation along my lines. But now I go further

---

4   Josef Hauer. *Vom Wesen des Musikalischen*. Robert Lienau. Berlin-Lichterfelde. 1966.

directly from Intuition into the realm of experience and observe, for example, that the ninth overtone is the decisive one for the violin, which is why its sound itself points to the tone-colour character of melos of the major second. Here two worlds confront each other, Intuition and experience; that I know very well. Up to now no physicist has stirred, for understandable reasons. Up to now no one has discriminated so finely, and at the moment there is no money to construct the equipment for the exact research into the overtone series of the different instruments. But let us assume that such an apparatus were already constructed and the results of experiments with good violins conclude that I have been in error. I would simply admit to have been led into error by my purely musical view of tone-colour, but from that moment would reject the sounds as such as pure sensory noise, which would deny from the beginning every *musical* character. The physicist then may no longer speak of the "'sound"-colour ("*Klang"farbe*), but in the case of the violin, at most from a sensory, especially delightful quality of noise, through which the musician is in fact mislead and into it places the light, intoxicating tone-colour character of melos, of the major second.

The case with Goethe is similar. Even if he should have been mislead a hundred times into such suppositions, this still does not concern the essence of his *Theory of Colours*, which touches realms that natural science does not reach. Goethe ignored mathematics, and this surely to the detriment of his *Theory of Colours*. But if you look into my theory of intervals you will find some suggestions with the help of the diagrams. You will also – even mathematically! – understand why Goethe speaks of the plus and minus side of colours, which for its part was taken amiss by the Newtonians. Through my theory of intervals several riddles in natural science are solved, because the musical element in man, Intuition, effects an impartial penetration into the essence of things than does the purely visual, Idealism.

Goethe, as the majority of Europeans, was a thoroughly visual person, an "Idealist"; *idein*—to see. He conceived spatially, conceptually, Idealistically, from the emotions, the senses, the erotic side, from the side of language and thought. In his *Theory of Colours*, however, he faces a problem, which is no longer soluble in the Idealistic conception alone, in the realm of movement itself, in the musical, Intuitive element. It is understandable that his musically estranged European society could not follow him, but it is also astonishing how this spirit knew how to move with decency and dignity in spheres in which it was not at home. Goethe's *Theory of Colours* is completely out of step, in the good sense, with the European manner. Goethe comes in his *Theory of Colours* as far as a visual person can penetrate into knowledge of the moment of movement, into the essence of things. It is noticeable that this spirit apparently so fixed, closed in himself, leaves his high pedestal, the sure ground of his art, and ventures into areas whose cultivation offers him no laurels. But it is precisely this initiative that for our time – which no longer stands in the sign of what is linguistic and Ideal but in the musical, Intuitive ideal – makes him so interesting and valuable. For what Goethe attempts in his *Theory of Colours* can only be completely solved and understood musically.

If we want to "enlighten" a European concerning the essence of the musical element, we have to approach him with concepts, ideas, Ideals. Well, pure musical, Intuitive, non-spatial, non-resting, immaterial, spiritual, living, movement itself is to be found *in the melos of atonal melody*. Everything else – colours, vowels, words, rhythm, and so on and so on – everything can be spiritually interpreted from pure melos; melos is the archetypal form of what is spiritual. Languages – and there are many – are daughters of melos, generated with the thoughts that the archetypally pure melodic element, the vowels and singing element of language, are rhythmically interpreted, emphasised (*beTONt*), accentuated, have been brought nearer to the moment of noise, the consonantal, notional, conceptual, material, spatial element. Now, a formed language – it could even be Chinese, which of all languages of the earth is the most melodic, most capable of intonation, that means, however, also the most spiritual, most rich in meaning, which is the least materialised, grown rigid, "dead", which resisted the longest the confusion from the tower of Babel, greediness and power, the national element – even this Chinese, compared with the "eternal", "unending" melos with its unlimited rhythmic possibilities of interpretation of thought, is a limitation, a narrowing. Goethe was caught up in the linguistic, conceptual, thought element, in the one-sided interpretation of melos conceived by the Greeks, and in 1800 still very incompletely explained by the researcher. He was the type of European who was a cultivated Hellenist, a civilised Roman, and as such – together with that spiritual impossibility, the "philosophers" – has burdened his conscience with many bad habits of our time. In reality, however, he could not understand a *Hölderlin*. Hölderlin, one of the most musical, spiritual people of Europe, had to fail because he did not find melos, pure movement, from the thinking-conceptual element of language, from that interpretation of the Greeks about which he was so enthusiastic, overwhelmed by it – as were several others after him. This was the greatest spiritual problem of the nineteenth century, this searching – amidst convulsions – after the archetypal, purely spiritual element, from which all languages proceed, to which all poetising and thinking is subject, after pure melos, after the moment of movement in things, after Intuition, after movement itself. In this battering against the Greek Idealistic wall – not against the Chinese walls: these open of themselves to the impartial and pure – shattered our strongest spirits, or they crouched before it like people thrown out.

Only Goethe, in a somewhat happier way, knew how to withdraw from this affair. Instinctively he took flight in the world of colours, to that which, it is true, is still spatial, resting, material appearance, but which stands the nearest to the immaterial ("etheric") of melos, movement, the purely musical, Intuition. I have included the essential passages of Goethe's *Theory of Colours* in my book *Vom Wesen des Musikalischen* ['The essence of music'], and left the rest to the "dogs". What Goethe says about the rainbow, the totality of colours, about the individual colours, is documentary for the whole spiritual history of Europe, even if it is not decisive. Let no one imagine that, as a purely Intuitive musician, I found it necessary to study Goethe's *Theory of Colours* in order as it were to be able to pick up something. The conception and writing of my theory of tone-colours was already tied up, even in its details, before I got to know Goethe's *Theory of Colours*. Of course, I was astonished and overjoyed at the same time to discover that my interpretation of melos of the individual intervals concerning colours agreed with Goethe's account of the moment of movement of colours, that he – following further on the way of intuition already begun – also came to the totality and the natural limits of the rainbow, to things which the musician initially chances upon, but once again are only able to be completely understood by musical people. You would think that after the appearance of Goethe's *Theory of Colours* painting would have begun an ascent, whereas in fact the exact opposite happened, it became engrossed with objects, became materialised. Why? Because colour is bound to the object, because the Intuitive, the moment of movement of colour – without object – does not find its complete, generally understood expression in painting, but solely in music, in melos. *Only proceeding from melos can you paint, interpret and "write" free from objects.* Consequently the enormous achievement of Goethe's *Theory of Colours* – from the spiritual-scientific standpoint – were ineffective for practical artistic life. Nevertheless, after pure melos has been found in atonal melody, these treasures can now be unearthed, and no Intuitive painter – who is occupied with the interpretation of atonal melos through the "script" of painting – will neglect spiritually to make Goethe's interpretation his own. There is nothing for it: when you want to interpret as a painter the melos of the minor sixth, that mournful, austere, anxious, yielding, full of longing, romantic interval, then you have to present it with blue, "cerulean" blue. This symbolism, the interpretation of melos through the "script" of the rhythmical element, of emphasis, of shades of colour, of the linguistic-conceptual element, of proportions, angles, curves, numbers, this interpretation of the immaterial, movement in the succession of time through the spatial, material signs of scripts, is genuine, real spiritual science. Against this, our European "pigeon-holes" with their dusty collections of music, books and collections of art, with their "business with scraps of paper" are like mortuaries and vaults in which spiritual life can never ever appear. So long as the world has existed, every spiritual person has been concerned with interpreting this primal form of movement, which now for the first time in Europe is embodied in atonal melos with its many-sidedness. And Goethe unconsciously attempted the first interpretation of melos in his *Theory of Colours*. Thereby he also partly came to know the spiritual need of someone who through millennia-long tradition, through his own prejudice and frenzied possession, wants to arrive into the pure sacrosanct, archetypal fields by traversing through a chaos erected by millions of others. In Goethe, someone who ends the whole Greek-European linguistic-Idealism has been found, but someone who for our time, orientated according to the purely musical element, is its forerunner.

Melos and Language

In my essays, when I speak about the highest spirituality that can be achieved by human beings, of the highest knowledge in the laying hold of pure melos, there is no need for a cognoscente of the gospels, nor a theologian, least of all a philosopher, to get agitated. I always speak briefly and to the point of human possibilities of ideation, of what the human being with his five senses at any time can control and grasp. I do not speak of that "spirit", the "only one" for emotional and fanatic people, nor of the Lord God, of His revelation and grace, but only about what the human being can lay hold of through thinking and feeling, by recognising and willing, through his imagination and its control through reason, through sensing and doing, Intuition and Idealism, and finally his ability to "comprehend". Actually I would have to write a new critique of knowledge which includes the musical realm of ideation, but in what language shall I present it? I know of only one, atonal melody. To deal completely with melos, to interpret it, several hundred years will pass, several thousand people will have to be occupied with it, and then one day when everything is over, finished, dead, then those people who call themselves philosophers can appear. My essays are only intended to draw the attention of the white races to what so far was strange to it, and that is the purely musical element in the human being. In these essays, in which I am forced to take a stand against all European cultural institutions, I use the expressions spiritual-bodily, musical-sensory, and so on, neither poetically nor absolutely but in the sense of contrary forms of movement. Everything about which I unfortunately have to write exists in atonal melos. This purely musical, purely spiritual element, however, is buried in such a way by the European cultural machinery, by its make-up, that in the first place I am forced to sift the grains of gold, the diamonds, from the mud.

If we recognise atonal melos as the purest form of movement, as movement itself, then everything else which somehow distances itself from it has to come nearer to material "movement", towards the bodily aspect, what is still, dead. It is also a fact that an unmusical person, that is, someone who does not possess spiritual movement within himself, who is not inwardly tremendously alive, full of imagination, awake, prepared to receive, talented, is creatively active, to whom the one case within a million possibilities which faces him does not say anything special, valid only for this case, that such a person faces atonal melos indifferently. It appears to him as arbitrary, chaotic, as a nothingness. Because there is nowhere on to which his instincts, his feeling can latch, he slides down and stands at a loss facing the purely spiritual, immaterial element. He cannot interpret the appearance, cannot come near to it rhythmically or melodically as a spiritual, organic entity. Interpretation, the rhythmical division of pure melos, of the atonal – for only this is free of all sensory elements – is a thoroughly spiritual act, the only one which exists in the scientific and artistic life of man. Opposing the interpretation of melos everything else deals with instinct, with the unconscious. Pure melos is like a magic mirror in which all the conceivable events of the world are to be seen. For a musical person melos is the telling of a story, a myth, an epic, in which the visible, spatial events grow out of the invisible, audible, through the rhythmical division of melos, through emphasis ("*BeTONung*") which brings him materially and physiologically into contact with the spiritual course of events, and places the further interpretation, thinking in visible terms, conceptual movement, gestures, the sound-gestures, *"language"* on his tongue.

This interpretative listening is the archetypally creative activity in the human being. Interpretation, thinking, speech and myth have their common root in melos. Melos is the "restlessness", the *"perpetuum mobile* [perpetual motion]" in the creative person. It must have been musical, intuitive people, singers, poets, thinkers in the true sense, who formed languages and myths, which the spiritual element in melos *composed* (*verDICHTETEN* = also lit. "condensed"), who, out of the physiological possibilities of producing sounds, sang *the sense*, recited (Got. *siggwan* = to sing, to read), heard, interpreted, indeed, interpreted and composed the meaning. Originally language was an inarticulate whimpering, singing, yodelling, gurgling, smacking of the lips, a stammering with syllables as small children do, the meaning of which is then comprehended by the intuitive, musical human being, articulated, rhythmically divided, conceptually interpreted. A human being who hears pure melos, takes part in the whole process from the first beginning of movement to its fully graspable elucidation in the spatial, conceptual world of objects; thereby are exerted all his spiritual forces – all that possibly exists and can exist. Only the musical, intuitive person experiences the world, the other person instinctively vegetates like the beasts; the spiritual half is missing. The musician in the true sense is his own creator of language and myth.

I would like still to indicate that moments of movement exist in language as in writing, which are understandable to all people on the earth: *i* (ee) and *u* (oo) are opposites, as in *oben - unten, spitz - stumpf, eckig - rund, licht - dunkel, weiss - schwarz, glänzend* (silver) - *matt* (dull); *e* (a), *o* (u), *eu* (u), *o* (ŏ) I feel on the passive, negative, cold, green-blue minus side, *ü*, *ai* (ei), *a* (ah), *au* (au) on the active, positive, warm, yellow-red plus side, the call 'oh' and 'ah' make this difference recognisable, moreover: *Meer, See, Ebene, Schnee, Kälte,* öde, *Heu, Fäulnis, Moos, Moor, hohl, tot, dürr, blühen, glühen, Frühling, heiss, reif, scheinen, warm, Flamme, Strahl, Glanz, braun, lau,* Skrt *usra* = red-brown, Skrt *hari* = yellowish; the protrusions of B and P are characterised through the words *Becken, Backe, backen, bähen, Bai, Balg, Ball, Apfel, Birne, Polster, Bann, Bau* (Old Indian *bhumi* = earth), *Bauch* (rounding), *bäumen, Baum, bauschen, Berg, Bett, Beule, beugen, biegen, bilden, blähen, blasen, bluhen, Blume, blöken, Bucht, Boden, Bogen, Bolle, Bombe, Born, Börse, Buch, Buckel, bücken, Bug, Bügel, Bühel, Bund, Bürde, Burg, Busen, Kopf, Koppe, Kuppel, Picke, Pilz, Pack, Panzer, pausbäckig, Beere, Perle, platzen, plötzlich, Pol, Pomp, Pracht, Prunk, prahlen, prangen, protzen, Punkt, oder,* über, *bin* (Skrt word *blu* = become); the indicative aspect in T t d is expressed in *Adel, edel, da, danken, denken, Datum,* Skrt *tantus* = thread, *deuten, dichten, Distil, Docht, Dolch, Dorn, dringen, der, die, das, dir, dich, du* (Sankt *tvam*), *Gitter, Kette, -tum, Lanze, Stab, Stachel, Licht, schneiden, Mitte, Nadel, Ort, sitzen, spitz, Stadt, stechen* (Skrt *tigma* = pointed), *stehen, Stern* (Skrt *stha*), *steigen* (Skrt *stigh* = walking), *stoßen, Stern* (Skrt *star*), *Stiel, stellen, Strahl* (arrow), *streiten* (Skrt *sridh* = fiend), *Tadel, Tag* (Sankt *dina*, to the word *dah* = burning), *tanzen, tasten, Tatze, tauchen, tunken, ducken, taufen, tief, tun* (Skrt *dha*), *tippen, Trotz, Zacke, Zinke, Zahn, Zange, zanken, Zapfen, Zaun, Zehe, Zeichen, seigen, seihen, Zepter, Zeit* (ancient German root *ti*), *zerren, ziehen, Ziel, Zipfel, Zunge, zu*; we find the expanding of F and V in *Dampf, Duft, dumpf, Eifer, Fanden, fahen, Fahne, fahren, fangen, Faser, fassen, faul, Feder, Fee, fegen, feilen, Feim, fein, Feld, Fell, fern, feucht, Feuer, Fieber, Filz, finden, flach, Flamme, flattern, Flaum, flechten, fliegen, fliehen, fliessen, flimmen, flittern, flimmern, Flocke, Flor, flüstern, Flut, Föhn, fort, frei, freuen, froh, fühlen, führen, fluchen, verfolgen, voll, füllen, Funken, Furche, fürchten, Furt, Luft, paffen, Pfeife, Pfeil, schlafen, viel, vor, für, von, ver-*; the letter forms K and G are symbolical for *Angel, ackern, Anker, Axt, Egge, Gaumen, Gier, begehren, ge-* (indicates joining together, completing), *gegen, gehen, Hacke, Haken, Kalk, Kampf, Kante, Kap, karg, keck, Keil, Kerker, Kern, Korn, Kkeule, kauen, Kiefer, Kinn, Kiel, Kies, Kiesel, klingen, knacken, knicken, Knie, Kegel, Kogel, Körper, kalt, kühl, kühn, merken, Ocker, Quader, Quadrat, Quarz, quer, schlagen, Zucker* (Sankt *carkara* = gravel, fine sand), (Ind. *khanda* = piece); we find the moment of movement of H: *Haar, Halle, Hölle, hauchen, Haus, Hut, Heil, heilig, Hülse, hohl, hell, hallen, hehr, Himmel, hie, hin, hoch, Höhe, hoffen, hören,* Skrt *hu* = sacrificially revering (God), *ich* (Skrt *aham*), *-heit, Uhr* (Lat. *hora* = hour), *heiter, keuchen, lachen, Loch, rauchen, riechen, Schlauch*; the J in: *ja, jach, jauchzen, juchzen, jubeln, Jugend, jung* (Skrt *yuvan*), *Jux* (Lat. *jocus* = joy), *Julfest, just* (Lat. *justus* = just, right, cf. *jungere* = bind, Sankt *ju*); the L in: *Leim, Lehm, fallen, glatt, Lack* (Skrt *laksa*), *laden, Last, liegen, lahm, Land, lang, Lab, laben, lax, leben, lecken* (Skrt *lih*), *leer* (Got. *lasiws* = weak), *Geleis, leisten, lehren, lernen, -lei, -lich, Leiche, Fleisch* (root *lih*), *leiden, Leid, leicht,* Lat. *liquor, liquere* = to be fluid, *Lende, lenken, lesen, Lein, Linie,* (Lat. *linum* = line, or thread), *licht, lieben* (Sankt *lubh* = strongly demand), *loben, geloben, glauben, ledig, gelind, los, lösen, Luft,* Öl, *Galle, Quelle, rollen*; the in: Sankt *mani* = string of pearls, *klammern, Gummi, Magen, mögen, vermögend,*

Macht, mahlen, Mulm, Müll, malmen, Mühle, Lat. *majus, magnus* = great (actually mighty), *Majestät, Mal, malen, Malz, Mammon, Masse, Menge, Mus, mästen, matt, müde, Meer, Moor, mein, mir, mich* (Sankt *ma*), *Mass, Milch, Molke,* Met (Sankt *madhu* = honey), *Moder, Mutter, nehmen, Schlamm, um-;* the N in: *Nacht, nüchtern, nach, nackt* (undressed), *Narr* (unreasonable), *Neid, nein, nörgeln, Nessel, nicht, nichts, nie, nieder, niemand, nimmer, nirgends, weder - noch, Not, null, nur, ohne, un-;* the rrr in: *Arbeit,* ärgern, *bohren, Borste, Bürste, brennen, braten, brechen, Bremse, Brust, drehen, dringen, drücken, graben, grob, krachen, Kraft, krallen, rackern, Rad, rauh, recken, reisen, reissen, reiten, reiben, reuten, roden, Rinde, Rippe, ritzen, roh, rollen, rühren, scharren, stark, streuen, streifen, trennen, Zorn;* the S in: *Blitz, brausen, Dunst,* Indo-Germ. word *as* = burning, *Eis, giessen, Glanz, Glas, gleissen, heiss, knistern, leise, lesen, sammeln, suchen, Nessel, prasseln, rösten, sagen, sägen, Sand, sanft, sausen, sehen, sehnen, seihen, Seil* (Sankt word *si* = bind), *senden, singen, Sense, seiden, Silber, sinnen, Sonne* (Sankt *svar*), *sorgen, summen, Sohn* (Sankt *sunu, su* = give birth); the sch in: *rauschen, kreischen, löschen, pantschen, schallen, rascheln, scnaben, schöpfen, schaudern, Schaum, scheuchen, scheuern, schiesen, schleifen, schliefen, Schlitten, schmecken, schmoren, schnauben, schnaufen, schreien, schütten, schwirren, spinnen, spritzen, sprudeln, spruhen, spülen;* the w in *wabern, wallen, wachsen, wild, wenden, walten, wieder, weben* (Sankt *vabh*), *wippen, wogen, wiegen, Weg, Welle* (Sankt *urmi*), *wallen wehen* (Sankt *va*), *werden, Weh, weinen, wehren, Wesen* (Sankt *vas* = remain), *wirken* (Zend *verez*), *werben, Wetter, wohnen* (Got. *wunan* = be happy, Sankt *van* = to love), *Wonne, wünschen, wissen* (Sankt *veda*), *wohl, wohlan, wollen* (Sankt *var* = choose), *wann, warum, was, welch, wer, wes, wie, wo, schweben, schwimmen, schwingen, Woche, Wechsel, walken* (Sankt *valg* = to move by hopping). The *moment of movement* in the interval (in colour, in the vowels, consonants, in the curve, proportion) can say everything and build a "world" for the poet, thinker, painter and musician. The individual arts can certainly not get out of their "skin", but through melos, through movement in itself, they become purified, illumined.

Nobody need be deterred by my attempt at a linguistic interpretation of melos, and it even may have totally failed. I did not state that my interpretations, even the musical, rhythmical ones, are necessarily the right ones, although always (and with everything) I keep in sight (hearing) all possibilities, the totality, and through this have refined my material nature (the aesthetic side) in such a way that a cruder error is almost out of the question. Anybody is free to do it better, and I will be the first person who will joyfully acknowledge this. The spring of melos out of which I have drawn is there for everybody. Everybody consequently can spiritually check it. Like myself, you can place yourself before the "nothingness" and wait if something starts to move within you. Do not unlimited possibilities of interpretation exist? But those who absolutely do not want to approach the spring, to the "fountain of wisdom", to the making conscious in interpretation, may stay with their crude art of instinct and emotional states (*Affekt*), whose roots we have to thank the Greek misunderstanding and non-understanding of melos. The Greeks produced for us the strongest emotional form of art, the tragedy, with the direct speech of the people acting, borne out of the *pathos*, the "faburden", the "noise-orchestra" of speech, which slowly kills its original progenitor, melos. A people who invented the problem – tragedy should not have deserved any language – although it was precisely the formed speech which has forgotten melos which made the Greek theatre possible. But the Greeks were the first who misused speech in the drama. In addition to all this evil there still developed with us in Europe the opera, which completely smothers the musical, intuitive element in the human being.

The Greek theatre is the typical appearance of the Idealism of speech, which is a *one-sided* interpretation of melos, inclining towards the physiological, thinking-conceptual element. In the Orient, where that highest knowledge in melos ("T A O"), that archetypal unchanging element in melody, that source out of which language and all the arts draw, where the archetypal form of movement itself is never lost out of sight (hearing!), in the Orient an appearance like the Greek theatre would have been unthinkable. The Greeks did the same to everything. The intuitively acquired and formed knowledge of the oriental people were taken over by them, and – without checking at their root, without the purifying influence of the musical element, without the continuous radiation through melos, through the archetypal part of movement – were simply used for its Idealistic effect. The untouchable, unmovable, ever freshly creating element in melos was forgotten, or never understood, and only the one interpretation, language – with its limited melody, its limited rhythm, its conceivable-conceptual character, in which the tendencies of the nation were reflected – became the norm, seen as the ideal and now employed in the service of the society united by that language – useful and biased. We can say that melos (the atonal) is the common possession of all, formed speech – the one-sided interpretation of melos – is but a part of people. Atonal melody as well has of course its Idealistic, sensory manifesting side, but it can only be effective in the sense-world when it first is conceived spiritually and musically. The conceptual, the already thought-out, the formed, the physical content of language is missing from the beginning, so that an unmusical, unspiritual person cannot be reached by the atonal melody. But for this reason it is also protected from every misuse. Formed speech, which is a one-sided interpretation of melos, directed towards the climatic, practical side, can work on the masses. With this we have laid hold of the root of Greek Idealism, which is built up on the usefulness of speech – and also out of tonal music arising out of the rhythm of speech and the dance – for sensory effect on the masses. The Greek theatre was a national, heathen, religious affair by which the big animal, that monster which grew into the "state", by which the national reproducing and maintaining organism proclaimed its will to the folk and under certain restraints celebrated its orgies. The theatre, Greek art in general, was geared to this, to the one-sided educative, tendentious influence on the masses facing the people's animalistic life of urges. It was a means to an end and conceived out of the Idea, from myth. The Greeks could not conceive of melos, those tremendous possibilities which have to be repeatedly freshly created and interpreted by every person; consequently they were subject to the single interpretation and creation in their myth. Their culture is a more or less realisable exposition of this myth and its ideas. The inner connection between myth-creating and the musical element, and the purely musical itself, Intuition, was missing with the Greeks. Somewhere, at sometime, these myths must have made their beginning, these stories of good and evil spirits, their deeds, forms and so on, this interpretation of transactions, *Affekte* [emotional states] in man, of the daemons. They must have derived from the Intuitive, that is "listening", musical peoples of the Orient. Perhaps Orpheus, too, was a creator of the Greek language and myth; Orpheus, who understood nature, the animals – namely people, as long as they still did not possess articulate speech. To him nature, too, the animals listened and obeyed – again the people who, because of his articulate, rhythmically formed speech, his telling of myths, epics, interpretations, venerated him as a higher being, who communed with spirits and gods. Just as everything was finished and beautifully constructed, just when out of the animal human beings slowly evolved, the "philosophers" arrived, who no longer understood the whole thing and consequently practised "criticism". This philosophical non-wisdom and non-method, this clerical and ecclesiastical abuse – preachers on Bach and Goethe, forming "churches", and so on –, this criticism-of-death on what is living, this impotent hate and envy against the creative, ever-present renewing element in the human being, this treason and discrediting of the spiritual, beginning with the Greeks up to our present-day critics, fault-finders, philosophical and literary dilettantes, traversed our entire Idealistic-possessed European manner. This manner always races to and fro between supermen and less than men, genius and madness, *pathos* and ridiculousness, hypocrisy and baseness, asceticism and craving for pleasure, tastelessness and aestheticism, without quietly coming to consciousness, without common point of meeting, without the uniting "melos" (T A O), that holds together the different discrepancy of "notes", without support (*Halt*), *without bearing* (*Haltung*). That the Greeks had philosophers, but did not have one single famous musician, apart from the splendid Orpheus, gives them the worst testimonial. It only goes to prove that they did not take a long, ascending Intuitive path, but took over everything already formed, finished, dead, misunderstood from the hands of ancient highly cultivated peoples. The linguistic Idealism, the descending movement from the highest knowledge of melos, is to be added to the bill of a tremendous rising upsurge of the Egyptians, Mesopotamians and Indians, as well as everything else which was good with the Greeks and with Europe. But everything which was bad in Europe – this had its model with the Greeks in their lack of understanding and misunderstanding of the Intuitive, musical element.

Out of melos any spiritual human being is able to build up for himself the forms of life from its primal origin, and create afresh, and learns to respect the immutable, the laws, the "*nomos*". He recognises the connection between things and becomes used to being responsible for his deeds. He never needs to take over anything which is finished, whose original meaning remains closed for him. Through melos he has at any time spiritual control for any event in the world. Melos cannot persuade him, cannot lie to him. It does not appeal to his sensual nature, to his weaknesses. The interpreter of melos, however, draws from the archetypal source, that health-giving spring from which everybody who wants to can drink. Proceeding from melos, anybody can repeatedly test the thoughtful-conceptual, the "dogmas"; he does not need the world to "demonstrate" anything to him. Language can deny its origin from melos and can become the tool of the seeker for power and the false prophets. Melos cannot be misused.

The Greeks fought melos with narrow-minded rules from their philosophers; they wanted to make music the servant of speech, of myth, that is, the producer subject to the product, the unchangeable to the changeable. They clogged up the source of melos and the result was they soon became high and dry. Because they did not properly trust their one-sided interpretation, cultural life began to totter – already some centuries later –, ever again laboriously propped up through effects, through display and staging. The theatre in its classical form was the most appropriate arena for this. (After the *pathos* of a Sophocles, Aeschylus and Euripides, there follows of necessity the irony of Aristophanes. Has this fact never opened the eyes of anyone in Europe concerning the "worth" of the theatre? Is it possible to treat Hölderlin's poems, Sophocles *choruses* ironically?) The dramatic element has killed the musical element, Intuition, in the human being. The dramatic poem is a misuse of speech, just as "polyphonic" music is the doing violence to melody.

In the Orient there exists a silhouette-theatre to music, without direct speech on the stage, but with a meaningful poem as the basis of the action. This is the only pure artistic possibility for a theatre. In Europe on the other hand the cinema is the consequence of the drama. People took it seriously and completely laid aside speech as art, contenting themselves with the externals of theatre.

Instinct and Interpretation

In order to form a clear picture of what we mean by spiritual creating, we have to proceed from a basis which is common to us all – from the purely animal side of the human being, from his nature, from instinct. Instinct is the feeling, the sensing of the spatial, material element, of resistance, friction, inhibition, like and dislike, but also the periodic returning, rhythmical side of material "movement" – in short, everything which takes its path from the purely sensory to melos, only this itself excluded. Melos alone lies outside the instinctive life, it can only be laid hold of, grasped, by the human being, and consequently with his language, thinking and interpreting he is above the animal. Interpretation, thinking means to show, to point to something, that is, to transform the inner, spiritual, immaterial movement into the outer, spatial, material "movement". For this it does not need speech alone, but *gesture* in general, that event in which the interpretation and thinking are expressed. The individual languages with their formed sound-gestures are already something interpreted, already something thought, and are consequently able to be understood even by animals and up to a certain degree answered as well – followed –, depending on how we approach their instinct with it. Certainly, animals are not able to comprehend the *meaning* of language, but even the fewest human beings, and not even all the poets do – because they are not able to grasp and interpret melos, which does *not* meet their instinct. Instinct reaches as far as sound, to noise, to the crude rhythmical element, to tonal music, which still is connected with the animal side of man and is also composed from the *Affekt* [emotional state]. Consequently everything can somehow be taken hold of and grasped with the animal instincts alone of the human being, everything, even formed language, tonal music – only not pure atonal melos, the only thing that cannot be misused for suggestive and hypnotic purposes, which is widest removed from *pathos*, which is the ethical part itself – the purely spiritual movement in the human being, the most purifying thing in human thinking and action. Languages, tonal music, the spatial arts are delivered up to the instincts, whereas atonal melody (its melos!) has *unconditionally* to be spiritually laid hold of before it can manifest in the sense world.

The animal side of man is the "movement" of his material, which he either can interpret himself, or which can be interpreted by others. The more complicated this movement is, the more chaotic, all the more difficult it is to interpret. People who cannot interpret their instinctive movements, who do not understand themselves, become unhappy and despair. And when chance does not come to help them – choice of profession, and so on – then they come to grief. Contemporary European humanity is stuck in this dilemma; it has refined and complicated to the utmost its instinctive, sensory life, and now – it can no longer interpret it. But just in the moment when the chaos intensified to fullest possession – through the "staged suicide attempt" of the Great War – in this moment of Europe's greatest spiritual need, pure melos, the source of everything spiritual, was opened up, out of which the greatest of all confusion can solely be interpreted – it might be that the Chinese were stuck in a similar decisive dilemma.

The animal instinct of the human being consequently reaches nearly as far as atonal melos. The latter cannot be conceived instinctively but only spiritually. As soon as a human being has spiritually grasped atonal melos, he can also interpret it *rhythmically*, conceptually, linguistically, pictorially, and therein, in the interpretation of an archetypal language with 479,001,600 "words" and their unlimited possibilities lies our cultural future. Atonal melos is a measure for the spirituality of every single person. Someone who is not able to grasp this should profess instinct, craft, experience and practice. Atonal melos is the peak of all spirituality in the human being, everything cultural, of all conceivable cultures in general. The Chinese have the high point of this pulsating spiritual life already behind them, they do not themselves today understand their works and – despite persistent warning of the best amongst themselves – slowly fall prey to big business. But Europe stands before a cultural task, for whose solution and development several centuries are required – the interpretation of *Melos*. Atonal melos is like that miraculous flower, those things in *1001 Nights* which millions of frenzied people pass by without noticing. But the one who does find it, for him it is as though scales fall from his eyes and he trembles before the mystery of truth. No sophisticated education, no instinct be it ever so complicated can help him here. The European has so far missed that which makes him fully human, "listening", Intuition.

Interpretation of melos is the crown of human knowledge and recognition, and you have to thank the intuitive peoples for those great secrets which they withheld from the human beings who are just instinctive. Our discoveries, inventions of modern times – except the purely technical ones – were for a long time known in China and India, but were kept strictly secret by the interpreters in order to avoid misuse. To the ancient Egyptians things were known – even technical things – which to us today are still a riddle.

Our scholastic and philosophic wisdom would never have dreamt that we Europeans have lived so far purely instinctively, that means actually like animals (ants, bees...) the excretions from whose glands, those substances, poisons, emotional states producing *pathos*, out of which, too, our European culture, though very complicated, was composed – without interpretation, without spiritual control. But now we have enough of this in our "pharmacy" and could slowly start with the "healing". Pure melos tames the demons of instinctive life and makes them serve the human being. Melos is like the diamond. It is found in amorphous stone, in the chaos of nature, whose complicated movements it has received into itself under tremendous pressure from without and formed the most beautiful and most splendid crystal.

The European stands at that turning point of culture which is in harmony with the beginning of every culture, as the animal-like, primitive human being of pre-history is indebted to the interpretation of the natural melos for the creation of his speech and the creations of myth, so now atonal melos forms the complicated and refined mechanism of the instinctive life, the highly organised animal in the human being into a recognising, interpreting, thinking being.

ARTISTS, THINKERS,

do you still want to rummage about in your emotions and extend the chaos further,

do you want to collect rubbish, left-overs, bones, instead of sitting at the richly set table of the manifold melos,

do you want to continue to work in the subconscious, although the source of knowledge has been shown you, the only one which is not yet clouded over and which cannot be clouded over,

do you not want a common language, a means of understanding, the possibility of spiritual control for your creating,

do you want thoroughly to uphold restriction, narrowness, or would you rather prefer to order yourselves to the *nomos* of movement,

do you want to serve with your craft the manifestation of the highest idea –

or do you want totally to throw yourselves into the arms of the official business, the fashion, the prostitution?

Vienna, December 1920

Fig. 75:   Alan Stott at his instrument.

A short note about the Compiler, Editor and Translator

Alan Stott (b. 1949, near Canterbury, England) played for eurythmy for the first time for members of the *London Eurythmy Stage Group* in 1967. He attended evening classes of Marguerite Lundgren and Eileen Wreford. After completing his teacher training at Dartington College of Arts, South Devon, College of St Matthias, Bristol, and Emerson College, Sussex (where he attended eurythmy courses given by Elizabeth Edmunds and Mollie von Heide), he helped found and taught as a class-teacher at the Bristol Waldorf School. Since 1976, he has played for eurythmy and taught music and anthroposophy in five eurythmy trainings and in four Steiner-Waldorf Schools, in England and Germany, and he has toured with eurythmy stage groups in Europe and the British Isles. Maren Weissenborn, who is a eurythmist, and Alan were married in 1982. Alan's musical life is divided between regular appearances as a solo pianist and accompanist (often with *The Anderida Ensemble*, which he founded in 1986, and *Eurythmy West Midlands*); as choir director; and as a player and subject teacher in the Eurythmy School, Stourbridge. He translates anthroposophical, musical and eurythmical studies, including the bi-annual *Newsletter* of the Section for the Arts of Eurythmy, Speech and Music (Dornach), and he edited the *Newsletter* of the Association of Eurythmists in Great Britain and Ireland until 2012.

For your notes

CPSIA information can be obtained
at www.ICGtesting.com
Printed in the USA
BVOW04s0802041217

501906BV00013B/552/P

9 780956 926616